Understanding GPS

Principles and Applications

Second Edition

Elliott D. Kaplan
Christopher J. Hegarty

Editors

ARTECH HOUSE

BOSTON | LONDON
artechhouse.com

Library of Congress Cataloging-in-Publication Data
Understanding GPS: principles and applications/[editors], Elliott Kaplan,
Christopher Hegarty.—2nd ed.
p. cm.
Includes bibliographical references.
ISBN 1-58053-894-0 (alk. paper)
1. Global Positioning System. I. Kaplan, Elliott D. II. Hegarty, C. (Christopher J.)

G109.5K36 2006
623.89'3—dc22   2005056270

British Library Cataloguing in Publication Data
Kaplan, Elliott D.
Understanding GPS: principles and applications.—2nd ed.
1. Global positioning system
I. Title II. Hegarty, Christopher J.
629'.045

ISBN-10: 1-58053-894-0

Cover design by Igor Valdman

Tables 9.11 through 9.16 have been reprinted with permission from ETSI. 3GPP TSs and TRs
are the property of ARIB, ATIS, ETSI, CCSA, TTA, and TTC who jointly own the copyright
to them. They are subject to further modifications and are therefore provided to you "as is"
for informational purposes only. Further use is strictly prohibited.

© 2006 ARTECH HOUSE, INC.
685 Canton Street
Norwood, MA 02062

International Standard Book Number: 1-58053-894-0

10 9 8 7 6 5 4 3 2 1

To my wife Andrea, whose limitless love and support enabled my contribution to this work. She is my shining star.

—Elliott D. Kaplan

To my family—Patti, Michelle, David, and Megan— for all their encouragement and support

—Christopher J. Hegarty

Contents

Preface

Since the writing of the first edition of this book, usage of the Global Positioning System (GPS) has become nearly ubiquitous. GPS provides the position, velocity, and timing information that enables many applications we use in our daily lives. GPS is in the midst of an evolutionary development that will provide increased accuracy and robustness for both civil and military users. The proliferation of augmentations and the development of other systems, including GALILEO, have also significantly changed the landscape of satellite navigation. These significant events have led to the writing of this second edition.

The objective of the second edition, as with the first edition, is to provide the reader with a complete systems engineering treatment of GPS. The authors are a multidisciplinary team of experts with practical experience in the areas that each addressed within this text. They provide a thorough treatment of each topic. Our intent in this new endeavor was to bring the first edition text up to date. This was achieved through the modification of some of the existing material and through the extensive addition of new material.

The new material includes satellite constellation design guidelines, descriptions of the new satellites (Block IIR, Block IIR-M, Block IIF), a comprehensive treatment of the control segment and planned upgrades, satellite signal modulation characteristics, descriptions of the modernized GPS satellite signals (L2C, L5, and M code), and advances in GPS receiver signal processing techniques. The treatment of interference effects on legacy GPS signals from the first edition is greatly expanded, and a treatment of interference effects on the modernized signals is newly added. New material is also included to provide in-depth discussions on multipath and ionospheric scintillation, along with the associated effects on the GPS signals.

GPS accuracy has improved significantly within the past decade. This text presents updated error budgets for both the GPS Precise Positioning and Standard Positioning Services. Also included are measured performance data, a discussion on continuity of service, and updated treatments of availability and integrity.

The treatment of differential GPS from the first edition has been greatly expanded. The variability of GPS errors with geographic location and over time is thoroughly addressed. Also new to this edition are a discussion of attitude determination using carrier phase techniques, a detailed description of satellite-based augmentation systems (e.g., WAAS, MSAS, and EGNOS), and descriptions of many other operational or planned code- and carrier-based differential systems.

The incorporation of GPS into navigation systems that also rely on other sensors continues to be a widespread practice. The material from the first edition on integrating GPS with inertial and automotive sensors is significantly expanded. New to the second edition is a thorough treatment on the embedding of GPS receivers within cellular handsets. This treatment includes an elaboration on network-assistance methods.

In addition to GPS, we now cover GALILEO with as much detail as possible at this stage in this European program's development. We also provide coverage of GLONASS, BeiDou, and the Japanese Quasi-Zenith Satellite System.

As in the first edition, the book is structured such that a reader with a general science background can learn the basics of GPS and how it works within the first few chapters, whereas the reader with a stronger engineering/scientific background will be able to delve deeper and benefit from the more in-depth technical material. It is this "ramp up" of mathematical/technical complexity, along with the treatment of key topics, that enable this publication to serve as a student text as well as a reference source. More than 10,000 copies of the first edition have been sold throughout the world. We hope that the second edition will build upon the success of the first, and that this text will prove to be of value to the rapidly increasing number of engineers and scientists that are working on applications involving GPS and other satellite navigation systems.

While the book has generally been written for the engineering/scientific community, one full chapter is devoted to Global Navigation Satellite System (GNSS) markets and applications. This is a change from the first edition, where we focused solely on GPS markets and applications. The opinions presented here are those of the authors and do not necessarily reflect the views of The MITRE Corporation.

Acknowledgments

Much appreciation is extended to the following individuals for their contributions to this effort. Our apologies are extended to anyone whom we may have inadvertently missed. We thank Don Benson, Susan Borgeson, Bakry El-Arini, John Emilian, Ranwa Haddad, Peggy Hodge, LaTonya Lofton-Collins, Dennis D. McCarthy, Keith McDonald, Jules McNeff, Tom Morrissey, Sam Parisi, Ed Powers, B. Rama Rao, Kan Sandhoo, Jay Simon, Doug Taggart, Avram Tetewsky, Michael Tran, John Ursino, A. J. Van Dierendonck, David Wolfe, and Artech House's anonymous peer reviewer.

Elliott D. Kaplan
Christopher J. Hegarty
Editors
Bedford, Massachusetts
November 2005

CHAPTER 1

Introduction

Elliott D. Kaplan
The MITRE Corporation

1.1 Introduction

Navigation is defined as the science of getting a craft or person from one place to another. Each of us conducts some form of navigation in our daily lives. Driving to work or walking to a store requires that we employ fundamental navigation skills. For most of us, these skills require utilizing our eyes, common sense, and landmarks. However, in some cases where a more accurate knowledge of our position, intended course, or transit time to a desired destination is required, navigation aids other than landmarks are used. These may be in the form of a simple clock to determine the velocity over a known distance or the odometer in our car to keep track of the distance traveled. Some other navigation aids transmit electronic signals and therefore are more complex. These are referred to as *radionavigation aids*.

Signals from one or more radionavigation aids enable a person (herein referred to as the *user*) to compute their position. (Some radionavigation aids provide the capability for velocity determination and time dissemination as well.) It is important to note that it is the user's radionavigation receiver that processes these signals and computes the position fix. The receiver performs the necessary computations (e.g., range, bearing, and estimated time of arrival) for the user to navigate to a desired location. In some applications, the receiver may only partially process the received signals, with the navigation computations performed at another location.

Various types of radionavigation aids exist, and for the purposes of this text they are categorized as either ground-based or space-based. For the most part, the accuracy of ground-based radionavigation aids is proportional to their operating frequency. Highly accurate systems generally transmit at relatively short wavelengths, and the user must remain within line of sight (LOS), whereas systems broadcasting at lower frequencies (longer wavelengths) are not limited to LOS but are less accurate. Early spaced-based systems (namely, the U.S. Navy Navigation Satellite System—referred to as Transit—and the Russian Tsikada system)[1] provided a two-dimensional high-accuracy positioning service. However, the frequency of obtaining a position fix is dependent on the user's latitude. Theoretically,

---

1. Transit was decommissioned on December 31, 1996, by the U.S. government. At the time of this writing, Tsikada was still operational.

a Transit user at the equator could obtain a position fix on the average of once every 110 minutes, whereas at 80° latitude the fix rate would improve to an average of once every 30 minutes [1]. Limitations applicable to both systems are that each position fix requires approximately 10 to 15 minutes of receiver processing and an estimate of the user's position. These attributes were suitable for shipboard navigation because of the low velocities, but not for aircraft and high-dynamic users [2]. It was these shortcomings that led to the development of the U.S. Global Positioning System (GPS).

1.2 Condensed GPS Program History

In the early 1960s, several U.S. government organizations, including the Department of Defense (DOD), the National Aeronautics and Space Administration (NASA), and the Department of Transportation (DOT), were interested in developing satellite systems for three-dimensional position determination. The optimum system was viewed as having the following attributes: global coverage, continuous/all weather operation, ability to serve high-dynamic platforms, and high accuracy. When Transit became operational in 1964, it was widely accepted for use on low-dynamic platforms. However, due to its inherent limitations (cited in the preceding paragraphs), the Navy sought to enhance Transit or develop another satellite navigation system with the desired capabilities mentioned earlier. Several variants of the original Transit system were proposed by its developers at the Johns Hopkins University Applied Physics Laboratory. Concurrently, the Naval Research Laboratory (NRL) was conducting experiments with highly stable space-based clocks to achieve precise time transfer. This program was denoted as Timation. Modifications were made to Timation satellites to provide a ranging capability for two-dimensional position determination. Timation employed a sidetone modulation for satellite-to-user ranging [3–5].

At the same time as the Transit enhancements were being considered and the Timation efforts were underway, the Air Force conceptualized a satellite positioning system denoted as System 621B. It was envisioned that System 621B satellites would be in elliptical orbits at inclination angles of 0°, 30°, and 60°. Numerous variations of the number of satellites (15–20) and their orbital configurations were examined. The use of pseudorandom noise (PRN) modulation for ranging with digital signals was proposed. System 621B was to provide three-dimensional coverage and continuous worldwide service. The concept and operational techniques were verified at the Yuma Proving Grounds using an inverted range in which pseudosatellites or *pseudolites* (i.e., ground-based satellites) transmitted satellite signals for aircraft positioning [3–6]. Furthermore, the Army at Ft. Monmouth, New Jersey, was investigating many candidate techniques, including ranging, angle determination, and the use of Doppler measurements. From the results of the Army investigations, it was recommended that ranging using PRN modulation be implemented [5].

In 1969, the Office of the Secretary of Defense (OSD) established the Defense Navigation Satellite System (DNSS) program to consolidate the independent development efforts of each military service to form a single joint-use system. The OSD also established the Navigation Satellite Executive Steering Group, which was charged with determining the viability of the DNSS and planning its development. From this effort, the system concept for NAVSTAR GPS was formed. The NAVSTAR GPS program was developed by the GPS Joint Program Office (JPO) in El Segundo, California [5]. At the time of this writing, the GPS JPO continued to oversee the development and production of new satellites, ground control equipment, and the majority of U.S. military user receivers. Also, the system is now most commonly referred to as simply *GPS*.

1.3   GPS Overview

Presently, GPS is fully operational and meets the criteria established in the 1960s for an optimum positioning system. The system provides accurate, continuous, world-wide, three-dimensional position and velocity information to users with the appropriate receiving equipment. GPS also disseminates a form of Coordinated Universal Time (UTC). The satellite constellation nominally consists of 24 satellites arranged in 6 orbital planes with 4 satellites per plane. A worldwide ground control/monitoring network monitors the health and status of the satellites. This network also uploads navigation and other data to the satellites. GPS can provide service to an unlimited number of users since the user receivers operate passively (i.e., receive only). The system utilizes the concept of one-way time of arrival (TOA) ranging. Satellite transmissions are referenced to highly accurate atomic frequency standards onboard the satellites, which are in synchronism with a GPS time base. The satellites broadcast ranging codes and navigation data on two frequencies using a technique called code division multiple access (CDMA); that is, there are only two frequencies in use by the system, called L1 (1,575.42 MHz) and L2 (1,227.6 MHz). Each satellite transmits on these frequencies, but with different ranging codes than those employed by other satellites. These codes were selected because they have low cross-correlation properties with respect to one another. Each satellite generates a short code referred to as the coarse/acquisition or C/A code and a long code denoted as the precision or P(Y) code. (Additional signals are forthcoming. Satellite signal characteristics are discussed in Chapter 4.) The navigation data provides the means for the receiver to determine the location of the satellite at the time of signal transmission, whereas the ranging code enables the user's receiver to determine the transit (i.e., propagation) time of the signal and thereby determine the satellite-to-user range. This technique requires that the user receiver also contain a clock. Utilizing this technique to measure the receiver's three-dimensional location requires that TOA ranging measurements be made to four satellites. If the receiver clock were synchronized with the satellite clocks, only three range measurements would be required. However, a crystal clock is usually employed in navigation receivers to minimize the cost, complexity, and size of the receiver. Thus, four measurements are required to determine user latitude, longitude, height, and receiver clock offset from internal system time. If either system time or height is accurately known, less than four satellites are required. Chapter 2 provides elaboration on TOA ranging as well as user position, velocity, and time (PVT) determination.

GPS is a dual-use system. That is, it provides separate services for civil and military users. These are called the Standard Positioning Service (SPS) and the Precise

Positioning Service (PPS). The SPS is designated for the civil community, whereas the PPS is intended for U.S. authorized military and select government agency users. Access to the GPS PPS is controlled through cryptography. Initial operating capability (IOC) for GPS was attained in December 1993, when a combination of 24 proto-type and production satellites was available and position determination/timing services complied with the associated specified predictable accuracies. GPS reached full operational capability (FOC) in early 1995, when the entire 24 production satel-lite constellation was in place and extensive testing of the ground control segment and its interactions with the constellation was completed. Descriptions of the SPS and PPS services are presented in the following sections.

1.3.1 PPS

The PPS is specified to provide a predictable accuracy of at least 22m (2 drms, 95%) in the horizontal plane and 27.7m (95%) in the vertical plane. The distance root mean square (drms) is a common measure used in navigation. Twice the drms value, or 2 drms, is the radius of a circle that contains at least 95% of all possible fixes that can be obtained with a system (in this case, the PPS) at any one place. The PPS pro-vides a UTC time transfer accuracy within 200 ns (95%) referenced to the time kept at the U.S. Naval Observatory (USNO) and is denoted as UTC (USNO) [7, 8]. Velocity measurement accuracy is specified as 0.2 m/s (95%) [4]. PPS measured per-formance is addressed in Section 7.7.

As stated earlier, the PPS is primarily intended for military and select govern-ment agency users. Civilian use is permitted, but only with special U.S. DOD approval. Access to the aforementioned PPS position accuracies is controlled through two cryptographic features denoted as antispoofing (AS) and selective availability (SA). AS is a mechanism intended to defeat deception jamming through encryption of the military signals. Deception jamming is a technique in which an adversary would replicate one or more of the satellite ranging codes, navigation data signal(s), and carrier frequency Doppler effects with the intent of deceiving a victim receiver. SA had intentionally degraded SPS user accuracy by *dithering* the satellite's clock, thereby corrupting TOA measurement accuracy. Furthermore, SA could have introduced errors into the broadcast navigation data parameters [9]. SA was discon-tinued on May 1, 2000, and per current U.S. government policy is to remain off. When it was activated, PPS users removed SA effects through cryptography [4].

1.3.2 SPS

The SPS is available to all users worldwide free of direct charges. There are no restrictions on SPS usage. This service is specified to provide accuracies of better than 13m (95%) in the horizontal plane and 22m (95%) in the vertical plane (global average; signal-in-space errors only). UTC (USNO) time dissemination accuracy is specified to be better than 40 ns (95%) [10]. SPS measured performance is typically much better than specification (see Section 7.7).

At the time of this writing, the SPS was the predominant satellite navigation ser-vice in use by millions throughout the world.

1.4   GPS Modernization Program

In January 1999, the U.S. government announced a new GPS modernization initiative that called for the addition of two civil signals to be added to new GPS satellites [11]. These signals are denoted as L2C and L5. The L2C signal will be available for nonsafety of life applications at the L2 frequency; the L5 signal resides in an aeronautical radionavigation service (ARNS) band at 1,176.45 MHz. L5 is intended for safety-of-life use applications. These additional signals will provide SPS users the ability to correct for ionospheric delays by making dual frequency measurements, thereby significantly increasing civil user accuracy. By using the carrier phase of all three signals (L1 C/A, L2C, and L5) and differential processing techniques, very high user accuracy (on the order of millimeters) can be rapidly obtained. (Ionospheric delay and associated compensation techniques are described in Chapter 7, while differential processing is discussed in Chapter 8.) The additional signals also increase the receiver's robustness to interference. If one signal experiences high interference, then the receiver can switch to another signal. It is the intent of the U.S. government that these new signals will aid civil, commercial, and scientific users worldwide. One example is that the combined use of L1 (which also resides in an ARNS band) and L5 will greatly enhance civil aviation.

During the mid to late 1990s, a new military signal called M code was developed for the PPS. This signal will be transmitted on both L1 and L2 and is spectrally separated from the GPS civil signals in those bands. The spectral separation permits the use of noninterfering higher power M code modes that increase resistance to interference. Furthermore, M code will provide robust acquisition, increased accuracy, and increased security over the legacy P(Y) code.

Chapter 4 contains descriptions of the legacy (C/A code and P(Y) code) and modernized signals mentioned earlier.

At the time of this writing, it was anticipated that both M code and L2C will be on orbit when the first Block IIR-M ("R" for replenishment, "M" for modernized) satellite is scheduled to be launched. (The Block IIR-M will also broadcast all legacy signals.) The Block IIF ("F" for follow on) satellite is scheduled for launch in 2007 and will generate all signals, including L5. Figure 1.1 provides an overview of GPS signal evolution. Figures 1.2 and 1.3 depict the Block IIR-M and Block IIF satellites, respectively.

At the time of this writing, the GPS III program was underway. This program was conceived in 2000 to reassess the entire GPS architecture and determine the necessary architecture to meet civil and military user needs through 2030. It is envisioned that GPS III will provide submeter position accuracy, greater timing accuracy, a system integrity solution, a high data capacity intersatellite crosslink capability, and higher signal power to meet military antijam requirements. At the time of this writing, the first GPS III satellite launch was planned for U.S. government fiscal year 2013.

1.5   GALILEO Satellite System

In 1998, the European Union (EU) decided to pursue a satellite navigation system independent of GPS designed specifically for civilian use worldwide. When com-

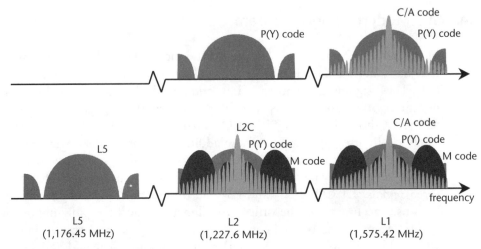

Figure 1.1   GPS signal evolution.

Figure 1.2   Block IIR-M satellite. (Courtesy of Lockheed Martin Corp. Reprinted with permission.)

pleted, GALILEO will provide multiple levels of service to users throughout the world. Five services are planned:

1. An *open* service that will be free of direct user charges;
2. A *commercial* service that will combine value-added data to a high-accuracy positioning service;
3. *Safety-of-life* (SOL) service for safety critical users;
4. *Public regulated* service strictly for government-authorized users requiring a higher level of protection (e.g., increased robustness against interference or jamming);
5. Support for *search and rescue*.

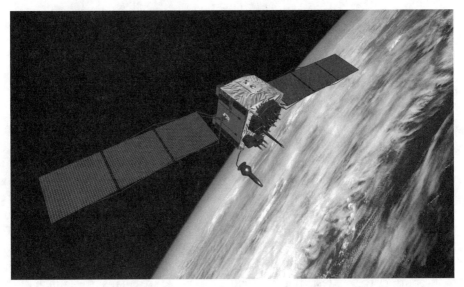

Figure 1.3   Block IIF satellite. (*Source:* The Boeing Company. Reprinted with permission.)

It is anticipated that the SOL service will authenticate the received satellite signals to assure that they are truly broadcast by GALILEO. Furthermore, the SOL service will include integrity monitoring and notification; that is, a timely warning will be issued to the users when the safe use of the SOL signals cannot be guaranteed according to specifications.

A 30-satellite constellation and full worldwide ground control segment is planned. Figure 1.4 depicts a GALILEO satellite. One key goal is to be fully compatible with the GPS system [12]. Measures are being taken to ensure interoperability between the two systems. Primary interoperability factors being addressed are signal structure, geodetic coordinate reference frame, and time reference system.

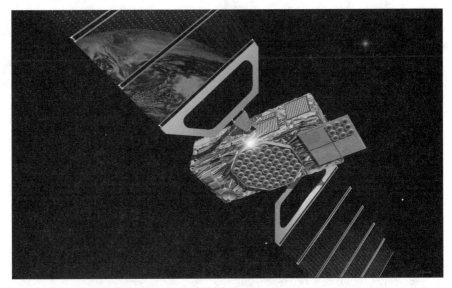

Figure 1.4   GALILEO satellite. (Courtesy of ESA.)

GALILEO is scheduled to be operational in 2008. Chapter 10 describes the GALILEO system, including satellite signal characteristics.

1.6 Russian GLONASS System

The Global Navigation Satellite System (GLONASS) is the Russian counterpart to GPS. It consists of a constellation of satellites in medium Earth orbit (MEO), a ground control segment, and user equipment, and it is described in detail in Section 11.1. At the time of this writing, GLONASS was being revamped and the system was undergoing an extensive modernization effort. The constellation had decreased to 7 satellites in 1991 but is currently at 14 satellites. The GLONASS program goals are to have 18 satellites in orbit in 2007 and 24 satellites in the 2010–2011 time frame. A new civil signal has been on orbit since 2003. This signal has been broadcast from two modernized satellites referred to as the GLONASS-M. These two satellites are reported to be test flight satellites. There are plans to launch a total of 8 GLONASS-M satellites. The follow-on satellite to the GLONASS-M is the GLONASS-K, which will broadcast all legacy signals plus a third civil frequency for SOL applications. The GLONASS-K class is scheduled for launch in 2008 [13].

As part of the modernization program, satellite reliability is being increased in both the GLONASS-M and GLONASS-K designs. Furthermore, the GLONASS-K is being designed to broadcast integrity data and wide area differential corrections [13]. Figures 1.5 and 1.6 depict the GLONASS-M and GLONASS-K satellites, respectively.

The Russian government has stated that, like GPS, GLONASS is a dual-use system and that there will be no direct user fees for civil users. The Russians are working with the EU and the United States to achieve compatibility between GLONASS and GALILEO, and GLONASS and GPS, respectively [13]. As in the case with

Figure 1.5 GLONASS-M satellite.

Figure 1.6 GLONASS-K satellite.

GPS/GALILEO interoperability, key elements to achieving interoperability are compatible signal structure, geodetic coordinate reference frame, and time reference system.

1.7 Chinese BeiDou System

The Chinese BeiDou system is a multistage satellite navigation program designed to provide positioning, fleet-management, and precision-time dissemination to Chinese military and civil users. Currently, BeiDou is in a semi-operational phase with three satellites deployed in geostationary orbit over China. The official Chinese press has designated the constellation as the BeiDou Navigation Test System (BNTS). The BNTS provides a radio determination satellite service (RDSS). Unlike GPS, GALILEO and GLONASS, which employ one-way TOA measurements, the RDSS requires two-way range measurements. That is, a system operations center sends out a polling signal through one of the BeiDou satellites to a subset of users. These users respond to this signal by transmitting a signal through at least two of the system's three geostationary satellites. The travel time is measured as the navigation signals loop from operations center to the satellite, to the receiver on the user platform, and back around. With this time-lapse information, the known locations of the two satellites, and an estimate of the user altitude, the user's location can be determined by the operations center. Once calculated, the operations center transmits the positioning information to the user. Since the operations center must calculate the positions for all subscribers to the system, BeiDou can also be used for fleet management and communications [14, 15].

Current plans call for the BNTS to also provide integrity and wide area differential corrections via a satellite-based augmentation system (SBAS) service. (SBAS is described in detail in Chapter 8.) At present, the RDSS capability is operational, and

SBAS is still under development. The BNTS provides limited coverage and only supports users in and around China. The BNTS should be operational through the end of the decade. In the long term, the Chinese plan is to deploy a regional or worldwide navigation constellation of 14–30 satellites under the BeiDou-2 program. The Chinese did not plan to finalize the design for BeiDou-2 until sometime in 2005 [14, 15]. Section 11.2 provides further details about BeiDou.

1.8 Augmentations

Augmentations are available to enhance stand-alone GPS performance. These can be space-based, such as a geostationary satellite overlay service that provides satellite signals to enhance accuracy, availability, and integrity, or they can be ground-based, as in a network that assists embedded GPS receivers in cellular telephones to compute a rapid position fix. Other forms of augmentations make use of inertial sensors for added robustness in the presence of interference. Inertial sensors are also used in combination with wheel sensors and magnetic compass inputs to provide vehicle navigation when the satellite signals are blocked in *urban canyons* (i.e., city streets surrounded by tall buildings). GPS receiver and sensor measurements are usually integrated by the use of a Kalman filter. (Chapter 9 provides in-depth treatment of inertial sensor integration and assisted-GPS network methods.)

Some applications, such as precision farming, aircraft precision approach, and harbor navigation, require far more accuracy than that provided by stand-alone GPS. They may also require integrity warning notifications and other data. These applications utilize a technique that dramatically improves stand-alone system performance, referred to as differential GPS (DGPS). DGPS is a method of improving the positioning or timing performance of GPS by using one or more reference stations at known locations, each equipped with at least one GPS receiver to provide accuracy enhancement, integrity, or other data to user receivers via a data link. There are several types of DGPS techniques, and, depending on the application, the user can obtain accuracies ranging from meters to millimeters. Some DGPS systems provide service over a local area (10–100 km) from a single reference station, while others service an entire continent. The European Geostationary Navigation Overlay Service (EGNOS) and U.S. Wide Area Augmentation System (WAAS) are examples of wide area DGPS services. EGNOS coverage is shown in Figure 1.7. Chapter 8 describes the underlying concepts of DGPS and details a number of operational and planned DGPS systems.

1.9 Markets and Applications

The first publication of this book referred to GPS as an *enabling* technology. It has truly become that but it is also a *ubiquitous* technology. Technology trends in component miniaturization and large-scale manufacturing have led to a proliferation of low-cost GPS receiver components. GPS receivers are embedded in many of the items we use in our daily lives. These items include cellular telephones, personal digital assistants (PDAs), and automobiles. Applications range from the provision of a reference time source for synchronizing computer networks to guidance of robotic

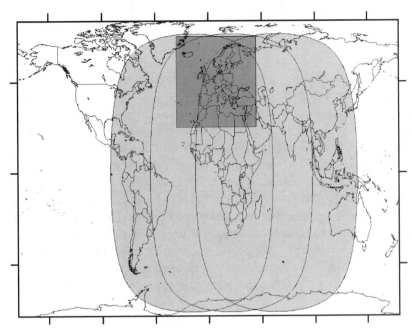

Figure 1.7   EGNOS geostationary satellite coverage.

vehicles. Market forecasts estimate Global Navigation Satellite System (GNSS) 2018 product sales and services to be $290 billion. (GNSS is defined as the world-wide set of satellite navigation systems.) By 2020, the GNSS market is expected to approach $310 billion with at least 3 billion chipsets in use [16, 17].

To illustrate the diverse use of satellite navigation technology, several examples of applications are presented next. Further discussion on applications and market projections is contained in Chapter 12.

1.9.1   Land

The majority of GNSS users are land-based. Applications range from leisure hiking to fleet vehicle management. The decreasing price of GNSS receiver components, coupled with the proliferation of telecommunications services, has led to the emergence of a variety of location-based services (LBS). LBS enables the *push and pull* of data from the user to a service provider. For example, a query can be made to find restaurants or lodging in a particular area, such as with General Motors' OnStar service. This request is sent over a datalink, along with the user's position, to the service provider. The provider searches a database for the information relevant to the user's position and returns it via the datalink. Another example is the ability of the user to request emergency assistance via forwarding his or her location to an emergency response dispatcher. Within the United States, this service has been mandated by the Federal Communications Commission and is called Emergency-911 (E-911). (Chapter 9 contains in-depth technical information regarding automotive applications as well as E-911 assisted GPS.)

An expanding worldwide market is the deployment of automatic vehicle location systems (AVLS) for fleet and emergency vehicle management. Fleet operators gain significant advantage with integrated GPS, communications, moving maps, and database technology for more efficient tracking and dispatch operations. One concept employed is called *geofencing*, where a vehicle's GPS is programmed with a fixed geographical area and alerts the fleet operator whenever the vehicle violates the prescribed "fence."

Since the writing of the first edition of this book, recreational usage has increased tremendously. A variety of low-cost GPS receivers are available from many sporting goods stores or through various Internet sources. Some have a digital map database and make an excellent navigation tool; however, the prudent user will still carry a traditional "paper" map and magnetic compass in the event of battery failure or receiver malfunction. Some recreational users participate in an adventure game known as *geocaching* [18]. Individuals or organizations set up caches throughout the world and post the cache locations on the Internet. Geocache players then use their GPS receivers to find the locations of the caches. Upon finding the cache, one usually signs the cache logbook indicating the date and time when one found the cache. Also, one may leave an item in the cache and then take an item in exchange.

Many of the world's military ground forces are GPS-equipped. Depending on the country and relationship to the United States, the receiver may be either SPS or PPS. Numerous countries have signed memoranda of understanding with the U.S. DOD and have access to the GPS military signals.

1.9.2 Aviation

The aviation community has propelled the use of GNSS and various augmentations to provide guidance for the en route through precision approach phases of flight. The continuous global coverage capability of GNSS permits aircraft to fly directly from one location to another, provided factors such as obstacle clearance and required procedures are adhered to. Incorporation of a data link with a GNSS receiver enables the transmission of aircraft location to other aircraft and to air traffic control (ATC). This function, called automatic dependent surveillance (ADS), is in use in various classes of airspace. In oceanic airspace, ADS is implemented using a point-to-point link from aircraft to oceanic ATC via satellite communications (SATCOM) or high-frequency datalink. Key benefits are ATC monitoring for collision avoidance and optimized routing to reduce travel time and, consequently, fuel consumption. ADS techniques are also being applied to airport surface surveillance of both aircraft and ground support vehicles.

A variant of ADS is automatic dependent surveillance-broadcast (ADS-B). This service employs a digital data link that broadcasts an aircraft's position, airspeed, heading, altitude and other information to multiple receivers on the ground as well as to other aircraft. (The ADS-B datalink can be thought of as a point-to-many link.) Thus, other aircraft equipped with ADS-B as well as ground controllers obtain a "picture" of the area air traffic situation. At the time of this writing, the U.S. Federal Aviation Administration (FAA) had implemented ADS-B and related data link technologies in a collaborative government/industry program called Safe Flight 21. The Safe Flight 21 initiative focuses on developing the required avionics, pilot procedures, and a compatible ground-based ADS system for air traffic control facilities.

Safe Flight 21 demonstration projects are in process in several areas within the United States, including Alaska and the Ohio River Valley.

GPS without augmentation now provides commercial and general aviation (GA) airborne systems with sufficient integrity to perform nonprecision approaches (NPA). NPA is the most common type of instrument approach performed by GA pilots. The FAA has instituted a program to develop NPA procedures using GPS. This so-called overlay program allows the use of a specially certified GPS receiver in place of a VHF omnidirectional range (VOR) or nondirectional beacon (NDB) receiver to fly the conventional VOR or NDB approach. New NPA overlays that define waypoints independent of ground-based facilities, and that simplify the procedures required for flight, are being put into service at the rate of about 500 to 1,000 approaches per year and are almost complete at the 5,000 public use airports in the United States. Other countries are implementing such procedures, and there is almost universal acceptance of some sort of GPS approach capability at most of the world's major airports.

In 2003, the FAA declared WAAS operational for instrument flight operations. WAAS broadcasts on the GPS L1 frequency so that signals are accessible to GPS receivers without the need for a dedicated DGPS corrections communications link. The performance of this system is sufficient for NPA and new types of vertically guided approaches that are only slightly less stringent than Category I precision approach. Further information regarding WAAS is provided in Chapter 8. Other SBASs [e.g., EGNOS, Multifunctional Transport Satelllite (MTSAT) Satellite Augmentation System (MSAS), and GPS and GEO Augmented Navigation (GAGAN)] are being fielded or considered to provide services equivalent to WAAS in other regions of the world and are described in Chapter 8.

DGPS is necessary to provide the performance required for vertically guided approaches. Traditional Category I, II, and III precision approaches involve guidance to the runway threshold in all three dimensions. Local area differential corrections, broadcast from an airport-deployed ground-based augmentation system (GBAS) reference station (see Chapter 8), are anticipated to meet all requirements for even the most demanding (Category III) approaches. Also, as GALILEO is deployed, the use of GNSS by aviation for en-route, approach, and landing is expected to become even more widespread.

1.9.3 Space Guidance

GPS enables various functions for spacecraft applications. These include attitude determination (i.e., heading, pitch, and roll), time synchronization, orbit determination, and absolute and relative position determination [19]. The German Space Agency (DARA) Challenging Microsatellite Payload (CHAMP) has been using GPS for attitude determination and time synchronization since 2000. In low Earth orbit (LEO), CHAMP also uses GPS measurements for atmospheric and ionospheric research and applications in weather prediction and space weather monitoring [20].

Since 1992, the Joint CNES-NASA TOPEX/POSEIDON satellite has used GPS in conjunction with ground processing for precise orbit determination with accuracies on the order of 3 cm [21] to conduct its mission of oceanographic research. The International Space Station employs GPS to provide position, velocity, and attitude determination [22]. Furthermore, pictures from NASA's LANDSAT of the Yucatan peninsula, coupled with a GPS-equipped airborne survey enabled a *National Geographic* expedition to find ruins of several heretofore unknown Mayan cities.

1.9.4 Maritime

GNSS has been embraced by both the commercial and recreational maritime communities. Navigation is enhanced on all bodies of waters, from oceanic travel to riverways, especially in inclement weather. Large pleasure craft and commercial ships may employ integrated navigation systems that include a digital compass, depth sounder, radar, and GPS. The integrated navigation solution is presented on a digital chart plotter as current ship position and intended route. For smaller vessels such as kayaks and canoes, handheld, waterproof, floatable units are available from paddle shops or the Internet. Maritime units can usually be augmented by WAAS, EGNOS, or maritime DGPS (MDGPS). MDGPS is a coastal network designed to broadcast DGPS corrections over coastal or waterway radiobeacons to suitably equipped users. MDGPS networks are employed in many countries, including Russia. Russian beacons transmit both DGPS and differential GLONASS corrections. The EGNOS Terrestrial Regional Augmentation Network (TRAN) is investigating the use of ground-based communications systems to rebroadcast EGNOS data to those maritime users with limited visibility to EGNOS geostationary satellites. Visibility may be limited for several reasons, including the location of the user at a latitude greater than that covered by the EGNOS satellites and the location of the user in a fjord where the receiver does not have line of sight to the satellite due to obscuring terrain [23]. Wide area differential GPS has been utilized by the offshore oil exploration community for several years. Also, highly accurate DGPS techniques are used in marine construction. Real-time kinematic (RTK) DGPS systems that produce centimeter-level accuracies for structure and vessel positioning are available. Chapter 8 contains descriptions of WAAS, EGNOS, MDGPS, and RTK.

1.10 Organization of the Book

This book is structured to first familiarize the reader with the fundamentals of PVT determination using GPS. Once this groundwork has been established, a description of the GPS system architecture is presented. Next, the discussion focuses on satellite signal characteristics and their generation. Received signal acquisition and tracking, as well as range and velocity measurement processes, are then examined. Signal acquisition and tracking is also analyzed in the presence of interference, multipath, and ionospheric scintillation. GPS performance (accuracy, availability, integrity, and continuity) is then assessed. A discussion of GPS differential techniques follows. Sensor-aiding techniques, including Intelligent Transport Systems (ITS) automotive applications and network-assisted GPS, are presented. These topics are followed by a comprehensive treatment of GALILEO. Details of GLONASS, BeiDou, and the Japanese Quasi-Zenith Satellite System (QZSS) are then provided. Finally, information on GNSS applications and their corresponding market projections is presented. Highlights of each chapter are summarized next.

Chapter 2 provides the fundamentals of user PVT determination. Beginning with the concept of TOA ranging, the chapter develops the principles for obtaining three-dimensional user position and velocity as well as UTC (USNO) from GPS. Included in this chapter are primers on GPS reference coordinate systems, Earth models, satellite orbits, and constellation design.

In Chapter 3, the GPS system architecture is presented. This includes descriptions of the space, control (i.e., worldwide ground control/monitoring network), and user (equipment) segments. Particulars of the constellation are described. The U.S. government nominal constellation is provided for those readers who need to conduct analyses using a validated reference constellation. Satellite types and corresponding attributes are provided, including the Block IIR, Block IIR-M, and Block IIF. One will note the increase in the number of transmitted civil and military navigation signals as the various satellite blocks progress. Of considerable interest are interactions between the control segment (CS) and the satellites. This section provides a thorough understanding of the measurement processing and building of the navigation data message. The navigation data message provides the user receiver with satellite ephemerides, satellite clock corrections, and other information that enable the receiver to compute PVT. An overview of user receiving equipment is presented, as well as related selection criteria relevant to both civil and military users.

Chapter 4 describes the GPS satellite signals and their generation. This chapter examines the properties of the GPS satellite signals, including frequency assignment, modulation format, navigation data, and the generation of PRN codes. This discussion is accompanied by a description of received signal power levels, as well as their associated autocorrelation characteristics. Cross-correlation characteristics are also described. The chapter is organized as follows. First, background information on modulations that are useful for satellite radionavigation, multiplexing techniques, and general signal characteristics, including autocorrelation functions and power spectra, is provided. Section 4.3 describes the *legacy* GPS signals, defined here as those signals broadcast by the GPS satellites up through the Block IIR space vehicles (SVs). Next, an overview of the GPS navigation data modulated upon the legacy GPS signals is presented. The new civil and military signals that will be broadcast by the Block IIR-M and later satellites are discussed in Section 4.5. Finally, Section 4.6 summarizes the chapter.

Receiver signal acquisition and tracking techniques are presented in Chapter 5. Extensive details of the numerous criteria that must be addressed when designing or analyzing these processes are offered. Signal acquisition and tracking strategies for various applications are examined, including those required for high-dynamic stress and indoor environments. The processes of obtaining pseudorange, delta range, and integrated Doppler measurements are described. These observables are used in the formulation of the navigation solution.

Chapter 6 discusses the effects of various channel impairments on GPS performance. The chapter begins with a discussion of intentional (i.e., jamming) and nonintentional interference. Degradations to the various receiver functions are quantified, and mitigation strategies are presented. A tutorial on link budget computations, needed for interference analyses and useful for other GPS systems engineering purposes, is included as an appendix to the chapter. Section 6.2 addresses multipath and shadowing. Multipath and shadowing can be significant and some-times dominant contributors to PVT error. These sources of error, their effects, and mitigation techniques are discussed. The chapter concludes with a discussion on ion-ospheric scintillation. Irregularities in the ionospheric layer of the Earth's atmo-sphere can at times lead to rapid fading in received GPS signal power levels. This phenomenon, referred to as ionospheric scintillation, can lead to a GPS receiver being unable to track one or more visible satellites for short periods of time.

GPS performance in terms of accuracy, availability, integrity, and continuity is examined in Chapter 7. It is shown how the computed user position error results from range measurement errors and user/satellite relative geometry. The chapter provides a detailed explanation of each measurement error source and its contribu-tion to overall error budgets. Error budgets for both the PPS and SPS are developed and presented.

Section 7.3 discusses a variety of important concepts regarding PVT estimation, beginning with an expanded description of the role of geometry in GPS PVT accu-racy determination and a number of accuracy metrics that are commonly used. This section also describes a number of advanced PVT estimation techniques, including the use of the weighted-least-squares (WLS) algorithm, the inclusion of additional estimated parameters (beyond the user x, y, z position coordinates and clock offset), and Kalman filtering.

Sections 7.4 through 7.6 discuss, respectively, the three other important perfor-mance metrics of availability, integrity, and continuity. Detailed examination of GPS availability is conducted using the nominal GPS constellation. This includes assessing availability as a function of mask angle and number of failed satellites. In addition to providing position, velocity, and timing information, GPS needs to pro-vide timely warnings to users when the system should not be used. This capability is known as integrity. Sources of integrity anomalies are presented, followed by a dis-cussion of integrity enhancement techniques including receiver consistency checks, such as receiver autonomous integrity monitoring (RAIM) and fault detection and exclusion (FDE), as well as SBAS and GBAS.

Section 7.7 discusses measured performance. The purpose of this section is to discuss assessments of GPS accuracy, which include but are not limited to direct measurements of PVT errors. This is a particularly complex topic due to the global nature of GPS, the wide variety of receivers, and how they are employed, as well as the complex environment in which the receivers must operate. The section con-cludes with a description of the range of typical performance users can expect from a cross-section of today's receivers, given current GPS constellation performance.

DGPS is discussed in Chapter 8. This chapter describes the underlying concepts of DGPS and details a number of operational and planned DGPS systems. A discus-sion of the spatial and time correlation characteristics of GPS errors (i.e., how GPS errors vary from location to location and how they change over time) is presented first. These characteristics are extremely important to understanding DGPS, since they directly influence the performance achievable from any type of DGPS system. Next, the underlying algorithms and performance of code- and carrier-based DGPS systems are described in detail. The Radio Technical Commission for Maritime Ser-vices (RTCM) Study Committee 104's message formats have been adopted through-out the world as a standard for many maritime and commercial DGPS applications.

A discussion of RTCM message formats for both code- and carrier-based applications is presented.

Chapter 8 also contains an in depth treatment of SBAS. The discussion first starts by reviewing the SBAS requirements as put forth by the International Civil Aviation Organization (ICAO). Next, SBAS architecture and functionality are described. This is followed by descriptions of the SBAS signal structure and user receiver algorithms. Present and proposed SBAS geostationary satellite locations and coverage areas are covered.

GBAS, in particular, the U.S. FAA's Local Area Augmentation System (LAAS), requirements and system details are then presented. The chapter closes with treatment and discussion of the data and products obtained from the U.S. National Geodetic Survey's Continuously Operating Reference Station (CORS) network and the International GPS Service.

In some applications, GPS is not robust enough to provide continuous user PVT. Receiver operation will most likely be degraded in an urban canyon where satellite signals are blocked by tall buildings or when intentional or nonintentional interference is encountered. Hence, other sensors are required to augment the user's receiver. This subject area is discussed in Chapter 9. The integration of GPS and inertial sensor technology is first treated. This is usually accomplished with a Kalman filter. A description of Kalman filtering is presented, followed by various descriptions of GPS/inertial navigation system (INS) integrated architectures including ultratight (i.e., deep integration). An elementary example is provided to illustrate the processing of GPS and INS measurements in a tightly coupled configuration. Inertial aiding of carrier and code tracking loops is then described in detail. Integration of adaptive antennas is covered next. Nulling, beam steering, and space-time adaptive processing (STAP) techniques are discussed.

Next, Section 9.2 covers ITS automotive applications. This section examines integrated positioning systems found in vehicle systems, automotive electronics, and mobile consumer electronics. Various integrated architectures for land vehicles are presented. A detailed review of low-cost sensors and methods used to augment GPS solutions are presented and example systems are discussed. Map matching is a key component of a vehicle navigation system. A thorough explanation is given regarding the confidence measures, including road shape correlation used in map-matching techniques that aid in determining a vehicle's true position. A thorough treatment of sensor integration principles is provided. Tradeoffs between position domain and measurement domain integration are addressed. The key aspects of Kalman filter designs for three integrated systems—an INS with GPS, three gyros, and two accelerometers; a system with GPS, a single gyro, and an odometer; and a system with GPS and differential odometers using an antilock brake system (ABS)—are detailed.

Chapter 9 concludes with an extensive elaboration of assisted-GPS network assistance methods (i.e., enhancing GPS performance using cellular network assistance). In applications in which the GPS receiver is part of an emergency response system, waiting 30 seconds for data demodulation can seem like an eternity. As such, methods to eliminate the need to demodulate the satellite navigation data message directly and to decrease the acquisition time of the signals in weak signal environments has been the basis for all assisted GPS work. The FCC requirements for

E-911 are presented. Extensive treatment of network assistance techniques, performance, and emerging standards is presented. This includes environment characterization in terms of median signal attenuation for rural, suburban, and urban areas.

Chapter 10 is dedicated to GALILEO. An overview of the system services is presented, followed by a detailed technical description of the transmitted satellite signals. Interoperability factors are considered next. The GALILEO system architecture is put forth with discussions on constellation configuration, satellite design, and launch vehicle description. Extensive treatment of the downlink satellite signal structure, ground segment architecture, interfaces, and processing is provided. This processing discussion covers clock and ephemeris predictions as well as integrity determination. The key design drivers for integrity determination and dissemination are highlighted. In addition to providing the navigation service, GALILEO will also contribute to the international search and rescue (SAR) architecture and its associated provided services. It is planned to provide a SAR payload on each GALILEO satellite, which will be backward compatible with the present COSPAS/SARSAT system. (The COSPAS/SARSAT system is the international satellite system for search and rescue [24].)

Chapter 11 contains descriptions of the Russian GLONASS, Chinese BeiDou, and Japanese QZSS satellite systems. An overview of the Russian GLONASS system is first presented, accompanied with significant historical facts. The constellation and associated orbital plane characteristics are then discussed. This is followed by a description of the ground control/monitoring network and current and planned spacecraft designs. The GLONASS coordinate system, Earth model, and time reference are also presented. GLONASS satellite signal characteristics are discussed. System performance in terms of accuracy and availability is covered. Elaboration is provided on intended GLONASS developments that will improve all system segments. Differential services are also presented.

The BeiDou program is discussed in Section 11.2. The history of the program is briefly described. Constellation and orbit attributes are provided. These are followed by spacecraft and RDSS service descriptions. User equipment classes and types are put forth. These include general user terminals such as an emergency reporting terminal that makes emergency reports to police and a general communications user terminal used for two-way text message correspondence. All classes of user terminals provide a real-time RDSS navigation service. The system architecture is described, followed by an overview of the five different types of BeiDou services. System coverage is put forth next. Future developments including BeiDou SBAS and BeiDou-2 are discussed.

At the time of this writing, the Japanese QZSS program was under development. When completed, QZSS will provide GPS augmentation and mobile satellite communications to Japan and its neighboring regions. The constellation, orbits, and satellite types have not been selected. The program goal is to address the shortfalls in GPS visibility in urban canyons and mountainous terrain, which, the Japanese assess, is a problem in 80% of the country. Concepts of spacecraft design and proposed orbital plane design are described. This is followed by an overview of the QZSS geodetic and time reference systems. Anticipated system coverage and accuracy performance complete the chapter.

Chapter 12 is dedicated to GNSS markets and applications. As mentioned earlier, GPS has been widely accepted in all sectors of transportation, and it is expected that GALILEO will be as well. While predicted values (euros/dollars) of the market for GNSS products and services vary with the prognosticator, it is certain that this market will be large. As other satellite systems come to fruition, this market will surely grow. This chapter starts with reviews of numerous market projections and continues with the process by which a company would target a specific market segment. Differences between the civil and military markets are discussed. It is of prime importance to understand these differences when targeting a specific segment of the military market. The influence of U.S. government and EU policy on the GNSS market is examined. Civil, government, and military applications are presented. The chapter closes with a discussion on financial projections for the GNSS industry.

References

[1] U.S. Department of Defense/Department of Transportation, *1994 Federal Radionavigation Plan*, Springfield, VA: National Technical Information Service, May 1995.

[2] Parkinson, B., "A History of Satellite Navigation," *NAVIGATION: Journal of The Institute of Navigation*, Vol. 42, No. 1, Spring 1995, pp. 109–164.

[3] GPS Joint Program Office, *NAVSTAR GPS User Equipment Introduction*, Public Release Version, February 1991.

[4] NAVSTAR GPS Joint Program Office, *GPS NAVSTAR User's Overview*, YEE-82-009D, GPS JPO, March 1991.

[5] McDonald, K., "Navigation Satellite Systems—A Perspective," *Proc. 1st Int. Symposium Real Time Differential Applications of the Global Positioning System*, Vol. 1, Braunschweig, Federal Republic of Germany, 1991, pp. 20–35.

[6] "Global View," *GPS World Magazine*, February 2002, p. 10.

[7] U.S. Department of Defense/Department of Transportation, *1999 Federal Radionavigation Plan*, Springfield, VA: National Technical Information Service, December 1999.

[8] https://gps.losangeles.af.mil/gpslibrary/FAQ.asp.

[9] Doucet, K., and Y. Georgiadou, "The Issue of Selective Availability," *GPS World Magazine*, September–October 1990, pp. 53–56.

[10] U.S. Department of Defense, *Standard Positioning System Performance Specification*, October 2001.

[11] U.S. Government Executive Branch, Vice Presidential Initiative, January 25, 1999.

[12] European Union Fact Sheet, "EU-US Co-Operation on Satellite Navigation Systems Agreement Between Galileo and the Global Positioning System (GPS)," June 2004.

[13] Federal Space Agency for the Russian Federation, "GLONASS: Status and Perspectives," *Munich Satellite Navigation Summit 2005*, Munich, Germany, March 9, 2005.

[14] "CTC—Civilian Service Provider BeiDou Navigation System" and associated Web sites in English, China Top Communications Web site, http://www.chinatopcom.com/english/gsii.htm, September 8, 2003.

[15] "BDStar Navigation—BeiDou Application the Omni-Directional Service Business" and associated Web sites in Chinese, BDStar Navigation Web site, http://www.navchina.com/pinpai/beidou.asp.

[16] Onidi, O., et al., "Directions 2004," *GPS World*, December 2003, p. 16.

[17] "Business in Satellite Navigation," *GALILEO Joint Undertaking*, Brussels, Belgium, 2003.

[18] http://www.geocaching.com.

[19]   Enderle, W., "Applications of GPS for Satellites and Sounding Rockets," *ASRI, 11th Annual Conference*, Sydney, Australia, December 1–3, 2001.

[20]   http://www.gfz-potsdam.de/pb1/op/champ/index_CHAMP.html.

[21]   http://topex-www.jpl.nasa.gov/technology/instrument-gps.html.

[22]   Gomez, S., "GPS on the International Space Station and Crew Return Vehicle," *GPS World*, June 2002, pp. 12–20.

[23]   "EGNOS TRAN Final Presentation," *GNSS Final Presentations ESTEC*, the Netherlands, April 21, 2004.

[24]   http://www.cospas-sarsat.org

CHAPTER 2

Fundamentals of Satellite Navigation

Elliott D. Kaplan and Joseph L. Leva
The MITRE Corporation

Dennis Milbert
NOAA (retired)

Mike S. Pavloff
Raytheon Company

2.1 Concept of Ranging Using TOA Measurements

GPS utilizes the concept of TOA ranging to determine user position. This concept entails measuring the time it takes for a signal transmitted by an emitter (e.g., foghorn, radiobeacon, or satellite) at a known location to reach a user receiver.

This time interval, referred to as the signal propagation time, is then multiplied by the speed of the signal (e.g., speed of sound or speed of light) to obtain the emitter-to-receiver distance. By measuring the propagation time of the signal broadcast from multiple emitters (i.e., navigation aids) at known locations, the receiver can determine its position. An example of two-dimensional positioning is provided next.

2.1.1 Two-Dimensional Position Determination

Consider the case of a mariner at sea determining his or her vessel's position from a foghorn. (This introductory example was originally presented in [1] and is contained herein because it provides an excellent overview of TOA position determination concepts.) Assume that the vessel is equipped with an accurate clock and the mariner has an approximate knowledge of the vessel's position. Also, assume that the foghorn whistle is sounded precisely on the minute mark and that the vessel's clock is synchronized to the foghorn clock. The mariner notes the elapsed time from the minute mark until the foghorn whistle is heard. The foghorn whistle propagation time is the time it took for the foghorn whistle to leave the foghorn and travel to the mariner's ear. This propagation time multiplied by the speed of sound (approximately 335 m/s) is the distance from the foghorn to the mariner. If the foghorn signal took 5 seconds to reach the mariner's ear, then the distance to the foghorn is 1,675m. Let this distance be denoted as $R1$. Thus, with only one measurement, the mariner knows that the vessel is somewhere on a circle with radius $R1$ centered about the foghorn, which is denoted as Foghorn 1 in Figure 2.1.

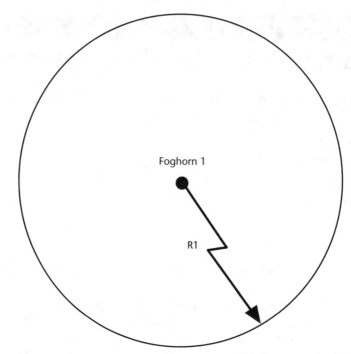

Figure 2.1   Range determination from a single source. (*After:* [1].)

Hypothetically, if the mariner simultaneously measured the range from a second foghorn in the same way, the vessel would be at range $R1$ from Foghorn 1 and range $R2$ from Foghorn 2, as shown in Figure 2.2. It is assumed that the foghorn transmissions are synchronized to a common time base and the mariner has knowledge of both foghorn whistle transmission times. Therefore, the vessel relative to the foghorns is at one of the intersections of the range circles. Since it was assumed that the mariner has approximate knowledge of the vessel's position, the unlikely fix can be discarded. Resolving the ambiguity can also be achieved by making a range measurement to a third foghorn, as shown in Figure 2.3.

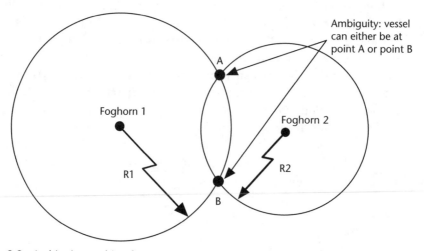

Figure 2.2   Ambiguity resulting from measurements to two sources. (*After:* [1].)

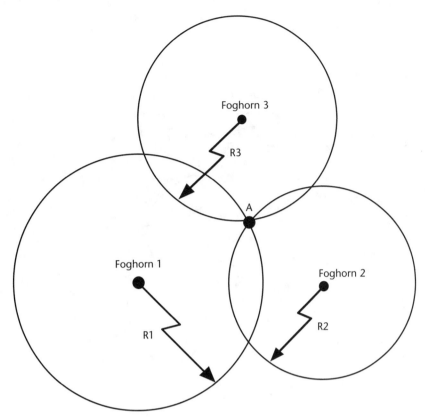

Figure 2.3 Position ambiguity removal by additional measurement. (*After:* [1].)

2.1.1.1 Common Clock Offset and Compensation

This development assumed that the vessel's clock was precisely synchronized with the foghorn time base. However, this might not be the case. Let us presume that the vessel's clock is advanced with respect to the foghorn time base by 1 second. That is, the vessel's clock believes the minute mark is occurring 1 second earlier. The propagation intervals measured by the mariner will be larger by 1 second due to the offset. The timing offsets are the same for each measurement (i.e., the offsets are common) because the same incorrect time base is being used for each measurement. The timing offset equates to a range error of 335m and is denoted as ε in Figure 2.4. The separation of intersections C, D, and E from the true vessel position, A, is a function of the vessel's clock offset. If the offset could be removed or compensated for, the range circles would then intersect at point A.

2.1.1.2 Effect of Independent Measurement Errors on Position Certainty

If this hypothetical scenario were realized, the TOA measurements would not be perfect due to errors from atmospheric effects, foghorn clock offset from the foghorn time base, and interfering sounds. Unlike the vessel's clock offset condition cited earlier, these errors would be generally independent and not common to all measurements. They would affect each measurement in a unique manner and result in inaccurate distance computations. Figure 2.5 shows the effect of independent

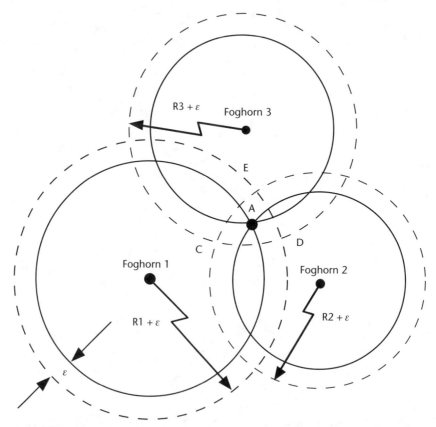

Figure 2.4 Effect of receiver clock offset on TOA measurements. (*After:* [1].)

errors (i.e., $\varepsilon_1, \varepsilon_2,$ and ε_3) on position determination assuming foghorn timebase/mariner clock synchronization. Instead of the three range circles intersecting at a single point, the vessel location is somewhere within the triangular error space.

2.1.2 Principle of Position Determination Via Satellite-Generated Ranging Signals

GPS employs TOA ranging for user position determination. By making TOA measurements to multiple satellites, three-dimensional positioning is achieved. We will observe that this technique is analogous to the preceding foghorn example; however, satellite ranging signals travel at the speed of light, which is approximately 3×10^8 m/s. It is assumed that the satellite ephemerides are accurate (i.e., the satellite locations are precisely known).

2.1.2.1 Three-Dimensional Position Location Via Intersection of Multiple Spheres

Assume that there is a single satellite transmitting a ranging signal. A clock onboard the satellite controls the timing of the ranging signal broadcast. This clock and others onboard each of the satellites within the constellation are effectively synchronized to an internal system time scale denoted as GPS system time (herein referred to as system time). The user's receiver also contains a clock that (for the moment) we assume

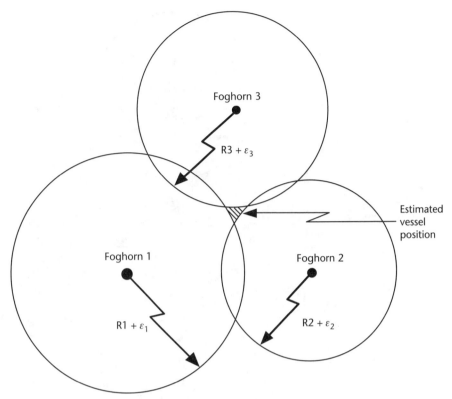

Figure 2.5   Effect of independent measurement errors on position certainty.

to be synchronized to system time. Timing information is embedded within the satellite ranging signal that enables the receiver to calculate when the signal left the satellite based on the satellite clock time. This is discussed in more detail in Section 2.4.1. By noting the time when the signal was received, the satellite-to-user propagation time can be computed. The product of the satellite-to-user propagation time and the speed of light yields the satellite-to-user range, R. As a result of this measurement process, the user would be located somewhere on the surface of a sphere centered about the satellite, as shown in Figure 2.6(a). If a measurement were simultaneously made using the ranging signal of a second satellite, the user would also be located on the surface of a second sphere that is concentric about the second satellite. Thus, the user would then be somewhere on the surface of both spheres, which could be either on the perimeter of the shaded circle in Figure 2.6(b) that denotes the plane of intersection of these spheres or at a single point tangent to both spheres (i.e., where the spheres just touch). This latter case could only occur if the user were collinear with the satellites, which is not the typical case. The plane of intersection is perpendicular to a line connecting the satellites, as shown in Figure 2.6(c).

Repeating the measurement process using a third satellite, the user is at the intersection of the perimeter of the circle and the surface of the third sphere. This third sphere intersects the shaded circle perimeter at two points; however, only one of the points is the correct user position, as shown in Figure 2.6(d). A view of the intersection is shown in Figure 2.6(e). It can be observed that the candidate locations are mirror images of one another with respect to the plane of the satellites. For

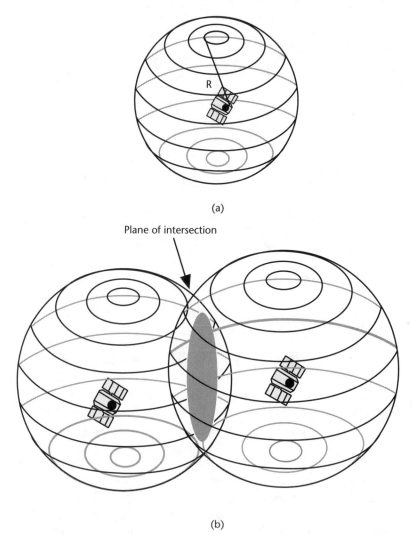

(a)

Plane of intersection

(b)

Figure 2.6   (a) User located on surface of sphere. (b) User located on perimeter of shaded circle. (*Source:* [2]. Reprinted with permission.) (c) Plane of intersection. (d) User located at one of two points on shaded circle. (*Source:* [2]. Reprinted with permission.) (e) User located at one of two points on circle perimeter.

a user on the Earth's surface, it is apparent that the lower point will be the true position. However, users that are above the Earth's surface may employ measurements from satellites at negative elevation angles. This complicates the determination of an unambiguous solution. Airborne/spaceborne receiver solutions may be above or below the plane containing the satellites, and it may not be clear which point to select unless the user has ancillary information.

2.2   Reference Coordinate Systems

To formulate the mathematics of the satellite navigation problem, it is necessary to choose a reference coordinate system in which the states of both the satellite and the

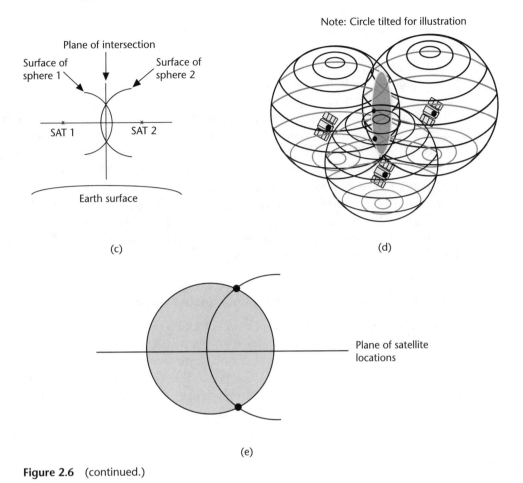

Note: Circle tilted for illustration

Plane of intersection

Surface of sphere 1

Surface of sphere 2

SAT 1   SAT 2

Earth surface

(c)

(d)

Plane of satellite locations

(e)

Figure 2.6 (continued.)

receiver can be represented. In this formulation, it is typical to describe satellite and receiver states in terms of position and velocity vectors measured in a Cartesian coordinate system. Two principal Cartesian coordinate systems are inertial and rotating systems. In this section, an overview is provided of the coordinate systems used for GPS.

2.2.1 Earth-Centered Inertial Coordinate System

For the purposes of measuring and determining the orbits of the GPS satellites, it is convenient to use an Earth-centered inertial (ECI) coordinate system, in which the origin is at the center of the mass of the Earth and whose axes are pointing in fixed directions with respect to the stars. A GPS satellite obeys Newton's laws of motion and gravitation in an ECI coordinate system. In typical ECI coordinate systems, the xy-plane is taken to coincide with the Earth's equatorial plane, the $+x$-axis is permanently fixed in a particular direction relative to the celestial sphere, the $+z$-axis is taken normal to the xy-plane in the direction of the north pole, and the $+y$-axis is chosen so as to form a right-handed coordinate system. Determination and subsequent prediction of the GPS satellite orbits are carried out in an ECI coordinate system.

One subtlety in the definition of an ECI coordinate system arises due to irregularities in the Earth's motion. The Earth's shape is oblate, and due largely to the gravitational pull of the Sun and the Moon on the Earth's equatorial bulge, the equatorial plane moves with respect to the celestial sphere. Because the x-axis is defined relative to the celestial sphere and the z-axis is defined relative to the equatorial plane, the irregularities in the Earth's motion would cause the ECI frame as defined earlier not to be truly inertial. The solution to this problem is to define the orientation of the axes at a particular instant in time, or *epoch*. The GPS ECI coordinate system uses the orientation of the equatorial plane at 1200 hours UTC (USNO) on January 1, 2000, denoted as the J2000 system. The $+x$-axis is taken to point from the center of the mass of the Earth to the direction of vernal equinox, and the y- and z-axes are defined as described previously, all at the aforementioned epoch. Since the orientation of the axes remains fixed, the ECI coordinate system defined in this way can be considered inertial for GPS purposes.

2.2.2 Earth-Centered Earth-Fixed Coordinate System

For the purpose of computing the position of a GPS receiver, it is more convenient to use a coordinate system that rotates with the Earth, known as an Earth-centered Earth-fixed (ECEF) system. In such a coordinate system, it is easier to compute the latitude, longitude, and height parameters that the receiver displays. As with the ECI coordinate system, the ECEF coordinate system used for GPS has its xy-plane coincident with the Earth's equatorial plane. However, in the ECEF system, the $+x$-axis points in the direction of 0° longitude, and the $+y$-axis points in the direction of 90°E longitude. The x-, y-, and z-axes therefore rotate with the Earth and no longer describe fixed directions in inertial space. In this ECEF system, the z-axis is chosen to be normal to the equatorial plane in the direction of the geographical North Pole (i.e., where the lines of longitude meet in the northern hemisphere), thereby completing the right-handed coordinate system.

GPS orbit computation software includes the transformations between the ECI and the ECEF coordinate systems. Such transformations are accomplished by the application of rotation matrices to the satellite position and velocity vectors in the ECI coordinate system, as described, for example, in [3]. The broadcast orbit computation procedure described in [4] and in Section 2.3 generates satellite position and velocity in the ECEF frame. Precise orbits from numerous computation centers also express GPS position and velocity in ECEF. Thus, with one exception, we may proceed to formulate the GPS navigation problem in the ECEF system without discussing the details of the orbit determination or the transformation to the ECEF system. This exception is consideration of the Sagnac effect on signal propagation in the rotating (noninertial) ECEF frame. (Section 7.2.3 contains an explanation of the Sagnac effect.)

As a result of the GPS navigation computation process, the Cartesian coordinates (x_u, y_u, z_u) of the user's receiver are computed in the ECEF system, as described in Section 2.4.2. It is typical to transform these Cartesian coordinates to latitude, longitude, and height of the receiver. In order to carry out this transformation, it is necessary to have a physical model describing the Earth.

2.2.3   World Geodetic System

The standard physical model of the Earth used for GPS applications is the DOD's World Geodetic System 1984 (WGS 84) [5]. One part of WGS 84 is a detailed model of the Earth's gravitational irregularities. Such information is necessary to derive accurate satellite ephemeris information; however, we are concerned here with estimating the latitude, longitude, and height of a GPS receiver. For this purpose, WGS 84 provides an ellipsoidal model of the Earth's shape, as shown in Figure 2.7. In this model, cross-sections of the Earth parallel to the equatorial plane are circular. The equatorial cross-section of the Earth has radius 6,378.137 km, which is the mean equatorial radius of the Earth. In the WGS 84 Earth model, cross-sections of the Earth normal to the equatorial plane are ellipsoidal. In an ellipsoidal cross-section containing the z-axis, the major axis coincides with the equatorial diameter of the Earth. Therefore, the semimajor axis, a, has the same value as the mean equatorial radius given previously. The minor axis of the ellipsoidal cross-section shown in Figure 2.7 corresponds to the polar diameter of the Earth, and the semiminor axis, b, in WGS 84 is taken to be 6,356.7523142 km. Thus, the eccentricity of the Earth ellipsoid, e, can be determined by

$$e = \sqrt{1 - \frac{b^2}{a^2}}$$

WGS 84 takes $e^2 = 0.00669437999014$. It should be noted that this figure is extremely close, but not identical, to the Geodetic Reference System 1980 (GRS 80) ellipsoid quantity of $e^2 = 0.00669438002290$. These two ellipsoids differ only by 0.1 mm in the semiminor axis, b.

Another parameter sometimes used to characterize the reference ellipsoid is the second eccentricity, e', which is defined as follows:

$$e' = \sqrt{\frac{a^2}{b^2} - 1} = \frac{a}{b}e$$

WGS 84 takes $e'^2 = 0.00673949674228$.

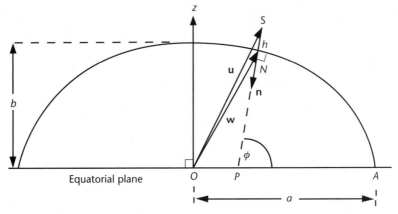

Figure 2.7   Ellipsoidal model of Earth (cross-section normal to equatorial plane).

2.2.3.1   Determination of User Geodetic Coordinates: Latitude, Longitude, and Height

The ECEF coordinate system is affixed to the WGS 84 reference ellipsoid, as shown in Figure 2.7, with the point O corresponding to the center of the Earth. We can now define the parameters of latitude, longitude, and height with respect to the reference ellipsoid. When defined in this manner, these parameters are called *geodetic*. Given a user receiver's position vector of $\mathbf{u} = (x_u, y_u, z_u)$ in the ECEF system, we can compute the geodetic longitude (λ) as the angle between the user and the x-axis, measured in the xy-plane

$$\lambda = \begin{cases} \arctan\left(\dfrac{y_u}{x_u}\right), & x_u \geq 0 \\[2ex] 180° + \arctan\left(\dfrac{y_u}{x_u}\right), & x_u < 0 \quad \text{and} \quad y_u \geq 0 \\[2ex] -180° + \arctan\left(\dfrac{y_u}{x_u}\right), & x_u < 0 \quad \text{and} \quad y_u < 0 \end{cases} \tag{2.1}$$

In (2.1), negative angles correspond to degrees west longitude. The geodetic parameters of latitude (φ) and height (h) are defined in terms of the ellipsoid normal at the user's receiver. The ellipsoid normal is depicted by the unit vector $\mathbf{n}$ in Figure 2.7. Notice that unless the user is on the poles or the equator, the ellipsoid normal does not point exactly toward the center of the Earth. A GPS receiver computes height relative to the WGS 84 ellipsoid. However, the height above sea level given on a map can be quite different from GPS-derived height due to the difference, in some places, between the WGS 84 ellipsoid and the geoid (local mean sea level). In the horizontal plane, differences between the local datum, such as North American Datum 1983 (NAD 83) and European Datum 1950 (ED 50), and WGS 84 can also be significant.

Geodetic height is simply the minimum distance between the user (at the endpoint of the vector $\mathbf{u}$) and the reference ellipsoid. Notice that the direction of minimum distance from the user to the surface of the reference ellipsoid will be in the direction of the vector $\mathbf{n}$. Geodetic latitude, φ, is the angle between the ellipsoid normal vector $\mathbf{n}$ and the projection of $\mathbf{n}$ into the equatorial (xy) plane. Conventionally, φ is taken to be positive if $z_u > 0$ (i.e., if the user is in the northern hemisphere), and φ is taken to be negative if $z_u < 0$. With respect to Figure 2.7, geodetic latitude is the angle NPA, where N is the closest point on the reference ellipsoid to the user, P is the point where a line in the direction of $\mathbf{n}$ intersects the equatorial plane, and A is the closest point on the equator to P. Numerous solutions, both closed-form and iterative, have been devised for the computation of geodetic curvilinear coordinates (φ, λ, h) from Cartesian coordinates (x, y, z). A popular and highly convergent iterative method by Bowring [6] is described in Table 2.1. For the computations shown in Table 2.1, a, b, e^2, and e'^2 are the geodetic parameters described previously. Note that the use of "N" in Table 2.1 follows Bowring [6] and does not refer to geoid height described in Section 2.2.4.

Table 2.1 Determination of Geodetic Height and Latitude in Terms of ECEF Parameters

$$p = \sqrt{x^2 + y^2}$$

$$\tan u = \left(\frac{z}{p}\right)\left(\frac{a}{b}\right)$$

Iteration Loop

$$\cos^2 u = \frac{1}{1 + \tan^2 u}$$

$$\sin^2 u = 1 - \cos^2 u$$

$$\tan\varphi = \frac{z + e'^2 b \sin^3 u}{p - e^2 a \cos^3 u}$$

$$\tan u = \left(\frac{b}{a}\right)\tan\varphi$$

until $\tan u$ converges, then

$$N = \frac{a}{\sqrt{1 - e^2 \sin^2 \phi}}$$

$$h = \frac{p}{\cos\phi} - N \qquad \varphi \neq \pm 90°$$

otherwise

$$h = \frac{z}{\sin\phi} - N + e^2 N \qquad \varphi \neq 0$$

2.2.3.2 Conversion from Geodetic Coordinates to Cartesian Coordinates in ECEF Frame

For completeness, equations for transforming from geodetic coordinates back to Cartesian coordinates in the ECEF system are provided later. Given the geodetic parameters λ, φ, and h, we can compute $\mathbf{u} = (x_u, y_u, z_u)$ in closed form as follows:

$$\mathbf{u} = \begin{bmatrix} \dfrac{a\cos\lambda}{\sqrt{1 + \left(1 - e^2\right)\tan^2\phi}} + h\cos\lambda\cos\phi \\[2em] \dfrac{a\sin\lambda}{\sqrt{1 + \left(1 - e^2\right)\tan^2\phi}} + h\sin\lambda\cos\phi \\[2em] \dfrac{a\left(1 - e^2\right)\sin\phi}{\sqrt{1 - e^2\sin^2\phi}} + h\sin\phi \end{bmatrix}$$

2.2.3.3 WGS 84 Reference Frame Relationships

There have been four realizations of WGS 84 as of this edition. The original WGS 84 was used for the broadcast GPS orbit beginning January 23, 1987. WGS 84 (G730), where the "G730" denotes GPS week, was used beginning on June 29, 1994. WGS 84 (G873) started on January 29, 1997 [5]. And, the current frame, WGS 84 (G1150), was introduced on January 20, 2002. These reference frame realizations have brought the WGS 84 into extremely close coincidence with the International Terrestrial Reference Frame (ITRF), administered by the International Association of Geodesy. For example, the WGS 84 (G1150) matches the ITRF2000 frame to better than 1 cm, one sigma [7].

The fact that there have been four realizations of WGS 84 has led to some confusion regarding the relationship between WGS 84 and other reference frames. In particular, care must be used when interpreting older references. For example, the original WGS 84 and NAD 83 were made coincident [8], leading to an assertion that WGS 84 and NAD 83 were identical. However, as stated above, WGS 84 (G1150) is coincident with ITRF2000. It is known that NAD 83 is offset from ITRF2000 by about 2.2m. Hence, the NAD 83 reference frame and the current realization of WGS 84 can no longer be considered identical.

2.2.4 Height Coordinates and the Geoid

The ellipsoid height, h, is the height of a point, P, above the surface of the ellipsoid, E, as described in Section 2.2.3.1. This corresponds to the directed line segment EP in Figure 2.8, where a positive sign denotes point P further from the center of the Earth than point E. Note that P need not be on the surface of the Earth, but could be above or below the Earth's surface. As discussed in the previous sections, ellipsoid height is easily computed from Cartesian ECEF coordinates.

Historically, heights have not been measured relative to the ellipsoid but, instead, relative to a surface called the *geoid*. The geoid is that surface of constant geopotential, $W = W_0$, which corresponds to global mean sea level in a least squares sense. Heights measured relative to the geoid are called *orthometric* heights, or, less formally, heights above mean sea level. Orthometric heights are important, because these are the type of height found on innumerable topographic maps and in paper and digital data sets.

The geoid height, N, is the height of a point, G, above the ellipsoid, E. This corresponds to the directed line segment EG in Figure 2.8, where positive sign denotes point G further from the center of the Earth than point E. And, the orthometric height, H, is the height of a point P, above the geoid, G. Hence, we can immediately write the equation

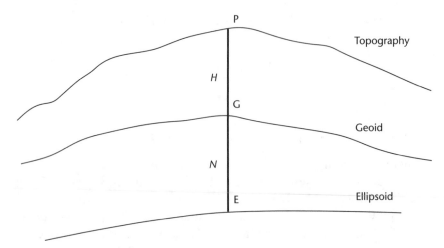

Figure 2.8 Relationships between topography, geoid, and ellipsoid.

$$h = H + N \qquad\qquad (2.2)$$

Note that Figure 2.8 is illustrative and that G and/or P may be below point E. Similarly, any or all terms of (2.2) may be positive or negative. For example, in the conterminous United States, the geoid height, N, is negative.

The geoid is a complex surface, with undulations that reflect topographic, bathymetric (i.e., measurements derived from bodies of water), and geologic density variations of the Earth. The magnitude of geoid height can be several tens of meters. Geoid height ranges from a low of about −105m at the southern tip of India to a high of about +85m at New Guinea. Thus, for many applications, the geoid is not a negligible quantity, and one must avoid mistaking an orthometric height for an ellipsoidal height.

In contrast to the ellipsoid, the geoid is a natural feature of the Earth. Like topography, there is no simple equation to describe the spatial variation of geoid height. Geoid height is modeled and tabulated by several geodetic agencies. Global geoid height models are represented by sets of spherical harmonic coefficients and, also, by regular grids of geoid height values. Regional geoid height models can span large areas, such as the entire conterminous United States, and are invariably expressed as regular grids. Recent global models typically contain harmonic coefficients complete to degree and order 360. As such, their resolution is 30 arc-minutes, and their accuracy is limited by truncation error. Regional models, by contrast, are computed to a much higher resolution. One arc-minute resolution is not uncommon, and truncation error is seldom encountered.

The best-known global geoid model is the National Geospatial-Intelligence Agency/National Aeronautical and Space Administration (NGA/NASA) WGS 84 EGM96 Geopotential Model [9], hereafter referred to as EGM96. This product is a set of coefficients complete to degree and order 360, a companion set of correction coefficients needed to compute geoid height over land, and a geoid height grid posted at 15 arc-minute spacing. EGM96 replaces an earlier global model denoted WGS 84 (180,180), which is complete only up to degree and order 180. Most of that WGS 84 coefficient set was originally classified in 1985, and only coefficients through degree and order 18 were released. Hence, the first public distributions of WGS 84 geoid height only had a 10 arc-degree resolution and suffered many meters of truncation error. Therefore, historical references to "WGS 84 geoid" values must be used with caution.

Within the conterminous United States, the current high-resolution geoid height grid is GEOID03, developed by the National Geodetic Survey, NOAA. This product is a grid of geoid heights, at 1 arc-minute resolution, and has an accuracy of 1 cm, one sigma [10]. Development is underway on a future geoid model series that will cover all U.S. states and territories.

When height accuracy requirements approach the meter level, then one must also become aware of the datum differences between height coordinates. For example, as discussed in Section 2.2.3.3, the origin of the NAD 83 reference frame is offset about 2.2m from the center of the Earth, causing about 0.5-m to 1.5-m differences in ellipsoidal heights in the conterminous United States. Current estimates place the origin of the U.S. orthometric height datum, NAVD 88, about 30 cm to 50 cm below the EGM96 reference geopotential surface. Because of these two datum offsets, GEOID03 was constructed to accommodate these origin differences and directly convert between NAD 83 and NAVD 88, rather than express a region of an idealized global geoid. In addition, offsets of 0.5m or more in national height datums are common, as tabulated in [11]. For these reasons, (2.2) is valid as a conceptual model but may be problematic in actual precision applications. Detailed treatment of height systems is beyond the scope of this text. However, more information may be found in [12, 13].

2.3   Fundamentals of Satellite Orbits

2.3.1   Orbital Mechanics

As described in Section 2.1, a GPS user needs accurate information about the positions of the GPS satellites in order to determine his or her position. Therefore, it is important to understand how the GPS orbits are characterized. We begin by describing the forces acting on a satellite, the most significant of which is the Earth's gravitation. If the Earth were perfectly spherical and of uniform density, then the Earth's gravitation would behave as if the Earth were a point mass. Let an object of mass m be located at position vector $\mathbf{r}$ in an ECI coordinate system. If G is the universal gravitational constant, M is the mass of the Earth, and the Earth's gravitation acts as a point mass, then, according to Newton's laws, the force, $\mathbf{F}$, acting on the object would be given by

$$\mathbf{F} = m\mathbf{a} = -G\frac{mM}{r^3}\mathbf{r} \tag{2.3}$$

where $\mathbf{a}$ is the acceleration of the object, and $r = |\mathbf{r}|$. The minus sign on the right-hand side of (2.3) results from the fact that gravitational forces are always attractive. Since acceleration is the second time derivative of position, (2.3) can be rewritten as follows:

$$\frac{d^2\mathbf{r}}{dt^2} = -\frac{\mu}{r^3}\mathbf{r} \tag{2.4}$$

where μ is the product of the universal gravitation constant and the mass of the Earth. In WGS 84, the original value of μ was 3986005×10^8 m³/s². Subsequently, the value of μ in WGS 84 was updated to 3986004.418×10^8 m³/s², but to maintain backward compatibility of the GPS navigation message, the original value of 3986005×10^8 m³/s² is still used. Equation (2.4) is the expression of so-called two-body or Keplerian satellite motion, in which the only force acting on the satellite is the point-mass Earth. Because the Earth is not spherical and has an uneven distribution of mass, (2.4) does not model the true acceleration due to the Earth's gravitation. If the function V measures the true gravitational potential of the Earth at an arbitrary point in space, then (2.4) may be rewritten as follows:

$$\frac{d^2\mathbf{r}}{dt^2} = \nabla V \tag{2.5}$$

where ∇ is the gradient operator, defined as follows:

$$\nabla V \underset{def}{=} \begin{bmatrix} \dfrac{\partial V}{\partial x} \\[6pt] \dfrac{\partial V}{\partial y} \\[6pt] \dfrac{\partial V}{\partial z} \end{bmatrix}$$

Notice that for two-body motion, $V = \mu/r$:

$$\nabla(\mu/r) = \mu \begin{bmatrix} \dfrac{\partial}{\partial x}\left(r^{-1}\right) \\[6pt] \dfrac{\partial}{\partial y}\left(r^{-1}\right) \\[6pt] \dfrac{\partial}{\partial z}\left(r^{-1}\right) \end{bmatrix} = -\dfrac{\mu}{r^2} \begin{bmatrix} \dfrac{\partial}{\partial x}\left(x^2 + y^2 + z^2\right)^{\frac{1}{2}} \\[6pt] \dfrac{\partial}{\partial y}\left(x^2 + y^2 + z^2\right)^{\frac{1}{2}} \\[6pt] \dfrac{\partial}{\partial z}\left(x^2 + y^2 + z^2\right)^{\frac{1}{2}} \end{bmatrix}$$

$$= -\dfrac{\mu}{2r^2}\left(x^2 + y^2 + z^2\right)^{-\frac{1}{2}} \begin{bmatrix} 2x \\ 2y \\ 2z \end{bmatrix} = -\dfrac{\mu}{r^3} \begin{bmatrix} x \\ y \\ z \end{bmatrix} = -\dfrac{\mu}{r^3}\mathbf{r}$$

Therefore, with $V = \mu/r$, (2.5) is equivalent to (2.4) for two-body motion. In the case of true satellite motion, the Earth's gravitational potential is modeled by a spherical harmonic series. In such a representation, the gravitational potential at a point P is defined in terms of the point's spherical coordinates (r, ϕ', α) as follows:

$$V = \dfrac{\mu}{r}\left[1 + \sum_{l=2}^{\infty}\sum_{m=0}^{l}\left(\dfrac{a}{r}\right)^l P_{lm}(\sin\phi')(C_{lm}\cos m\alpha + S_{lm}\sin m\alpha)\right] \qquad (2.6)$$

where:

r = distance of P from the origin

ϕ' = geocentric latitude of P (i.e., angle between $\mathbf{r}$ and the xy-plane)

α = right ascension of P

a = mean equatorial radius of the Earth (6,378.137 km in WGS 84)

P_{lm} = associated Legendre function

C_{lm} = spherical harmonic cosine coefficient of degree l and order m

S_{lm} = spherical harmonic sine coefficient of degree l and order m

Notice that the first term of (2.6) is the two-body potential function. Also notice that geocentric latitude in (2.6) is different from geodetic latitude defined in Section 2.2. WGS 84 not only defines a reference coordinate frame and ellipsoid, but it also has a companion geopotential model called WGS 84 EGM96. This model provides the spherical harmonic coefficients C_{lm} and S_{lm} through 360th degree and order. For GPS orbit computations, however, coefficients are used only through degree and order 12.

Additional forces acting on satellites include the so-called third-body gravitation from the Sun and Moon. Modeling third-body gravitation requires knowledge of the solar and lunar positions in the ECI coordinate system as a function of time. Polynomial functions of time are generally used to provide the orbital elements of the Sun and Moon as functions of time. A number of alternative sources and formulations exist for such polynomials with respect to various coordinate systems (for example, see [14]). Another force acting on satellites is solar radiation pressure, which results from momentum transfer from solar photons to a satellite. Solar radiation pressure is a function of the Sun's position, the projected area of the satellite in the plane normal to the solar line of sight, and the mass and reflectivity of the satellite. There are additional forces acting on a satellite, including outgassing (i.e., the slow release of gases trapped in the structure of a satellite), the Earth's tidal variations, and orbital maneuvers. To model a satellite's orbit very accurately, all of these perturbations to the Earth's gravitational field must be modeled. For the purposes of this text, we will collect all of these perturbing accelerations in a term $\mathbf{a}_d$, so that the equations of motion can be written as

$$\frac{d^2\mathbf{r}}{dt^2} = \nabla V + \mathbf{a}_d \tag{2.7}$$

There are various methods of representing the orbital parameters of a satellite. One obvious representation is to define a satellite's position vector, $\mathbf{r}_0 = \mathbf{r}(t_0)$, and velocity vector, $\mathbf{v}_0 = \mathbf{v}(t_0)$, at some reference time, t_0. Given these initial conditions, we could solve the equations of motion (2.7) for the position vector $\mathbf{r}(t)$ and the velocity vector $\mathbf{v}(t)$ at any other time t. Only the two-body equation of motion (2.4) has an analytical solution, and even in that simplified case, the solution cannot be accomplished entirely in closed form. The computation of orbital parameters from the fully perturbed equations of motion (2.7) requires numerical integration.

Although many applications, including GPS, require the accuracy provided by the fully perturbed equations of motion, orbital parameters are often defined in terms of the solution to the two-body problem. It can be shown that there are six constants of integration, or *integrals*, for the equation of two-body motion, (2.4). Given six integrals of motion and an initial time, one can find the position and velocity vectors of a satellite on a two-body orbit at any point in time from the initial conditions.

In the case of the fully perturbed equation of motion, (2.7), it is still possible to characterize the orbit in terms of the six integrals of two-body motion, but those six parameters will no longer be constant. A reference time is associated with two-body orbital parameters used to characterize the orbit of a satellite moving under the influence of perturbing forces. At the exact reference time, the reference orbital parameters will describe the true position and velocity vectors of the satellite, but as time progresses beyond (or before) the reference time, the true position and velocity of the satellite will increasingly deviate from the position and velocity described by the six two-body integrals or parameters. This is the approach taken in formulating the GPS ephemeris message, which includes not only six integrals of two-body motion, but also the time of their applicability (reference time) and a characterization of how those parameters change over time. With this information, a GPS receiver can compute the "corrected" integrals of motion for a GPS satellite at the time when it is solving the navigation problem. From the corrected integrals, the position vector of the satellite can be computed, as we will show. First, we present the definitions of the six integrals of two-body motion used in the GPS system.

There are many possible formulations of the solution to the two-body problem, and GPS adopts the notation of the classical solution, which uses a particular set of six integrals of motion known as the Keplerian orbital elements. These Keplerian elements depend on the fact that for any initial conditions $\mathbf{r}_0$ and $\mathbf{v}_0$ at time t_0, the solution to (2.4) (i.e., the orbit), will be a planar conic section. The first three Keplerian orbital elements, illustrated in Figure 2.9, define the shape of the orbit. Figure 2.9 shows an elliptical orbit that has semimajor axis a and eccentricity e. (Hyperbolic and parabolic trajectories are possible but not relevant for Earth-orbiting satellites, such as in GPS.) In Figure 2.9, the elliptical orbit has a focus at point F, which corresponds to the center of the mass of the Earth (and hence the origin of an ECI or ECEF coordinate system). The time t_0 at which the satellite is at some reference point A in its orbit is known as the *epoch*. As part of the GPS ephemeris message, where the epoch corresponds to the time at which the Keplerian elements define the actual location of the satellite, the epoch is called *reference time of ephemeris*. The point, P, where the satellite is closest to the center of the Earth is known as perigee, and the time at which the satellite passes perigee, τ, is another Keplerian orbital parameter. In summary, the three Keplerian orbital elements that define the shape of the elliptical orbit and time relative to perigee are as follows:

a = semimajor axis of the ellipse

e = eccentricity of the ellipse

τ = time of perigee passage

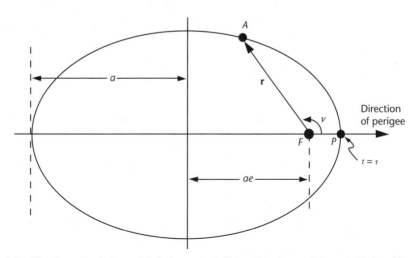

Figure 2.9   The three Keplerian orbital elements defining the shape of the satellite's orbit.

Although the Keplerian integrals of two-body motion use time of perigee passage as one of the constants of motion, an equivalent parameter used by the GPS system is known as the mean anomaly at epoch. Mean anomaly is an angle that is related to the true anomaly at epoch, which is illustrated in Figure 2.9 as the angle v. After defining true anomaly precisely, the transformation to mean anomaly and the demonstration of equivalence to time of perigee passage will be shown.

True anomaly is the angle in the orbital plane measured counterclockwise from the direction of perigee to the satellite. In Figure 2.9, the true anomaly at epoch is $v = \angle PFA$. From Kepler's laws of two-body motion, it is known that true anomaly does not vary linearly in time for noncircular orbits. Because it is desirable to define a parameter that does vary linearly in time, two definitions are made that transform the true anomaly to the mean anomaly, which is linear in time. The first transformation produces the eccentric anomaly, which is illustrated in Figure 2.10 with the true anomaly. Geometrically, the eccentric anomaly is constructed from the true anomaly first by circumscribing a circle around the elliptical orbit. Next, a perpendicular is dropped from the point A on the orbit to the major axis of the orbit, and this perpendicular is extended upward until it intersects the circumscribed circle at point B. The eccentric anomaly is the angle measured at the center of the circle, O, counterclockwise from the direction of perigee to the line segment OB. In other words, $E = \angle POB$. A useful analytical relationship between eccentric anomaly and true anomaly is as follows [14]:

$$E = 2\arctan\left[\sqrt{\frac{1-e}{1+e}}\tan\left(\frac{1}{2}v\right)\right] \qquad (2.8)$$

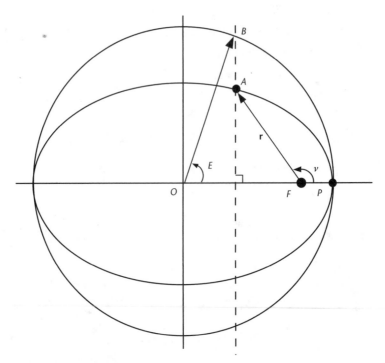

Figure 2.10   Relationship between eccentric anomaly and true anomaly.

Once the eccentric anomaly has been computed, the mean anomaly is given by Kepler's equation

$$M = E - e\sin E \qquad (2.9)$$

As stated previously, the importance of transforming from the true to the mean anomaly is that time varies linearly with the mean anomaly. That linear relationship is as follows:

$$M - M_0 = \sqrt{\frac{\mu}{a^3}}(t - t_0) \qquad (2.10)$$

where M_0 is the mean anomaly at epoch t_0, and M is the mean anomaly at time t. From Figures 2.9 and 2.10, and (2.8) and (2.9), it can be verified that $M = E = v = 0$ at the time of perigee passage. Therefore, if we let $t = \tau$, (2.10) provides a transformation between mean anomaly and time of perigee passage:

$$M_0 = -\sqrt{\frac{\mu}{a^3}}(\tau - t_0) \qquad (2.11)$$

From (2.11), it is possible to characterize the two-body orbit in terms of the mean anomaly, M_0, at epoch t_0, instead of the time of perigee passage τ. GPS makes use of the mean anomaly at epoch in characterizing orbits.

GPS also makes use of a parameter known as *mean motion*, which is given the symbol n and is defined to be the time derivative of the mean anomaly. Since the mean anomaly was constructed to be linear in time for two-body orbits, mean motion is a constant. From (2.10), we find the mean motion as follows:

$$n \underset{def}{=} \frac{dM}{dt} = \sqrt{\frac{\mu}{a^3}}$$

From this definition, (2.10) can be rewritten as $M - M_0 = n(t - t_0)$.

Mean motion can also be used to express the orbital period P of a satellite in two-body motion. Since mean motion is the (constant) rate of change of the mean anomaly, the orbital period is the ratio of the angle subtended by the mean anomaly over one orbital period to the mean motion. It can be verified that the mean anomaly passes through an angle of 2π radians during one orbit. Therefore, the orbital period is calculated as follows:

$$P = \frac{2\pi}{n} = 2\pi\sqrt{\frac{a^3}{\mu}} \qquad (2.12)$$

Figure 2.11 illustrates the three additional Keplerian orbital elements that define the orientation of the orbit. The coordinates in Figure 2.11 could refer either to an ECI or to an ECEF coordinate system. In the case of GPS, the Keplerian parameters are defined in relation to the ECEF coordinate system described in Section 2.2. In this case, the xy-plane is always the Earth's equatorial plane. The following three Keplerian orbital elements define the orientation of the orbit in the ECEF coordinate system:

i = inclination of orbit

Ω = longitude of the ascending node

ω = argument of perigee

Inclination is the dihedral angle between the Earth's equatorial plane and the satellite's orbital plane. The other two Keplerian orbital elements in Figure 2.11 are defined in relation to the *ascending node*, which is the point in the satellite's orbit where it crosses the equatorial plane with a +z component of velocity (i.e., going from the southern to the northern hemisphere). The orbital element that defines the angle between the +x-axis and the direction of the ascending node is called the right ascension of the ascending node (RAAN). Because the +x-axis is fixed in the direction of the prime meridian (0° longitude) in the ECEF coordinate system, the right ascension of the ascending node is actually the *longitude* of the ascending node, Ω. The final orbital element, known as the argument of perigee, ω, measures the angle from the ascending node to the direction of perigee in the orbit. Notice that Ω is measured in the equatorial plane, whereas ω is measured in the orbital plane.

In the case of GPS satellites, the orbits are nearly (but not quite) circular, with eccentricities of no larger than 0.02 and semimajor axes of approximately 26,560 km. From (2.12), we compute the orbital period to be approximately 43,080 seconds or 11 hours, 58 minutes. The orbital inclinations are approximately 55° for the

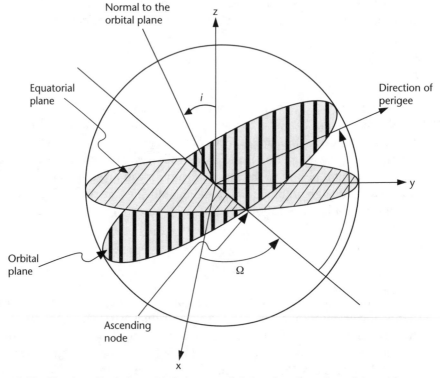

Figure 2.11 The three Keplerian orbital elements defining the orientation of the orbit.

GPS constellation. The remaining orbital parameters vary between satellites, so that the constellation provides coverage of the entire Earth.

As previously indicated, the actual motion of a satellite is described by (2.7) rather than (2.4). However, the Keplerian orbital elements may be computed for a satellite at a particular instant in time from its true position and velocity vectors. In this case, the orbital elements are known as *osculating*; if all forces perturbing the point-mass force of the Earth were to cease at the time of the osculating orbital elements, the satellite would follow the two-body orbit described by those osculating elements. Because of the perturbing accelerations in (2.7), the osculating orbital elements of a satellite will change slowly over time. The osculating orbital elements do not change quickly because the first term of the Earth's gravitational harmonic series, (2.6), is still the dominant element in the force field acting on a satellite.

GPS almanac data and ephemeris data transmitted by the satellites include the osculating Keplerian orbital elements, with the exception that the time of perigee passage is converted to mean anomaly at epoch by (2.11). In order to be useful, it is necessary for the osculating elements to include the reference time, known as the time of epoch or time of ephemeris, at which the orbital elements were valid. Only at epoch are the orbital elements exactly as described by the osculating values; at all later times, the true orbital elements deviate slightly from the osculating values.

Because it is necessary for the GPS ephemeris message to contain very accurate information about the satellite's position and velocity, it is insufficient to use only the osculating Keplerian orbital elements for computing the position of a GPS satellite, except very near the epoch of those elements. One solution to this problem would be to update the GPS ephemeris messages very frequently. Another solution would be for the GPS receiver to integrate the fully perturbed equation of motion, (2.7), which would include a detailed force model, from epoch to the desired time. Because both of these solutions are computationally intensive, they are impractical for real-time operations. Therefore, the osculating Keplerian orbital elements in the GPS ephemeris message are augmented by "correction" parameters that allow the user to estimate the Keplerian elements fairly accurately during the periods of time between updates of the satellite's ephemeris message. (Particulars on ephemeris message updating are provided in Section 3.3.1.4.) Any time after the epoch of a particular ephemeris message, the GPS receiver uses the correction parameters to estimate the true orbital elements at the desired time.

Table 2.2 summarizes the parameters contained in the GPS ephemeris message. These parameters are found in IS-GPS-200 [4], which is the interface specification between the GPS space segment and GPS user segment. As can be seen, the first seven parameters of the GPS ephemeris message are time of epoch and, essentially, the osculating Keplerian orbital elements at the time of epoch, with the exceptions that the semimajor axis is reported as its square root and that mean anomaly is used instead of time of perigee passage. The next nine parameters allow for corrections to the Keplerian elements as functions of time after epoch.

Table 2.3 provides the algorithm by which a GPS receiver computes the position vector of a satellite (x_s, y_s, z_s) in the ECEF coordinate system from the orbital elements in Table 2.2. For computation (3) in Table 2.3, t represents the GPS system time at which the GPS signal was transmitted. In the notation of Table 2.3, the subscript k appearing in computation (3) and below means that the subscripted vari-

Table 2.2   GPS Ephemeris Data Definitions

t_{0e}	Reference time of ephemeris
$\sqrt{a}$	Square root of semimajor axis
e	Eccentricity
i_0	Inclination angle (at time t_{0e})
Ω_0	Longitude of the ascending node (at weekly epoch)
ω	Argument of perigee (at time t_{0e})
M_0	Mean anomaly (at time t_{0e})
di/dt	Rate of change of inclination angle
$\dot{\Omega}$	Rate of change of longitude of the ascending node
Δn	Mean motion correction
C_{uc}	Amplitude of cosine correction to argument of latitude
C_{us}	Amplitude of sine correction to argument of latitude
C_{rc}	Amplitude of cosine correction to orbital radius
C_{rs}	Amplitude of sine correction to orbital radius
C_{ic}	Amplitude of cosine correction to inclination angle
C_{is}	Amplitude of sine correction to inclination angle

Table 2.3   Computation of a Satellite's ECEF Position Vector

(1)	$a = \left(\sqrt{a}\right)^2$	Semimajor axis
(2)	$n = \sqrt{\dfrac{\mu}{a^3}} + \Delta n$	Corrected mean motion, $\mu = 398{,}600.5 \times 10^8 \text{ m}^3/\text{s}^2$
(3)	$t_k = t - t_{0e}$	Time from ephemeris epoch
(4)	$M_k = M_0 + n(t_k)$	Mean anomaly
(5)	$M_k = E_k - e \sin E_k$	Eccentric anomaly (must be solved iteratively for E_k)
(6)	$\sin v_k = \dfrac{\sqrt{1-e^2}\,\sin E_k}{1 - e \cos E_k}$ $\cos v_k = \dfrac{\cos E_k - e}{1 - e \cos E_k}$	True anomaly
(7)	$\phi_k = v_k + \omega$	Argument of latitude
(8)	$\delta\phi_k = C_{us} \sin(2\phi_k) + C_{uc} \cos(2\phi_k)$	Argument of latitude correction
(9)	$\delta r_k = C_{rs} \sin(2\phi_k) + C_{rc} \cos(2\phi_k)$	Radius correction
(10)	$\delta i_k = C_{is} \sin(2\phi_k) + C_{ic} \cos(2\phi_k)$	Inclination correction
(11)	$u_k = \phi_k + \delta\phi_k$	Corrected argument of latitude
(12)	$r_k = a(1 - e \cos E_k) + \delta r_k$	Corrected radius
(13)	$i_k = i_0 + (di/dt)t_k + \delta i_k$	Corrected inclination
(14)	$\Omega_k = \Omega_0 + \left(\dot{\Omega} - \dot{\Omega}_e\right)(t_k) - \dot{\Omega}_e t_{0e}$	Corrected longitude of node
(15)	$x_p = r_k \cos u_k$	In-plane x position
(16)	$y_p = r_k \sin u_k$	In-plane y position
(17)	$x_s = x_p \cos \Omega_k - y_p \cos i_k \sin \Omega_k$	ECEF x-coordinate
(18)	$y_s = x_p \sin \Omega_k + y_p \cos i_k \cos \Omega_k$	ECEF y-coordinate
(19)	$z_s = y_p \sin i_k$	ECEF z-coordinate

able is measured at time t_k, the time (in seconds) from epoch to the GPS system time of signal transmission.

There are a few additional subtleties in the computations described in Table 2.3. First, computation (5), which is Kepler's equation, (2.9), is transcendental in the desired parameter, E_k. Therefore, the solution must be carried out numerically. Kepler's equation is readily solved either by iteration or Newton's method. A second subtlety is that computation (6) must produce the true anomaly in the correct quadrant. Therefore, it is necessary either to use both the sine and the cosine or to use a *smart* arcsine function. Also, to carry out computation (14), it is also necessary to know the rotation rate of the Earth. According to IS-GPS-200, this rotation rate is $\dot{\Omega}_\varepsilon = 7.2921151467 \times 10^{-5}$ rad/s, which is consistent with the WGS 84 value to be used for navigation, though WGS 84 also provides a slightly different value in defining the ellipsoid. Finally, IS-GPS-200 defines the value of π to be used by GPS user equipment as exactly 3.1415926535898.

As can be seen from the computations in Table 2.3, the variations in time of the orbital parameters are modeled differently for particular parameters. For example, mean motion is given a constant correction in computation (2), which effectively corrects the mean anomaly computed in (4). On the other hand, latitude, radius, and inclination are corrected by truncated harmonic series in computations (8), (9), and (10), respectively. Eccentricity is given no correction. Finally, longitude of the node is corrected linearly in time in computation (14). It is a misnomer of GPS system terminology, as in Table 2.2, that the longitude of the node, Ω_0, is given "at weekly epoch." In reality, Ω_0 is given at the reference time of ephemeris, t_{0e}, the same as the other GPS parameters. This can be verified by inspection of computation (14) from Table 2.3. Reference [15] provides an excellent description of the tradeoffs that resulted in the use of ephemeris message parameters and computations described in Tables 2.2 and 2.3.

2.3.2   Constellation Design

A satellite "constellation" is characterized by the set of orbital parameters for the individual satellites in that constellation. The design of a satellite constellation entails the selection of those orbital parameters to optimize some objective function of the constellation (typically to maximize some set of performance parameters at minimum cost—i.e., with the fewest satellites). The design of satellite constellations has been the subject of numerous studies and publications. Our purpose here is to provide a general overview of satellite constellation design to summarize the salient considerations in the design of constellations for satellite navigation, to provide some perspective on the selection of the original 24-satellite GPS constellation, and to set the ground work for discussions of future satellite navigation constellations such as GALILEO.

2.3.2.1   Overview of Constellation Design

Given innumerable combinations of orbital parameters for each satellite in a constellation, it is convenient to segregate orbits into categories. One categorization of orbits is by eccentricity:

- Circular orbits have zero (or nearly zero) eccentricity.
- Highly elliptical orbits (HEO) have large eccentricities (typically with $e > 0.6$).

Another categorization of orbits is by altitude:

- Geosynchronous Earth orbit (GEO) is an orbit with a period equal to the duration of the sidereal day—substituting $P = 23$ hours, 56 minutes, 4.1 seconds into (2.12) yields $a = 42,164.17$ km as the orbital semimajor axis for GEO, or an altitude of 35,786 km;
- LEO is a class of orbits with altitude typically less than 1,500 km;
- MEO is a class of orbits with altitudes below GEO and above LEO, with most practical examples being in the range of roughly 10,000–25,000 km altitude;
- Supersynchronous orbits are those with altitude greater than GEO (greater than 35,786 km).

Note that GEO defines an orbital altitude such that the period of the orbit equals the period of rotation of the Earth in inertial space (the sidereal day). A *geostationary* orbit is a GEO orbit with zero inclination and zero eccentricity. In this special case, a satellite in geostationary orbit has no apparent motion to an observer on Earth, because the relative position vector from the observer to the satellite (in ECEF coordinates) remains fixed over time. In practice, due to orbital perturbations, satellites never stay in exactly geostationary orbit; therefore, even so-called geostationary satellites have some small residual motion relative to users on the Earth.

Another categorization of orbits is by inclination:

- Equatorial orbits have zero inclination; hence, a satellite in equatorial orbit travels in the Earth's equatorial plane.
- Polar orbits have 90° inclination; hence, a satellite in polar orbit passes through the Earth's axis of rotation.
- Prograde orbits have nonzero inclination with a value less than 90° (and hence have ground tracks that go in general from west to east).
- Retrograde orbits have nonzero inclination with a value greater than 90° and less than 180° (and hence have ground tracks that go in general from east to west).
- Collectively, prograde and retrograde orbits are known as *inclined*.

Theoretical studies of satellite constellations typically focus on some particular subset of orbital categories. For example, Walker extensively studied inclined circular orbits [16], Rider further studied inclined circular orbits to include both global and zonal coverage [17], and Adams and Rider studied circular polar orbits [18]. These studies all focus on determining the set of orbits in their categories that require the fewest satellites to provide a particular level of coverage (i.e., the number of satellites in view from some region on Earth). The studies determine optimal orbital inclinations for their category of orbits and then determine the configuration of satellites in planes (i.e., for a given orbital altitude, how many satellites are required in what set of orbital planes to provide a given level of coverage with the fewest satellites). The level of coverage is usually characterized by the minimum number of satellites required to be visible in some region of the world above a minimum elevation angle.

2.3.2.2 Inclined Circular Orbits

As an example of how to use one of these constellation design studies, consider Rider's work [17] on inclined circular orbits. Rider studied the class of orbits that are circular and of equal altitude and inclination. This specific study further limited its analysis to constellations of P orbital planes with S satellites per plane and equal phasing between planes (i.e., satellite 1 in plane 1 passes through its ascending node at the same time as satellite 1 in plane 2). Figure 2.12 illustrates equal versus unequal phasing between planes in the case of two orbital planes with three equally spaced satellites per plane ($P = 2$, $S = 3$). The orbital planes are equally spaced around the equatorial plane so that the difference in right ascension of ascending node between planes equals $360°/P$, and satellites are equally spaced within each orbital plane.

Rider [17] made the following definitions:

α = elevation angle
R_e = spherical radius of the Earth (these studies all assume a spherical Earth)
h = orbital altitude of the constellation being studied

Then the Earth central angle, θ, as shown in Figure 2.13, is related to these parameters as follows:

$$\cos(\theta + \alpha) = \frac{\cos \alpha}{1 + h/Re} \tag{2.13}$$

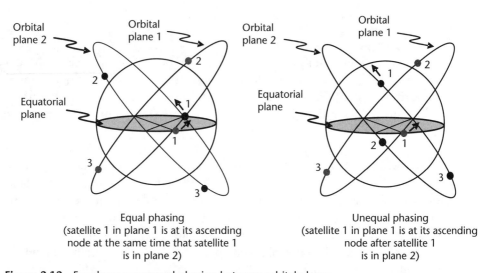

Equal phasing
(satellite 1 in plane 1 is at its ascending node at the same time that satellite 1 is in plane 2)

Unequal phasing
(satellite 1 in plane 1 is at its ascending node after satellite 1 is in plane 2)

Figure 2.12 Equal versus unequal phasing between orbital planes.

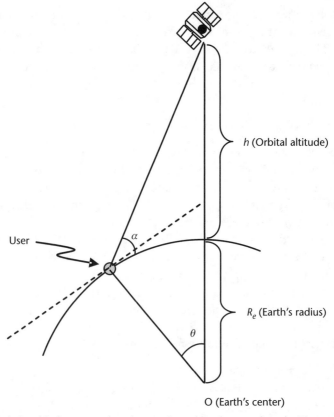

Figure 2.13 Relationship between elevation angle and Earth central angle (θ).

From (2.13), given an orbital altitude, h, and a minimum elevation angle, α, the corresponding Earth central angle, θ, can be computed. Rider then defines a so-called half street width parameter, c, which is related to the Earth central angle, θ, and the number of satellites per orbital plane, S, as follows:

$$\cos \theta = \left(\cos c \right)\left(\cos \frac{\pi}{S} \right) \tag{2.14}$$

Finally, Rider's analysis produces a number of tables that relate optimal combinations of orbital inclination, i, half street width, c, and number of orbital planes, P, for various desired Earth coverage areas (global versus mid-latitude versus equatorial versus polar) and various levels of coverage (minimum number of satellites in view).

Practical applications of the theoretical work [16–18] have included the IRIDIUM LEO mobile satellite communications constellation, which was originally planned to be an Adams/Rider 77-satellite polar constellation and ended up as a 66-satellite polar constellation, the ICO MEO mobile satellite communications constellation, which was originally planned to be a Rider 10-satellite inclined circular constellation, and the Globalstar LEO mobile satellite communications constellation, which was originally planned to be a Walker 48-satellite inclined circular constellation of 8 planes.

Selection of a class of orbits for a particular application is made based on the requirements of that application. For example, in many high-bandwidth satellite communications applications (e.g., direct broadcast video or high-rate data trunking), it is desirable to have a nearly geostationary orbit to maintain a fixed line of sight from the user to the satellite to avoid the need for the user to have an expensive steerable antenna. On the other hand, for lower bandwidth mobile satellite service applications, where lower data latency is desirable, it is preferable to use LEO or MEO satellites to reduce range from the user to the satellite.

As a specific example of constellation design using this body of work ([16–18]), consider the design of a constellation of MEO satellites providing worldwide continuous coverage above a minimum 10° elevation angle. The objective is to minimize the number of satellites providing this level of coverage within the class of Rider orbits. Specifically, consider the case with $h = 10{,}385$ km (corresponding to an orbital period of 6 hours). With $\alpha = 10°$, the Earth central angle θ can be computed from (2.13) to be 58.0°.

Rider's results in Table 4 of [17] then show that with two orbital planes, the optimal inclination is 45°, and $c = 45°$. We now have enough information to solve (2.14) for S. This solution is $S = 4.3$, but since satellites come only in integer quantities, one must round up to 5 satellites per plane. Hence, Rider's work indicates that with 2 orbital planes, one must have 5 satellites per plane to produce continuous worldwide coverage with a minimum of 1 satellite above a minimum 10° elevation angle. With 3 orbital planes of the same altitude and with the same coverage requirement, Rider's work shows $c = 35.26°$, and $S = 3.6$, or 4 satellites per plane. In this case, 12 total satellites would be required to provide the same level of coverage if one were to use 3 planes. Clearly it is more cost effective (by 2 satellites) to use a 2 × 5 constellation ($P = 2$, $S = 5$) versus a 3 × 4 constellation ($P = 3$, $S = 4$). As it turns out, this example yielded exactly the constellation design envisioned by Inmarsat in its original concept for the ICO satellite communications system (a 2 × 5 constellation of 6-hour orbits inclined 45°). The ICO system added a spare satellite in each plane for robustness, but the baseline operational constellation was the 2 × 5 Rider constellation discussed here.

2.3.2.3   Walker Constellations

It turns out that the more generalized Walker constellations [16] can produce a given level of coverage with fewer satellites in general than the Rider constellations [17]. Walker constellations use circular inclined orbits of equal altitude and inclination, where the orbital planes are equally spaced around the equatorial plane and satellites are equally spaced within orbital planes, as with Rider constellations. However, Walker constellations allow more general relationships between the number of satellites per plane and the phasing between planes. To that end, Walker introduced the notation $T/P/F$, where T is the total number of satellites in the constellation, P is the number of orbital planes, and F is the phase offset factor that determines the phasing between adjacent orbital planes (see Figure 2.12 for an illustration of the concept of phasing between orbital planes). With the number of satellites per plane, S, it is obvious that $T = S \times P$. F is an integer such that $0 \le F \le P - 1$, and the offset in mean anomaly between the first satellite in each adjacent orbital plane is $360° \times F / P$. That is, when the first satellite in plane 2 is at its ascending node, the first satellite in plane 1 will have covered an orbital distance of $(360° \times F/P)°$ within its orbital plane.

Typically with one satellite per plane, a value of F can be found such that a Walker constellation can provide a given level of coverage with fewer satellites than a Rider constellation. However, such Walker constellations with one satellite per plane are less robust against failure than Rider constellations, because it is virtually impossible to spare such a constellation. For example, with a spare orbital plane, it would be required to reposition the satellite from the spare plane into the plane of a failed satellite, but the cost in fuel is extremely prohibitive to execute such an orbital maneuver. Realistically, satellites can be repositioned only within an orbital plane; hence the greater application of Rider-type constellations versus the more generalized Walker constellations.

Another significant issue in constellation design is the requirement to maintain orbital parameters within a specified range. Such orbital maintenance is called *stationkeeping*, and it is desirable to minimize the frequency and magnitude of maneuvers required over the lifetime of a satellite. This is true in all applications because of the life-limiting factor of available fuel on the satellite, and it is particularly true for satellite navigation applications because satellites are not immediately available to users after a stationkeeping maneuver while orbital and clock parameters are stabilized and ephemeris messages are updated. Therefore, more frequent stationkeeping maneuvers both reduce the useful lifetime of satellites in a constellation and reduce the overall availability of the constellation to users. Some orbits have a *resonance* effect, in which there is an increasing perturbation in a satellite's orbit due to the harmonic effects of (2.6). Such orbits are undesirable because they require more stationkeeping maneuvers to maintain a nominal orbit.

2.3.2.4 Constellation Design Considerations for Satellite Navigation

Satellite navigation constellations have very different geometrical constraints from satellite communications systems, the most obvious of which is the need for more multiplicity of coverage (i.e., more required simultaneous satellites in view for the navigation applications). As discussed in Section 2.4, the GPS navigation solution requires a minimum of four satellites to be in view of a user to provide the minimum of four measurements necessary for the user to determine three-dimensional position and time. Therefore, a critical constraint on the GPS constellation is that it must provide a minimum of fourfold coverage at all times. In order to ensure this level of coverage robustly, the actual nominal GPS constellation was designed to provide more than fourfold coverage so that the minimum of four satellites in view can be maintained even with a satellite failure. Also, more than fourfold coverage is useful for user equipment to be able to determine autonomously if a GPS satellite is experiencing a signal or timing anomaly (see Section 7.5.3.1). Therefore, the practical constraint for coverage of the GPS constellation is minimum sixfold coverage above 5° minimum elevation angle.

The problem of constellation design for satellite navigation has the following major constraints and considerations:

1. Coverage needs to be global.
2. At least six satellites need to be in view of any user position at all times.
3. To provide the best navigation accuracy, the constellation needs to have good geometric properties, which entails a dispersion of satellites in both azimuth and elevation angle from a user (a discussion of the effects of geometric properties on navigation accuracy is provided in Sections 7.1 and 7.3).
4. The constellation needs to be robust against single satellite failures.
5. The constellation must be maintainable given the increased frequency of satellite failures with a large constellation. That is, it must be relatively inexpensive to reposition satellites within the constellation.
6. Stationkeeping requirements need to be manageable. In other words, it is preferable to minimize the frequency and magnitude of maneuvers required to maintain the satellites within the required range of their orbital parameters.
7. There are tradeoffs between the distance of the satellite from the Earth's surface versus payload weight, determined, in part, by the transmitter power required to send a signal to Earth with minimum received power.

2.3.2.5   Selection of the GPS Constellation

The need for global coverage (1) and the need for good geometric diversity world-wide (3) eliminate the use of geostationary satellites for navigation, though a con-stellation of geosynchronous satellites with enough inclination could theoretically be used to provide global coverage including the poles. Considerations weighing against the use of an inclined GEO constellation to provide global coverage for nav-igation include constraint (7) and the increased satellite power (and thus payload weight) required from GEO to provide the necessary power flux density at the sur-face of the Earth relative to satellites at lower altitudes and the regulatory coordina-tion issues associated with GEO orbits. Thus, the constraint of global coverage (1) plus practical considerations drive the satellite navigation constellation to inclined LEO or MEO orbits.

Constraint (2) for minimum sixfold coverage, plus the need to minimize the size of the constellation for cost reasons, drives the desired constellation to higher alti-tude for satellite navigation. With satellites costing in the $20 million–$80 million range, even for relatively small satellites such as GPS, the differences in constellation size drive the desired altitude as high as possible. To first approximation, an order of magnitude more satellites would be required to provide the necessary sixfold cov-erage from LEO versus that with MEO. When launch costs are factored in, the over-all cost differential between LEO and MEO is billions of dollars. Moreover, constellations of LEO satellites tend to have worse geometric properties from a dilu-tion of precision perspective than MEOs—consideration (3). With LEO and GEO altitudes shown to be undesirable, MEO altitudes were determined to be preferable for GPS.

Ultimately, inclined 12-hour orbits were selected for GPS as the best compro-mise between coverage, dilution of precision characteristics, and cost. Some desir-able characteristics of this orbital altitude include repeating ground tracks, a relatively high altitude (which in turn produces good dilution of precision properties), and a relatively low number of satellites required to provide the redundancy of coverage required for navigation. It is true that stationkeeping is more frequent at the GPS 12-hour orbital altitude than other potential altitudes in the 20,000- to 25,000-km range due to the resonance issue discussed is Section 2.3.2.3, and so newer satellite navigation architectures, such as that for GALILEO, consider criterion (6) and make slight modifications to the exact orbital altitude of the MEO constellation. (GALILEO is discussed in Chapter 10.)

The robustness considerations of (4) and (5) drove the desire for multiple satellites per orbital plane, versus a more generalized Walker-type constellation that could provide the same level of coverage with fewer satellites but in separate orbital planes (see the discussion at the end of Section 2.3.2.3). Ultimately, a 6-plane configuration was selected with four satellites per plane. The orbital planes are inclined by 55°, in accordance with Walker's results, but due in part to early plans to use the Space Shuttle as the primary launch vehicle. The planes are equally spaced by 60° in right ascension of the ascending node around the equator. Satellites are not equally spaced within the planes, and there are phase offsets between planes to achieve improved geometric dilution of precision characteristics of the constellation. Hence, the GPS constellation can be considered a tailored Walker constellation.

In reality, more than 24 satellites are operated on orbit today, in part to provide greater accuracy and robustness of the constellation and, at the time of this writing, in part because a relatively large number of Block IIR satellites exist in storage on the ground, so "overpopulation" of the constellation has been possible.

2.4 Position Determination Using PRN Codes

GPS satellite transmissions utilize direct sequence spread spectrum (DSSS) modulation. DSSS provides the structure for the transmission of ranging signals and essential navigation data, such as satellite ephemerides and satellite health. The ranging signals are PRN codes that binary phase shift key (BPSK) modulate the satellite carrier frequencies. These codes look like and have spectral properties similar to random binary sequences but are actually deterministic. A simple example of a short PRN code sequence is shown in Figure 2.14. These codes have a predictable pattern, which is periodic and can be replicated by a suitably equipped receiver. At the time of this writing, each GPS satellite broadcasted two types of PRN ranging codes: a "short" coarse/acquisition (C/A)-code and a "long" precision (P)-code. (Additional signals are planned to be broadcast. They are described in Chapter 4.) The C/A code has a 1-ms period and repeats constantly, whereas the P-code satellite transmission is a 7-day sequence that repeats approximately every Saturday/Sunday midnight. Presently, the P-code is encrypted. This encrypted code is denoted as the Y-code. The Y-code is accessible only to PPS users through cryptography. Further details regard-

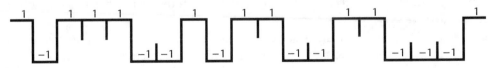

Figure 2.14 PRN ranging code.

ing PRN code properties, frequency generation, and associated modulation processes are contained in Chapter 4.

2.4.1   Determining Satellite-to-User Range

Earlier, we examined the theoretical aspects of using satellite ranging signals and multiple spheres to solve for user position in three dimensions. That example was predicated on the assumption that the receiver clock was perfectly synchronized to system time. In actuality, this is generally not the case. Prior to solving for three-dimensional user position, we will examine the fundamental concepts involving satellite-to-user range determination with nonsynchronized clocks and PRN codes. There are a number of error sources that affect range measurement accuracy (e.g., measurement noise and propagation delays); however, these can generally be considered negligible when compared to the errors experienced from nonsynchronized clocks. Therefore, in our development of basic concepts, errors other than clock offset are omitted. Extensive treatment of these error sources is provided in Section 7.2.

In Figure 2.15, we wish to determine vector $\mathbf{u}$, which represents a user receiver's position with respect to the ECEF coordinate system origin. The user's position coordinates x_u, y_u, z_u are considered unknown. Vector $\mathbf{r}$ represents the vector offset from the user to the satellite. The satellite is located at coordinates x_s, y_s, z_s within the

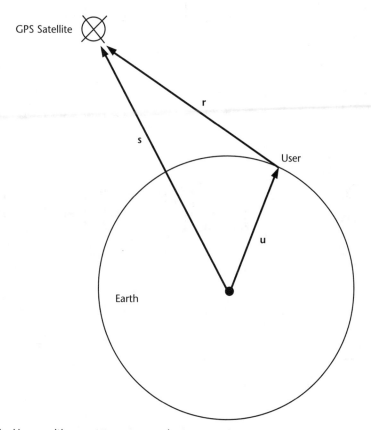

Figure 2.15   User position vector representation.

ECEF Cartesian coordinate system. Vector **s** represents the position of the satellite relative to the coordinate origin. Vector **s** is computed using ephemeris data broadcast by the satellite. The satellite-to-user vector **r** is

$$\mathbf{r} = \mathbf{s} - \mathbf{u} \qquad\qquad (2.15)$$

The magnitude of vector **r** is

$$\|\mathbf{r}\| = \|\mathbf{s} - \mathbf{u}\| \qquad\qquad (2.16)$$

Let r represent the magnitude of **r**

$$r = \|\mathbf{s} - \mathbf{u}\| \qquad\qquad (2.17)$$

The distance r is computed by measuring the propagation time required for a satellite-generated ranging code to transit from the satellite to the user receiver antenna. The propagation time measurement process is illustrated in Figure 2.16. As an example, a specific code phase generated by the satellite at t_1 arrives at the

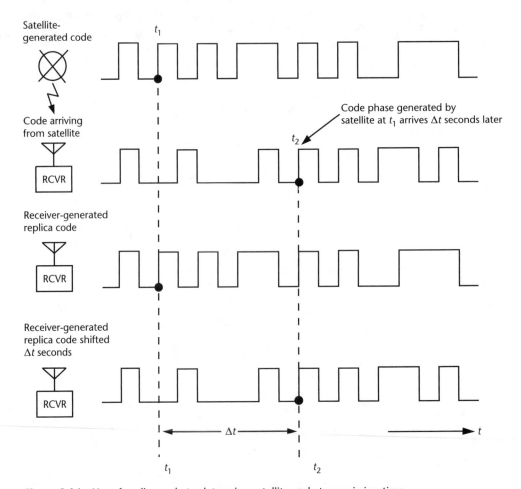

Figure 2.16   Use of replica code to determine satellite code transmission time.

receiver at t_2. The propagation time is represented by Δt. Within the receiver, an identical coded ranging signal is generated at t, with respect to the receiver clock. This replica code is shifted in time until it achieves correlation with the received satellite-generated ranging code. If the satellite clock and the receiver clock were perfectly synchronized, the correlation process would yield the true propagation time. By multiplying this propagation time, Δt, by the speed of light, the true (i.e., geometric) satellite-to-user distance can be computed. We would then have the ideal case described in Section 2.1.2.1. However, the satellite and receiver clocks are generally not synchronized.

The receiver clock will generally have a bias error from system time. Further, satellite frequency generation and timing is based on a highly accurate free running cesium or rubidium atomic clock, which is typically offset from system time. Thus, the range determined by the correlation process is denoted as the pseudorange ρ. The measurement is called *pseudorange* because it is the range determined by multiplying the signal propagation velocity, c, by the time difference between two nonsynchronized clocks (the satellite clock and the receiver clock). The measurement contains (1) the geometric satellite-to-user range, (2) an offset attributed to the difference between system time and the user clock, and (3) an offset between system time and the satellite clock. The timing relationships are shown in Figure 2.17, where:

T_s = System time at which the signal left the satellite

T_u = System time at which the signal reached the user receiver

δt = Offset of the satellite clock from system time [advance is positive; retardation (delay) is negative]

t_u = Offset of the receiver clock from system time

$T_s + \delta t$ = Satellite clock reading at the time that the signal left the satellite

$T_u + t_u$ = User receiver clock reading at the time the signal reached the user receiver

c = speed of light

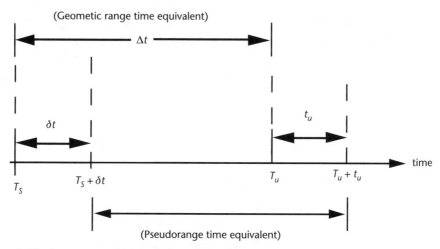

Figure 2.17   Range measurement timing relationships.

$$\textit{Geometric range, } r = c(T_u - T_s) = c\Delta t$$

$$\textit{Pseudorange, } \rho = c\left[(T_u + t_u) - (T_S + \delta t)\right]$$
$$= c(T_u - T_S) + c(t_u - \delta t)$$
$$= r + c(t_u - \delta t)$$

Therefore, (2.15) can be rewritten as:

$$\rho - c(t_u - \delta t) = \|\mathbf{s} - \mathbf{u}\|$$

where t_u represents the advance of the receiver clock with respect to system time, δt represents the advance of the satellite clock with respect to system time, and c is the speed of light.

The satellite clock offset from system time, δt, is composed of bias and drift contributions. The GPS ground-monitoring network determines corrections for these offset contributions and transmits the corrections to the satellites for rebroadcast to the users in the navigation message. These corrections are applied within the user receiver to synchronize the transmission of each ranging signal to system time. Therefore, we assume that this offset is compensated for and no longer consider δt an unknown. (There is some residual offset, which is treated in Section 7.2.1, but in the context of this discussion we assume that this is negligible.) Hence, the preceding equation can be expressed as

$$\rho - ct_u = \|\mathbf{s} - \mathbf{u}\| \qquad (2.18)$$

2.4.2 Calculation of User Position

In order to determine user position in three dimensions (x_u, y_u, z_u) and the offset t_u, pseudorange measurements are made to four satellites resulting in the system of equations

$$\rho_j = \|\mathbf{s}_j - \mathbf{u}\| + ct_u \qquad (2.19)$$

where j ranges from 1 to 4 and references the satellites. Equation (2.19) can be expanded into the following set of equations in the unknowns x_u, y_u, z_u, and t_u:

$$\rho_1 = \sqrt{(x_1 - x_u)^2 + (y_1 - y_u)^2 + (z_1 - z_u)^2} + ct_u \qquad (2.20)$$

$$\rho_2 = \sqrt{(x_2 - x_u)^2 + (y_2 - y_u)^2 + (z_2 - z_u)^2} + ct_u \qquad (2.21)$$

$$\rho_3 = \sqrt{(x_3 - x_u)^2 + (y_3 - y_u)^2 + (z_3 - z_u)^2} + ct_u \qquad (2.22)$$

$$\rho_4 = \sqrt{(x_4 - x_u)^2 + (y_4 - y_u)^2 + (z_4 - z_u)^2} + ct_u \qquad (2.23)$$

where x_j, y_j, and z_j denote the jth satellite's position in three dimensions.

These nonlinear equations can be solved for the unknowns by employing either (1) closed-form solutions [19–22], (2) iterative techniques based on linearization, or (3) Kalman filtering. (Kalman filtering provides a means for improving PVT estimates based on optimal processing of time sequence measurements and is described in Sections 7.3.5 and 9.1.3.) Linearization is illustrated in the following paragraphs. (The following development regarding linearization is based on a similar development in [23].) If we know approximately where the receiver is, then we can denote the offset of the true position (x_u, y_u, z_u) from the approximate position $(\hat{x}_u, \hat{y}_u, \hat{z}_u)$ by a displacement $(\Delta x_u, \Delta y_u, \Delta z_u)$. By expanding (2.20) to (2.23) in a Taylor series about the approximate position, we can obtain the position offset $(\Delta x_u, \Delta y_u, \Delta z_u)$ as linear functions of the known coordinates and pseudorange measurements. This process is described next.

Let a single pseudorange be represented by

$$\rho_j = \sqrt{\left(x_j - x_u\right)^2 + \left(y_j - y_u\right)^2 + \left(z_j - z_u\right)^2} + ct_u \tag{2.24}$$
$$= f\left(x_u, y_u, z_u, t_u\right)$$

Using the approximate position location $(\hat{x}_u, \hat{y}_u, \hat{z}_u)$ and time bias estimate $\hat{t}_u$, an approximate pseudorange can be calculated:

$$\hat{\rho}_j = \sqrt{\left(x_j - \hat{x}_u\right)^2 + \left(y_j - \hat{y}_u\right)^2 + \left(z_j - \hat{z}_u\right)^2} + c\hat{t}_u \tag{2.25}$$
$$= f\left(\hat{x}_u, \hat{y}_u, \hat{z}_u, \hat{t}_u\right)$$

As stated earlier, the unknown user position and receiver clock offset is considered to consist of an approximate component and an incremental component:

$$x_u = \hat{x}_u + \Delta x_u$$
$$y_u = \hat{y}_u + \Delta y_u$$
$$z_u = \hat{z}_u + \Delta z_u \tag{2.26}$$
$$t_u = \hat{t}_u + \Delta t_u$$

Therefore, we can write

$$f\left(x_u, y_u, z_u, t_u\right) = f\left(\hat{x}_u + \Delta x_u, \hat{y}_u + \Delta y_u, \hat{z}_u + \Delta z_u, \hat{t}_u + \Delta t_u\right)$$

This latter function can be expanded about the approximate point and associated predicted receiver clock offset $(\hat{x}_u, \hat{y}_u, \hat{z}_u, \hat{t}_u)$ using a Taylor series:

$$f\left(\hat{x}_u + \Delta x_u, \hat{y}_u + \Delta y_u, \hat{z}_u + \Delta z_u, \hat{t}_u + \Delta t_u\right) = f\left(\hat{x}_u, \hat{y}_u, \hat{z}_u, \hat{t}_u\right)$$
$$+ \frac{\partial f\left(\hat{x}_u, \hat{y}_u, \hat{z}_u, \hat{t}_u\right)}{\partial \hat{x}_u} \Delta x_u + \frac{\partial f\left(\hat{x}_u, \hat{y}_u, \hat{z}_u, \hat{t}_u\right)}{\partial \hat{y}_u} \Delta y_u \tag{2.27}$$
$$+ \frac{\partial f\left(\hat{x}_u, \hat{y}_u, \hat{z}_u, \hat{t}_u\right)}{\partial \hat{z}_u} \Delta z_u + \frac{\partial f\left(\hat{x}_u, \hat{y}_u, \hat{z}_u, \hat{t}_u\right)}{\partial \hat{t}_u} \Delta t_u + \ldots$$

The expansion has been truncated after the first-order partial derivatives to eliminate nonlinear terms. The partials derivatives evaluate as follows:

$$\frac{\partial f\left(\hat{x}_u,\hat{y}_u,\hat{z}_u,\hat{t}_u\right)}{\partial \hat{x}_u} = -\frac{x_j - \hat{x}_u}{\hat{r}_j}$$

$$\frac{\partial f\left(\hat{x}_u,\hat{y}_u,\hat{z}_u,\hat{t}_u\right)}{\partial \hat{y}_u} = -\frac{y_j - \hat{y}_u}{\hat{r}_j}$$

$$\frac{\partial f\left(\hat{x}_u,\hat{y}_u,\hat{z}_u,\hat{t}_u\right)}{\partial \hat{z}_u} = -\frac{z_j - \hat{z}_u}{\hat{r}_j}$$

$$\frac{\partial f\left(\hat{x}_u,\hat{y}_u,\hat{z}_u,\hat{t}_u\right)}{\partial \hat{t}_u} = c$$

(2.28)

where

$$\hat{r}_j = \sqrt{\left(x_j - \hat{x}_u\right)^2 + \left(y_j - \hat{y}_u\right)^2 + \left(z_j - \hat{z}_u\right)^2}$$

Substituting (2.25) and (2.28) into (2.27) yields

$$\rho_j = \hat{\rho}_j - \frac{x_j - \hat{x}_u}{\hat{r}_j}\Delta x_u - \frac{y_j - \hat{y}_u}{\hat{r}_j}\Delta y_u - \frac{z_j - \hat{z}_u}{\hat{r}_j}\Delta z_u + ct_u \qquad (2.29)$$

We have now completed the linearization of (2.24) with respect to the unknowns Δx_u, Δy_u, Δz_u, and Δt_u. (It is important to remember that we are neglecting secondary error sources such as Earth rotation compensation, measurement noise, propagation delays, and relativistic effects, which are treated in detail in Section 7.2.)

Rearranging this expression with the known quantities on the left and unknowns on right yields

$$\hat{\rho}_j - \rho_j = \frac{x_j - \hat{x}_u}{\hat{r}_j}\Delta x_u + \frac{y_j - \hat{y}_u}{\hat{r}_j}\Delta y_u - \frac{z_j - \hat{z}_u}{\hat{r}_j}\Delta z_u - ct_u \qquad (2.30)$$

For convenience, we will simplify the previous equation by introducing new variables where

$$\Delta\rho = \hat{\rho}_j - \rho_j$$

$$a_{xj} = \frac{x_j - \hat{x}_u}{\hat{r}_j}$$

$$a_{yj} = \frac{y_j - \hat{y}_u}{\hat{r}_j}$$

$$a_{zy} = \frac{z_j - \hat{z}_u}{\hat{r}_j}$$

(2.31)

The a_{xj}, a_{yj}, and a_{zj} terms in (2.31) denote the direction cosines of the unit vector pointing from the approximate user position to the jth satellite. For the jth satellite, this unit vector is defined as

$$\mathbf{a}_j = \left(a_{xj}, a_{yj}, a_{zj} \right)$$

Equation (2.30) can be rewritten more simply as

$$\Delta\rho_j = a_{xj}\Delta x_u + a_{yj}\Delta y_u + a_{zj}\Delta z_u - c\Delta t_u$$

We now have four unknowns: Δx_u, Δy_u, Δz_u, and Δt_u, which can be solved for by making ranging measurements to four satellites. The unknown quantities can be determined by solving the set of linear equations that follow:

$$
\begin{aligned}
\Delta\rho_1 &= a_{x1}\Delta x_u + a_{y1}\Delta y_u + a_{z1}\Delta z_u - c\Delta t_u \\
\Delta\rho_2 &= a_{x2}\Delta x_u + a_{y2}\Delta y_u + a_{z2}\Delta z_u - c\Delta t_u \\
\Delta\rho_3 &= a_{x3}\Delta x_u + a_{y3}\Delta y_u + a_{z3}\Delta z_u - c\Delta t_u \\
\Delta\rho_4 &= a_{x4}\Delta x_u + a_{y4}\Delta y_u + a_{z4}\Delta z_u - c\Delta t_u
\end{aligned}
\tag{2.32}
$$

These equations can be put in matrix form by making the definitions

$$
\Delta\boldsymbol{\rho} = \begin{bmatrix} \Delta\rho_1 \\ \Delta\rho_2 \\ \Delta\rho_3 \\ \Delta\rho_4 \end{bmatrix}
\quad
\mathbf{H} = \begin{bmatrix} a_{x1} & a_{y1} & a_{z1} & 1 \\ a_{x2} & a_{y2} & a_{z2} & 1 \\ a_{x3} & a_{y3} & a_{z3} & 1 \\ a_{x4} & a_{y4} & a_{z4} & 1 \end{bmatrix}
\quad
\Delta\mathbf{x} = \begin{bmatrix} \Delta x_u \\ \Delta y_u \\ \Delta z_u \\ -c\Delta t_u \end{bmatrix}
$$

One obtains, finally,

$$\Delta\boldsymbol{\rho} = \mathbf{H}\Delta\mathbf{x} \tag{2.33}$$

which has the solution

$$\Delta\mathbf{x} = \mathbf{H}^{-1}\Delta\boldsymbol{\rho} \tag{2.34}$$

Once the unknowns are computed, the user's coordinates x_u, y_u, z_u and the receiver clock offset t_u are then calculated using (2.26). This linearization scheme will work well as long as the displacement (Δx_u, Δy_u, Δz_u) is within close proximity of the linearization point. The acceptable displacement is dictated by the user's accuracy requirements. If the displacement does exceed the acceptable value, this process is reiterated with $\hat{\rho}$ being replaced by a new estimate of pseudorange based on the calculated point coordinates x_u, y_u, and z_u. In actuality, the true user-to-satellite measurements are corrupted by uncommon (i.e., independent) errors, such as measurement noise, deviation of the satellite path from the reported ephemeris, and multipath. These errors translate to errors in the components of vector $\Delta\mathbf{x}$, as shown here:

$$\boldsymbol{\epsilon}_x = \mathbf{H}^{-1}\boldsymbol{\epsilon}_{\text{meas}} \tag{2.35}$$

where $\boldsymbol{\epsilon}_{meas}$ is the vector containing the pseudorange measurement errors and $\boldsymbol{\epsilon}_x$ is the vector representing errors in the user position and receiver clock offset.

The error contribution $\boldsymbol{\epsilon}_x$ can be minimized by making measurements to more than four satellites, which will result in an overdetermined solution set of equations similar to (2.33). Each of these redundant measurements will generally contain independent error contributions. Redundant measurements can be processed by least squares estimation techniques that obtain improved estimates of the unknowns. Various versions of this technique exist and are usually employed in today's receivers, which generally employ more than four user-to-satellite measurements to compute user PVT. Appendix A provides an introduction to least squares techniques.

2.5 Obtaining User Velocity

GPS provides the capability for determining three-dimensional user velocity, which is denoted $\dot{\mathbf{u}}$. Several methods can be used to determine user velocity. In some receivers, velocity is estimated by forming an approximate derivative of the user position, as shown here:

$$\dot{\mathbf{u}} = \frac{d\mathbf{u}}{dt} = \frac{\mathbf{u}(t_2) - \mathbf{u}(t_1)}{t_2 - t_1}$$

This approach can be satisfactory provided the user's velocity is nearly constant over the selected time interval (i.e., not subjected to acceleration or jerk) and that the errors in the positions $\mathbf{u}(t_2)$ and $\mathbf{u}(t_1)$ are small relative to difference $\mathbf{u}(t_2) - \mathbf{u}(t_1)$.

In many modern GPS receivers, velocity measurements are made by processing carrier-phase measurements, which enable precise estimation of the Doppler frequency of the received satellite signals. The Doppler shift is produced by the relative motion of the satellite with respect to the user. The satellite velocity vector $\mathbf{v}$ is computed using ephemeris information and an orbital model that resides within the receiver. Figure 2.18 is a curve of received Doppler frequency as a function of time measured by a user at rest on the surface of the Earth from a GPS satellite. The received frequency increases as the satellite approaches the receiver and decreases as it recedes from the user. The reversal in the curve represents the time when the Doppler shift is zero and occurs when the satellite is at its closest position relative to the user. At this point, the radial component of the velocity of the satellite relative to the user is zero. As the satellite passes through this point, the sign of Δf changes. At the receiver antenna, the received frequency, f_R, can be approximated by the classical Doppler equation as follows:

$$f_R = f_T \left(1 - \frac{(\mathbf{v}_r \cdot \mathbf{a})}{c} \right) \tag{2.36}$$

where f_T is the transmitted satellite signal frequency, $\mathbf{v}_r$ is the satellite-to-user relative velocity vector, $\mathbf{a}$ is the unit vector pointing along the line of sight from the user to the satellite, and c is the speed of propagation. The dot product $\mathbf{v}_r \cdot \mathbf{a}$ represents the

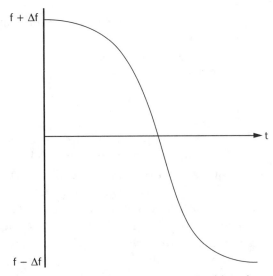

Figure 2.18 Received Doppler frequency by user at rest on Earth's surface.

radial component of the relative velocity vector along the line of sight to the satellite. Vector $\mathbf{v}_r$ is given as the velocity difference

$$\mathbf{v}_r = \mathbf{v} - \dot{\mathbf{u}} \tag{2.37}$$

where $\mathbf{v}$ is the velocity of the satellite, and $\dot{\mathbf{u}}$ is the velocity of the user, both referenced to a common ECEF frame. The Doppler offset due to the relative motion is obtained from these relations as

$$\Delta f = f_R - f_T = -f_T \frac{(\mathbf{v} - \dot{\mathbf{u}}) \cdot \mathbf{a}}{c}$$

At the GPS L1 frequency, the maximum Doppler frequency for a stationary user on the Earth is approximately 4 kHz, corresponding to a maximum line-of-sight velocity of approximately 800 m/s.

There are several approaches for obtaining user velocity from the received Doppler frequency. One technique is described herein. This technique assumes that the user position $\mathbf{u}$ has been determined and its displacement $(\Delta x_u, \Delta y_u, \Delta z_u)$ from the linearization point is within the user's requirements. In addition to computing the three-dimensional user velocity $\dot{\mathbf{u}} = (\dot{x}_u, \dot{y}_u, \dot{z}_u)$, this particular technique determines the receiver clock drift $\dot{t}_u$.

For the jth satellite, substituting (2.37) into (2.36) yields

$$f_{Rj} = f_{Tj}\left\{1 - \frac{1}{c}\left[(\mathbf{v}_j - \dot{\mathbf{u}}) \cdot \mathbf{a}_j\right]\right\} \tag{2.38}$$

The satellite transmitted frequency f_{Tj} is the actual transmitted satellite frequency.

As stated in Section 2.4.1, satellite frequency generation and timing is based on a highly accurate free running atomic standard, which is typically offset from system time. Corrections are generated by the ground-control/monitoring network periodically to correct for this offset. These corrections are available in the navigation message and are applied within the receiver to obtain the actual satellite transmitted frequency. Hence,

$$f_{Tj} = f_0 + \Delta f_{Tj} \qquad (2.39)$$

where f_0 is the nominal transmitted satellite frequency (i.e., L1), and Δf_{Tj} is the correction determined from the navigation message update.

The measured estimate of the received signal frequency is denoted f_j for the signal from the jth satellite. These measured values are in error and differ from the f_{Rj} values by a frequency bias offset. This offset can be related to the drift rate $\dot{t}_u$ of the user clock relative to GPS system time. The value $\dot{t}_u$ has the units seconds/second and essentially gives the rate at which the user's clock is running fast or slow relative to GPS system time. The clock drift error, f_j, and f_{Rj}, are related by the formula

$$f_{Rj} = f_j\left(1 + \dot{t}_u\right) \qquad (2.40)$$

where $\dot{t}_u$ is considered positive if the user clock is running fast. Substitution of (2.40) into (2.38), after algebraic manipulation, yields

$$\frac{c\left(f_j - f_{Tj}\right)}{f_{Tj}} + \mathbf{v}_j \cdot \mathbf{a}_j = \dot{\mathbf{u}} \cdot \mathbf{a}_j - \frac{c f_j \dot{t}_u}{f_{Tj}}$$

Expanding the dot products in terms of the vector components yields

$$\frac{c\left(f_j - f_{Tj}\right)}{f_{Tj}} + v_{xj}a_{xj} + v_{yj}a_{yj} + v_{zj}a_{zj} = \dot{x}_u a_{xj} + \dot{y}_u a_{yj} + \dot{z}_u a_{zj} - \frac{c f_j \dot{t}_u}{f_{Tj}} \qquad (2.41)$$

where $\mathbf{v}_j = (v_{xj}, v_{yj}, v_{zj})$, $\mathbf{a}_j = (a_{xj}, a_{yj}, a_{zj})$, and $\dot{\mathbf{u}} = (\dot{x}_u, \dot{y}_u, \dot{z}_u)$. All of the variables on the left side of (2.41) are either calculated or derived from measured values. The components of $\mathbf{a}_j$ are obtained during the solution for the user location (which is assumed to precede the velocity computation). The components of $\mathbf{v}_j$ are determined from the ephemeris data and the satellite orbital model. The f_{Tj} can be estimated using (2.39) and the frequency corrections derived from the navigation updates. (This correction, however, is usually negligible, and f_{Tj} can normally be replaced by f_0.) The f_j can be expressed in terms of receiver measurements of delta range (see Chapter 5 for a more detailed description of receiver processing). To simplify (2.41), we introduce the new variable d_j, defined by

$$d_j = \frac{c\left(f_j - f_{Tj}\right)}{f_{Tj}} + v_{xj}a_{xj} + v_{yj}a_{yj} + v_{zj}a_{zj} \qquad (2.42)$$

The term f_j / f_{Tj} on the right side in (2.41) is numerically very close to 1, typically within several parts per million. Little error results by setting this ratio to 1. With these simplifications, (2.41) can be rewritten as

$$d_j = \dot{x}_u a_{xj} + \dot{y}_u a_{yj} + \dot{z}_u a_{zj} - c\dot{t}_u$$

We now have four unknowns: $\dot{\mathbf{u}} = \dot{x}_u, \dot{y}_u, \dot{z}_u, \dot{t}_u$ which can be solved by using measurements from four satellites. As before, we calculate the unknown quantities by solving the set of linear equations using matrix algebra. The matrix/vector scheme is

$$\mathbf{d} = \begin{bmatrix} d_1 \\ d_2 \\ d_3 \\ d_4 \end{bmatrix} \quad \mathbf{H} = \begin{bmatrix} a_{x1} & a_{y1} & a_{z1} & 1 \\ a_{x2} & a_{y2} & a_{z2} & 1 \\ a_{x3} & a_{y3} & a_{z3} & 1 \\ a_{x4} & a_{y4} & a_{z4} & 1 \end{bmatrix} \quad \mathbf{g} = \begin{bmatrix} \dot{x}_u \\ \dot{y}_u \\ \dot{z}_u \\ -c\dot{t}_u \end{bmatrix}$$

Note that $\mathbf{H}$ is identical to the matrix used in Section 2.4.2 in the formulation for the user position determination. In matrix notation,

$$\mathbf{d} = \mathbf{Hg}$$

and the solution for the velocity and time drift are obtained as

$$\mathbf{g} = \mathbf{H}^{-1}\mathbf{d}$$

The phase measurements that lead to the frequency estimates used in the velocity formulation are corrupted by errors such as measurement noise and multipath. Furthermore, the computation of user velocity is dependent on user position accuracy and correct knowledge of satellite ephemeris and satellite velocity. The relationship between the errors contributed by these parameters in the computation of user velocity is similar to (2.35). If measurements are made to more than four satellites, least squares estimation techniques can be employed to obtain improved estimates of the unknowns.

2.6   Time and GPS

GPS disseminates a realization of coordinated universal time (UTC) that provides the capability for time synchronization of users worldwide. Applications range from data *time tagging* to communications system packet switching synchronization. Worldwide time dissemination is an especially useful feature in military frequency hopping communications systems, where time synchronization permits all users to change frequencies simultaneously.

2.6.1   UTC Generation

UTC is a composite time scale. That is, UTC is comprised of inputs from a time scale derived from atomic clocks and information regarding the Earth's rotation rate. The time scale based on atomic standards is called International Atomic Time (TAI). TAI is a uniform time scale based on the atomic second, which is defined as the fundamental unit of time in the International System of Units. The atomic second is defined as "the duration of 9,192,631,770 periods of the radiation corresponding to the transition between two hyperfine levels of the ground state of the cesium 133 atom" [24]. The Bureau International des Poids et Mesures (BIPM) is the international body responsible for computing TAI. TAI is derived from an ensemble of atomic standards located at more than 50 timing laboratories in various countries. The BIPM statistically processes these inputs to calculate definitive TAI [25]. TAI is referred to as a "paper" time scale since it is not kept by a physical clock.

The other time scale used to form UTC is called Universal Time 1 (UT1). UT1 is a measure of the Earth's rotation angle with respect to the Sun. It is one component of the Earth orientation parameters that define the actual orientation of the ECEF coordinate system with respect to space and celestial bodies and is treated as a time scale in celestial navigation [24]. UT1 remains a nonuniform time scale due to variations in the Earth's rotation. Also, UT1 drifts with respect to atomic time. This is on the order of several milliseconds per day and can accumulate to 1 second in a 1-year period. The International Earth Rotation and Reference System Service (IERS) is responsible for definitively determining UT1. Civil and military timekeeping applications require knowledge of the Earth's orientation as well as a uniform time scale. UTC is a time scale with these characteristics. The IERS determines when to add or subtract leap seconds to UTC such that the difference between UTC and UT1 does not exceed 0.9 second. Thus, UTC is synchronized with solar time [25] at the level of approximately 1 second. The USNO maintains an ensemble of approximately 50 cesium standards and forms its own version of UTC, denoted as UTC (USNO) that is kept to within 50 ns of the international standard UTC, provided by the BIPM approximately 1 month in arrears.

2.6.2 GPS System Time

GPS system time (previously referred to as system time) is referenced to UTC (USNO).

GPS system time is also a paper time scale; it is based on statistically processed readings from the atomic clocks in the satellites and at various ground control segment components. GPS system time is a continuous time scale that is not adjusted for leap seconds. GPS system time and UTC (USNO) were coincident at 0h January 6, 1980. At the time of this writing, GPS system time led UTC (USNO) by 13 seconds. The GPS control segment is required to steer GPS system time within 1 μs of UTC (USNO) (modulo 1 second) [26], but the difference is typically within 50 ns (modulo 1 second). An epoch in GPS system time is distinguished by the number of seconds that have elapsed since Saturday/Sunday midnight and the GPS week number. GPS weeks are numbered sequentially and originate with week 0, which began at 0h January 6, 1980 [25].

2.6.3 Receiver Computation of UTC (USNO)

2.6.3.1 Static Users

It can be observed from (2.20) that if the user's position (x_u, y_u, z_u) and satellite ephemerides (x_1, y_1, z_1) are known, a static receiver can solve for t_u by making a single pseudorange measurement, ρ_1. Once t_u is determined, it can be subtracted from the receiver clock time, t_{rcv}, to obtain GPS system time, t_E. (Note that in the development of the user position solution in Section 2.4.1, GPS system time was denoted as T_u, which represented the instant in system time when the satellite signal reached the user receiver. However, we need to represent GPS system time at *any particular time* and will use the parameter t_E to do so.)

Expressing receiver clock time at any particular time:

$$t_{rcv} = t_E + t_u$$

So that:

$$t_E = t_{rcv} - t_u$$

From IS-GPS-200 [4], UTC (USNO), t_{UTC}, is computed as follows:

$$t_{UTC} = t_E - \Delta t_{UTC}$$

where Δt_{UTC} represents the number of integer leap seconds Δt_{LS} and a fractional estimate of the difference between GPS system time and UTC (USNO) modulo 1 second denoted herein as δt_A. [The control segment provides polynomial coefficients (A_0, A_1, and A_2) in the navigation data message that are used to compute the fractional difference between GPS system time and UTC (USNO) [4].]

Therefore, UTC (USNO), t_{UTC}, can be computed by the receiver as follows:

$$\begin{aligned}
t_{UTC} &= t_E - \Delta t_{UTC} \\
&= t_{rcv} - t_u - \Delta t_{UTC} \\
&= t_{rcv} - t_u - \Delta t_{LS} - \delta t_A
\end{aligned}$$

2.6.3.2   Mobile Users

Mobile users compute UTC (USNO) using the exact methodology described earlier except that they need to solve the system of (2.20)–(2.23) to determine the receiver clock offset, t_u.

References

[1]   NAVSTAR GPS Joint Program Office (JPO), *GPS NAVSTAR User's Overview*, YEE-82-009D, GPS JPO, El Segundo, CA, March 1991.

[2]   Langley, R., "The Mathematics of GPS," *GPS World Magazine*, Advanstar Communications, July–August 1991, pp. 45–50.

[3]   Long, A. C., et al., (eds.), *Goddard Trajectory Determination System (GTDS) Mathematical Theory*, Revision 1, FDD/552-89/001, Greenbelt, MD: Goddard Space Flight Center, July 1989.

[4]   GPS Navstar Joint Program Office, *Navstar GPS Space Segment/Navigation User Interfaces, IS-GPS-200*, Revision D, GPS Navstar Joint Program Office, El Segundo, CA, December 7, 2004.

[5]   National Imagery and Mapping Agency, Department of Defense, *World Geodetic System 1984 (WGS 84): Its Definition and Relationships with Local Geodetic Systems*, NIMA TR8350.2, 3rd ed., Bethesda, MD: National Imagery and Mapping Agency, January 2000.

[6]   Bowring, B. R., "Transformation from Spatial to Geographical Coordinates," *Survey Review*, Vol. XXIII, 181, July 1976, pp. 323–327.

[7]   Merrigan, M. J., et al., "A Refinement to the World Geodetic System 1984 Reference Frame," *Proc. of The Institute of Navigation ION GPS 2002*, Portland, OR, September 24–27, 2002, pp.1519–1529.

[8]   Schwarz, C. R., "Relation of NAD 83 to WGS 84," *North American Datum of 1983*, C. R. Schwarz, (ed.), NOAA Professional Paper NOS 2, National Geodetic Survey, Silver Spring, MD: NOAA, December 1989, pp. 249–252.

[9]   Lemoine, F. G., et al., *The Development of the Joint NASA GSFC and NIMA Geopotential Model EGM96*, NASA/TP-1998-206861, Greenbelt, MD: NASA Goddard Space Flight Center, July 1998.

[10] Roman, D. R., et al., "Assessment of the New National Geoid Height Model, GEOID03," *Proc. of American Congress on Surveying and Mapping 2004 Meeting*, Nashville, TN, April 16–21, 2004.

[11] Rapp, R. H., "Separation Between Reference Surfaces of Selected Vertical Datums," *Bulletin Geodesique*, Vol. 69, No. 1, 1995, pp. 26–31.

[12] Milbert, D. G., "Computing GPS-Derived Orthometric Heights with the GEOID90 Geoid Height Model," *Technical Papers of the 1991 ACSM-ASPRS Fall Convention*, Atlanta, GA, October 28–November 1, 1991, pp. A46–A55.

[13] Parker, B., et al., "A National Vertical Datum Transformation Tool," *Sea Technology*, Vol. 44, No. 9, September 2003, pp. 10–15, http://chartmaker.ncd.noaa.gov/bathytopo/vdatum.htm.

[14] Battin, R. H., *An Introduction to the Mathematics and Methods of Astrodynamics*, New York: AIAA, 1987.

[15] Van Dierendonck, A. J., et al., "The GPS Navigation Message," *GPS Papers Published in Navigation*, Vol. I, Washington, D.C.: Institute of Navigation, 1980.

[16] Walker, J. G., "Satellite Constellations," *Journal of the British Interplanetary Society*, Vol. 37, 1984, pp. 559–572.

[17] Rider, L., "Analytical Design of Satellite Constellations for Zonal Earth Coverage Using Inclined Circular Orbits," *The Journal of the Astronautical Sciences*, Vol. 34, No. 1, January–March 1986, pp. 31–64.

[18] Adams, W. S., and L. Rider, "Circular Polar Constellations Providing Continuous Single or Multiple Coverage Above a Specified Latitude," *The Journal of the Astronautical Sciences*, Vol. 35, No. 2, April–June 1987, pp. 155–192.

[19] Leva, J., "An Alternative Closed Form Solution to the GPS Pseudorange Equations," *Proc. of The Institute of Navigation (ION) National Technical Meeting*, Anaheim, CA, January 1995.

[20] Bancroft, S., "An Algebraic Solution of the GPS Equations," *IEEE Trans. on Aerospace and Electronic Systems*, Vol. AES-21, No. 7, January 1985, pp. 56–59.

[21] Chaffee, J. W., and J. S. Abel, "Bifurcation of Pseudorange Equations," *Proc. of The Institute of Navigation National Technical Meeting*, San Francisco, CA, January 1993, pp. 203–211.

[22] Fang, B. T., "Trilateration and Extension to Global Positioning System Navigation," *Journal of Guidance, Control, and Dynamics*, Vol. 9, No. 6, November–December 1986, pp. 715–717.

[23] Hofmann-Wellenhof, B., et al., *GPS Theory and Practice*, 2nd ed., New York: Springer-Verlag Wien, 1993.

[24] Seeber, G., *Satellite Geodesy: Foundations, Methods, and Applications*, New York: Walter De Gruyter, 1993.

[25] Langley, R., "Time, Clocks, and GPS," *GPS World Magazine*, Advanstar Communications, November–December 1991, pp. 38–42.

[26] Parker, T., and D. Mataskis, "Time and Frequency Dissemination Advances in GPS Transfer Techniques," *GPS World Magazine*, Advanstar Communications, November 2004, pp. 32–38.

CHAPTER 3

GPS System Segments

Arthur J. Dorsey and Willard A. Marquis
Lockheed Martin Corporation

Peter M. Fyfe
The Boeing Company

Elliott D. Kaplan and Lawrence F. Wiederholt
The MITRE Corporation

3.1 Overview of the GPS System

GPS is comprised of three segments: satellite constellation, ground-control/monitoring network, and user receiving equipment. Formal GPS JPO programmatic terms for these components are space, control, and user equipment segments, respectively. The satellite constellation is the set of satellites in orbit that provide the ranging signals and data messages to the user equipment. The control segment (CS) tracks and maintains the satellites in space. The CS monitors satellite health and signal integrity and maintains the orbital configuration of the satellites. Furthermore, the CS updates the satellite clock corrections and ephemerides as well as numerous other parameters essential to determining user PVT. Finally, the user receiver equipment (i.e., user segment) performs the navigation, timing, or other related functions (e.g., surveying). An overview of each system segment is provided next, followed by further elaboration on each segment starting in Section 3.2.

3.1.1 Space Segment Overview

The space segment is the constellation of satellites from which users make ranging measurements. The SVs (i.e., satellites) transmit a PRN-coded signal from which the ranging measurements are made. This concept makes GPS a passive system for the user with signals only being transmitted and the user passively receiving the signals. Thus, an unlimited number of users can simultaneously use GPS. A satellite's transmitted ranging signal is modulated with data that includes information that defines the position of the satellite. An SV includes payloads and vehicle control subsystems. The primary payload is the navigation payload used to support the GPS PVT mission; the secondary payload is the nuclear detonation (NUDET) detection system, which supports detection and reporting of Earth-based radiation phenomena.

The vehicle control subsystems perform such functions as maintaining the satellite pointing to Earth and the solar panels pointing to the Sun.

3.1.2 Control Segment (CS) Overview

The CS is responsible for maintaining the satellites and their proper functioning. This includes maintaining the satellites in their proper orbital positions (called stationkeeping) and monitoring satellite subsystem health and status. The CS also monitors the satellite solar arrays, battery power levels, and propellant levels used for maneuvers. Furthermore, the CS activates spare satellites (if available) to maintain system availability. The CS updates each satellite's clock, ephemeris, and almanac and other indicators in the navigation message at least once per day. Updates are more frequently scheduled when improved navigation accuracies are required. (Frequent clock and ephemeris updates result in reducing the space and control contributions to range measurement error. Further elaboration on the effects of frequent clock and ephemeris updates is provided in Sections 3.3.1.4 and 7.2).

The ephemeris parameters are a precise fit to the GPS satellite orbits and are valid only for a time interval of 4 hours with the once-per-day normal upload schedule. Depending on the satellite block, the navigation message data can be stored for a minimum of 14 days to a maximum of a 210-day duration in intervals of 4 hours or 6 hours for uploads as infrequent as once per two weeks and intervals of greater than 6 hours in the event that an upload cannot be provided for over 2 weeks. The almanac is a reduced precision subset of the ephemeris parameters. The almanac consists of 7 of the 15 ephemeris orbital parameters. Almanac data is used to predict the approximate satellite position and aid in satellite signal acquisition. Furthermore, the CS resolves satellite anomalies, controls SA and AS (see Sections 1.3.1 and 7.2.1), and collects pseudorange and carrier phase measurements at the remote monitor stations to determine satellite clock corrections, almanac, and ephemeris. To accomplish these functions, the CS is comprised of three different physical components: the master control station (MCS), monitor stations, and the ground antennas, each of which is described in more detail in Section 3.3.

3.1.3 User Segment Overview

The user receiving equipment comprises the user segment. Each set of equipment is typically referred to as a *GPS receiver*, which processes the L-band signals transmitted from the satellites to determine user PVT. While PVT determination is the most common use, receivers are designed for other applications, such as computing user platform attitude (i.e., heading, pitch, and roll) or as a timing source. Section 3.4 provides further discussion on the user segment.

3.2 Space Segment Description

The space segment has two principal aspects: One aspect is the constellation of satellites in terms of the orbits and positioning within the orbits. The other aspect is the features of the satellites that occupy each orbital slot. Each aspect is described next.

3.2.1 GPS Satellite Constellation Description

The U.S. government baseline configuration for the constellation consists of 24 satellites. Within this configuration, the satellites are positioned in six Earth-centered orbital planes with four satellites in each plane. The nominal orbital period of a GPS satellite is one-half of a sidereal day or 11 hours, 58 minutes [1]. The orbits are nearly circular and equally spaced around the equator at a 60° separation with a nominal inclination relative to the equatorial plane of 55°. Figure 3.1 depicts the GPS constellation. The orbital radius (i.e., nominal distance from the center of mass of the Earth to the satellite) is approximately 26,600 km. This satellite constellation provides a 24-hour global user navigation and time determination capability. Figure 3.2 presents the satellite orbits in a planar projection referenced to the epoch time of 0000h July 1, 1993 UTC (USNO). Thinking of an orbit as a ring, this figure opens each orbit and lays it flat on a plane. Similarly, for the Earth's equator, it is like a ring that has been opened and laid on a flat surface. The slope of each orbit represents its inclination with respect to the Earth's equatorial plane, which is nominally 55°.

The orbital plane locations with respect to the Earth are defined by the longitude of the ascending node, while the location of the satellite within the orbital plane is defined by the mean anomaly. The longitude of the ascending node is the point of intersection of each orbital plane with the equatorial plane. The Greenwich meridian is the reference point where the longitude of the ascending node has the value of zero. Mean anomaly is the angular position of each satellite within the orbit, with the Earth's equator being the reference or point with a zero value of mean anomaly. It can be observed that the relative phasing between most satellites in adjoining orbits is approximately 40°. The Keplerian parameters for the 24-SV constellation are defined in Section 2.3.1.

The orbital slot assignments of this baseline design are contained in [2] and are provided in Table 3.1. (Note that RAAN is the Right Ascension of the Ascending Node, as defined in Section 2.3.1.)

The remaining reference orbit values (with tolerances) are:

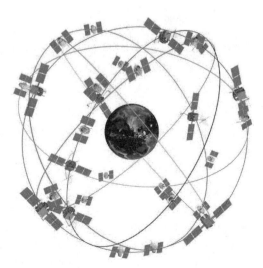

Figure 3.1 GPS satellite constellation. (*Source:* Lockheed Martin Corp. Reprinted with permission.)

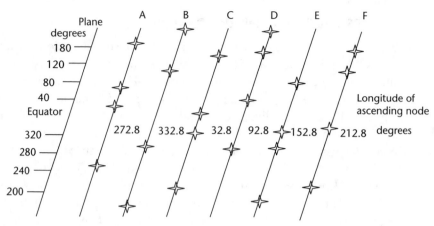

Figure 3.2 GPS constellation planar projection.

Table 3.1 Reference Orbit Slot Assignments as of the Defined Epoch

Slot	RAAN (°)	Argument of Latitude (°)	Slot	RAAN (°)	Argument of Latitude (°)
A1	272.847	268.126	D1	92.847	135.226
A2	272.847	161.786	D2	92.847	265.446
A3	272.847	11.676	D3	92.847	35.136
A4	272.847	41.806	D4	92.847	167.356
B1	332.847	80.956	E1	152.847	197.046
B2	332.847	173.336	E2	152.847	302.596
B3	332.847	309.976	E3	152.847	66.066
B4	332.847	204.376	E4	152.847	333.686
C1	32.847	111.876	F1	212.847	238.886
C2	32.847	11.796	F2	212.847	345.226
C3	32.847	339.666	F3	212.847	105.206
C4	32.847	241.556	F4	212.847	135.346

Defined epoch: 0000Z, July 1, 1993; Greenwich hour angle: 18 hours, 36 minutes, 14.4 seconds referenced to FK5/J2000.00 coordinates.

- Groundtrack equatorial crossing: ±2°;
- Eccentricity: 0.00–0.02;
- Inclination: 55° ± 3°;
- Semimajor axis: 26,559.7 km ± 50 km for Block IIR, ± 17 km for Block II/IIA;
- Longitude of the ascending node: ±2°;
- Argument of perigee: ±180°.

Several different notations are used to refer to the satellites in their orbits. One nomenclature assigns a letter to each orbital plane (i.e., A, B, C, D, E, and F) with each satellite within a plane assigned a number from 1 to 4. Thus, a satellite referenced as B3 refers to satellite number 3 in orbital plane B. A second notation used is a NAVSTAR satellite number assigned by the U.S. Air Force. This notation is in the form of space vehicle number (SVN); for example, 60 refers to NAVSTAR satellite 60. The third notation represents the configuration of the PRN code generators onboard the satellite. These PRN code generators are configured uniquely on each satellite, thereby producing unique versions of both C/A code and P(Y) code. Thus, a satellite can be identified by the PRN codes that it generates. Occasionally, the PRN assignment for a given SVN can change during the satellite's mission duration.

3.2.2 Constellation Design Guidelines

As discussed in Section 2.3.2, several tradeoffs are involved in the design of the GPS constellation. One primary concern is the geometric contribution to navigation accuracy; in other words, is the satellite geometry sufficiently diverse to provide good observability to users throughout the world. This geometry is measured by a parameter called dilution of precision (DOP) and is described in more detail in Section 7.3. Studies continue concerning tradeoffs on different possible satellite configurations. Some studies have investigated the use of 30 satellites in three orbital planes as well as the utility of geostationary satellites. Most of this work is done with a nominal constellation assuming all satellites are healthy and operational, but a new dimension for study is introduced when satellite failures are considered. Single or multiple satellite failures provide a new dimension around which to optimize performance from a geometry consideration. Another design consideration is line-of-sight observability of the satellites by the ground stations to maintain the ephemeris of the satellites and the uploading of this data.

3.2.3 Space Segment Phased Development

The continuing development of the control and space segments has been phased in over many years, starting in the mid-1970s. This development started with a concept validation phase and has progressed to several production phases. The satellites associated with each phase of development are called a *block* of satellites. Characteristics of each phase and block are presented in the following sections.

3.2.3.1 Satellite Block Development

Five satellite blocks have been developed to date. The initial concept validation satellites were called Block I. The last remaining prototype Block I satellite was disposed of in late 1995. Block II satellites are the initial production satellites, while Block IIA refers to upgraded production satellites. All Block I, II, and IIA satellites have been launched. Block IIR satellites, denoted as the replenishment satellites, are being deployed. At the time of this writing, modified Block IIR versions denoted as Block IIR-M were scheduled for launch in 2005. Block IIF satellites, referred to as the follow-on or sustainment satellites, are being built. GPS III satellites are in the planning stage for a post-2010 deployment. Since satellites are launched only as replacements for a satellite failure, their scheduling is difficult to predict, especially when most satellites have far outlived their design lifetime. At the time of this writing, the constellation consisted of 27 operational satellites. Table 3.2 describes the configuration of the current satellite constellation. Thus, the current optimized constellation has up to seven orbital slots unevenly spaced around each plane, with some satellites in relatively close proximity to provide redundant coverage for near-term predicted failures. Since the state of the constellation varies, the Internet is the best source for current status information. One such Web site is operated and maintained by the U.S. Coast Guard Navigation Center [3].

3.2.3.2 Navigation Payload Overview

The navigation payload is responsible for the generation and transmission of ranging codes and navigation data on the L1, L2, and (starting with Block IIF) L5 carrier frequencies to the user segment. Control of the navigation payload is taken from

Table 3.2 Satellite Constellation Configuration (as of January 29, 2005)

Block/Launch Order	PRN Number	SVN	Launch Date	Orbital Slot
II-5	17	17	December 11, 1989	D6
II-9	15	15	October 1, 1990	D5
IIA-11	24	24	July 4, 1991	D1
IIA-12	25	25	February 23, 1992	A2
IIA-14	26	26	July 7, 1992	F2
IIA-15	27	27	September 9, 1992	A4
IIA-16	01	32	November 22, 1992	F6
IIA-17	29	29	December 18, 1992	F5
IIA-19	31	31	March 30, 1993	C5
IIA-20	07	37	May 13, 1993	C4
IIIA-21	09	39	June 26, 1993	A1
IIA-22	05	35	August 30, 1993	B4
IIA-23	04	34	October 26, 1993	D4
IIA-24	06	36	March 10, 1994	C1
IIA-25	03	33	March 28, 1996	C2
IIA-26	10	40	July 16, 1996	E3
IIA-27	30	30	September 12, 1996	B2
IIA-28	08	38	November 6, 1997	A3
IIR-2	13	43	July 23, 1997	F3
IIR-3	11	46	October 7, 1999	D2
IIR-4	20	51	May 11, 2000	E1
IIR-5	28	44	July 16, 2000	B3
IIR-6	14	41	November 10, 2000	F1
IIR-7	18	54	January 30, 2001	E4
IIR-8	16	56	January 29, 2003	B1
IIR-9	21	45	March 31, 2003	D3
IIR-10	22	47	December 21, 2003	E2
IIR-11	19	59	March 20, 2004	C3
IIR-12	23	60	June 23, 2004	F4
IIR-13	02	61	November 6, 2004	D7

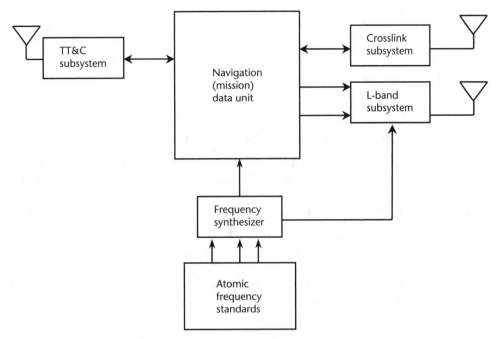

Figure 3.3 Satellite navigation payload.

reception of the predicted navigation data and other control data from the CS via the tracking, telemetry, and control (TT&C) links. The navigation payload is only one part of the spacecraft, with other systems being responsible for such functions as attitude control and solar panel pointing. Figure 3.3 is a generic block diagram of a navigation payload. Atomic frequency standards (AFSs) are used as the basis for generating the extremely stable ranging codes and carrier frequencies transmitted by the payload. Each satellite contains multiple AFSs to meet the mission reliability, with only one operating at any time. Since the AFSs operate at their natural frequencies, a frequency synthesizer, phase-locked to the AFS, generates the basic 10.23-MHz reference that serves as the timing reference within the payload for ranging signal and transmit frequency generation. The navigation data unit (NDU), known as the mission data unit in the Block IIR design, contains the ranging code generators that generate the C/A code and P(Y) codes (plus new civil and military signals in later payloads) for modulo-2 addition with the navigation message data. The NDU also contains a processor that stores the uploads received from the CS containing multiple days of navigation message data, and it assures that the current issue of navigation message data is provided for this modulo-2 addition. The combined baseband ranging signals are then sent to the L-band subsystem where they are modulated onto the L-band carrier frequencies and amplified for transmission to the user. (Chapter 4 describes the signal-generation process in detail.) The L-band subsystem contains numerous components, including the L1 and L2 transmitters and associated antenna. The NDU processor also interfaces to the crosslink receiver/transmitter for intersatellite communication, as well as ranging, on Block IIR and later versions. This crosslink receiver/transmitter uses a separate antenna and feed system. (It should be noted that the intersatellite ranging is functional on the Block IIR, Block IIR-M, and Block IIF space vehicles; however, the U.S. government has chosen so far not to add this capability to the CS.) As stated previously, the primary and secondary SV payloads are navigation and NUDET, respectively. Occasionally, the satellites carry additional payloads, such as laser reflectors for satellite laser ranging (i.e., validation of predicted ephemeris), and free electron measurement experiments.

3.2.3.3 Block I—Initial Concept Validation Satellites

Block I satellites were developmental prototypes to validate the initial GPS concept, so only 11 satellites were built. The Block I satellites, built by Rockwell International, were launched between 1978 and 1985 from Vandenberg Air Force Base, California. A picture of the Block I satellite is presented in Figure 3.4. The onboard storage capability was for about 3.5 days of navigation messages. The navigation message data was transmitted for a 1-hour period and was valid for an additional 3 hours. Since there was no onboard momentum dumping, frequent ground contact was required for momentum management. Without momentum dumping, the satellites would lose attitude control after a short time interval. Two cesium and two rubidium AFSs were employed. These satellites were designed for a mean mission duration (MMD) of 4.5 years, a design life of 5 years and inventory expendable (e.g., fuel, battery life, and solar panel power capacity) of 7 years. Reliability improvements were made to the atomic clocks on later satellites based on failure analysis from earlier launches. Some Block I satellites operated for more than double their design life.

3.2.3.4 Block II—Initial Production Satellites

On-orbit operation of the Block I satellites provided valuable experience that led to several significant capability enhancements in subsystem design for the Block II operational satellites. These improvements included radiation hardening to prevent random memory upset from such events as cosmic rays to improve reliability and survivability. Besides these enhancements, several other refinements were incorporated to support the fully operational GPS system requirements. Since the NDU processor would not be programmable on-orbit, flexibility was designed into the flight

Figure 3.4 Block I satellite.

software via changeable databases. Thus, no reprogramming has been required on the Block II satellites since the first launch. While most of the changes affected only the CS/space interface, some also affected the user signal interface. The significant changes are identified as the following: To provide security, SA and AS capabilities were added. (SA and AS are discussed in Sections 1.3.1 and 7.2.1.) System integrity was improved by the addition of automatic error detection for certain error conditions. After detection of these error conditions, there is a changeover to the transmission of nonstandard PRN codes (NSCs) to prevent the usage of a corrupted signal or data. Nine Block II satellites were built by Rockwell International, and the first was launched in February 1989 from Cape Canaveral Air Force Station in Florida. The onboard navigation message storage capacity was expanded to allow for a 14-day mission. Autonomous onboard momentum control was implemented in the satellite within the attitude and velocity control system, thus eliminating the need for ground contact to perform momentum dumping. Again, for reliability and survivability, multiple rubidium and cesium AFSs were onboard. These satellites were designed for a MMD of 6 years, a design life of 7.5 years, and inventory expendables (e.g., fuel, battery life, and solar panel power capacity) of 10 years. At the time of this writing, one Block II satellite remained in the constellation. The Block II average life to date is 11.8 years, with SVN 15 having the greatest longevity at nearly 15 years. Figure 3.5 depicts a Block II satellite.

3.2.3.5   Block IIA—Upgraded Production Satellites

The Block IIA satellites are very similar to the Block II satellites, but with a number of system enhancements to allow an extended operation period of 180 days. Spacecraft autonomous momentum control was extended. The onboard navigation data storage capability was tested to assure retention for the 180-day period. For approximately the first day on-orbit, the navigation message data is broadcast for a

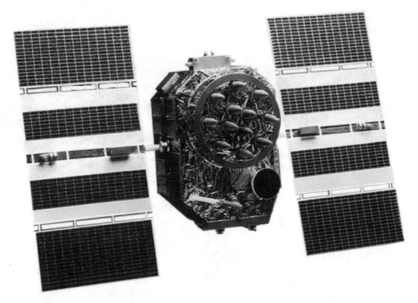

Figure 3.5   Block II satellite.

2-hour period and is valid over a 4-hour interval. For the remainder of the first 14 days, the navigation message is broadcast for a 4-hour period with a validity period of 6 hours (2 additional hours). Following this initial 14-day period, the navigation message data broadcast periods gradually extend from 6 hours to 144 hours. With this additional onboard storage retention capability, the satellites can function continuously for a period of 6 months without ground contact. However, the accuracy of the CS ephemeris and clock predictions and thus the accuracy of the navigation message data gracefully degrade over time such that the user range error (URE) will be bounded by 10,000m after 180 days. (The URE is the contribution of the pseudorange error from the CS and space segment.) Typically, the URE is 1.4m (1σ). (Pseudorange errors are extensively discussed in Section 7.2.) With no general onboard processing capability, no updates to stored reference ephemeris data are possible. So, as a result, full system accuracy is only available when the CS is functioning properly and navigation messages are uploaded on a daily basis. Block IIA electronics are radiation-hardened. Nineteen Block IIA satellites were built by Rockwell International, with the first launched in November 1990 from Cape Canaveral Air Force Station in Florida and the last launched in November 1997. The life expectancy of the Block IIA is the same as that of the Block II. At the time of this writing, 16 Block IIA satellites remained in the constellation, with a projected MMD of over 10.3 years. A Block IIA satellite is shown in Figure 3.6.

3.2.3.6 Block IIR—Replenishment Satellites

The GPS Block IIR (replenishment) satellites (Figure 3.7) represent an ever-growing presence in the GPS constellation. Over half of the original 21 IIR SVs have been

Figure 3.6 Block IIA satellite.

Figure 3.7 Block IIR satellite. (*Source:* Lockheed Martin Corp. Reprinted with permission.)

launched since 1997 (the first Block IIR satellite was lost in a launch accident early that year). Lockheed Martin and its navigation payload subcontractor, ITT Aerospace/Communications, are building these satellites.

The Block IIR began development following contract award in 1989 as a totally compatible upgrade and replacement to the Block II and Block IIA SVs. All of the basic GPS features are supported: C/A and P(Y) code on L1, P(Y) on L2, ultra-high frequency (UHF) crosslink capability, attitude determination system to stabilize the SV bus platform, reaction control system to maintain the on-orbit location in the constellation, and sufficient power capacity for the life of the vehicle.

There are two versions of the Block IIR SV. The "classic" IIR and its AFSs, autonomy, reprogrammability, and improved antenna panel will be described first. The features of the "modernized" IIR will be covered later in this section.

Classic IIR
The baseline (nonmodernized) GPS Block IIR has now been dubbed the *classic IIR*.

The Block IIR satellites are designed for a MMD of 6 years, a design life of 7.5 years, and inventory expendables (e.g., fuel, battery life, and solar panel power capacity) of 10 years. As of August 2005, there were 12 IIR SVs in the 30-SV constellation. The oldest IIR SV (SVN 43) was over 8 years old at time of this writing, exceeding the required 7.5-year design life.

Figure 3.8 shows some of the main components of the Block IIR SV. Several of these will be highlighted in the remainder of this section.

Advanced Atomic Frequency Standards
All IIR SVs contain three next generation rubidium AFSs (RAFS). The IIR design has a significantly enhanced physics package that improves stability and reliability [4].

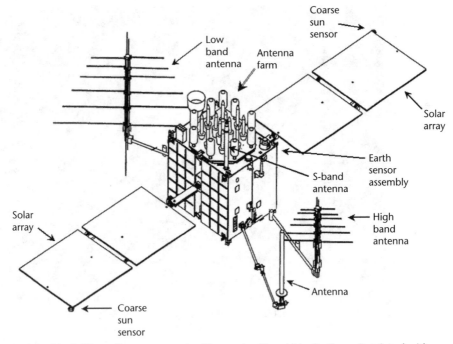

Figure 3.8 Block IIR satellite components. (*Source:* Lockheed Martin Corp. Reprinted with permission.)

The RAFS has a MMD of 7.5 years. It is coupled with a redundant voltage controlled crystal oscillator (VCXO) and software functionality into what is called the time keeping system (TKS). The TKS loop provides a timing tuning capability to stabilize and control satellite clock performance.

IIR Accuracy

An accurate onboard AFS provides the key to good GPS PVT accuracy [5]. Figure 3.9 shows the 1-day Hadamard deviation for mid-2004. Hadamard deviation measures frequency stability—the lower the number, the more stable the AFS. Hadamard deviation (as opposed to Allan deviation) currently provides the best way to measure frequency stability in AFS with nonzero frequency drift. (Appendix B provides descriptions of both the Hadamard and Allan deviations.)

The IIR specification requires that the total IIR URE (defined in Section 3.2.3.5) value should be less than 2.2m when operating a RAFS. The URE performance for GPS IIR has averaged approximately 0.8m or better for several years [6]. Thus, the required specification is easily surpassed.

There is also a significantly improved solar pressure model (by an order of magnitude compared to the II/IIA model) used in the MCS when computing the orbit of the IIR [7, 8]. This increases the accuracy of the ephemeris modeling on the ground.

Enhanced Autonomy

The advanced capabilities of the Block IIR SV include a redundancy management system called REDMAN, which monitors bus subcomponent functionality and provides for warning and component switching to maintain SV health.

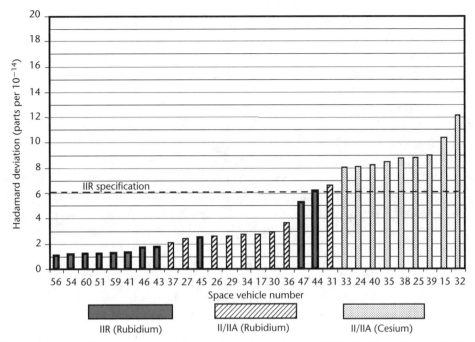

Figure 3.9 One-day Hadamard stability ranking. (*Source:* Lockheed Martin Corp. Reprinted with permission.)

The Block IIR uses nickel hydrogen (NiH_2) batteries, which require no reconditioning and accompanying operator burden.

When in Earth eclipse, automatic pointing of the solar array panels is accomplished via an onboard orbit propagation algorithm to enable quiescent reacquisition of the Sun following eclipse exit. This provides a more stable and predictive SV bus platform and orientation for the L-band signal.

Block IIR has an expanded NSC capability to protect the user from spurious signals. It is enabled automatically in response to the detection of the most harmful on-orbit RAFS and VCXO discontinuities.

Block IIR has a capability to perform autonomous navigation via intersatellite crosslink ranging. This function is called AutoNav. It provides 180-day independent navigation performance without ground contact. Although the CS currently cannot support full AutoNav operation, portions of this capability are undergoing on-orbit testing. There is potential for increased accuracy when using AutoNav.

In addition to intersatellite ranging, other communications with on-orbit SVs consist of crosslink commanding and data transfer to other SVs in the constellation. The Block IIR SVs were also designed to operate through laser and nuclear threats.

Reprogrammability

There are several reprogrammable computers on board: the redundant SV bus spacecraft processor unit (SPU) and the redundant navigation system mission data unit (MDU). Reprogrammability allows the CS to change the flight software in on-orbit SVs. This feature has already been employed on-orbit in several instances. The MDU was provided with diagnostic buffers to give detailed insight into the behavior of the TKS. It was also given a jumpstart capability allowing current TKS parameters to be saved to a special area of memory and reused following the load of a new program. This feature reduces, by about 4 hours, the time required to recover from a new program load. The SPU was provided with new rolling buffers to save high-speed telemetry data for SV functions even when not in contact with the CS.

Improved Antenna Panel

Lockheed Martin, under an internal research and development effort, developed new L-band and UHF antenna element designs. The new L1 power received on the ground will be at least −154.5 dBW (edge-of-Earth, as compared to the current typical IIR performance of −155.5 dBW) and the new L2 power received on the ground will be −159.5 dBW (edge-of-Earth, as compared to the current typical IIR performance of −161.5 dBW). This provides greater signal power to the user. The last 4 of the 12 classic IIRs and all of the modernized IIRs have the improved antenna panel.

Block IIR-M—Modernized Replenishment Satellites

The modernized GPS IIR (IIR-M) (see Figure 3.10) will bring new services to military and civilian users [9, 10]. The IIR-M is the result of an effort to bring modernized functionality to IIR SVs that were built several years ago and placed into storage until they were needed for launch. The Air Force contracted Lockheed Martin in 2000 to modernize several of the unlaunched IIR SVs. This modernization program has been accomplished within existing solar array capability, available on-board processor margins, and current vehicle structural capabilities.

As many as eight Block IIR SVs will be modernized. Maintaining constellation health could interfere with this goal, but current predictions are optimistic as the

Figure 3.10   Block IIR-M satellite. (*Source:* Lockheed Martin Corp. Reprinted with permission.)

older Block II/IIA SVs continue to surprise with their longevity. IIR-M brings the new military and civilian services to users at least 3 years earlier than if modernized capabilities were to wait for just Block IIF and Block III.

At the time of this writing, the IIR-M SVs were undergoing the design modifications and were available for launch in 2005. Early testing of L2C and M code (new civil and military signals, respectively) will occur for some time following the first IIR-M launch while more modernized SVs are added to the constellation.

Modernized Signals

New L-band signals and increased L-band power will significantly improve navigation performance for users worldwide. Three new signals will be provided: two new military codes on L1 and on L2, and a new civilian code on L2. The new L2 civil signal denoted as L2C will be an improved signal sequence over L1 C/A, enabling ionospheric error correction to be done by civilian users. It will be ground-selectable, allowing selection of either L2 C/A or a proposed new L2C code or L2C off. The new signal structure will be totally backward-compatible with existing L1 C/A and P(Y), and L2 P(Y). (Refer to Section 4.5.1 for further details.)

The M code on L1 and L2 for the military user will also be ground-selectable and will include a pseudo-M code to be used during testing activities. The new M code will provide the authorized user with more signal security.

Modernized Hardware

The new navigation panel boxes consist of a redesigned L1 transmitter, a redesigned L2 transmitter, and the new waveform generator/modulator/intermediate power amplifier/converter (WGMIC) (Figure 3.11). The WGMIC is a new box developed by ITT coupling the brand-new waveform generator with the functionality of the L1 signal modulator/intermediate power amplifier (IPA), the L2 signal modulator/IPA, and the dc-to-dc converter. The waveform generator provides much of the new modernized signal structure and controls the power settings on the new transmitters. To manage the thermal environment of these higher-power boxes, heat pipes were incorporated into the fabrication of the structural panel. Lockheed Martin has used similar heat pipes on other satellites it has built.

The improved IIR antenna panel discussed earlier in this section will also be installed on all IIR-M SVs. This will provide greater signal power to the user. The antenna redesign effort was begun prior to the modernization decision but will significantly enhance the new IIR-M features. L-band power will be increased on both L1 and L2 frequencies. L1 will be increased by at least double the power, and L2 will be increased by at least quadruple power at low elevation angles.

The UHF performance has also been improved. This does not directly affect the user, but it enhances intersatellite communication: data transfer, commanding, and crosslink ranging.

Other total navigation payload (TNP) modifications include new MDU software that is also useable in the classic IIR SVs. Table 3.3 highlights some of the other SV modifications, including the new antenna array (which includes the downlink signal L-band array), new power switching capability, as well as other component and harness changes.

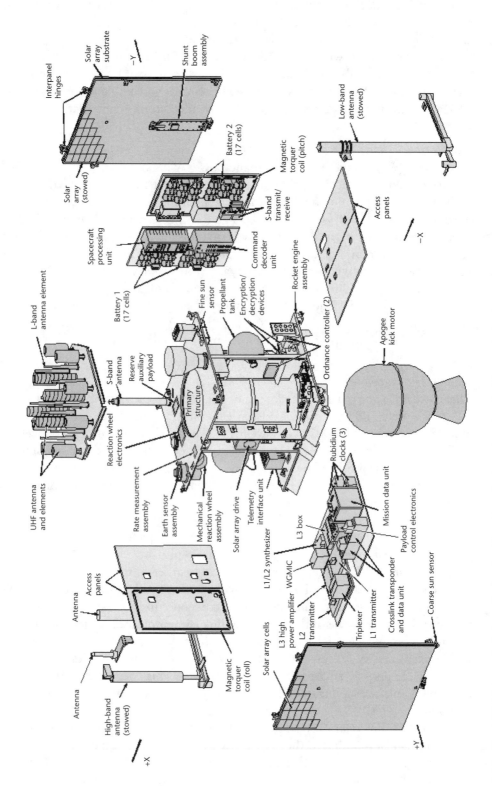

Figure 3.11 Block IIR-M expanded view. (*Source:* Lockheed Martin Corp. Reprinted with permission.)

Table 3.3 IR-M Modification Summary

Component	Magnitude of Change	Description of Change
Antenna panel	Moderate redesign	Replace L-band elements with broadband proprietary elements
L-band subsystem	Technology upgrade	Replace five separate components with three multifunction assemblies (L1 and L2 high-power amplifiers and a WGMIC)
L-band structural panel	New design, similar to those flown on communication SVs	Higher-power dissipation requires integral heat pipes in the panel honeycomb structure
Payload control electronics	Minor modification	Add power switching and fusing to accommodate additional power
Power regulation unit	Minor modification	Spare pins connected to additional power and return lines for higher power

3.2.3.7 Block IIF—Follow-On Sustainment Satellites

In 1995, the Air Force (GPS JPO) released a request for proposal (RFP) for a set of satellites to sustain the GPS constellation, designated as Block II follow-on, or IIF. The RFP also requested the provider to include the modifications to the GPS CS necessary to operate the IIF SV. While necessary for service sustainment, the IIF SV procurement afforded the Air Force the opportunity to start adding new signals and additional flexibility to the system beyond the capabilities and improvements of the IIR SV. A new military acquisition code on L2 was required, as well as an option for a new civil L5 signal at a frequency within 102.3 MHz of the existing L2 frequency of 1,227.6 MHz. The L5 frequency that was eventually settled upon was 1,176.45 MHz, placing it in a frequency band that is protected for ARNS. (The L5 signal is described in Section 4.5.2.)

The RFP also allowed the provider to offer additional "best value" features that could be considered during the proposal evaluation. Boeing (then Rockwell) included several best value features in its proposal and was awarded the IIF contract in April 1996. Several of these features were to improve service performance, including a URE 3m or less in AutoNav mode, an age of data for the URE of less than 3 hours using the UHF crosslink to update the navigation message, and design goals for AFS Allan variance performance better than specification. (Appendix B contains details on the Allan variance.) Other features supported the addition of auxiliary payloads on the IIF SV and reduction of operational complexity for the operators via greater use of the UHF crosslink communication system.

The original planned launch date for the first IIF SV was April 2001. However, due to the longevity of the Block II and IIA SVs and projected service life of the IIR SVs, the need date for a IIF launch was extended sufficiently to allow the Air Force to direct modifications to the IIF SV that resulted in the present design. The first modification was enabled when the Delta II launch vehicle (LV) was deselected for IIF, leaving the larger evolved expendable launch vehicle (EELV) as the primary LV. The larger fairing of the EELV enabled the "Big Bird" modification to the IIF SV, which expanded the spacecraft volume, nadir surface area, power generation, and thermal dissipation capability. Around the same time, extensive studies were performed by the GPS Modernization Signal Development Team (GMSDT) to evaluate new capabilities needed from GPS, primarily to add new military and civil ranging signals. The GMSDT was formed as a government/Federally Funded Research and Development Center (FFRDC)/industry team to evaluate the deficiencies of the existing signal structure and recommend a new signal structure that would address the key areas of modulation and signal acquisition, security, data message structure, and system implementation. Today's M code signal structure is the result of those studies. (M code is discussed in Section 4.5.3.) The complete list of ranging signals provided by the IIF SV is shown in Table 3.4. It should be noted that the new ranging signals also carry improved versions of the clock and ephemeris data in their respective navigation messages. This eliminates some of the resolution limitations the original navigation message had imposed as the URE has continued to improve.

The original flexibility and expandability features of the IIF SV in both the spacecraft and navigation payload designs allowed the addition of these new signals without major revisions to the IIF design. An exploded view of the Block IIF SV is depicted in Figure 3.12. The figure shows all of the components of the spacecraft subsystems. These include the attitude determination and control subsystem, which keeps the antennas pointing at the Earth and the solar panels at the Sun; the electrical power subsystem that generates, regulates, stores, and shunts the DC power for the satellite; and the TT&C subsystem, which allows the MCS operators to communicate with and control the satellite on-orbit. To support the increase in DC power requirements due to the increased transmit power, the solar arrays were switched from silicon technology to higher efficiency triple-junction gallium arsenide. Additionally, the thermal design had to be revised to accommodate the additional transmitter thermal loads. Other than some realignment to maintain weight and thermal balance, no other modifications were required for the spacecraft.

The navigation payload on the Block IIF SV includes two RAFSs and one cesium AFS per the contract requirement for dual technology. These AFSs provide the tight frequency stability necessary to generate high-accuracy ranging signals. The NDU generates all of the baseband forms of the ranging signals. The original NDU design included a spare slot that allowed the addition of M code and the L5 signal within the same envelope. The original NDU computer was designed with 300% expansion memory margin and 300% computational reserve (throughput margin), so that there was sufficient reserve to support the generation of the new navigation messages for M code and L5 plus other modernization requirements. The computer program is reprogrammable on-orbit and is loaded from onboard electrically erasable programmable read-only memory (EEPROM) when power is applied, avoiding the need for large blocks of contact time with the ground antennas. The L-band subsystem generates about 350W of radio frequency (RF) power for transmitting the three sets of signals in Table 3.4.

Table 3.4 Block IIF Ranging Signal Set

Link (Frequency)	L1 (1,575.42 MHz)	L2 (1,227.6 MHz)	L5 (1,176.45 MHz)
Civil (open) signals	C/A code	L2C	L5
Military (restricted) signals	P(Y) code M code	P(Y) code M code	—

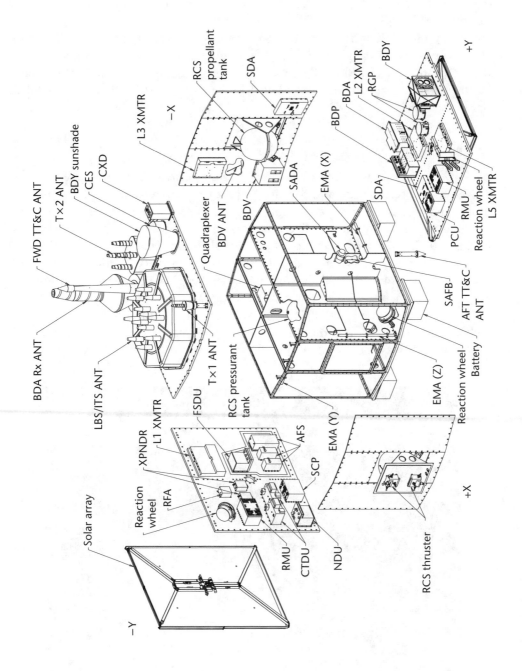

Figure 3.12 Expanded view of the Block IIF. (*Source:* The Boeing Company. Reprinted with permission.)

The Block IIF SV is designed for a life of 12 years with a MMD of 9.9 years. It is backward compatible with the Block IIR capabilities described in Section 3.2.3.6, including the capability to operate in AutoNav mode. An on-orbit depiction of the Block IIF SV is shown in Figure 3.13. The nadir-facing side contains a set of UHF and L-band antennas and other components that are very reminiscent of all of the previous GPS satellites.

The original IIF contract was for a basic buy of 6 SVs and two options of 15 and 12 SVs for a possible total of 33 SVs. At the time of this writing, GPS JPO projections indicated that 16 Block IIF SVs will be procured and launched to maintain the constellation prior to the start of GPS III. The first Block IIF launch is scheduled for 2007.

3.2.3.8 Block III—Next Generation Satellites

The GPS III program was conceived to reassess the entire GPS architecture as it has evolved to its present state and determine the correct architecture to lead into the future. The program has two main goals: reduce the government's total ownership costs and provide sufficient architectural flexibility to satisfy evolving requirements through 2030. On a more technical side, GPS III is expected to provide submeter position accuracy, greater timing accuracy, a system integrity solution, a high data capacity intersatellite crosslink capability, and higher signal power to meet military antijam requirements. Two system architecture/requirements development (SARD) studies were performed in 2001–2002 by contractor teams led by Boeing and Lockheed Martin, resulting in a baseline concept description from each team. (An unfunded study was conducted by Spectrum Astro.) After a short extension on those

Figure 3.13   Block IIF SV (*Source:* The Boeing Company. Reprinted with permission.)

contracts and a brief planning period for the government, GPS III entered phase A development with two contracts, again to Boeing and Lockheed Martin teams. Each team completed a system requirements review in 2005. At the time of this writing, the first GPS III satellite launch was planned for fiscal year 2013.

3.3 Control Segment

The control segment (CS) is responsible for monitoring, commanding, and controlling the GPS satellite constellation. Functionally, the CS monitors the downlink L-band navigation signals, updates the navigation messages, and resolves satellite anomalies. Additionally, the CS monitors each satellite's state of health, manages tasks associated with satellite stationkeeping maneuvers and battery recharging, and commands the satellite payloads, as required [11].

The major elements of the CS consist of the MCS, L-band monitor stations, and S-band ground antennas. The primary CS functions are performed at the MCS, under the operation of the U.S. Air Force Space Command, Second Space Operation Squadron (2SOPS), located at Schriever Air Force Base (AFB) in Colorado Springs, Colorado. It provides continuous GPS services, 24 hours per day, 7 days a week, and serves as the mission control center for GPS operations. A backup MCS, located at a contractor facility in Gaithersburg, Maryland, provides redundancy of the MCS. The major elements of the CS and their functional allocation are shown in Figure 3.14.

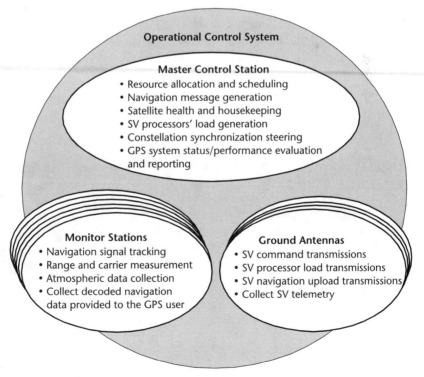

Figure 3.14 CS overview.

The 2SOPS supports all crew-action required operations of the GPS constellation, including daily uploading of navigation information to the satellites and monitoring, diagnosis, reconfiguration, and stationkeeping of all satellites in the GPS constellation. Spacecraft prelaunch, launch, and insertion operations are performed by a different ground control system under the command of the First Space Operations Squadron (1SOPS), also located at Schriever AFB. If a given SV is determined to be incapable of normal operations, the satellite commanding is transferred to 1SOPS for anomaly resolution or test monitoring.

3.3.1 Current Configuration

At the time of this writing, the CS configuration consisted of dual MCSs, six monitor stations, and four ground antennas (see Figure 3.15). The MCS data processing software, hosted on an IBM mainframe under the Multiple Virtual Storage operating system, commands and controls the CS with multiple high-definition textual displays. The monitor stations and ground antennas are unmanned and are operated remotely from the active MCS. The monitor stations' and ground antennas' data processing software, hosted on Sun workstations under the UNIX operating system, communicate with the MCS using transmission control processing/Internet processing (TCP/IP) communication protocols. The MCS also has numerous internal and external communication links. The majority of these links use the IBM's System Network Architecture communication protocol. There are plans to transition all of these links to TCP/IP.

The CS configuration is in transition. Two major upgrades are in development: the Legacy Accuracy Improvement Initiative (L-AII) and the Architecture Evolution Plan (AEP). The L-AII upgrade adds up to 14 NGA monitor stations. Therefore, there can be a total of 20 Air Force and NGA monitoring stations within the CS. These additional NGA stations will provide the CS with continuous L-band tracking coverage of the constellation. (The current six monitor station configuration can have satellite L-band coverage outages of up to 2 hours.) The AEP upgrade replaces

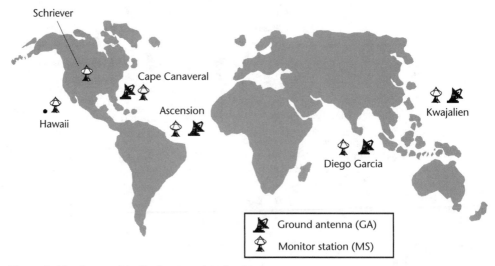

Figure 3.15 Geographic distribution of CS facilities.

the MCS legacy mainframe with a distributed Sun workstation configuration. The AEP upgrade provides an integrated suite of commercial off-the-shelf products and improved graphical user interface displays. As AEP evolves, the CS will have additional features and functionality, including support for the IIF satellites and the modernized signals (further discussion is found in Section 3.3.2).

3.3.1.1   MCS Description

The MCS provides the central command and control of the GPS constellation. Specific functions include:

- Monitoring and maintaining satellite state of health;
- Monitoring the satellite orbits;
- Estimating and predicting satellite clock and ephemeris parameters;
- Generating GPS navigation messages;
- Maintaining GPS timing service and its synchronization to UTC (USNO);
- Monitoring the navigation service integrity;
- End-around verifying and logging the navigation data delivered to the GPS user;
- Commanding satellite maneuvers to maintain the GPS orbit and repositioning due to vehicle failures.

All ground facilities necessary to support the GPS constellation are contained within the CS, as shown in Figure 3.14. The CS shares a ground antenna with the Air Force Satellite Control Network and additional monitor stations with NGA, under the L-AII and AEP upgrade. The MCS consists of data processing, control, display, and communications equipment to support these functions. The discussion here is limited to the navigation service, with no discussion related to the satellite maintenance activities.

The primary task of the MCS is to generate and distribute the navigation data message (sometimes referred to as the NAV Data message). (Details of the NAV Data message are contained in Section 4.4.) The MCS uses a sequence of steps, including collecting and processing the monitor station measurements, generating satellite ephemeris and clock estimates and predictions, and constructing and distributing the NAV Data messages. The monitor stations provide the raw pseudorange, carrier phase, and meteorological measurements that are smoothed by the MCS. A Kalman filter generates the precise satellite ephemeris and clock estimates, using these smoothed measurements. The CS filter is a linearized Kalman filter, with the ephemeris estimates linearized around a nominal reference trajectory. The reference trajectory is computed using accurate models to describe each satellite's motion. These ephemeris estimates, together with the reference trajectory, construct the precise ephemeris predictions that form the basis of the NAV Data message ephemeris parameters. Specifically, a least squares fit routine converts the predicted positions into the navigation orbital elements, in accordance with IS-GPS-200 (see Section 2.3.1). The resulting orbital elements are uploaded into the satellite's navigation payload memory and transmitted to the GPS user.

Fundamentally, GPS navigation accuracy is derived from a coherent time scale, known as GPS system time, with one of the critical components being the satellite's AFS, which provides the stable reference for the satellite clock. As discussed earlier, each satellite carries multiple AFSs. The MCS commands the satellite AFSs, monitors their performance, and maintains estimates of satellite clock bias, drift, and drift rate (for rubidium only) to support the generation of clock corrections for the NAV Data message. As stated in Section 2.6, GPS system time is defined relative to an ensemble of all active SV and MS AFSs. The ensemble or composite AFS improves GPS time stability and minimizes its dependency on any single AFS failure in defining such a coherent time scale.

Another important task of the MCS is to monitor the integrity of the navigation service. Throughout the entire data flow from MCS to satellite and back, the MCS ensures that all NAV Data message parameters are uploaded and transmitted correctly. The MCS maintains a complete memory image of the NAV Data message and compares each downlink message (received from its monitor stations) against the expected message. Significant differences between the downlink versus expected navigation message result in an alert and corrective action by 2SOPS. Along with navigation bit errors, the MCS monitors the L-band ranging data for consistency across satellites and across monitor stations. When an inconsistency is observed across satellites or monitor stations, the MCS generates an L-band alert within 60 seconds of detection [12].

The CS depends on several external data sources for coordination with the UTC (USNO) absolute time scale, precise monitor station coordinates, and Earth-orientation parameters. NGA and USNO provide the CS with such external data.

3.3.1.2 Monitor Station Description

To perform the navigation tracking function, the CS has a dedicated, globally distributed, L-band monitor station network. At the time of this writing, the CS network consisted of six Air Force monitor stations: Ascension Island, Diego Garcia, Kwajalein, Hawaii, Colorado Springs, and Cape Canaveral. These stations are located near the equator to maximize L-band coverage and are shown in Figure 3.16.

Each monitor station operates under the control of the MCS and consists of the equipment and computer programs necessary to collect satellite-ranging data, satellite status data, and local meteorological data. This data is forwarded to the MCS for processing. Specifically, a monitor station consists of a single dual-frequency receiver, dual cesium AFSs, meteorological sensors, and local workstations and communication equipment. Each receiver's antenna element consists of a conical ground plane with annular chokes at the base to produce a 14-dB multipath-to-direct signal rejection ratio for signal paths above 15° elevation. (An in-depth discussion on multipath is contained in Section 6.2.) The HP5071 cesium AFSs provide a 5-MHz reference to the receiver. Continuous-phase measurements between the AFSs are provided to the MCS for independent monitoring of the active atomic clock and for support of AFS switchovers. The MCS maintains a coherent monitor station time scale. At AFS switchovers, the MCS provides the phase and frequency difference estimates (between AFSs) to the CS Kalman filter to minimize any time

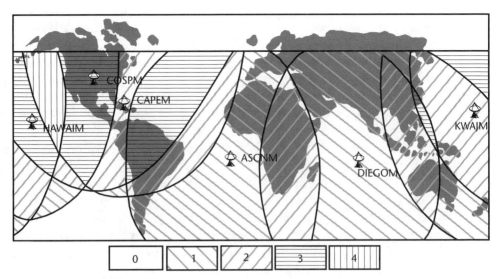

Figure 3.16   CS monitor station coverage.

scale disruptions. Meteorological sensors provide surface pressure, temperature, and dew point measurements to the CS Kalman filter to model the troposphere delay. However, these meteorological sensors are in disrepair, and their measurements have been replaced by monthly tabular data [13]. The local workstations provide commands and data collection between the monitor station and the MCS.

The Air Force monitor stations use a 12-channel, survey-grade, all-in-view receiver. These receivers, developed by Allen Osbourne Associates (AOA), are based on proven Jet Propulsion Laboratory (JPL) Turbo Rogue technology. The AOA receiver is designed with complete independence of the L1 and L2 tracking loops, with each tracking loop commanded by the MCS under various track acquisition strategies. With such a design, the overall receiver tracking performance can be maintained, even when tracking abnormal satellites (e.g., nonstandard code or satellite initialization, which require additional acquisition processing). These all-digital receivers have no detectable interchannel bias errors. (An earlier CS receiver required external interchannel bias compensation due to its analog design with separate correlation and data processing cards. Interchannel bias is a time-delay difference incurred when processing a common satellite signal through different hardware and data processing paths in a receiver.)

The CS receivers differ from normal receivers in several areas. First, these receivers require external commands for acquisition. Although most user equipment is only designed to acquire and track GPS signals that are in compliance with applicable specifications, the CS receiver needs to track signals even when they are not in compliance. The external commands allow the CS receiver to acquire and track abnormal signals from unhealthy satellites. Second, all measurements are time tagged to the satellite X1 epoch (see Section 4.3.1.1 for further details on the X1 epoch), whereas a typical user receiver time tags range measurements relative to the receiver's X1 epoch. Synchronizing measurements relative to the satellite's X1 epochs facilitates the MCS's processing of data from the entire distributed CS L-band Monitor Station Network. The CS receivers provide the MCS with 1.5-

second pseudorange and accumulated delta range measurements (also known as P-code and carrier phase measurements, respectively). Third, the MCS receives all of the raw demodulated navigation bits from each monitor station (without processing of the Hamming code used for error detection) so that problems in the NAV Data message can be observed. The returned NAV Data message is compared bit by bit against expected values to provide a complete system-level verification of the MCS-ground antenna-satellite-monitor station data path. Additionally, the CS receivers provide the MCS with various internal signal indicators, such as time of lock of the tracking loops and internally measured signal-to-noise ratio (SNR). This additional data is used by the MCS to discard questionable measurements from the CS Kalman filter. As noted earlier, the CS maintains the monitor station time scale to accommodate station time changes, failures, and reinitialization of the station equipment. The Air Force monitor station coverage of the GPS satellites is shown in Figure 3.16, with the grayscale code denoting the number of monitor stations visible to a satellite [14]. Satellite coverage varies from zero in the region west of South America to as many as three in the continental United States.

3.3.1.3 Ground Uplink Antenna Description

To perform the satellite commanding and data transmission function, the CS includes a dedicated, globally distributed, ground antenna network. Currently, the CS network, colocated with the Air Force monitor stations, consists of Ascension Island, Diego Garcia, Kwajalein, and Cape Canaveral. The Cape Canaveral facility also serves as part of the prelaunch compatibility station supporting prelaunch satellite compatibility testing. Additionally, one automated remote tracking station ground antenna located in Colorado, from the Air Force Satellite Control Network, serves as a GPS ground antenna. These ground antennas provide the TT&C interface between the CS and the space segment for uploading the navigation data.

These ground antennas are full-duplex, S-band communication facilities that have dedicated command and control sessions with a single SV at a time. Under MCS control, multiple simultaneous satellite contacts can be performed. Each ground antenna consists of the equipment and computer programs necessary to transmit commands, navigation data uploads, and payload control data received from the MCS to the satellites and to receive satellite telemetry data that is forwarded to the MCS. All CS ground antennas are dual-threaded for system redundancy and integrity. The CS ground antennas have been recently upgraded to support S-band ranging. The S-band ranging provides the CS with the capability to perform satellite early orbit and anomaly resolution support. The ground antenna coverage of the GPS satellites is shown in Figure 3.17, with the grayscale code denoting the number of ground antennas visible to a satellite [14].

3.3.1.4 MCS Data Processing

MCS Measurement Processing
To support the MCS estimation and prediction function, the CS continuously tracks the L1 and L2 P(Y) codes. At track acquisition, the L1 C/A code is sampled during the handover to P(Y) code to ensure that it is being broadcast (however, the

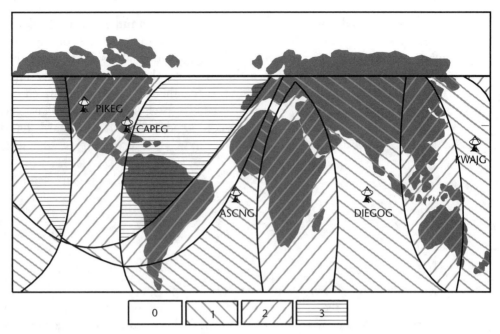

Figure 3.17   CS ground antenna coverage.

CS does not continuously track the L1 C/A code). The raw 1.5-second L1 and L2 pseudorange and carrier phase (also known as accumulated delta range) measurements are converted at the MCS into 15-minute smoothed measurements. The smoothing process uses the carrier phase measurements to smooth the pseudorange data to reduce the measurement noise. The process provides smoothed pseudorange and sampled carrier phase measurements for use by the CS Kalman filter.

The smoothing process consists of data editing to remove outliers and cycle slips, converting raw dual-frequency measurements to ionosphere-free observables, and generating smoothed measurements once a sufficient number of validated measurements are available. Figure 3.18 shows a representative data smoothing interval consisting of 600 pseudorange and carrier phase observations, with 595 observations used to form a smoothed pseudorange minus carrier phase offset and the 5 remaining observations used to form a carrier phase polynominal.

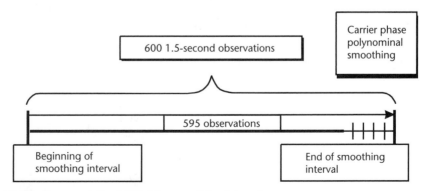

Figure 3.18   Representative MCS data-smoothing interval.

The CS data editing limit checks the pseudoranges and performs third-difference tests on the raw L1 and L2 observables. The third-difference test compares consecutive sequences of L1 and L2 observables against thresholds. If the third-difference test exceeds these thresholds, then those observables are discarded for subsequent use in that interval. Such data editing protects the CS Kalman filter from questionable measurements. Ionosphere-corrected, L1 pseudorange, and phase measurements, ρ_c and ϕ_c, respectively, are computed using the standard ionosphere correction (see Section 7.2.4.1):

$$\rho_c = \rho_1 - \frac{1}{(1-\alpha)} \cdot (\rho_1 - \rho_2)$$

$$\phi_c = \phi_1 + \frac{1}{(1-\alpha)} \cdot (\phi_1 - \phi_2)$$

(3.1)

where $\alpha = (154/120)^2$, and ρ_i and ϕ_i for $i = 1, 2$ are the validated L1 and L2 pseudorange and phase measurements, respectively.

Ionosphere-corrected pseudorange and carrier-phase measurements are related by a constant offset. By exploiting this fact, a smoothed pseudorange measurement, $\overline{\rho}_c$, is formed from a carrier phase as follows:

$$\overline{\rho}_c = \phi_c + B$$

(3.2)

where B is an unknown constant computed by averaging the L1 ionosphere-corrected pseudorange and carrier-phase measurement, ρ_c and ϕ_c, differences

$$B = \sum \left(\rho_c(z_j) - \phi_c(z_j) \right)$$

(3.3)

over all validated measurements in the smoothing interval. The CS pioneered such carrier-aided smoothing of pseudoranges in the early 1980s.

The CS Kalman filter performs measurement updates every 15 minutes based on its uniform GPS time scale (i.e., GPS system time). The smoothing process generates second-order pseudorange and carrier-phase measurement polynomials in the neighborhood of these Kalman update times. A phase measurement polynomial, consisting of bias, drift, and drift rate, $\hat{\mathbf{X}}_c$, is formed using a least-squares fit of the last five phase measurements in the smoothing interval, $\vec{\boldsymbol{\phi}}_c$:

$$\hat{\mathbf{X}}_c = \left(\mathbf{A}^T \mathbf{W} \mathbf{A} \right)^{-1} \cdot \mathbf{A}^T \mathbf{W} \vec{\boldsymbol{\phi}}_c$$

(3.4)

where

$$\mathbf{A} = \begin{bmatrix} 1 & -2\tau & 4\tau^2 \\ 1 & -\tau & \tau^2 \\ 1 & 0 & 0 \\ 1 & \tau & \tau^2 \\ 1 & 2\tau & 4\tau^2 \end{bmatrix}, \quad \vec{\boldsymbol{\phi}}_c = \begin{bmatrix} \phi_c(z_{-2}) \\ \phi_c(z_{-1}) \\ \phi_c(z_0) \\ \phi_c(z_1) \\ \phi_c(z_2) \end{bmatrix}$$

(3.5)

where τ equals 1.5 seconds and $\{z_i$, for $i = -2, -1, 0, 1, 2\}$ denotes the time tags associated with the last five phase measurements in the interval. The weighting matrix, $\mathbf{W}$ in (3.4), is diagonal with weights derived from the receiver's reported SNR value. The pseudorange measurement polynomial, $\hat{\mathbf{X}}_p$, is formed using the constant offset in (3.3) as follows:

$$\hat{\mathbf{X}}_p = \hat{\mathbf{X}}_c + \begin{bmatrix} B \\ 0 \\ 0 \end{bmatrix} \tag{3.6}$$

These smoothed pseudorange and phase measurements, in (3.6) and (3.4) respectively, are interpolated by the CS Kalman filter to a common GPS time scale, using the satellite clock estimates.

MCS Ephemeris and Clock Processing
The MCS ephemeris and clock processing software continuously estimates the satellite ephemeris and clock states, using a Kalman filter with 15-minute updates based on the smoothed measurements described earlier. The MCS ephemeris and clock estimates are used to predict the satellite's position and clock at future times to support the generation of the NAV Data message.

The MCS ephemeris and clock processing is decomposed into two components: offline processing for generating reference trajectories, inertial-to-geodetic coordinate transformations, and Sun/Moon ephemeris, and real-time processing associated with maintaining the CS Kalman filter estimates. The MCS offline processing depends on highly accurate models. The CS reference trajectory force models [15, 16] include the WGS-84 Earth gravitational harmonics (truncated to degree 8 and order 8), the satellite-unique solar radiation models, the solar and lunar gravitational effects (derived from the JPL Solar Ephemeris, DE200), and the solar and lunar solid tidal effects (second-degree Legendre polynomials). The magnitude of these various forces and their corresponding effect on the GPS orbits has been analyzed and is summarized in Table 3.5 [17].

The differences on the left- and right-hand sides of Table 3.5 quantify the positional error due to that component on the ephemeris trajectory and orbit determination, respectively. Since the equations of motion describing GPS orbits are nonlinear, the CS linearizes the ephemeris states around a nominal reference trajectory [18, 19]. To support ephemeris predictions, these ephemeris estimates are maintained relative to the reference trajectory's epoch states and the trajectory partials (relative to the epoch) used to propagate to current or future times.

The CS Kalman filter tracks the satellite ephemeris in ECI coordinates and transforms the satellite positions into ECEF coordinates using a series of rotation matrices (as described in Section 2.2). These ECI-to-ECEF coordinate rotation matrices account for luni-solar and planetary precession, nutation, Earth rotation, polar motion, and UT1-UTC effects. (Polar motion and UT1-UTC Earth orientation predictions are provided weekly to the CS by the NGA.)

The CS Kalman state estimate consists of three ECI positions and velocities, two solar pressures, and up to three clock states for each satellite, along with a tropospheric wet height and two clock states for each monitor station. The two solar

Table 3.5 Acceleration Forces Perturbing Satellite Orbit

Perturbing Acceleration	RMS Orbit Differences over 3 Days (m)				RMS Orbit Determination (m)			
	Radial	Along Track	Cross Track	Total	Radial	Along Track	Cross Track	Total
Earth oblateness (C_{20})	1,341	36,788	18,120	41,030	1,147	1,421	6,841	7,054
Moon gravitation	231	3,540	1,079	3,708	87	126	480	504
Sun gravitation	83	1,755	431	1,809	30	13	6	33
C_{22}, S_{22}	80	498	10	504	3	3	4	5
C_{nm}, S_{nm} (n,m = 3..8)	11	204	10	204	4	13	5	15
C_{nm}, S_{nm} (n,m = 4..8)	2	41	1	41	1	2	1	2
C_{nm}, S_{nm} (n,m = 5..8)	1	8	0	8	0	0	0	0
Solar radiation pressure	90	258	4	273	0	0	0	0.001

pressure states consist of a scaling parameter to the a priori solar pressure model and a Y-body axis acceleration. The Kalman filter clock states include a bias, drift, and draft rate (for Rubidium only). To avoid numerical instability, the CS Kalman filter is formulated in U-D factored form, where the state covariance (e.g., **P**) is maintained as:

$$P = U \cdot D \cdot U^T \tag{3.7}$$

with **U** and **D** being upper triangular and diagonal matrices, respectively [19]. The U-D filter improves the numerical dynamic range of the CS filter estimates, whose time constants vary from several hours to several weeks. The CS Kalman time update has the form:

$$\tilde{U}(t_{k+1})\tilde{D}(t_{k+1})\tilde{U}(t_{k+1})^T = \left[B(t_k) | \hat{U}(t_k) \right] \begin{bmatrix} Q(t_k) & \\ & \hat{D}(t_k) \end{bmatrix} \begin{bmatrix} B(t_k)^T \\ \hat{U}(t_k)^T \end{bmatrix} \tag{3.8}$$

where $\hat{U}(\cdot), \hat{D}(\cdot)$ and $\tilde{U}(\cdot), \tilde{D}(\cdot)$ denote the a priori and a posteriori covariance factors, respectively; $Q(\cdot)$ denotes the state process noise matrix; and $B(\cdot)$ denotes the matrix that maps the process noise to the appropriate state domain. The CS process noises include the satellite and ground station clocks, troposphere-wet height, solar pressure, and ephemeris velocity (with the latter being in radial, along-track, and cross-track coordinates [20]). Periodically, the 2SOPS retunes the satellite and ground station clock process noises, using on-orbit GPS Allan and Hadamard clock characterization, as provided by the Naval Research Laboratory [21, 22]. The CS Kalman filter performs scalar measurement updates, with a statistically consistent test to detect outliers (based on the measurement residuals or innovation process [18]). The CS measurement model includes a clock polynomial model (up to second order), the Hopfield/Black troposphere model [23, 24], the IERS station tide displacement model (vertical component only), and periodic relativity and satellite phase center corrections.

Since a pseudorange measurement is simply the signal transit time between the transmitting satellite and the receiving monitor station, the CS Kalman filter can estimate both the ephemeris and clock errors. However, any error common to all of the clocks remains unobservable. Essentially, given a system of n clocks, there are only equivalently $n - 1$ separable clock observables, leaving one unobservable state. An early CS Kalman filter design avoided this unobservablity by artificially forcing a single monitor station clock as the *master* and referencing all CS clock estimates to that station. Based on the theory of composite clocks, developed in [25], the CS Kalman filter was upgraded to exploit this unobservability and established GPS system time as the ensemble of all active AFSs. At each measurement update, the composite clock reduces the clock estimate uncertainties [20]. Also with the composite clock, GPS time is steered to UTC (USNO) absolute time scale for consistency with other timing services. Common view of the satellites from multiple monitor stations is critical to the estimation process. This closure of the time-transfer function provides the global time scale synchronization necessary to achieve submeter estimation performance. Given such advantages of the composite clock, the International GPS Service (IGS) has recently transitioned its products to IGS system time along the lines of the composite clocks [26].

The CS Kalman filter has several unique features. First, the CS Kalman filter is decomposed into smaller minifilters, known as partitions. The CS partitioned Kalman filter was required due to computational limitations in the 1980s. In a single partition, the Kalman filter estimates up to six satellites and all ground states, with logic across partitions to coordinate the alignment of the redundant ground estimates. Second, the CS Kalman filter has constant state estimates (i.e., filter states with zero covariance). (This feature is used in the cesium and rubidium AFS models, which are linear and quadratic polynomials, respectively). Classically, Kalman theory requires the state covariance to be positive-definite. However, given the U-D time update in (3.8) and its associated Gram-Schmidt factorization [19], the a posteriori covariance factors, $\tilde{U}(\cdot), \tilde{D}(\cdot)$, are constructed to be positive semidefinite with selected states having zero covariance. Third, the CS Kalman filter supports Kalman backups. The CS Kalman backup consists of retrieving prior filter states and covariances (up to the past 24 hours) and reprocessing the smoothed measurement under different filter configurations. This backup capability is critical to 2SOPS for managing satellite, ground station, or operator-induced abnormalities. The CS Kalman filter has various controls available to 2SOPS to manage special events, including AFS runoffs, autonomous satellite jet firings, AFS reinitializations and switchovers of AFSs, reference trajectories, and Earth orientation parameter changes. The CS Kalman filter has been continuously running since the early 1980s with no filter restarts.

MCS Upload Message Formulation

The MCS upload navigation messages are generated by a sequence of steps. First, the CS generates predicted ECEF satellite antenna phase center positions, denoted as $[\tilde{r}_{sa}(\cdot | t_k)]_E$, using the most recent Kalman filter estimate at time, t_k. Next, the CS performs a least squares fit of these predicted positions using the NAV Data message ephemeris parameters. The least squares fits are over either 4-hour or 6-hour time intervals, also known as a subframe. (Note that the subframe fitting intervals are longer for the extended operation uploads.) The 15 orbital elements (see Section 2.3.1, Table 2.2) can be expressed in vector form as

$$\mathbf{X}(t_{oe}) \equiv \left[\sqrt{a}, e, M_0, \omega, \Omega_0, i_0, \dot{\Omega}, \dot{i}, \Delta n, C_{uc}, C_{us}, C_{ic}, C_{is}, C_{rc}, C_{rs} \right]^T \qquad (3.9)$$

with an associated ephemeris reference time, t_{oe}, and are generated using a nonlinear weighted least squares fit.

For a given subframe, the orbital elements, $\mathbf{X}(t_{oe})$, are chosen to minimize the performance objective:

$$\sum_{\ell} \left\{ \begin{array}{c} \left(\left[\bar{r}_{sa}(t_\ell | t_k) \right]_E - g_{eph}(t_\ell, \mathbf{X}(t_{oe})) \right)^T \mathbf{W}(t_\ell) \\ \left(\left[\bar{r}_{sa}(t_\ell | t_k)_E \right] - g_{eph}(t_\ell, \mathbf{X}(t_{oe})) \right) \end{array} \right\} \qquad (3.10)$$

where $g_{eph}( )$ is a nonlinear function mapping the orbital elements, $\mathbf{X}(t_{oe})$, to an ECEF satellite antenna phase center position (see Section 2.3.1, Table 2.3) and $\mathbf{W}( )$ is a weighting matrix.

As defined in (3.10), all position vectors and associated weighting matrices are in ECEF coordinates. Since the CS error budget is defined relative to the user range error (see Section 7.2), the weighting matrix is resolved into radial, along-track, and cross-track (RAC) coordinates, with the radial given the largest weight. The weighting matrix of (3.10) has the form:

$$\mathbf{W}(t_\ell) = \mathbf{M}_{E \leftarrow RAC}(t_\ell) \cdot \mathbf{W}_{RAC}(t_\ell) \cdot \mathbf{M}_{E \leftarrow RAC}(t_\ell)^T \qquad (3.11)$$

where $\mathbf{M}_{E \leftarrow RAC}(\cdot)$ is a coordinate transformation from RAC to ECEF coordinates, and $\mathbf{W}_{RAC}$ is a diagonal RAC weighting matrix.

For the orbital elements in (3.9), the performance objective in (3.10) can become ill conditioned for small eccentricity, e. An alternative orbital set is introduced to remove such ill conditioning; specifically, three auxiliary elements defined as follows:

$$\alpha = e \cos \omega, \quad \beta = e \sin \omega, \quad \gamma = M_0 + \omega \qquad (3.12)$$

Thus, the objective function in (3.10) is minimized relative to the alternative orbital elements, $\overline{\mathbf{X}}(\cdot)$ having the form:

$$\overline{\mathbf{X}}(t_{oe}) \equiv \left[\sqrt{a}, \alpha, \beta, \gamma, \Omega_0, i_0, \dot{\Omega}, \dot{i}, \Delta n, C_{uc}, C_{us}, C_{ic}, C_{is}, C_{rc}, C_{rs} \right]^T \qquad (3.13)$$

The three orbital elements (e, M_0, ω) are related to the auxiliary elements, (α, β, γ) by the inverse mapping

$$e = \sqrt{\alpha^2 + \beta^2}, \omega = \tan^{-1}(\beta/\alpha), M_0 = \gamma - \omega \qquad (3.14)$$

The advantage of minimizing (3.10) with respect to $\overline{\mathbf{X}}(\cdot)$ in (3.13) versus $\mathbf{X}(\cdot)$ in (3.9) is that the auxiliary orbital elements are well defined for small eccentricity.

The minimization problem in (3.10) and (3.14) is simplified by linearizing $g_{eph}( )$ about a nominal orbital element set, denoted by $\overline{\mathbf{X}}_{nom}(t_{oe})$ such that

$$g_{eph}\left(t_\ell,\overline{\mathbf{X}}(t_{oe})\right)=g_{eph}\left(t_\ell,\overline{\mathbf{X}}_{nom}(t_{oe})\right)$$
$$+\left.\frac{\partial\,g_{eph}\left(t_\ell,\lambda\right)}{\partial\,\lambda}\right|\lambda=\overline{\mathbf{X}}_{nom}(t_{oe})\cdot\left(\overline{\mathbf{X}}(t_{oe})-\overline{\mathbf{X}}_{nom}(t_{oe})\right) \quad (3.15)$$

and then (3.10) becomes equivalently

$$\sum_\ell\left\{\begin{array}{l}\left(\left[\Delta\overline{r}_{sa}\left(t_\ell|t_k\right)\right]_E-\mathbf{P}\left(t_\ell,\overline{\mathbf{X}}_{nom}(t_{oe})\right)\cdot\Delta\overline{\mathbf{X}}(t_{oe})\right)^T\\ \cdot\mathbf{W}(t_\ell)\cdot\left(\left[\Delta\overline{r}_{sa}\left(t_\ell|t_k\right)\right]_E-\mathbf{P}\left(t_\ell,\overline{\mathbf{X}}_{nom}(t_{oe})\right)\cdot\Delta\overline{\mathbf{X}}(t_{oe})\right)\end{array}\right\} \quad (3.16)$$

where

$$\left[\Delta\overline{r}_{sa}\left(t_\ell|t_k\right)\right]_E=\left[\overline{r}_{sa}\left(t_\ell|t_k\right)\right]_E-g_{eph}\left(t_\ell,\mathbf{X}_{nom}(t_{oe})\right) \quad (3.17)$$

$$\mathbf{P}\left(t_\ell,\mathbf{X}_{nom}(t_{oe})\right)=\left.\frac{\partial\,g_{eph}\left(t_\ell,\lambda\right)}{\partial\,\lambda}\right|\lambda=\overline{\mathbf{X}}_{nom}(t_{oe}) \quad (3.18)$$

$$\Delta\overline{\mathbf{X}}(t_{oe})=\overline{\mathbf{X}}(t_{oe})-\overline{\mathbf{X}}_{nom}(t_{oe}) \quad (3.19)$$

Following classical least square techniques (see description in Appendix A) applied to the performance objective in (3.16) yields

$$\sum_\ell\left\{\mathbf{P}\left(t_\ell,\overline{\mathbf{X}}_{nom}(t_{oe})\right)^T\mathbf{W}(t_\ell)\mathbf{P}\left(t_\ell,\overline{\mathbf{X}}_{nom}(t_{oe})\right)\right\}\Delta\overline{\mathbf{X}}(t_{oe})$$
$$=\sum_\ell\left\{\mathbf{P}\left(t_\ell,\overline{\mathbf{X}}_{nom}(t_{0r})\right)^T\mathbf{W}(t_\ell)\left[\Delta\overline{r}_{sa}\left(t_\ell|t_k\right)\right]_E\right\} \quad (3.20)$$

where the solution, $\Delta\overline{\mathbf{X}}(t_{oe})$, is referred to as the differential correction. Since $g_{eph}(\ )$ is nonlinear, the optimal orbital elements in (3.16) are obtained by successive iteration: first, a nominal orbital vector, $\overline{\mathbf{X}}_{nom}(t_{oe})$, followed by a series of the differential correction, $\Delta\overline{\mathbf{X}}(t_{oe})$ using (3.20), until the differential correction converges to zero. Following a similar approach, the almanac and clock navigation parameters are also generated. These resulting orbital elements, $\overline{\mathbf{X}}(\cdot)$, are then scaled and truncated in compliance with the NAV Data message format. Note, these orbital elements, $\overline{\mathbf{X}}(\cdot)$, are quasi-Keplerian and represent a local fit of the satellite ECEF trajectory, and they are not acceptable for overall orbit characterization.

Representative curve fit errors, associated with the NAV Data message generation described earlier, are shown in Figure 3.19. For 4-hour utilization intervals, three performance metrics are depicted: RMS URE, the maximum URE, and the root sum squared (RSS) position errors. For the June–July 2000 period and across all satellites, the constellation RMS-URE, Max-URE, and Max-RSS errors were 8.72, 14.7, and 52.9 cm (RMS), respectively, with along-track component being the dominant error.

MCS Upload Message Dissemination
Nominally, each satellite's NAV Data message is uploaded at least once per day. Before each new upload transmission, the NAV Data message is verified to be in

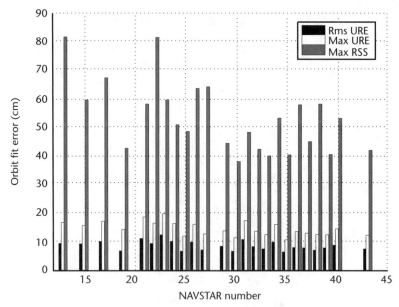

Figure 3.19 MCS upload message fit errors.

compliance with IS-GPS-200, with navigation bits populating the subframes. Additionally, the MCS-ground antenna-satellite uploads are checked, after the navigation data is locked into the satellite's memory and prior to authorizing the L-band transmission. Error protection codes exist along the entire path of navigation service for integrity. The satellite upload communication protocol is enforced to assure proper and error-free data content onboard the satellite before its use is authorized.

The NAV Data is based on predictions of the CS Kalman filter estimates, which degrade with age of data. The 2SOPS monitors the navigation accuracy and performs contingency uploads when the accuracy exceeds specific thresholds. Unfortunately, the dissemination of the NAV Data message is a tradeoff of upload frequency to navigation accuracy. Various upload strategies have been evaluated to minimize upload frequency while maintaining an acceptable navigation service [6, 27]. Figure 3.20 shows the basis tradeoff curve: an increase in upload frequency reduces the prediction age of data and thus improves the signal-in-space URE (see Section 7.2). GPS navigation accuracy depends on many factors, including performance of the satellite AFSs, the number and placement of the monitor stations, measurement errors, ephemeris modeling, and filter tuning.

3.3.2 CS Planned Upgrades

Over the next several years, the CS will field two major upgrades: the L-AII and the AEP. The L-AII upgrade modifies the existing MCS mainframe implementation to support additional monitor stations and satellites in a partitioned Kalman filter. Since the 1980s, the MCS has used a partitioned Kalman filter consisting of up to six satellites and up to six monitor stations per partition. This partition filter design was due to computational limitations and hindered CS navigation accuracy. The L-AII upgrade will enable the MCS to support up to 20 monitor stations and up to 32 satellites in a partition. (Note: The CS Kalman filter will maintain the partitioning and

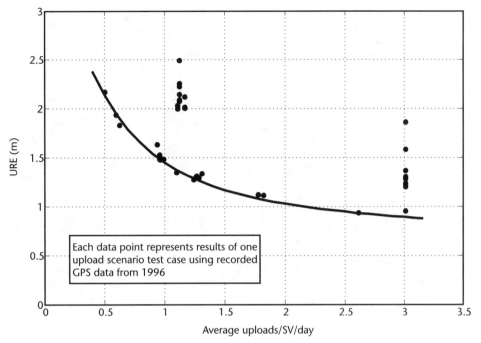

Figure 3.20   MCS uploads versus navigation accuracy. (*From:* [27]. 1997 IONS. Reprinted with permission.)

backup capabilities to support satellite abnormalities.) NGA will provide additional monitoring stations for the MCS with 15-minute smoothed and 1.5-second raw pseudorange and carrier phase measurements from Ashtech geodetic-quality receivers. These smoothed and raw measurements will be used in the CS Kalman filter and L-band monitor [12] processing, respectively. Once operational, the CS Kalman filter zero-age-of-data URE will be reduced approximately by one-half [6, 28] and the L-band monitor visibility coverage will be increased from 1.5 monitor stations/satellite to 3 to 4 monitor stations/satellite. The combined Air Force and NGA monitor station network is shown in Figure 3.21.

The L-AII upgrade includes several model improvements to the MCS processing. The existing and planned model updates are summarized in Table 3.6.

Various U.S. government agencies, research laboratories, and the international GPS community have developed improved GPS models over the past 20 years. These L-AII model updates of geopotential, station-tide displacement, and Earth orientation parameters enable the MCS processing to be compliant with the conventions of the IERS [29]. The recently developed JPL solar pressure model improves the satellite ephemeris dynamic modeling with the inclusion of Y-axis, β-dependent force, where β is the angle between the Sun-Earth line and the satellite orbital plane. The Neill/Saastamoinen model improves tropospheric modeling at low elevations.

The AEP upgrade replaces the MCS mainframe with a distributed Sun workstation configuration. The AEP upgrade extends beyond the L-AII upgrade to include an integrated suite of commercial off-the-shelf products and an improved graphical user interface. The AEP update is an object-oriented software design using TCP/IP communication protocols across workstations connected by a 1-GB Ethernet local

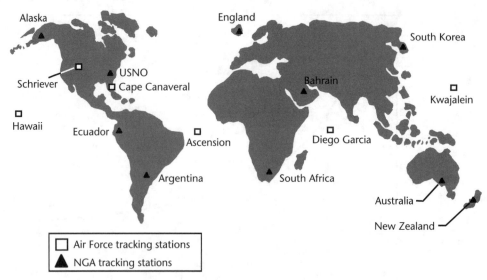

Figure 3.21   Combined Air Force and NGA monitor station network.

Table 3.6   Existing and Planned Model Upgrades

Model	Existing MCS Capability [15, 20]	Planned MCS Upgrade
Geopotential model	WGS84 (8×8) gravitational harmonics	EGM 96 (12×12) gravitational harmonics [29]
Station tide displacement	Solid tide displacement accounting for lunar and solar vertical component only	IERS 2003, including vertical and horizontal components [29]
Earth orientation parameters	No zonal or diurnal/semidiurnal tidal compensation	Restoration of zonal tides and application of diurnal/semidiurnal tidal corrections [29]
Solar radiation pressure model	Rockwell Rock42 model for Block II/IIA and Lockheed Martin Lookup model for IIR	JPL empirically derived solar pressure model [30]
Troposphere model	Hopfield/Black model	Neill/Saastamoinen model [31, 32]

area network (LAN). The AEP distributed architecture maintains the MCS operational data in an Oracle database (with a standby failover strategy).

The AEP upgrade provides the infrastructure for incremental MCS improvements, including support for the IIF satellites and the modernized signals (see Sections 3.2.3.7 and 4.5, respectively). Regarding the modernized signals, an alternative NAV Data message representation will be deployed with additional parameters and reduced quantization errors. Representative curve fit errors associated with the modernized NAV Data message are shown in Figure 3.22. For 3-hour utilization intervals, three performance metrics are depicted: RMS URE, the maximum URE, and the RSS position errors. For the June–July 2000 period and across all satellites, the constellation RMS-URE, Max-URE, and Max-RSS errors were 0.543, 0.943, and 3.56 cm (RMS), respectively. A comparison with the results of Figure 3.19 shows that the modernized signals curve fit errors will be significantly reduced.

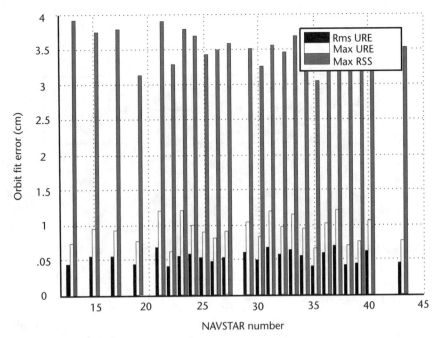

Figure 3.22 Modernized signal message fit errors.

3.4 User Segment

The user receiving equipment, typically referred to as a GPS receiver, processes the L-band signals transmitted from the satellites to determine PVT. Technology trends in component miniaturization and large-scale manufacturing have led to a proliferation of low-cost GPS receiver components. GPS receivers are embedded in many of the items we use in our daily lives. These items include cellular telephones, PDAs, and automobiles. This is in contrast to the initial receiving sets manufactured in the mid-1970s as part of the system concept validation phase. These first receivers were primarily analog devices for military applications and were large, bulky, and heavy. Today, receivers take on many form factors, including chipsets, handheld units, and Industry Standard Architecture (ISA) compatible cards. In fact, there are many single-chip GPS receivers that have leveraged low-voltage bipolar complementary metal oxide semiconductor (BiCMOS) processes and power-management techniques to meet the need for small size and low battery drain of handheld devices. Selection of a GPS receiver depends on the user's application (e.g., civilian versus military, platform dynamics, and shock and vibration environment). Following a description of a typical receiver's components, selection criteria are addressed. Detailed information regarding GPS receiver architectures and integrations for cellular telephone and automotive applications is contained in Chapter 9.

3.4.1 GPS Set Characteristics

A block diagram of a GPS receiving set is shown in Figure 3.23. The GPS set consists of five principal components: antenna, receiver, processor, input/output (I/O) device such as a control display unit (CDU), and a power supply.

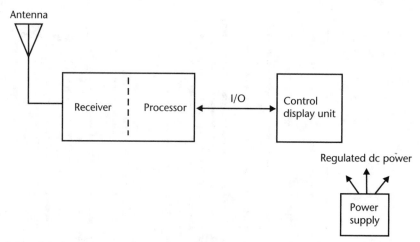

Figure 3.23 Principal GPS receiver components.

3.4.1.1 Antenna

Satellite signals are received via the antenna, which is right-hand circularly polarized (RHCP) and provides near hemispherical coverage. Typical coverage is 160° with gain variations from about 2.5 dBic at zenith to near unity at an elevation angle of 15°. (The RHCP antenna unity gain also can be expressed as 0 dBic = 0 dB with respect to an isotropic circularly polarized antenna.) Below 15°, the gain is usually negative. An example antenna pattern is shown in Figure 3.24. This pattern was pro-

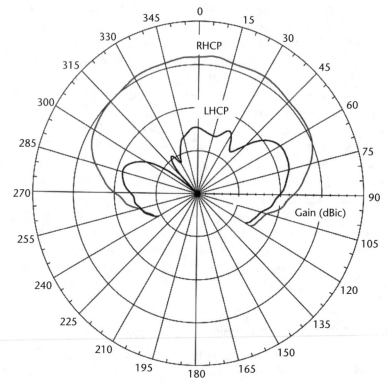

Figure 3.24 Example of RHCP hemispherical antenna pattern.

duced by a stacked-patch antenna element embedded in a dielectric substrate. This particular antenna is designed to operate at both L1 and L2, but only the L1 pattern has been provided for illustration. Even well-designed GPS antennas will exhibit a small but nonzero cross-polarized left-hand circularly polarized (LHCP) response in addition to the desired RHCP pattern shown in Figure 3.24. It can be observed that the RHCP response is nearly perfect at boresight, but as the elevation angle decreases the response is attenuated (i.e., the antenna gain decreases). This gain decrease is attributed to the horizontal electric field component being attenuated by the conducting ground plane. Therefore, a typical GPS antenna tends to be predominantly vertically polarized for low elevation angles. At zenith, the ratio of the vertical electric field to the horizontal electric field response is near unity. This ratio is referred to as the axial ratio. As the elevation angle decreases, the axial ratio increases.

Another GPS antenna design factor is transfer response. So that the signal is undistorted, it is desirable for the magnitude response to be nearly constant as a function of frequency and for the phase response to be linear with frequency within the passband of interest. (GPS signal bandwidths are discussed later as well as in Chapter 4.)

Furthermore, when we compute position with a GPS receiver, we are truly estimating the position of the electrical phase center of the antenna. There is both a physical and an electrical realization of this phase center. The physical realization is just that. One can actually use a ruler to measure the physical center of the antenna. However, the electrical phase center is often not collocated with the physical phase center and may vary with the direction of arrival of the received signal. The electrical and physical phase centers for survey-grade GPS antennas may vary by centimeters. Calibration data describing this difference may be required for high-accuracy applications.

Finally, a low-noise amplifier may be embedded in the antenna housing (or radome) in some GPS antennas. This is referred to as an active antenna. The purpose of this is to maintain a low-noise figure within the receiver. One must note that the amplifier requires power, which is usually supplied by the receiver front end thru the RF coaxial cable.

The antenna (and receiver front end) must have sufficient bandwidth to pass the signals of interest. Typically, the bandwidth of a GPS patch or helix antenna ranges from 1% to 2% of the center frequency. Two percent bandwidths for L1, L2, and L5 center frequencies are 31.5 MHz, 24.6 MHz, and 23.5 MHz, respectively. GPS receivers that track P(Y) code on both L1 and L2 need to accommodate on the order of 20.46-MHz bandwidths on both frequencies. If the set only tracks C/A code or L1C on L1, the antenna (and receiver) need to accommodate bandwidths of approximately 2.046 and 4.092 MHz, respectively. It should be noted that the receiver's antenna/front-end bandwidth is directly proportional to the accuracy required for the specific application of the receiver. That is, the more frequency content of the received satellite signal that is processed, the better the accuracy performance will be. For example, a survey receiver antenna/front end will most likely be designed to pass the full 20.46 MHz of the P(Y) code. Whereas, a low-cost hiking receiver designed for C/A code may only have a front-end bandwidth of 1.7 MHz instead of the full 2.046 MHz. (Further elaboration on bandwidth and accuracy performance is contained in Chapter 5.)

New civil signals L2C and L5 have null-to-null bandwidths of 2.046 MHz and 20.46 MHz, respectively. The military M code can be processed within the existing L1 and L2 24-MHz bandwidths. Since M code signal power is defined within a 30.69-MHz band around the center frequency, approximately 92% of this power is within the 24-MHz band. (GPS signal characteristics are contained in Chapter 4.)

The addition of new signals (M code, L1C, L2C, and L5) will require new antennas for some users. For example, those utilizing L1 C/A code and L2C will need a dual-band antenna. (Dual frequency measurements enable determination of the ionospheric delay and provide robustness to interference. Ionospheric delay determination and compensation are discussed in Chapter 7.) SOL signal users that require operation in the ARNS bands will need antennas to receive C/A code on L1 and the L5 signal on L5. At the time of this writing, RTCA was developing aviation standards for a dual-band L1/L5 antenna. Some receivers may be tri-band. That is, they will receive and process the signals broadcast on all three GPS frequencies, L1, L2, and L5, which will require a tri-band antenna. Reference [33] provides details on one approach for a tri-band (L1/L2 M code and L5) antenna design.

Antenna designs vary from helical coils to thin microstrip (i.e., patch) antennas. High-dynamic aircraft prefer low-profile, low–air resistance patch antennas, whereas land vehicles can tolerate a larger antenna. Antenna selection requires evaluation of such parameters as antenna gain pattern, available mounting area, aerodynamic performance, multipath performance, and stability of the electrical phase center of the antenna [34].

Another issue regarding antenna selection is the need for resistance to interference. (In the context of this discussion, any electronic emission, whether friendly or hostile, that interferes with the reception and processing of GPS signals is considered an interferer.) Some military aircraft employ antenna arrays to form a null in the direction of the interferer. Another technique to mitigate the effects of interference is to employ a beam-steering array. Beam-steering techniques electronically concentrate the antenna gain in the direction of the satellites to maximize link margin. Finally, beam forming combines both nulling and beam steering for interferer mitigation. (References [35–37] provide detailed descriptions of the theory and practical applications of nulling, beam steering, and beam forming.)

3.4.1.2 Receiver

Chapter 5 provides a detailed description of receiver signal acquisition and tracking operation; however, some high-level aspects are described herein to aid our discussion. Two basic receiver types exist today: (1) those that track L1 C/A code and P(Y) code on L1 and L2 and (2) those that only track C/A code. In light of the GPS modernization effort, these are referred to as legacy receivers. Forthcoming military receivers are being referred to as YMCA. That is, they will track L1 C/A, L1 and L2 P(Y), and L1 and L2 M code. The forthcoming civil signals, L1C, L2C, and L5, will require new receivers to be built. It is envisioned that a number of receiver types will be available. Most likely, these will be dual band to achieve ionospheric compensation and increased interference immunity. As mentioned earlier, ARNS band users will require dual band (L1 and L5) receivers and antennas.

Legacy PPS users generally employ sets that track P(Y) code on both L1 and L2. These sets initiate operation with receivers tracking C/A code on L1 and then transition to tracking P(Y) code on both L1 and L2. Y-code tracking occurs only with the aid of cryptographic equipment. (If the satellite signal is encrypted and the receiver does not have the proper cryptographic equipment, the receiver generally defaults to tracking C/A code on L1.) It is anticipated that the forthcoming YMCA receivers will perform a direct acquisition of the M code signal. Following M code acquisition, the receivers will then track M code on both L1 and L2 if the receiver is capable of dual-frequency operation. Otherwise, it will operate on either L1 or L2.

Alternatively, legacy SPS users employ sets that track the C/A code exclusively on L1, since that is the only frequency on which the C/A code is generally broadcast. Forthcoming L1C, L2C, and L5 receivers will track signals on these respective frequencies.

In addition to the receiver types mentioned earlier, there are other variations, such as civilian semicodeless tracking receivers, which track the C/A code on L1 and carrier phase of both the L1 and L2 frequencies. These receivers employ signal-processing techniques that to do not require cryptographic access to the P(Y) code. Utilizing the carrier phase as a measurement observable enables centimeter-level (or even millimeter-level) measurement accuracy. (Carrier-phase measurements are described extensively in Section 8.4.) Most receivers have multiple channels whereby each channel tracks the transmission from a single satellite. A simplified block diagram of a multichannel generic SPS receiver is shown in Figure 3.25. The

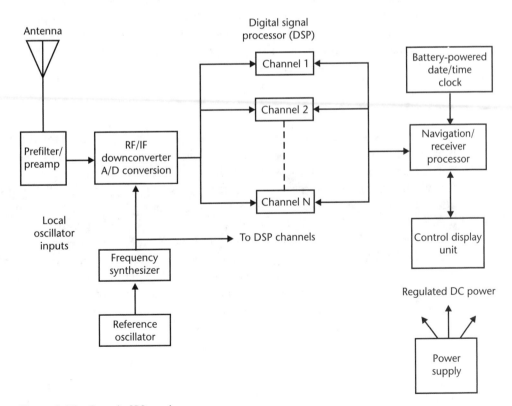

Figure 3.25   Generic SPS receiver.

received RF CDMA satellite signals are usually filtered by a passive bandpass prefilter to reduce out-of-band RF interference.

This is normally followed by a preamplifier. The RF signals are then downconverted to an intermediate frequency (IF). The IF signals are sampled and digitized by an analog to digital (A/D) converter. The A/D sampling rate is typically 2 to 20 times the PRN code chipping rate [1.023 MHz for L1 C/A code and 10.23 MHz for L1 and L2 P(Y) code]. The minimum sampling rate is twice the stopband bandwidth of the codes to satisfy the Nyquist criterion. For L1 C/A code only sets, the stopband bandwidth may be slightly greater than 1 MHz. Alternatively, the stopband bandwidth is slightly more than 10 MHz for P(Y) code sets. Oversampling reduces the receiver sensitivity to A/D quantization noise, thereby reducing the number of bits required in the A/D converter. The samples are forwarded to the digital signal processor (DSP). The DSP contains N parallel channels to simultaneously track the carriers and codes from up to N satellites. (N generally ranges from 8 to 12 in today's receivers.) Each channel contains code and carrier tracking loops to perform code and carrier-phase measurements, as well as navigation message data demodulation. The channel may compute three different satellite-to-user measurement types: pseudoranges, delta ranges (sometimes referred to as delta pseudorange), and integrated Doppler, depending on the implementation. The desired measurements and demodulated navigation message data are forwarded to the processor.

Note that GPS receivers designed for use in handheld devices need to be power efficient. Depending on the implementation, these receivers may trade off susceptibility to high-power in-band interferers to achieve minimum power supply (e.g., battery) drain. High dynamic range receiver front ends are needed in interference-resistant receivers, and the necessary components (e.g., amplifiers and mixers with high intermodulation product levels) require high bias voltage levels.

3.4.1.3 Navigation/Receiver Processor

A processor is generally required to control and command the receiver through its operational sequence, starting with channel signal acquisition and followed by signal tracking and data collection. (Some GPS sets have an integral processing capability within the channel circuitry to perform these signal-processing functions.) In addition, the processor may also form the PVT solution from the receiver measurements. In some applications, a separate processor may be dedicated to the computation of both PVT and associated navigation functions. Most processors provide an independent PVT solution on a 1-Hz basis. However, receivers designated for autoland aircraft precision approach and other high-dynamic applications normally require computation of independent PVT solutions at a minimum of 5 Hz. The formulated PVT solution and other navigation-related data is forwarded to the I/O device.

3.4.1.4 I/O Device

The I/O device is the interface between the GPS set and the user. I/O devices are of two basic types: integral or external. For many applications, the I/O device is a

CDU. The CDU permits operator data entry, displays status and navigation solution parameters, and usually accesses numerous navigation functions, such as waypoint entry and time to go. Most handheld units have an integral CDU. Other installations, such as those onboard an aircraft or ship, may have the I/O device integrated with existing instruments or control panels. In addition to the user and operator interface, applications such as integration with other sensors (e.g., INS) require a digital data interface to input and output data. Common interfaces are ARINC 429, MIL-STD-1553B, RS-232, and RS-422.

3.4.1.5   Power Supply

The power supply can be either integral, external, or a combination of the two. Typically, alkaline or lithium batteries are used for integral or self-contained implementations, such as handheld portable units; whereas an existing power supply is normally used in integrated applications, such as a board-mounted receiver installed within a server to provide accurate time. Airborne, automotive, and shipboard GPS set installations normally use platform power but typically have built-in power converters (ac to dc or dc to dc) and regulators. There usually is an internal battery to maintain data stored in volatile random access memory (RAM) integrated circuits (ICs) and to operate a built-in timepiece (date/time clock) in the event platform power is disconnected.

3.4.2   GPS Receiver Selection

At the time of this writing, there were well over 100 GPS set manufacturers in the United States and abroad. While some, like SiRF, offer a few different chip set receivers for integration with other electronic functions, other companies like GARMIN and Trimble Navigation have many different end products ranging from handhelds to automobile and aircraft navigators to complex survey receivers. GPS receiver selection is dependent on user application. The intended application strongly influences receiver design, construction, and capability. For each application, numerous environmental, operational, and performance parameters must be examined. A sampling of these parameters follows:

- What are the shock and vibration requirements, temperature and humidity extremes, as well as atmospheric salt content?
- If the receiver is to be used by government or military personnel, PPS operation may be required. PPS operation usually dictates that a dual-frequency set with a cryptographic capability is needed.
- The necessary independent PVT update rate must be determined. As an example, this rate is different for aircraft precision approach than it is for marine oil tanker guidance.
- Will the receiver have to operate in a high-multipath environment (i.e., near buildings or on an aircraft where satellite signals are reflected by various fuselage surfaces)? If so, multipath mitigation signal-processing techniques may be required. (Detailed descriptions of multipath and multipath-mitigation

techniques are contained in Chapter 6. The contribution to the GPS error budget is described in Chapter 7.)

- Under what type of dynamic conditions (e.g., acceleration and velocity) will the set have to operate? GPS sets for fighter aircraft applications are designed to maintain full performance even while experiencing multiple "Gs" of acceleration, whereas sets designated for surveying are not normally designed for severe dynamic environments.
- Is a DGPS capability required? (DGPS is an accuracy-enhancement technique covered in Chapter 8.) DGPS provides greater accuracy than stand-alone PPS and SPS. Most receivers are manufactured with a DGPS capability.
- Does the application require reception of the geostationary satellite-based overlay service referred to as SBAS broadcasting satellite integrity, ranging, and DGPS information? (SBAS is discussed in Chapter 8.)
- Waypoint storage capability as well as the number of routes and legs need to be assessed.
- Does the GPS set have to operate in an environment that requires enhanced interference rejection capabilities? Chapter 6 describes several techniques to achieve this.
- If the receiver has to be interfaced with an external system, does the proper I/O hardware and software exist? An example would be a user who requires a blended solution consisting of GPS and other sensors, such as an IMU and vision system.
- In terms of data input and display features, does the receiver require an external or integral CDU capability? Some aircraft and ships use *repeater* units such that data can be entered or extracted from various physical locations. Display requirements such as sunlight-readable or night-vision-goggle-compatible must be considered.
- Are local datum conversions required, or is WGS-84 sufficient? If so, does the receiver contain the proper transformations?
- Is portability for field use required?
- Economics, physical size, and power consumption must also be considered.

As stated earlier, these are only a sampling of GPS set selection parameters. One must carefully review the requirements of the user application prior to selecting a receiver. In most cases, the selection will be a tradeoff that requires awareness of the impact of any GPS set deficiencies for the intended application.

References

[1]   Bate, R., et al., *Fundamentals of Astrodynamics*, New York: Dover Publications, 1971.
[2]   U.S. Department of Defense, *Global Positioning System Standard Positioning Service Performance Standard*, Washington, D.C., October 2001.
[3]   U.S. Coast Guard Navigation Center, http://www.navcen.uscg.gov.
[4]   Riley, W. J., *Rubidium Atomic Frequency Standards for GPS Block IIR*, ION-GPS-92, Albuquerque, NM, September 1992.

[5]   Marquis, W., "Increased Navigation Performance from GPS Block IIR," *NAVIGATION: Journal of The Institute of Navigation*, Vol. 50, No. 4, Winter 2003–2004.

[6]   Taylor, J., and E. Barnes, "GPS Current Signal-In-Space Performance," *ION 2005 Annual Technical Meeting*, San Diego, CA, January 24–26, 2005.

[7]   Marquis, W., and C. Krier, *Examination of the GPS Block IIR Solar Pressure Model*, ION-GPS-2000, Salt Lake City, UT, September 2000.

[8]   Swift, E. R., *GPS REPORTS: Radiation Pressure Scale and Y-Axis Acceleration Estimates for 1998–1999*, Naval Surface Warfare Center, report #3900 T10/006, March 9, 2000.

[9]   Hartman, T., et al., "Modernizing the GPS Block IIR Spacecraft," *ION-GPS-2000*, Salt Lake City, UT, September 2000.

[10] Marquis, W., "M Is for Modernization: Block IIR-M Satellites Improve on a Classic," *GPS World Magazine*, Vol. 12, No. 9, September 2001, pp. 38–44.

[11] Parkinson, B., et al., *Global Positioning System: Theory and Applications*, Vol. I, Washington, D.C.: American Institute of Aeronautics and Astronautics, 1996.

[12] Brown, K., et al., "L-Band Anomaly Detection in GPS," *Proc. of the 51st Annual Meeting, Inst. of Navigation*, Washington, D.C., 1995.

[13] Hay, C., and J. Wong, "Improved Tropospheric Delay Estimation at the Master Control Station," *GPS World*, July 2000, pp. 56–62.

[14] Mendicki, P., "GPS Ground Station Coverage—Visibility Gap Analysis," Aerospace Corporation, October 2002, unpublished.

[15] "GPS OCS Mathematical Algorithms, Volume GOMA-S," DOC-MATH-650, Operational Control System of the NAVSTAR Global Positioning System, June 2001.

[16] Cappelleri, J., C. Velez, and A. Fucha, *Mathematical Theory of the Goddard Trajectory Determination System*, Goddard Space Flight Center, April 1976.

[17] Springer, T., *Modeling and Validating Orbits and Clocks Using the Global Positioning System*, Ph.D. Dissertation, Astronomical Institute, University of Bern, November 1999.

[18] Maybeck, P. S., *Stochastic Models, Estimation and Control*, Vol. 1, New York: Academic Press, 1979.

[19] Bierman, G. J., *Factorization Methods for Discrete Sequential Estimation*, Orlando, FL: Academic Press, 1977.

[20] "GPS OCS Mathematical Algorithms, Volume GOMA-E," DOC-MATH-650, Operational Control System of the NAVSTAR Global Positioning System, June 2001.

[21] Buisson, J., "NAVSTAR Global Positioning System: Quarterly Reports," Naval Research Laboratory, Quarterly, Washington, D.C., July 31, 2004.

[22] Van Dierendonck, A., and R. Brown, "Relationship Between Allan Variances and Kalman Filter Parameters," *Proc. of 16th Annual PTTI Meeting*, Greenbelt, MD, 1984.

[23] Hopfield, H., "Tropospheric Effects on Electromagnetically Measured Range, Prediction from Surface Water Data," *Radio Science*, Vol. 6, No. 3, March 1971, pp. 356–367.

[24] Black, H., "An Easily Implemented Algorithm for Tropospheric Range Correction," *Journal of Geophysical Research*, Vol. 83, April 1978, pp. 1825–1828.

[25] Brown, K., "The Theory of the GPS Composite Clock," *Proc. of ION GPS-91*, Institute of Navigation, Washington, D.C., 1991.

[26] Senior, K., et al., "Developing an IGS Time Scale," *IEEE Trans. on Ferroelectronics and Frequency Control*, June 2003, pp. 585–593.

[27] Brown, K., et al., "Dynamic Uploading for GPS Accuracy," *Proc. of ION GPS-97*, Institute of Navigation, Washington, D.C., 1997.

[28] Yinger, C., et al., "GPS Accuracy Versus Number of NIMA Stations," *Proc. of ION GPS 03*, Institute of Navigation, Washington, D.C., 2003.

[29] McCarthy, D., (ed.), *IERS Technical Note*, 21, U.S. Naval Observatory, July 1996.

[30] Bar-Sever, Y., and D. Kuang, "New Empirically Derived Solar Radiation Pressure Model for GPS Satellites," *JPL Interplanetary Network Progress Report*, Vol. 24-159, November

2004; addendum: "New Empirically Derived Solar Radiation Pressure Model for Global Positioning System Satellites During Eclipse Seasons," *JPL Interplanetary Network Progress Report,* Vol. 42-160, February 2005.

[31]   Saastamoinen, J., "Contributions to the Theory of Atmospheric Refraction," *Bulletin Géodésique,* No. 105, pp. 270–298; No. 106, pp. 383–397; No. 107, pp. 13–34, 1973.

[32]   Niell, A., "Global Mapping Functions for the Atmosphere Delay at Radio Wavelengths," *Journal of Geophysical Research,* Vol. 101, No. B2, 1996, pp. 3227–3246.

[33]   Rama Rao, B., et al., "Triple Band GPS Trap Loaded Inverted L Antenna Array," The MITRE Corporation, 2002, http://www.mitre.org/work/tech_papers/tech_papers_02/rao_triband.

[34]   Seeber, G., *Satellite Geodesy: Foundations, Methods, and Applications,* New York: Walter De Gruyter, 1993.

[35]   Klemm, R., *Principles of Space-Time Adaptive Processing,* London: The Institution of Electrical Engineers, 2002.

[36]   Klemm, R., *Applications of Space-Time Adaptive Processing,* London: The Institution of Electrical Engineers, 2004.

[37]   Fante, R., and J. Vaccaro, "Wideband Cancellation of Interference in a GPS Receive Array," *IEEE Trans. on Aerospace and Electronic Systems,* Vol. AES-36, April 2000, pp. 549–564.

CHAPTER 4

GPS Satellite Signal Characteristics

Phillip W. Ward
NAVWARD GPS Consulting

John W. Betz and Christopher J. Hegarty
The MITRE Corporation

4.1 Overview

In this chapter, we examine the properties of the GPS satellite signals, including frequency assignment, modulation format, navigation data, and the generation of PRN codes. This discussion is accompanied by a description of received signal power levels as well as their associated autocorrelation characteristics. Cross-correlation characteristics are also described. The chapter is organized as follows. First, background information on modulations that are useful for satellite radio-navigation, multiplexing techniques, and general signal characteristics including autocorrelation functions and power spectra are discussed in Section 4.2. Section 4.3 describes the *legacy* GPS signals, defined here as those signals broadcast by the GPS satellites up through the Block IIR SVs. Section 4.4 presents an overview of the GPS navigation data modulated upon the legacy GPS signals. As discussed in Chapter 3, civil and military signals will be broadcast by the Block IIR-M and later satellites. These new signals are discussed in Section 4.5. Finally, Section 4.6 summarizes the chapter.

4.2 Modulations for Satellite Navigation

4.2.1 Modulation Types

Binary phase shift keying (BPSK) is a simple digital signaling scheme in which an RF carrier is either transmitted "as is" or with a 180° phase shift over successive intervals in time depending on whether a digital 0 or 1 is being conveyed (e.g., see [1]). A BPSK signal, as illustrated in Figure 4.1, can be thought of as the product of two time waveforms—the unmodulated RF carrier and a data waveform that takes on a value of either +1 or −1 for each successive interval of $T_b = 1/R_b$ seconds, where R_b is the data rate in bits per second. The data waveform amplitude for the kth interval of T_b seconds can be generated from the kth data bit to be transmitted using either the mapping $[0, 1] \rightarrow [-1, +1]$ or $[0, 1] \rightarrow [+1, -1]$. In many systems, *forward error cor-*

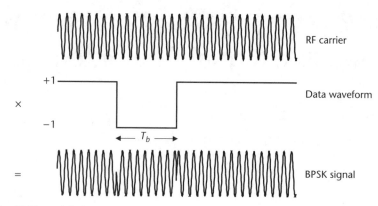

Figure 4.1 BPSK modulation.

rection (FEC) is employed, whereby redundant bits (more than the original information bits) are transmitted over the channel according to some prescribed method, enabling the receiver to detect and correct some errors that may be introduced by noise, interference, or fading. When FEC is employed, common convention is to replace T_b with T_s and R_b with R_s to distinguish data symbols (actually transmitted) from data bits (that contain the information before FEC). The data waveform alone is considered a *baseband* signal, meaning that its frequency content is concentrated around 0 Hz rather than the carrier frequency. Modulation by the RF carrier centers the frequency content of the signal about the carrier frequency, creating what is known as a *bandpass* signal.

Direct sequence spread spectrum (DSSS) is an extension of BPSK or other phase shift keyed modulation used by GPS and other satellite navigation systems discussed in this text. As shown in Figure 4.2, DSSS signaling adds a third component, referred to as a *spreading* or PRN waveform, which is similar to the data waveform but at a much higher symbol rate. This PRN waveform is completely known, at least to the intended receivers. The PRN waveform is often periodic, and the finite sequence of bits used to generate the PRN waveform over one period is referred to as a *PRN*

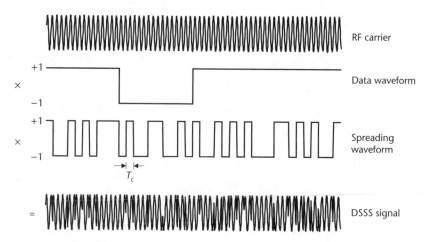

Figure 4.2 DSSS modulation.

sequence or *PRN code*. An excellent overview of PRN codes, including their generation, characteristics, and code families with good properties is provided in [2]. The
minimum interval of time between transitions in the PRN waveform is commonly
referred to as the *chip period*, T_c; the portion of the PRN waveform over one chip
period is known as a *chip* or *spreading symbol*; and the reciprocal of the chip period
is known as the *chipping rate*, R_c. The independent time parameter for the PRN
waveform is often expressed in units of chips and referred to as *codephase*.

The signal just described is called *spread spectrum,* because of the wider bandwidth occupied by the signal after modulation by the high-rate PRN waveform. In
general, the bandwidth is proportional to the chipping rate.

There are three primary reasons why DSSS waveforms are employed for satellite navigation. First and most importantly, the frequent phase inversions in the signal introduced by the PRN waveform enable precise ranging by the receiver.
Second, the use of different PRN sequences from a well-designed set enables multiple satellites to transmit signals simultaneously and at the same frequency. A
receiver can distinguish among these signals, based on their different codes. For this
reason, the transmission of multiple DSSS signals having different spreading
sequences on a common carrier frequency is referred to as *code division multiple
access* (CDMA). Finally, as detailed in Chapter 6, DSSS provides significant rejection of narrowband interference.

It should be noted that the chip waveform in a DSSS signal does not need to be
rectangular (i.e., a constant amplitude over the chip period), as we have assumed
earlier. In principle, any shape could be used and different shapes can be used for
different chips. Henceforth, we will denote DSSS signals generated using BPSK signaling with rectangular chips as *BPSK-R* signals. Several variations of the basic
DSSS signal that employ nonrectangular symbols have been investigated for satellite
navigation applications in recent years. *Binary offset carrier* (BOC) signals [3] are
generated using DSSS techniques but employ portions of a square wave for the
spreading symbols. A generalized treatment of the use of arbitrary binary patterns
to generate each spreading symbol is provided in [4]. Spreading symbol shapes, such
as raised cosines, whose amplitudes vary over a wide range of values, are used
extensively in digital communications. These shapes have also been considered for
satellite navigation but to date have not been used for practical reasons. For precise
ranging, it is necessary for the satellite and user equipment to be able to faithfully
reproduce the spreading waveform, which is facilitated through the use of signals
that can be generated using simple digital means. Furthermore, spectral efficiency,
which has motivated extensive studies in symbol shaping for communications applications, is generally not a concern for satellite navigation. Finally, DSSS signals with
constant envelope (e.g., those that employ binary-valued—one magnitude with two
possible polarities—spreading symbols) can be efficiently transmitted using
switching-class amplifiers.

4.2.2 Multiplexing Techniques

In navigation applications, it is frequently required to broadcast multiple signals
from a satellite constellation, from a single satellite, and even upon a single carrier
frequency. There are a number of techniques to facilitate this sharing of a common

transmission channel without the broadcast signals interfering with each other. The use of different carrier frequencies to transmit multiple signals is referred to as *frequency division multiple access* (FDMA) or *frequency division multiplexing* (FDM). Sharing a transmitter over time among two or more signals is referred to as *time division multiple access* (TDMA) or *time division multiplexing* (TDM). CDMA, or the use of different spreading codes to allow the sharing of a common carrier frequency, was introduced previously in Section 4.2.1.

When a common transmitter is used to broadcast multiple signals on a single carrier, it is desirable to combine these signals in a manner that forms a composite signal with a constant envelope for the reason discussed in Section 4.2.1. Two binary DSSS signals may be combined using *quadrature phase shift keying* (QPSK). In QPSK, the two signals are generated using RF carriers that are in phase *quadrature* (i.e., they have a relative phase difference of 90°, such as cosine and sine functions of the same time parameter) and are simply added together. The two constituents of a QPSK signal are referred to as the *in-phase* and *quadraphase* components.

When it is desired to combine more than two signals on a common carrier, more complicated multiplexing techniques are required. *Interplexing* combines three binary DSSS signals on a common carrier while retaining constant envelope [5]. To accomplish this feat, a fourth signal that is completely determined by the three desired signals, is also transmitted. The overall transmitted signal may be expressed in the form of a QPSK signal:

$$s(t) = s_I(t)\cos(2\pi f_c t) - s_Q(t)\sin(2\pi f_c t) \tag{4.1}$$

with in-phase and quadra-phase components, $s_I(t)$ and $s_Q(t)$, respectively, as:

$$\begin{aligned} s_I(t) &= \sqrt{2P_I}\, s_1(t)\cos(m) - \sqrt{2P_Q}\, s_2(t)\sin(m) \\ s_Q(t) &= \sqrt{2P_Q}\, s_3(t)\cos(m) + \sqrt{2P_I}\, s_1(t)s_2(t)s_3(t)\sin(m) \end{aligned} \tag{4.2}$$

where $s_1(t)$, $s_2(t)$, and $s_3(t)$ are the three desired signals, f_c is the carrier frequency, and m is an index that is set in conjunction with the power parameters P_I and P_Q to achieve the desired power levels for the four multiplexed (three desired plus one additional) signals.

Other techniques for multiplexing more than two binary DSSS signals while retaining constant envelope include *majority vote* [6] and *intervoting* [7]. In majority vote, an odd number of DSSS signals are combined by taking the majority of their underlying PRN sequence values at every instant in time to generate a composite DSSS signal. Intervoting consists of the simultaneous application of interplexing and majority vote.

4.2.3 Signal Models and Characteristics

In addition to the general quadrature signal representation in (4.1) for GNSS signals, we will find it occasionally convenient to use the *complex-envelope* or *lowpass* representation, $s_l(t)$, defined by the relation:

$$s(t) = \text{Re}\left\{s_l(t)e^{j2\pi f_c t}\right\} \tag{4.3}$$

where Re{·} denotes the real part of. The in-phase and quadraphase components of the real signal $s(t)$ are related to its complex envelope by:

$$s_l(t) = s_I(t) + js_Q(t) \tag{4.4}$$

Two signal characteristics of great importance for satellite navigation applications are the *autocorrelation function* and *power spectral density*. The autocorrelation function for a lowpass signal with constant power is defined as:

$$R(\tau) = \lim_{T\to\infty} \frac{1}{2T} \int_{-T}^{T} s_l^*(t)s_l(t+\tau)dt \tag{4.5}$$

where * denotes complex conjugation. The power spectral density is defined to be the Fourier transform of the autocorrelation function:

$$S(f) = \int_{-\infty}^{\infty} R(\tau)e^{-j2\pi f\tau} dt \tag{4.6}$$

The power spectral density describes the distribution of power within the signal with regard to frequency.

It is often convenient to model some portions of a DSSS signal as being random. For instance, the data symbols and PRN code are often modeled as *coin-flip sequences* (i.e., they randomly assume values of either +1 or −1 with each outcome occurring with equal probability and with each value being independent of other values). The autocorrelation function for a DSSS signal with random components is generally taken to be the average or expected value of (4.5). The power spectral density remains as defined by (4.6).

As an example, consider a baseband DSSS signal without data employing rectangular chips with a perfectly random binary code, as shown in Figure 4.3(a). The autocorrelation function illustrated in Figure 4.3(b) is described in equation form as [8]:

$$R(\tau) = A^2\left(1 - \frac{|\tau|}{T_c}\right) \quad \text{for } |\tau| \le T_c \tag{4.7}$$
$$= 0 \quad\quad\quad\quad \text{elsewhere}$$

The power spectrum of this signal shown in Figure 4.3(c) (as a function of angular frequency $\omega = 2\pi f$) may be determined using (4.6) to be:

$$S(f) = A^2 T_c \text{sinc}^2\left(\pi f T_c\right) \tag{4.8}$$

where $\text{sinc}(x) = \dfrac{\sin x}{x}$. What is important about a DSSS signal using a random binary code is that it correlates with itself in one and only one place, and it is uncorrelated with any other random binary code. Satellite navigation systems

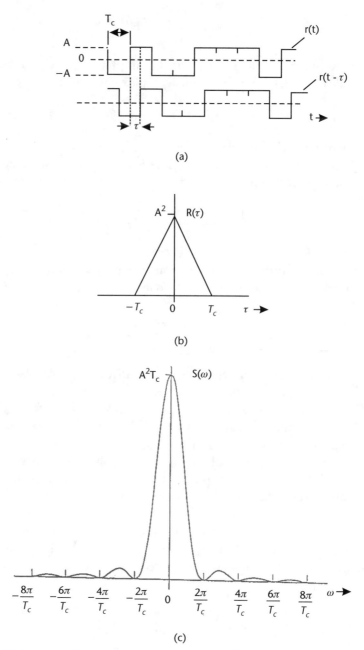

Figure 4.3 (a) A random binary code producing (b) the autocorrelation function, and (c) power spectrum of a DSSS signal.

employing rectangular chips have similar autocorrelation and power spectrum properties to those described for the random binary code case, but they employ PRN codes that are perfectly predictable and reproducible. This is why they are called *pseudo* random codes.

To illustrate the effects of finite-length PRN codes, consider a DSSS signal without data employing a PRN sequence that repeats every N bits. Further let us assume that this sequence is generated using a *linear feedback shift register* that is of *maxi-*

mum length. A linear feedback shift register is a simple digital circuit that consists of n bits of memory and some feedback logic [2], all clocked at a certain rate. Every clock cycle, the nth bit value is output from the device, the logical value in bit 1 is moved to bit 2, the value in bit 2 to bit 3, and so on. Finally, a linear function is applied to the prior values of bits 1 to n to create a new input value into bit 1 of the device. With an n-bit linear feedback shift register, the longest length sequence that can be produced before the output repeats is $N = 2^n - 1$. A linear feedback shift register that produces a sequence of this length is referred to as maximum length. During each period, the n bits within the register pass through all 2^n possible states, except the all-zeros state, since all zeros would result in a constant output value of 0. Because the number of negative values (1s) is always one larger than the number of positive values (0s) in a maximum-length sequence, the autocorrelation function of the spreading waveform $PN(t)$ outside of the correlation interval is $-A^2/N$. Recall that the correlation was 0 (uncorrelated) in this interval for the DSSS signal with random code in the previous example. The autocorrelation function for a maximum-length PRN sequence is the infinite series of triangular functions with period NT_c (seconds) shown in Figure 4.4(a). The negative correlation amplitude $(-A^2/N)$ is shown in Figure 4.4(a), when the time shift, τ, is greater than $\pm T_c$ or multiples of $\pm T_c(N \pm 1)$ and represents a zero-frequency term in the series. Expressing the equation for the periodic autocorrelation function mathematically [9] requires the use of the unit impulse function shifted in time by discrete (m) increments of the PRN sequence period NT_c: $\delta(\tau + mNT_c)$. Simply stated, this notation (also called a Dirac delta function) represents a unit impulse with a discrete phase shift of mNT_c seconds. Using this notation, the autocorrelation function can be expressed as the sum of the zero-frequency term and an infinite series of the triangle function, $R(\tau)$, defined by (4.7). The infinite series of the triangle function is obtained by the convolution (denoted by $\otimes$) of $R(\tau)$ with an infinite series of the phase shifted unit impulse functions as follows:

$$R_{PN}(\tau) = \frac{-A^2}{N} + \frac{N+1}{N}R(\tau) \otimes \sum_{m=-\infty}^{\infty}\delta(\tau + mNT_c) \qquad (4.9)$$

The power spectrum of the DSSS signal generated from a maximum-length PRN sequence is derived from the Fourier transform of (4.9) and is the line spectrum shown in Figure 4.4(b). The unit impulse function is also required to express this in equation form as follows:

$$S_{PN}(f) = \frac{A^2}{N^2}\left(\delta(f) + \sum_{m=-\infty \neq 0}^{\infty}(N+1)\text{sinc}^2\left(\frac{m\pi}{N}\right)\delta\left(2\pi f + \frac{m2\pi}{NT_c}\right)\right) \qquad (4.10)$$

where $m = \pm 1, \pm 2, \pm 3, \ldots$

Observe in Figure 4.4(b) that the envelope of the line spectrum is the same as the continuous power spectrum obtained for the random PRN code, except for the small zero-frequency term in the line spectrum and the scale factor T_c. As the period, N (chips), of the maximum-length sequence increases, then the line spacing,

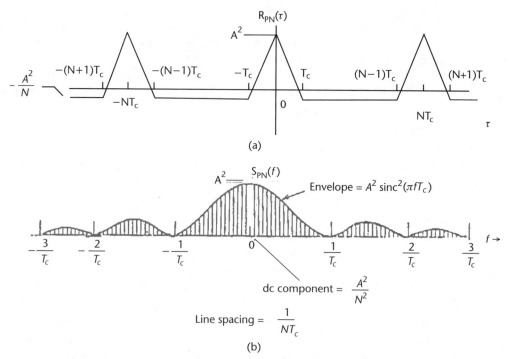

Figure 4.4 (a) The autocorrelation function of a DSSS signal generated from a maximum-length PRN sequence, and (b) its line spectrum.

$1/NT_c$ (Hz), of the line spectrum decreases proportionally, so that the power spectrum begins to approach a continuous spectrum.

Next consider the general baseband DSSS signal that uses the arbitrary symbol $g(t)$:

$$s(t) = \sum_{k=-\infty}^{\infty} a_k g(t - kT_c) \tag{4.11}$$

If the PRN code values $\{a_k\}$ are assumed to be generated as a random coin-flip sequence, then the autocorrelation function for this signal may be found by taking the mean value of (4.5), resulting in:

$$R(\tau) = \int_{-\infty}^{\infty} g(t)g*(t-\tau)dt \tag{4.12}$$

Although data was neglected in (4.11), its introduction does not change the result for a nonrepeating coin-flip sequence. Using this result, along with (4.6) for power spectral density, we can express the autocorrelation function and power spectrum for unit-power BPSK-R signals, for which

$$g_{BPSK-R}(t) = \begin{cases} 1/\sqrt{T_c}, & 0 \le t \le T_c \\ 0, & \text{elsewhere} \end{cases} \tag{4.13}$$

as:

$$R_{BPSK-R}(\tau) = \begin{cases} 1 - |\tau|/T_c, & |\tau| \le T_c \\ 0, & \text{elsewhere} \end{cases} \tag{4.14}$$

$$S_{BPSK-R}(f) = T_c \operatorname{sinc}^2(\pi f T_c)$$

The notation BPSK-R(n) is often used to denote a BPSK-R signal with $n \times$ 1.023-MHz chipping rate. As will be discussed in Sections 4.3 and 4.5 and Chapter 10, GPS and GALILEO employ frequencies that are multiples of 1.023 MHz.

A BOC signal may be viewed as being the product of a BPSK-R signal with a square wave subcarrier. The autocorrelation and power spectrum are dependent on both the chip rate and characteristics of the square wave subcarrier. The number of square wave half-periods in a spreading symbol is typically selected to be an integer:

$$k = \frac{T_c}{T_s} \tag{4.15}$$

where $T_s = 1/(2f_s)$ is the half-period of a square wave generated with frequency f_s. When k is even, a BOC spreading symbol can be described as:

$$g_{BOC}(t) = g_{BPSK-R}(t) \operatorname{sgn}\left[\sin(\pi t/T_s + \psi)\right] \tag{4.16}$$

where sgn is the signum function (1 if the argument is positive, −1 if the argument is negative) and ψ is a selectable phase angle. When k is odd, a BOC signal may be viewed as using two symbols over every two consecutive chip periods—that given in (4.16) for the first spreading symbol in every pair and its inverse for the second. Two common values of ψ are 0° or 90°, for which the resultant BOC signals are referred to as *sine phased* or *cosine phased*, respectively.

With a perfect coin-flip spreading sequence, the autocorrelation functions for cosine- and sine-phased BOC signals resemble saw teeth, piecewise linear functions between the peak values as shown in Table 4.1. The expression for the autocorrelation function applies for k odd and k even when a random code is assumed. The notation BOC(m,n) used in the table is shorthand for a BOC modulation generated using an $m \times$ 1.023-MHz square wave frequency and an $n \times$ 1.023-MHz chipping rate. The BOC subscripts s and c refer to sine-phased and cosine- phased, respectively.

The power spectral density for a sine-phased BOC modulation is [3]:

$$S_{BOC_s}(f) = \begin{cases} T_c \operatorname{sinc}^2(\pi f T_c) \tan^2\left(\dfrac{\pi f}{2f_s}\right) & , k \text{ even} \\[3ex] T_c \dfrac{\cos^2(\pi f T_c)}{(\pi f T_c)^2} \tan^2\left(\dfrac{\pi f}{2f_s}\right) & , k \text{ odd} \end{cases} \tag{4.17}$$

and the power spectral density for a cosine-phased BOC modulation is:

Table 4.1 Autocorrelation Function Characteristics for BOC Modulations

Modulation	Number of Positive and Negative Peaks in Autocorrelation Function	Delay Values of Peaks (Seconds)	Autocorrelation Function Values for Peak at $\tau = jT_s/2$	
			j even	j odd
$BOC_s(m, n)$	$2k - 1$	$\tau = jT_s/2,$ $-2k + 2 \le j \le 2k - 2$	$(-1)^{j/2}(k-|j/2|)/k$	$(-1)^{(|j|-1)/2}/(2k)$
$BOC_c(m, n)$	$2k + 1$	$\tau = jT_s/2,$ $-2k + 1 \le j \le 2k - 1$	$(-1)^{j/2}(k-|j/2|)/k$	$(-1)^{(|j|+1)/2}/(2k)$

$$S_{BOC_c(m,n)}(f) = \begin{cases} 4T_c \operatorname{sinc}^2(\pi f T_c) \left(\dfrac{\sin^2\left(\dfrac{\pi f}{4f_s}\right)}{\cos\left(\dfrac{\pi f}{2f_s}\right)} \right)^2 & ,k \text{ even} \\[4em] 4T_c \dfrac{\cos^2(\pi f T_c)}{(\pi f T_c)^2} \left(\dfrac{\sin^2\left(\dfrac{\pi f}{4f_s}\right)}{\cos\left(\dfrac{\pi f}{2f_s}\right)} \right)^2 & ,k \text{ odd} \end{cases} \tag{4.18}$$

A binary coded symbol (BCS) modulation [4] uses a spreading symbol defined by an arbitrary bit pattern $\{c_m\}$ of length M as:

$$g_{BCS}(t) = \sum_{m=0}^{M-1} c_m p_{T_c/M}(t - mT_c/M) \tag{4.19}$$

where $p_{T_c/M}(t)$ is a pulse taking on the value $1/\sqrt{T_c}$ over the interval $[0, T_c/M]$ and zero elsewhere. The notation BCS($[c_0, c_1, ..., c_{M-1}], n$) is used to denote a BCS modulation that uses the sequence $[c_0, c_1, ..., c_{M-1}]$ for each symbol and a chipping rate of $R_c = n \times 1.023$ MHz $= 1/T_c$. As shown in [4], the autocorrelation function for a BCS($[c_0, c_1, ..., c_{M-1}], n$) modulation with perfect spreading code is a piecewise linear function between the values:

$$R_{BCS}(nT_c/M) = \frac{1}{M}\sum_{m=0}^{M-1} c_m c_{m-n} \tag{4.20}$$

where n is an integer with magnitude less than or equal to M and where it is understood that $c_m = 0$ for $m \notin [0, M-1]$. The power spectral density is:

$$S_{BCS}(f) = T_c \left| \frac{1}{M}\sum_{m=0}^{M-1} c_m e^{-j2\pi mfT_c/M} \right|^2 \operatorname{sinc}^2(\pi f T_c/M) \tag{4.21}$$

Given the success of BPSK-R modulations, why consider more advanced modulations like BOC or BCS? Compared to BPSK-R modulations, which only allow the signal designer to select carrier frequency and chip rate, BOC and BCS modulations provide additional design parameters for waveform designers to use. The resulting modulation designs can provide enhanced performance when bandwidth is limited (due to implementation constraints at transmitter and receiver, or due to spectrum allocations). Also, modulations can be designed to better share limited frequency bands available for use by multiple GNSS. The spectra can be shaped in order to limit interference and otherwise spectrally separate different signals. In order to obtain adequate performance, such modulation design activities must carefully consider a variety of signal characteristics in the time and frequency domains, and they should not concentrate exclusively on spectrum shape.

4.3   Legacy GPS Signals

This section details the legacy GPS navigation signals—that is, those navigation signals that are broadcast by the GPS SVs up through the Block IIR class (see Chapter 3). The legacy GPS SVs transmit navigation signals on two carrier frequencies called L1, the primary frequency, and L2, the secondary frequency. The carrier frequencies are DSSS modulated by spread spectrum codes with unique PRN sequences associated with each SV and by a common navigation data message. All SVs transmit at the same carrier frequencies in a CDMA fashion. In order to track one SV in common view with several other SVs by the CDMA technique, a GPS receiver must replicate the PRN sequence for the desired SV along with the replica carrier signal, including Doppler effects. Two carrier frequencies are required to measure the ionospheric delay, since this delay is related by a scale factor to the difference in signal TOA for the two carrier frequencies. Single frequency users must estimate the ionospheric delay using modeling parameters that are broadcast to the user in the navigation message. (Further information on ionospheric delay compensation is contained in Section 7.2.4.1.) The characteristics of the legacy GPS signals are further explained in the following sections.

4.3.1   Frequencies and Modulation Format

A block diagram that is representative of the SV signal structure for L1 ($154f_0$) and L2 ($120f_0$) is shown in Figure 4.5 (where f_0 is the fundamental frequency: 10.23 MHz). As shown in Figure 4.5, the L1 frequency ($154f_0$) is modulated by two PRN codes (plus the navigation message data), the C/A code, and the P code. The L2 frequency ($120f_0$) is modulated by only one PRN code at a time. One of the P code modes has no data modulation. The nominal reference frequency, f_0, as it appears to an observer on the ground, is 10.23 MHz. To compensate for relativistic effects, the output of the SV's frequency standard (as it appears from the SV) is 10.23 MHz offset by a $\Delta f/f$ of 4.467×10^{-10} (see Section 7.2.3). This results in a Δf of 4.57×10^{-3} Hz and $f_0 = 10.22999999543$ MHz [10]. To the GPS receiver on the ground, the C/A code has a chipping rate of 1.023×10^6 chips/s ($f_0/10 = 1.023$ MHz) and the P code has a chipping rate of 10.23×10^6 chips/s ($f_0 = 10.23$ MHz). Using the notation introduced in Section 4.2.3, the C/A code signal uses a BPSK-R(1) modulation and the P code uses a BPSK-R(10) modulation. The P code is available to PPS users but not to SPS users since the CS normally configures an AS mode in the SV. When AS is

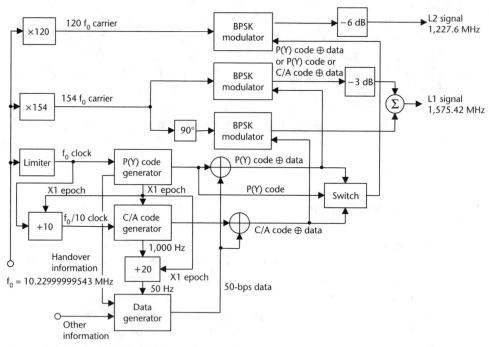

Figure 4.5 Legacy GPS satellite signal structure.

activated, the P code is encrypted to form what is known as the Y-code. The Y-code has the same chipping rate as the P code. Thus, the acronym often used for the precision (encrypted) code is P(Y) code.

Since the PPS (primarily military) users have access to the cryptographic keys and algorithms used in the AS process but the SPS (primarily civil) users do not, then AS denies access to the P code by SPS users. In the past, both the C/A code and the P(Y) code, as well as the L1 and L2 carrier frequencies, were subjected to an encrypted time-varying frequency offset (referred to as *dither*) plus an encrypted ephemeris and almanac offset error (referred to as *epsilon*) known as SA. SA denied the full accuracy of GPS to the stand-alone SPS users. However, SA has been deactivated on all GPS satellites since May 1, 2000, so this subject will not be further discussed in this chapter.

Note in Figure 4.5 that the same 50-bps navigation message data is combined with both the C/A code and the P(Y) code prior to modulation with the L1 carrier. An exclusive-or logic gate is used for this modulation process, denoted by ⊕. Since the C/A code ⊕ data and P(Y) code ⊕ data are both synchronous operations, the bit transition rate cannot exceed the chipping rate of the PRN codes. Also note that BPSK modulation is used with the carrier signals. The P(Y) code ⊕ data is modulated in phase quadrature with the C/A code ⊕ data on L1. As shown in Figure 4.5, the L1 carrier is phase shifted 90° before being BPSK modulated by the C/A code ⊕ data. Then this result is combined with the attenuated output of the BPSK modulation of L1 by the P(Y) code ⊕ data. The 3-dB amplitude difference and phase relationship between P code and C/A code on L1 are illustrated by the vector phase diagram in Figure 4.6. Figure 4.7 illustrates the result of P code ⊕ data and C/A ⊕ data. As observed in Figure 4.7, the exclusive-or process is equivalent to binary multiplica-

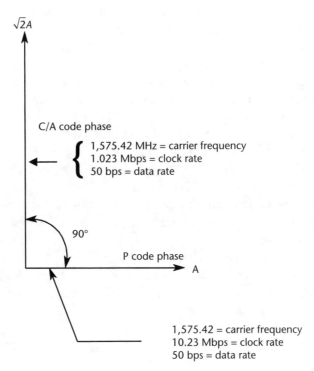

P(Y) code signal = long secure code with 50-bps data
C/A code signal = 1023 chip Gold code with 50-bps data

$$L_i(\omega_1 t) = A[P_i(t) \oplus D_i(t)]\cos(\omega_1 t) + \sqrt{2}A[G_i(t) \oplus D_i(t)]\sin(\omega_1 t)$$

Figure 4.6 GPS signal structure for L1.

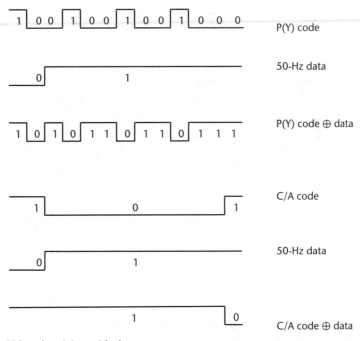

Figure 4.7 GPS code mixing with data.

tion of two 1-bit values yielding a 1-bit product using the convention that logical 0 is plus and logical 1 is minus. There are 204,600 P(Y) code epochs between data epochs and 20,460 C/A code epochs between data epochs, so the number of times that the phase could change in the PRN code sequences due to data modulation is relatively infrequent, but the spectrum changes due to this modulation are very significant.

Figure 4.8 illustrates how the signal waveforms would appear before and after the BPSK modulation of one P(Y) code ⊕ data transition and one C/A code ⊕ data transition. There are 154 carrier cycles per P(Y) code chip and 1,540 carrier cycles per C/A code chip on L1, so the phase shifts on the L1 carrier are relatively infrequent. The L2 frequency (1,227.60 MHz) can be modulated by either the P(Y) code ⊕ data or the C/A code ⊕ data or by the P(Y) code alone as selected by the CS. The P(Y) code and C/A codes are never present simultaneously on L2 prior to GPS modernization (see Section 4.5), unlike the case with L1. In general, the P(Y) code ⊕ data is the one selected by the CS. There are 120 carrier cycles per P(Y) code chip on L2, so the phase transitions on the L2 carrier are relatively infrequent. Table 4.2 summarizes the GPS signal structure on L1 and L2.

The PPS user has the algorithms, the special Y-code hardware per channel, and the key to gain access to the Y-code. PPS receivers formerly included a precise positioning service security module (PPSSM) to store and process the cryptographic keys and an auxiliary output chip (AOC) to produce the Y-code. Current generation PPS receivers are built around a security architecture referred to as the selective availabil-

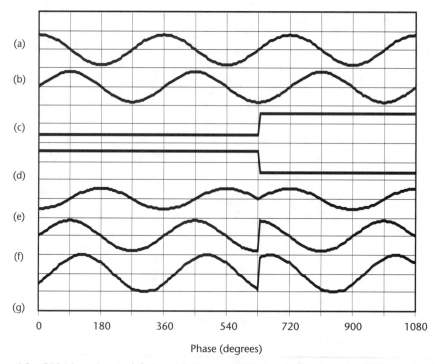

Figure 4.8 GPS L1 carrier modulation: (a) L1 carrier (0° phase), (b) L1 carrier (90° phase), (c) P(Y) code ⊕ data, (d) C/A code ⊕ data, (e) P(Y) code ⊕ data BPSK modulated on L1 carrier (0° phase) with 3-dB attenuation, (f) C/A code ⊕ data BPSK modulated on L1 carrier (90° phase), and (g) composite modulated L1 carrier signal.

Table 4.2 Legacy GPS Signal Structure

Signal Priority	Primary	Secondary
Signal designation	L1	L2
Carrier frequency (MHz)	1,575.42	1,227.60
PRN codes (Mchip/s)	P(Y) = 10.23 and C/A = 1.023	P(Y) = 10.23 or C/A = 1.023 (Note 1)
Navigation message data modulation (bps)	50	50 (Note 2)

1. The code usually selected by the CS on L2 is P(Y) code.
2. The 50-Hz navigation data message is usually modulated on L2 P(Y) code but can be turned off by the CS. There are three possibilities on L2: P(Y) code with data, P(Y) code with no data, and C/A code with data.

ity/antispoofing module (SAASM). The use of the AS Y-code denies direct (SPS GPS receiver) access to the precision code. This significantly reduces the possibility of an enemy spoofing a PPS receiver (i.e., transmitting a stronger, false precise code that captures and misleads the receiver). However, AS also denies direct access to the precision code to all SPS users, friendly or otherwise. Indirect access is still possible as discussed in [11] and Section 5.14.

4.3.1.1 Direct Sequence PRN Code Generation

Figure 4.9 depicts a high-level block diagram of the direct sequence PRN code generation used for GPS C/A code and P code generation to implement the CDMA technique. Each synthesized PRN code is derived from two other code generators. In each case, the second code generator output is delayed with respect to the first before their outputs are combined by an exclusive-or circuit. The amount of delay is different for each SV. In the case of P code, the integer delay in P-chips is identical to the PRN number. For C/A code, the delay is unique to each SV, so there is only a table lookup relationship to the PRN number. These delays are summarized in Table 4.3. The C/A code delay can be implemented by a simple but equivalent technique that eliminates the need for a delay register. This technique is explained in the following paragraphs.

The GPS C/A code is a Gold code [12] with a sequence length of 1,023 bits (chips). Since the chipping rate of the C/A code is 1.023 MHz, the repetition period of the pseudorandom sequence is $1,023/(1.023 \times 10^6 \text{ Hz})$ or 1 ms. Figure 4.10 illustrates the design architecture of the GPS C/A code generator. Not included in this diagram are the controls necessary to set or read the phase states of the registers or the counters. There are two 10-bit shift registers, G1 and G2, which generate maximum length PRN codes with a length of $2^{10} - 1 = 1,023$ bits. (The only state not used is the all-zero state). It is common to describe the design of linear code generators by means of polynomials of the form $1 + \Sigma X^i$, where X^i means that the output of the ith cell of the shift register is used as the input to the modulo-2 adder (exclusive-or), and the 1 means that the output of the adder is fed to the first cell [8]. The design specification for C/A code calls for the feedback taps of the G1 shift register to be connected to stages 3 and 10. These register states are combined with each other by an exclusive-or circuit and fed back to stage 1. The polynomial that describes this shift register architecture is: $G1 = 1 + X^3 + X^{10}$. The polynomials and initial states for both

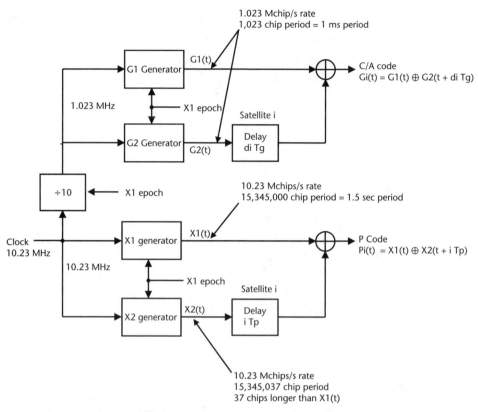

Figure 4.9 GPS code generators.

the C/A-code and P-code generator shift registers are summarized in Table 4.4. The unique C/A code for each SV is the result of the exclusive-or of the G1 direct output sequence and a delayed version of the G2 direct output sequence. The equivalent delay effect in the G2 PRN code is obtained by the exclusive-or of the selected positions of the two taps whose output is called G21. This is because a maximum-length PRN code sequence has the property that adding a phase-shifted version of itself produces the same sequence but at a different phase. The function of the two taps on the G2 shift register in Figure 4.10 is to shift the code phase in G2 with respect to the code phase in G1 without the need for an additional shift register to perform this delay. Each C/A code PRN number is associated with the two tap positions on G2. Table 4.3 describes these tap combinations for all defined GPS PRN numbers and specifies the equivalent direct sequence delay in C/A code chips. The first 32 of these PRN numbers are reserved for the space segment. Five additional PRN numbers, PRN 33 to PRN 37, are reserved for other uses, such as ground transmitters (also referred to as pseudosatellites or *pseudolites*). Pseudolites were used during Phase I (concept demonstration phase) of GPS to validate the operation and accuracy of the system before any satellites were launched and in combination with the earliest satellites. C/A codes 34 and 37 are identical.

The GPS P code is a PRN sequence generated using four 12-bit shift registers designated X1A, X1B, X2A, and X2B. A detailed block diagram of this shift register architecture is shown in Figure 4.11 [10]. Not included in this diagram are the controls necessary to set or read the phase states of the registers and counters. Note that

Table 4.3   Code Phase Assignments and Initial Code Sequences for C/A Code and P Code

SV PRN Number	C/A Code Tap Selection	C/A Code Delay (Chips)	P Code Delay (Chips)	First 10 C/A Chips (Octal)[1]	First 12 P Chips (Octal)
1	2 ⊕ 6	5	1	1440	4444
2	3 ⊕ 7	6	2	1620	4000
3	4 ⊕ 8	7	3	1710	4222
4	5 ⊕ 9	8	4	1744	4333
5	1 ⊕ 9	17	5	1133	4377
6	2 ⊕ 6	18	6	1455	4355
7	1 ⊕ 8	139	7	1131	4344
8	2 ⊕ 9	140	8	1454	4340
9	3 ⊕ 10	141	9	1626	4342
10	2 ⊕ 3	251	10	1504	4343
11	3 ⊕ 4	252	11	1642	4343
12	5 ⊕ 6	254	12	1750	4343
13	6 ⊕ 7	255	13	1764	4343
14	7 ⊕ 8	256	14	1772	4343
15	8 ⊕ 9	257	15	1775	4343
16	9 ⊕ 10	258	16	1776	4343
17	1 ⊕ 4	469	17	1156	4343
18	2 ⊕ 5	470	18	1467	4343
19	3 ⊕ 6	471	19	1633	4343
20	4 ⊕ 7	472	20	1715	4343
21	5 ⊕ 8	473	21	1746	4343
22	6 ⊕ 9	474	22	1763	4343
23	1 ⊕ 3	509	23	1063	4343
24	4 ⊕ 6	512	24	1706	4343
25	5 ⊕ 7	513	25	1743	4343
26	6 ⊕ 8	514	26	1761	4343
27	7 ⊕ 9	515	27	1770	4343
28	8 ⊕ 10	516	28	1774	4343
29	1 ⊕ 6	859	29	1127	4343
30	2 ⊕ 7	860	30	1453	4343
31	3 ⊕ 8	861	31	1625	4343
32	4 ⊕ 9	862	32	1712	4343
33[2]	5 ⊕ 10	863	33	1745	4343
34[2]	4 ⊕ 10[3]	950[3]	34	1713[3]	4343
35[2]	1 ⊕ 7	947	35	1134	4343
36[2]	2 ⊕ 8	948	36	1456	4343
37[2]	4 ⊕ 10[3]	950[3]	37	1713[3]	4343

1. In the octal notation for the first 10 chips of the C/A code, as shown in this column, the first digit (1) represents a 1 for the first chip and the last three digits are the conventional octal representation of the remaining 9 chips. For example, the first 10 chips of the SV PRN number 1 C/A code are 1100100000.

2. PRN codes 33 through 37 are reserved for other uses (e.g., pseudolites).

3. C/A codes 34 and 37 are identical.

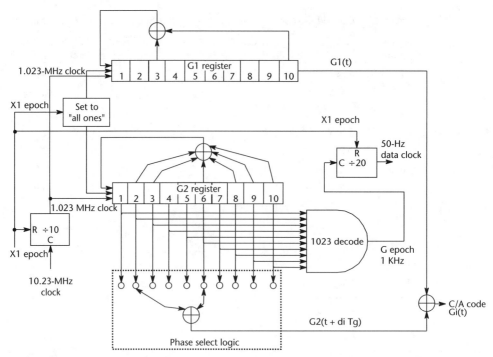

Figure 4.10   C/A code generator.

the X1A register output is combined by an exclusive-or circuit with the X1B register output to form the X1 code generator and that the X2A register output is combined by an exclusive-or circuit with the X2B register output to form the X2 code generator. The composite X2 result is fed to a shift register delay of the SV PRN number in chips and then combined by an exclusive-or circuit with the X1 composite result to generate the P code.

The design specification for the P code calls for each of the four shift registers to have a set of feedback taps that are combined by an exclusive-or circuit with each other and fed back to their respective input stages. The polynomials that describe the architecture of these feedback shift registers are shown in Table 4.4, and the logic diagram is shown in detail in Figure 4.11.

Referring to Figure 4.11, note that the natural cycles of all four feedback shift registers are truncated. For example, X1A and X2A are both reset after 4,092 chips, eliminating the last three chips of their natural 4,095 chip sequences. The registers X1B and X2B are both reset after 4,093 chips, eliminating the last two chips of their natural 4,095 chip sequences. This results in the phase of the X1B sequence lagging by one chip with respect to the X1A sequence for each X1A register cycle. As a result, there is a relative phase precession between the X1A and X1B registers. A similar phase precession takes place between X2A and X2B. At the beginning of the GPS week, all of the shift registers are set to their initial states simultaneously, as shown in Table 4.4. Also, at the end of each X1A epoch, the X1A shift register is reset to its initial state. At the end of each X1B epoch, the X1B shift register is reset to its initial state. At the end of each X2A epoch, the X2A shift register is reset to its initial state. At the end of each X2B epoch, the X2B shift register is reset to its initial state. The outputs (stage 12) of the A and B registers are combined by an exclu-

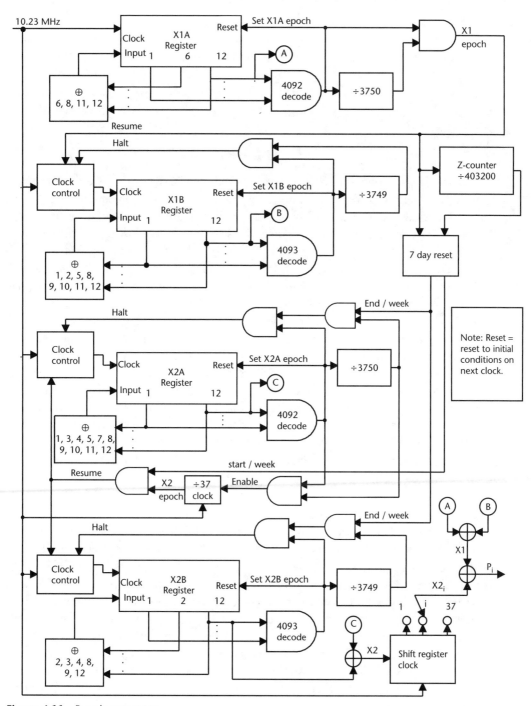

Figure 4.11 P code generator.

sive-or circuit to form an X1 sequence derived from X1A $\oplus$ X1B, and an X2 sequence derived from X2A $\oplus$ X2B. The X2 sequence is delayed by i chips (corresponding to SVi) to form X2i. The P code for SVi is Pi = X1 $\oplus$ X2i.

Table 4.4   GPS Code Generator Polynomials and Initial States

Register	Polynomial	Initial State
C/A code G1	$1 + X^3 + X^{10}$	1111111111
C/A code G2	$1 + X^2 + X^3 + X^6 + X^8 + X^9 + X^{10}$	1111111111
P code X1A	$1 + X^6 + X^8 + X^{11} + X^{12}$	001001001000
P code X1B	$1 + X^1 + X^2 + X^5 + X^8 + X^9 + X^{10} + X^{11} + X^{12}$	010101010100
P code X2A	$1 + X^1 + X^3 + X^4 + X^5 + X^7 + X^8 + X^9 + X^{10} + X^{11} + X^{12}$	100100100101
P code X2B	$1 + X^2 + X^3 + X^4 + X^8 + X^9 + X^{12}$	010101010100

There is also a phase precession between the X2A/X2B shift registers with respect to the X1A/X1B shift registers. This is manifested as a phase precession of 37 chips per X1 period between the X2 epochs (shown in Figure 4.11 as the output of the divide by 37 counter) and the X1 epochs. This is caused by adjusting the X2 period to be 37 chips longer than the X1 period. The details of this phase precession are as follows. The X1 epoch is defined as 3,750 X1A cycles. When X1A has cycled through 3,750 of these cycles, or $3,750 \times 4,092 = 15,345,000$ chips, a 1.5-second X1 epoch occurs. When X1B has cycled through 3,749 cycles of 4,093 chips per cycle, or 15,344,657 chips, it is kept stationary for an additional 343 chips to align it to X1A by halting its clock control until the 1.5-second X1 epoch resumes it. Therefore, the X1 registers have a combined period of 15,345,000 chips. X2A and X2B are controlled in the same way as X1A and X1B, respectively, but with one difference: when 15,345,000 chips have completed in exactly 1.5 seconds, both X2A and X2B are kept stationary for an additional 37 chips by halting their clock controls until the X2 epoch or the start of the week resumes it. Therefore, the X2 registers have a combined period of 15,345,037 chips, which is 37 chips longer than the X1 registers.

Note that if the P code were generated by $X1 \oplus X2$, and if it were not reset at the end of the week, it would have the potential sequence length of $15,345,000 \times 15,345,037 = 2.3547 \times 10^{14}$ chips. With a chipping rate of 10.23×10^6, this sequence has a period of 266.41 days or 38.058 weeks. However, since the sequence is truncated at the end of the week, each SV uses only one week of the sequence, and 38 unique one-week PRN sequences are available. The sequence length of each P code, with the truncation to a 7-day period, is 6.1871×10^{12} chips. As in the case of C/A code, the first 32 PRN sequences are reserved for the space segment and PRN 33 through 37 are reserved for other uses (e.g., pseudolites). The PRN 38 P code is sometimes used as a test code in P(Y) code GPS receivers, as well as to generate a reference noise level (since, by definition, it cannot correlate with any used SV PRN signals). The unique P code for each SV is the result of the different delay in the X2 output sequence. Table 4.3 shows this delay in P code chips for each SV PRN number. The P code delays (in P code chips) are identical to their respective PRN numbers for the SVs, but the C/A code delays (in C/A code chips) are different from their PRN numbers. The C/A code delays are typically much longer than their PRN numbers. The replica C/A codes for a conventional GPS receiver are usually synthesized by programming the tap selections on the G2 shift register.

Table 4.3 also shows the first 10 C/A code chips and the first 12 P code chips in octal format, starting from the beginning of the week. For example, the binary sequence for the first 10 chips of PRN 5 C/A code is 1001011011 and for the first 12 chips of PRN 5 P code is 100011111111. Note that the first 12 P code chips of PRN 10 through PRN 37 are identical. This number of chips is insignificant for P code, so the differences in the sequence do not become apparent until later in the sequence.

4.3.2 Power Levels

Table 4.5 summarizes the minimum received power levels for the three GPS signals. The levels are specified in terms of decibels with respect to 1W (dBW). The specified received GPS signal power levels [10] are based on a user antenna that is linearly polarized with 3-dB gain. Since the GPS SVs transmit RHCP signals, the table is adjusted for a typical RHCP antenna with unity gain and also accounts for the polarization mismatch adjustment that is included in the SV link budget for their RHCP antenna array (see Table 4.6). The RHCP antenna unity gain can be expressed as: 0 dBic = 0 dB with respect to an isotropic circularly polarized antenna. The resulting RHCP antenna received signal levels are slightly stronger than the minimum specified received signal, since the linear polarization mismatch is not double counted in the receiver RHCP antenna. However, this should be considered as receiver design margin and the specified minimum received power levels used for worst-case analysis.

Figure 4.12 illustrates that the minimum received power is met when the SV is at two elevation angles: 5° from the user's horizon and at the user's zenith. In between

Table 4.5 Minimum Received GPS Signal Power

	L1 C/A Code	L1 P(Y) Code	L2 P(Y) Code or C/A Code
User minimum received power at 3-dB gain linearly polarized antenna (dBW)	−158.5	−161.5	−164.5
Adjustment for unity gain antenna (dB)	−3.0	−3.0	−3.0
Adjustment for typical RHCP antenna versus linearly polarized antenna (dB)	3.4	3.4	4.4
User minimum received power at unity gain RHCP antenna (dBW)	−158.1	−161.1	−163.1

Table 4.6 L1 and L2 Navigation Satellite Signal Power Budget

	L1 C/A Code	L1 P Code	L2
User minimum received power	−158.5 dBW	−161.5 dBW	−164.5 dBW
Users linear antenna gain	3.0 dB	3.0 dB	3.0 dB
Free space propagation loss	184.4 dB	184.4 dB	182.3 dB
Total atmospheric loss	0.5 dB	0.5 dB	0.5 dB
Polarization mismatch loss	3.4 dB	3.4 dB	4.4 dB
Required satellite EIRP	26.8 dBW	23.8 dBW	19.7 dBW
Satellite antenna gain at 14.3° worst-case BLK II off-axis angle (dB)	13.4 dB	13.4 dB	11.5 dB
Required minimum satellite antenna input power	13.4 dBW 21.9W	10.4 dBW 11.1W	8.2 dBW 6.6W

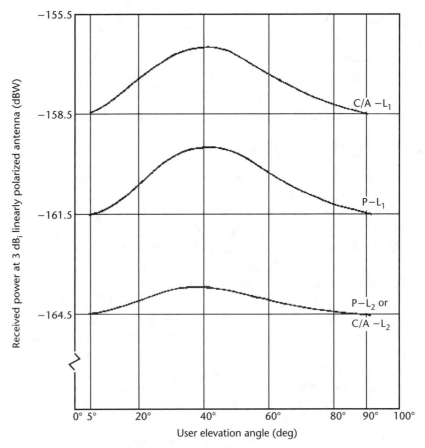

Figure 4.12 User received minimum signal power levels.

these two elevation angles, the minimum received signal power levels gradually increase up to 2 dB maximum for the L1 signals and up to 1 dB maximum for the L2 signal and then decrease back to the specified minimums. This characteristic occurs because the shaped beam pattern on the SV transmitting antenna arrays can only match the required gain at the angles corresponding to the center of the Earth and near the edge of the Earth, resulting in slightly increasing transmitting antenna array gain in between these nadir angles. The user's antenna gain pattern is typically maximum at the zenith and minimum at 5° above the horizon and for lower elevation angles.

The received signal levels are not expected to exceed −153 dBW and −155.5 dBW, respectively, for the C/A code and P(Y) code components on the L1 and L2 channels [10]. Typically, the signal powers for the SVs are from 1 to 5 dB higher than the minimum specified levels, depending on elevation angle and SV block, and they remain nearly constant until their ends of life.

Table 4.6 tabulates the navigation satellite signal power budget for the Block II GPS satellites adapted from [13] using the minimum user received power levels as the starting point. It shows the output power levels at the worst-case off-axis angle of 14.3° and for the assumed worst-case atmospheric loss of 0.5 dB. Referring to Table 4.6, the link budget for the L1 C/A code to provide the signal power with a unity gain transmitting antenna is: −158.5 − 3.0 + 184.4 + 0.5 + 3.4 = 26.8 dBW.

Since the satellite L1 antenna array has a minimum gain of 13.4 dB for C/A code at the worst-case off-axis angle of 14.3°, the minimum L1 antenna transmitter power for C/A code is $\log_{10}^{-1}[(26.8-13.4)/10]=21.9\text{W}$. Note that a minimum of 32.9W of L1 power and 6.6W of L2 power (for a total of 39.5W) must be delivered to the satellite antenna arrays to maintain the specification. The efficiency of the high-power amplifier (HPA) subassembly determines how much actual power must be provided in the satellite.

4.3.3 Autocorrelation Functions and Power Spectral Densities

The autocorrelation characteristics of the GPS PRN codes are fundamental to the signal demodulation process. The power spectral densities of the GPS PRN codes determine the channel bandwidths required to transmit and receive the spread spectrum signals

As would be expected, the GPS PRN codes have periodic correlation triangles and a line spectrum that closely resemble the characteristics of maximum-length shift register PN sequences, but with several subtle differences. This is because the GPS PRN codes are *not* shift register sequences of maximum length. For example, for the C/A code 10-bit shift register, there are only 30 usable maximum-length sequences, and among these available maximum-length sequences, the cross-correlation properties between different codes are not as good as that desired for GPS. Another problem is that the autocorrelation function of maximum-length sequences has sidelobes when the integration time is one (or a few) code periods. (This can be a problem to a lesser extent with the C/A codes as well.) In a GPS receiver, the integration and dump time associated with the correlation of its replica C/A code with the incoming SV C/A code (similar to autocorrelation) is typically 1 to 5 ms (i.e., 1 to 5 C/A code periods). Except for a highly specialized mode of operation called data wipeoff, the integration and dump time never exceeds the 50-Hz data period of 20 ms. During search modes, these short integration and dump periods for the maximum-length sequences increase the probability of high sidelobes leading to the receiver locking onto a wrong correlation peak (a sidelobe). For these reasons, the Gold codes described earlier were selected for the C/A codes.

Using the exclusive-or of two maximum length shift registers, G1 and G2 (with a programmable delay), there are 2^n-1 possible delays. Therefore, there are 1,023 possible Gold codes for the GPS C/A code generator architecture (plus two additional maximum-length sequences if the G1 and G2 sequences were used independently). However, there are only 45 Gold code combinations for the architecture of the C/A code generator defined in [10], using two taps on the G2 register to form the delay. The 32 Gold codes with the best properties were selected for the GPS space segment. (There were only four more unique two-tap combinations selected for the pseudolites since two of these codes are redundant.) Extensions of the GPS C/A code for such applications as the WAAS, wherein augmentation C/A code signals are transmitted from geostationary satellites, required a careful analysis of their properties and their effect on the space segment codes before their implementation. (Refer to Chapter 8 for details on the WAAS C/A code generation.)

Neglecting the navigation data, the autocorrelation function of the GPS C/A code signal is:

$$R_G(\tau) = \frac{1}{1{,}023 T_{CA}} \int_{t=0}^{1023} G_i(t) G_i(t+\tau)\, d\tau \qquad (4.22)$$

where:

$G_i(t)$ = C/A code Gold code sequence as a function of time, t, for SVi

T_{CA} = C/A code chipping period (977.5 ns)

τ = phase of the time shift in the autocorrelation function

The C/A code autocorrelation function is a series of correlation triangles with a period of 1,023 C/A code chips or 1 ms, as shown in Figure 4.13(a). As observed in Figure 4.13(a), the autocorrelation function of the GPS C/A (Gold) codes has the same period and the same shape in the correlation interval as that of a maximum-

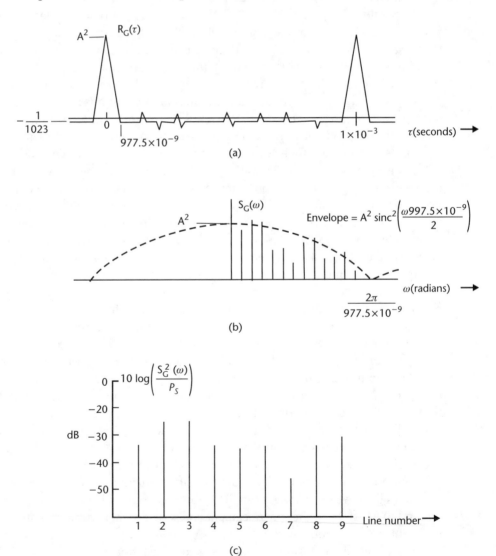

Figure 4.13 (a) The autocorrelation function, (b) spectrum, and (c) power ratio of a typical C/A code.

length sequence (see Section 4.2.3). There are small fluctuations in the intervals between the correlation intervals rather than the uniform minimum correlation level of 1/1,023 for the maximum-length sequence using a 10-bit feedback shift register [14]. This is because the C/A code correlation process cannot be synchronously clocked, as was assumed for the maximum-length sequence. These small fluctuations in the autocorrelation function of the C/A codes result in the deviation of the line spectrum from the $\text{sinc}^2(x)$ envelope, as shown in Figure 4.13(b). Recall that the power line spectrum of the maximum-length sequences matched the $\text{sinc}^2(x)$ envelope exactly, except for the zero-frequency term. However, the line spectrum spacing of 1,000 Hz is the same for both the C/A code and the 10-bit maximum-length sequence code. Figure 4.13(c) illustrates that the ratio of the power in each C/A line to the total power in the spectrum plotted in decibels can fluctuate significantly (nearly 8 dB) with respect to the −30 dB levels that would be obtained if every line contained the same power. Every C/A code has a few *strong* lines [i.e., lines above the $\text{sinc}^2(x)$ envelope], which render them more vulnerable to a continuous wave (CW) RF interference at this line frequency than their maximum length sequence counterpart. For example, the correlation process between a CW line and a PRN code ordinarily spreads the CW line, but the mixing process at some strong C/A code line results in the RF interference line being minimally suppressed. As a result, the CW energy "leaks" through the correlation process at this strong line frequency. The presence of the navigation data mitigates this leakage to a certain extent. (The effects of RF interference will be discussed further in Chapter 6.)

Keeping in mind that the GPS C/A codes have these limitations, it is often convenient and approximately correct to illustrate their autocorrelation functions as following ideal maximum-length sequences, as shown in Figure 4.14. Note that there are other typical simplifications in this figure. The τ-axis is represented in C/A code chips instead of seconds and the peak amplitude of the correlation function has been normalized to unity (corresponding to the PRN sequence amplitude being ±1).

The autocorrelation function of the GPS P(Y) code is:

$$R_P(\tau) = \frac{1}{6.1871 \times 10^{12}\, T_{CP}} \int_{t=0}^{6.1871 \times 10^{12}} P_i(t) P_i(t + \tau)\, dt \tag{4.23}$$

where:

$P_i(t)$ = P(Y) code PRN sequence as a function of time, t, for SVi

T_{CP} = P(Y) code chipping period (97.8 ns)

τ = phase of the time shift in the autocorrelation function

The P(Y) code is also not a maximum-length sequence code, but because its period is so long and its chipping rate is so fast, its autocorrelation characteristics are essentially ideal. The P(Y) code was designed to have a one-week period made up of 403,200 periods of its 1.5-second X1 epochs, called Z-counts. Figure 4.15 depicts a normalized autocorrelation function for P(Y) code (amplitude $A = ±1$) with the phase shift axis, τ, shown in units of P(Y) code chips. The autocorrelation function for P(Y) code has similar characteristics to the C/A code, but with signifi-

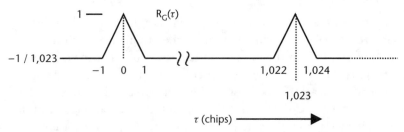

Figure 4.14 Normalized and simplified autocorrelation function of a typical C/A code with τ in chips.

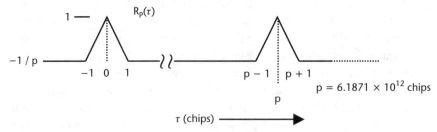

Figure 4.15 Normalized and simplified autocorrelation function of a typical P(Y) code with τ in chips.

Table 4.7 Comparisons Between C/A Code and P(Y) Code Autocorrelation

	C/A Code	P(Y) Code
Maximum autocorrelation amplitude	1	1
Typical autocorrelation amplitude outside the correlation interval	$-\dfrac{1}{1,023}$	$-\dfrac{1}{6.1871 \times 10^{12}}$
Typical autocorrelation in decibels with respect to maximum correlation	-30.1	-127.9
Autocorrelation period	1 ms	1 week
Autocorrelation interval (chips)	2	2
Autocorrelation time interval (ns)	1,955.0	195.5
Autocorrelation range interval (m)	586.1	58.6
R_c = chipping rate (Mchip/s)	1.023	10.23
T_c = chipping period (ns)	977.5	97.8
Range of one chip (m)	293.0	29.3

cant differences in values. Table 4.7 compares these characteristics. From Table 4.7, it can be observed that P(Y) code can be considered essentially uncorrelated with itself (typically −127.9 dB) for all intervals outside the correlation interval, whereas, the C/A code is adequately uncorrelated with itself (typically −30.1 dB) outside its correlation interval. However, the C/A codes can be as poorly uncorrelated with themselves as −21.1 dB outside the correlation interval—fortunately this occurs only a small percentage of the time.

When the GPS codes are combined with the 50-Hz navigation message data, there is essentially an imperceptible effect on the resulting autocorrelation functions and the power spectrum. When these are modulated onto the L-band carrier, there is a translation to L-band of the power spectrum from the baseband frequencies that have been described so far. Assuming that the PRN waveform is BPSK modulated onto the carrier and that the carrier frequency and the code are not coherent, the resulting power spectrum is given by [9]:

$$S_L(\omega) = \frac{1}{2}\left[P_c S_{PN}(\omega + \omega_c) + P_c S_{PN}(\omega - \omega_c)\right]$$ (4.24)

where:

P_c = unmodulated carrier power

ω_c = carrier frequency (radians)

$S_{PN}(\omega_c)$ = power spectrum of the PRN code(s) (plus data) at baseband

As can be observed from (4.24), the baseband spectra are shifted up to the carrier frequency (and down to the negative carrier frequency). In the following GPS L-band power spectrum illustrations, only the (upper) single-sided frequency is considered. The GPS signals were synthesized by a GPS signal generator and measured by a Hewlett-Packard spectrum analyzer.

Figure 4.16 is a plot of the power spectrum of the GPS P(Y) code and C/A code (plus 50-Hz data) BPSK modulated onto the L1 carrier. The spectrum analyzer performed the plot using a 300-kHz resolution bandwidth, so it is impossible to observe the line spectrum characteristics of either code. Therefore, the power spectrums appear to be continuous. The center frequency is at the L1 carrier, 1,575.42

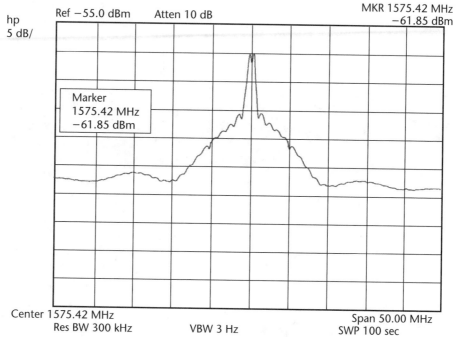

Figure 4.16   Power spectrum of L1 P(Y) code and C/A code from a GPS signal generator.

MHz. The combined power spectra of C/A code and P(Y) codes are centered at the L1 carrier frequency. The first nulls of the C/A code power spectrum are at ±1.023 MHz from the center frequency and the first nulls of the P(Y) code power spectrum are at ±10.23 MHz from the center frequency.

Figure 4.17 is a plot of the power spectrum of the GPS P(Y) code (plus 50-Hz data) BPSK modulated onto the L2 carrier. The plot is virtually identical to Figure 4.15, except the center frequency is at the L2 carrier, 1,227.60 MHz, and the C/A code modulation is removed. The first null of the P(Y) code is at ±10.23 MHz.

Figure 4.18 is a plot of the power spectrum of the GPS C/A code (plus 50-Hz data) BPSK modulated onto the L1 carrier with the P(Y) code turned off. The frequency scale has been adjusted to be narrower than Figure 4.16 by a factor of ten in order to inspect the C/A code power spectrum more closely. The resolution bandwidth of the spectrum analyzer has been reduced to 3 kHz so that the line spectrum of the C/A code is just beginning to be visible in the plot. The strong lines of the C/A code [those above the nominal $\text{sinc}^2(x)$ envelope] are also somewhat observable. It would be impossible to observe the line spectrum of the P(Y) code with a spectrum analyzer because the resolution bandwidth corresponding to its extremely fine line spacing would be unreasonably narrow.

4.3.4 Cross-Correlation Functions and CDMA Performance

The GPS modulation/demodulation concept is based on the use of a different PRN code in each SV, but with the same code chipping rates and carrier frequencies on each SV. This modulation/demodulation technique is called CDMA, as discussed in Section 4.2.1. The CDMA technique requires the user GPS receiver to synthesize a

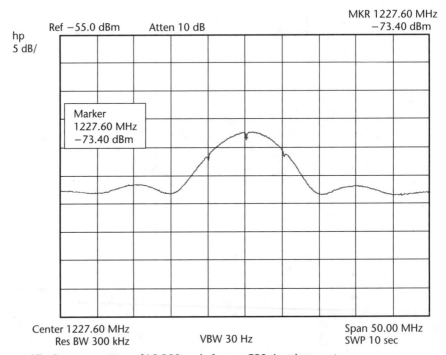

Figure 4.17 Power spectrum of L2 P(Y) code from a GPS signal generator.

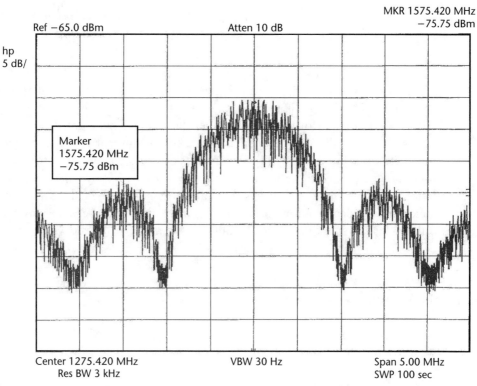

Figure 4.18   Power spectrum of L1 C/A code from a GPS signal generator showing the line spectrum of the C/A code.

replica of the SV-transmitted PRN code and to shift the phase of the replica PRN code so that it correlates with a unique PRN code for each SV tracked. Each SV PRN code used in the CDMA system must be minimally cross-correlated with another SV's PRN code for any phase or Doppler shift combination within the entire code period. The autocorrelation characteristics of the GPS codes have already been discussed. The ideal cross-correlation functions of the GPS codes are defined by the following equation:

$$R_{ij}(\tau) = \int_{-\infty}^{\infty} PN_i(t)PN_j(t+\tau)d\tau = 0 \qquad (4.25)$$

where:

$PN_i(t)$ = PRN waveform for satellite i

$PN_j(t)$ = PRN waveform for all other satellites j where $j \neq i$

Equation (4.25) states that the PRN waveform of satellite i does not correlate with the PRN waveform of any other satellite for any phase shift τ. In practice this is impossible, just as it is impossible for a satellite to have the desirable characteristic of zero autocorrelation outside its correlation interval. In order for the CDMA discrimination technique to work, a certain level of cross-correlation signal rejection performance must be achieved among all of the used PRN codes. Because the code length is 6.1871×10^{12} chips and the chipping rate is 10.23 Mchip/s (1-week period), the cross-correlation level of the GPS P(Y) codes with any other GPS P(Y) code approaches −127 dB with respect to maximum autocorrelation. Hence, the cross-correlation of the P(Y) code of any GPS SV can be treated as uncorrelated with any other GPS SV signals for any phase shift. Because of this excellent P(Y) code cross-correlation performance, no further discussion is warranted.

Because the GPS C/A code length was a compromise at 1,023 chips with a chipping rate of 1.023 Mchip/s (1-ms period), the cross-correlation properties can be poor under certain circumstances. As shown in Table 4.8, the C/A code cross-correlation functions have peak levels that can be as poor as −24 dB with respect to its maximum autocorrelation for a zero Doppler difference between any two codes. Table 4.9 shows that for higher Doppler difference levels at the worst-case intervals of 1 kHz, the cross-correlation levels can be as poor as −21.1 dB.

4.4 Navigation Message Format

As described in Section 4.3, both the C/A code and P(Y) code signals are modulated with 50-bps data. This data provides the user with the information necessary to compute the precise locations of each visible satellite and time of transmission for each navigation signal. The data also includes a significant set of auxiliary information that may be used, for example, to assist the equipment in acquiring new satellites, to translate from GPS system time to UTC (see Section 2.6), and to correct for a number of errors that affect the range measurements. This section outlines the main features of the GPS navigation message format. For a more complete description, the interested reader is referred to [10].

Table 4.8 C/A Code Maximum Cross-Correlation Power (Zero Doppler Differences)

Cumulative Probability of Occurrence	Cross-Correlation for Any Two Codes (dB)
0.23	−23.9
0.50	−24.2
1.00	−60.2

Table 4.9 C/A Code Maximum Cross-Correlation Power Summed for All 32 Codes (Increments of 1-kHz Doppler Differences)

Cumulative Probability of Occurrence	Cross-Correlation at $\Delta = 1\ kHz\ (dB)$	Cross-Correlation at $\Delta = 2\ kHz\ (dB)$	Cross-Correlation at $\Delta = 3\ kHz\ (dB)$	Cross-Correlation at $\Delta = 4\ kHz\ (dB)$	Cross-Correlation at $\Delta = 5\ kHz\ (dB)$
0.001	−21.1	−21.1	−21.6	−21.1	−21.9
0.02	−24.2	−24.2	−24.2	−24.2	−24.2
0.1	−26.4	−26.4	−26.4	−26.4	−26.4
0.4	−30.4	−30.4	−30.4	−30.4	−30.4

The GPS navigation message is transmitted in five 300-bit subframes, as shown in Figure 4.19. Each subframe is itself composed of ten 30-bit words. The last 6 bits in each word of the navigation message are used for parity checking to provide the user equipment with a capability to detect bit errors during demodulation. A (32, 26) Hamming code is employed. The five subframes are transmitted in order beginning with subframe 1. Subframes 4 and 5 consist of 25 pages each, so that the first time through the five subframes, page 1 of subframes 4 and 5 are broadcast. In the next cycle through the five subframes, page 2 of subframes 4 and 5 are broadcast and so on.

Although there are provisions for a loss of ground contact, normally the control segment uploads critical navigation data elements once or twice per day per satellite. In this nominal mode of operation, the same critical navigation data elements (e.g., satellite ephemeris and clock correction data) are broadcast repeatedly over 2-hour time spans (except if an upload occurs during this interval). On 2-hour boundaries, each satellite switches to broadcasting a different set of these critical elements, which are stored in tables in the satellite's RAM. The control segment generates these message elements based upon its current estimates of each satellite's position and clock error and prediction algorithms on how these parameters will change over time.

The first two words of each subframe (bits 1–60) contain telemetry (TLM) data and a handover word (HOW). The TLM word is the first of the 10 words in each subframe and includes a fixed preamble, a fixed 8-bit pattern 10001011 that never changes. This pattern is included to assist the user equipment in locating the beginning of each subframe. Each TLM word also includes 14 bits of data that are only meaningful to authorized users. The HOW, so-named because it allows the user

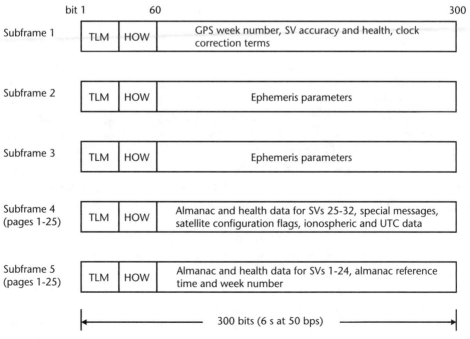

Figure 4.19 Navigation message format.

equipment to "handover" from C/A code tracking to P(Y) code tracking, provides the GPS time-of-week (TOW) modulo 6 seconds corresponding to the leading edge of the following subframe. The HOW also provides two flag bits, one that indicates whether antispoofing is activated (see Section 4.3.1), and one that serves as an alert indicator. If the alert flag is set, it indicates that the signal accuracy may be poor and should be processed at the user's own risk. Finally, the HOW provides the subframe number (1–5).

Subframe 1 provides the GPS transmission week number, which is the number of weeks modulo 1,024 that have elapsed since January 5, 1980. The first rollover of the GPS week number occurred on August 22, 1999. The next rollover will occur in April 2019. It is prudent that the GPS receiver designer keep track of these rare but inevitable rollover epochs in nonvolatile memory. Subframe 1 also provides the following satellite clock correction terms: a_{f0}, a_{f1}, a_{f2}, and time of clock, t_{oc}. These terms are extremely important for precise ranging, since they account for the lack of perfect synchronization between the timing of the SV broadcast signals and GPS system time (see Section 7.2.1). A 10-bit number referred to as issue of data, clock (IODC) is included in subframe 1 to uniquely identify the current set of navigation data. User equipment can monitor the IODC field to detect changes to the navigation data. The current IODC is different from IODCs used over the past seven days. Subframe 1 also includes a group delay correction, T_{gd}, a user range accuracy (URA) indicator, a SV health indicator, an L2 code indicator, and an L2 P data flag. T_{gd} is needed by single-frequency (L1- or L2-only) users since the clock correction parameters refer to the timing of the P(Y) code on L1 and L2, as apparent to a user that is using a linear combination of dual-frequency L1/L2 P(Y) code measurements to mitigate ionospheric errors (see Section 7.2.4.1). The URA indicator provides the user with an estimate of the 1-sigma range errors to the satellite due to satellite and control segment errors (and is fully applicable only for L1/L2 P-code users). The SV health indicator is a 6-bit field that indicates whether the satellite is operating normally or whether components of the signal or navigation data are suspected to be erroneous. The L2 code indicator field indicates whether the P(Y) code or C/A code is active on L2. Finally, the L2 P data flag indicates whether navigation data is being modulated onto the L2 P(Y) code.

Subframes 2 and 3 include the osculating Keplerian orbital elements described in Section 2.3 that allow the user equipment to precisely determine the location of the satellite. Subframe 2 also includes a fit interval flag and an age of data offset (AODO) term. The fit interval flag indicates whether the orbital elements are based upon a nominal 4-hour curve fit (that corresponds to the 2-hour nominal data transmission interval described earlier) or a longer interval. The AODO term provides an indication of the age of the elements based on a navigation message correction table (NMCT) that has been included in the GPS navigation data since 1995 [15]. Both subframes 2 and 3 also include an issue of data ephemeris (IODE) field. IODE consists of the 8 least significant bits (LSBs) of IODC and may be used by the user equipment to detect changes in the broadcast orbital elements.

Pages 2–5 and 7–10 of subframe 4 and pages 1–24 of subframe 5 contain almanac data (coarse orbital elements that allow the user equipment to determine approximate positions of other satellites to assist acquisition) for SVs 1–32 (see Section 2.3). Page 13 of subframe 4 includes the NMCT range corrections. Page 18 of subframe 4 includes ionospheric correction parameters for single-frequency users (see Section 7.1.2.5) and parameters so that user equipment can relate UTC to GPS system time (see Section 2.6.3). Page 25 of subframes 4 and 5 provide configuration and health flags for SVs 1–32. The data payloads of the remaining pages of subframes 4 and 5 are currently reserved.

4.5   Modernized GPS Signals

At the time of this writing, three additional signals were anticipated to be broadcast by GPS satellites by 2006. As illustrated in Figure 4.20, these include two new civil signals, an L2 civil (L2C) signal [10, 16] and a signal at 1,176.45 MHz (115 f_0) referred to as L5 [17, 18]. A new military signal, M code, will also be added at L1 and L2 [19]. This section provides an overview of each of these new signals.

4.5.1   L2 Civil Signal

As shown in Figure 4.20, the L2 civil (L2C) signal has a similar power spectrum (i.e., 2.046 MHz null-to-null bandwidth) to the C/A code. L2C is very different from the C/A code in many other ways, however. First, L2C uses two different PRN codes per satellite. The first PRN code is referred to as the civil moderate (CM) code because it employs a sequence that repeats every 10,230 chips, which is considered to be of moderate length. The second code, the civil long (CL) code, is extremely long with a length of 767,250 chips. As shown in Figure 4.21, these two codes are generated, each at a 511.5-kchip/s rate, and are used in the following manner to generate the overall L2C signal: First, the CM code is modulated by a 25-bps navigation data stream after the data is encoded into a 50-baud stream with a rate one-half constraint-length 7 FEC code. The 25-bps data rate is one-half the rate of the navigation data on the C/A code and P(Y) code signals and was chosen so that the data on the L2C signal can be demodulated in challenged environments (e.g., indoors or under heavy foliage) where 50-bps data could not be. Next, the baseband

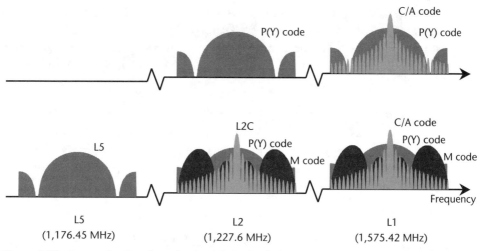

Figure 4.20   Legacy (top) and modernized GPS signals (bottom).

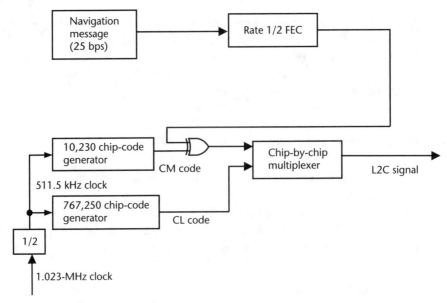

Figure 4.21   Baseband L2C signal generator.

L2C signal is formed by the chip-by-chip multiplexing of the CM (with data) and CL codes. The fact that L2C devotes one-half its power to a component without data (CL) is an important design feature shared by the other modernized GPS signals. This feature enables very robust tracking of the signal by a GPS receiver (see Section 5.3.1).

The L2C signal has an overall chip rate of 2×511.5-kchip/s rate = 1.023 Mchip/s, which accounts for its similar power spectrum to the C/A code. There are important differences between the L2C and C/A code signal power spectra, however. Since both CM and CL are much longer than the length-1,023 C/A code, the maximum lines in the L2C power spectrum are far lower than the maximum lines in the C/A code power spectrum. As will be discussed in Chapter 6, the lower lines in the L2C power spectrum lead to greatly increased robustness in the presence of narrowband interference.

The CM and CL codes are generated using the same 27-stage linear feedback shift register shown in Figure 4.22. A shorthand notation is used in the diagram. The number that appears in each block in the figure represents the number of stages (each holding 1 bit) between feedback taps. CM and CL codes for different satellites

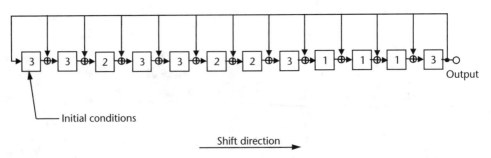

Figure 4.22   CM and CL PRN code generation.

are generated by different initial loads of the register. The register is reset every 10,230 chips for CM and every 767,250 chips for CL. The CM code repeats 75 times for each repetition of the CL code. At the 511.5-kchip/s rate, the period of the CM code is 20 ms (one P(Y) code data bit period) and the period of the CL code is 1.5 seconds (one X1 epoch or Z-count).

The rate one-half constraint-length FEC scheme used to encode the 25-bps L2C navigation data into a 50-baud bit stream is shown in Figure 4.23.

The minimum specified received L2C power level for signals broadcast from the Block IIR-M and IIF satellites is −160 dBW [10].

4.5.2 L5

The GPS L5 signal is generated as shown in Figure 4.24. QPSK is used to combine an in-phase signal component (I5) and a quadraphase signal component (Q5). Different length-10,230 PRN codes are used for I5 and Q5. I5 is modulated by 50-bps navigation data that, after the use of FEC using the same convolutional encoding as L2C, results in an overall symbol rate of 100 baud. A 10.23-MHz chipping rate is employed for both the I5 and Q5 PRN codes resulting in a 1-ms code repetition period.

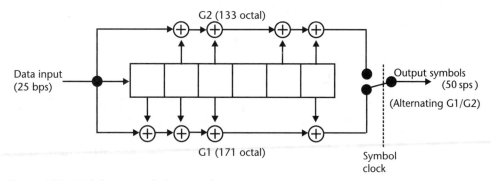

Figure 4.23 L2C data convolution encoder.

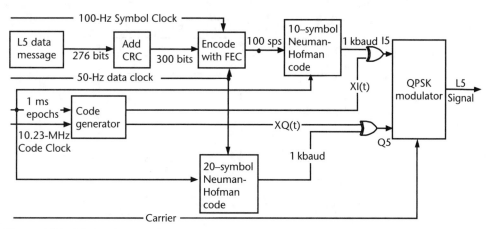

Figure 4.24 L5 signal generation.

Neuman-Hofman (NH) synchronization codes [6] are modulated upon I5 and Q5 at a 1-kbaud rate. For I5, the 10-symbol NH code 0000110101 is generated over a 10-ms interval and repeated. For Q5, the 20-symbol NH code 00000100110101001110 is used. Every 1 ms, the current NH code bit is modulo-2 added to the PRN code chip. For example, on I5, the PRN code repeats 10 times over each 10-ms interval. During this interval, the PRN code is generated normally (upright) for repetitions 1–4, 7, and 9 (the zero bits in the I5 NH code 0000110101) and is inverted over repetitions 5, 6, 8, and 10 (corresponding to the set bits in the I5 NH code). The start of the I5 NH code is aligned with the start of each 10-ms data symbol that results from the FEC encoding. The Q5 NH code is synchronized with the 20-ms data bits.

The I5 and Q5 PRN codes are generated using the logic circuit shown in Figure 4.25, which is built around three 13-bit linear feedback shift registers. Every 1 ms, the XA coder is initialized to all 1s. Simultaneously, the XBI and XBQ coders are initialized to different values, specified in [18], to yield the I5 and Q5 PRN codes.

The minimum specified received L5 power level for signals broadcast from the Block IIF satellites is −154.9 dBW [18].

4.5.3 M Code

The modernized military signal (M code) is designed exclusively for military use and is intended to eventually replace the P(Y) code [19]. During the transition period of

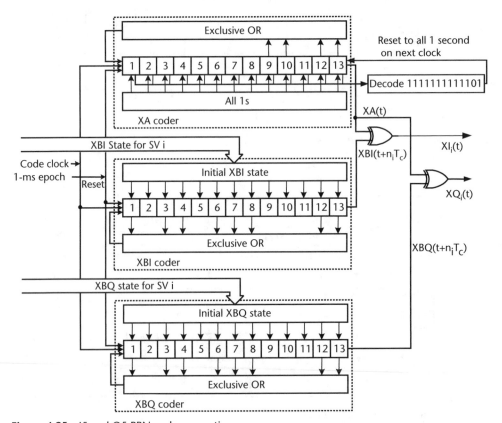

Figure 4.25 I5 and Q5 PRN code generation.

replacing the GPS constellation with modernized SVs, the military user equipment will combine P(Y) code, M code, and C/A code operation in the so-called YMCA receiver. The primary military benefits that M code provides are improved security plus spectral isolation from the civil signals to permit noninterfering higher power M code modes that support antijam resistance. Other benefits include enhanced tracking and data demodulation performance, robust acquisition, and compatibility with C/A code and P(Y) code. It accomplishes these objectives within the existing GPS L1 (1,575.42 MHz) and L2 (1,227.60 MHz) frequency bands.

To accomplish the spectral separation shown in Figure 4.20, the new M code employs BOC modulation [3]. Specifically, M code is a BOC_s (10,5) signal. The first parameter denotes the frequency of an underlying squarewave subcarrier, which is 10×1.023 MHz, and the second parameter denotes the underlying M code generator code chipping rate, which is 5×1.023 Mchip/s. Figure 4.26 depicts a very high level block diagram of the M code generator. It illustrates the BOC square wave modulation of the underlying M code generator that results in the split spectrum signals of Figure 4.20.

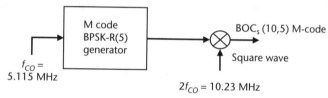

Figure 4.26   M code signal generation.

Table 4.10   Summary of GPS Signal Characteristics

Signal	Center Frequency (MHz)	Modulation Type	Data Rate (bps)	Null-to-Null Bandwidth (MHz)*	PRN Code Length
L1 C/A code	1,575.42	BPSK-R(1)	50	2.046	1023
L1 P(Y) code	1,575.42	BPSK-R(10)	50	20.46	P: 6187104000000 Y: cryptographically generated
L2 P(Y) code	1,227.6	BPSK-R(10)	50	20.46	P: 6187104000000 Y: cryptographically generated
L2C	1,227.6	BPSK-R(1)	25	2.046	CM: 10,230 CL: 767,250 (2 PRN sequences are chip-by-chip multiplexed)
L5	1,176.45	BPSK-R(10)	50	20.46	I5: 10,230 Q5: 10,230 (two components are in phase quadrature)
L1 M code	1,575.42	BOC(10,5)	N/A	30.69*	Cryptographically generated
L2 M code	1,227.6	BOC(10,5)	N/A	30.69*	Cryptographically generated
L1C	1,575.42	BOC(1,1)	N/A	4.092*	N/A

* For binary offset carrier modulations, null-to-null bandwidth is defined here as bandwidth between the outer nulls of the largest spectral lobes.

The M code signal will be broadcast through the Earth-coverage L-band antenna on the Block IIR-M and later GPS satellites. The minimum anticipated Earth-coverage M code power level is −158 dBW on L1 [19]. For Block III and later GPS satellites, a higher power M code signal is also planned to be broadcast in limited geographic regions. The minimum received power for this higher powered signal, referred to as *spot beam* M code, is anticipated to be −138 dBW [19].

4.5.4   L1 Civil Signal

The United States is planning to add a modernized civil signal upon the L1 frequency within the Block III time frame [20]. The design of this new signal, referred to as L1C, was still underway at the time of this writing. The modulation will likely be $BOC_s(1,1)$, based upon the recommendations from [20].

4.6   Summary

This chapter has described the current and planned GPS signals. A summary of key characteristics of each of the signals is presented in Table 4.10.

References

[1]   Proakis, J., *Digital Communications*, 4th ed., New York: McGraw-Hill, 2000.

[2]   Simon, M., et al., *Spread Spectrum Communications Handbook*, New York: McGraw-Hill, 1994.

[3]   Betz, J., "Binary Offset Carrier Modulations for Radionavigation," *NAVIGATION: Journal of The Institute of Navigation*, Vol. 48, No. 4, Winter 2001–2002.

[4]   Hegarty, C., J. Betz, and A. Saidi, "Binary Coded Symbol Modulations for GNSS," *Proceedings of The Institute of Navigation Annual Meeting*, Dayton, OH, June 2004.

[5]   Butman, S., and U. Timor, "Interplex—An Efficient Multichannel PSK/PM Telemetry System," *IEEE Trans. on Communication Technology*, Vol. COM-20, No. 3, June 1972.

[6]   Spilker, J. J., Jr., *Digital Communications by Satellite*, Englewood Cliffs, NJ: Prentice-Hall, 1977.

[7]   Cangiani, G., R. Orr, and C. Nguyen, *Methods and Apparatus for Generating a Constant-Envelope Composite Transmission Signal*, U.S. Patent Application Publication, Pub. No. U.S. 2002/0075907 A1, June 20, 2002.

[8]   Forssell, B., *Radionavigation Systems*, Upper Saddle River, NJ: Prentice-Hall, 1991, pp. 250–271.

[9]   Holmes, J. K., *Coherent Spread Spectrum Systems*, Malabar, FL: Krieger Publishing Company, 1990, pp. 344–394.

[10] ARINC, *NAVSTAR GPS Space Segment/Navigation User Interfaces*, IS-GPS-200D, ARINC Research Corporation, Fountain Valley, CA, December 7, 2004.

[11] Woo, K. T., "Optimum Semicodeless Processing of GPS L2," *NAVIGATION: Journal of The Institute of Navigation*, Vol. 47, No. 2, Summer 2000, pp. 82–99.

[12] Gold, R., "Optimal Binary Sequences for Spread Spectrum Multiplexing," *IEEE Trans. on Information Theory*, Vol. 33, No. 3, 1967.

[13] Czopek, F. M., "Description and Performance of the GPS Block I and II L-Band Antenna and Link Budget," *Proc. 6th International Technical Meeting of the Satellite Division of the Institute of Navigation*, Vol. I, Salt Lake City, UT, September 22–24, 1993, pp. 37–43.

[14]   Spilker, J. J., Jr., "GPS Signal Structure and Performance Characteristics," *NAVIGATION: Journal of The Institute of Navigation*, Vol. 25, No. 2, 1978.

[15]   Shank, C., B. Brottlund, and C. Harris, "Navigation Message Correction Tables: On-Orbit Results," *Proc. of the Institute of Navigation Annual Meeting*, Colorado Springs, CO, June 1995.

[16]   Fontana, R. D., W. Cheung, and T. Stansell, "The New L2 Civil Signal," *GPS World*, September 2001, pp. 28–34.

[17]   Van Dierendonck, A. J., and C. Hegarty, "The New Civil GPS L5 Signal," *GPS World*, September 2000, pp. 64–71.

[18]   ARINC Engineering Services, LLC, IS-GPS-705, *Navstar GPS Space Segment/User Segment L5 Interfaces*, El Segundo, CA, January 5, 2005.

[19]   Barker, B., et al., "Overview of the GPS M Code Signal," *Proc. of The Institute of Navigation National Technical Meeting*, Anaheim, CA, January 2000.

[20]   Hudnut, K., and B. Titus, *GPS L1 Civil Signal Modernization*, Stewardship Project #204, Interagency GPS Executive Board, Washington, D.C., July 30, 2004.

CHAPTER 5

Satellite Signal Acquisition, Tracking, and Data Demodulation

Phillip W. Ward
NAVWARD GPS Consulting

John W. Betz and Christopher J. Hegarty
The MITRE Corporation

5.1 Overview

In practice, a GPS receiver must first replicate the PRN code that is transmitted by the SV being acquired by the receiver; then it must shift the phase of the replica code until it correlates with the SV PRN code. When cross-correlating the transmitted PRN code with a replica code, the same correlation properties occur that occurs for the mathematical autocorrelation process for a given PRN code. As will be seen in this chapter, the mechanics of the receiver correlation process are very different from the autocorrelation process because only selected points of the correlation envelope are found and examined by the receiver. When the phase of the GPS receiver replica code matches the phase of the incoming SV code, there is maximum correlation. When the phase of the replica code is offset by more than 1 chip on either side of the incoming SV code, there is minimum correlation. This is indeed the manner in which a GPS receiver detects the SV signal when acquiring or tracking the SV signal in the code phase dimension. It is important to understand that the GPS receiver must also detect the SV in the carrier phase dimension by replicating the carrier frequency plus Doppler (and usually eventually obtains carrier phase lock with the SV signal by this means). Thus, the GPS signal acquisition and tracking process is a two-dimensional (code and carrier) signal replication process.

In the code or range dimension, the GPS receiver accomplishes the cross-correlation process by first searching for the phase of the desired SV and then tracking the SV code state. This is done by adjusting the nominal spreading code chip rate of its replica code generator to compensate for the Doppler-induced effect on the SV PRN code due to LOS relative dynamics between the antenna phase centers of the receiver and the SV. There is also an apparent Doppler effect on the code tracking loop caused by the frequency offset in the receiver's reference oscillator with respect to its specified frequency. This common mode error effect, which is the time bias rate that is ultimately determined by the navigation solution, is quite small for the code tracking loop and is usually neglected for code tracking and measurement purposes. The code correlation process is implemented as a real-time multiplication of the phase-shifted replica code with the incoming SV code, followed by an integration and dump process. The objective of the GPS receiver is to keep the prompt phase of its replica code generator at maximum correlation with the desired SV code phase. Typically, three correlators are used for tracking purposes, one at the prompt or on-time correlation position for carrier tracking and the other two located symmetrically early and late with respect to the prompt phase for code tracking. Modern receivers use multiple (even massively multiple) correlators to speed up the search process and some use multiple correlators for robust code tracking.

However, if the receiver has not simultaneously adjusted (tuned) its replica carrier signal so that it matches the frequency of the desired SV carrier, then the signal correlation process in the range dimension is severely attenuated by the resulting frequency response roll-off characteristic of the GPS receiver. This has the consequence that the receiver never acquires the SV. If the signal was successfully acquired because the SV code and frequency were successfully replicated during the search process, but the receiver subsequently loses track of the SV frequency, then the receiver subsequently loses code track as well. Thus, in the carrier Doppler frequency dimension, the GPS receiver accomplishes the carrier matching (wipeoff) process by first searching for the carrier Doppler frequency of the desired SV and then tracking the SV carrier Doppler state. It does this by adjusting the nominal carrier frequency of its replica carrier generator to compensate for the Doppler-induced effect on the SV carrier signal due to LOS relative dynamics between the receiver and the SV. There is also an apparent Doppler error effect on the carrier loop caused by the frequency offset in the receiver's reference oscillator with respect to its specified frequency. This error, which is common to all satellites being tracked by the receiver, is determined by the navigation filter as the time bias rate in units of seconds per second. This error in the carrier Doppler phase measurement is important to the search process (if known) and is an essential correction to the carrier Doppler phase measurement process.

The two-dimensional search and tracking process can best be explained and understood in progressive steps. The clearest explanation is in reverse sequence from the events that actually take place in a typical real world GPS receiver, namely signal search and acquisition followed by steady state tracking. The two-dimensional search and acquisition process is easier to understand if the two-dimensional steady state tracking process is explained first (Section 5.2). Once in steady state tracking, the two-dimensional code and carrier tracking process is easier to understand if the carrier tracking process is explained first even though both the code and carrier tracking processes are taking place simultaneously. This is the explanation sequence that will be used. The explanation will first be given in the context of a generic GPS receiver architecture with minimum use of equations. This high-level overview will then be followed by more detailed explanations of the carrier (Section 5.3) and code tracking loops (Section 5.4), including the most useful equations. Sections 5.5 through 5.7 cover additional topics regarding the tracking loops. Section 5.5 addresses the design of loop filters. Section 5.6 discusses measurement errors and tracking thresholds. Section 5.7 describes how the pseudorange, delta pseudorange, and integrated Doppler measurements are formed from the natural measurements of a GPS receiver.

The remainder of the chapter addresses acquisition (Section 5.8); other functions performed by the receiver including the sequence of initial operations (Section 5.9), data demodulation (Section 5.10), and special baseband functions (Section 5.11) such as SNR estimation and lock detection; and some special topics. The special topics include the use of digital processing (Section 5.12), considerations for indoor use (Section 5.13), and techniques to track the Y code without cryptographic access to this signal (Section 5.14). Throughout the chapter, extensive use of spreadsheet approximation equations and some experience-proven, rule-of-thumb, tracking threshold criteria are presented that will make it practical for the reader to not only understand but actually design the baseband portion of a GPS receiver.

5.2   GPS Receiver Code and Carrier Tracking

Most modern GPS receiver designs are digital receivers. These receiver designs have evolved rapidly toward higher and higher levels of digital component integration, and this trend is expected to continue. Also, microprocessors and their specialized cousin, DSPs, are becoming so powerful and cost effective that software defined receivers (SDRs) are being developed that use no custom digital components. For this reason, a high-level block diagram of a modern generic digital GPS receiver will be used to represent a generic GPS receiver architecture, as shown in Figure 5.1. The GPS RF signals of all SVs in view are received by a RHCP antenna with nearly hemispherical (i.e., above the local horizon) gain coverage. These RF signals are amplified by a low noise preamplifier (preamp), which effectively sets the noise figure of the receiver. There may be a passive bandpass prefilter between the antenna and preamp to minimize out-of-band RF interference. These amplified and signal condi-

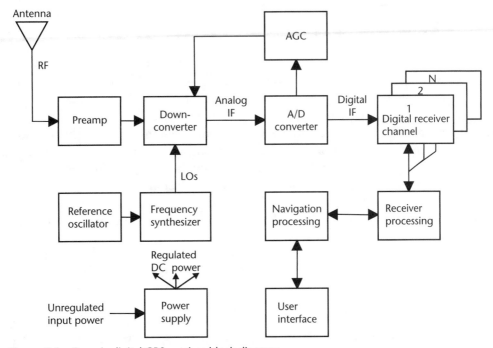

Figure 5.1   Generic digital GPS receiver block diagram.

tioned RF signals are then down-converted to an IF using signal mixing frequencies from local oscillators (LOs). The LOs are derived from the reference oscillator by the frequency synthesizer, based on the frequency plan of the receiver design. One LO per downconverter stage is required. Two-stage down-conversion to IF is typical, but one-stage down-conversion and even direct L-band digital sampling have also been used. However, since nearly 100 dB of signal gain is required prior to digitization, placing all of this gain at L-band is conducive to self-jamming in the receiver front end, so downconversion is assumed here. The LO signal mixing process generates both upper and lower sidebands of the SV signals, so the lower sidebands are selected and the upper sidebands and leak-through signals are rejected by a postmixer bandpass filter. The signal Dopplers and the PRN codes are preserved after the mixing process. Only the carrier frequency is lowered, but the Doppler remains referenced to the original L-band signal. The A/D conversion process and automatic gain control (AGC) functions take place at IF. Not shown in the block diagram are the baseband timing signals that are provided to the digital receiver channels by the frequency synthesizer phase locked to the reference oscillator's stable frequency. The IF must be high enough to provide a single-sided bandwidth that will support the PRN code chipping frequency. An antialiasing IF filter must suppress the stopband noise (unwanted out-of-band signals) to levels that are acceptably low when this noise is aliased into the GPS signal passband by the A/D conversion process. The signals from all GPS satellites in view are buried in thermal noise at IF.

At this point the digitized IF signals are ready to be processed by each of the N digital receiver channels. No demodulation has taken place, only signal gain and conditioning plus A/D conversion into the digital IF. Traditionally, these digital receiver channel functions are implemented in one or more application-specific integrated circuits (ASICs), but SDRs would use field programmable gate arrays (FPGAs) or even DSPs. This is why these functions are shown as separate from the receiver processing function in the block diagram of Figure 5.1. The name *digital receiver channel* is somewhat misleading since it is neither the ASIC nor FPGA but the receiver processing function that usually implements numerous essential but complex (and fortunately less throughput-demanding) baseband functions, such as the loop discriminators and filters, data demodulation, SNR meters, and phase lock indicators. The receiver processing function is usually a microprocessor. The microprocessor not only performs the baseband functions, but also the decision-making functions associated with controlling the signal preprocessing functions of each digital receiver channel. It is common that a single high-speed microprocessor supports the receiver, navigation, and user interface functions.

Figure 5.2 illustrates a high-level block diagram typical of one of the digital receiver channels where the digitized received IF signal is applied to the input. For simplification, only the functions associated with the code and carrier tracking loops are illustrated, and the receiver channel is assumed to be tracking the SV signal in steady state. Referring to Figure 5.2, first the digital IF is stripped of the carrier (plus carrier Doppler) by the replica carrier (plus carrier Doppler) signals to produce in-phase (I) and quadraphase (Q) sampled data. Note that the replica carrier signal is being mixed with all of the in-view GPS SV signals (plus noise) at the digital IF. The I and Q signals at the outputs of the mixers have the desired phase relationships

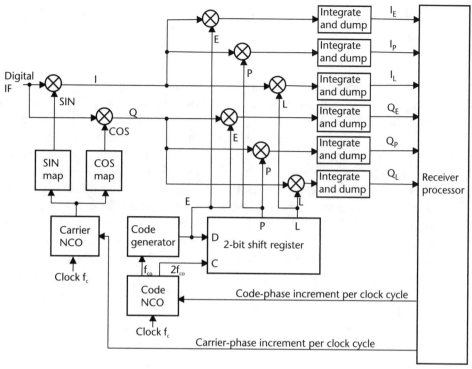

Figure 5.2   Generic digital receiver channel block diagram.

with respect to the detected carrier of the desired SV. However, the code stripping processes that collapse these signals to baseband have not yet been applied. Therefore, the I and Q signals at the output of the carrier mixers are dominated by noise. The desired SV signal remains buried in noise until the I and Q signals are collapsed to baseband by the code stripping process that follows. The replica carrier (including carrier Doppler) signals are synthesized by the carrier numerically controlled oscillator (NCO) and the discrete sine and cosine mapping functions.

The code wipeoff function could have been implemented before the carrier wipeoff function in this design, but this would increase the carrier wipeoff complexity with no improvement in receiver performance. The wipeoff sequence presented in Figure 5.2 is the least complex design.

Later, it will be shown that the NCO produces a staircase function whose period is the desired replica carrier plus Doppler period. The sine and cosine map functions convert each discrete amplitude of the staircase function to the corresponding discrete amplitude of the respective sine and cosine functions. By producing I and Q component phases 90° apart, the resultant signal amplitude can be computed from the vector sum of the I and Q components, and the phase angle with respect to the I-axis can be determined from the arctangent of Q/I. In closed loop operation, the carrier NCO is controlled by the carrier tracking loop in the receiver processor. In phase lock loop (PLL) operation, the objective of the carrier tracking loop is to keep the phase error between the replica carrier and the incoming SV carrier signals at zero. Any misalignment in the replica carrier phase with respect to the incoming SV signal carrier phase produces a nonzero phase angle of the prompt I and Q vector magnitude, so that the amount and direction of the phase change can be detected and corrected by the carrier tracking loop. When the PLL is phase locked, the I signals are maximum (signal plus noise) and the Q signals are minimum (containing only noise).

In Figure 5.2, the I and Q signals are then correlated with early, prompt, and late replica codes (plus code Doppler) synthesized by the code generator, a 2-bit shift register, and the code NCO. In closed loop operation, the code NCO is controlled by the code tracking loop in the receiver processor. In this example, the code NCO produces twice the code generator clocking rate, $2f_{co}$, and this is fed to the clock input of the 2-bit shift register. The code generator clocking rate, f_{co}, that contains the nominal spreading code chip rate (plus code Doppler) is fed to the code generator. The NCO clock, f_c, should be a much higher frequency than the shift register clock, $2f_{co}$. With this combination, the shift register produces two phase-delayed versions of the code generator output. As a result, there are three replica code phases designated as early (E), prompt (P), and late (L). E and L are typically separated in phase by 1 chip and P is in the middle. Not shown are the controls to the code generator that permit the receiver processor to preset the initial code tracking phase states that are required during the code search and acquisition (or reacquisition) process.

The prompt replica code phase is aligned with the incoming SV code phase producing maximum correlation if it is tracking the incoming SV code phase. Under this circumstance, the early phase is aligned a fraction of a chip period early, and the late phase is aligned the same fraction of the chip period late with respect to the incoming SV code phase, and these correlators produce about half the maximum correlation. Any misalignment in the replica code phase with respect to the incoming SV code phase produces a difference in the vector magnitudes of the early and late correlated outputs so that the amount and direction of the phase change can be detected and corrected by the code tracking loop.

5.2.1 Predetection Integration

Predetection is the signal processing after the IF signal has been converted to baseband by the carrier and code stripping processes, but prior to being passed through a signal discriminator (i.e., prior to the nonlinear signal detection process). Extensive digital predetection integration and dump processes occur after the carrier and code stripping processes. This causes very large numbers to accumulate, even though the IF A/D conversion process is typically with only 1 to 3 bits of quantization resolution with the carrier wipeoff process involving a matching multiplication precision and the code wipeoff process that follows usually involving only 1-bit multiplication.

Figure 5.2 shows three complex correlators required to produce three in-phase components, which are integrated and dumped to produce I_E, I_P, I_L and three quadraphase components integrated and dumped to produce Q_E, Q_P, Q_L. The carrier wipeoff and code wipeoff processes must be performed at the digital IF sample rate, which is of the order of 50 MHz for a military P(Y) code receiver (that also operates with C/A code), 5 MHz for civil C/A code receivers that use 1-chip E-L correlator spacing, and up to 50 MHz for civil C/A code receivers that use narrow correlator spacing for improved multipath error performance. The integrate and dump accumulators provide filtering and resampling at the processor baseband input rate, which can be at 1,000 Hz during search modes or as low as 50 Hz during track modes, depending on the desired dwell time during search or the desired predetection integration time during track. The 50- to 1,000-Hz rates are well within the servicing capability of modern high-speed microprocessors, but the 5- or 50-MHz rates are challenging even for modern DSPs. This further explains why the high-speed but simple processes are implemented in a custom digital ASIC or FPGA, while the low-speed but complex processes are implemented in a microprocessor.

The hardware integrate and dump process in combination with the baseband signal processing integrate and dump process (described next) defines the predetection integration time. Later, it will be shown that the predetection integration time is a compromise design. It must be as long as possible to operate under weak or RF interference signal conditions, and it must be as short as possible to operate under high dynamic stress signal conditions.

5.2.2   Baseband Signal Processing

Figure 5.3 illustrates typical baseband code and carrier tracking loops for one receiver channel in the closed loop mode of operation. The functions are typically performed by the receiver processor shown in Figure 5.2. The combination of these carrier and code tracking baseband signal processing functions and the digital receiver channel carrier and code wipeoff and predetection integration functions form the carrier and code tracking loops of one GPS receiver channel.

The baseband functions are usually implemented in firmware. Note that the firmware need only be written once, since the microprocessor runs all programs sequentially. This is contrasted to the usual parallel processing that takes place in the

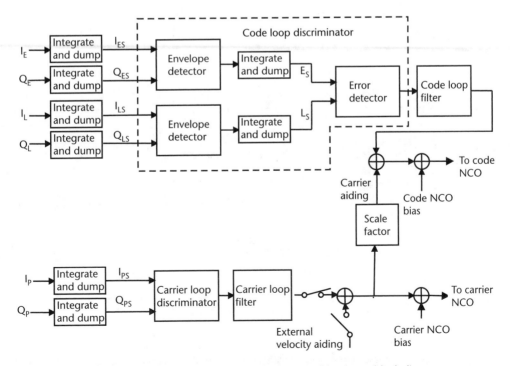

Figure 5.3   Generic baseband processor code and carrier tracking loops block diagram.

digital receiver ASIC(s) or FPGA(s), but even these devices can multiplex their digital processes sequentially in order to reduce gate count if they are capable of running faster than real time. Therefore, the ASIC, FPGA, and microprocessor programs can be designed to be reentrant with a unique variable area for each receiver channel so that only one copy of each algorithm is required to service all receiver channels. This reduces the gate count or program memory requirements and ensures that every receiver baseband processing function is identical. Digital multiplexing also eliminates interchannel bias in the ASIC or FPGA (hardware portion of the digital receiver) with no performance loss. (Section 7.2.7.2 further discusses interchannel biases.)

The three complex pairs of baseband I and Q signals from the digital receiver may be resampled again by the integrate and dump accumulators. The total combined duration of the receiver and processor integrate and dump functions establishes the predetection integration time for the signal. Normally, this cannot exceed 20 ms, which is the 50-Hz navigation message data bit period for the GPS C/A and P(Y) code signals. Figure 5.4 illustrates the phase alignment needed to prevent the predetection integrate and dump intervals from integrating across a SV data transition boundary. The start and stop boundaries for these integrate and dump functions should not straddle the data bit transition boundaries because each time the SV data bits change signs, the signs of the subsequent integrated I and Q data may

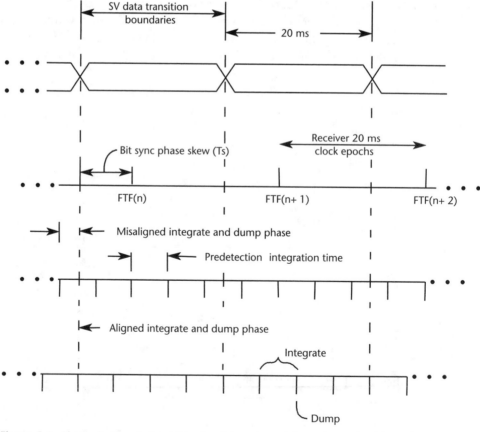

Figure 5.4 Phase alignment of predetection integrate and dump intervals with SV data transition boundaries.

change. If the boundary is straddled and there is a data transition, the integration and dump result for that interval will be degraded. In the worst case, if the data transition occurs at the halfway point, the signal will be totally canceled for that interval. Usually, during initial C/A code signal search, acquisition, and loop closure, the receiver does not know where the SV data bit transition boundaries are located because each C/A code epoch is only 1 ms in duration but the data bit is 20 ms in duration. Then, the performance degradation has to be accepted until the bit synchronization process locates the data bit transitions. During these times, short predetection integration times are used in order to ensure that most of the integrate and dump operations do not contain a data transition boundary. With signals that have spreading code periods that are as long or longer than the data bit period, receivers can choose longer predetection time intervals that are aligned with data bit edges.

As shown in Figure 5.4, the SV data transition boundary usually does not align with the receiver's 20-ms clock boundary, which will hereafter be called the fundamental time frame (FTF). The phase offset is shown as *bit sync phase skew*. A bit synchronization process determines this phase offset shortly after the signal has been acquired when the receiver does not know its position and precise GPS time. In general, the bit sync phase skew is different for every SV being tracked because even though the data transitions are well aligned at SV transmit time, the difference in range to the user causes them to be skewed at receive time. This range difference amounts to about a 20-ms variation from zenith to horizon. The receiver design must accommodate these data bit phase skews if an optimum predetection integration time is used. This optimization is assumed in the generic receiver design, but some receiver designs do not implement this added complexity. They use short (suboptimal) predetection integration times.

5.2.3 Digital Frequency Synthesis

In this generic design example, both the carrier and code tracking loops use an NCO for precision replica carrier and code generation. The NCO provides measurements that contain negligible quantization noise [1].

One replica carrier cycle and one replica code cycle are completed each time the NCO overflows. A block diagram of the carrier loop NCO and its sine and cosine mapping functions are shown in Figure 5.5 [1]. In Figure 5.3, note that there is a code NCO bias and a carrier NCO bias applied to their respective NCOs. These biases set the NCO frequency to the nominal code spreading code chip rate and IF carrier frequency, respectively, because they are constants. As an NCO bias computational example using the equation for output frequency in Figure 5.5, assume that the bias is set for the P(Y) code nominal spreading code chip rate of 10.23 MHz. Assume a 32-bit NCO with a clock $f_s = 200$ MHz, then the code NCO bias is $M = 10.23 \times 2^{32}/200 = 2.1969 \times 10^8$. This value of M sets the NCO output frequency to 10.23 MHz with a resolution of $200 \times 10^6/2^{32} = 0.046566$ Hz.

For the carrier NCO, the map functions convert the amplitude of the NCO staircase output [Figure 5.6(a)] into the appropriate trigonometric functions as shown in Figure 5.6(b, c). Figure 5.7 illustrates the basic idea of digital frequency synthesizer design.

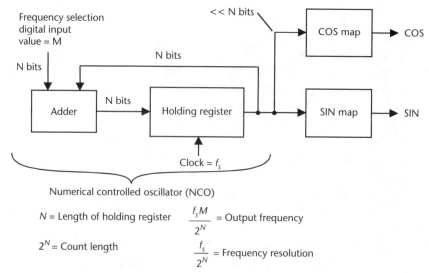

Figure 5.5 Digital frequency synthesizer block diagram.

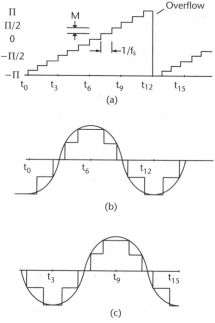

Figure 5.6 Digital frequency synthesizer waveforms: (a) NCO phase state, (b) COS map output, and (c) SIN map output.

5.2.4 Carrier Aiding of Code Loop

In Figure 5.3, the carrier loop filter output is adjusted by a scale factor and added to the code loop filter output as aiding. This is called a *carrier-aided* code loop. The scale factor is required because the Doppler effect on the signal is inversely proportional to the wavelength of the signal. Therefore, for the same relative velocity between the SV and the GPS receiver, the Doppler on the spreading code chip rate is much smaller than the Doppler on the L-band carrier. (Keep in mind that even

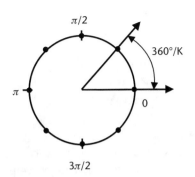

Degrees	Holding register (binary)	SIN map (sign magnitude)	COS map (sign magnitude)
0	1 0 0...	0 0 0	0 1 1
45	1 0 1...	0 1 0	0 1 0
90	1 1 0...	0 1 1	0 0 0
135	1 1 1...	0 1 0	1 1 0
180	0 0 0...	0 0 0	1 1 1
225	0 0 1...	1 1 0	1 1 0
270	0 1 0...	1 1 1	0 0 0
315	0 1 1...	1 1 0	0 1 0

Maps for J = 3, K = 2^J = 8

Notes:
1. The number of bits, J, is determined for the SIN and COS outputs. The phase plane of 360 degrees is subdivided into 2^J = K phase points.
2. K values are computed for each waveform, one value per phase point. Each value represents the amplitude of the waveform to be generated at that phase point. The upper J bits of the holding register are used to determine the address of the waveform amplitude.
3. Rate at which phase plane is traversed determines the frequency of the output waveform.
4. The upper bound of the amplitude error is 2ΠK.
5. The approximate amplitude error is: 2ΠK cos ϕ(t), where ϕ(t) is the phase angle.

Figure 5.7   Digital frequency synthesizer design.

though the carrier has been downconverted to IF and the NCO carrier bias is set to the IF, the carrier Doppler effect remains referenced to L-band.) The scale factor that compensates for this difference in frequency is given by:

$$Scale\ factor = \frac{R_c}{f_L} \text{ (dimensionless)} \tag{5.1}$$

where:

R_c = spreading code chip rate (Hz) plus Doppler effect

= R_0 for P(Y) code = 10.23 Mchip/s + P(Y) Doppler effect

= R_0/10 for C/A code = 1.023 Mchip/s + C/A Doppler effect

f_L = L-band carrier (Hz)

= 154 R_0 for L1

= 120 R_0 for L2

Table 5.1 shows the three practical combinations of this scale factor.

The carrier loop output should always provide Doppler aiding to the code loop because the carrier loop jitter is orders of magnitude less noisy than the code loop and thus much more accurate. The carrier loop aiding removes virtually all of the LOS dynamics from the code loop, so the code loop filter order can be made smaller, its update rate slower, and its bandwidth narrower than for the unaided case, thereby reducing the noise in the code loop measurements. In fact, the code loop only tracks the dynamics of the ionospheric delay plus noise. When both the

Table 5.1 Scale Factors for Carrier Aided Code

Carrier Frequency (Hz)	Code Rate (chips/s)	Scale Factor
$L1 = 154\,R_0$	$R_0/10$ for C/A	$1/1540 = 0.00064935$
$L1 = 154\,R_0$	R_0 for P(Y)	$1/154 = 0.00649350$
$L2 = 120\,R_0$	R_0 for P(Y)	$1/120 = 0.00833333$

code and carrier loops must maintain track, nothing is lost in tracking performance by using carrier aiding for an unaided GPS receiver, even though the carrier loop is the weakest link.

5.2.5 External Aiding

As shown in Figure 5.3, external velocity aiding, say from an inertial measurement unit (IMU), can be provided to the receiver channel in closed carrier loop operation. The switch, shown in the unaided position, must be closed when external velocity aiding is applied. At the instant that external aiding is injected, the loop filter state must be set to the time bias rate if known; otherwise, it is zeroed. The external rate aiding must be converted into LOS velocity aiding with respect to the GPS satellite. The lever arm effects on the aiding must be computed with respect to the GPS antenna phase center, which requires knowledge of the vehicle attitude and the location of the antenna phase center with respect to the navigation center of the external source of velocity aiding. For closed carrier loop operation, the aiding must be very precise and have little or no latency or the tracking loop must be delay-compensated for the latency. If open carrier loop aiding is implemented, less precise external velocity aiding is required, but there are no meaningful delta range measurements available. Also, it is not likely that the SV navigation message data can be demodulated in this mode, so it is a short-term, weak signal hold-on strategy. In this open-loop weak signal hold-on case, the output of the carrier loop filter is not combined with the external velocity aiding to control the carrier NCO, but the open-loop output of the filter can be used to provide a SNR computation. (External aiding using IMU and other sensor measurements is discussed further in Chapter 9.)

5.3 Carrier Tracking Loops

Figure 5.8 presents a block diagram of a GPS receiver carrier tracking loop. The programmable designs of the carrier predetection integrators, the carrier loop discriminators, and the carrier loop filters characterize the receiver carrier tracking loop. These three functions determine the two most important performance characteristics of the receiver carrier loop design: the carrier loop thermal noise error and the maximum LOS dynamic stress threshold. Since the carrier tracking loop is always the weak link in a stand-alone GPS receiver, its threshold characterizes the unaided GPS receiver performance.

The carrier loop discriminator defines the type of tracking loop as a PLL, a Costas PLL (which is a PLL-type discriminator that tolerates the presence of data

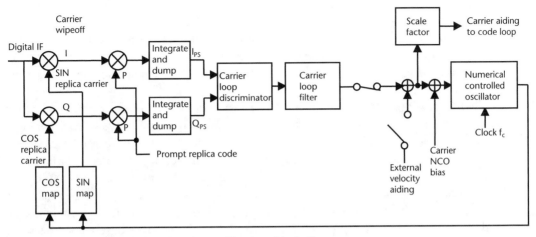

Figure 5.8   Generic GPS receiver carrier tracking loop block diagram.

modulation on the baseband signal), or a frequency lock loop (FLL). The PLL and the Costas loop are the most accurate, but they are more sensitive to dynamic stress than the FLL. The PLL and Costas loop discriminators produce phase error estimates at their outputs. The FLL discriminator produces a frequency error estimate. Because of this, there is also a difference in the architecture of the loop filter, described later.

There is a paradox that the GPS receiver designer must solve in the design of the predetection integration time and the discriminator and loop filter functions of the carrier tracking loop. To tolerate dynamic stress, the predetection integration time should be short, the discriminator should be an FLL, and the carrier loop filter bandwidth should be wide. However, for the carrier measurements to be accurate (have low noise), the predetection integration time should be long, the discriminator should be a PLL, and the carrier loop filter noise bandwidth should be narrow. In practice, some compromise must be made to resolve this paradox. A well-designed GPS receiver should close its carrier tracking loops with short predetection integration times, using an FLL and a wideband carrier loop filter. Assuming there is data modulation on the carrier, it should then systematically transition into a Costas PLL, gradually adjusting the predetection integration time equal to the period of the data transitions while also gradually adjusting the carrier tracking loop bandwidth as narrow as the maximum anticipated dynamics permits. Later, an FLL-assisted-PLL carrier tracking loop will be described that automatically adjusts to dynamic stress.

5.3.1   Phase Lock Loops

If there was no 50-Hz data modulation on the GPS signal, the carrier tracking loop discriminator could use a pure PLL discriminator. For example, a P(Y) code receiver could implement a pure PLL discriminator for use in the L2 carrier tracking mode if the control segment turns off data modulation. Although this mode is specified as a possibility, it is unlikely to be activated. This mode is specified in IS-GPS-200 [2] because pure PLL operation enables an improved signal tracking threshold by up to 6 dB. All modernized GPS signals make provisions for dataless carrier tracking in addition to providing data, but the provision involves sharing the total signal power between a half-power component that contains the data and another half-power component that is dataless. The sharing technique loses 3 dB from the dataless component used for tracking, but there is a net gain of 3 dB when tracking the dataless signal with a pure PLL.

It is also possible to implement short-term pure PLL modes by a process called data wipeoff. The GPS receiver typically acquires a complete copy of the full navigation message after 25 iterations of the 5 subframes (12.5 minutes), or the current data can be provided by some external means. The receiver then can compute the navigation message sequence until the GPS control segment uploads a new message or until the SV changes the message. Until the message changes significantly, the GPS receiver can perform data wipeoff of each bit of the incoming 50-Hz navigation data message and use a pure PLL discriminator. The receiver baseband processing function does this by reversing the sign of the integrated prompt I and Q components in accordance with a consistent algorithm. For example, if I_{PS} and Q_{PS} have predetection integration times of 5 ms, then there are four samples of I_{PS} and Q_{PS} between each SV data bit transition that are assured to have the same sign. This sign will be the sign of the data bit known by the receiver a priori for that data interval. Each 5-ms sample may fluctuate in sign due to noise. If the known data bit for this interval is a "0," then the data wipeoff process does nothing to all four samples. If the known data bit for this interval is a "1," then the sign is reversed on all four samples.

Table 5.2 illustrates the four-quadrant arctangent discriminator algorithm and a simple approximation using Q normalized by a long-term average of the prompt envelope. Interestingly, the Q approximation has been proven experimentally to slightly outperform the theoretically optimal and more complex ATAN2 function. Figure 5.9(a) compares the phase error outputs of these PLL discriminators assuming no noise in the I and Q signals. Note that the ATAN2 discriminator is the only one that remains linear over the full input error range of ±180°. However, in the presence of noise, both of the discriminator outputs are linear only near the 0° region. These PLL discriminators will achieve the 6-dB improvement in signal tracking threshold (by comparison with the Costas discriminators described next) for the dataless carrier because they track the full four quadrant range of the input signal.

5.3.2 Costas Loops

Any carrier loop that is insensitive to the presence of data modulation is usually called a Costas loop since Costas was the original inventor. Table 5.3 summarizes several GPS receiver Costas PLL discriminators, their output phase errors, and their characteristics. Figure 5.9(b) compares the phase error outputs of these Costas PLL discriminators, assuming no noise in the I and Q signals. As shown, the two-quadrant ATAN Costas discriminator of Table 5.3 is the only Costas PLL discriminator that remains linear over half of the input error range (± 90°). In the presence of noise, all of the discriminator outputs are linear only near the 0° region.

Referring to the carrier tracking loop block diagram of Figure 5.8, the phase derotation (carrier wipeoff) process used in the generic receiver design requires only two multiples. Assuming that the carrier loop is in phase lock and that the replica

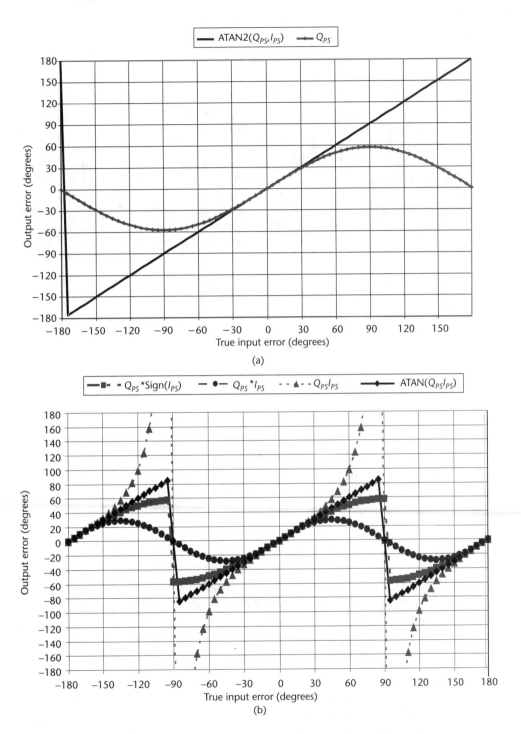

Figure 5.9 (a) Comparison of PLL discriminators, and (b) comparison of Costas PLL discriminators.

sine function is in-phase with the incoming SV carrier signal (converted to IF), this results in a sine squared product at the I output, which produces maximum I_{PS}

Table 5.2 PLL Discriminator

Discriminator Algorithm	Output Phase Error	Characteristics
$ATAN2(Q_{PS}, I_{PS})$	ϕ	Four-quadrant arctangent. Optimal (maximum likelihood estimator) at high and low SNR. Slope not signal amplitude dependent. High computational burden. Usually table lookup implementation.
$\dfrac{Q_{PS}}{Ave\sqrt{I_{PS}^2 + Q_{PS}^2}}$	$\sin\phi$	Q_{PS} normalized by averaged prompt envelope. Slightly outperforms four-quadrant arctangent. Q_{PS} approximates ϕ to $\pm 45°$. Normalization provides insensitivity at high and low SNR. Also keeps slope not signal amplitude dependent. Low computational burden.

Table 5.3 Common Costas Loop Discriminators

Discriminator Algorithm	Output Phase Error	Characteristics
$Q_{PS} \times I_{PS}$	$\sin 2\phi$	Classic Costas analog discriminator. Near optimal at low SNR. Slope proportional to signal amplitude squared A^2. Moderate computational burden.
$Q_{PS} \times \text{Sign}(I_{PS})$	$\sin\phi$	Decision directed Costas. Near optimal at high SNR. Slope proportional to signal amplitude A. Least computational burden.
Q_{PS}/I_{PS}	$\tan\phi$	Suboptimal but good at high and low SNR. Slope not signal amplitude dependent. Higher computational burden. Divide by zero error at $\pm 90°$.
$ATAN(Q_{PS}/I_{PS})$	ϕ	Two-quadrant arctangent. Optimal (maximum likelihood estimator) at high and low SNR. Slope not signal amplitude dependent. Highest computational burden. Usually table lookup implementation.

amplitude (signal plus noise) following the code wipeoff and integrate and dump process. The replica cosine function is 90° out of phase with the incoming SV carrier. This results in a cosine × sine product at the Q output, which produces minimum Q_{PS} amplitude (noise only). For this reason, I_{PS} will be near its maximum (and will flip 180° each time the data bit changes sign), and Q_{PS} will be near its minimum (and will also flip 180° each time the data bit changes sign).

Note that the classical complex pair carrier phase derotation scheme is not used in this generic receiver design because the natural GPS IF signal is real. The classical phase derotation scheme requires an I and Q input signal at IF. This, in turn, requires the real IF signal be phase shifted 90° to produce the quadrature component. This is a design penalty of added IF circuit complexity. If this is done on the analog side, the Nyquist sample rate is half that of the generic A/D converter requirement. This is a design benefit if the A/D converter speed presents a design limitation, but this is not likely with today's technology. But two A/D converters are required to digitize the I and Q input signals. This is a design penalty that doubles the A/D components. A single A/D converter can be used to produce the I and Q signals if a technique referred to as *quadrature sampling* (also known as *pseudosampling* or *IF sampling*) is employed. However, the classical phase derotation process still requires four multiplies and two additions with no additional performance improvement. This is a phase derotation design penalty of two additional multiplies and two adds. The generic design is therefore the preferred carrier phase derotation scheme.

These PLL characteristics are illustrated in Figure 5.10, where the phasor, A (the vector sum of I_{PS} and Q_{PS}), tends to remain aligned with the I-axis and switches 180° during each data bit reversal.

It is straightforward to detect the bits in the SV data message stream using a Costas PLL. The I_{PS} samples are simply accumulated for one data bit interval, and the sign of the result is the data bit. Since there is a 180° phase ambiguity with a Costas PLL, the detected data bit stream may be normal or inverted. This ambiguity is resolved during the frame synchronization process by comparing the known preamble at the beginning of each subframe both ways (normal and inverted) with the bit stream. If a match is found with the preamble pattern inverted, the bit stream is inverted and the subframe synchronization is confirmed by parity checks on the TLM and HOW. Otherwise, the bit stream is normal. Once the phase ambiguity is resolved, it remains resolved until the PLL loses phase lock or slips cycles. If this

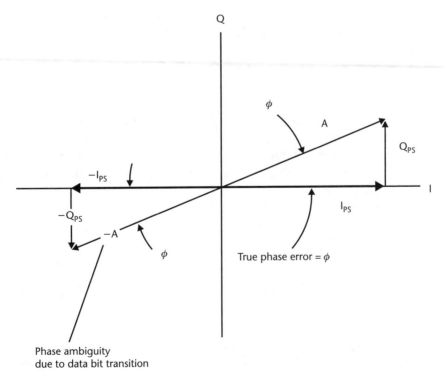

Figure 5.10 I, Q phasor diagram depicting true phase error between replica and incoming carrier phase.

happens, the ambiguity must be resolved again. The 180° ambiguity of the Costas PLL can be resolved by referring to the phase detection result of the data bit demodulation. If the data bit phase is normal, then the carrier Doppler phase indicated by the Costas PLL is correct. If the data bit phase is inverted, then the carrier Doppler phase indicated by the Costas PLL phase can be corrected by adding 180°.

Costas PLLs as well as conventional PLLs are sensitive to dynamic stress, but they produce the most accurate velocity measurements. For a given signal power level, Costas PLLs also provide the most error-free data demodulation in comparison to schemes used with FLLs. Therefore, this is the desired steady state tracking mode of the GPS receiver carrier tracking loop. It is possible for a PLL to close in a false phase lock mode if there is excess frequency error at the time of loop closure. Therefore, a well-designed GPS receiver carrier tracking loop will close the loop with a more dynamically robust FLL operated at wideband. Then it will gradually reduce the carrier tracking loop bandwidth and transition into a wideband PLL operation in order to systematically reduce the pull-in frequency error. Finally, it will narrow the PLL bandwidth to the steady state mode of operation. If dynamic stress causes the PLL to lose lock, the receiver will detect this with a sensitive phase lock detector and transition back to the FLL. The PLL closure process is then repeated.

5.3.3 Frequency Lock Loops

PLLs replicate the exact phase and frequency of the incoming SV (converted to IF) to perform the carrier wipeoff function. FLLs perform the carrier wipeoff process by replicating the approximate frequency, and they typically permit the phase to rotate with respect to the incoming carrier signal. For this reason, they are also called *automatic frequency control* (AFC) loops. The FLLs of GPS receivers must be insensitive to 180° reversals in the I and Q signals. Therefore, the sample times of the I and Q signals should not straddle the data bit transitions. During initial signal acquisition, when the receiver does not know where the data transition boundaries are, it is usually easier to maintain frequency lock than phase lock with the SV signal while performing bit synchronization. This is because the FLL discriminators are less sensitive to situations where some of the I and Q signals do straddle the data bit transitions. When the predetection integration times are small compared to the data bit transition intervals, fewer integrate and dump samples are corrupted, but the squaring loss is higher. Table 5.4 summarizes several GPS receiver FLL discriminators, their output frequency errors, and their characteristics.

Figure 5.11 compares the frequency error outputs of each of these discriminators assuming no noise in the I_{PS} and Q_{PS} samples. Figure 5.11(a) illustrates that the frequency pull-in range with a 5-ms predetection integration time (200-Hz bandwidth) has twice the pull-in range of Figure 5.11(b) with a 10-ms predetection integration time (100-Hz bandwidth). Note in both figures that the single-sided frequency pull-in ranges of the cross and ATAN2(dot, cross) FLL discriminators are equal to half the predetection bandwidths. The (cross) × sign(dot) FLL discriminator frequency pull-in ranges are only one-fourth of the predetection bandwidths. Also note that the (cross) × sign(dot) and the cross FLL discriminator outputs, whose outputs are sine functions divided by the sample time

Table 5.4 Common Frequency Lock Loop Discriminators

Discriminator Algorithm	Output Frequency Error	Characteristics
$\dfrac{cross}{(t_2 - t_1)}$ where: $cross = I_{PS1} \times Q_{PS2} - I_{PS2} \times Q_{PS1}$	$\dfrac{\sin[(\phi_2 - \phi_1)]}{t_2 - t_1}$	Near optimal at low SNR. Slope proportional to signal amplitude squared A^2. Least computational burden.
$\dfrac{(cross) \times sign(dot)}{(t_2 - t_1)}$ where: $dot = I_{PS1} \times I_{PS2} + Q_{PS1} \times Q_{PS2}$ $cross = I_{PS1} \times Q_{PS2} - I_{PS2} \times Q_{PS1}$	$\dfrac{\sin[2(\phi_2 - \phi_1)]}{t_2 - t_1}$	Decision directed. Near optimal at high SNR. Slope proportional to signal amplitude A. Moderate computational burden
$\dfrac{ATAN2(dot, cross)}{(t_2 - t_1)}$	$\dfrac{\phi_2 - \phi_1}{t_2 - t_1}$	Four-quadrant arctangent. Maximum likelihood estimator. Optimal at high and low SNR. Slope not signal amplitude dependent. Highest computational burden. Usually table lookup implementation.

Note: Integrated and dumped prompt samples I_{PS1} and Q_{PS1} are the samples taken at time t_1, just prior to the samples I_{PS2} and Q_{PS2} taken at a later time t_2. These two adjacent samples should be within the same data bit interval. The next pair of samples are taken starting $(t_2 - t_1)$ seconds after t_2 (i.e., no I and Q samples are reused in the next discriminator computation).

interval $(t_2 - t_1)$ in seconds, are also divided by 4 to more accurately approximate the true input frequency error. The ATAN2 (x, y) function returns the answer in radians, is converted to degrees, divided by the sample time interval $(t_2 - t_1)$ in seconds, and is also divided by 360 to produce at its output a true representation of the input frequency error within its pull-in range. The amplitudes of all of the discriminator outputs are reduced (their slopes tend to flatten), and they tend to start rounding off near the limits of their pull-in range as the noise levels increase.

The I, Q phasor diagram in Figure 5.12 depicts the change in phase, $\phi_2 - \phi_1$, between two adjacent samples of I_{PS} and Q_{PS}, at times t_1 and t_2. This phase change over a fixed time interval is proportional to the frequency error in the carrier tracking loop. The figure also illustrates that there is no frequency ambiguity in the GPS receiver FLL discriminator because of data transitions, provided that the adjacent I and Q samples are taken within the same data bit interval. However, it is possible for the FLL loop to close with a false frequency lock in a high dynamic environment. For this reason, very short predetection integration times (wider pull-in range) are important for initial FLL loop closure. For example, if the search dwell time was 1 ms or 2 ms, then the initial predetection integration time in FLL should be the same. Note that with a FLL, the phasor, A, which is the vector sum of I_{PS} and Q_{PS}, rotates at a rate directly proportional to the frequency error (between the replica carrier and the incoming carrier). When true frequency lock is actually achieved, the vector stops rotating, but it may stop at any angle with respect to the I-axis. For this reason, coherent code tracking, as will be discussed in the following section, is not possible while in FLL because it depends on the I components being maximum (signal plus noise) and the Q components to be minimum (noise only) (i.e., in phase lock). It is possible to demodulate the SV data bit stream in FLL by a technique called *differential demodulation*. Because the demodulation technique involves a differentia-

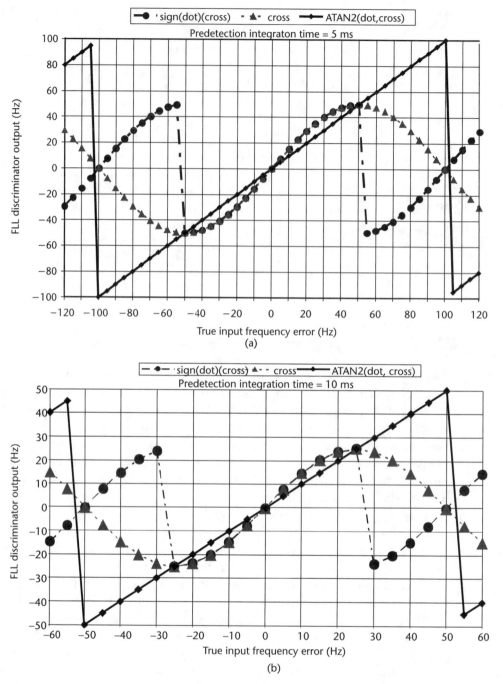

Figure 5.11 Comparison of frequency lock loop discriminators: (a) 5-ms predetection integration time, and (b) 10-ms predetection integration time.

tion (noisy) process, detecting the change in sign of the phasor in a FLL is noisier than detecting the sign of the integrated (lower noise) I_{ps} in a PLL. Therefore, for the same signal quality, FLL data detection has a much higher bit and word error rate than PLL data detection.

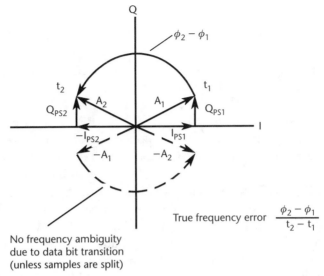

Figure 5.12 *I, Q* phasor diagram depicting true frequency error between replica and incoming carrier frequency.

5.4 Code Tracking Loops

Figure 5.13 shows a block diagram of a GPS receiver code tracking loop. The design of the programmable predetection integrators, the code loop discriminator, and the code loop filter characterizes the receiver code tracking loop. These three functions determine the most important two performance characteristics of the receiver code loop design: the code loop thermal noise error and the maximum LOS dynamic stress threshold. Even though the carrier tracking loop is the weak link in terms of the receiver's dynamic stress threshold, it would be disastrous to attempt to aid the

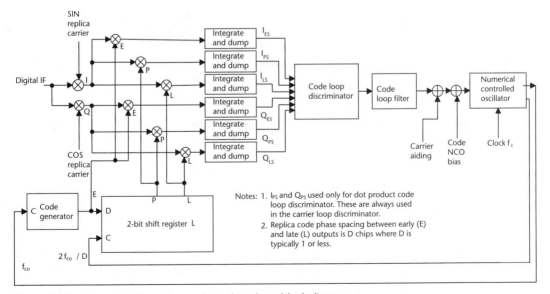

Figure 5.13 Generic GPS receiver code tracking loop block diagram.

carrier loop with the code loop output. This is because, unaided, the code loop thermal noise is orders of magnitude larger than the carrier loop thermal noise.

Table 5.5 summarizes four GPS receiver delay lock loop (DLL) discriminators and their characteristics. The fourth DLL discriminator is called a coherent dot product DLL. A more linear version can be implemented using only the E and L components, but the dot product slightly outperforms it. The coherent DLL provides superior performance when the carrier loop is in PLL. Under this condition, there is signal plus noise in the I components and mostly noise in the Q components. However, this high-precision DLL mode fails if there are frequent cycle slips or total loss of phase lock because the phasor rotates, causing the signal power to be shared in both the I and Q components, which consequently causes power loss in the coherent DLL. Successful operation requires a sensitive phase lock detector and rapid transition to the quasi-coherent DLL. All of the DLL discriminators can be normalized. Normalization removes the amplitude sensitivity, which improves performance under rapidly changing SNR conditions. Therefore, normalization helps the DLL tracking and threshold performance to be independent of AGC performance. However, normalization does not prevent reduction of the gain (slope) when SNR decreases. As SNR is reduced, the DLL slope approaches zero. Since loop bandwidth

Table 5.5 Common Delay Lock Loop Discriminators

Discriminator Algorithm	Characteristics
$\frac{1}{2}\frac{E-L}{E+L}$ where: $E = \sqrt{I_{ES}^2 + Q_{ES}^2}, L = \sqrt{I_{LS}^2 + Q_{LS}^2}$	Noncoherent early minus late envelope normalized by $E+L$ to remove amplitude sensitivity. High computational load. For 1-chip $E-L$ correlator spacing, produces true tracking error within ±0.5 chip of input error (in the absence of noise). Becomes unstable (divide by zero) at ±1.5-chip input error, but this is well beyond code tracking threshold in the presence of noise.
$\frac{1}{2}(E^2 - L^2)$	Noncoherent early minus late power. Moderate computational load. For 1-chip $E-L$ correlator spacing, produces essentially the same error performance as 0.5 $(E-L)$ envelope within ±0.5 chip of input error (in the absence of noise). Can be normalized with $E^2 + L^2$.
$\frac{1}{2}[(I_{ES}-I_{LS})I_{PS} + (Q_{ES}-Q_{LS})Q_{PS}]$ (dot product) $\frac{1}{4}[(I_{ES}-I_{LS})/I_{PS} + (Q_{ES}-Q_{LS})/Q_{PS}]$ (normalized with I_{PS}^2 and Q_{PS}^2)	Quasi-coherent dot product power. Uses all three correlators. Low computational load. For 1-chip $E-L$ correlator spacing, it produces nearly true error output within ±0.5 chip of input (in the absence of noise). Normalized version shown second using I_{PS}^2 and Q_{PS}^2, respectively.
$\frac{1}{2}(I_{ES}-I_{LS})I_{PS}$ (dot product) $\frac{1}{4}\frac{(I_{ES}-I_{LS})}{I_{PS}}$ (normalized with I_{PS}^2)	Coherent dot product. Can be used only when carrier loop is in phase lock. Low computational load. Most accurate code measurements. Normalized version shown second using I_{PS}^2.

Note: The code loop discriminator outputs may be summed to reduce the iteration rate of the code loop filter as compared to that of the carrier loop filter when the code loop is aided by the carrier loop. The rule-of-thumb limit is that total integration time must be less than one-fourth the DLL bandwidth. Note that this does not increase the predetection integration time for the code loop but does reduce noise. However the code loop NCO must be updated every time the carrier loop NCO is updated, even though the code loop filter output has not been updated. The last code loop filter output is combined with the current value of carrier aiding.

is roughly proportional to loop gain, loop bandwidth approaches zero at low SNR. This results in poor DLL response to dynamic stress and can result in instability if a third-order DLL filter is used (never used with carrier-aided code implementation). Carrier aiding (including externally provided carrier aiding) minimizes this problem, but the phenomena may produce unexpected DLL behavior at very low SNR.

Figure 5.14 compares the four DLL discriminator outputs. The plots assume 1-chip spacing between the early and late correlators. This means that the 2-bit shift register is shifted at twice the clock rate of the code generator. Also assumed is an ideal correlation triangle (infinite bandwidth) and that there is no noise on the I and Q measurements. For typical receiver bandwidths, the correlation peak tends to be rounded, the ramps on either side of the peak are nonlinear, and the correlation amplitudes at ± 0.5-chip from the correlation peak are slightly higher than for the infinite bandwidth case, while the prompt correlation amplitude is slightly lower.

The normalized early minus late envelope discriminator is very popular because its output error is linear over a 1-chip range, but the dot product power discriminator slightly outperforms it. Some GPS receiver designs synthesize the early minus late replica code as a combined replica signal. The benefit is that only one complex correlator is required to generate an early minus late output. This can be normalized with the prompt signal, but linear operation in the 1-chip range can only be achieved with $E + L$ normalization. This requires dedicated E and L correlators.

To reduce the computational burden of forming the GPS signal envelopes (the magnitude of the I and Q vectors), approximations are often used. Two of the most popular approximations (named after their originators) are the JPL approximation and the Robertson approximation.

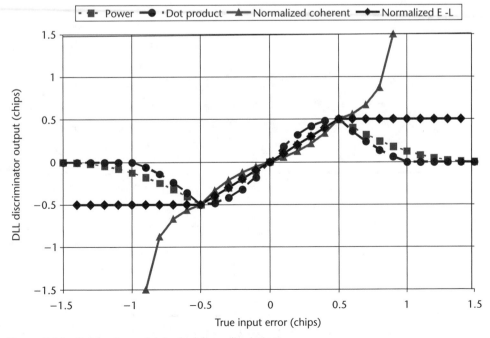

Figure 5.14   Comparison of delay lock loop discriminators.

The JPL approximation to $A = \sqrt{I^2 + Q^2}$ is defined by:

$$A_{ENV} = X + 1/8Y \qquad \text{if } X \geq 3Y$$
$$A_{ENV} = 7/8\,X + 1/2Y \quad \text{if } X < 3Y$$

where   (5.2)

$$X = MAX(|I|,|Q|)$$
$$Y = MIN(|I|,|Q|)$$

The Robertson approximation is:

$$A_{ENV} = MAX(|I| + 1/2\,|Q|, |Q| + 1/2|I|)$$ (5.3)

The JPL approximation is more accurate but has a greater computational burden.

Figure 5.15 illustrates the envelopes that result for three different replica code phases being correlated simultaneously with the same incoming SV signal. For ease of visualization, the in-phase component of the incoming SV signal is shown without noise. The three replica phases are 1/2 chip apart and are representative of the early, prompt, and late replica codes that are synthesized in the code loop of Figure 5.13.

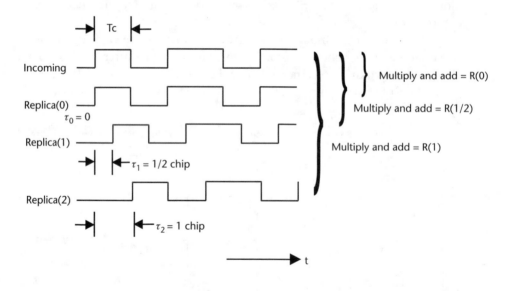

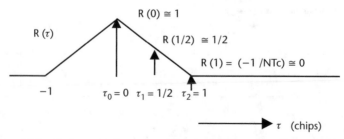

Figure 5.15 Code correlation process for three different replica code phases.

Figure 5.16 illustrates how the early, prompt, and late envelopes change as the phases of the replica code signals are advanced with respect to the incoming SV signal. For ease of visualization, only 1 chip of the continuous PRN signal is shown, and the incoming SV signal is shown without noise. Figure 5.17 illustrates the normalized early minus late envelope discriminator error output signals corresponding to the four replica code offsets in Figure 5.16. The closed code loop operation becomes apparent as a result of studying these replica code phase changes, the envelopes that they produce, and the resulting error output generated by the early minus late envelope code discriminator. If the replica code is aligned, then the early and late envelopes are equal in amplitude and no error is generated by the discriminator. If the replica code is misaligned, then the early and late envelopes are unequal by an amount that is proportional to the amount of code phase error between the replica and the incoming signal (within the limits of the correlation interval). The code discriminator senses the amount of error in the replica code and the direction (early or late) from the difference in the amplitudes of the early and late envelopes. This error is filtered and then applied to the code loop NCO, where the output frequency is increased or decreased as necessary to correct the replica code generator phase with respect to the incoming SV signal code phase.

The discriminator examples given thus far have assumed that each channel of the GPS receiver contains three complex code correlators to provide early, prompt, and late correlated outputs. In early generations of GPS receiver designs, analog correlators were used instead of digital correlators. There was strong emphasis on reducing the number of expensive and power-hungry analog correlators, so there were numerous code tracking loop design innovations that minimized the number of correlators. The *tau-dither* technique time shares the early and late replica code with one complex (*I* and *Q*) correlator. This suffers a 3-dB loss of tracking threshold in the code loop because only half the energy is available from the early and late signals. This loss of threshold is unimportant in an unaided GPS receiver design because there is usually more than a 3-dB difference between the conventional code

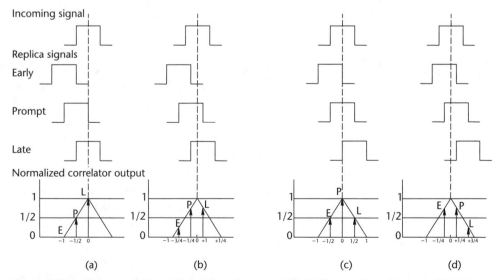

Figure 5.16 Code correlation phases: (a) replica code 1/2-chip early, (b) replica code 1/4-chip early, (c) replica code aligned, and (d) replica code 1/4-chip late.

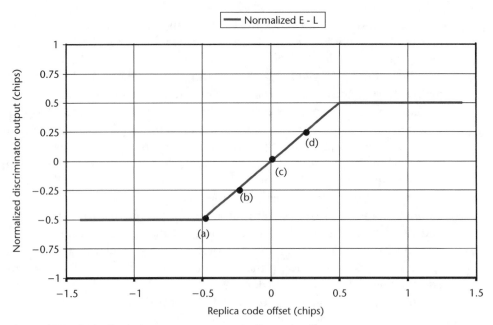

Figure 5.17   Code discriminator output versus replica code offset.

loop and carrier tracking loop thresholds. The extra margin in the code loop threshold only pays off for aided GPS receivers. The Texas Instruments TI 4100 GPS receiver [3] not only used the tau-dither technique, but also time shared only two analog correlators and the same replica code and carrier generators to simultaneously and continuously track (using 2.5-ms dwells) the L1 P code and L2 P code signals of four GPS satellites. It also simultaneously demodulated the 50-Hz navigation messages. Because the L2 tracking was accomplished by tracking L1-L2, this signal with nearly zero dynamics permitted very narrow bandwidth tracking loops and therefore suffered only a little more than 6 dB of tracking threshold losses instead of the expected 12 dB. Since the same circuits were time shared across all channels and frequencies, there was zero interchannel bias error in the TI 4100 measurements.

Modern digital GPS receivers often contain many more than three complex correlators because digital correlators are relatively inexpensive (e.g., only one exclusive-or circuit is required to perform the 1-bit multiply function). The innovations relating to improved performance through the use of more than three complex correlators include faster acquisition times [4], multipath mitigation (e.g., see [5], and also Section 6.3), and a wider discriminator correlation interval that provides jamming robustness when combined with external (IMU) aiding [6]. However, there is no improvement in tracking error due to thermal noise or improvement in tracking threshold using multiple correlators. Reducing parts count and power continue to be important, so multiplexing is back in vogue. The speed of digital circuits has increased to the point that correlators, NCOs, and other high-speed baseband functions can be digitally multiplexed without a significant power penalty because of the reduction in feature size of faster digital components. The multiplexing is faster than the real-time digital sampling of the GPS signals by a factor of N, where N is the number of channels sharing the same device. Since there is no loss of energy, there is no loss of signal processing performance, as was the case with the TI 4100 analog multiplexing. There is also no interchannel bias error.

5.5   Loop Filters

The objective of the loop filter is to reduce noise in order to produce an accurate estimate of the original signal at its output. The loop filter order and noise bandwidth also determine the loop filter's response to signal dynamics. As shown in the receiver block diagrams, the loop filter's output signal is effectively subtracted from the original signal to produce an error signal, which is fed back into the filter's input in a closed loop process. There are many design approaches to digital filters. The design approach described here draws on existing knowledge of analog loop filters, then adapts these into digital implementations. Figure 5.18 shows block diagrams of first, second, and third-order analog filters.[1] Analog integrators are represented by $1/s$, the Laplace transform of the time domain integration function. The input signal is multiplied by the multiplier coefficients, then processed as shown in Figure 5.18. These multiplier coefficients and the number of integrators completely determine the loop filter's characteristics. Table 5.6 summarizes these filter characteristics and provides all of the information required to compute the filter coefficients for first, second, and third-order loop filters. Only the filter order and noise bandwidth must be chosen to complete the design.

Figure 5.19 depicts the block diagram representations of analog and digital integrators. The analog integrator of Figure 5.19(a) operates with a continuous time domain input, $x(t)$, and produces an integrated version of this input as a continuous time domain output, $y(t)$. Theoretically, $x(t)$ and $y(t)$ have infinite numerical resolution, and the integration process is perfect. In reality, the resolution is limited by noise, which significantly reduces the dynamic range of analog integrators. There are also problems with drift.

The boxcar digital integrator of Figure 5.19(b) operates with a sampled time domain input, $x(n)$, which is quantized to a finite resolution and produces a discrete integrated output, $y(n)$. The time interval between each sample, T, represents a unit delay, z^{-1}, in the digital integrator. The digital integrator performs discrete integration perfectly with a dynamic range limited only by the number of bits used in the accumulator, A. This provides a dynamic range capability much greater than can be achieved by its analog counterpart, and the digital integrator does not drift. The boxcar integrator performs the function $y(n) = T[x(n)] + A(n-1)$, where n is the discrete sampled sequence number.

Figure 5.19(c) depicts a digital integrator that linearly interpolates between input samples and more closely approximates the ideal analog integrator. This is called the bilinear z-transform integrator. It performs the function $y(n) = T/2[x(n)] + A(n-1) = 1/2[A(n) + A(n-1)]$. The digital filters depicted in Figure 5.20 result when the Laplace integrators of Figure 5.18 are each replaced with the digital

---

1.   Jerry D. Holmes originally developed these analog and digital loop filter architectures and filter parameters. They were used in the first commercial GPS receiver design, the TI 4100 NAVSTAR Navigator, Texas Instruments, Inc., 1982.

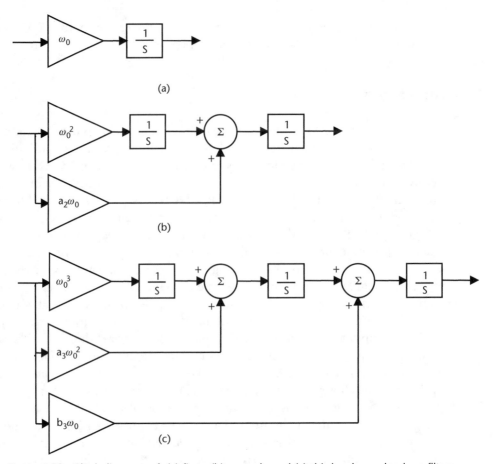

Figure 5.18 Block diagrams of: (a) first-, (b) second-, and (c) third-order analog loop filters.

Table 5.6 Loop Filter Characteristics

Loop Order	Noise Bandwidth B_n (Hz)	Typical Filter Values	Steady State Error	Characteristics
First	$\dfrac{\omega_0}{4}$	ω_0 $B_n = 0.25\,\omega_0$	$\dfrac{(dR/dt)}{\omega_0}$	Sensitive to velocity stress. Used in aided code loops and sometimes used in aided carrier loops. Unconditionally stable at all noise bandwidths.
Second	$\dfrac{\omega_0(1 + a_2^2)}{4a_2}$	ω_0^2 $a_2\omega_0 = 1.414\omega_0$ $B_n = 0.53\,\omega_0$	$\dfrac{(d^2R/dt^2)}{\omega_0^2}$	Sensitive to acceleration stress. Used in aided and unaided carrier loops. Unconditionally stable at all noise bandwidths.
Third	$\dfrac{\omega_0(a_3b_3^2 + a_3^2 - b_3)}{4(a_3b_3 - 1)}$	ω_0^3 $a_3\omega_0^2 = 1.1\omega_0^2$ $b_3\omega_0 = 2.4\omega_0$ $B_n = 0.7845\,\omega_0$	$\dfrac{(d^3R/dt^3)}{\omega_0^3}$	Sensitive to jerk stress. Used in unaided carrier loops. Remains stable at $B_n \leq 18$ Hz.

Source: [7].

Note: The loop filter natural radian frequency, ω_0, is computed from the value of the loop filter noise bandwidth, B_n, selected by the designer. R is the LOS range to the satellite. The steady state error is inversely proportional to the nth power of the tracking loop bandwidth and directly proportional to the nth derivative of range, where n is the loop filter order. Also see footnote 1.

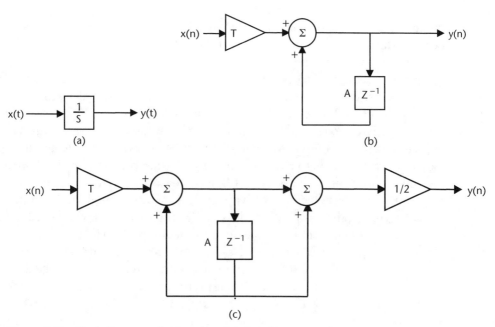

Figure 5.19 Block diagrams of: (a) analog, (b) digital boxcar, and (c) digital bilinear transform integrators.

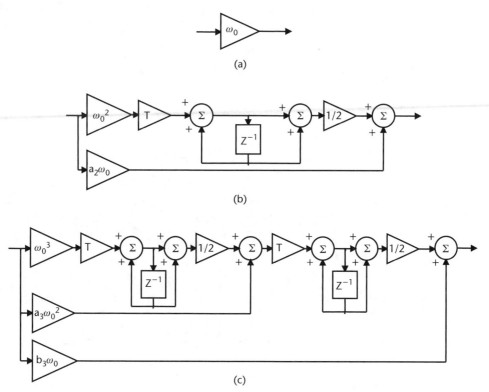

Figure 5.20 Block diagrams of (a) first-, (b) second-, and (c) third-order digital loop filters excluding the last integrator (the NCO).

bilinear integrator shown in Figure 5.19(c). The last digital integrator is not included because this function is implemented by the NCO. The NCO is equivalent to the boxcar integrator of Figure 5.19(b).

Figure 5.21 illustrates two FLL-assisted PLL loop filter designs (see footnote 1). Figure 5.21(a) depicts a second-order PLL filter with a first-order FLL assist. Figure 5.21(b) depicts a third-order PLL filter with a second-order FLL assist. If the PLL error input is zeroed in either of these filters, the filter becomes a pure FLL. Similarly, if the FLL error input is zeroed, the filter becomes a pure PLL. The lowest noise loop closure process is to close in pure FLL, then apply the error inputs from both discriminators as an FLL-assisted PLL until phase lock is achieved, then convert to pure PLL until phase lock is lost. However, if the noise bandwidth parameters are chosen correctly, there is very little loss in the ideal carrier tracking threshold performance when both discriminators are continuously operated [7]. In general, the natural radian frequency of the FLL, ω_{0f}, is different from the natural radian frequency of the PLL, ω_{0p}. These natural radian frequencies are determined from the desired loop filter noise bandwidths, B_{nf} and B_{np}, respectively. The values for the second-order coefficient a_2 and third-order coefficients a_3 and b_3 can be determined from Table 5.6. These coefficients are the same for FLL, PLL, or DLL applications if the loop order and the noise bandwidth, B_n, are the same. Note that the FLL coefficient insertion point into the filter is one integrator back from the PLL and DLL insertion points. This is because the FLL error is in units of hertz (change in range per unit of time), whereas the PLL and DLL errors are in units of phase (range).

A loop filter parameter design example will clarify the use of the equations in Table 5.6. Suppose that the receiver carrier tracking loop will be subjected to high

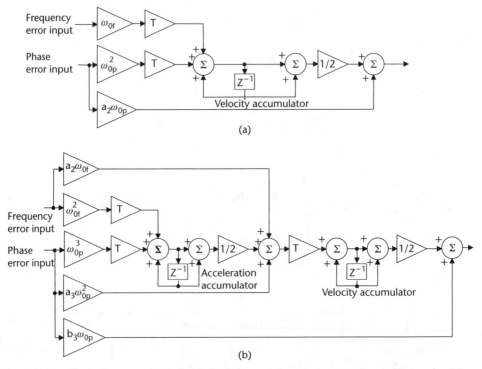

(a)

(b)

Figure 5.21 Block diagrams of FLL-assisted PLL filters: (a) second-order PLL with first-order FLL assist, and (b) third-order PLL with second-order FLL assist.

acceleration dynamics and will not be aided by an external navigation system, but must maintain PLL operation. A third-order loop is selected because it is insensitive to acceleration stress. To minimize its sensitivity to jerk stress, the noise bandwidth, B_n, is chosen to be the widest possible consistent with stability. Table 5.6 indicates that $B_n \leq 18$ Hz is safe. This limitation has been determined through extensive Monte Carlo simulations and is related to the maximum predetection integration time (which is typically the same as the reciprocal of the carrier loop iteration rate) plus extremes of noise and dynamic range. If $B_n = 18$ Hz, then $\omega_0 = B_n/0.7845 = 22.94455$ rad/s. The three multipliers shown in Figure 5.20(c) are computed as follows:

$$\omega_0^3 = 12,079.21$$
$$a_3\omega_0^2 = 1.1\omega_0^2 = 579.10$$
$$b_3\omega_0 = 2.4\omega_0 = 55.07$$

If the carrier loop is updated at a 200-Hz rate, then $T = 0.005$ second for use in the digital integrators. This completes the third-order filter parameter design. The remainder of the loop filter design is the implementation of the digital integrator accumulators to ensure that they will never overflow (i.e., that they have adequate dynamic range). The use of floating point arithmetic in modern microprocessors with built-in floating point hardware greatly simplifies this part of the design process. Note that in Figure 5.21(b), the velocity accumulator contains the loop filter estimate of LOS velocity between the antenna phase center and the SV. This estimate includes a self-adjusting bias component that compensates the carrier tracking loop for the reference oscillator frequency error (i.e., the time bias rate error that is in common with all tracking channels). Similarly, the acceleration accumulator contains the loop filter estimate of LOS acceleration that includes a self-adjusting bias component, which compensates the carrier tracking loop for the time rate of change of the reference oscillator frequency error. These accumulators should be initialized to zero just before initial loop closure unless good estimates of the correct values are known a priori. Also, they should be reset to their bias components (as learned by the navigation process) or to zero if unknown at the exact instance of injecting external carrier velocity aiding into the closed loop.

It should be noted that the loop filters described in this section, and in general any loop filters that are based on an adaptation of analog designs, only achieve the design noise bandwidth, B_n, when the product B_nT is very small (well below unity). As this product increases, the true noise bandwidth tends to be larger than the target value, and eventually the loop becomes unstable. An alternative loop formulation described in [8] overcomes some of these limitations. However, instability for extremely large values of the product B_nT is inevitable for any loop filter.

5.6   Measurement Errors and Tracking Thresholds

The GPS measurement errors and tracking thresholds are closely related because the receiver loses lock when the measurement errors exceed a certain boundary. Because the code and carrier tracking loops are nonlinear, especially near the threshold regions, only Monte Carlo simulations of the GPS receiver under the combined dynamic and SNR conditions will determine the true tracking performance [9]. However, general rules that approximate the measurement errors of the tracking loops can be used based on closed form equations. Numerous sources of measurement errors are in each type of tracking loop. However, it is sufficient for rule-of-thumb tracking thresholds to analyze only the dominant error sources.

5.6.1   PLL Tracking Loop Measurement Errors

The dominant sources of phase error in a GPS receiver PLL are phase jitter and dynamic stress error. A conservative rule of thumb for tracking threshold is that the 3-sigma jitter must not exceed one-fourth of the phase pull-in range of the PLL discriminator. Only arctangent carrier phase discriminators are considered for the generic receiver design. In the case of a dataless PLL four-quadrant arctangent discriminator whose phase pull-in range is 360°, the 3-sigma rule threshold is therefore 90°. For the case where there is data modulation, the PLL two-quadrant arctangent discriminator must be used and has a phase pull-in range of 180°. Therefore the 3-sigma rule threshold is 45°. Therefore, the PLL rule thresholds are stated as follows:

$$3\sigma_{PLL} = 3\sigma_j + \theta_e \leq 90° \text{ (dataless)}$$

$$3\sigma_{PLL} = 3\sigma_j + \theta_e \leq 45° \text{ (data present)}$$

(5.4)

where:

σ_j = 1-sigma phase jitter from all sources except dynamic stress error

θ_e = dynamic stress error in the PLL tracking loop

Equation (5.4) implies that dynamic stress error is a 3-sigma effect and is additive to the phase jitter. The phase jitter is the RSS of every source of uncorrelated phase error, such as thermal noise and oscillator noise. Oscillator noise includes vibration-induced jitter and Allan deviation–induced jitter. It also includes satellite oscillator phase noise. Even though IS-GPS-200 [2] specifies that this is no greater than 0.1 rad (5.7°) 1-sigma tracking error in a 10-Hz PLL, the operational SVs exhibit about an order of magnitude lower error than this to date. This external source of noise jitter is not included in the foregoing analysis but should be considered in very narrowband PLL applications.

In the P(Y) code and C/A code examples to follow, the presence of data modulation is assumed. Expanding on (5.4), the 1-sigma rule threshold for the PLL tracking loop for the two-quadrant arctangent discriminator is therefore:

$$\sigma_{PLL} = \sqrt{\sigma_{tPLL}^2 + \sigma_v^2 + \theta_A^2} + \frac{\theta_e}{3} \leq 15° \quad \text{(data present)}$$

(5.5)

where:

σ_{tPLL} = 1-sigma thermal noise in degrees

σ_v = 1-sigma vibration-induced oscillator jitter in degrees

θ_A = Allan variance–induced oscillator jitter in degrees

5.6.1.1 PLL Thermal Noise

Often the PLL thermal noise is treated as the only source of carrier tracking error, since the other sources of PLL jitter may be either transient or negligible. The thermal noise jitter for an arctangent PLL is computed as follows:

$$\sigma_{PLLt} = \frac{360}{2\pi} \sqrt{\frac{B_n}{C/N_0} \left(1 + \frac{1}{2T\,C/N_0}\right)} \quad \text{(degrees)} \tag{5.6}$$

$$\sigma_{PLLt} = \frac{\lambda_L}{2\pi} \sqrt{\frac{B_n}{C/N_0} \left(1 + \frac{1}{2T\,C/N_0}\right)} \quad \text{(m)} \tag{5.7}$$

where:

B_n = carrier loop noise bandwidth (Hz)

C/N_0 = carrier to noise power expressed as a ratio (Hz)

$\quad = 10^{\frac{(C/N_0)_{dB}}{10}}$ for $(C/N_0)_{dB}$ expressed in dB-Hz

T = predetection integration time (seconds)

λ_L = GPS L-band carrier wavelength (m)

$\quad$ = (299,792,458 m/s)/(1,575.42 MHz) = 0.1903 m/cycle for L1

$\quad$ = (299,792,458 m/s)/(1,227.6 MHz) = 0.2442 m/cycle for L2

Note that (5.6) and (5.7) do not include factors relating to C/A code or P(Y) code or the loop filter order. Also note that (5.6) is independent of carrier frequency when the error is expressed in units of degrees. The carrier thermal noise error standard deviation is strictly dependent on the carrier–to-noise power ratio, C/N_0, the noise bandwidth, B_n, and the predetection integration time, T. The carrier-to-noise power ratio, C/N_0, is an important factor in many GPS receiver performance measures. It is computed as the ratio of recovered power, C, (in W) from the desired signal to the noise density N_0 (in W/Hz). Methods for determining C/N_0 with and without external interference are described in Section 6.2.2. If C/N_0 increases (e.g., the recovered signal power is increased or the noise level is decreased), the standard deviation decreases. Decreasing the noise bandwidth reduces the standard deviation. The part of the equation involving the predetection integration time, T, is called the squaring loss. Increasing the predetection integration time reduces the squaring loss, which in turn decreases the standard deviation.

It is a common misconception that the GPS P(Y) (precision) codes always produce more accurate measurements than the C/A (coarse) codes. While the P(Y) code signal provides the potential for better code tracking accuracy, the PLL thermal noise error is the same for either code for the same C/N_0, since PLL processing uses quantities after the spreading code has been stripped off. Further, since the C/A code is 3 dB stronger than P(Y) code, the carrier thermal noise error is smaller for C/A code receivers than for P(Y) code receivers, assuming no signal jamming and that all other things in the receiver designs are equal. It is another common misconception that the carrier loop measurement is a velocity measurement, when actually it is a range measurement. The PLL thermal noise error is in units of range because it is part of the carrier Doppler phase measurement (i.e., a measurement of some fraction of the carrier wavelength). The velocity is approximated using the change in carrier Doppler phase between two carrier range measurements over a short time. Any single PLL measurement is a precise phase measurement of the carrier Doppler phase within one cycle. The differential measurement must also account for the integer number of carrier Doppler phase cycles that occur between measurements.

Figure 5.22 illustrates the PLL thermal noise jitter plotted as a function of $(C/N_0)_{dB}$ for three different noise bandwidths assuming the maximum 20-ms predetection integration time. Even though the thermal noise jitter is not directly dependent on the loop order, there is an indirect relationship. The loop order is sensitive to the same order of dynamics (first order to velocity stress, second order to acceleration stress, and third order to jerk stress), and the loop bandwidth must be wide enough to accommodate these higher-order dynamics. In general, when the loop order is made higher, there is an improvement in dynamic stress performance. Thus, the thermal noise can be reduced for the same minimum C/N_0 by increasing the loop order and reducing the noise bandwidth while also improving the dynamic performance.

5.6.1.2 Vibration-Induced Oscillator Phase Noise

Vibration-induced oscillator phase noise is a complex analysis problem. In some cases, the expected vibration environment is so severe that the reference oscillator

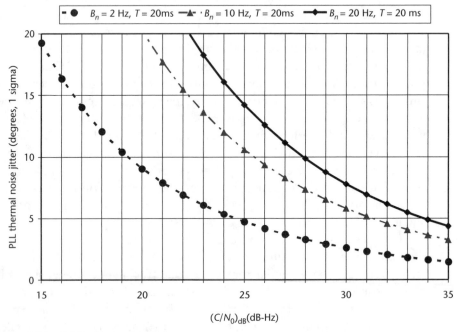

Figure 5.22   PLL thermal noise jitter.

must be mounted using vibration isolators in order for the GPS receiver to success-fully operate in PLL. The equation for vibration induced oscillator jitter is:

$$\sigma_v = \frac{360 f_L}{2\pi} \sqrt{\int_{f\,min}^{f\,max} S_v^2(f_m) \frac{P(f_m)}{f_m^2} df_m} \quad \text{(degrees)} \tag{5.8}$$

where:

f_L = L-band input frequency in Hz

$S_v(f_m)$ = oscillator vibration sensitivity of $\Delta f/f_L$ per g as a function of f_m

f_m = random vibration modulation frequency in Hz

$P(f_m)$ = power curve of the random vibration in g^2/Hz as a function of f_m

g = the acceleration due to gravity $\approx$ 9.8 m/s^2

If the oscillator vibration sensitivity, $S_v(f_m)$, is not variable over the range of the random vibration modulation frequency, f_m, then (5.8) can be simplified to:

$$\sigma_v = \frac{360 f_L S_v}{2\pi} \sqrt{\int_{f\,min}^{f\,max} \frac{P(f_m)}{f_m^2} df_m} \quad \text{(degrees)} \tag{5.9}$$

As a simple computational example, assume that the random vibration power curve is flat from 20 Hz to 2,000 Hz with an amplitude of 0.005 g^2/Hz. If $S_v = 1 \times 10^{-9}$ parts/g and f_L = L1 = 1,575.42 MHz, then the vibration-induced phase jitter using (5.9) is:

$$\sigma_v = 90.265 \sqrt{0.005 \int_{20}^{2000} \frac{df_m}{f_m^2}} = 90.265 \sqrt{0.005 \left(\frac{1}{20} - \frac{1}{200} \right)} = 1.42°$$

5.6.1.3 Allan Deviation Oscillator Phase Noise

The equations used to determine Allan deviation phase noise are empirical. They are stated in terms of what the requirements are for the short-term stability of the reference oscillator as determined by the Allan variance method of stability mea-surement. (Appendix B contains a description of the Allan variance.) The equation for short-term Allan deviation for a second-order PLL is [10]:

$$\sigma_A(\tau) = 2.5 \frac{\Delta\theta}{\omega_L \tau} \quad \text{(dimensionless units of } \Delta f/f) \tag{5.10}$$

where:

$\Delta\theta$ = rms jitter into phase discriminator due to the oscillator (rad)

ω_L = L-band input frequency = $2\pi f_L$ (rad/s)

τ = short-term stability gate time for Allan variance measurement (seconds).

The equation for a third-order PLL is similar [10]:

$$\sigma_A(\tau) = 2.25 \frac{\Delta\theta}{\omega_L \tau} \text{(dimensionless units of } \Delta f/f) \tag{5.11}$$

If the Allan variance, $\sigma_A^2(\tau)$, has already been determined for the oscillator for the short-term gate time, τ, then the Allan deviation–induced jitter in degrees, $\theta_A = 360\Delta\theta/2\pi$, can be computed from the previous equations. Usually $\sigma_A^2(\tau)$ changes very little for the short-term gate times involved. These gate times must include the reciprocal of the range of noise bandwidths used in the carrier loop filters, $\tau = 1/B_n$. A short-term gate-time range of 5 ms to 1,000 ms should suffice for all PLL applications. Rearranging (5.10) using these assumptions, the equation for the second-order loop is:

$$\theta_{A2} = 144 \frac{\sigma_A(\tau) f_L}{B_n} \text{ (degrees)} \tag{5.12}$$

Rearranging (5.11) using these assumptions, the equation for the third-order loop is:

$$\theta_{A3} = 160 \frac{\sigma_A(\tau) f_L}{B_n} \text{ (degrees)} \tag{5.13}$$

For example, assume that the loop filter is third-order with a noise bandwidth, $B_n = 18$ Hz, tracking the L1 signal, and the Allan deviation is specified to be $\sigma_A(\tau) = 1 \times 10^{-10}$ or better for gate times that include $\tau = 1/B_n = 56$ ms. The phase jitter contribution due to this error is $\theta_{A3} = 1.40°$ or less. Obviously, a reference oscillator with a short-term Allan deviation characteristic that is more than an order of magnitude worse than this example will cause PLL tracking problems.

Figure 5.23 graphically portrays the sensitivity of a third-order PLL to changes in short-term Allan deviation performance of the reference oscillator, especially as the noise bandwidth, B_n, is narrowed. The objective of narrowing the bandwidth is to reduce the thermal noise error to improve the tracking threshold. However, as Figure 5.23 illustrates, the Allan deviation effects begin to dominate at the narrower noise bandwidths. This effect is usually the primary source of aided GPS receiver narrowband PLL tracking problems, assuming that the external velocity aiding accuracy is not the limiting factor. However, even for an unaided GPS receiver, a reference oscillator with a poor Allan deviation characteristic, say a $\Delta f/f$ of less than 1×10^{-9}, will prevent reliable PLL operation. Therefore, the oscillator specification for Allan deviation is important for all GPS receiver designs.

5.6.1.4 Dynamic Stress Error

The dynamic stress error is obtained from the steady state error formulas shown in Table 5.6. This error depends on the loop bandwidth and order. The maximum dynamic stress error may be slightly larger than the steady state error if the loop filter response to a step function has overshot, but the steady state error formula will

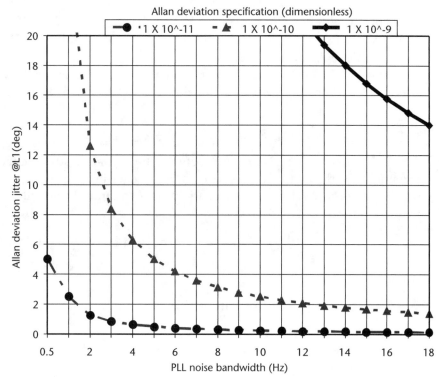

Figure 5.23   Allan deviation jitter in third-order PLL at L1.

suffice. There should be no more than about a 7% overshoot if the filter is designed for minimum mean square error, which is the case for the typical loop filter coefficients shown in the table. From Table 5.6, a second-order loop with minimum mean square error, the dynamic stress error is:

$$\theta_{e2} = \frac{d^2R/dt^2}{\omega_0^2} = \frac{d^2R/dt^2}{\left(\dfrac{B_n}{0.53}\right)^2} = 0.2809\frac{d^2R/dt^2}{B_n^2} \quad \text{(degrees)} \qquad (5.14)$$

where d^2R/dt^2 = maximum LOS acceleration dynamics (°/s^2).

From Table 5.6, a third-order loop with minimum mean square error, the dynamic stress error is defined as follows:

$$\theta_{e3} = \frac{d^3R/dt^3}{\omega_0^3} = \frac{d^3R/dt^3}{\left(\dfrac{B_n}{0.7845}\right)^3} = 0.4828\frac{d^3R/dt^3}{B_n^3} \quad \text{(degrees)} \qquad (5.15)$$

where d^3R/dt^3 = maximum LOS jerk dynamics (°/s^3).

Note that (5.15) is a 3-sigma error. As an example of how this error is computed, suppose the third-order loop noise bandwidth is 18 Hz and the maximum LOS jerk dynamic stress to the SV is 10 g/s = 98 m/s^3. To convert this to °/s^3, multiply the jerk dynamics by the number of carrier wavelengths contained in 1m in units of

°/m. For L1, $d^3R/dt^3 = (98 \text{ m/s}^3) \times (360°/\text{cycle}) \times (1{,}575.42 \times 10^6 \text{ cycles/s})/c = 185{,}398°/s^3$ where $c = 299{,}792{,}458$ m/s is the speed of light. For L2, $d^3R/dt^3 = 98 \times 360 \times 1{,}227.60 \times 10^6/c = 144{,}666°/s^3$.

Using (5.15), the 3-sigma stress error for an 18-Hz third-order PLL is 15.35° for L1 and 11.96° for L2. These are well below the 45° 3-sigma rule-of-thumb levels.

5.6.1.5 Reference Oscillator Acceleration Stress Error

The PLL cannot tell the difference between the dynamic stress induced by real dynamics and the dynamic stress caused by changes in frequency in the reference oscillator due to acceleration sensitivity of the oscillator. The oscillator change in frequency due to dynamic stress is:

$$\Delta f_g = 360\, S_g f_L G(t) \quad (°/s) \tag{5.16}$$

where:

S_g = g-sensitivity of the oscillator ($\Delta f/f$ per g)

f_L = L-band input frequency (Hz)

= 1,575.42 MHz for L1

= 1,227.76 MHz for L2

$G(t)$ = acceleration stress in g as a function of time

For the components of $G(t)$ due to acceleration (g), the units of Δf_g are °/s, a velocity error as sensed by the loop filter. For an unaided second-order carrier tracking loop, this acceleration-induced oscillator error can be ignored because it is insensitive to velocity stress. For the components of $G(t)$ due to jerk stress (g/s), the units of Δf_g are °/s², an acceleration error as sensed by the loop filter. For an unaided third-order carrier tracking loop, this jerk-induced oscillator error can be ignored because it is insensitive to acceleration stress. In reality, there will always be some level of dynamic stress that will adversely affect tracking loop regardless of the loop filter order because there are always higher order components of dynamic stress when the host vehicle is subjected to dynamics. Nothing can be done about this for an unaided tracking loop except to align the least sensitive S_g axis of the reference oscillator along the direction of the anticipated maximum dynamic stress, but this is often impractical. For an externally aided tracking loop where the LOS dynamic stress can be measured and S_g is known, it is prudent to model this acceleration stress sensitivity and apply the correction to the aiding. Note that, like all oscillator-induced errors, the error is common mode to all receiver tracking channels, so one correction applies to all aided channels.

5.6.1.6 Total PLL Tracking Loop Measurement Errors and Thresholds

Figure 5.24 illustrates the total PLL jitter as a function of $(C/N_0)_{dB}$ for a third-order PLL, including all effects described in (5.5), (5.6), (5.9), (5.13), and (5.15). Equation (5.5) can be rearranged to solve for the dynamic stress error, and this can be solved

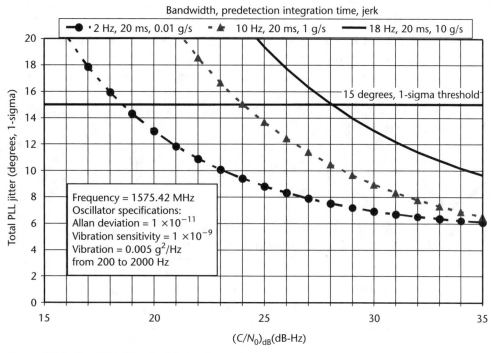

Figure 5.24   Total PLL jitter for third-order carrier loop.

for the dynamic stress at threshold. Figure 5.25 illustrates the dynamic stress at threshold as a function of noise bandwidth for a third-order PLL.

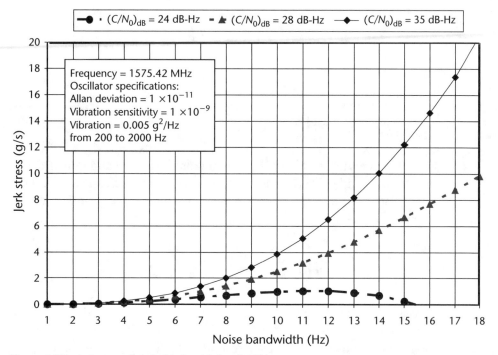

Figure 5.25   Jerk stress thresholds for third-order PLL.

5.6.2 FLL Tracking Loop Measurement Errors

The dominant sources of frequency error in a GPS receiver FLL are frequency jitter due to thermal noise and dynamic stress error. The rule of thumb for tracking threshold is that the 3-sigma jitter must not exceed one-fourth of the frequency pull-in range of the FLL discriminator. As observed in Figure 5.11, the FLL discriminator pull-in range is $1/T$ Hz. Therefore, the general rule of thumb for FLL tracking threshold is:

$$3\sigma_{FLL} = 3\sigma_{tFLL} + f_e \leq 1/4T \quad (Hz) \tag{5.17}$$

where:

$3\sigma_{tFLL}$ = 3-sigma thermal noise frequency jitter

f_e = dynamic stress error in the FLL tracking loop

Equation (5.17) shows that the dynamic stress frequency error is a 3-sigma effect and is additive to the thermal noise frequency jitter. The reference oscillator vibration and Allan deviation–induced frequency jitter are small-order effects on the FLL and are considered negligible. The 1-sigma frequency jitter threshold would be $1/(12T) = 0.0833/T$ Hz.

The FLL tracking loop jitter due to thermal noise is:

$$\sigma_{tFLL} = \frac{1}{2\pi T} \sqrt{\frac{4FB_n}{C/N_0}\left[1 + \frac{1}{T\,C/N_0}\right]} \quad (Hz) \tag{5.18}$$

$$\sigma_{tFLL} = \frac{\lambda_L}{2\pi T} \sqrt{\frac{4FB_n}{C/N_0}\left[1 + \frac{1}{T\,C/N_0}\right]} \quad (m/s) \tag{5.19}$$

where:

$F = 1$ at high C/N_0

$\quad = 2$ near threshold

Note that (5.17) is independent of modulation design and loop order. It is independent of L-band carrier frequency if the error units are expressed in hertz.

Because the FLL tracking loop involves one more integrator than the PLL tracking loop of the same order, the dynamic stress error is:

$$f_e = \frac{d}{dt}\left(\frac{1}{360\omega_0^n}\frac{d^n R}{dt^n}\right) = \frac{1}{360\omega_0^n}\frac{d^{n+1}R}{dt^{n+1}} \quad (Hz) \tag{5.20}$$

As an example of how the dynamic stress error is computed from (5.20), assume a second-order FLL with a noise bandwidth of 2 Hz and a predetection integration time of 5 ms. From Table 5.6, for a second-order loop $B_n = 0.53\omega_0$, so $\omega_0^2 = (2/0.53)^2$

$= 14.24\ \text{Hz}^2$. If the maximum LOS jerk dynamics is $10\ g/s = 98\ \text{m/s}^3$, then this translates into $d^3R/dt^3 = 98 \times 360 \times 1,575.42 \times 10^6/c = 185,398°/\text{s}^3$ for L1. Substituting these numbers into (5.20) results in a maximum dynamic stress error of $f_e = 185,398/(14.24 \times 360) = 36\ \text{Hz}$. Since the 3-sigma threshold is $1/(4 \times 0.005) = 50$ Hz, the FLL noise bandwidth is acceptable. Figure 5.26 illustrates the FLL thermal noise tracking jitter and tracking thresholds, assuming a second-order loop under $10\ g/s$ jerk dynamics with typical noise bandwidths and predetection integration times.

Figure 5.27 illustrates the jerk stress thresholds for a second-order FLL as a function of noise bandwidth with $(C/N_0)_{dB}$ as a running parameter. Comparing the thresholds in Figure 5.27 for the second-order FLL with those of Figure 5.25 for a third-order PLL, notice that the FLL has much better dynamic stress performance than the PLL at the same noise bandwidths and C/N_0. For example, at 10 Hz and 35 dB-Hz, the FLL can tolerate up to $240\ g/s$ while the PLL can only tolerate up to $4\ g/s$. The spread is much smaller for weaker C/N_0. The PLL would have performed moderately better under dynamic stress if the predetection integration time had been reduced from 20 ms to 5 ms, as was the case for the FLL. This comparison reinforces the earlier statements that a robust GPS receiver design will use an FLL as a backup to the PLL during initial loop closure and during high dynamic stress with loss of phase lock but will revert to pure PLL for the steady state low to moderate dynamics in order to produce the highest accuracy carrier Doppler phase measurements. Also note that the maximum predetection integration time for FLL with C/A code or P(Y) code is 10 ms, since two samples within one data transition interval are required for the FLL discriminator.

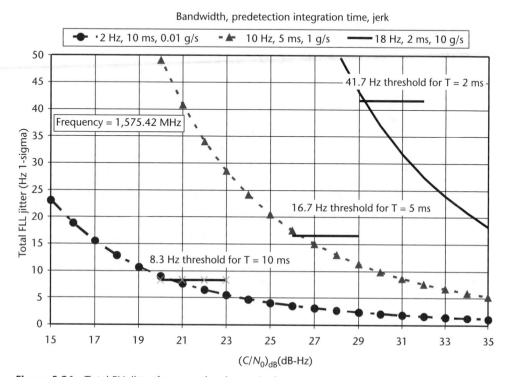

Figure 5.26   Total FLL jitter for second-order carrier loop.

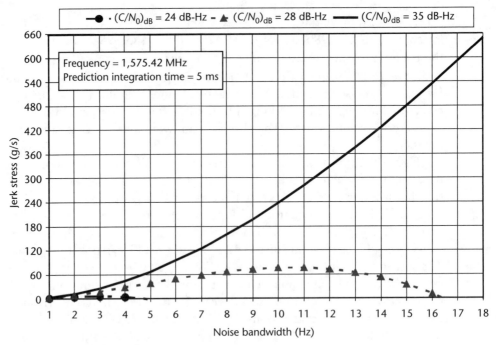

Figure 5.27   Jerk stress thresholds for second-order FLL.

5.6.3   C/A and P(Y) Code Tracking Loop Measurement Errors

When there is no multipath or other distortion of the received signal and no interference, the dominant sources of range error in a GPS receiver code tracking loop (DLL) are thermal noise range error jitter and dynamic stress error. The rule-of-thumb tracking threshold for the DLL is that the 3-sigma value of the jitter due to all sources of loop stress must not exceed half of the linear pull-in range of the discriminator. Therefore, the rule-of-thumb tracking threshold is:

$$3\sigma_{DLL} = 3\sigma_{tDLL} + R_e \leq D/2 \qquad (5.21)$$

where:

σ_{tDLL} = 1-sigma thermal noise code tracking jitter (chips)

R_e = dynamic stress error in the DLL tracking loop (chips)

D = early-to-late correlator spacing (chips)

A general expression for thermal noise code tracking jitter for a noncoherent DLL discriminator is [11]:

$$\sigma_{tDLL} \cong \frac{1}{T_c} \sqrt{\frac{B_n \displaystyle\int_{-B_{fe}/2}^{B_{fe}/2} S_s(f)\sin^2(\pi f D T_c)\,df}{(2\pi)^2\, C/N_0 \left(\displaystyle\int_{-B_{fe}/2}^{B_{fe}/2} f S_s(f)\sin(\pi f D T_c)\,df\right)^2}}$$

(5.22)

$$\times \sqrt{\left[1 + \frac{\displaystyle\int_{-B_{fe}/2}^{B_{fe}/2} S_s(f)\cos^2(\pi f D T_c)\,df}{TC/N_0 \left(\displaystyle\int_{-B_{fe}/2}^{B_{fe}/2} S_s(f)\cos(\pi f D T_c)\,df\right)^2}\right]} \quad \text{(chips)}$$

where:

B_n = code loop noise bandwidth (Hz)

$S_s(f)$ = power spectral density of the signal, normalized to unit area over infinite bandwidth

B_{fe} = double-sided front-end bandwidth (Hz)

T_c = chip period (seconds) = $1/R_c$ where R_c is the chipping rate

For BPSK-R(n) modulations (see Section 4.2.3) such as P(Y) code ($n = 10$) and C/A code ($n = 1$), and when using a noncoherent early-late power DLL discriminator, the thermal noise code tracking jitter can be found by substituting (4.14) into (5.22). The result can be approximated by [12]:

$$\sigma_{tDLL} \cong \begin{cases} \sqrt{\dfrac{B_n}{2C/N_0} D\left[1 + \dfrac{2}{TC/N_0(2-D)}\right]}, & D \ge \dfrac{\pi R_c}{B_{fe}} \\[2em] \sqrt{\dfrac{B_n}{2C/N_0}\left(\dfrac{1}{B_{fe}T_c} + \dfrac{B_{fe}T_c}{\pi-1}\left(D - \dfrac{1}{B_{fe}T_c}\right)^2\right)} \\[0.5em] \quad \times \left[1 + \dfrac{2}{TC/N_0(2-D)}\right], & \dfrac{R_c}{B_{fe}} < D < \dfrac{\pi R_c}{B_{fe}} \\[2em] \sqrt{\dfrac{B_n}{2C/N_0}\left(\dfrac{1}{B_{fe}T_c}\right)\left[1 + \dfrac{1}{TC/N_0}\right]}, & D \le \dfrac{R_c}{B_{fe}} \end{cases} \quad \text{(chips)} \quad (5.23)$$

The part of the right-hand side of (5.22) and (5.23) in brackets involving the predetection integration time, T, is called the squaring loss. Hence, increasing T reduces the squaring loss in noncoherent DLLs. When using a coherent DLL discriminator, the bracketed term on the right is equal to unity (no squaring loss) [12]. As seen in (5.23), the DLL jitter is directly proportional to the square root of the filter noise bandwidth (lower B_n results in a lower jitter, which, in turn, results in a lower C/N_0 threshold). Also, increasing the predetection integration time, T, results in a lower C/N_0 threshold, but with less effect than reducing B_n. Reducing the correlator spacing, D, also reduces the DLL jitter at the expense of increased code tracking sensitivity to dynamics. Narrowing D should be accompanied by increasing the front-end bandwidth B_{fe} to avoid "flattening" of the DLL correlation peak in the region where the narrow correlators are being operated. In fact, (5.23) shows that there is no benefit to reducing D to less than the spreading code rate divided by the front-end bandwidth.

As D becomes vanishingly small, the trigonometric functions in (5.22) can be replaced by their first-order Taylor Series expansions about zero, and this equation becomes

$$\sigma_{tDLL} \cong \frac{1}{T_c}\sqrt{\frac{B_n}{(2\pi)^2(C/N_0)\int\limits_{-B_{fe}/2}^{B_{fe}/2}f^2 S_s(f)df}\left[1+\frac{1}{T(C/N_0)\int\limits_{-B_{fe}/2}^{B_{fe}/2}S_s(f)df}\right]}\qquad\text{(chips)}\quad(5.24)$$

The term $\sqrt{\int\limits_{-B_{fe}/2}^{B_{fe}/2}f^2 S_S(f)df}$ is called the root-mean-squared (RMS) bandwidth of the signal, and it is a measure of the "sharpness" of the correlation peak. Clearly, signals with larger RMS bandwidths offer the potential for more accurate code tracking. In fact, the frequency-squared term in the RMS bandwidth indicates that even very small amounts of high frequency content in the signal can enable more accurate code tracking. Intuitively, these high frequency components produce sharper edges and more distinct zero crossings in the waveform, enabling more accurate code tracking.

The use of carrier-aided code (practically a universal design practice) effectively removes the code dynamics, so the use of narrow correlators is an excellent design tradeoff for C/A code receivers. For C/A code receivers where the correlation interval in units of time is an order of magnitude greater than for P(Y) code, reducing the correlator spacing reduces the effects of thermal noise and multipath (see Section 6.3) on C/A, but this also requires increasing the front-end bandwidth, which increases the vulnerability to in-band RF interference.

Note that the thermal noise is independent of tracking loop order in (5.23) Also note that the thermal noise is the same for either C/A code or P(Y) code when expressed in units of chips. However, all other things being equal, the thermal noise is ten times larger for the C/A code than the P(Y) code because the chip wavelength of the C/A code is ten times longer than for P(Y) code. For example, from (5.23), this is readily observed if the measurement is converted to meters. To convert to meters, multiply (5.23) by $c \cdot T_c$ (e.g., by 293.05 m/chip for C/A code or by 29.305 m/chip for P(Y) code).

Figure 5.28(a) uses (5.23) to compare C/A code and P(Y) code accuracy in units of meters. (Figure 5.28 also includes results for the M code that will be explained in Section 5.6.4.) A one-chip correlator E-L spacing (e.g., $D = 1$) and normalized receiver bandwidth $b \equiv B_{fe}/R_c = 2$ (i.e., the front-end receiver bandwidth is equal to twice the chip rate) is used for each BPSK-R result. Figure 5.28(b) uses (5.23) to

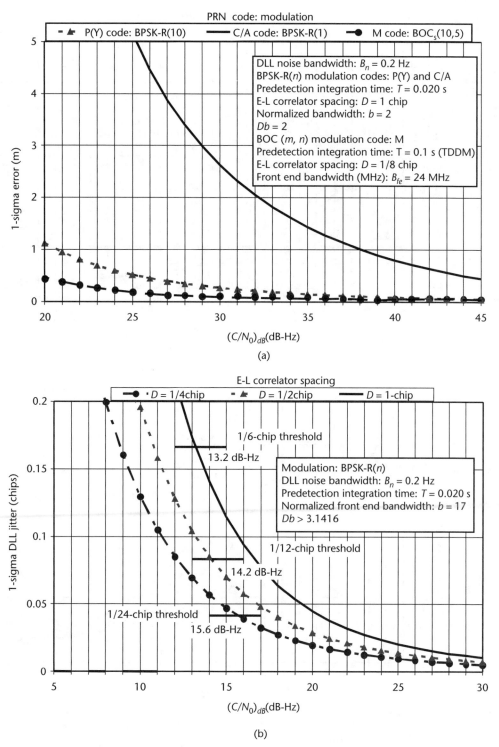

Figure 5.28 Delay lock loop jitter versus $(C/N_0)_{dB}$: (a) comparison of P(Y) code, C/A code, and M code DLL accuracy, (b) comparison of DLL jitter for different correlator spacing, (c) effect of noise bandwidth on DLL jitter, and (d) effect of predetection integration time on DLL jitter.

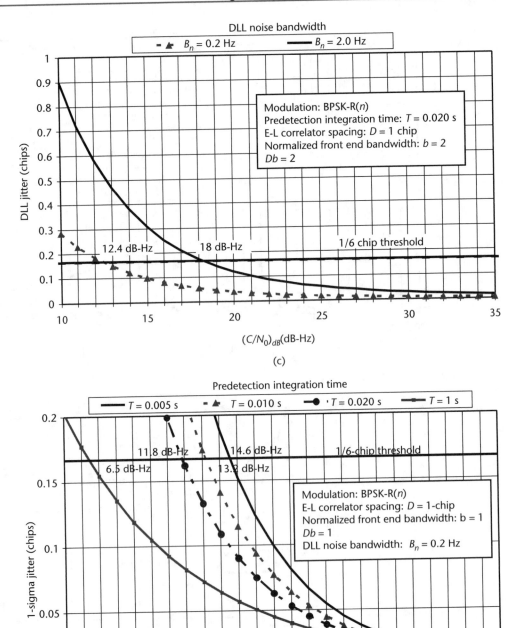

Figure 5.28 (Continued.)

compare the DLL performance for BPSK-R modulations with different correlator spacings and an extremely wide receiver bandwidth ($b = 17$). Note that both the thermal noise jitter and the rule-of-thumb thresholds are reduced when the correlator spacing is reduced, but that there is only a slight loss of tracking threshold as the correlator spacing is reduced (provided that the receiver front end bandwidth is increased appropriately).

Figure 5.28(c) uses (5.23) with $Db = 2$ to demonstrate the improved DLL tracking threshold by reducing the noise bandwidth. Figure 5.28(d) uses (5.23) with $Db = 2$ to illustrate the improved DLL tracking threshold by increasing the predetection integration time. The 1-second predetection integration time provides the lowest code tracking threshold. To support a predetection integration time greater than 20 ms (the navigation message data bit interval), the data wipeoff process must be implemented for C/A code and the normal mode of P(Y) code. Recall that this technique uses the GPS receiver's a priori knowledge of the navigation message data bit stream to remove the 180° data transitions. This data wipeoff technique permits longer than 20-ms predetection integration times and, if properly implemented, can achieve nearly 6 dB of additional $(C/N_0)_{dB}$ threshold improvement [see Figure 5.28(d) at threshold crossings]. This is a short-term "desperation" DLL weak signal hold-on strategy for an externally aided GPS receiver when the carrier is aided open loop. Data wipeoff also improves the PLL tracking threshold when the carrier loop is closed-loop aided, but not to the extent that the code loop tracking threshold is improved. Changes in any part of the SV navigation message data stream by a GPS control segment upload or autonomously by the SV will cause errors in the data wipeoff, which, in turn, will cause deterioration in the tracking threshold.

The DLL tracking loop dynamic stress error is determined by:

$$R_e = \frac{d^n R / dt^n}{\omega_0^n} \quad \text{(chips)} \tag{5.25}$$

where $d^n R / dt^n$ is expressed in chips/s^n.

As an example of how the dynamic stress error is computed from (5.25), assume that the code loop is an unaided third-order C/A code DLL with $B_n = 2$ Hz and $D = 1$ chip. From Table 5.6, for a third-order loop $\omega_0 = B_n / 0.7845$. If the maximum LOS jerk stress is 10 g/s, then this is equivalent to $d^3 R / dt^3 = 98$ m/s^3/293.05 m/chip = 0.3344 chips/s^3. Substituting these numbers into (5.25) results in a maximum dynamic stress error of $R_e = 0.02$ chip, a 3-sigma effect. Since the 3-sigma threshold is 1/2-chip, this would indicate that the DLL noise bandwidth is more than adequate for C/A code. If the receiver was P(Y) code, then $R_e = 0.2$ chip, which is still adequate. Note that carrier-aided code techniques removes virtually all the dynamic stress from the code tracking loop. Therefore, as long as the carrier loop remains stable, the code loop experiences negligible dynamic stress, and this effect is not included in the code loop tracking threshold analysis.

5.6.4   Modernized GPS M Code Tracking Loop Measurement Errors

The modernized GPS M code uses a $BOC_s(10,5)$ modulation technique (see Sections 4.2.3 and 4.5.3). By substituting (4.17) into (5.22), the following approximation for M code DLL jitter in the presence of thermal noise can be determined [13]:

$$\sigma_{tM} \cong \begin{cases} \dfrac{1}{T_c}\sqrt{\dfrac{B_n}{(2\pi)^2 \dfrac{C}{N_0}\left(0.66B_{fe}-7.7E6\right)^2}\left[1+\dfrac{1}{\left(B_{fe}\cdot 7.3E-8-0.96\right)T\dfrac{C}{N_0}}\right]}, & 16\text{ MHz} \le B_{fe} \le 24.5\text{ MHz} \\[40pt] \dfrac{1}{T_c}\sqrt{\dfrac{B_n}{(2\pi)^2 \dfrac{C}{N_0}\left(0.007B_{fe}+8.4E6\right)^2}\left[1+\dfrac{1}{0.837T\dfrac{C}{N_0}}\right]}, & 24.5\text{ MHz} < B_{fe} \le 30\text{ MHz} \end{cases}$$

$$(\text{chips}) \quad (5.26)$$

where $\dfrac{1}{T_c} = R_c = 5.115$ Mchips/s.

To obtain the 1-sigma jitter in meters, multiply (5.26) by 58.610 m/chip. Figure 5.28(a) uses (5.26) in units of meters to compare the modernized M code accuracy with the P(Y) and C/A codes. Note that the correlator spacing, D (in M chips), does not appear in (5.26), but this approximation is restricted to an E–L spacing of 1/4 M code chips or less. The rule of thumb for M code DLL tracking threshold is identical to (5.21). M code has a provision for dataless tracking that permits extended predetection integration times, but this mode also loses 3 dB because every other code bit is dataless. Reduce $(C/N_0)_{dB}$ by 3 dB before converting to C/N_0 both places in (5.26) to account for this loss in signal (increase in jitter) when using the M code time division data multiplexing (TDDM) mode.

5.7   Formation of Pseudorange, Delta Pseudorange, and Integrated Doppler

Contrary to popular belief, the natural measurements of a GPS receiver are not pseudorange or delta pseudorange [14]. This section describes the natural measurements of a GPS receiver and describes how they may be converted into pseudorange, delta pseudorange, and integrated carrier Doppler phase measurements. The natural measurements are replica code phase and replica carrier Doppler phase (if the GPS receiver is in phase lock with the satellite carrier signal) or replica carrier Doppler frequency (if the receiver is in frequency lock with the satellite carrier signal). The replica code phase can be converted into satellite transmit time, which can be used to compute the pseudorange measurement. The replica carrier Doppler phase or frequency can be converted into delta pseudorange. The replica carrier Doppler phase measurements can also be converted into integrated carrier Doppler phase measurements used for ultraprecise (differential) static and kinematic surveying or positioning.

The most important concept presented in this section is the measurement relationship between the replica code phase state in the GPS receiver and the satellite transmit time. This relationship is unambiguous for P(Y) code, but can be ambiguous for C/A code. Every C/A code GPS receiver is vulnerable to this ambiguity problem and, under weak signal acquisition conditions, the ambiguity will occur. When the ambiguity does occur in a C/A code GPS receiver, it causes serious range measurement errors, which, in turn, result in severe navigation position errors.

5.7.1   Pseudorange

The definition of pseudorange to SV_i, where i is the PRN number is as follows:

$$\rho_i(n) = c\left[T_R(n) - T_{Ti}(n)\right] \quad (\text{m}) \tag{5.27}$$

where:

c = speed of light = 299,792,458 (m/s)

$T_R(n)$ = receive time corresponding to epoch n of the GPS receiver's clock (seconds)

$T_{Ti}(n)$ = transmit time based on the SV_i clock (seconds)

Figure 5.29 depicts the GPS satellite SV_i transmitting its PRN code PRN_i starting at the end of the GPS week. Corresponding to each chip of the PRN_i code is a linear SV_i clock time. When this signal reaches the GPS receiver, the transmit time, $T_{Ti}(n)$, is the SV_i time corresponding to the PRN code state that is being replicated at receiver epoch n. The pseudorange derived from this measurement corresponds to a

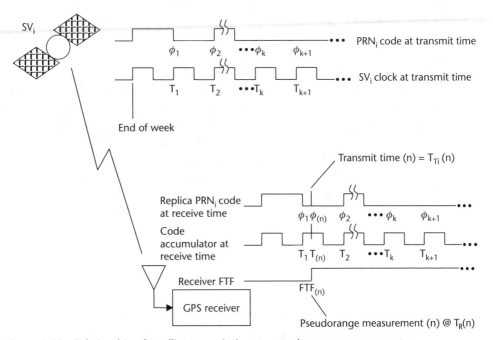

Figure 5.29   Relationship of satellite transmit time to pseudorange measurements.

particular receive time epoch (epoch n) in the GPS receiver. Every epoch in the PRN code that is transmitted by SV_i is precisely aligned to the GPS time of week as maintained inside SV_i's time-keeping hardware. When this transmitted PRN code reaches the user GPS receiver, which is successfully correlating a replica PRN code with it, the phase offset of the replica code with respect to the beginning of the GPS week represents the transmit time of SV_i. The first thing that the navigation process needs for position measurement incorporation is the SV_i transmit time corrected to true GPS time. It is therefore logical that the natural measurement (SV_i transmit time) should be sent to the navigation process (along with the receive time) and not the pseudorange measurement (along with the receive time). This is because the SV_i transmit time is lost after this artificial computation is performed. This forces the navigation process into a wasteful iterative process of computing the SV_i transmit time. Highly sophisticated GPS receivers implement vector tracking of the SVs instead of scalar tracking described herein. This overcomes this problem because either the raw I and Q measurements or the discriminator outputs are sent to the navigation process as measurements for Kalman filtering by the navigation process. Thus, the navigation process dynamically changes the noise bandwidth of the tracking loops in an optimal manner.

Typically, the GPS receiver will take a set of measurements at the same receive time epoch. This is why the receive time is not identified with any particular SV PRN number in (5.27). When the GPS receiver schedules a set of measurements, it does this based on its own internal clock, which contains a bias error with respect to true GPS time. Eventually the navigation process learns this bias error as a byproduct of the GPS navigation solution. The SV transmit time also contains a bias error with respect to true GPS time, although the control segment ensures that this is maintained at less than 1 ms. This correction is transmitted to the receiver by SV_i as clock correction parameters via the navigation message. However, neither of these corrections is included in the pseudorange measurement of (5.27). These corrections and others are determined and applied by the navigation process.

5.7.1.1 Pseudorange Measurement

From (5.27), it can be concluded that if the receiver baseband process can extract the SV transmit time from the code tracking loop, then it can provide a pseudorange measurement. The precise transmit time measurement for SV_i is equivalent to its code phase offset with respect to the beginning of the GPS week. There is a one-to-one relationship between the SV_i replica code phase and the GPS time. Thus, for every fractional and integer chip advancement in the code phase of the PRN code generator since the initial (reset) state at the beginning of the week, there is a corresponding fractional and integer chip advancement in the GPS time. The fractional and integer chip codephase will hereafter be called the code state. The receiver baseband process time keeper, which contains the GPS time corresponding to this code state, will hereafter be called the code accumulator.

The replica code state corresponds to the receiver's best estimate of the SV transmit time. The receiver baseband process knows the code state because it sets the initial states during the search process and keeps track of the changes in the code state thereafter. The receiver baseband code tracking loop process keeps track of the GPS

transmit time corresponding to the phase state of the code NCO and the replica
PRN code generator state after each code NCO update. It does this by discrete integration of every code phase increment over the interval of time since the last NCO
update and adds this number to the code accumulator. The combination of the replica code generator state (integer code state) and the code NCO state (fraction code
state) is the replica code state. Since the code phase states of the PRN code generator
are pseudorandom, it would be impractical to read the code phase state of the PRN
code generator and then attempt to convert this nonlinear code state into a linear
GPS time state, say, by a table lookup.

   There are too many possible code states, especially for the P code generator. A
very practical way to maintain the GPS time in a GPS receiver is to use a separate
code accumulator in the GPS receiver baseband process and to synchronize this
accumulator to the replica PRN code generator phase state. Figure 5.30 (derived
from the code tracking loop of Figure 5.13) illustrates the high-level block diagram
relationship between the replica PRN code generator and the code accumulator
(which is not included in Figure 5.13) in the code tracking loop of one GPS receiver
channel.

   A typical GPS navigation measurement incorporation rate is once per second. A
typical GPS receiver FTF for scheduling measurements is 20 ms, which is the same
as the 50-Hz navigation message data period. The receiver baseband process schedule for updating the code and carrier NCOs is usually some integer subset of the

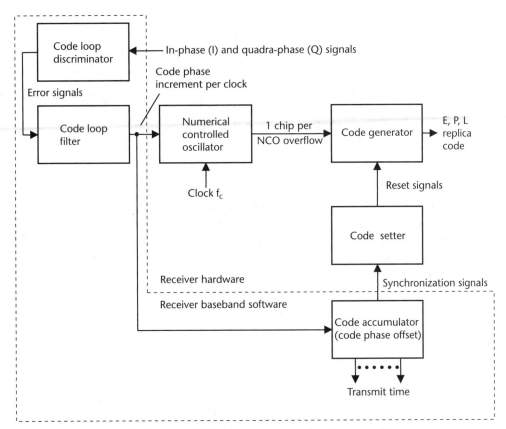

Figure 5.30   Relationship between PRN code generator and code accumulator.

FTF, such as 20, 10, 5, 2, or 1 ms. Assuming that the FTF is 20 ms, the receiver measurement process maintains a monotone counter (call it the FTF counter) in 20-ms increments derived from the receiver's reference oscillator. The FTF counter is set to zero at power up, counts up, rolls over, counts up, and so on. Assuming that the navigation measurement incorporation rate is 1 Hz, the navigation process will schedule measurements to be extracted from the code and carrier tracking loops every fiftieth FTF (i.e., based on the receiver's time epochs). When the receiver baseband process extracts the measurements from the code and carrier tracking loops, it time tags the measurements with the FTF count. The navigation process assigns and maintains a GPS receive time corresponding to the FTF count. The receive time initialization can be the first SV's transmit time plus a nominal propagation time of, say, 76 ms if the navigation process does not know the GPS time accurately. This will set the initial receive time accurate to within 20 ms.

When a pseudorange measurement is scheduled on FTF(n), the receiver baseband code tracking loop process extracts the SV_i transmit time from its code accumulator and propagates this time forward to FTF(n). The result is the SV_i transmit time with a measurement resolution of 2^{-N} of a code chip, where N is the number of bits in the code NCO adder. If the code NCO adder uses a 32-bit register, this measurement resolution is less than a quarter of a nanochip, which makes the code measurement quantization noise negligible. The receiver baseband process can compute the pseudorange measurement from the SV_i transmit time using (5.27) and time tag the measurement with FTF(n) before sending the result to the navigation process. However, the navigation process needs the (corrected) SV_i transmit time to compute the location of SV_i when it transmitted the measurement. Hence, the best measurement to send to the GPS navigation process is the (uncorrected) SV transmit time, along with the FTF time tag. The navigation process applies the clock correction (including relativity correction), uses the corrected SV_i transmit time to compute the SV_i position, then computes the pseudorange plus other corrections before incorporation of the measurement. (Satellite clock and relativistic corrections are discussed in Sections 7.2.1 and 7.2.3, respectively.)

5.7.1.2 Measurement Time Skew

Figure 5.4 illustrates the bit sync phase skew, T_s, which exists between the SV data transition boundaries and the receiver 20-ms clock epochs (i.e., the FTFs). The control segment ensures that every SV transmits every epoch within 1 ms of true GPS time (i.e., the SV clocks are aligned to within 1 ms of true GPS time). Therefore, all of the SV data transition boundaries are approximately aligned to true GPS time at transmit time. However, at the GPS receiver the SV data transition boundaries are, in general, skewed with respect to each other and with respect to the receiver's FTF boundary. This is because the SVs are at different ranges with respect to the user GPS receiver antenna phase center. The user GPS receiver must adjust the phases of its integrate and dump boundaries in order to avoid integrating across the SV data bit transition boundaries. The time skew, T_s, is different for each SV being tracked, and it changes with time because the range to the SVs change with time. Therefore, the epochs from each replica code generator, such as the C/A code 1-ms epochs, are skewed with respect to each other and to the FTF. As a result, the integrate and dump times and the updates to the code and carrier NCOs are performed on a changing skewed time phase with respect to the FTF time phase, but the receiver baseband process learns and controls this time skew in discrete phase increments. The code accumulator is normally updated on the skewed time schedule that matches the code NCO update schedule. Therefore, if all of the GPS receiver measurements of a multiple channel GPS receiver are to be made on the same FTF, the contents of the code accumulator, when extracted for purposes of obtaining a measurement, must be propagated forward by the amount of the time skew between the code NCO update events and the FTF.

5.7.1.3   Maintaining the Code Accumulator

Although there are many code accumulator time-keeping conventions that would work, the following convention is convenient for setting the initial code generator and NCO phase states [1]. Three counters, Z, X1, and P, are maintained as the code accumulator. The Z counter (19 bits) accumulates in GPS time increments of 1.5 seconds, then is reset one count short of the maximum Z count of 1 week = 403,200. Hence, the maximum Z count is 403,199. The X1 counter (24 bits) accumulates in GPS time increments of integer P chips, then is reset one count short of the maximum X1 count of 1.5 seconds = 15,345,000. Hence, the maximum X1 count is 15,344,999. The P counter accumulates in GPS time increments of fractions of a P chip, then rolls over one count short of one P chip. The P counter is the same length as the code NCO adder. A typical length is 32 bits.

Note in Figure 5.13 that the code NCO synthesizes a code clock rate that is an integer multiple, $2/D$, faster than the code generator spreading code chip rate, where D is the E-L code correlator spacing in chips (often $D = 1$). This is required in order to generate phase shifted replica codes, which are necessary for error detection in the code discriminator. The P counter tracks the fractional part of the code phase state, which is the code NCO state. Using this convention and assuming that the code NCO and code accumulator are updated every T seconds, the algorithm for maintaining the code accumulator is as follows. Note that the equals sign means "is replaced with."

$$P_{temp} = P + f_c \Delta\phi_{co} T$$
$$P = \text{fractional part of } P_{temp} \qquad\qquad \text{(chips)}$$
$$X_{temp} = (X1 + \text{whole part of } P_{temp})/15,345,000$$
$$X1 = \text{remainder of } X_{temp} \qquad\qquad \text{(chips)}$$
$$Z = \text{remainder of } [(Z + \text{whole part of } X_{temp})/403,200] \quad \text{(1.5 seconds)} \qquad (5.28)$$

where:

P_{temp} = temporary P register

f_c = code NCO clock frequency (Hz)

$\Delta\phi_{co}$ = code NCO phase increment per clock cycle

$\qquad$ = code NCO bias + code loop filter velocity correction

T = time between code NCO updates (seconds)

The earlier definition of $\Delta\phi_{CO}$ contains two components, the code NCO bias and the code loop filter velocity correction. The code NCO bias (see Figure 5.13) is the phase increment per clock that accounts for the marching of time in the P code replica code generator. When applied to the P replica code generator, this is 10.23 Mchip/s. When applied to the C/A replica code generator, this is 1.023 Mchip/s. The code E-L correlator spacing, D, requires a second output from the NCO to be $2/D$ faster than the spreading code chip rate to clock the 2-bit shift register. Algorithm (5.29) assumes that the NCO produces the code generator clock. If the code generator clock is produced by dividing the NCO shift register clock by $2/D$, then algorithm (5.29) and the NCO bias must be scaled accordingly. The code loop filter velocity correction is the combination of carrier aiding and code loop filter output. This combined output corrects the P replica code generator for Doppler (and a small order effect due to changes in ionospheric delay) referenced to the P code chip rate. Usually the code generator provides the divide-by-10 function required for the C/A code generator if both P and C/A codes are generated. This is the correct factor for the spreading code chip rate and the code Doppler/ionospheric delay components.

5.7.1.4 Obtaining a Measurement from the Code Accumulator

To obtain a measurement, the code accumulator must be propagated to the nearest FTF(n). This results in the set of measurements $P_i(n)$, $X1_i(n)$, and $Z_i(n)$ for SV_i. When converted to time units of seconds, the result is $T_{Ti}(n)$, the transmit time of SV_i at the receiver time epoch n. This is done very much like (5.28), except the time T is replaced with the skew time, T_s, and the code accumulator is not updated.

$$P_{temp} = P + f_c\,\Delta\phi_{co}\,T_s$$
$P_i(n)$ = fractional part of P_{temp} (chips)
X_{temp} = ($X1$ + whole part of P_{temp})/15,345,000
$X1_i(n)$ = remainder of X_{temp} (chips)
$Z_i(n)$ = remainder of [(Z + whole part of X_{temp})/403,200]   (1.5 seconds)   (5.29)

Note that (5.29) produces no error due to the measurement propagation process for the code accumulator measurements because the code NCO is running at a constant rate, $\Delta\phi_{CO}$ per clock, during the propagation interval. The following equation converts the code accumulator measurements to the SV_i transmit time, $T_{Ti}(n)$. Double precision floating point computations are assumed.

$$T_{Ti}(n) = \left[P_i(n) + X1_i(n)\right]/\left(10.23\times10^6\right) + Z_i(n)\times1.5 \quad \text{(seconds)} \qquad (5.30)$$

5.7.1.5 Synchronizing the Code Accumulator to the C/A code and P Code Generators

Synchronizing the code accumulator to the C/A code and P code generators is the most complicated part of the pseudorange measurement process. This is because the count sequences taking place in the code generator shift registers are PRN sequences, while the count sequence taking place in the code accumulator is a linear sequence. Fortunately, predictable reset timing events in the PRN shift registers permit them to be synchronized to the code accumulator. The first thought might be to design the code generator shift registers such that they contain the linear counters that are synchronized by the hardware and read by the receiver baseband process. However, the phase states of the code generators must be controlled by the receiver baseband process. So a better design is to use code setters in the hardware and maintain the code accumulator in the receiver baseband processor. By far, the simplest case is the C/A code generator setup, described first.

C/A Code Setup

Figure 5.31 illustrates a high-level block diagram of the P and C/A code generators, including their code setters. (Details of code generation were discussed in Chapter 4.) Recall from Section 4.3.1.1 that the C/A code generator consists of two 10-bit linear feedback shift registers called the G1 and G2 registers [2]. The C/A code setup requires one 10-bit code setter to initialize both the G1 and G2 registers in the C/A code generator. The phase states of the G1 and G2 registers are the same for every SV for the same GPS time of week. It is the tap combination on the G2 register (or equivalently, the delay added to the G2 register) in combination with the G1 register that determines the PRN number. A typical C/A code setter is capable of setting the G1 and G2 registers to their initial states and to their midpoint states. Since it requires only 1 ms for the C/A code generator to cycle through its complete state, this code setter design example holds the maximum delay to 1/2 ms until the C/A code generator is synchronized to the code accumulator after initialization of the code setter. This code setter design counts from 0 to 511 (1/2 C/A code epoch) and then rolls over.

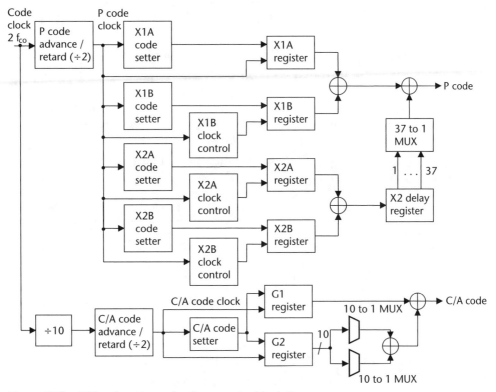

Figure 5.31   GPS code setter and code generator block diagram.

With the code setter hardware described earlier, the C/A code setup process works as follows. In accordance with a future time delay equal to a fixed number of code NCO reference clock cycles later, the code accumulator value for that future time is loaded into the code setter. This value matches the desired C/A code time after the scheduled time delay. The value for the code setter is computed just as if the 1,023 state C/A code generator had the same linear counting properties as a 1,023 bit counter. The code setter begins counting after the scheduled time delay, starting with the loaded count value. The code setter sets the G1 and G2 registers when the count rolls over. If the value sent from the code accumulator was greater than 511, the C/A code setter resets the G1 and G2 registers to their initial states. If the value sent from the code accumulator was less than or equal to 511, the code setter sets the G1 and G2 registers to their halfway points. As a result, the C/A replica code generator phase state matches the code accumulator GPS time state when the code setter rolls over and is synchronized to the code accumulator thereafter. When the receiver is tracking the SV after initialization, the code setter process can be repeated as often as desired without altering the C/A replica code generator phase state, because both the code accumulator and the code generator are ultimately synchronized by the same reference clock, the code NCO clock. If the receiver is in the search process, the C/A code advance/retard feature shown in Figure 5.31 provides the capability to add or remove clock cycles in half-chip increments. The code accumulator must keep track of these commanded changes. If the receiver can predict the satellite transmit time to within a few chips during the search process, it can use the code setter to perform a direct C/A code search. This condition is satisfied if the receiver has previously acquired four or more satellites and its navigation solution has converged. Ordinarily, all 1,023 C/A code chips are searched.

Some commercial C/A code receiver designs do not use a code NCO, but instead propagate the code generator at the nominal spreading code chip rate between code loop updates, tolerating the error build up due to code Doppler and ionospheric delay changes. Instead of the code NCO, a counter with a fractional chip advance/retard capability is used to adjust the phase of the C/A replica code generator in coarse phase increments. This results in a very low-resolution code measurement (large quantization noise) and a noisy pseudorange measurement in comparison to the code NCO technique.

The algorithm for the code accumulator output to the C/A code setter is as follows:

$$G = \text{remainder of} \left[\left\{ \text{whole part of} \left[(X1/10) \right] \right\} / 1{,}023 \right] \tag{5.31}$$

where:

G = future scheduled C/A code time value sent to the code setter

$X1$ = future scheduled GPS time of week in P chips ($0 \leq X1 \leq 15{,}344{,}999$)

An alternative design to the code setter timing technique is to precompute and store all 1,023 10-bit PRN states for G1 and G2 in two tables, then use the value G from (5.31) as the index to these tables. This would result in two 10-bit words being transferred into a G1 buffer register and a G2 buffer register. At the instance of the future code clock that corresponds to the computation of G, the buffer contents would be parallel transferred into the C/A code generator. This instantly aligns the replica code generator to the C/A code portion of the code accumulator. The ambiguity in the code accumulator must be removed by reading the handover word and placing it into the code accumulator at the correct epoch. This is described later.

P Code Setup
Figure 5.31 illustrates the high-level block diagram for the P code setup. (Details of P code generation were discussed in Chapter 4.) Recall from Chapter 4 that the P code generator contains four 12-bit linear feedback shift registers, called X1A, X1B, X2A, and X2B [2]. The PRN phase states of these four registers are the same for every SV PRN number at the same GPS time of the week. The unique PRN code is determined by the delay of the X2 output. Each of the four shift registers must have a corresponding 12-bit code setter. The P code setup is similar to the C/A code setup, but involves a much more complex code setter process, since, in general, all four shift registers must be reset at different time phases. There are two unusual code setter timing patterns that involve additional delays in the X1B, X2A, and X2B shift registers. The first occurs at the end of every X1 and X2 cycle. The second occurs at the end of the X2 cycle at the end of the GPS week.

Table 5.7 shows the count states for the first cycle of the GPS week for the four registers, starting with the 3,749th and 3,750th cycles of the X1A and X2A registers. After each cycle of X1A and X1B, the X1B epoch advances 1 chip ahead of X1A. The same pattern occurs between X2A and X2B. For the P code phases shown in Table 5.7, the X1 and X2 counts match during the first X1 cycle of the week (i.e., the X1A and X2A registers and the X1B and X2B registers are aligned to each other

Table 5.7   Count States for 3,749th and 3,750th Cycles of X1A in First X1 Cycle of Week

Z	X1	X1A	X1B	D1B	X2	X2A	D2A	X2B	D2B
0	15340563	3747	4092	0	15340563	3747	0	4092	0
0	15340564	3748	0	343	15340564	3748	0	0	380
.	.	.	.	.	.	.	.	.	.
0	15340907	4091	343	343	15340907	4091	0	343	380
0	15340908	0	344	343	15340908	0	37	344	380
.	.	.	.	.	.	.	.	.	.
0	15344655	3747	4091	343	15344655	3747	37	4091	380
0	15344656	3748	4092	343	15344656	3748	37	4092	380
0	15344657	3749	4092	342	15344657	3749	37	4092	379
.	.	.	.	.	.	.	.	.	.
0	15344998	4090	4092	1	15344998	4090	37	4092	38
0	15344999	4091	4092	0	15344999	4091	37	4092	37
1	0	0	0	0	15345000	4091	36	4092	36
.	.	.	.	.	.	.	.	.	.
1	35	35	35	0	15345035	4091	1	4092	1
1	36	36	36	0	15345036	4091	0	4092	0
1	37	37	37	0	0	0	0	0	0

Note: These count states are not the PRN code states contained in the shift registers.

in phase). This is the only time during the GPS week that they are aligned. As can be observed in Table 5.7, they become misaligned immediately after the first X1 cycle of the week completes. This is because following each X1 cycle, the X2 cycle continues for an additional 37 chips. These last two cycles are chosen for the most representative timing illustration because the X1 period is defined as 3,750 X1A cycles, which equals 1.5 seconds or one Z count. When the X1B code reaches its last chip in the last X1A cycle of an X1 cycle, the X1B register is held in its final state (4092) for 344 chips until the X1A register reaches its final state. Then X1A and X1B are reset. The Z count is incremented by one, and the X1 cycle starts over.

The X2 period is defined by 3,750 X2A cycles plus 37 chips. In the last X2A cycle of the X2 cycle, the X2B register is held in its final state (4092) until X2A reaches its final state, and then the X2A register is held in its final state (4091) and the X2B register continues to be held in its final state (4092) for an additional 37 chips. During this last X2A cycle, X2B is held in it final state (4092) for a total of 381 chips. Then X2A and X2B are reset and their cycles start over. Thus, the X2 epochs are delayed by 37 chips per Z count, with respect to the X1 epochs, until the end of the GPS week.

Note in Table 5.7 that the values for the X1A, X1B, X2A, and X2B registers are their count states, not their PRN code states. The PRN code states corresponding to the last two count states and the reset states are shown in Table 5.8. The only PRN code states that are important to the P code setters are the reset states, but the last two PRN code states prior to reset are useful for code generator verification purposes.

The previous description for X2 is correct except for the last X1A cycle of the GPS week shown in Table 5.9. During this last cycle, the X2A register holds in its final state (4091) and then the X2B register holds in its final state (4092) until the end of the last X1 cycle of the week. The X1B final state holding count is the same as for the rest of the week (compare with Table 5.7).

The same future scheduling must be performed to accomplish the code setup process for the P code generator as was used in the C/A code setup. The X1A and X2A code setters count P code clock cycles from 0 to 4,091 and the X1B and X2B code setters count from 0 to 4,092. This simplified code setter design example uses three countdown delay counters, D1B for X1B, D2A for X2A, and D2B for X2B, which are set by flags from the receiver baseband process at the end of an X1 or X2 cycle. Note that X1A is never delayed. It is possible to design the code setter so that the receiver baseband process does not have to set flags, but this simplified design example suffices to explain the principles involved. As observed in Tables 5.7 and

Table 5.8 PRN Code States Corresponding to Final Two and Reset Count States

Code Setter States (Decimal)	X1A Code (Hexadecimal)	X1B Code (Hexadecimal)	X2A Code (Hexadecimal)	X2B Code (Hexadecimal)
4090	892	·	E49	·
4091	124	955	C92	155
4092	·	2AA	·	2AA
0 (reset)	248	554	925	554

Table 5.9 Count States for 3,749th and 3,750th Cycles of X1A in Last X1 Cycle of Week

Z	X1	X1A	X1B	D1B	X2	X2A	D2A	X2B	D2B
403199	15339838	3022	3367	0	421475	4091	0	3989	0
403199	15339839	3023	3368	0	421476	0	1069	3990	0
.	.	.	.	.	.	.	.	.	.
403199	15339941	3125	3470	0	421578	102	1069	4092	0
403199	15339942	3126	3471	0	421579	103	1069	0	965
.	.	.	.	.	.	.	.	.	.
403199	15340563	3747	4092	0	422200	724	1069	621	965
403199	15340564	3748	0	343	422201	725	1069	622	965
.	.	.	.	.	.	.	.	.	.
403199	15340907	4091	343	343	422544	1068	1069	965	965
403199	15340908	0	344	343	422545	1069	1069	966	965
.	.	.	.	.	.	.	.	.	.
403199	15343929	3021	3365	343	425566	4090	1069	3987	965
403199	15343930	3022	3366	343	425567	4091	1069	3988	965
403199	15343931	3023	3367	343	425568	4091	1068	3989	965
.	.	.	.	.	.	.	.	.	.
403199	15344033	3125	3469	343	425670	4091	966	4091	965
403199	15344034	3126	3470	343	425671	4091	965	4092	965
403199	15344035	3127	3471	343	425672	4091	964	4092	964
.	.	.	.	.	.	.	.	.	.
403199	15344655	3747	4091	343	426292	4091	344	4092	344
403199	15344656	3748	4092	343	426293	4091	343	4092	343
403199	15344657	3749	4092	342	426294	4091	342	4092	342
.	.	.	.	.	.	.	.	.	.
403199	15344998	4090	4092	1	426635	4091	1	4092	1
403199	15344999	4091	4092	0	426636	4091	0	4092	0
0	0	0	0	0	0	0	0	0	0

Note: These count states are not the PRN code states contained in the shift registers.

5.9, D1B is always set to a count of 343 chips. D2A is set to 37 and D2B is set to 380 unless it is at the end of the last X2 cycle of the week, in which case they are set to 1,069 and 965, respectively. The rule followed by the code setters is that if their delay counter is nonzero, they hold their final states until the delay counter counts down to zero, then they rollover to the zero (reset) states. The delay counters rule is that if their code setters are not in the final state, they hold their delay counts until the code setter reaches its final state, then they begin counting down. The receiver baseband rule is that if the code setter counts to the reset state can be reached without using the delay counter, the receiver baseband process adjusts the code setter to the appropriate value and does not set the delay counter flag. Otherwise, it sets the appropriate delay counter flags (which instructs the code setter hardware to put the appropriate maximum delays into the counters). This rule avoids the need for the code setter hardware to set any other count state into the delay counters other than their maximum delay counts.

The code setters are loaded with the timing state valid at the first epoch that the counting process begins. As each code setter rolls over to zero, it resets its corresponding code register to that register's initial code state. In addition, the X1A divide-by-3,750 counter and the Z counter must be set to their correct states when the X1A register is reset. Similarly, the X1B divide-by-3,749 counter, the X2A divide-by-3,750 counter, and the X2B divide-by-3,749 counter must be set to their correct states when their respective registers are reset by their code setters. Thus, when all four code setters have rolled over, the code generator is synchronized to the code accumulator. This requires approximately 500 μs in the worst case.

The final step in the explanation of the P code setter operation is the algorithm for converting the code accumulator into P code setter states and the setting of the three flags, D1B, D2A, and D2B. The code setter timing and the rules have already been explained. Figure 5.32 depicts the logical flow diagram that covers all P code setter timing conditions. This diagram should be compared to the count states in Tables 5.7 and 5.9. Note that if the P code generator is already synchronized to the code accumulator, the action of the P code setter does not alter the replica code state, since the reset pulses occur at exactly the same times that they naturally occur in the code generator. However, to ensure that the receiver baseband software code accumulator always matches the P code generator code state, it is prudent for the software to periodically repeat the code setup process.

Alternatively, all 4,092 PRN states of the 12-bit X1A and X1B shift registers and all 4,093 PRN states of the 12-bit X2A and X2B shift registers can be precomputed and stored as lookup tables that are indexed by the delays computed in Figure 5.32 (without the need for the flag setting logic). These PRN values can then be transferred to buffer code setter registers and their contents transferred into their respective registers at the appropriate epoch.

With Y code operation, the same P code processes are implemented in the same manner and then encrypted by a specialized hardware design. In the original military receivers, this was called the AOC. The AOC output, when combined with P code, synthesizes the Y code function before correlation with the incoming SV Y code signals. The AOC implements a classified encryption algorithm, and each receiver channel requires one AOC. The component that synchronizes all of the AOCs to their respective replica P code generators is the PPSSM. In newer military receivers, the AOC and the PPSSM functions are integrated into the receiver design. The new military GPS receiver engine is the SAASM. The SAASM is a more secure advanced military GPS receiver design. Only keyed PPS receivers can replicate the Y code.

This code setter design example supports direct P(Y) code acquisition. Direct P(Y) code acquisition is used if the receiver can accurately predict the satellite transmit time so that less time is required to acquire the P(Y) code by direct sequence than to perform a C/A code search and handover. The direct P(Y) code acquisition condition is satisfied if the receiver has previously acquired four or more satellites and its

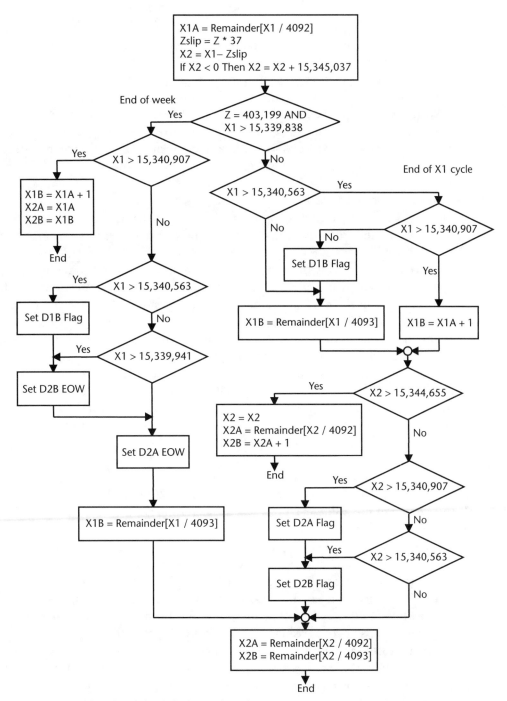

Figure 5.32 Flowchart of P code setter algorithm.

navigation solution has converged. Under certain jamming conditions, it may be impossible to acquire the C/A code but possible to acquire P(Y) code. Then, direct P(Y) code acquisition is essential. This is possible only if the navigation state has sufficient position, velocity, and time precision, plus the ephemeris data for all SVs to be acquired, or this information is transferred to the receiver by an operating host

GPS receiver. The most sensitive navigation state parameter is usually precise time because there is 1m of range uncertainty to each SV that must be searched for every 3 ns of time uncertainty. Massively parallel correlators help to minimize the sensitivity to time and position uncertainty. Reference [6] describes a multiple correlator/search detector architecture that supports rapid direct P(Y) code acquisition. If the receiver is engaged in the direct P(Y) code search process, the P code advance/retard function shown in Figure 5.31 provides the capability to add clock cycles or remove clock cycles in 1/2-chip increments. The code accumulator keeps track of these changes.

Obtaining Transmit Time from the C/A Code

Figure 5.33[2] illustrates the GPS timing relationships that enable a C/A code receiver to determine the true GPS transmit time. The C/A code repeats every 1 ms and is therefore ambiguous every 1 ms of GPS time (about every 300 km of range). There is a HOW at the beginning of every one of the five subframes of the satellite navigation message. The HOW contains the Z count of the first data bit transition boundary at the beginning of the next subframe. This is the first data bit of the TLM that precedes every HOW. The beginning of this 20-ms data bit is synchronized with the beginning of one of the satellite's C/A code 1-ms epochs, but there are 20 C/A code epochs in every data bit period. At this subframe epoch, the X1 register has just produced a carry to the Z-count, so the X1 count is zero. The C/A code ambiguity is resolved by setting the Z count to the HOW value and the X1 count to zero at the beginning of the next subframe. In practice, the actual values of the Z count and X1 count are computed for a near-term C/A code epoch without waiting for the next subframe.

The Z-count and X1-count will be correct if the GPS receiver has determined its bit synchronization to within 1 ms or better accuracy. This level of accuracy will perfectly align the 1-ms C/A code epoch with the 20-ms data bit transition point of the first bit in the following TLM word. Therefore, the C/A code transmit time will be unambiguous and correct. If the bit synchronization process makes an error in the alignment of the 1-ms replica C/A code epoch with the 20-ms data bit epoch, then the X1 count will be off by some integer multiple of 1 ms. If the receiver attempts a handover to P code and fails, the typical strategy is to try the handover again with 1-ms changes in the value used for X1, then 2-ms changes, and so on, before attempting to redetermine bit synchronization, which can take 6 seconds or longer and prevents processing of GPS measurements until complete.

A successful handover to P code verifies the bit synchronization process. However, if the GPS receiver is a C/A code receiver, the verification for correct bit synchronization is more difficult. This verification task must be performed by the navigation process. Since 1 ms of GPS time error is equivalent to about 300 km of pseudorange error, the navigation error can be quite serious. In the unlikely case that every channel makes the identical bit sync error, the navigation position error washes out of the position solution into the time bias solution, and the GPS time is in error by 1 ms. The typical bit sync error manifestations in the navigation solution are unrealistic local level velocity and elevation computations. The latitude and lon-

---

2.   Jerry D. Holmes originally developed a similar GPS timing chart for use by the GPS Systems Engineering staff at Texas Instruments, Inc., during the GPS phase I development program, circa 1976.

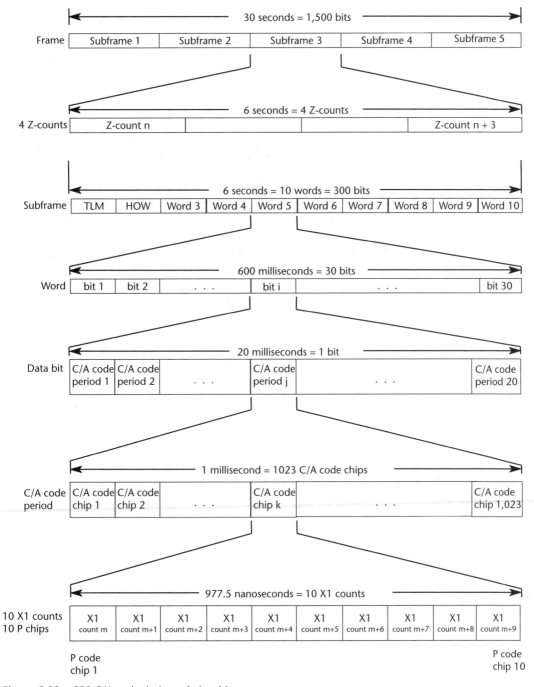

Figure 5.33   GPS C/A code timing relationships.

gitude computations are also unrealistic, but there is usually no boundary condition for comparison. However, the velocity and elevation computations can be compared to acceptable boundary conditions.

The bit synchronization process is a statistical process that is dependent on C/N_0. It will occasionally be incorrect. It will be incorrect almost every time the

C/N_0 drops below the bit synchronization design threshold. This causes serious navigation integrity problems for C/A code receivers under conditions of signal attenuation or RF interference. This problem is compounded if there is no design provision to adapt the bit synchronization process for poor C/N_0 conditions or for the navigation process to check for bit synchronization errors.

5.7.2 Delta Pseudorange

The definition of delta pseudorange to SV_i is as follows.

$$\Delta\rho_i(n) = \rho_i(n+J) - \rho_i(n-K) \quad (m) \tag{5.32}$$

where:

$\rho_i(n+J)$ = pseudorange at J FTF epochs later than FTF(n) (m)

$\rho_i(n-K)$ = pseudorange at K FTF epochs earlier than FTF(n) (m)

$J = 0$ or K depending on design preferences (dimensionless)

Even though (5.32) implies that delta pseudorange could be derived from the code tracking loop, the result would be a very noisy measurement. This differential measurement will be more than two orders of magnitude less noisy if taken from the carrier tracking loop operated as a PLL. If the carrier loop is operated as a FLL, the measurement is taken the same way, but the FLL is only about 100 times less noisy than code measurements.

The carrier Doppler phase measurements are extracted by the receiver baseband process from the carrier tracking loop using a carrier accumulator. It is more simple but similar to using the code accumulator to extract transmit time measurements from the code tracking loop. The carrier accumulator consists of the integer cycle count, N_{CA}, and the fractional cycle count, Φ_{CA}, of the carrier Doppler phase measurement.

The carrier accumulator is updated after each carrier loop output to the carrier NCO using the following algorithm (remembering that the equal sign means that the right-hand side replaces the value on the left-hand side):

$$\begin{aligned}
\Phi_{temp} &= \Phi_{CA} + f_c\Delta\Phi_{CA}T \\
\Phi_{CA} &= \text{fractional part of } \Phi_{temp} \quad (\text{cycles}) \\
N_{CA} &= N_{CA}(\text{last value}) + \text{integer part of } \Phi_{temp} \quad (\text{cycles})
\end{aligned} \tag{5.33}$$

where:

Φ_{temp} = temporary Φ_{CA} register

f_c = carrier NCO clock frequency (Hz)

$\Delta\Phi_{CA}$ = carrier NCO carrier Doppler phase increment per clock cycle

= carrier loop filter velocity correction + velocity aiding (if any)

T = time between carrier NCO updates (seconds)

N_{CA} = integer carrier Doppler phase cycles since some starting point

The fractional part of the carrier accumulator, Φ_{CA}, is initialized to the same state as the carrier NCO at the beginning of the search process, which is typically zero. The integer number of carrier Doppler phase cycles, N_{CA}, is ambiguous. Since only differential measurements are taken from this register, the ambiguity does not matter. The carrier integer accumulator is usually set to zero when the carrier loop is first closed following a successful search operation. Note that the marching of time carrier NCO bias (see Figure 5.2) is not included in the carrier accumulator because it is simply a bias term to match the carrier at IF. Since only differential measurements are extracted from the carrier accumulator, this bias term, if included, would cancel out. The counter rolls over when the Doppler cycle count exceeds the count capacity or underflows if the Doppler count is in the reverse direction and drops below the zero count. The differential measurement comes out correct if the counter capacity is large enough to ensure that this happens no more than once between any set of differential measurements extracted from the carrier accumulator.

To extract a carrier Doppler phase measurement, $N_{CAi}(n)$, $\Phi_{CAi}(n)$, for SV_i corresponding to the carrier accumulator, it must be propagated forward to the nearest FTF(n) by the skew time, T_s, similar to the technique used in the code tracking loop.

$$\Phi_{temp} = \Phi_{CA} + f_c \Delta\Phi_{CA} T_S$$
$$\Phi_{CAi} = \text{fractional part of } \Phi_{temp} \quad (\text{cycles}) \tag{5.34}$$
$$N_{CAi} = \text{integer part of } \Phi_{temp} \quad (\text{cycles})$$

Note that there is no error due to the measurement propagation process for the carrier Doppler phase measurement because the carrier NCO is running at a constant rate, $\Delta\Phi_{CA}$ per clock, during the propagation interval.

The precise delta pseudorange is simply the change in phase in the carrier accumulator during a specified time. The formula for extracting the delta pseudorange from the carrier accumulator is as follows.

$$\Delta\rho_i(n) = \left\{ \begin{array}{l} \left[N_{CAi}(n+J) - N_{CAi}(n-K) \right] + \\ \left[\Phi_{CAi}(n+J) - \Phi_{CAi}(n-K) \right] \end{array} \right\} \lambda_L \quad (\text{m}) \tag{5.35}$$

where:

λ_L = wavelength of the L-band carrier frequency

= 0.1903 m/cycle for L1

= 0.2442 m/cycle for L2

As a design example, suppose the navigation measurement incorporation rate is 1 Hz (a very typical rate), then the delta pseudorange measurement should begin and end with each range measurement. To accommodate this for an FTF period of 20 ms, $J = 0$ and $K = -50$. Alternatively, if the navigation throughput permits, the delta pseudorange measurement could be incorporated at a 50-Hz rate with $J = 0$ and $K = 1$. In either case, the delta range measurement should be modeled by the navigation process as a change in range over the previous second, not as an average velocity over the interval.

5.7.3 Integrated Doppler

The definition of integrated Doppler is obtained from (5.34). The integrated Doppler measurement for SV_i at FTF(n) can be converted to units of meters as follows.

$$ID_i(n) = \left[N_{CAi}(n) + \Phi_{CAi}(n) \right] \lambda_L \quad \text{(m)} \tag{5.36}$$

This measurement, when derived from a PLL, is used for ultraprecise differential interferometric GPS applications, such as static and kinematic surveying or for attitude determination. Note that when the integer cycle count ambiguity is resolved by the interferometric process, this measurement is equivalent to a pseudorange measurement with more than two orders of magnitude less noise than the transmit time (pseudorange) measurements obtained from the code loop. The integrated Doppler noise for a high-quality GPS receiver designed for interferometric applications typically is about 1 mm (1 sigma) under good signal conditions. A transmit time (pseudorange) measurement typically will have about 1m of noise (1 sigma). Once the integer cycle ambiguity is resolved, as long as the PLL does not slip cycles, the ambiguity remains resolved thereafter. (Further information on differential interferometric processing and ambiguity resolution is provided in Section 8.4.)

Two GPS receivers that are making transmit time and carrier Doppler phase measurements on their respective receiver epochs will in general be time skewed with respect to one another. For ultraprecise differential applications, it is possible to remove virtually all of the effects of time-variable bias by eliminating this time skew between GPS receivers (i.e., spatially separated GPS receivers can make synchronous measurements). This is accomplished by precisely aligning the measurements to GPS time epochs instead of to (asynchronous) receiver FTF epochs. Initially, of course, the measurements must be obtained with respect to the receiver FTF epochs. After the navigation process determines the time bias between its FTF epochs and true GPS time, each navigation request for a set of receiver measurements should include the current estimate of the time bias with respect to the FTF (a very slowly changing value if the reference oscillator is stable). The receiver measurement process then propagates the measurements to the FTF plus the time bias as nearly perfect (within nanoseconds) of true GPS time. These measurements are typically on the GPS 1-second time of week epoch. This is important for precision differential operation since as little as 1 second of time skew between receivers corresponds to satellite position changes of nearly 4,000m. Of course, the differential measurements can be propagated to align to the same time epoch if the GPS receiver's measurements are time skewed, but not with the accuracy that can be obtained if they are aligned to a common GPS time epoch within each GPS receiver during the original measurement process. The carrier Doppler measurement must be corrected for the frequency error in the satellite's atomic standard (i.e., reference oscillator) before measurement incorporation. This correction is broadcast in the satellite's navigation message as the a_{f1} term (see Sections 4.4 and 7.2.1). The measurement also includes the receiver's reference oscillator frequency error. This error is determined as a time bias rate correction by the navigation solution. For some applications, it is also corrected for the differential ionospheric delay, but this is usually a negligible error.

5.8 Signal Acquisition

There is a large amount of literature on PRN code acquisition in direct sequence receivers. For an extensive historical survey and descriptions on time domain search detectors, [15] is recommended. Reference [16] describes the use of modern frequency domain search techniques for rapid acquisition. The following GPS signal acquisition material is based on traditional time domain search techniques.

GPS signal acquisition is a search process. This search process, like the tracking process, requires replication of both the code and the carrier of the SV to acquire the SV signal (i.e., the signal match for success is two dimensional). The range dimension is associated with the replica code. The Doppler dimension is associated with the replica carrier. The initial search process is always a C/A code search for C/A code receivers and usually begins with a C/A code search for P(Y) code receivers. The initial C/A code search usually involves replicating all 1,023 C/A code phase states in the range dimension. The criteria for direct C/A code and direct P(Y) code acquisitions were discussed in the previous section. If the range and Doppler uncertainty are known, then the search pattern should cover the 3-sigma values of the uncertainty. If the uncertainty is large in either or both dimensions, the search pattern is correspondingly large, and the expected search time increases. Some criteria must be established to determine when to terminate the search process for a given SV and select another candidate SV. Fortunately, the range dimension for C/A code search is bounded by the ambiguity of C/A code to only 1,023 chips total range uncertainty, but it is essentially unbounded for direct P(Y) code search.

The following example assumes that a C/A code search is being performed and that all 1,023 C/A code phases are being examined. The code phase is typically searched in increments of 1/2 chip. Each code phase search increment is a code bin. Each Doppler bin is roughly $2/(3T)$ Hz, where T is the search dwell time (the longer the dwell time, the smaller the Doppler bin). The combination of one code bin and one Doppler bin is a cell. Figure 5.34 illustrates the two-dimensional search process. If the Doppler uncertainty is unknown and the SV Doppler cannot be computed from a knowledge of the user position and time plus the SV orbit data, then the maximum user velocity plus just less than 800 m/s maximum SV Doppler (for worst case, see Section 2.5) for a stationary user must be searched in both directions about zero Doppler.

As stated earlier, one Doppler bin is defined as approximately $2/(3T)$, where $T =$ signal integration time per cell or dwell time per cell. Dwell times can vary from less than 1 ms (Doppler bins of about 667 Hz) for strong signals up to 10 ms (67-Hz Doppler bins) for weak signals. The poorer the expected C/N_0, then the longer the dwell time (and overall search time) must be in order to have reasonable success of signal acquisition. Unfortunately, the actual C/N_0 is unknown until after the SV sig-

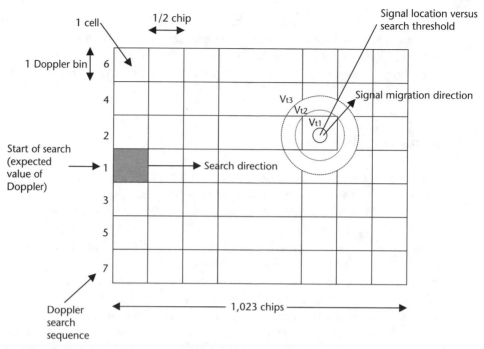

Figure 5.34   Two-dimensional C/A code search pattern.

nal is acquired. Signal obscuration (trees, buildings, snow or ice on the antenna, and so forth), RF interference, ionospheric scintillation, and antenna gain roll-off can all significantly reduce C/N_0 (see Chapter 6).

Referring to Figure 5.34, the search pattern usually follows the range direction from early to late in order to avoid multipath with Doppler held constant until all range bins are searched for each Doppler value. The direct arrival of a signal subject to multipath is always ahead in time of the reflected arrivals. In the Doppler bin direction, the search pattern typically starts from the mean value of the Doppler uncertainty (zero Doppler if the actual LOS velocity estimate is unknown) and then goes symmetrically one Doppler bin at a time on either side of this value until the 3-sigma Doppler uncertainty has been searched. Then the search pattern is repeated, typically with a reduction in the search threshold scale factor. It is important to recognize that the C/A code autocorrelation and crosscorrelation sidelobes can cause false signal detections if these sidelobes are strong enough. The sidelobes tend to increase as the search dwell time is decreased. To counter this problem, a combination of both increased dwell time (to minimize sidelobes) and a high detector threshold setting (to reject sidelobes) can be used for the initial search pass. On subsequent search passes, the dwell time and threshold can be decreased. The penalty for this scheme is increased search time when the C/N_0 is low.

During the dwell time, T, in each cell, the I and Q signals are integrated and dumped and the envelope $\sqrt{I^2 + Q^2}$ is computed or estimated. Each envelope is compared to a threshold to determine the presence or absence of the SV signal. The detection of the signal is a statistical process because each cell either contains noise with the signal absent or noise with the signal present. Each case has its own probability density function (pdf). Figure 5.35 illustrates a single trial (binary) decision

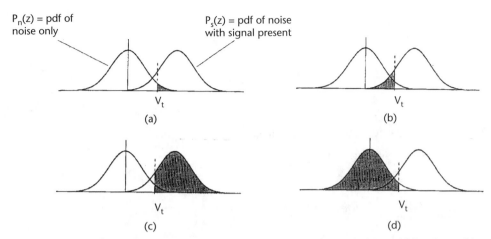

Figure 5.35   Pdfs for a binary decision: (a) shaded area represents probability of false alarm, (b) shaded area represents probability of false dismissal, (c) shaded area represents probability of detection, and (d) shaded area represents probability of correct dismissal.

example where both pdfs are shown. The pdf for noise with no signal present, $p_n(z)$, has a zero mean. The pdf for noise with the signal present, $p_s(z)$, has a nonzero mean. The single trial threshold is usually based on an acceptable single trial probability of false alarm, P_{fa}. For the chosen threshold, V_t, any cell envelope that is at or above the threshold is detected as the presence of the signal. Any cell envelope that is below the threshold is detected as noise. There are four outcomes of the single trial (binary) decision processes illustrated in Figure 5.35, two wrong and two right. By knowing the pdfs of the envelopes, the single trial probability can be computed by an appropriate integration with the threshold as one limit and infinity as the other. These integrations are shown as the shaded areas in Figure 5.35. The two statistics that are of most interest for the signal detection process are the single trial probability of detection, P_d, and the single trial probability of false alarm, P_{fa}. These are determined as follows:

$$P_d = \int_{V_t}^{\infty} p_s \, dz \tag{5.37}$$

$$P_{fa} = \int_{V_t}^{\infty} p_n \, dz \tag{5.38}$$

where:

$p_s(z)$ = pdf of the envelope in the presence of the signal

$p_n(z)$ = pdf of the envelope with the signal absent

To determine these pdfs, assume that I and Q have a Gaussian distribution. Assuming that the envelope is formed by $\sqrt{I^2 + Q^2}$, then $p_s(z)$ is a Ricean distribution [17] defined by:

$$p_s(z) = \begin{cases} \dfrac{z}{\sigma_n^2} e^{-\left(\frac{z^2+A^2}{2\sigma_n^2}\right)} I_0\left(\dfrac{zA}{\sigma_n^2}\right), & z \geq 0 \\ 0, & z < 0 \end{cases} \tag{5.39}$$

where:

z = value of the random variable

σ^2 = RMS noise power

A = RMS signal amplitude

$I_0\left(\dfrac{zA}{\sigma_n}\right)$ = modified Bessel function of zero order

$I_0(x) \approx \dfrac{e^x}{\sqrt{2\pi x}}$ for $x \gg 1$

Equation (5.39) for $z \geq 0$ can be expressed in terms of the predetection SNR as presented to the envelope detector, C/N (dimensionless), as follows:

$$p_s(z) = \dfrac{z}{\sigma_n^2} e^{-\left(\frac{z^2}{2\sigma_n^2}+C/N\right)} I_0\left(\dfrac{z\sqrt{2C/N}}{\sigma_n}\right) \tag{5.40}$$

where:

C/N = predetection signal to noise ratio

$C/N = A^2 / 2\sigma_n^2$

$\quad = (C/N_0)T$

T = search dwell time

For the case where there is no signal present, then evaluating (5.39) for $A = 0$ yields a Rayleigh distribution for $p_n(z)$, which is defined by:

$$p_n(z) = \dfrac{z}{\sigma_n^2} e^{-\left(\frac{z^2}{2\sigma_n^2}\right)} \tag{5.41}$$

The result of integrating (5.38) using the pdf of (5.41) is:

$$p_{fa} = e^{-\left(\frac{V_t^2}{2\sigma_n^2}\right)} \tag{5.42}$$

Rearranging (5.42) yields the threshold in terms of the desired single trial probability of false alarm and the measured 1-sigma noise power:

$$V_t = \sigma_n \sqrt{-2 \ln P_{fa}} = X\sigma_n \tag{5.43}$$

For example, if it is desired that $P_{fa} = 16\%$, then $V_t = X\sigma_n = 1.9144615\,\sigma_n$. Using this result, the single trial probability of detection, P_d, is computed for the expected C/N_0 and dwell time, T, using (5.37) and (5.40) with $\sigma_n = 1$ (normalized). Some examples of the single trial probability of detection are shown in Table 5.10 for various SNRs.

Figure 5.36, taken from [18], illustrates the structure of search detectors used for signal acquisition. Referring to Figure 5.36, two types of search detectors used in GPS receiver designs will be described. A variable dwell time detector makes a "yes" or "no" decision in a variable interval of time if "maybe" conditions are present. A fixed dwell time detector makes a "yes" or "no" decision in a fixed interval of time. The probability of detection and especially the poor false alarm rate from single dwell time detectors (single trial decisions as shown in Table 5.10) are usually unsatisfactory for GPS applications. So, single dwell time search detector schemes are seldom used. All other things being equal, a properly tuned variable dwell time (sequential) multiple trial detector will search faster than a fixed dwell time multiple trial detector.

5.8.1   Tong Search Detector

The first example of a search algorithm is a sequential variable dwell time search detector called the Tong detector. Figure 5.37 illustrates the block diagram of the Tong detector. Search algorithms are typically implemented as a receiver baseband process. Because of its simplicity, the Tong detector can be implemented as part of the receiver correlation and preprocessing hardware, with its search parameters programmed by the baseband process. The Tong detector has a reasonable computational burden and is excellent for detecting signals with an expected $(C/N_0)_{dB}$ of 25 dB-Hz or higher. If acquisition is to be performed under heavy jamming conditions where the $(C/N_0)_{dB}$ will be less than this, then a hybrid maximum-likelihood search detector should be used. A pure maximum-likelihood search detector would require the receiver hardware to produce the results of all of the search dwells in parallel, which is usually impractical. The Tong detector is a suboptimal search algorithm that requires an average factor of only 1.58 longer to make a decision than a maximum-likelihood (optimum) search algorithm [19].

Table 5.10   Single Trial Probability of Detection

C/N	P_d	$(C/N_0)_{dB} = (C/N)_{dB} - 10\log_{10}T\ (dB\text{-}Hz)$			
(ratio)	(dimensionless)	$T = 1\ ms$	$T = 2.5\ ms$	$T = 5\ ms$	$T = 10\ ms$
1.0	0.431051970	30.00	26.02	23.01	20.00
2.0	0.638525844	33.01	29.03	26.02	23.01
3.0	0.780846119	34.77	30.79	27.78	24.77
4.0	0.871855378	36.02	32.04	29.03	26.02
5.0	0.927218854	36.99	33.01	30.00	26.99
6.0	0.959645510	37.78	33.80	30.79	27.78
7.0	0.978075147	38.45	34.47	31.46	28.45
8.0	0.988294542	39.03	35.05	32.04	29.03
9.0	0.993845105	39.54	35.56	32.55	29.54

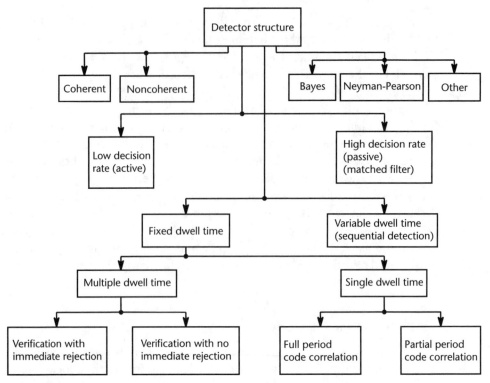

Figure 5.36 Structure of search detectors. (*Source:* [18].)

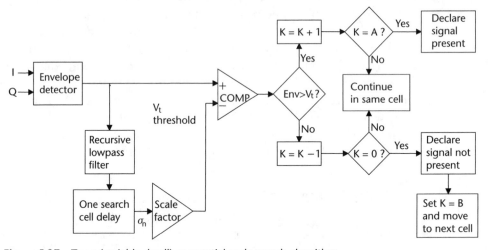

Figure 5.37 Tong (variable dwell) sequential code search algorithm.

The operation of the Tong detector is as follows:

1. Every T seconds an integrated correlation envelope is formed as $\sqrt{I^2 + Q^2}$ (or its approximation). If there are three correlators in the receiver, each correlator is typically spaced 1/2-chip apart and three Tong detectors are used. In this manner, three code bins at a time are searched, and the search

process speeds up by (almost) a factor of three. It is not quite a factor of three because all three search cells must be dismissed before the search process can proceed to the next three cells. In order to generate the I and Q signals, the receiver baseband search process has synthesized the correct Doppler (the center frequency of the respective search process Doppler bin in the search pattern) and the correct replica C/A code phase with the corresponding spreading code chip rate plus code Doppler. For example, the C/A code phase corresponding to the first of its 1,023 states is where the C/A code setter resets the G1 and G2 registers at the beginning of the cell integrate and dump time. The marching of time for the C/A code generator plus the code Doppler keeps its phase aligned to this cell. If the cell is dismissed, then the C/A code generator phase is advanced by 1/2 chip (times the number of correlators), and the search process is continued for that Doppler bin until the last C/A code phase state has been reached. Then the Doppler center frequency is shifted to the next bin in the search pattern and the process is repeated.

2. At each cell the up/down counter (K) is initialized to $K = B = 1$. Where a higher probability of detection and lower probability of false alarm are desired at the expense of search speed, then $B = 2$. If the envelope sample exceeds the threshold, V_t, then the up/down counter is incremented by one. If the sample does not exceed the threshold, then the up/down counter is decremented by one. As shown in Figure 5.37, one technique for obtaining the RMS noise, σ_n, which is used to set the threshold, is to pass the correlation envelopes into a recursive lowpass filter with a delay of one search cell. A better technique is for the receiver to synthesize the RMS noise by correlating the input signal with an unused PRN code (e.g., the G1 register output for C/A code search). The RMS output is multiplied by a scale factor, X, to obtain the threshold, V_t. Assuming that the envelope is formed by $\sqrt{I^2 + Q^2}$, then the scale factor is determined from (5.43), $X = \sqrt{-2\ln(P_{fa})}$, where P_{fa} is the single trial probability of false alarm. Typically, the envelope is determined from the Robertson approximation. In this case, it has been determined [17] that a multiplier factor of 1.08677793 must be used for the scale factor, so that: $X_R = 1.08677793\ X = \sqrt{-2.3621724\ln(P_{fa})}$.

   The determination of the most suitable single trial probability of false alarm, the overall false alarm, and the overall probability of detection is a tuning process. The final determination must be obtained by simulation. Assuming the Robertson envelope approximation, the scale factor range is typically from 1.8 ($P_{fa} = 25\%$) for low expected $(C/N_0)_{dB}$ (≥ 25 dB-Hz) to 2.1 ($P_{fa} = 16\%$) for high expected $(C/N_0)_{dB}$ (≥ 39 dB-Hz).

3. If the counter contents reach the maximum value, A, then the signal is declared present, and the Tong search is terminated. This is typically followed by additional vernier search processes designed to find the code phase and Doppler combination that produces the peak detection of the signal before the code/carrier loop closure process is begun. If the counter reaches 0, then the signal is declared absent and the search process is

advanced to the next cell. The determination of A must be by simulation. Its selection is a tradeoff between search speed and probability of detection, but a typical range is $A = 12$ for low expected C/N_0 to $A = 8$ for high expected C/N_0. Note that it is possible for the Tong detector to get trapped into an extended dwell in the same cell under certain poor signal conditions. For this reason, a *mush* counter should be used that counts every test within the same cell then declares the signal not present when the mush count exceeds A by some reasonable amount.

The mean number of dwell times to dismiss a cell containing noise only is determined as follows:

$$N_n = \frac{1}{1 - 2P_{fa}} \tag{5.44}$$

Since most of the time is spent searching cells that contain only noise, the Tong detector search speed can be estimated from:

$$R_S = \frac{d}{N_n T} = \frac{d(1 - 2P_{fa})}{T} \quad \text{(chips/s)} \tag{5.45}$$

where d = chips per cell (typically 1/2 chip per cell)

For example, for $P_{fa} = 16\%$, a dwell time of 5 ms, and 1/2 chip per cell, the code search rate is = 68 chips/s. Note that the search speed increases when the probability of false alarm decreases.

The overall probability of false alarm for the Tong detector is [19]:

$$P_{FA} = \frac{\left(\frac{1 - P_{fa}}{P_{fa}}\right)^B - 1}{\left(\frac{1 - P_{fa}}{P_{fa}}\right)^{A + B - 1} - 1} \tag{5.46}$$

The overall probability of detection for the Tong detector is [19]:

$$P_D = \frac{\left(\frac{1 - P_d}{P_d}\right)^B - 1}{\left(\frac{1 - P_d}{P_d}\right)^{A + B - 1} - 1} \tag{5.47}$$

Figure 5.38 is a plot of (5.47) as a function of the Tong detector input SNR, $(C/N)_{dB}$, $= 10\log_{10}(C/N)$ expressed in units of decibels, with $B = 1$ and A as a running parameter ranging from 2 to 12, and with the overall probability of false alarm set equal to 1×10^{-6} for every case [17]. Figure 5.38 illustrates the excellent search detector performance of the Tong detector and the increased sensitivity of the detector

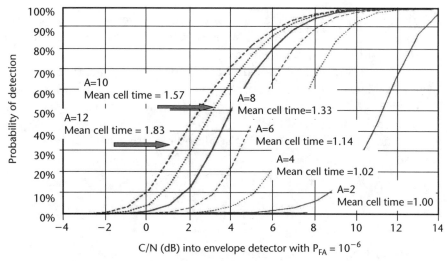

Figure 5.38   Probability of detection for Tong search detector.

with the increase of A. The cost of increasing A is shown as a decrease in the search rate.

5.8.2   *M* of *N* Search Detector

The second example of a search algorithm is a fixed interval detector called the M of N search detector. Figure 5.39 depicts the M of N search algorithm. The M of N search detector takes N envelopes and compares them to the threshold for each cell. If M or more of them exceed the threshold, then the signal is declared present. If not, the signal is declared absent, and the process is repeated for the next cell in the search pattern. These are treated as Bernoulli trials, and the number of envelopes, n, that exceed the threshold has a binomial distribution. The same threshold-setting technique is used and the same formula applies for the single trial probability of

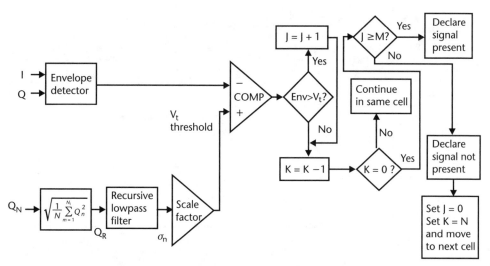

Figure 5.39   *M* of *N* (fixed interval) sequential code search algorithm.

false alarm, P_{fa}, as was described for the Tong detector. Note that the M of N algorithm in Figure 5.39 contains a superior reference noise source technique compared to that of the Tong algorithm in Figure 5.37. This requires a preplanned receiver design that provides the same PRN code for each channel that is not used by (does not correlate with) any SV in the constellation—such as G1(t) for C/A code and PRN 38 for P(Y) code—and one component of a spare complex correlator (shown as Q_N component in Figure 5.39).

The overall probability of false alarm in N trials is [17]:

$$P_{FA} = \sum_{n=M}^{N} \binom{N}{n} P_{fa}^{n} \left(1 - P_{fa}\right)^{N-n} = 1 - \sum_{n=0}^{M-1} \binom{N}{n} P_{fa}^{n} \left(1 - P_{fa}\right)^{N-n}$$

$$= 1 - B\left(M - 1; N, P_{fa}\right) \tag{5.48}$$

where $B(k;N,p)$ is the cumulative pdf.

The overall probability of detection in N trials is [17]:

$$P_{D} = \sum_{n=M}^{N} \binom{N}{n} P_{d}^{n} \left(1 - P_{d}\right)^{N-n} = 1 - B\left(M - 1; N, P_{d}\right) \tag{5.49}$$

Figure 5.40 illustrates the M of N probability of detection versus C/N into the detector for $N = 8$ and $M = 3, 4, 5,$ and 6 when $P_{FA} = 1 \times 10^{-6}$. By inspection of Figure 5.40, it is clear that $M = 5$ is the optimum value. The data were generated by computing P_{fa} given M, N, and P_{FA} using the following equation [17]:

$$P_{fa} = B^{-1}\left(M - 1; N, 1 - P_{FA}\right) \tag{5.50}$$

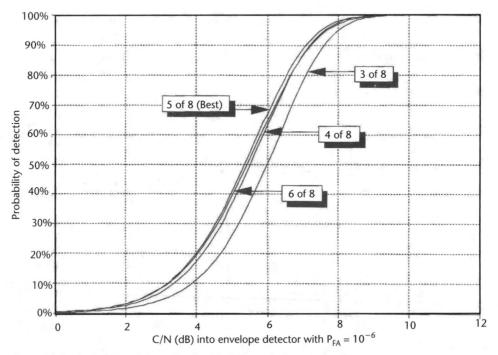

Figure 5.40 Probability of detection for M of N search detector.

The value for P_{fa} is then substituted into (5.43) to compute the threshold, V_t (assuming the signal is absent). V_t sets the lower limit of the integration when (5.40) is substituted into (5.37) as follows:

$$P_d = \int_{V_t}^{\infty} \frac{z}{\sigma_n^2} e^{-\left(\frac{z^2}{2\sigma_n^2} + C/N\right)} I_0 \left(\frac{z\sqrt{2\,C/N}}{\sigma_n}\right) dz \qquad (5.51)$$

Using (5.51), P_d is evaluated for each C/N with σ_n normalized to unity. Finally, P_D is computed for the M and N values using (5.49). The search speed for this example, assuming a dwell time of 5 ms, is $R_s = 1/(N\,2T) = 12.5$ chips/s, which is more than five times slower than the Tong search speed.

5.8.3   Direct Acquisition of GPS Military Signals

While P(Y) code was designed for acquisition through C/A code, efforts have been made to develop direct P(Y) acquisition capabilities, and such capabilities are provided in some modern P(Y) code receivers. Direct P(Y) code acquisition is used if the receiver can accurately predict the satellite transmit time so that less time is required to acquire the P(Y) code by direct sequence than to perform a C/A code search and handover. The direct P(Y) code acquisition condition is satisfied if the receiver has previously acquired four or more satellites and its navigation solution has converged. Under certain jamming conditions, it may be impossible to acquire the C/A code but possible to acquire P(Y) code. Then, direct P(Y) code acquisition is essential and can be supported if the navigation state has been transferred to the receiver with sufficient precision and the ephemeris data for all SVs to be acquired are present. The most sensitive navigation state parameter is precise time. Reference [6] describes a multiple correlator/search detector architecture that supports rapid direct P(Y) code acquisition.

In contrast to the P(Y) code signal, the M code signal was designed so that direct acquisition would be the primary means of acquisition, drawing on advances in acquisition algorithms and integrated circuit technology. The $BOC_s(10,5)$ modulation allows separate acquisition processing on upper and lower sidebands (with processing at the 5.115-MHz spreading code chip rate) and noncoherent integration of the results from the two sidebands, as illustrated in Figure 5.41 [20]. Note that the two sidebands may be selected and processed at the digital IF part of the receiver rather than by two L-band downconverters. Also note that the replica M code does not contain the square wave component. This approach suffers only a fraction of a decibel in performance compared to coherent processing of both sidebands.

Interestingly, when the sideband acquisition processing approach is used, M code signal direct acquisition processing uses approximately half the arithmetic operations and half the storage of Y code signal direct acquisition processing [20]. An integrated circuit based on this processing approach has been designed, built, and tested, displaying the ability to acquire even with relatively large initial time uncertainties in significant levels of jamming [21]. The processing architecture is based on computation of short-time correlations, followed by FFT backend processing for parallel search of multiple frequency values.

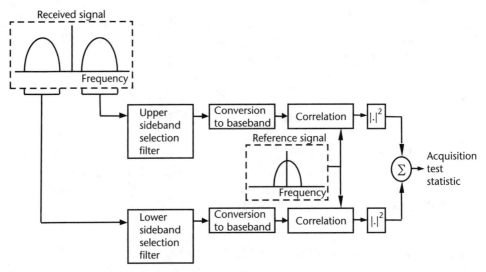

Figure 5.41 Sideband acquisition processing of the M code signal.

Acquisition in jamming requires long integration times. Coherent integration times are limited by data bit boundaries, oscillator stability, and dynamics. They also lead to narrow Doppler bins. Consequently, a large number of noncoherent integrations is employed in jamming. Detection performance is readily predicted using standard theory. The output signal-to-noise plus interference ratio (SNIR) after correlation is given by

$$\rho_o = \frac{T}{L}\frac{0.25C}{N_0 + J_0} \tag{5.52}$$

where T is the coherent integration time used in the correlations, L is the implementation loss expressed as a number greater than or equal to unity, the factor of 0.25 accounts for splitting the received signal power into four distinct segments (upper and lower sidebands, even and odd spreading symbols) in each coherent integration time, and J_0 is the effective power spectral density of the received jamming signal (see Section 6.2).

The detection probability is found using the generalized Marcum Q function. Using the notation $P_N(X, Y)$ [22] as the probability that the random variable with $2N$ degrees of freedom and SNIR of X exceeds threshold value of Y allows the detection probability to be expressed

$$P_d = P_{4N_n}\left(\rho_o, V_t\right) \tag{5.53}$$

where N_n is the number of coherent integrations times used, and V_t is the detection threshold calculated to provide the needed false alarm probability for the given number of noncoherent integrations. The factor of four in the subscript in (5.53) accounts for the fact that the number of complex quantities being noncoherently combined is four times the number of coherent integration times used, reflecting the combination of upper and lower sidebands, and even and odd spreading symbols.

The expressions (5.52) and (5.53) can be used to determine the number of coherent integration times needed to achieve a specific detection probability at a given false alarm probability.

The time (in seconds) to search the initial time uncertainty of $\pm\Delta$ seconds and an initial frequency uncertainty of $\pm\Phi$ Hz is then

$$T_{\text{search}} = N_n \left\lceil \frac{\Delta}{T} \right\rceil \left\lceil \frac{\Phi T}{N_{STC}} \right\rceil \tag{5.54}$$

where T is the coherent integration time, N_{STC} is the number of short-time correlations within the coherent integration time, and $\lceil x \rceil$ is the smallest integer greater than x.

5.9   Sequence of Initial Receiver Operations

The sequence of initial GPS receiver operations depends on the design of the receiver and the past history of the receiver operation. Obviously, the first operation is to select the satellites and then to conduct a search for the selected satellites. There is usually strong emphasis on how fast the receiver will acquire the selected satellites. To determine which satellites are visible and which constellation of visible satellites is the most suitable, three things are needed: (1) an up-to-date almanac; (2) rough estimates of user position and velocity; and (3) an estimate of user GPS time. If any of these parameters are missing or obsolete, the receiver has no choice but to perform what is called a *sky search*, described later. If all are available, then using the user position, the GPS time estimate, and the almanac, the SV positions and LOS Doppler can be computed. Using the estimated user position and the SV positions, the visible SVs can be determined. From the list of visible SVs and the user position, typically the best constellation geometry for good dilution of precision is determined. The best constellation might be selected based on some criteria other than dilution of precision depending on the application. When the constellation has been selected, the search process begins. From the user velocity and the SV LOS Doppler, the total LOS Doppler can be determined. This is used in the Doppler search pattern for the SV. If the approximate time and position are known and the ephemeris data has been obtained during a recent previous operation, the time to first fix can be around 30 seconds for a typical multichannel GPS receiver if the signals are unobstructed. It can require up to 30 seconds just to read the ephemeris data for the SV following signal acquisition. If the ephemeris is not available for the first fix, the almanac data is ordinarily used until the more precise data become available. Reading the almanac data following signal acquisition takes 12.5 minutes. The almanac data, used for SV selection and acquisition, is valid for several days, whereas the ephemeris data, used for navigation, begins to deteriorate after about 3 hours. For the best navigation accuracy, the ephemeris data should be updated each time newer data is available from the space segment.

A critical piece of information is time. Most modern GPS receivers have a built-in timepiece that continues to run even when the set is powered down. They also have nonvolatile memory that stores the last user position, velocity, and time when the set was powered down, plus the ephemeris data for the last SVs tracked and the most recent almanac. These memory features support fast initial acquisition the next time the GPS receiver is powered up, assuming that the receiver has not been transported hundreds of miles to a new location while powered down or that several days elapse between operation. The stored ephemeris can be used to compute the first fix if it has been 3 hours or less since the receiver was last powered down.

The sky search is actually a bootstrap mode of operation to get the GPS receiver into operation when one or more of the almanac, position/velocity, and time parameters are missing or obsolete. Sky search is a remarkable feature made possible by the GPS C/A code design that permits the receiver to enter into the navigation mode without any a priori knowledge or any external help from the operator. Bootstrapping is virtually impossible for P(Y) code or M code without help from C/A code. The sky search mode requires the receiver to search the sky for all possible PRN codes, in all possible Doppler bins, and for all 1,023 code states of each PRN code until at least four SVs are acquired. This cold start process can require many minutes for the receiver to find visible SVs. The first four SVs found by sky search are unlikely to provide the best geometric performance, but after the almanac, position/velocity, and time information has been restored by using the first four SVs, the navigation process can then determine which SVs are visible and what is the best subset for navigation. For *all-in-view* GPS receivers that track up to 12 SVs simultaneously, good geometry is assured if all SVs in view have been acquired and their measurements incorporated into the navigation solution. This multiple channel feature significantly improves the time to first fix for the sky search mode, since there is significant parallelism in the search process and current almanac data is not required to determine the best geometry.

5.10   Data Demodulation

As noted in Section 5.3.2, when a Costas loop is operating, demodulating the navigation data bits is accomplished by accumulating the I_{PS} samples across one data bit interval and seeing if the result is positive or negative. The resultant bit error rate for the C/A code and P(Y) code signals is:

$$P_b = \frac{1}{2} erfc\left(\sqrt{(C/N_0)/R_b}\right) \tag{5.55}$$

where R_b is the data rate (in bits per second) and

$$erfc(x) = \frac{2}{\sqrt{\pi}} \int_{t=x}^{\infty} e^{-t^2} dt \tag{5.56}$$

is the complementary error function.

For the modernized GPS signals (L2C, L5, and the M code) and SBAS signals (discussed in Section 8.6.1.2), a rate half constraint length 7 convolutional code is employed for more robust data demodulation. With soft decision Viterbi decoding, the bit error rate (BER) may be tightly upper bounded for values of interest using [15]:

$$P_b \le \frac{1}{2}\left(36D^{10} + 211D^{12} + 1404D^{14} + 11633D^{16}\right)$$

$$D = \exp\left(-\frac{1}{2R_b}\frac{C}{N_0}\right)$$

(5.57)

It should be noted that both of these BER expressions presume that the PLL is perfectly tracking carrier phase without any slips. At low C/N_0's, phase tracking errors degrade the BER. If the C/N_0 is too low or if the signal dynamics are too severe, then as discussed in Section 5.6.1 the PLL is unable to track carrier phase, and data demodulation can no longer be performed.

Before detection of the data bits can commence, bit synchronization must be performed. This function may be performed by accumulating I_{PS} outputs over all possible start/end points and then comparing the power seen in each possibility. For instance, with the C/A code and P(Y) code signals, the I_{PS} outputs are normally based upon 1-ms integrations. There are 20 I_{PS} outputs per data bit and 20 possible bit edge timing possibilities to explore. It should be noted that if the receiver makes an error of 1 ms or more in estimating the location of a data bit edge, the results could be catastrophic. As noted in Section 5.7.1.5, a 300-km pseudorange error would be seen for a 1-ms error. Fortunately, robust detection of the correct bit edge location is not difficult via the previously mentioned technique if the power in the 20-ms accumulated I_{PS} outputs (i.e., the square of the 20-ms accumulations) for each of the 20 bit edge possibilities are compared over many bit durations.

5.11   Special Baseband Functions

Numerous special baseband functions must be implemented in a GPS receiver design, but the following three design examples are among the most important.

5.11.1   Signal-to-Noise Power Ratio Meter

An accurate measure of C/N_0 in each receiver tracking channel is probably the most important mode and quality control parameter in the receiver baseband area. The basic C/N_0 meter design in Figure 5.42 shows that prompt I and Q signals and noise samples from the same channel are integrated and dumped using K samples (typically over the maximum 20-ms predetection integration time). A power envelope is formed from the averaged prompt I and Q signals. This is passed through a lowpass filter (LPF) and output as an estimate of the carrier power for the numerator (even though it also contains noise). The averaged quadraphase components of the noise samples is scaled, then squared and passed through a LPF to form an estimate of the noise power for the denominator. The C/N_0 (ratio-Hz) estimate is formed by dividing the numerator (C) by the denominator (N_0).

5.11.2   Phase Lock Detector with Optimistic and Pessimistic Decisions

Many receiver control decisions are made based on the phase lock detector. Some applications require more certainty of phase lock than others. Figure 5.43 illustrates

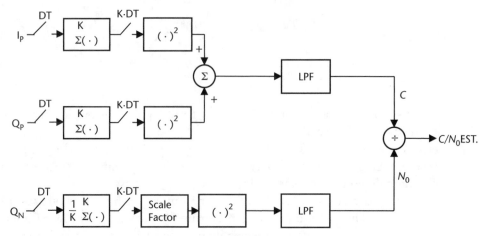

Figure 5.42 Basic carrier-to-noise power ratio meter.

a basic phase lock indicator design, which provides an *optimistic* phase lock indicator that decides quickly and changes its mind slowly but is not as reliable as the *pessimistic* phase lock indicator, which decides slowly and changes its mind quickly.

The phase lock indicator concept is simple: if the loop is in phase lock, then I_{PS} will be maximum and Q_{PS} will be minimum. The phase of the envelope tends to stay near the I-axis. As the phase jitter increases in the loop due to noise, dynamic stress, and so forth, the phase of the envelope jitters around the I-axis. Eventually, the jitter will reach a level where a cycle will be slipped or complete loss of phase lock occurs.

In Figure 5.43 the absolute values of the prompt I and Q signals and passes these through a LPF. The in-phase filtered result, I_p, is divided by a scale factor, K_2, and this result is compared to the unscaled quadraphase filtered result, Q_p. The decision is made that phase lock has been achieved if the scaled average absolute amplitude of I_p is greater than the average absolute amplitude of Q_p. This decision is based on the averaged phase being less than about 15° one sigma.

Observe in Figure 5.43 that the first positive decision results in an optimistic decision. The pessimistic decision that phase lock has been achieved does not occur until several optimistic decisions in a row are made. The first time that the threshold criteria is not met, the pessimistic phase lock indicator is set false. The optimistic

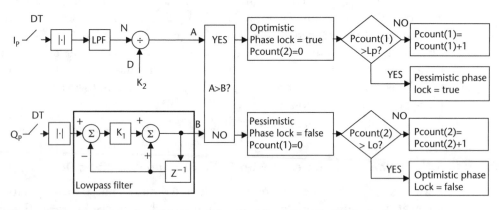

Figure 5.43 Basic phase lock detector with optimistic and pessimistic indicators.

phase lock indicator is not reset until several loss of phase lock comparisons are made in a row. Typical values for the design parameters are: $DT = 20$ ms, $K_1 = 0.0247$, $K_2 = 1.5$, $L_p = 50$, and $L_0 = 240$.

5.11.3 False Frequency Lock and False Phase Lock Detector

False frequency lock can occur in FLL. This can be detected when the DLL velocity state does not match the FLL velocity state. Since both exist, only a comparison check is necessary in FLL to correct the FLL velocity state.

False phase lock can occur in PLL operation when the phase lock indicator declares phase lock but the PLL replica frequency state is incorrect. The incorrect frequency is typically some multiple of 25 Hz for the C/A and P(Y) code signals. The FLL-assisted PLL loop design ordinarily prevents false phase lock, but it is prudent to implement a false phase lock indicator to detect this possible false carrier loop condition. The false phase lock indicator is used only when the phase lock indicator declares that a phase lock condition exists.

Figure 5.44 is a design example of a false phase lock indicator. It performs a frequency discriminator function on a pair of prompt in-phase and quadraphase samples, I_{Pi-1}, Q_{Pi-1}, I_{Pi} and Q_{Pi} formed into the cross product, C, and dot product, D, functions shown as inputs into the detector. Typically, the in-phase and quadraphase samples are collected every 10 ms and the C and D products are formed every $DT = 20$ ms, then applied to the input. These are integrated and dumped for N samples (typically $N = 50$). Typically, at $N \times DT = 1$ second intervals, the four-quadrant arctangent is computed with output E. The absolute value of E represents the change in phase in 1 second, F, which is in units of hertz; this is compared to a threshold, G (for this example, this is 15.5 Hz). If D exceeds G, then the pessimistic phase lock indicator is set to "false" and a 25-Hz correction is applied to the carrier accumulator based on the sign of E.

5.12 Use of Digital Processing

The use of digital processing was as important to the feasibility of the GPS navigation concept as the advancement of reliable space qualified atomic standards. The computational burdens in the GPS space segment, control segment, and user segment are such that digital signal processing is an indispensable asset. Even the earli-

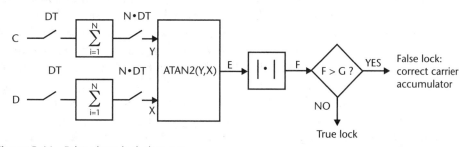

Figure 5.44 False phase lock detector.

est GPS receivers with high analog front end design content utilized digital processing in the receiver baseband processing, receiver control, navigation, and user interface areas. The custom component digital technology known as ASICs, FPGAs, DSPs, and general purpose microprocessors are advancing so rapidly that all GPS receiver manufacturers currently use digital processing at higher levels of the signal processing functions. Also, the processing speed along with built-in floating point processors enables the modern GPS receiver designer to use optimum algorithms rather than approximations. Fortunately, as the feature sizes of ASICs and FPGAs become smaller, their power consumption is reduced and their speed is increased. These advances in technology not only reduce the component count, which reduces cost and power and increases reliability, but also can greatly improve performance. For this reason, outdated analog GPS receiver processing techniques were not discussed.

The partitioning between the microprocessor or DSP and the custom digital components depends on the digital signal processing throughput capability (bit manipulation and computational speed) of the microprocessor or DSP. Eventually DSPs may take over the role of ASICs and FPGAs. It is important to keep in mind that every process performed in the microprocessor is performed in sequential steps, whereas the custom digital components (ASICs or FPGAs) typically perform their processing in parallel. However, the speed of ASICs and FPGAs has increased to the point where digital multiplexing (time sharing of the same function) is now used.

The digital data is sampled data, and there is real time between these samples in which the DSP or microprocessor can process the previous data. The processor is interrupted every time the sampled data is updated. This is called real-time processing, and the real-time processor must have completed all of the tasks within the interrupt time line and have some throughput resources left over for additional processes that are scheduled for completion on longer time lines. Fortunately, the nature of GPS digital signal processing is such that as the processing steps become more complex, there is also more real time allowed between the processes to complete the signal processing. For example, in a C/A code digital GPS receiver, the digital samples containing the spread spectrum signals at IF of all of the visible SVs must be processed at a rate of 2 to 6 MHz (and even faster for modern wideband narrow correlator designs). The replica C/A code generators (one per SV tracked) must operate at 1.023 MHz. At these processing speeds, it is unlikely that the speed-power product of general purpose microprocessors will make them the suitable choice to perform the carrier and code wipeoff functions in the very near future—perhaps never—but specialized DSPs might eventually make a showing. However, after the SV signals have been despread, the processing rate per SV seldom exceeds 1 kHz and typically is of the order of 50 to 200 Hz per SV, which is well within the real-time signal processing capability of a modern microprocessor. The navigation process in a GPS receiver seldom exceeds 1 Hz, even for a high dynamics application.

Since extensive use is made of non-real-time computer modeling and simulations for all aspects of a GPS receiver design, including external aiding, the ideal design environment is one that permits the stripping away of test features not required for real-time operation and the porting of the real-time programs into the actual GPS receiver hardware without modification of the source code [23].

5.13 Considerations for Indoor Applications

The generic receiver design described in the previous sections is a continuously tracking design for outdoor (direct LOS) applications where the C/N_0 may be modestly deteriorated by signal attenuation due to foliage, multipath, antenna gain roll-off, and so on, or by signal interference due to unwanted in-band RF signals. The principles described thus far assume that the carrier and code loops are closed after the search process, and, as long as the C/N_0 remains above the tracking threshold, the receiver will operate satisfactorily. The E-911 requirement for autonomous cellular phone location has motivated the development of highly specialized GPS receivers that can obtain range measurements indoors where the C/N_0 is 20 dB or more lower than the normal situation. These receivers, which are integrated with cellular phone handsets, maximize the use of aiding from communication networks to avoid the need to read the satellite navigation message data or any other tracking mode that requires continuous satellite signal tracking. The objective of these specialized designs is to obtain a reasonable estimate of the user position by extensive averaging of the code correlations with several weak GPS SV signals until there is enough signal processing gain to obtain a set of transmit time measurements from them. The indoor measurements do not have to be nearly as accurate as is expected for the continuously tracking GPS receiver designs. In indoor applications, it is often acceptable for the position determination to only be sufficiently accurate so as to identify the building location. As a result, indoor GPS applications are probably the only operational situation where multipath signals are considered to be friendly signals by the GPS receiver since there is little or no direct GPS signal energy inside most buildings.

There are numerous variations of network-aided GPS techniques. This section outlines some basic principles to obtain the high sensitivities needed for indoor applications. Section 9.4 provides a detailed overview of network-assistance techniques, including industry standards.

One common practice for GPS receivers in cellular handsets is to never close any tracking loops, but rather to dwell on the GPS signals in a controlled (network-aided) search mode long enough to extract enough crude range measurements to provide a snapshot position. The rover receivers utilize communications aiding in order to dwell within the correlation range of the C/A code (about 300m per correlator) and within the carrier Doppler bin in a signal search mode. To accomplish this, they utilize a reference receiver with a clear view of the sky within the cellular network to provide the information needed to replicate their code phase and to synthesize their Doppler estimate during an extended search dwell. If the aiding is such that the SV signals remain within the Doppler bin and the correlation window during the extended search dwell, then sufficient processing gain is achieved to produce valid transmit time measurements. A number of factors make this practical. The user dynamics are small inside buildings, and their distance from the relay (GPS reference) station is not large; therefore, the difference between the user LOS range and Doppler to the SVs is not much different from that of the reference station. Extending the correlator range and the Doppler tolerance is part of the innovative designs of these specialized receivers. Also, the latency of aiding is tolerable to the user receiver since the aiding is applied open loop to the carrier wipeoff process (i.e., the total Doppler error from all sources must not exceed the Doppler bin width, and this width is determined by the dwell time for each coherent set of code correlations). Unless data wipeoff information is provided (and this is seldom used), this limits the coherent dwell times to 20 ms or less depending on the sophistication of the aiding. The coherent results are summed together noncoherently for as long as possible—typically less than 600 ms. The greatest limitation to the amount of noncoherent integration that can take place in the rover receiver is the stability of the reference oscillator, which is usually provided by the cellular phone. These reference oscillators are not normally specified with the stringent stability requirements of GPS receivers, but there is more tolerance in this case because there is no attempt to achieve phase lock with the satellite signals.

The methods for obtaining pseudorange measurements in indoor applications are similar to the techniques for acquisition described in Section 5.8. A major difference is that, as described earlier, the communications aiding typically results in a very narrow window in the two-dimensional codephase/Doppler parameter space. This restricted space allows much longer dwells than would be practical for an unaided receiver. As an example of the sensitivities that can be achieved by various levels of coherent and further noncoherent integration, Figure 5.45 presents the probabilities of detecting a GPS signal as a function of $(C/N_0)_{dB}$ for various values of the coherent integration period, T, and the number, K, of successive I and Q outputs

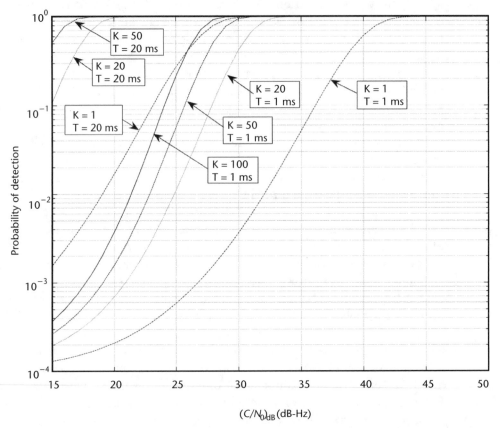

Figure 5.45 Probability of detection as a function of $(C/N_0)_{dB}$ using K noncoherent integrations at T ms dwells for 10^{-4} probability of false alarm.

that are squared and summed. As noted in Section 5.8, over one coherent integration period the envelope $\sqrt{I^2 + Q^2}$ has a Ricean pdf when the signal is present and a Rayleigh distribution when the signal is not present. Further noncoherent integration is typically achieved by summing $I^2 + Q^2$ from each of K successive coherent integration periods. The total resultant dwell time is KT. The sum of $I^2 + Q^2$ over the K periods has a central chi-square pdf with $2K$ degrees of freedom when the signal is not present and a noncentral chi-square pdf with $2K$ degrees of freedom when the signal is present (e.g., [24]). Figure 5.45 assumes that the thresholds for each pair of (T, K) values is set to achieve a false alarm probability of 10^{-4}.

The curves in Figure 5.45 ignore some practical issues such as cross-correlation among C/A code signals, which generally require the thresholds to be inflated somewhat to avoid excessive false alarms. As noted in Section 4.3.4, the cross-correlation levels of the C/A code signals can be as high as -21 dB. This can cause false acquisitions under certain Doppler differences and antenna gain conditions. For example, a user in a building might receive one C/A code signal through a window with very little attenuation and a second C/A signal through several floors of a building with very high attenutation. Discrimination among signals received with great strength differences can be very difficult for a C/A code receiver, resulting in an occasional false acquisition. Fortunately, the unwanted SV signal cannot usually be tracked for long because both the correlation properties and the Doppler change rapidly, resulting in loss of lock and a reacquisition process for the GPS receiver. It is important that the GPS receiver design implement sophisticated C/A code search procedures that avoid cross-correlation and autocorrelation sidelobe acquisitions. If the receiver successfully hands over from C/A code to P(Y) code, then this success provides a built-in assurance of the integrity of the C/A code measurements. However, if the receiver remains in C/A code, then there is always concern that false tracking has occurred under such marginal signal conditions.

It is also important to note that significant implementation losses can result from Doppler frequency errors in the carrier NCO and timing errors in the replica PRN code, particularly for large values of T. Thus, the curves in Figure 5.45 should really be viewed as upper bounds on achievable detection probabilities.

The numerous design tradeoffs and solutions that have been adopted within industry for indoor applications are discussed further in Section 9.4.

5.14 Codeless and Semicodeless Processing

Since only the P(Y) code signal is normally broadcast on L2 by the GPS SVs up through the Block IIR-Ms, this denies direct two-frequency operation to SPS users when AS is activated by the control segment (see Section 4.3.1). Two-frequency carrier-phase measurements are highly desirable for surveying applications (see Section 8.4) and dual-frequency pseudoranges are needed to accurately compensate for ionospheric delays in navigation applications (see Section 7.2.4.1). This has motivated the development of techniques to obtain L2 Y code pseudorange and carrier-phase measurements without the cryptographic knowledge for full access to this signal. These techniques are referred to as either *codeless* or *semicodeless* processing. Codeless techniques only utilize the known 10.23-MHz chip rate of the Y code signal, and the fact that [2] assures that the same Y code signal is broadcast on both L1 and L2, whereas the semicodeless techniques further exploit a deduced relationship between the Y code and P code.

Since they operate without full knowledge of the Y code signal, the codeless and semicodeless designs operate at significantly reduced SNRs, which requires the tracking loop bandwidths to be extremely narrow. This, in turn, reduces their ability to operate in a high dynamic environment without aiding. Fortunately, robust aiding is generally available from tracking loops operating upon the C/A code signal. Typical codeless and semicodeless receiver designs use L1 C/A carrier tracking loops to effectively remove the LOS dynamics from the L1 and L2 Y code signals, and then extract the L1-L2 differential measurements by some variation of a signal squaring technique that does not require full knowledge of the replica code. Codeless techniques effectively treat the Y code PRN as 10.23-Mbps data, which can be removed through squaring or by cross-correlation of the L1 and L2 signals. Semicodeless techniques exploit some known features of the Y code (e.g., [25]). In addition to the signal-to-noise disadvantage mentioned earlier, codeless receivers suffer from other robustness problems. Although the parallel C/A-code processing provides access to the GPS navigation message, codeless processing of L2 does not allow decoding of the navigation data for the purpose of verifying that the desired SV is being tracked. Also, two SVs with the same Doppler will interfere with each other in the codeless mode; therefore, the scheme fails for this temporary tracking condition. Modern semicodeless receivers, on the other hand, provide relatively robust tracking of the L2 Y code signal with assistance from the L1 C/A code. These concepts will become obsolete when the modernized GPS civil signals become available.

References

[1]   Ward, P. W., "An Inside View of Pseudorange and Delta Pseudorange Measurements in a Digital NAVSTAR GPS Receiver," *Proc. of ITC/USA/'81 International Telemetering Conference, GPS-Military and Civil Applications*, San Diego, CA, October 1981.

[2]   IS-GPS-200, *NAVSTAR GPS Space Segment/Navigation User Interfaces (Public Release Version)*, ARINC Research Corporation, El Segundo, CA, December 7, 2004.

[3]   Ward, P. W., "An Advanced NAVSTAR GPS Multiplex Receiver," *Proc. of IEEE PLANS '80, Position Location and Navigation Symposium*, December 1980.

[4]   Kohli, S., "Application of Massively Parallel Signal Processing Architectures to GPS/Inertial Systems," *IEEE PLANS '92 Position Location and Navigation Symposium*, April 1992.

[5]   Townsend, B., et al., "Performance Evaluation of the Multipath Estimating Delay Lock Loop," *Proc. of ION National Technical Meeting*, January 1995, pp. 277–283.

[6]   Przyjemski, J., E. Balboni, and J. Dowdle, "GPS Anti-Jam Enhancement Techniques," *Proc. of ION 49th Annual Meeting*, June 1993, pp. 41–50.

[7]   Ward, P., "Performance Comparisons Between FLL, PLL and a Novel FLL-Assisted-PLL Carrier Tracking Loop Under RF Interference Conditions," *Proceedings of the 11th International Technical Meeting of The Satellite Division of The Institute of Navigation*, Nashville, TN, September 1998, pp. 783–795.

[8]   Stephens, S. A., and J. C. Thomas, "Controlled-Root Formulation for Digital Phase-Locked Loops," *IEEE Trans. on Aerospace and Electronic Systems*, January 1995.

[9]   Ward, P., "Using a GPS Receiver Monte Carlo Simulator to Predict RF Interference Performance," *Proc. of 10th International Technical Meeting of The Satellite Division of The Institute of Navigation*, Kansas City, MO, September 1997, pp. 1473–1482.

[10] Fuchser, T. D., "Oscillator Stability for Carrier Phase Lock," *Internal Memorandum G(S)-60233,* Texas Instruments Incorporated, February 6, 1976.

[11] Betz, J. W., and K. R. Kolodziejski, "Generalized Theory of GPS Code-Tracking Accuracy with an Early-Late Discriminator," 2000, unpublished.

[12] Betz, J. W., and K. R. Kolodziejski, "Extended Theory of Early-Late Code Tracking for a Bandlimited GPS Receiver," *NAVIGATION: Journal of The Institute of Navigation,* Vol. 47, No. 3, Fall 2000, pp. 211–226.

[13] Betz, J. W., "Design and Performance of Code Tracking for the GPS M Code Signal," *Proc. of 13th International Technical Meeting of The Satellite Division of The Institute of Navigation,* Salt Lake City, UT, September 2000, pp. 2140–2150.

[14] Ward, P., "The Natural Measurements of a GPS Receiver," *Proc. of The Institute of Navigation 51st Annual Meeting,* Colorado Springs, CO, June 5–7, 1995, pp. 67–85.

[15] Simon, M. K., et al., *Spread Spectrum Communications Handbook,* rev. ed., New York: McGraw-Hill, 1994, pp. 751–900.

[16] Scott, L., A. Jovancevic, and S. Ganguly, "Rapid Signal Acquisition Techniques for Civilian and Military User Equipments Using DSP Based FFT Processing," *Proc. of 14th International Technical Meeting of The Satellite Division of The Institute of Navigation,* Salt Lake City, UT, September 2001, pp. 2418–2427.

[17] Ward, P., "GPS Receiver Search Techniques," *Proc. of IEEE PLANS '96,* Atlanta, GA, April 1996.

[18] Polydoros, A., "On the Synchronization Aspects of Direct-Sequence Spread Spectrum Systems," Ph.D. dissertation, Department of Electrical Engineering, University of Southern California, August 1982.

[19] Tong, P. S., "A Suboptimum Synchronization Procedure for Pseudo Noise Communication Systems" *Proc. of National Telecommunications Conference,* 1973, pp. 26D-1–26D-5.

[20] Fishman, P., and J. W. Betz, "Predicting Performance of Direct Acquisition for the M Code Signal," *Proc. of ION 2000 National Technical Meeting,* Institute of Navigation, January 2000.

[21] Betz, J. W., J. D. Fite, and P. T. Capozza, "DirAc: An Integrated Circuit for Direct Acquisition of the M-Code Signal," *Proc. of The Institute of Navigation ION GNSS 2004,* Long Beach, CA, September 2004.

[22] Shnidman, D. A., "The Calculation of the Probability of Detection and the Generalized Marcum Q-Function," *IEEE Trans. on Information Theory,* Vol. 35, No. 2, March 1989.

[23] Jovancevic, A., et al., "Open Architecture GPS Receiver," *Proc. of ION 57th Annual Meeting,* Albuquerque, NM, June 2001.

[24] Van Dierendonck, A. J., "GPS Receivers," in *Global Positioning System: Theory and Applications, Vol. I,* B. Parkinson and J. J. Spilker, Jr., (eds.), Washington, D.C.: American Institute of Aeronautics and Astronautics, 1996.

[25] Woo, K. T., "Optimum Semicodeless Processing of GPS L2," *NAVIGATION: Journal of The Institute of Navigation,* Vol. 47, No. 2, Summer 2000, pp. 82–99.

CHAPTER 6
Interference, Multipath, and Scintillation

Phillip W. Ward
NAVWARD GPS Consulting

John W. Betz and Christopher J. Hegarty
The MITRE Corporation

6.1 Overview

This chapter discusses three general classes of RF channel impairments that can degrade GNSS performance. The first class of impairments discussed is *interference*, which is the focus of Section 6.2. RF signals from any undesired source that are received by a GNSS receiver are considered interference. The interference is often unintentional (e.g., out-of-band emissions from other licensed RF systems). The interference may also be intentional, in which case it is commonly referred to as *jamming*.

Section 6.3 discusses the second class of RF channel impairments, which is *multipath*. Invariably there are reflective surfaces between each GNSS spacecraft and the user receiver that result in RF echoes arriving at the receiver after the desired (LOS) signal. These echoes are referred to as multipath, a term that originated from the fact that each transmitted signal is transiting over multiple paths to the receiver—the single direct path and a number of indirect (reflected) paths.

The third and final class of channel impairments considered in this chapter, in Section 6.4, is *ionospheric scintillation*. Ionospheric scintillation is a signal-fading phenomenon that is caused by irregularities in the ionospheric layer of the Earth's atmosphere.

6.2 Radio Frequency Interference

Because GNSS receivers rely on external RF signals, they are vulnerable to RF interference (unintentional interference or jamming). RF interference can result in degraded navigation accuracy or complete loss of receiver tracking. This section first describes types and sources of interference in Section 6.2.1. Next, the effects of interference on receiver performance are discussed in Section 6.2.2. Finally, Section 6.2.3 discusses mitigation techniques.

6.2.1 Types and Sources of RF Interference

Table 6.1 summarizes various types and potential sources of RF interference. Interference is normally classified as either *wideband* or *narrowband*, depending on whether its bandwidth is large or small relative to the bandwidth of the desired GNSS signal. Note that what might be considered wideband interference to the GPS L1 C/A code or L2C might be narrowband to P(Y) code, M code, or L5. The ultimate limit in narrowband interference is a signal consisting of a single tone, referred to as a *continuous wave* (CW).[1] The RF interference may be unintentional or intentional (jamming). There is a certain level of interference among signals of the same type, where signals from different satellites within one system interfere with one another's reception. Such interference is referred to as *self-interference* or *intrasystem interference*. Interference between two satellite navigation systems such as between GPS and GALILEO signals is referred to as *intersystem interference*. If pseudolites are used, operation at close range to these ground transmitters will almost certainly result in interference to the satellite signals, although the effects of such interference can be reduced through use of burst (pulse) techniques by the pseudolites to reduce the duty cycle. In fact, an efficient wideband jamming technique uses a waveform based on the same modulation, at the same carrier frequency, to form *matched spectrum* interference. If the intent of the intentional transmission is to not just disrupt GNSS operation, but rather to produce a false position within the victim receiver through the broadcast of false GNSS signals, the transmission is referred to as *spoofing*. As a benign example of spoofing, when a GPS receiver is connected to a GPS satellite signal simulator for testing, that receiver under test is being spoofed.

6.2.1.1 Jamming and Spoofing

Intentional jamming and spoofing must be anticipated in the design of military receivers. Hence, all classes of in-band jammers, including multiple access jammers (i.e., jammers from a strategic array of multiple locations), must be considered in the design. *Smart spoofers* track the location of the target GNSS receiver and use this information along with a quasi-real-time GNSS signal generator to create strong GNSS signals that initially match the actual weaker signals in TOA until loop capture is assured, then lead the target receiver astray. The smart spoofer must be able to synthesize (duplicate) the target PRN code. *Repeat-back spoofers* utilize an array of steered very high gain antennas to track all satellites in view, then rebroadcast an amplified version toward the target receiver. The end effect on the target receiver navigation solution (if captured by these signals) is a location and velocity of the repeat-back spoofer antenna array phase center with a time bias solution that includes the common mode range between the spoofer and the victim receiver. The major weakness of both spoofing techniques is that all of the spoofing signals arrive from the same direction (unless spatial diversity is also used), so that directional null-steering antenna techniques can be used to defeat spoofers. The encrypted AS Y code is used to replace the public P code for military applications to minimize the

---

1. In the literature, this term is sometimes defined differently to mean continuously transmitting, as opposed to pulsed.

Table 6.1   Types of RF Interference and Potential Sources

Class—Type	Potential Sources
Wideband—band-limited Gaussian	Intentional matched bandwidth noise jammers
Wideband—phase/frequency modulation	Television transmitters' harmonics or near-band microwave link transmitters overcoming the front end filter of a GNSS receiver
Wideband—matched spectrum	Intentional matched-spectrum jammers, spoofers, or nearby pseudolites
Wideband—pulse	Any type of burst transmitters such as radar or ultrawideband (UWB)
Narrowband—phase/frequency modulation	Intentional chirp jammers or harmonics from an amplitude modulation (AM) radio station, citizens band (CB) radio, or amateur radio transmitter
Narrowband—swept continuous wave	Intentional swept CW jammers or frequency modulation (FM) stations transmitters' harmonics
Narrowband—continuous wave	Intentional CW jammers or near-band unmodulated transmitter's carriers

potential for spoofing military GPS receivers. The encrypted M code is even more secure.

6.2.1.2   Unintentional Interference

Unintentional RF interference can be expected at low levels for a GNSS receiver operating practically anywhere in the world. There are a large number of systems that we depend on in daily life that rely on the transmission of RF energy within L-band. Table 6.2 shows abridged versions of U.S. and international tables of allocations for frequencies near those used by the GPS signals. The services shown in all capital letters are *primary*, and the ones shown with initial capitals are *secondary*. Secondary services are permitted to operate in their designated bands but are not generally provided protection from the primary services and further are not allowed to provide harmful levels of interference to the primary services.

GPS L1 is in a band that is designated for use only by other satellite navigation signals in most regions of the world. The GPS L2 and L5 signals are in less pristine spectrum. L2 is in the 1,215–1,240-MHz band, which has a coprimary radiolocation allocation worldwide. Radiolocation services that operate in the band include a large number of radars that are used for air traffic control, military surveillance, and drug interdiction. Although some of these radars operate with very high transmit power (kilowatts to megawatts), fortunately they are pulsed systems, and, as will be discussed in Section 6.2.2, GPS receivers can be very robust against pulsed interference due to the clipping that occurs in their A/D converters if their front-end design does not saturate and their automatic gain control has a very fast attack and recovery rate. Additionally, a number of countries permit fixed and mobile services to operate in the 1,215–1,240-MHz band.

L5 is located within a portion of the 960–1,215-MHz band that is used worldwide for electronic aids to air navigation. DME and TACAN ground beacons transmit at power levels up to 10 kW on frequencies that fall within a GPS L5 receiver passband. Some nations also permit the use of Link 16, a tactical military communications system with radios that nominally transmit 200W over 51 frequencies

Table 6.2 Frequency Allocations Near GPS

International Table	U.S. Table	Notes
960–1,164 MHz AERONAUTICAL RADIONAVIGATION	AERONAUTICAL RADIONAVIGATION	Used worldwide for electronic aids to air navigation, including distance measuring equipment (DME), tactical air navigation (TACAN), secondary surveillance radars (SSR), and ADS. Some nations permit Link 16 (a military communication system) usage on a noninterference basis. GPS L5 and GALILEO E5A are at 1,176.45 MHz, GALILEO E5B is at 1,207.14 MHz. A number of other radionavigation-satellite signals are planned for the 1,164–1,215-MHz band.
1,164–1,215 MHz AERONAUTICAL RADIONAVIGATION RADIONAVIGATION-SATELLITE	AERONAUTICAL RADIONAVIGATION	
1,215–1,240 MHz EARTH EXPLORATION-SATELLITE (active) RADIOLOCATION RADIONAVIGATION-SATELLITE SPACE RESEARCH (active)	EARTH EXPLORATION-SATELLITE (active) RADIOLOCATION RADIONAVIGATION-SATELLITE SPACE RESEARCH (active)	Used worldwide for primary radars for purposes including air traffic control, military surveillance, and drug interdiction. Thirty-one countries have coprimary allocations for fixed and mobile services. Band also used for active spaceborne sensors (e.g., for ocean surface measurements). GPS L2 is at 1,227.6 MHz. GLONASS L2 and GALILEO E6 frequencies are within the 1,240–1,300-MHz band.
1,240–1,300 MHz EARTH EXPLORATION-SATELLITE (active) RADIOLOCATION RADIONAVIGATION-SATELLITE SPACE RESEARCH (active) Amateur	AERONAUTICAL RADIONAVIGATION EARTH EXPLORATION-SATELLITE (active) RADIOLOCATION SPACE RESEARCH (active) Amateur	
1,300–1,350 MHz AERONAUTICAL RADIONAVIGATION RADIOLOCATION RADIONAVIGATION-SATELLITE	AERONAUTICAL RADIONAVIGATION Radiolocation	
1,350–1,400 MHz FIXED* MOBILE* RADIOLOCATION	FIXED* LAND MOBILE* MOBILE* RADIOLOCATION*	Varied band usage worldwide among fixed services, land mobile, mobile, and radiolocation.
1,535–1,559 MHz MOBILE-SATELLITE (space-to-Earth)	MOBILE-SATELLITE (space-to-Earth)	Downlink frequencies for satellite communications services (e.g., INMARSAT).
1,559–1,610 MHz AERONAUTICAL RADIONAVIGATION RADIONAVIGATION-SATELLITE	AERONAUTICAL RADIONAVIGATION RADIONAVIGATION-SATELLITE	GPS, GLONASS, and GALILEO L1 signals are within this band.

Table 6.2   (Continued)

International Table	U.S. Table	Notes
1,610–1,626.5 MHz MOBILE-SATELLITE (Earth-to-space) AERONAUTICAL RADIONAVIGATION RADIO ASTRONOMY* RADIODETERMINATION- SATELLITE*	MOBILE-SATELLITE (Earth-to-space) AERONAUTICAL RADIONAVIGATION RADIO ASTRONOMY* RADIODETERMINATION- SATELLITE	Uplink frequencies for commercial satellite communications services. Portions of the band are protected for radio astronomy sensors.

*Only in some nations or portions of the band.

throughout the 960–1,215-MHz band. Fortunately, DME/TACAN and Link 16 are pulsed.

It is inevitable that some out-of-band energy from the signals in adjacent bands will at times fall within the range of frequencies processed by GNSS receivers. This energy can originate from the spillover of energy from bands immediately above or below one of the GNSS carrier frequencies, from *harmonics,* or from *intermodulation products.* Harmonics are signals at integer multiples of the carrier frequency of a transmitter that are caused by nonlinearities (e.g., saturation of an amplifier that leads to clipping) upon transmission. Intermodulation products occur when two or more signals at different frequencies are passed through a nonlinearity.

Even if interfering signals are out of the nominal band processed by a GNSS receiver, strong RF signals can still deteriorate GNSS receiver performance (e.g., by saturating the low-noise amplifiers used in the receiver front end). Although regulations are in place within the United States and internationally to protect GNSS spectrum, there are occasionally instances of equipment malfunctions or equipment misuse that can lead to intolerable levels of interference. Nonlinear effects (e.g., amplifier saturation) may accidentally occur in high-powered transmitters causing lower power harmonics that become in-band RF interference to GNSS receivers. The offending transmitter source has to be located and corrected before normal GNSS operation in that vicinity can resume. Some regions of the world experience more frequent problems with interference to GNSS than others. For example, in the Mediterranean, there have been a number of reports of GPS L1 C/A code receivers failing to operate properly because of strong in-band harmonics from television transmitters in the region.

6.2.2   Effects of RF Interference on Receiver Performance

6.2.2.1   Front-End Considerations

Since the GNSS signals of all of the SVs in view of the antenna are below the thermal noise level, the receiver front-end (analog) hardware requires considerable gain (approximately 100 dB) and very little dynamic range if the design excludes the effects of RF interference on the receiver hardware. It is essential that the receiver front-end hardware have a dynamic range that will tolerate the front-end gain variations due to component tolerance and aging plus temperature variations. A prudent commercial GNSS receiver front-end design should also accommodate the RF interference levels that their digital baseband tracking loops can tolerate. For military GPS receivers, it is essential that the front-end dynamic range accommodate the maximum expected levels of RF interference (i.e., the specified levels). The digital tracking portion of the military receiver must be designed to match the front-end performance. This means that none of the front-end gain stages go into gain compression for the specified nonburst-type jamming. For burst-type (pulse) jammers, such as on-board radars, the front-end design must prevent any gain stage from going into saturation, and the receiver must adjust its gain to instantly blank (compress) when excessive burst energy is present, then instantly recover (expand back to linear operation) when the burst energy disappears.

The RF susceptibility characteristics of GNSS receivers to adjacent-band RF interference must be considered when evaluating the overall effectiveness of the system for any potential application. Only front-end filtering or antenna cancellation techniques can prevent the GNSS receiver from being overdriven by these adjacent out-of-band signals. One advantage of multistage down conversion is the opportunity to not only isolate the gain stages, but also add increasingly higher-Q filters as the IF is lowered. Surface acoustic wave (SAW) filters are highly effective with high-Q characteristics even at L-band. But SAWs also have large insertion loss, so they must be used well past the front-end preamplifier that sets the noise figure of the receiver. Low insertion loss passive bandpass filters can and should be used prior to the preamp. Cavity filters are a very suitable passive filter choice but tend to be physically large. Because of this, they are often physically included inside the passive GNSS antenna. The preferred conventional filter for GNSS at lower IF stages is one that is maximally flat in-band and has the sharpest stop-band roll-off characteristics, such as a Chebyshev bandpass filter. The front-end filtering not only prevents unwanted out-of-band interference but also reduces aliasing (discussed later in the A/D conversion section). The front-end filtering problem is particularly difficult on platforms where high-powered transmitter antennas are near the GNSS receiver antenna. Highly specialized signal cancellation antenna design techniques that actually use samples of the interfering signals or deep null steering front-end filters are often the only possible solutions to this problem.

6.2.2.2 AGC

The gain objective of the front-end design is that the RMS amplitude of the thermal noise plus jamming noise must remain essentially constant at the input of the analog-to-digital converter (ADC). The optimum RMS levels are discussed in Section 6.2.2.3. This must be accomplished without any analog gain stages being driven into compression. High-powered burst jammers will drive these stages into compression, but all of the gain stages must be prevented from saturating. Otherwise, they will be slow to recover to their linear gain when the burst energy disappears.

The effect of continuous gain compression (or saturation) is the suppression of the GNSS signals in a manner that is highly disproportional to the level of the noise that caused the effect (i.e., a very nonlinear detrimental effect). This nonlinear effect renders the linear circuit theory presented elsewhere in this book meaningless. It does not matter what elegant algorithms have been implemented in the digital part of the receiver to accomplish acquisition and tracking if the analog GNSS signals have been totally corrupted by the nonlinear behavior of the front end.

The constant RMS amplitude feature is usually provided by one or more AGC stages or one AGC stage and one or more switchable attenuators upstream from the AGC. Normally, the AGC operates on the receiver's thermal noise level, and this corresponds to the highest gain mode of the receiver. If this were always the case, the AGC time constant would not be critical. However, a prudent AGC design should assume that there will be occasions where in-band RF interference will appear above this thermal noise level that can be mitigated with proper AGC and ADC design. When RF interference occurs, the action of the AGC is to rapidly reduce the gain in order to maintain the original RMS level at the input of the ADC. There is probably no optimum AGC time constant for all possible types of RF interference. As a design guideline, the attack/recovery times should be much shorter than the shortest integrate and dump times following the correlation process. The range of acceptable AGC attack and recovery times is typically much shorter than 1 ms but no shorter than $50\,\mu s$. The actual time should be as close to $50\,\mu s$ as possible consistent with AGC amplifier stability. The AGC amplifier is usually the last gain stage of the receiver. Figure 6.1 illustrates such an AGC amplifier along with a non-uniform 2-bit quantization ADC and a digital jamming-to-noise ratio (J/N) meter that will be described later. As shown in Figure 6.1, the analog gain control voltage has a nonlinear effect on the gain, G_A, of the AGC amplifier as follows:

$$G_A = \alpha e^{\beta V_{AGC}} \tag{6.1}$$

where:

V_{AGC} = AGC control voltage

α = AGC gain coefficient

β = AGC control voltage coefficient

Equation (6.1) can be expressed in terms of the control voltage

$$V_{AGC} = \frac{1}{\beta} \ln\left(\frac{G_{AGC}}{\alpha}\right) \tag{6.2}$$

The two coefficients can be calibrated at the factory and stored as constants. For higher precision that accounts for aging and other drift factors, the calibration can be performed during built-in test immediately following power-up operation but prior to receiver operation. This built-in test requires that the front end be muted and a built-in tone at two precise amplitudes injected, one at the upper end and the other at the lower end of the AGC range. The built-in calibration and muting are important only if it is desired that the J/N meter (described later) is accurate.

Many commercial GPS receivers are not designed to account for RF interference; they are designed to provide enough gain (usually distributed over one or two downconversion stages) to raise the RMS thermal noise amplitude to a value suitable for A/D conversion at the IF. Direct L-band sampling, with all the gain and bandpass antialiasing filtering confined to one stage, is highly vulnerable to self-jamming (i.e., self-induced oscillation due to leak-through feedback from the

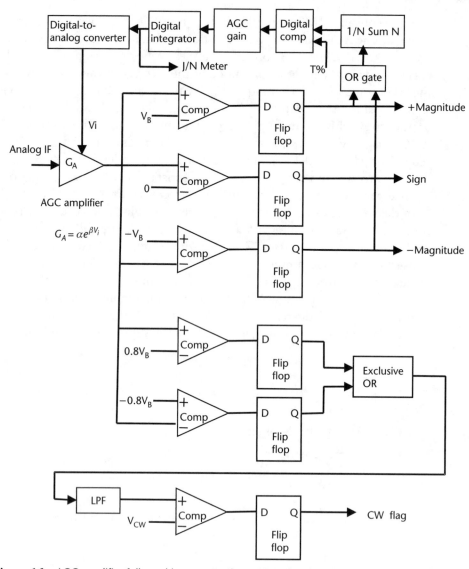

Figure 6.1 AGC amplifier followed by a nonuniform ADC, CW detector, and digital *J/N* meter.

extremely high-level output to the nearby extremely low-level input signals).
Self-jamming has the same detrimental effect as continuous gain compression (or
saturation) of the receiver front end, except that no external RF interference is
required.

If a 1-bit ADC is used, no AGC is required because the ADC is simply a limiter.
However, 1-bit ADCs are extremely vulnerable to being captured by very low levels of
CW interference (see the following section). AGC is always used with multibit ADCs.

6.2.2.3 A/D Conversion Effects

A/D conversion consists of two distinct processes: signal sampling and signal
quantization. If the quantization process is instantaneous and continuous, as in a

flash ADC, then the digital sampling process can follow the A/D quantization process. If the quantization process is sequential (time-consuming), as in a successive approximation ADC, then an analog sample-and-hold (zero-order-hold) process must precede the A/D quantization process in order to hold the sampled analog signal constant until the quantization process completes.

The sampling process always introduces aliasing noise into the digitized signal because it is impossible to completely filter out higher frequency components to fully comply with the Nyquist sampling theorem. The Nyquist sampling theorem says that all information is contained in the sampled data if the continuous analog data is sampled at twice the highest frequency content of the data. For example, if there is no frequency content beyond B_s-Hz bandwidth of a given signal, then sampling this signal at $2B_s$ Hz preserves all of its information and there is no aliasing. Obviously antialiasing filtering can only "reduce" the levels of the higher frequency signal components outside of B_s Hz to an RMS level that is small but not zero. These low-level out-of-band signal components are all aliased (folded back) into the in-band signals by the sampling process. Once aliased, no postprocessing technique can remove this noise.

A common misunderstanding is the belief that B_s Hz is the passband B_p of the desired GNSS signal (buried in noise), when, in fact, B_s Hz is the (much wider) stopband (i.e., the bandwidth at which the undesired higher frequency signals, which may or may not be buried in noise, have all been reduced by the antialiasing filter to a low level). For P(Y) code, the usual assumption is that the front-end bandwidth B_p should be about twice the spreading code rate, or 20 MHz. Since there is zero P(Y) code energy at the spreading code rate frequency nulls, there is less than 0.1 dB loss of additional signal-to-thermal-noise ratio incurred by using a very sharp cutoff bandpass filter of 17 MHz. Assuming the stopband, B_s, for the antialiasing filter is achieved at 25 MHz, this implies a sample rate of $R_s = 50$ MHz, not 34 MHz. Contrast this with the 20-MHz passband case with the same antialiasing filter roll-off rate, resulting in a stopband of 28 MHz and $R_s = 56$ MHz, not 40 MHz. The 17-MHz bandwidth design choice is an excellent tradeoff to reduce the ADC sampling rate with negligible increase of antialiasing filter implementation loss.

It is common practice in high-end commercial C/A code receiver designs to widen the front-end bandwidth in order to operate them with narrow correlators for improved pseudorange accuracy in thermal noise as well as to mitigate multipath effects. In this case, the front-end bandwidth and ADC sample rates must both be increased to include multiple C/A code sidelobes.

Misunderstanding of the fundamental requirement for ADC sampling rate based on the stopband of the antialiasing filter can result in tens of decibels of aliasing noise. For a well-designed GNSS receiver, the antialiasing filtering and the sampling rate are both appropriately designed so that the effect of aliasing noise is negligible.

The quantization process introduces additional interference into the signal in the form of quantization noise and clipping noise. The quantization noise is caused by the finite amplitude resolution as defined by the least significant bit in the ADC. The clipping noise is related to that portion of the analog signal amplitude that is beyond the peak-to-peak value of the reference voltage range of the ADC. If digital frequency excision or frequency domain search techniques are used following the

ADC, then high-precision ADCs are required because precise amplitude information is essential to these processes. Time domain transversal filter or frequency domain FFT techniques are commonly used for frequency excision. Typically these ADCs are 12-bit for military and 10-bit for commercial frequency excision applications. In these cases, both the quantization noise and clipping noise are negligible.

The vast majority of GPS receivers use fewer than 4 bits in the ADC because there is little signal degradation improvement beyond 3 bits. With appropriate sampling ($R_s \geq 2B_s$), the ADC degradations for wideband Gaussian noise are 1.96 dB for 1-bit, 0.55 dB for 2-bit, and 0.16 dB for 3-bit ADCs [1]. This assumes antialiasing filtering that suppresses the RMS noise levels well below the ADC degradation levels at and beyond B_s. By contrast, with undersampling ($R_s = 2B_p$), the ADC degradations for wideband Gaussian noise with mismatched sample rates result in degradations of approximately 3.5 dB for 1-bit, 1.2 dB for 2-bit, and 0.6 dB for 3-bit ADCs [2]. These results were based on a P(Y) code receiver design with passband bandwidth of twice the spreading code rate ($B_p = 2R_c$) and an optimum AGC signal amplitude into the ADC. No AGC is required for the 1-bit (limiter) case. Assuming a typical ADC voltage reference of +/– 5 VDC (a 10-V peak-to-peak ADC range), the optimum RMS level outputs from the AGC into the ADC to achieve these minimum ADC signal degradations for the P(Y) code receiver example are approximately 12.5V for 2-bit and 7.7V for 3-bit ADCs. A second example in [2] illustrates the same mismatched sample rate ($R_s = 2B_p$) for a wideband C/A code receiver design with $B_p = 5R_c$. In this case, the degradations are somewhat reduced to approximately 2.3 dB for 1-bit, 0.7 dB for 2-bit, and 0.3 dB for 3-bit ADCs. The 1-bit ADC is clipped all of the time. The approximate RMS level outputs from the AGC into the ADC to achieve these minimum ADC signal degradations for this C/A-code example (still assuming a 10-V peak-to-peak ADC voltage reference) are approximately 10.1V for 2-bit and 5.6V for 3-bit ADCs. This illustrates that the optimum AGC levels for the 2-bit ADC is clipped a high percentage of the time and the 3-bit ADC is seldom clipped. This is in accordance with the reduction in the quantization noise as the number of ADC bits is increased. Obviously, both designs suffer additional signal degradations due to aliasing noise caused by undersampling. Reference [2] also includes 4-bit and 5-bit ADC degradations (not discussed here) that serve to illustrate the diminishing returns for more quantization precision in GPS applications that do not perform digital frequency excision or frequency domain processing. They also illustrate that the AGC level must be adapted to the antialiasing filtering, the sample rate, and the number of bits in the ADC in order to achieve minimum signal degradation in the presence of wideband Gaussian noise.

The preferred low-precision ADC embodiment in a GPS receiver is the nonuniform 2-bit quantization design included in Figure 6.1. This ADC design is adapted from [3, 4] for GPS applications because of its substantial processing gain in the presence of CW interference plus thermal noise.[2] As a result of CW jamming, the statistics of the zero crossings of the signal are no longer determined by a combination of thermal noise and the GPS signals buried in this random noise, but become domi-

---

2.   H. Logan Scott originally adapted Amoroso's nonuniform ADC design [3] for military GPS receivers. This
       design was first used in the TI 4XOP family of military GPS receiver designs, Texas Instruments, Inc., 1985.

nated by the statistics of the CW signal. The probability density of a CW signal amplitude is

$$P(x) = \frac{1}{\pi\sqrt{1-x^2}} \tag{6.3}$$

This function is plotted in Figure 6.2. Observe in this plot that the CW signal spends most of its time near the peak amplitudes rather than in the vicinity of the zero crossing. The result is that the combination of the signals plus thermal noise plus a strong CW signal spends very little time near the zero crossing.

Virtually all modern receivers are precorrelation ADC designs, so the ADC process takes place prior to the digital correlation process. If the ADC is properly designed, the digital correlation process that follows spreads the CW signal into a wideband signal, while despreading the signal into a narrowband (data modulation) signal with a bandwidth that is essentially the reciprocal of the predetection integration time. This is a significant signal bandwidth reduction and CW interference bandwidth expansion. Filtering the resulting narrowband signal provides significant processing gain against the CW, but this is only true if the CW signal does not first capture the ADC. The ADC is subjected to the full amplitude of CW interference in a precorrelation ADC receiver. In the case of a 1-bit ADC (limiter), there is very little correlation possible in the presence of CW interference. The CW interference essentially captures the 1-bit ADC in a precorrelation ADC receiver design. This increases the 1-bit ADC SNR degradation from 1.96 dB in the presence of Gaussian noise to 6.0 dB in the presence of any constant envelope (including CW) interference [3]. The nonuniform 2-bit ADC of Figure 6.1 reduces this degradation to less than 0.6 dB in the presence of Gaussian noise, and in the presence of CW

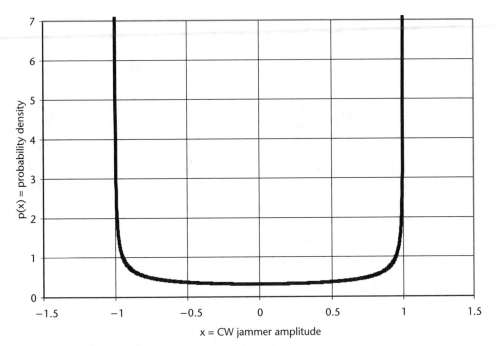

Figure 6.2   Probability density of a CW (sinusoidal) signal.

interference it can outperform an infinite-bit linear ADC by more than 10 dB at high jamming-to-desired signal (*J/S*) power ratios (60 dB or higher) (see footnote 2). It performs well for modulated CW, such as swept CW and narrowband jammers.

The principle of operation of the nonlinear ADC in the presence of CW is as follows. In the design in [3], the application is for very short period PRN codes that are BPSK modulated and received at the much higher SNRs typical of spread spectrum communications systems. Thus, the upper and lower magnitude comparator voltages are changed dynamically by complementary digital counters at the ADC output, while the AGC attack and recovery rate is slow. Referring to the Figure 6.1 adaptation of this concept for receiver applications, the upper and lower magnitude comparator voltages, V_B, are held constant, the AGC attack and recovery rate is fast, and the feedback to the AGC controls the RMS amplitude for proper clipping of the ADC. As part of the AGC feedback control, the weighting factor, N, adjusts the statistical averaging time to properly follow fluctuations in the noise level of the signal plus noise that exceeds the plus and minus magnitude bit comparators. A comparator passes the output of the weighting factor function that exceeds a certain percentage (*T%*). The result is an AGC control error that is digitally integrated, then converted to an analog AGC control voltage (see footnote 2). Figure 6.3 depicts the GPS signal buried in (dominated by) thermal noise being added to (riding on top of) a CW signal, along with typical complementary threshold settings of $T = 5\%$. The *T%* threshold adjusts the signal statistics such that a similar effect is taking place at the plus magnitude and minus magnitude comparators as would occur at the sign bit comparator with only thermal noise present. In this manner, the nonuniform ADC provides correlation in the presence of constant envelope interference. The values of *T%* and N can be constants or variable, depending on the level of sophistication

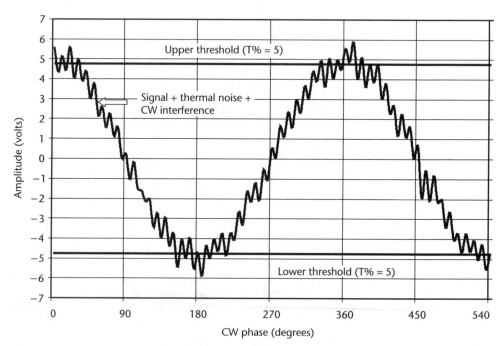

Figure 6.3 Setting nonuniform ADC threshold to exploit constant envelope interference statistics.

desired. If variable, then the J/N meter (described in the following section) and the CW signal detector in Figure 6.1 are used to make the adjustments dynamically. The range of $T\%$ is adjusted typically between 5% and 15% and N between 4 and 16, depending on the presence of the CW and the level of CW interference as indicated by these built-in monitors. The best CW performance at the highest J/N is achieved when $T\%$ is 5 and N is 16. There is less signal degradation at the lowest J/N conditions if $T\%$ is 15% and N is 4. The specific design requires tuning (see footnote 2).

6.2.2.4   Receiver Jamming Situational Awareness—J/N Meter

Figure 6.1 illustrates the circuit simplicity of adding a J/N meter to a receiver design containing an AGC amplifier that is controlled by a digital feedback loop. To achieve this simplicity, the addition of the J/N meter must be part of the original receiver AGC design plan. Since the addition of a J/N meter is seldom preplanned, there have been numerous papers published on interference measurement techniques performed within the tracking loops or the navigation solution of a receiver. The main problem with these concepts is that the receiver must be tracking to measure jamming. It is important to have situational awareness about jamming during the search modes and adapt the search strategy accordingly, then adapt the tracking strategy accordingly if tracking is possible. It is also important to have situational awareness when the receiver fails to navigate. In this case, a situational display can inform the user that the jamming level exceeds the search or tracking capability of the receiver. Only an AGC J/N meter can perform this function because the J/N meter continues to operate even if the search and tracking functions are incapable of operating at the measured jamming levels. The bottom line is that measuring the control voltage levels to the AGC to determine jamming is superior to any other method, but the provision for this measurement must be preplanned in the original AGC design. For military GPS receivers, this means that the situational awareness requirement must be specified.

As demonstrated for the simple case of detecting CW interference in Figure 6.1, the digital IF signal statistics can be analyzed and characterized for other classes of interference. So, not only can the AGC and ADC areas of a receiver provide situational awareness with respect to the jamming level that is actually being experienced by the receiver regardless of whether the receiver is capable of operating at that jamming level, but also the jamming type can be identified if these designs are preplanned.

The principle of operation of the J/N meter in Figure 6.1 is as follows. In the absence of interference, the signals are buried in thermal noise. Under this condition, the AGC adjusts the RMS signal amplitude for optimal ADC performance based on thermal noise. If the AGC control voltage changes from this level, that change is an indication that the noise level has increased. This increase can only be caused by interference, and the measure of this interference is the change in the AGC control voltage. As depicted in Figure 6.1, the AGC gain is reduced in the presence of increased interference. Because of the logarithmic nature of the AGC control voltage, J/N is equal to the change in AGC control voltage times a scale factor. Obviously, J/N is unity (0 dB) in the presence of thermal noise. The digital design in Figure 6.1 that ultimately provides the analog control voltage to the AGC can be a very accurate measurement of J/N if the amplifier is calibrated as described in Section 6.2.2.2.

6.2.2.5 Effects of Interference on Acquisition, Carrier Tracking, and Data Demodulation

The performance of signal acquisition, carrier tracking, and data demodulation all depend on the SNIR at the output of each correlator in a receiver. Consequently, evaluating the effect of RF interference on correlator output SNIR provides the basis for assessing the effect of this interference on these three receiver functions. This section describes the underlying theory behind this effect and then presents approximation techniques for such analysis.

When the aggregate interference can be modeled as statistically stationary, and when the spectra of either the interference or the desired signal (or both) are well approximated by a straight line over a bandwidth that is the reciprocal of the integration time used in the correlation, the correlator output SNIR is as follows [5]:

$$\rho_c(\tau,\theta) = \frac{2TC_S \Big/ N_0 \left[\Re\left\{ e^{j\theta} \int_{-\infty}^{\infty} S_S(f) H_T(f) H_R(f) e^{j2\pi f\tau} df \right\} \right]^2}{\int_{-\infty}^{\infty} |H_R(f)|^2 S_S(f) df + C_i \Big/ N_0 \int_{-\infty}^{\infty} |H_R(f)|^2 S_i(f) S_S(f) df} \tag{6.4}$$

where τ is the delay of the locally generated replica code relative to the true TOA of the received signal in space, θ is the carrier phase of the replica carrier signal relative to the phase of the received signal, T is the integration time of the correlator, C_s is the received power of the desired signal (in watts), N_0 is the power spectral density of the white noise (in W/Hz), $\Re\{\cdot\}$ denotes the real part of the enclosed function, $S_s(f)$ is the power spectral density of the signal, normalized to unit area over infinite bandwidth, $H_T(f)$ is the transfer function of the SV signal transmitter, $H_R(f)$ is the transfer function of the receiver filter, C_i is the power of the received interference signal (in watts), and $S_i(f)$ is the power spectral density of the aggregate interference, normalized to unit area over infinite bandwidth.

The quality of a received GNSS signal is commonly described in terms of its *carrier-power-to-noise-density ratio*, implying that the noise is white and thus can be described by a scalar noise density. Yet (6.4) shows that any nonwhite interference must be accounted for as well and must be described by its power spectral density, including its power. Thus, analyzing the correlator output SNIR in interference is extremely cumbersome. However, if a fictitious white noise density is formulated that produces the same output SNIR as the combination of the actual white noise and interference, then the resulting effective carrier-power-to-noise-density ratio is both correct and straightforward to analyze using the fiction of effective white noise.

To derive an *effective* C_s/N_0, or $(C_s/N_0)_{eff}$, observe that (6.4) with no interference is:

$$
\rho_c(\tau,\theta) = \frac{2TC_S \Big/ N_0 \left[\Re\left\{ e^{j\theta} \int\limits_{-\infty}^{\infty} S_S(f)H_T(f)H_R(f)e^{j2\pi f\tau}\,df \right\} \right]^2}{\int\limits_{-\infty}^{\infty} |H_R(f)|^2 S_S(f)\,df}
\tag{6.5}
$$

Typically, the delay and phase values of most interest are when the output SNIR is highest. At this point, C_S/N_0 is:

$$
C_S/N_0 = \frac{\max\limits_{\tau,\theta}[\rho_c(\tau,\theta)]\int\limits_{-\infty}^{\infty}|H_R(f)|^2 S_S(f)\,df}{2T\left[\Re\left\{ e^{j\hat{\theta}} \int\limits_{-\infty}^{\infty} S_S(f)H_T(f)H_R(f)e^{j2\pi f\hat{\tau}}\,df \right\}\right]^2}
\tag{6.6}
$$

where $(\hat{\tau},\hat{\theta}) = \arg\max\limits_{\tau,\theta}[\rho_c(\tau,\theta)]$, the values that maximize the output SNIR.

When there is both interference and white noise, $(C_S/N_0)_{eff}$ is defined in a way analogous to (6.6) as follows

$$
(C_S/N_0)_{eff} = \frac{\max\limits_{\tau,\theta}[\rho_c(\tau,\theta)]\int\limits_{-\infty}^{\infty}|H_R(f)|^2 S_S(f)\,df}{2T\left[\Re\left\{ e^{j\hat{\theta}} \int\limits_{-\infty}^{\infty} S_S(f)H_T(f)H_R(f)e^{j2\pi f\hat{\tau}}\,df \right\}\right]^2}
$$

$$
= (C_S/N_0)\frac{\int\limits_{-\infty}^{\infty}|H_R(f)|^2 S_S(f)\,df}{\int\limits_{-\infty}^{\infty}|H_R(f)|^2 S_S(f)\,df + \dfrac{C_I}{N_0}\int\limits_{-\infty}^{\infty}|H_R(f)|^2 S_I(f)S_S(f)\,df}
\tag{6.7}
$$

$$
= \frac{1}{\dfrac{1}{(C_S/N_0)} + \dfrac{C_I/C_S}{\dfrac{\int\limits_{-\infty}^{\infty}|H_R(f)|^2 S_S(f)\,df}{\int\limits_{-\infty}^{\infty}|H_R(f)|^2 S_I(f)S_S(f)\,df}}}
$$

Observe that (6.7) can be expressed as [6]:

$$
(C_S/N_0)_{eff} = \frac{1}{\dfrac{1}{(C_S/N_0)} + \dfrac{C_I/C_S}{QR_c}}
\tag{6.8}
$$

where C_S/N_0 is the unjammed carrier-to-noise-power ratio of the received signal inside the receiver, C_I/C_S is the jamming-to-received-signal power ratio inside the receiver, Q is a dimensionless jamming resistance quality factor to be determined for various types of jammers and signal modulators, and R_c is the spreading code rate of the code generator in chips per second. Note that increasing the value of Q in (6.8) improves $(C_s/N_0)_{eff}$. Therefore, higher jamming resistance quality factor, Q, results in increased jamming effectiveness. Comparing (6.7) and (6.8) yields

$$Q = \frac{\int_{-\infty}^{\infty}|H_R(f)|^2 S_S(f)df}{R_c\int_{-\infty}^{\infty}|H_R(f)|^2 S_I(f)S_S(f)df} \tag{6.9}$$

To assist in the interpretation of (6.9), define the receiver transfer function to have maximum magnitude of unity, so $\max_f|H_R(f)|=1$, which can be achieved by multiplying the filter transfer function by a scalar without changing (6.9) in the process. With this definition, the numerator of (6.9) is the fraction of signal power passed by the receiver front end. (Recall that the signal power spectral density is defined to have unit area over all frequencies.)

Then, (6.9) can be expressed succinctly as

$$Q = \frac{\int_{-\infty}^{\infty}|H_R(f)|^2 S_S(f)df}{R_c\kappa_{IS}} \tag{6.10}$$

where κ_{IS} is called the spectral separation coefficient (SSC) [7], which is defined as

$$\kappa_{IS} = \int_{-\infty}^{\infty}|H_R(f)|^2 S_I(f)S_S(f)df \tag{6.11}$$

Equation (6.11) has units of reciprocal hertz or seconds. Observe that the SSC depends on the spectrum of the desired signal as well as the spectrum of the interference. Different interferers may have the same SSC with a given desired signal, and when they do, the different interferers affect $(C_s/N_0)_{eff}$ the same way. It follows then that different interferers may have a different SSC with a given desired signal. For example, if interferer A has x dB smaller SSC with the desired signal than interferer B, then interferer A has the same effect on $(C_s/N_0)_{eff}$ as interferer B when the power in A is increased by x dB.

Computing Jamming Resistance Quality Factor Q
To consider interference effects further for some nominal situations, suppose that the receive filter is very wide, so that $H_R(f)$ can be treated as approximately unity in (6.9) at frequencies where the desired signal has appreciable power, and the limits on the integrals can be approximated by infinity, so that (6.9) is approximated by

$$Q \cong \frac{1}{R_c\int_{-\infty}^{\infty}S_I(f)S_S(f)df} \tag{6.12}$$

Examples of different types of interference can now be evaluated.

Case 1—Narrowband Interference.   For narrowband interference centered at f_i, the power spectrum can be modeled as $S_i(f) = \delta(f - f_i)$, where $\delta(\cdot)$ is the Dirac delta function having infinite amplitude, vanishing width, and unit area. Substituting for this interference power spectral density in (6.12) yields

$$Q = \frac{1}{R_c S_S (f_i)} \tag{6.13}$$

In general, narrowband interference affects $(C_s/N_0)_{eff}$ more when the interference frequency is at or near the maximum of the signal power spectrum. Moreover, when the normalized power spectrum of the desired signal has a smaller maximum, the desired signal is degraded less by narrowband interference at the worst-case frequency.

BPSK-R(n) is the modulation notation introduced in Section 4.2.3 for received signals that have been synthesized by BPSK with rectangular spreading symbols at a chip rate of $R_c = 1.023 \times n$ MHz. Using this notation, P(Y) code is BPSK-R(10) while L1 C/A code and L2C are BPSK-R(1), but M code is a $BOC_s(m,n) = BOC_s(10,5)$ modulation (see Sections 4.2.3 and 4.5.3). The baseband power spectral density functions for BPSK-R(n) and $BOC_s(m,n)$ signals are given, respectively, in (4.14) and (4.17).

If the narrowband interference is placed at the spectral maximum of a BPSK-R(n) signal ($f = 0$ for the baseband power spectral density), $S_s(f = 0) = 1/R_c$, and (6.13) becomes $Q = \dfrac{1}{R_C / R_C} = 1$. If instead the interference is placed at a frequency other than the signal's spectral peak, Q is greater than unity, meaning that the interference has less effect.

For a BOC(m,n) modulation, if the interferer is located at one or both of the spectral peaks, Q takes on values in the range $1.9 \le Q \le 2.5$, depending upon the subcarrier frequency, the spreading code rate, and whether cosine phasing or sine phasing is used. If the narrowband interferer is at any other frequency, Q again takes on larger values, indicating that interference of fixed power has less effect on $(C_s/N_0)_{eff}$.

Case 2—Matched Spectrum Interference.   Consider now when the interference has the same power spectral density as the desired signal. This situation could arise from multiple access interference or from a jamming waveform whose spectrum is matched to that of the desired signal.

$$Q = \frac{1}{R_c \displaystyle\int_{-\infty}^{\infty} [S_S(f)]^2 \, df} \tag{6.14}$$

When the signal is BPSK-R(n), substituting (4.14) into (6.14) yields

$$Q = \cfrac{1}{R_c \int\limits_{-\infty}^{\infty} T_c^2 \, \text{sinc}^4\left(\pi f T_c\right) df} = 1.5 \qquad (6.15)$$

For a BOC(m,n) modulation, Q takes on values in the range $3 \le Q \le 4.5$, depending upon the subcarrier frequency, the spreading code rate, and whether cosine-phasing or sine-phasing is used.

Case 3—Bandlimited White Noise Interference.   When the interference has flat spectrum centered at f_i and extending from $f_i - \beta_i/2 \le f \le f_i + \beta_i/2$, its spectrum is expressed as

$$S_i(f) = \begin{cases} \cfrac{1}{\beta_i}, & f_i - \beta_i/2 \le f \le f_i + \beta_i/2 \\ 0, & \text{elsewhere.} \end{cases} \qquad (6.16)$$

Substituting (6.16) into (6.12) yields

$$Q = \cfrac{1}{\cfrac{R_c}{\beta_i} \int\limits_{f_i-\beta_i/2}^{f_i+\beta_i/2} S_S(f) df} \qquad (6.17)$$

If β_i becomes small, (6.17) approaches (6.13), the result for narrowband interference.

If β_i is large enough so that almost all of the signal power is included within $f_i - \beta_i/2 \le f \le f_i + \beta_i/2$, then (6.17) becomes

$$Q = \frac{\beta_i}{R_c} \qquad (6.18)$$

Rearranging (6.18), $QR_c = \beta_i$, which shows that modulation design, and in particular higher spreading code rates, provide no benefit to $(C_s/N_0)_{eff}$ when the noise spectrum is flat over the frequency range occupied by the signal. Moreover, for fixed interference power, the wider the interference bandwidth, the larger the value of Q, and hence the smaller influence of the interference on $(C_s/N_0)_{eff}$.

When the signal is BPSK-R(n) and the interference spectrum is centered on the signal spectrum so that $f_i = 0$, substituting (4.14) into (6.17) yields

$$Q = \cfrac{1}{\cfrac{1}{\beta_i} \int\limits_{\beta_i/2}^{\beta_i/2} \text{sinc}^2\left(\pi f T_c\right) df} \qquad (6.19)$$

When in addition $\beta_i = 2R_c$ so that the interference covers the null-to-null main lobe of the signal spectrum, (6.19) becomes

$$Q = \frac{2}{\displaystyle\int_{-R_c}^{R_c} \mathrm{sinc}^2\left(\pi f T_c\right) df} \cong 2.22 \tag{6.20}$$

When the modulation is BOC(m, n) and the interference spectrum is centered on one or both of the subcarrier frequencies so that $f_i = \pm m \times 1.023$ MHz, Q is slightly more than twice the value of the corresponding Q for a BPSK-R(n) modulation. In particular, when $\beta_i = 2R_c$ so that the interference covers one or both null-to-null main lobes of the signal spectrum, Q takes on values in the range $4.6 \le Q \le 5.5$, depending on the subcarrier frequency, the spreading code rate, and whether cosine phasing or sine phasing is used.

Table 6.3 summarizes these Qs for C/A code, P(Y) code, and M code, along with their associated modulation types and spreading code rates for the three classes of jammer types analyzed earlier.

Computing J/S and Tolerable Jamming Power
When expressed in units of dB-Hz, (6.8) becomes

$$\left(C_S/N_0\right)_{eff,dB} \overset{\Delta}{=} 10\log_{10}\left(C_S/N_0\right)_{eff}$$

$$= -10\log_{10}\left[10^{-\frac{(C_S/N_0)_{dB}}{10}} + \frac{10^{\frac{(C_i/C_s)_{dB}}{10}}}{QR_c} \right] \tag{6.21}$$

where:

$(C_s/N_0)_{dB} = 10\log_{10}(C_s/N_0)$ (dB-Hz)

$(C_i/C_s)_{dB} = 10\log_{10}(C_i/C_s)$ (dB)

$R_c = 1.023$ Mchip/s for L1 C/A code and L2C

$\quad = 5.115$ Mchip/s for M code

$\quad = 10.23$ Mchip/s for P(Y) code and L5 code

Equation (6.21) shows that the effect of jamming is to reduce the unjammed $(C_s/N_0)_{dB}$ in a receiver to a lower value, $(C_s/N_0)_{eff, dB}$. As shown in Chapter 5, signal

Table 6.3   Summary of Jamming Resistance Quality Factors (Q)

Signal/Jammer Type	Q (Dimensionless)		
PRN code	C/A Code	P(Y) Code	M Code
Spreading code rate	$R_c = 1.023$ MHz	$R_c = 10.23$ MHz	$R_c = 5.115$ MHz
Modulation type	BPSK-R(1)	BPSK-R(10)	BOC$_s$(10,5)
Bandlimited white noise null to null	2.22	2.22	5.3
Matched spectrum	1.5	1.5	4.0
Narrowband at spectral peak(s)	1	1	2.3

acquisition, carrier tracking, and data demodulation deteriorate as the $(C_s/N_0)_{eff}$ is reduced until these receiver functions are lost. Chapter 5 shows that the effect of interference on code tracking is not described by $(C_s/N_0)_{eff}$, so a separate assessment must be performed to evaluate the effect on code tracking and loss of lock.

Equation (6.21) can be rearranged to solve for $(C_i/C_s)_{dB}$ as follows:

$$(C_i/C_s)_{dB} = 10\log_{10}\left[QR_c\left(10^{-\frac{(C_s/N_0)_{eff,dB}}{10}} - 10^{-\frac{(C_s/N_0)_{dB}}{10}}\right)\right] \tag{6.22}$$

Computing the unjammed $(C_s/N_0)_{dB}$ in (6.21) and (6.22) in units of dB-Hz involves numerous parameters and is presented piecewise as follows:

$$
\begin{aligned}
(C_s/N_0)_{dB} &= (C_s)_{dB} - (N_0)_{dB} && \text{(dB-Hz)} \\
(C_s)_{dB} &= (C_{Ri})_{dB} + (G_{Svi})_{dB} - L_{dB} && \text{(dBW)} \\
(N_0)_{dB} &= 10\log_{10}\left[k(T_{ant} + T_{amp})\right] && \text{(dBW)} \\
T_{amp} &= 290\left(10^{\frac{(N_f)_{dB}}{10}} - 1\right) && \text{(K)}
\end{aligned}
\tag{6.23}
$$

where:

$(C_s)_{dB}$ = recovered signal power received from SV_i (dBW)

$(N_0)_{dB}$ = thermal noise power component in a 1-Hz bandwidth (dBW)

$(C_{Ri})_{dB}$ = received signal power from SV_i at antenna input (dBW)

$(G_{Svi})_{dB}$ = antenna gain toward SV_i (dBic)

L_{dB} = receiver implementation loss, including A/D converter loss (dB)

k = Boltzmann's constant = 1.38×10^{-23} (J/K)

T_{ant} = antenna noise temperature (K)

T_{amp} = amplifier temperature (K)

Q = jamming resistance quality factor (dimensionless)

R_c = spreading code rate (chips/s)

$(N_f)_{dB}$ = amplifier noise figure at 290K (dB)

As a computation example of (6.23), assume $(C_{Ri})_{dB} = -158.5$ dBW (i.e., the IS-GPS-200 minimum specified received signal power level for L1 C/A code) (see Section 4.3.2 for details). Further assume that a fixed reception pattern antenna (FRPA) is used with a typical gain roll off to about -3 dBic at the elevation mask angle of 5° above the horizon. This is the elevation angle where the minimum GPS received power specification is met. It is also typical for the antenna gain to increase to 1.5 dBic or more at zenith, where the GPS minimum received power specification is also met. In between these two elevation angles, the received signal power tends to increase slightly due to the satellite antenna array gain pattern. In other words, the received signal power and antenna gain combination tends to be lower by about -3 dB near the elevation mask angle of $5°$ and higher by about 1.5 dB at zenith with a fluctuation range of more than 4.5 dB in the approximately hemispherical gain coverage region of a typical FRPA. Antenna tilt can significantly increase this gain fluctuation range. In this example, the antenna is assumed to have $(G_{SVi})_{dB} = 1.5\,dB$ gain toward the SV to allow for the higher SV signal levels that exist most of the time, counting the gains of both the receiver antenna and the SV antenna. The implementation loss is assumed to be 2 dB ($L_{dB} = 2$) for a high-quality receiver design and A/D converter. Using these assumptions in (6.23), the total recovered signal power is $(C_s)_{dB} = -158.5 + 1.5 - 2 = -159.0$ dBW. Next assume that the receiver noise figure $(N_f)_{dB} = 4.3$ dB at 290 K, so $T_{amp} = 290 \times (10^{0.43} - 1) = 490.5$ K. Assuming that the antenna noise temperature is 100K, then the thermal noise can be computed as $N_0 = 10\log_{10}[k \times (100 + 490.5)] = -200.9$ dBW. Therefore, the unjammed $(C_s/N_0)_{dB} = -159.0 + 200.9 = 41.9$ dB-Hz.

Note that the unjammed $(C_s/N_0)_{dB}$ in (6.23) accounts for the antenna gain in the direction of the satellite as well as the implementation loss of the receiver. Similarly, if the antenna gain in the direction of the jammer, $(G_J)_{dB}$, is accounted for in (6.22), then

$$(C_i/C_S)_{dB} = (C_\ell)_{dB} - (C_S)_{dB}$$
$$(C_i)_{dB} = J_{dB} + (G_J)_{dB} - L_{dB}$$
$$(C_S)_{dB} = (C_{Ri})_{dB} + (G_{SVi})_{dB} - L_{dB} = S_{dB} + (G_{SVi})_{dB} - L_{dB} \qquad (6.24)$$
$$(C_i/C_S)_{dB} = J_{dB} - S_{dB} + (G_J)_{dB} - (G_{SVi})_{dB} = (J/S)_{dB} + (G_J)_{dB} - (G_{SVi})_{dB}$$

where $(J/S)_{dB}$ is the jamming to signal power ratio at the antenna input in decibels. Substituting this into (6.22)

$$(J/S)_{dB} = (G_{SVi})_{dB} - (G_J)_{dB} + 10\log_{10}\left[QR_c\left(10^{-\frac{(C_S/N_0)_{eff,dB}}{10}} - 10^{-\frac{(C_S/N_0)_{dB}}{10}}\right)\right] \quad (6.25)$$

From (6.25), the receiver $(J/S)_{dB}$ performance can be computed for a given QR_c using the unjammed $(C_s/N_0)_{dB}$ from (6.23) and obtaining the value of $(C_s/N_0)_{eff,dB}$ by simply equating it to the receiver tracking threshold as determined from the approximation methods presented in Chapter 5. Recall that the carrier tracking threshold $(C_s/N_0)_{eff,dB}$ is the weak link for an unaided GPS receiver and even for an externally aided receiver if the carrier loop is closed.

As a computational example of (6.24) using the unjammed C/A code example where $(C_s/N_0)_{dB} = 41.9$ dB-Hz, assume the antenna gain toward the jammer, $(G_J)_{dB}$, is -3 dB. Note that the jammer signal may or may not be RHCP. If RHCP, then the antenna gain toward the jammer would be the same as its gain in that direction for an SV. But if the jammer is linearly polarized, then an additional 3-dB loss or more must be included in the gain toward the jammer, depending on the polarization mismatch of the GPS antenna. Since the desired signal is C/A code with a BPSK-R(1) modulation, $R_c = 1.023$ Mchip/s. Assume a bandlimited white noise (BLWN) jamming waveform whose spectrum is rectangular, centered at the C/A center frequency, and approximately 2 MHz wide (null to null), so that $Q \cong 2.22$. If the PLL carrier tracking threshold example from Section 5.6.1 is used, then the tolerable $(C_s/N_0)_{eff,dB} = 28$ dB-Hz. Substituting these and the unjammed $(C_s/N_0)_{dB}$ from the previous computational example into (6.25)

$$(J/S)_{dB} = 1.5 + 3.0 + 10\log_{10}\left[2.22 \times 1.023 \times 10^6 \left(10^{-2.8} - 10^{-4.19}\right)\right]$$
$$= 39.9\,\text{dB}$$

For L1 P(Y) code, there is BPSK-R(10) modulation with $R_c = 10.23$ Mchip/s and $(C_{Ri})_{dB} = -161.5$ dBW. Assume the jamming waveform has a BLWN rectangular spectrum centered on L1 with width of 20.46 MHz (null to null) so that $Q = 2.22$ (and the remaining assumptions the same). The unjammed $(C_s/N_0)_{dB} = 38.9$ dB-Hz, so

$$(J/S)_{dB} = 1.5 + 3.0 + 10\log_{10}\left[2.22 \times 10.23 \times 10^6 \left(10^{-2.8} - 10^{-3.89}\right)\right]$$
$$= 49.7\,\text{dB}$$

Note that if the unjammed $(C_s/N_0)_{dB}$ for Y code were the same as for C/A code above, the $(J/S)_{dB}$ would be exactly 10 dB greater, reflecting the factor of 10 increase in spreading code chip rate.

For the normal power M code with BOC$_s$(10,5) modulation and $R_c = 5.115$ Mcps, $(C_{Ri})_{dB} = -158.0$ dBW. Assume that the BLWN jamming spectrum consists of two (null to null) rectangles, centered ±10.23 MHz away from L1, each with width of 10.23 MHz so that $Q \cong 5.3$ (and the remaining assumptions the same). The unjammed $(C_s/N_0)_{dB} = 43.4$ dB-Hz so

$$(J/S)_{dB} = 1.5 + 3.0 + 10\log_{10}\left[5.3 \times 5.115 \times 10^6 \left(10^{-2.8} - 10^{-4.34}\right)\right]$$
$$= 50.7\,\text{dB}$$

Table 6.4 summarizes the receiver $(J/S)_{dB}$ performance for L1 C/A code, L1 P(Y) code, and M code for all three types of jamming with the same assumptions for antenna gain toward the satellite (1.5 dB), gain toward the jammer (−3 dB), implementation loss (2 dB), and noise figure (4.3 dB) for a receiver tracking threshold $(C_s/N_0)_{eff,dB} = 28$ dB-Hz. The applicable Q used to compute each entry is shown in

Table 6.4 J/S Performance (with Appropriate Q) for 28-dB-Hz Carrier Tracking Threshold

Jammer Type	$(J/S)_{dB}$ (Q, Dimensionless)		
	L1 C/A Code	L1 P(Y) Code	L1 M Code (Normal)
Bandlimited white noise null to null	39.9 (2.22)	49.7 (2.22)	50.7 (5.3)
Matched spectrum	38.2 (1.5)	48.0 (1.5)	49.5 (4.0)
Narrowband at spectral peak(s)	36.4 (1)	46.2 (1)	47.1 (2.3)

parenthesis for reference. Note that this produces nine different values of J/S performance for the same receiver tracking threshold.

Figure 6.4 depicts the $(J/S)_{dB}$ performance as a function of the $(C_s/N_0)_{eff,dB}$ (receiver tracking threshold) for L1 C/A, L1 P(Y), and M code receivers for null-to-null jammers customized to each signal. The same assumptions were made as in the earlier examples to determine the unjammed $(C_s/N_0)_{dB}$.

Tolerable jamming (tolerable J) is a better way than J/S of comparing receiver jamming performance when there are multiple levels of signal power involved. Since the values of $(J/S)_{dB}$ in Table 6.4 are based on the receiver tracking threshold, the tolerable J_{dB} (dBW) is $(J/S)_{dB}$ (dB) plus the specified minimum received signal power level, $(C_{Ri})_{dB}$(dBW). Table 6.5 compares the receiver tolerable J performance for L1 C/A code, L1 P(Y) code, and M code for BLWN null-to-null(s) jammer assuming that all three receivers have the same 28-dB-Hz tracking threshold. (Actually, the M-code signal should have an even lower tracking threshold because of TDDM, as discussed in Chapter 5.) This comparison example reveals that the M code receiver outperforms the P(Y) code receiver by 4.5 dB and the P(Y) code receiver outperforms the C/A code receiver by 6.8 dB when all three receivers have the same tracking threshold (28 dB-Hz). With the 3-dB reduction in threshold from TDDM in M code, M code would outperform P(Y) code by 7.5 dB in tolerable jamming.

Figure 6.5 depicts the tolerable J_{dB} performance as a function of the $(C_s/N_0)_{eff,dB}$ (receiver tracking threshold) for L1 C/A, L1 P(Y), and M code receivers for BLWN null-to-null(s) jammers customized to each signal. The same assumptions were made as in the previous examples to determine the unjammed C_s/N_0.

Computing RF Interference Signal Levels
Even though the J/S performance of a GNSS receiver sounds impressive when the ratio is reported in decibels, it becomes less impressive when the actual jammer sig-

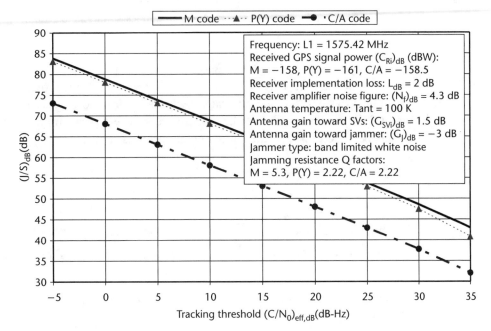

Figure 6.4 J/S performance as a function of receiver tracking threshold.

Table 6.5 Tolerable Jamming for 28-dB-Hz Carrier Tracking Threshold

	Jammer Type = BLWN Null to Null(s)		
	L1 C/A code	L1 P(Y) code	L1 M code (normal)
$(J/S)_{dB}$ (dB) with (Q)	39.9 (2.22)	49.7 (2.22)	50.7 (5.4)
Minimum specified $(S_r)_{dB}$ (dBW)	−158.5	−161.5	−158.0
Tolerable J_{dB} (dBW)	−118.6	−111.8	−107.3

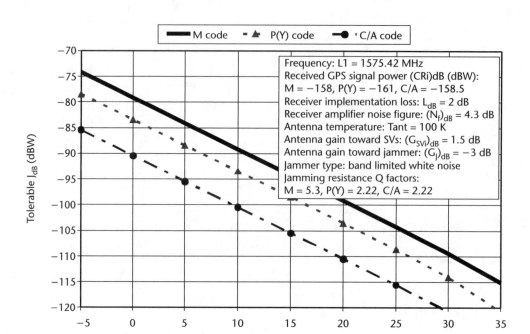

Figure 6.5 Tolerable *J* performance as a function of carrier tracking threshold, assuming all signals have the same tracking threshold.

nal levels are considered. This is because the GNSS signal power received at the antenna input is so small. To demonstrate how little jammer power is required at the input of a GNSS receiver to disable it when the receiver *J/S* performance in units of decibels has been determined, the following equation is required:

$$(J/S)_{dB} = (J_r)_{dB} - (S_r)_{dB} \tag{6.26}$$

where:

$(J_r)_{dB}$ = incident jammer power at the receiver antenna input (dBW)

$(S_r)_{dB}$ = incident signal power at the receiver antenna input (dBW)

Rearranging (6.26), $(J_r)_{dB} = (J/S)_{dB} + (S_r)_{dB}$. Since $(J_r)_{dB} = 10\log_{10} J_r$, then the jammer power in watts at the antenna input is

$$J_r = 10^{\frac{(J/S)_{dB} + (S_r)_{dB}}{10}} \tag{6.27}$$

Using the minimum specified received signal power level for C/A code at normal power, $(S_r)_{dB} = -158.5$ dBW and the jamming performance for the C/A code receiver in the previous section where $(C_s/N_0)_{eff,dB} = 28$ dB-Hz and $(J/S)_{dB} = 39.9$ dB for a BLWN null-to-null white noise jammer, the incident jammer power is determined from (6.27) as follows:

$$J_r = 10^{\frac{39.9 + (-158.5)}{10}} = 1.38 \times 10^{-12} \quad \text{W}$$

This demonstrates that for the FRPA design assumed in the previous section, less than 1.5 pW of incident RF interference power is required to disable a C/A code receiver with a moderate $(J/S)_{dB}$ performance of 39.9 dB.

Table 6.6 depicts the disabling incident power (along with the tolerable J and J/S performance for easy comparison). Note that even though the J/S performance of M code is about the same as that for P(Y) code, the disabling incident power and tolerable J are significantly larger for M code. Table 6.6 also shows clearly how much more robust P(Y) code and M code are than C/A code in the presence of jamming. Disabling incident power and tolerable J both provide insight into receiver antijam performance when there are different received signal powers and different values of R_c and Q involved. For example, one might think that M code would have a 3-dB lower J/S performance than P(Y) code since its spreading code rate is half that of P(Y) code. Since the Q for M code is more than double that of P(Y) code and its power is 3.5 dB stronger, the M code J/S performance is higher, as shown in brackets in Table 6.6. In fact, Table 6.6 shows that M code is more robust in the presence of jamming than P(Y) code for all three jammer types.

Computing Range to RF Interference

Usually, the receiver operating range from the source of the RF interference is desired given the effective isotropic radiated power (EIRP) of the interference source. (Refer to Appendix C for greater insight into propagation loss.)

The formula for the link budget for the transmitted jammer power is given by:

$$\left(EIRP_j\right)_{dB} = \left(J_r\right)_{dB} - \left(G_i\right)_{dB} + \left(L_p\right)_{dB} + \left(L_f\right)_{dB} \quad \text{dBW} \tag{6.28}$$

Table 6.6   Disabling Incident Power, Tolerable J, and J/S for 28-dB-Hz Carrier Tracking Threshold

Jammer Type	Incident Power in pW (Tolerable J_{dB} (dBW)) [($J/S)_{dB}$ (dB)]		
	L1 C/A Code	L1 P(Y) Code	M Code (Normal)
Wideband null to null	1.38 (−118.6) [39.9]	6.61 (−111.8)[49.7]	18.62 (−107.3) [50.7]
Wideband matched spectrum	0.93 (−120.3) [38.2]	4.47 (−113.5) [48.0]	14.13 (−108.5) [49.5]
Narrowband at spectral peak(s)	0.62 (−122.1) [36.4]	2.95 (−115.3) [46.2]	8.13 (−110.9) [47.1]

where:

$(EIRP_j)_{dB}$ = EIRP of the jammer

$$= (J_t)_{dB} + (G_t)_{dB}$$

$(J_t)_{dB}$ = jammer transmit power into its antenna (dBW)

$$= 10 \log_{10} J_t \ (J_t \text{ expressed in W})$$

$(G_t)_{dB}$ = jammer transmitter antenna gain (dBic)

$(J_r)_{dB}$ = incident (received) jammer power (dBW)

$$= 10 \log_{10} J_r \ (J_r \text{ expressed in W})$$

$(L_p)_{dB}$ = free space propagation loss (dB)

$$= 20 \log_{10} \left(\frac{4\pi d}{\lambda_j} \right) \text{(see Appendix C)}$$

d = range to jammer (m)

λ_j = wavelength of jammer frequency (m)

$(G_j)_{dB}$ = receiver antenna gain toward jammer (dBic)

$(L_f)_{dB}$ = jammer power loss due to receiver front-end filtering (dB)

As a computational example for L1 P(Y) code and a BLWN null-to-null jammer, assume that the propagation loss between jammer and GNSS receiver can be modeled as free space, that jammer transmitter power $J_t = 2W$, so $(J_t)_{dB} = 10 \log_{10} 2 = 3.0$ dBW, and the jammer antenna gain $(G_t)_{dB} = 3$ dB. Then $(EIRP_j)_{dB} = 6$ dBW, and the EIRP is $EIRP_t = 10^{0.6} = 4.0W$. Since the jammer frequency is in-band, the wavelength, λ_j, will be assumed to be the same as L1, and $(L_f)_{dB}$ is therefore assumed to be 0 dB. The receiver antenna gain toward the jammer, $(G_j)_{dB}$, is assumed to be −3 dBic (i.e., a power ratio of one-half representing the antenna gain with respect to a unity gain isotropic circularly polarized antenna). Using the J/S from Table 6.4 for the example of an L1 P(Y) code receiver with the third-order 18-Hz noise bandwidth carrier tracking loop for a BLWN null-to-null jammer, $(J/S)_{dB} = 49.7$ dB, and the minimum guaranteed received signal $(S_r)_{dB} = -161.5$ dBW then from (6.26), the tolerable J is

$$(J_r)_{dB} = (J/S)_{dB} + (S_r)_{dB} = 49.7 + (-161.5) = -111.8 \text{ dBW}$$

The LOS range to the antenna at which the receiver reaches its loss of track threshold can now be determined from (6.28), rearranged to solve for d

$$(L_p)_{dB} = 20 \log_{10} \left(\frac{4\pi d}{\lambda_j} \right)$$

$$= (J_t)_{dB} + (G_t)_{dB} - (J_r)_{dB} + (G_j)_{dB} - (L_f)_{dB}$$

$$= (3 + 3) + 111.8 + (-3) - 0 = 114.8 \text{ dB}$$

Next, we solve for the range, d, to the jammer to attenuate the 4-W transmitted jamming signal to the threshold level at the receiver input. This corresponds to the range from the jammer for the receiver to reach its tolerable J level:

$$d = \frac{\lambda_j 10^{\frac{(L_p)_{dB}}{20}}}{4,000\pi} = 8.3 \text{ km} \qquad (4.5 \text{ nmi})$$

Table 6.7 illustrates this distance computation for all three jammer types and L1 C/A code, L1 P(Y) code, and L1 M code receivers using the same assumptions for $EIRP_j$ and the receiver antenna gain toward the jammer, G_j. Note that the narrowband jammer is the most effective (lowest Q) for a given power, but it is also the easiest to mitigate.

Using the same equations and assumptions in the previous example, Figure 6.6(a–c) are plots of the range to the jammer as a function of the EIRP of a BLWN null-to-null(s) jammer with $(J/S)_{dB}$ as a running parameter for L1 C/A code, L1 P(Y) code, and M code receivers, respectively. Using the $(C_s/N_0)_{eff}$ obtained from the rule of thumb for carrier tracking threshold analysis or by using Monte Carlo simulations, the actual J/S performance of a receiver can be determined from Figure 6.4. Using the actual J/S performance, the LOS range to the jammer can be determined from Figure 6.6 for a wideband jammer, given the EIRP of the jammer. Alternatively, for a given range to the jammer, the tolerable EIRP can be determined.

6.2.2.6 Vulnerability of C/A Code to CW Interference

The GPS C/A code is a Gold code with a short 1-ms period (i.e., the PRN sequence repeats every 1 ms). Therefore, the C/A code (neglecting the navigation data) has a line spectrum with lines that are 1 kHz apart. Although it is typical for each line in the C/A code power spectrum to be down 24 dB or more with respect to the total power, there are some lines in every C/A code that are stronger. The C/A code line spectrum characteristic is inferior to a maximum-length PRN sequence with the same number of shift register bits [8]. As a result, a CW jammer can mix with a strong C/A code line and leak through the correlator. Table 6.8 summarizes the worst line frequency and the worst line (strongest) amplitude for every C/A code [9]. These phenomena cause more of a problem during C/A code search and acquisition modes than in tracking modes. If the receiver has a CW jammer detector such as the

Table 6.7 Tolerable J Distance to 4-W Jammer, Assuming Free-Space Propagation

Jammer Type	Distance, km (nmi)		
	L1 C/A Code	L1 P(Y) Code	M Code (Normal)
Wideband null to null	18.2 (10.0)	8.3 (4.5)	4.9 (2.7)
Wideband matched spectrum	22.1 (12.1)	10.1 (5.5)	5.7 (3.1)
Narrowband at spectral peak(s)	27.2 (14.4)	12.5 (6.8)	7.4 (4.1)

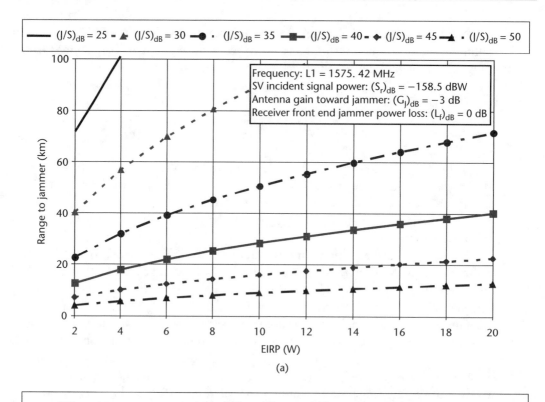

(a)

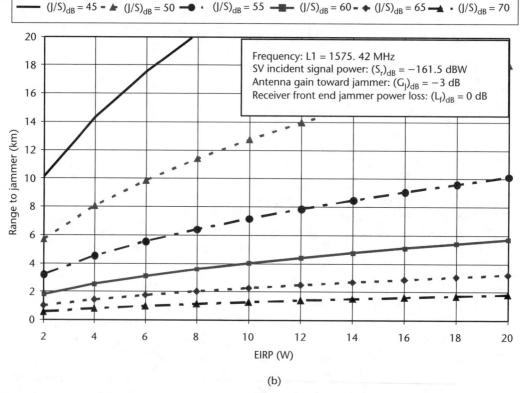

(b)

Figure 6.6 Range to jammer as a function of EIRP: (a) L1 C/A code receiver, (b) L1 P(Y) code receiver, and (c) M code receiver.

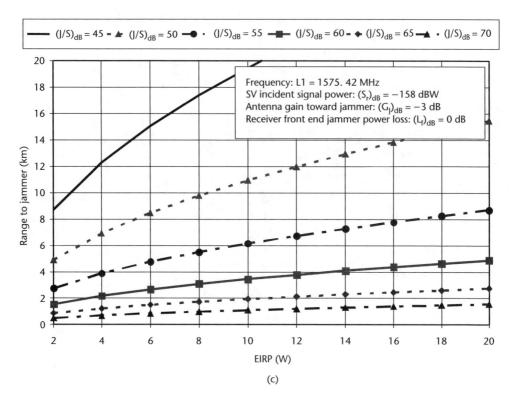

Figure 6.6   (continued.)

one shown in Figure 6.1, this can provide a warning that special (time-consuming) search measures must be taken, such as increasing the search dwell time and adjusting the search detector parameters for best C/A code search operation in the presence of CW. The new L2C and L5 signals have design features that minimize this vulnerability. The line spectra of the P(Y) code and M code have line spacing so narrow that they essentially take on attributes of continuous spectrum, so these signals do not exhibit this vulnerability.

Even if an adaptive antenna array or temporal filtering are used to reduce CW interference to the thermal noise level, there remains a vulnerability of C/A code to CW interference. The thermal noise floor can be determined from the following equation:

$$\left(N_{ther}\right)_{dB} = \left(N_0\right)_{dB} + 10\log_{10}\left(B\right) \quad \text{dBW} \tag{6.29}$$

where B = receiver front-end bandwidth (Hz).

Assume that the C/A code receiver is a narrow correlator design with a 15-MHz bandwidth. Substituting the thermal noise density, $(N_0)_{dB}$, value from the example in Section 6.2.2.5 into (6.29) yields:

$$\left(N_{ther}\right)_{dB} = -200.9 + 71.8 = -129.1 \quad \text{dBW}$$

Table 6.8 Worst C/A Line for Each of the 37 Codes

C/A Code PRN Number	Worst Line Frequency (kHz)	Worst Line Amplitude (dB)	C/A Code PRN Number	Worst Line Frequency (kHz)	Worst Line Amplitude (dB)
1	42	−22.71	20	30	−22.78
2	263	−23.12	21	55	−23.51
3	108	−22.04	22	12	−22.12
4	122	−22.98	23	127	−23.08
5	23	−21.53	24	123	−21.26
6	227	−21.29	25	151	−23.78
7	78	−23.27	26	102	−23.06
8	66	−21.50	27	132	−21.68
9	173	−22.09	28	203	−21.73
10	16	−22.45	29	176	−22.22
11	123	−22.64	30	63	−22.14
12	199	−22.08	31	72	−23.13
13	214	−23.52	32	74	−23.58
14	120	−22.01	33	82	−21.82
15	69	−21.90	34	55	−24.13
16	154	−22.58	35	43	−21.71
17	138	−22.50	36	23	−22.23
18	183	−21.40	37	55	−24.13
19	211	−21.77			

If an adaptive antenna array or temporal filter takes the CW interference down to this thermal noise floor, then $(J_r)_{dB} = (N_{ther})_{dB}$. Substituting this into (6.26) and using the minimum received L1 C/A code received power $(S_r)_{dB} = 158.5$ dBW give:

$$\left(J/S\right)_{dB} = \left(J_r\right)_{dB} - \left(S_r\right)_{dB} = \left(N_{ther}\right)_{dB} - \left(S_r\right)_{dB} = -129.1 - (-158.5) = 29.4 \text{ dB}$$

This would not be a problem for most unaided C/A code receiver designs if the source were wideband noise RF interference or even narrowband RF interference if the bandwidth were, say, 100 kHz. However, CW interference at this level could cause problems with the C/A code receiver because of the leak-through phenomena described earlier [compare 29.4 dB $(J/S)_{dB}$ with the worst-case leak-through levels shown in Table 6.8]. If the C/A code receiver were a standard correlator design, then $B = 1.7$ MHz and the $(J/S)_{dB}$ decreases to 19.9 dB. Thus, increasing the receiver front-end bandwidth increases the intrinsic vulnerability of C/A code to CW interference.

A C/A code (Gold code) jammer can also be a problem for this same situation because temporal side lobes are produced. In both cases, the problem is more serious during C/A code search and acquisition modes than for tracking modes.

6.2.2.7   Effects of RF Interference on Code Tracking

The effect of RF interference on code tracking is different from its effect on signal acquisition, carrier tracking, and data demodulation. While the latter three functions depend on the output SNIR at the output of a prompt correlator, as described in Section 6.2.2.5, code tracking relies on the difference between an early correlator and a late correlator, as described in Section 5.2.

The interference considered here is modeled as Gaussian and zero-mean, but not necessarily having a white (flat) spectrum. The analysis assumes that the receiver front end does not saturate or respond nonlinearly in some other way to the interference, as discussed in Section 6.2.2.1, and that there is no multipath, so that code tracking errors are caused by noise and interference. While the effects of white noise on code tracking error are considered in Section 5.6.3, this section evaluates the effect of nonwhite interference, which produces additional random, zero-mean, code tracking error. The effect of interference is quantified in terms of the standard deviation of the code tracking error.

As described in Section 5.4, there are many different designs for discriminators and tracking loops, and interference may have different effects on each. However, a lower bound on the code tracking error has been developed that is independent of code tracking circuit design, yet is a tight bound in the sense that it provides reasonably accurate predictions of code tracking performance for well-designed tracking circuits. This lower bound (in units of seconds) is given by [10]:

$$
\sigma_{LB} \cong \frac{\sqrt{B_n}}{2\pi \sqrt{\int_{-\beta_r/2}^{\beta_r/2} f^2 \left[\frac{S_S(f)}{\left(\frac{C_S}{N_0}\right)^{-1} + \frac{C_I}{C_S} S_I(f)} \right] df}}
\tag{6.30}
$$

where the code-tracking loop has a (one-sided) equivalent rectangular bandwidth of B_n Hz that is much smaller than the reciprocal of the correlation integration time, the power spectral density of white noise, and any spectrally flat interference is N_0 W/Hz, and the nonwhite component of the interference has power spectral density $C_I S_I(f)$ W/Hz, with normalized power spectral density $\int_{-\infty}^{\infty} S_I(f)df = 1$ and interference power over infinite bandwidth of C_I W (the aggregate interference carrier power and power spectral density may result from the aggregation of multiple interfering signals). The signal has power spectral density $S_S(f)$ normalized to unit power over infinite bandwidth, $\int_{-\infty}^{\infty} S_I(f)df = 1$, and C_S is the recovered desired signal power, also defined over an infinite bandwidth, so that the signal has a carrier power to noise density ratio of C_S/N_0 Hz, in white noise. The ratio of interference power to signal power is C_I/C_S. It is assumed that the power spectral densities are symmetric about $f = 0$. Precorrelation filtering in the receiver is approximated by an ideal filter with linear phase and rectangular passband having total bandwidth β_r Hz.

Now consider a code tracking loop whose discriminator uses coherent early-late processing, where the carrier phase of the reference signal tracks that of the received signal, so that the in-phase or real outputs of early and late correlations drive the discriminator, with early-to-late spacing of D spreading code periods. Using the same notation and assumptions as in (6.30), the standard deviation (in units of seconds) for the coherent early-late processing in interference is [10]:

$$
\begin{aligned}
\sigma_{CELP} & \cong \frac{\sqrt{B_n}}{2\pi \int_{-\beta_r/2}^{\beta_r/2} fS_S(f)\sin(\pi fDT_c)df} \sqrt{\int_{-\beta_r/2}^{\beta_r/2}\left[\left(\frac{C_S}{N_0}\right)^{-1}+\frac{C_I}{C_S}S_I(f)\right]S_S(f)\sin^2(\pi fDT_c)df} \\
& = \frac{\sqrt{B_n}}{2\pi \int_{-\beta_r/2}^{\beta_r/2} fS_S(f)\sin(\pi fDT_c)df} \\
& \times \sqrt{\left(\frac{C_S}{N_0}\right)^{-1}\int_{-\beta_r/2}^{\beta_r/2} S_S(f)\sin^2(\pi fDT_c)df + \frac{C_I}{C_S}\int_{-\beta_r/2}^{\beta_r/2} S_I(f)S_S(f)\sin^2(\pi fDT_c)df}
\end{aligned}
$$

(6.31)

The second line in (6.31) shows that the code tracking error is the RSS of a term that only involves the signal in white noise and a term that involves the spectra of the interference and the desired signal, scaled by the ratio of interference power to signal power.

In the limit as D becomes vanishingly small,[3] the trigonometric expressions in (6.31) can be replaced by Taylor Series expansions around $D = 0$, and (6.31) becomes

$$
\sigma_{CELP,D\to 0} \cong \frac{\sqrt{B_n}}{2\pi\beta_S}\left[\left(\frac{C_S}{N_0}\right)^{-1}+\frac{C_I}{C_S}\frac{\chi_{IS}}{\beta_S^2}\right]^{1/2}
$$

(6.32)

where

$$
\beta_S = \sqrt{\int_{-\beta_r/2}^{\beta_r/2} f^2 S_S(f)df}
$$

(6.33)

is the RMS bandwidth of the signal computed over the precorrelation bandwidth and χ_{IS} is the code tracking SSC defined by

3. In practice, how small D needs to be depends upon the specific spectra of signal and interference. Examination of the Taylor Series expansions shows that the criterion $DT_c\beta_r \ll \frac{2\sqrt{3}}{\pi} \cong 1.1$ is sufficient but not always necessary.

$$\chi_{\iota S} = \int_{-\beta_r/2}^{\beta_r/2} f^2 S_\iota(f) S_S(f) df \tag{6.34}$$

which includes a frequency-squared weighting in the integral that is not found in the SSC used for correlator output SNR defined in (6.11).

The expression (6.33) shows that neither the output SNIR nor merely the RMS bandwidth of the modulation is sufficient to describe code tracking accuracy for CELP; instead the quantity $\dfrac{C_\iota}{C_S} \dfrac{\chi_{\iota S}}{\beta_S^2}$ is needed. When this quantity is small, CELP with small early-late spacing approaches the lower bound on code-tracking error.

The interference spectrum affects code-tracking accuracy in a fundamentally different way from the way it affects effective C/N_0. The frequency-squared weighting inside the integral in (6.34) indicates that interference power away from the center frequency can have much greater effect on code-tracking accuracy than on effective C/N_0, which has no such frequency-squared weighting.

In many applications, early-late processing uses the power difference between early and late taps, rather than relying on carrier phase tracking to support coherent processing. The code tracking error for the resulting noncoherent early-late processing is [10]:

$$\sigma_{NELP} \cong \sigma_{CELP} \sqrt{1 + \frac{\displaystyle\int_{-\beta_r/2}^{\beta_r/2} S_S(f)\cos^2(\pi f D T_c)df}{T\dfrac{C_S}{N_0}\left(\displaystyle\int_{-\beta_r/2}^{\beta_r/2} S_S(f)\cos(\pi f D T_c)df\right)^2} + \frac{\displaystyle\int_{-\beta_r/2}^{\beta_r/2} S_\iota(f)S_S(f)\cos^2(\pi f D T_c)df}{T\dfrac{C_S}{C_\iota}\left(\displaystyle\int_{-\beta_r/2}^{\beta_r/2} S_S(f)\cos(\pi f D T_c)df\right)^2}} \tag{6.35}$$

which reveals the same behavior of noncoherent early-late processing (NELP) that is well known for infinite front-end bandwidth and white noise—the standard deviation of NELP code tracking error is the product of the standard deviation of CELP code tracking error and a *squaring loss* that is greater than unity, but approaches unity as the signal power increases relative to both the white noise level and the interference power.

In the limit as D becomes vanishingly small, the trigonometric expressions in (6.35) can be replaced by Taylor Series expansions around zero, and (6.35) becomes

$$\sigma_{NELP,D\to 0} \cong \sigma_{CELP,D\to 0} \left[1 + \frac{\displaystyle\int_{-\beta_r/2}^{\beta_r/2} S_\iota(f)S_S(f)df}{TC_S \left(\displaystyle\int_{-\beta_r/2}^{\beta_r/2} S_S(f)df \right)^2} \right]^{1/2} \qquad (6.36)$$

$$\sigma_{CELP,D\to 0} \left[1 + \frac{1}{T\dfrac{C_S}{N_0}\eta} + \frac{\kappa_{\iota S}}{T\dfrac{C_S}{C_\iota}\eta^2} \right]^{1/2}$$

where η is the fraction of signal power passed by the precorrelation bandwidth,

$$\eta = \int_{-\beta_r/2}^{\beta_r/2} S_S(f)df \qquad (6.37)$$

and $\kappa_{\iota S}$ is the SSC describing the effect of interference on correlator output SNR, defined in (6.11).

Clearly, quantifying the effect of interference on code tracking accuracy is different and more complicated than evaluating its effect on signal acquisition, carrier tracking, and data demodulation. Not only does the effect depend on the spectra of signal and interference and on the precorrelation filter, but also on details of the discriminator design and the bandwidth of the code tracking loop.

As an example, consider narrowband interference centered at $\pm f_\iota$, whose spectrum is modeled as $S_\iota(f) = 0.5[\delta(f+f_\iota) + \delta(f-f_\iota)]$, where $\delta(\cdot)$ is the Dirac function having infinite amplitude, vanishing width, and unit area. Substituting for this interference power spectral density in the code tracking SSC (6.34), assuming the interference is within the precorrelation bandwidth, yields

$$\chi_{\iota S} = f_\iota^2 S_S(f_\iota) \qquad (6.38)$$

The lower bound on code tracking accuracy with narrowband interference is obtained by substituting the interference spectrum into (6.30), yielding

$$\sigma_{LB} \cong \frac{\sqrt{B_n}}{2\pi \sqrt{\dfrac{C_S}{N_0} \displaystyle\int_{-\beta_r/2}^{\beta_r/2} f^2 S_S(f)df}} \qquad (6.39)$$

$$= \frac{1}{2\pi\beta_S} \sqrt{\frac{B_n}{C_S/N_0}}$$

This result shows that optimal code tracking in narrowband interference produces the same code tracking error as with no narrowband interference. It is readily shown that this processing is closely approximated by narrowband excision followed by CELP with very small early-late processing.

When narrowband excision is not employed and NELP is used, the effect of narrowband interference is obtained using (6.36) and (6.32), assuming small early-late spacing,

$$\sigma_{NELP,D\to 0} \cong \frac{\sqrt{B_n}}{2\pi\beta_s} \sqrt{\left[\left(\frac{C_s}{N_0}\right)^{-1} + \frac{C_i}{C_s}\frac{f_i^2 S_s(f_i)}{\beta_s^2}\right]\left[1 + \frac{1}{T\frac{C_s}{N_0}\eta} + \frac{S_s(f_i)}{T\frac{C_s}{C_i}\eta^2}\right]}$$ (6.40)

Figure 6.7 plots (6.39) and (6.40) for four different modulations, calculated with B_n of 0.1 Hz, $(C_s/N_0)_{dB}$ of 30 dB-Hz, $(C/C_s)_{dB}$ of 40 dB, precorrelation bandwidth of 24 MHz, correlation integration time of 20 ms, and very small early-spacing. The results for NELP approach the lower bound for certain interference frequencies. Interference very near band center degrades NELP code tracking accuracy less than interference further away from band center. The oscillatory behavior of the NELP error for BPSK-R(1) and BOC(1,1) demonstrates that narrowband interference away from band center can have the same effect on code tracking error as interference nearer to band center, reflecting the frequency-squared weighting in (6.34). The result for NELP BPSK-R(10) shows that the maximum error occurs

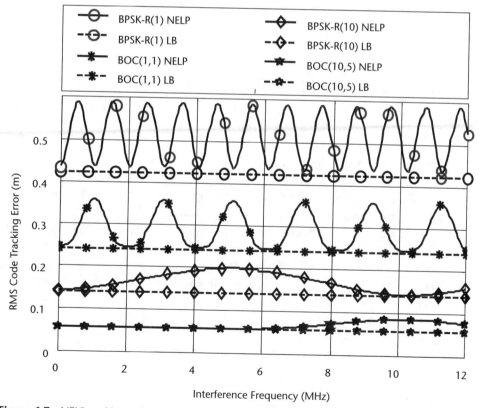

Figure 6.7 NELP and lower bound (LB) code tracking error of different modulations in narrowband interference, for different frequency interference, with 0 MHz corresponding to band center, and 12 MHz corresponding to the edge of the band.

when the narrowband interference is placed halfway between the spectral peak at band center and the first spectral null at 10.23 MHz.

6.2.3 Interference Mitigation

The three primary means of interference mitigation are: (1) enhancements of the receiver tracking threshold, especially by means of external velocity aiding from an IMU, (2) frequency excision techniques to remove narrowband energy by hardware means (transversal filters) or by signal processing means (FFT techniques), usually at the digital IF stage, and (3) antenna null-steering toward jammers or gain steering toward the SVs or preferably both. In addition to these controlled design features, a number of factors help to reduce the RF interference effects. The RF interference can only have the full effect of this analysis on the receiver if it is in the LOS of the receiver antenna and unobstructed. For commercial aviation applications, the RF interference sources will typically be at ground level, while the receiver antenna will be elevated during en route navigation. This increases the LOS range, but because the source of the interference will, in general, be from below the aircraft's horizon, the body of the aircraft will help to block the interference. Also, the gain pattern of the antenna rolls off significantly below the aircraft horizon, unless pseudolites are being used to support local differential operation. In this case, the receiver antenna used with gain toward the ground will be vulnerable to RF interference from the ground. However, as the aircraft approaches for landing or for ground-based operation of receivers in general, the RF interference signals can be attenuated due to Earth curvature, foliage, buildings, and so on.

6.2.3.1 Mitigating Narrowband and Pulse RF Interference

Narrowband interference can be mitigated by spectrum excision techniques. These techniques essentially suppress the narrowband energy down to the thermal noise level, but that also suppresses the signal in those frequency regions. This loss of energy will have a small effect on the receiver's tracking performance if only a small percentage of the spectrum is suppressed. C/A code receivers can still experience acquisition problems with CW interference if suppressed to the thermal noise level due to the strong spectral lines of the C/A code (see Section 6.2.2.6).

Pulsed interference can be easily mitigated by instant recovery analog design techniques, such as front-end clipping, front-end saturation prevention, and fast attack, fast recovery AGC design. *Pulse blanking*, or the zeroing of the received signal when strong pulsed interference is detected, is a particularly effective mitigation technique [11]. The receiver cannot correlate with the signals during these bursts, but the duty cycle of most burst jammers is usually so low that correlations take place most of the time (unless saturation is permitted to take place in the front end). Thus, a well-designed receiver front end renders the overall receiver immune to most burst jammers [e.g., a pulse jammer with 50% duty cycle blanks out half the received signal power, but that will degrade the $(C_s/N_0)_{dB}$ by only 3 dB]. It is relatively inexpensive in terms of cost or size, weight, and power to build in pulse-jamming mitigation features in a receiver, but most commercial receivers do not have such protection.

6.2.3.2 Mitigating Gaussian and Spectrum Matching Wideband Interference

Encrypted military signals such as Y code or M code provide no intrinsic advantage against enemy jamming owing to encryption. The most difficult military jamming threats to mitigate are bandlimited Gaussian noise jammers whose bandwidths are matched to the null-to-null signal spectrum of the target signal and jammers whose spectrum characteristics exactly match the target signal. For these wideband jammers, there are only two mitigation techniques available, receiver tracking threshold enhancements and antenna directional gain control. The latter consists of directional null steering toward the jammers and gain steering toward the SVs. The most advanced controlled reception pattern antenna (CRPA) technology that combines both techniques is STAP. It is possible to steer nulls toward the jammers without assistance from the receiver, but to steer gain toward the SVs requires direction cosines. This, in turn, requires an attitude and heading reference system for the CRPA, preferably from an inertial measurement unit. The typical military CRPA uses seven elements and can therefore steer up to six nulls toward enemy jammers. It is possible to obtain 30 dB or more null steering with a high-performance CRPA, but the null depth decreases as the number of jammers increase. With so few antenna elements, STAP cannot provide much, if any, beam steering or gain toward each SV, but it helps to minimize the adverse effects of the jammer null-steering process. Obviously, if the jammer direction is colocated with the SV direction, that SV will be lost. But it is much better to lose that SV than all of the SVs, as would be the case with a FRPA. Also, the most advanced STAP will remove all narrowband jamming energy by frequency excision techniques from each antenna element so as not to lose wideband nulls to narrowband jammers.

There are also low-cost antenna null-steering techniques that depend on the jammers to be ground located (or some a priori known location). One example is the analog cancellation technique that senses the jamming energy from a "bow-tie" antenna element that has a sector antenna gain coverage at and slightly above the horizon and then subtracts this energy from the FRPA portion of the GPS antenna. Another technique assumes and senses nonpolarized jammer energy and removes it from the RHCP GPS signals. All of these low-cost antenna techniques require that the enemy cooperate with the a priori restrictions of the antenna design.

6.3 Multipath

Improvements due to GNSS augmentations and GNSS modernization are reducing many sources of error, leaving multipath and shadowing as significant and sometimes dominant contributors to error. This section discusses these sources of error, their effects, and ways to mitigate their effects.

Multipath is the reception of reflected or diffracted replicas of the desired signal. Since the path traveled by a reflection is always longer than the direct path, multipath arrivals are delayed relative to the direct path. When the multipath delay is large (e.g., greater than twice the spreading code symbol period for a BPSK-R modulation), a receiver can readily resolve the multipath. As long as the receiver tracks the direct path (which always arrives earlier than any multipath), such resolvable multipaths have little effect on performance. However, multipath reflections from nearby objects, or even grazing multipaths reflected from distant objects, can arrive at short delays (e.g., tens or hundreds of nanoseconds) after the arrival of the direct path. Such multipaths distort the correlation function between the received composite (direct path plus multipaths) signal and the locally generated reference in the receiver. They also distort the composite phase of the received signal, introducing errors in pseudorange and carrier phase measurements that are different among the signals from different satellites, and thus produce errors in position, velocity, and time.

Shadowing is excess attenuation of the direct path, typically introduced when the direct path propagates through foliage or a structure. When the multipath does not experience the same excess attenuation, the received power of the multipath may be even greater than the received power of the shadowed direct path. Such a phenomenon can occur in outdoor situations as that portrayed in Figure 6.8, and also in indoor situations, such as when the direct path passes through walls or ceiling and roof, while the multipath is reflected from another building and arrives through a window or other opening. Consequently, shadowing of the direct path and multipath has combined effects on the relative amplitudes of direct path and multipaths. In some cases, shadowing of the direct path may be so severe that the receiver can only track the multipath(s).

The error introduced by multipaths depends upon their delays, but also their power and carrier phase relative to those of the direct path. Multipaths with received power much less than that of the direct path produce little distortion of the received signal and consequently produce little error. The received carrier phase of the multipath relative to that of the direct path also has a direct influence on the degree and character of the distortion.

Typically, consideration of multipath in a GNSS context emphasizes its effect on signal code and carrier tracking accuracies, since these receiver functions are more sensitive to multipath degradation than signal acquisition or data demodulation—under most situations, multipath conditions that would cause observable degradation to acquisition or data demodulation also introduce large degradations to pseudorange accuracy. Effects on acquisition and data demodulation are assessed using techniques developed in digital communications [12], and so the remainder of this discussion focuses on tracking performance.

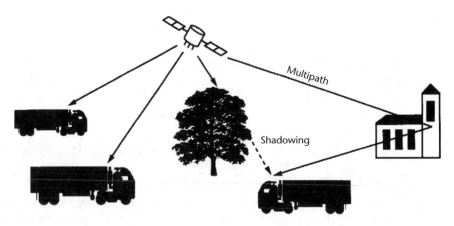

Figure 6.8 Outdoor multipath situation.

Section 6.3.1 describes different models and characteristics of multipath and shadowing. Section 6.3.2 relates the effect of multipath on signal tracking accuracy for situations involving different signal modulations, different precorrelation bandwidths, and different early-late spacings in the code tracking discriminator. Section 6.2.3 discusses some specialized techniques for multipath mitigation.

6.3.1 Multipath Characteristics and Models

The simplest model of multipath is a set of discrete reflected signals having larger delays and different amplitudes and carrier phases from the direct path. If the signal with no multipath is described in analytic signal form as

$$s(t) = \alpha_0 x(t - \tau_0) e^{-j\phi_0} e^{j2\pi f_c (t - \tau_0)} \tag{6.41}$$

where $x(t)$ is the complex envelope of the transmitted signal, τ_0 is the time for the signal to propagate from satellite to receiver, and f_c is the carrier frequency in hertz, then a simple model for the complex envelope of a received signal with multipath (neglecting noise and interference) after frequency down conversion (neglecting any intentional IF) is

$$r(t) = \alpha_0 e^{-j\phi_0} x(t - \tau_0) e^{-j2\pi f_c \tau_0} + \sum_{n=1}^{N} \alpha_n e^{-j\phi_n} x(t - \tau_n) e^{j2\pi f_n t} \tag{6.42}$$

where there are N multipaths, α_0 is the received amplitude of the direct path and the α_n are the received amplitudes of the multipath returns, τ_0 is the propagation delay of the direct path, the τ_n are the propagation delays of the multipath returns, ϕ_0 is the received carrier phase of the direct path, the ϕ_n are the received carrier phases of the multipath returns, and the f_n are the received frequencies of the multipath returns relative to the carrier frequency.

In general, each of the parameters in (6.42) is time varying due to motion of the satellites and the receiver, as well as motion of objects that produce the multipath. This time variation is not shown explicitly in (6.42) because it complicates the notation. However, it is accounted for in some of the multipath models discussed next.

The expression (6.42) can be rewritten using parameters that relate the multipaths to the direct path:

$$r(t) = \alpha_0 e^{-j\tilde{\phi}_0} \left[x(t - \tau_0) + \sum_{n=1}^{N} \tilde{\alpha}_n e^{-j\tilde{\phi}_n} x(t - \tau_0 - \tilde{\tau}_n) \right] \tag{6.43}$$

where $\tilde{\alpha}_n = \alpha_n / \alpha_0$ is the multipath-to-direct ratio (MDR) of amplitudes, $\tilde{\tau}_n = \tau_n - \tau_0$ is the excess delay of the multipath returns, and the $\tilde{\phi}_n$ are the received carrier phases of the different signal components. The multipath profile producing (6.43) can be portrayed graphically as a power-delay profile (PDP) by plotting the points $\{(\tilde{\tau}_n, \tilde{\alpha}_n^2)\}_{n=1}^{N}$.

The expression (6.43) implies that the received carrier frequencies of the multipaths are equal to the received carrier frequency of the direct path. This representation may not be adequate when relative motion between satellites, scatterers, and receiver is different from relative motion between satellites and receiver, causing multipath arrivals at different Doppler shifts from the direct path. When the Doppler differences are significant (greater than the reciprocal of the coherent integration time in the correlator), however, they cause the received multipath signals to be essentially uncorrelated with the direct path, and thus can often be neglected since they do not correlate well with the reference signal used to track the direct path.

A special case of (6.43) occurs when the propagation geometry is such that the direct path is nearly tangent to the Earth's surface (such as when the satellite is near the horizon). Then there can be a single dominant multipath arrival that reflects from a large object near the horizon, with excess delay orders of magnitude less than the reciprocal of the signal bandwidth and only a small fraction of the carrier period—often smaller than a picosecond. When the reflection coefficient is sufficiently high and there are no other multipaths, then $x(t - \tau_0 - \tilde{\tau}_1) \cong x(t - \tau_0)$. Consequently, (6.43) can be approximated (when the reflection introduces a 180° rotation of the carrier phase) as

$$r(t) \cong \alpha_0 e^{-j\tilde{\phi}_0} \left[1 - \alpha_1 e^{-j\tilde{\phi}_1} \right] x(t - \tau_0) \qquad (6.44)$$

where $\tilde{\phi}_1 = 2\pi f_c \tilde{\tau}_1$ is very small, so that when the reflection is strong enough for α_1 to be near unity, the magnitude of the quantity in square brackets is very much less than unity. The delay of this multipath is so small that it causes negligible pseudorange error, but by nearly canceling the direct path, it causes significant reduction in received signal power, relative to what would be observed with free-space propagation. This phenomenon is well known in land mobile radio [13], and not addressed further in this section.

More general models of multipath channels [12] do not represent the fine structure as models discussed previously, but instead represent the effect of the multipath channel—in our case, relative to the direct path, as in (6.43)—as a slowly time-varying linear system. The impulse response falls off with excess delay, and the range of excess delays where the impulse response is essentially nonzero is called the channel's *multipath spread*. In turn, the multipath spread can be represented by the RMS delay spread of the channel. This linear system has a time-varying transfer function that describes how it passes different frequency components of the signal.

Since the transfer function at a given frequency randomly varies over time, the correlation between transfer functions at different times and the same frequency [12] describes the time variation of the channel. If the time variation is fast relative to time constants in the receiver tracking loops, the multipath errors are smoothed by the receiver processing. Otherwise, they produce a time-invariant error term. The power spectral density resulting from the Fourier transform of this correlation is called the Doppler power spectrum of the channel, and the range of frequencies over which it is essentially nonzero is called the *Doppler spread* of the channel. The reciprocal of the Doppler spread is the coherence time of the channel—the time over which the multipath structure does not change much relative to the direct path. Two fundamental quantities introduced by this channel model—the multipath spread and the Doppler spread—provide succinct yet useful high-level representations of the multipath characteristics.

Despite its limited realism, (6.43) with $N = 1$ and time-invariant parameters is widely used in theoretical assessments of multipath performance due to its ease of use. This time-invariant distortion produces a bias error in pseudorange. If the multipath is specular, the MDR remains independent of range from receiver to reflector, and hence independent of the multipath's excess delay. For a reflection to be truly specular, the reflector must be very large, the reflecting surface must be smooth (surface roughness less than a few centimeters for L-band signals), and have consistent electrical properties. Observe that the one-path specular multipath model provides the limiting case of zero Doppler spread (time-invariant impulse response) and infinite delay spread.

On airplanes at altitude, multipath typically involves reflections from surfaces such as the wings and tail, sometimes accompanied by creeping waves over the aircraft skin. Aircraft multipath may be characterized as a discrete number of reflections all occurring with relative delays less than 20 ns and relative amplitudes less than 0.3 for vehicles as large as a Boeing 747 [14]. The model (6.43) can be employed for this situation; since the reflecting surfaces are close to the receive antenna and share the same motion, the multipath parameters, including the phases $\tilde{\phi}_n$, may remain constant over time periods exceeding the reciprocal of tracking loop bandwidths, motivating use of time-invariant parameters over durations longer than the reciprocal of the signal tracking loops. For this case, the delay spread is very short (20 ns) and the Doppler spread is also small (perhaps thousandths of a hertz).

In terrestrial applications, there have been extensive efforts to measure, model, and predict the diverse multipath environments that may be encountered. For some applications, multipath can be characterized as a large number of reflections from objects in the proximity of the user. A general model for this diffuse multipath is presented in [15]. In this model, 500 small reflectors are randomly located within 100m of the user. Since the reflectors are small, each emanates a spherical wave, and thus the received power from each reflector varies with the square of the distance between the reflector and the user. Moreover, the large number of signal reflections, spaced so closely in delay, make the multipath arrivals appear to result from passing through a linear filter with continuous impulse response amplitude decreasing with excess delay, rather than the discrete delays in (6.42) and (6.43). This diffuse scatterer model has been found to closely emulate measured multipath for an aviation differential GPS reference station application with the receiver located in an open environment. Here, the delay spread is hundreds of nanoseconds, and the Doppler spread is tenths or hundredths of a hertz.

Among many attempts to measure and model real-world multipath environments, [16] stands out as offering a particularly comprehensive and useful representation of complex terrestrial multipath. As shown in Figure 6.9, the parametric model is based on (6.42), with the arrivals grouped into three components: the direct path, a discrete set of near echoes, and a discrete set of far echoes. Shadowing of the direct path is represented by a Rice distribution of amplitude when LOS visibility exists between the receiver and the transmitter, and a Rayleigh distribution when LOS visibility does not exist. The mean received power of the near echoes falls off exponentially with delay. The number of far echoes is typically much smaller than the number of near echoes, and the mean value of the far echoes does not vary over the range of delays. The numbers of near echoes and number of far echoes are

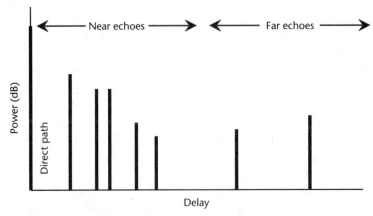

Figure 6.9 Canonical power-delay-profile for land-mobile satellite channel.

each Poisson distributed, described by different Poisson parameters. Multipath phases are modeled as independent and identically distributed over 360°. Extensive tables of statistical parameters for these components are provided in [16] for many different environments (e.g., open, rural, urban, highway) and satellite elevations. Time variation of the multipath characteristics is described in [16] using second-order statistics based on Doppler spectra, with bandwidth established by the movement of satellites and the receiver.

As noted in [16], the LOS does not always exist between the receiver and transmitter, particularly for low-elevation angles. For instance, trees or buildings along a road may block signals from below a certain elevation angle. In urban environments, 97% of signals were blocked when the transmitter was at an elevation angle of 15°, and blockage of lower-elevation satellites was also not uncommon even in rural environments, due to shadowing by trees. In these circumstances, it is entirely possible for a receiver to track a reflection rather than the direct signal, causing large pseudorange errors.

Over the range of environments and elevation angles considered in [16], the average power of the near echoes never exceeds −16.5 dB relative to the average power of the direct path. The mean power levels of the near echoes fall off at a wide variety of rates, ranging from 1 to 37 dB/μs depending on the elevation angle and environment. The range of delays associated with the near echoes is from 0 to 0.6 μs. No significant far echoes occur beyond 5 to 15 μs, and the mean power levels of the far echoes are within the range of −20 to −30 dB (relative to an unshadowed direct path). Doppler spreads are dominated either by the satellite motion or the receiver motion. Delay spreads are often multiple microseconds, while Doppler spreads for a stationary receiver can be tenths of hertz—but for a receiver in a vehicle, it can be many hertz, particularly for multipaths with small excess delay.

Indoor multipath has very different characteristics depending on the placement of the building relative to other buildings, satellite elevation, whether the receiver is in an interior area deep within the building or near a window, what floor the receiver is on, and the building materials. Except in cases where the direct path is shadowed, multipath with significant values of MDR typically arises from reflections near the receive antenna, thus having small excess delay. Indoor data discussed in [17] has RMS delay spread less than 50 ns, with delay spread less than 250 ns. The Doppler spread is often dominated by the motion of the receiver and can be millihertz for stationary receivers or multipaths with large excess delay, and hertz for multipaths with small excess delay and receivers being carried by a person.

While it is difficult to make any generalizations about phenomena as highly variable as multipath and shadowing, several observations can be made. Shadowing exacerbates any multipath effects, and severe shadowing can cause the receiver to track a multipath rather than a direct path, causing potentially large ranging errors. Near-in multipaths are often the most stable over time for a receiver that does not move relative to its local environment, but the fastest varying in time for a receiver that moves relative to its local environment. Near-in multipaths often have the greatest MDR, but typically introduce smaller ranging errors than multipaths with larger excess delays.

6.3.2 Effects of Multipath on Receiver Performance

Since received signals from different satellites typically encounter different multipath channels, the resulting pseudorange errors are not common to signals received from different satellites, and thus produce errors in position, velocity, and time. Further, the size of the multipath errors in tracking different satellites may also be very different, since signals received from higher-elevation satellites tend to experience less multipath in many applications. Ironically, the contributions of lower-elevation satellites to improved dilution of precision can provide an important incentive to use these signals, in spite of their larger multipath errors.

As discussed in Section 6.3.1, actual multipath environments are both complicated and diverse, making it difficult to quantify the effects of multipath in ways that are both generally applicable yet accurate. Computer simulations that synthesize waveforms, and then employ high-fidelity channel models and specific receiver processing approaches, can provide accurate and realistic assessments, yet they provide little insight into underlying issues and characteristics. In contrast, the multipath model (6.43) has limited realism but provides useful insights. In fact, extensive assessments have been made using the one-path specular multipath version of (6.43). While the numerical results obtained are often not representative of real-world multipath conditions, they provide useful diagnostic insights. Further, it is sufficient, although it may not be necessary, to perform well under these simple conditions.

For the one-path specular multipath model, (6.43) can be rewritten (continuing to neglect noise and interference), as

$$r(t) = \alpha_0 e^{-j\tilde{\phi}_0} \left[x(t - \tau_0) + \tilde{\alpha}_1 e^{-j\tilde{\phi}_1} x(t - \tau_0 - \tilde{\tau}_1) \right] \tag{6.45}$$

When the locally generated reference $e^{-j\theta}x(t)$ is correlated against this received signal, the statistical mean of the result is

$$\bar{\lambda}(\tau) = \alpha_0 e^{-j(\tilde{\phi}_0 - \theta)} \left[R_x(\tau - \tau_0) + \tilde{a}_1 e^{-j\tilde{\phi}_1} R_x(\tau - \tau_0 - \tilde{\tau}_1) \right]$$
$$= \alpha_0 e^{-j(\tilde{\phi}_0 - \theta)} \hat{R}_x(\tau - \tau_0) \tag{6.46}$$

The term $\hat{R}_x(\tau - \tau_0) = R_x(\tau - \tau_0) + \tilde{\alpha}_1 e^{-j\tilde{\phi}_1} R_x(\tau - \tau_0 - \tilde{\tau}_1)$ is a *composite correlation function*, which is the sum of the ideal correlation function and a second version of the ideal correlation function that is scaled in amplitude, rotated in phase, and delayed. When the receiver attempts to estimate delay and carrier phase from this composite correlation function, its estimates are in error, even in the absence of noise and interference.

Figure 6.10 illustrates the effect of one-path multipath on noncoherent early-late processing for a signal with BPSK-R(1) modulation strictly bandlimited to 4 MHz. The top row shows results with no multipath, while subsequent rows show

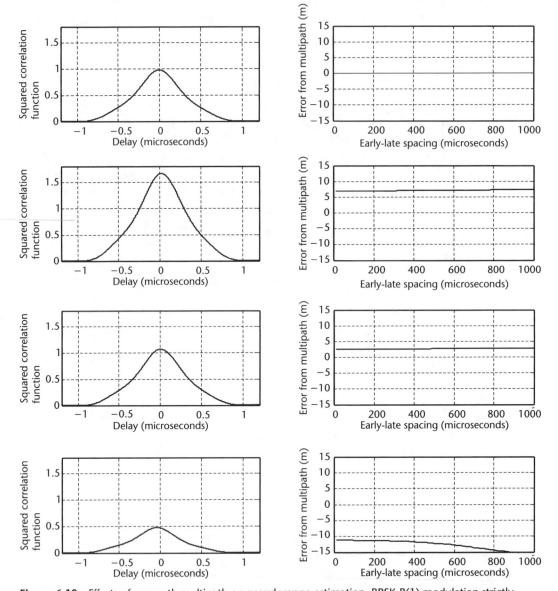

Figure 6.10 Effects of one-path multipath on pseudorange estimation, BPSK-R(1) modulation strictly bandlimited to 4 MHz. Top row shows no multipath, while in subsequent rows MDR is –10 dB and excess delay is 0.1 μs, while phase is 0°, 90°, and 180°. Left-hand column shows distorted correlation functions, while right-hand column shows dependence of range error on early-late spacing.

results for multipath phase (relative to phase of the direct path) of 0°, 90°, and 180°. The left-hand columns show magnitude-squared correlation functions, while the right-hand columns show the pseudorange error introduced by the multipath for different values of early-late spacing. The phase of the multipath dictates whether the error is positive or negative. With the narrow precorrelation bandwidth in this case, narrower early-late spacings examined here have little effect on the error in most cases.

Figure 6.11 shows the same results as in Figure 6.10, for a signal with BPSK-R(1) modulation bandlimited to 24 MHz. With the wider precorrelation bandwidth, narrower early-late spacing significantly reduces the error in most cases.

Figure 6.12 shows the same results as in Figure 6.10, for a signal with BPSK-R(10) modulation bandlimited to 24 MHz. Since the sharper correlation function peak resolves this multipath better, the ranging errors tend to be smaller. When these results are repeated for multipath excess delay of 0.4 μs, the errors for BPSK-R(1) modulation are similar to those in Figures 6.10 and 6.11, while BPSK-R(10) modulation displays no errors, since its sharper correlation function peak completely resolves the multipath with larger excess delay.

For a more comprehensive depiction of ranging error caused by one-path multipath, recognize that for a given modulation and receiver design (including precorrelation bandwidth and code tracking discriminator), multipath error is determined by the MDR, phase, and delay of the multipath. When the MDR is constant (independent of delay and phase) as in specular multipath, the error for a given multipath delay varies with multipath phase, as seen in Figures 6.10 through 6.12. For a given MDR, the maximum and minimum errors at each delay are taken over all multipath phase values, producing a range of possible delay estimates for each value of excess delay. If $\hat{\tau}_o(\tilde{\alpha}_1, \tilde{\tau}_1, \tilde{\phi}_1)$ is the estimated delay for a specific MDR, excess delay, and multipath phase, then denote the error in delay estimation by $\varepsilon(\tilde{\alpha}_1, \tilde{\tau}_1, \tilde{\phi}_1) = \tau_0 - \hat{\tau}_0(\tilde{\alpha}_1, \tilde{\tau}_1, \tilde{\phi}_1)$. The maximum and minimum errors for a specific excess delay are respectively $\max_{\tilde{\phi}_1} \varepsilon(\tilde{\alpha}_1, \tilde{\tau}_1, \tilde{\phi}_1)$ and $\min_{\tilde{\phi}_1} \varepsilon(\tilde{\alpha}_1, \tilde{\tau}_1, \tilde{\phi}_1)$; the envelope of delay errors at a given excess delay is defined by

$$\left(\max_{\tilde{\phi}_1} \varepsilon\left(\tilde{\alpha}_1, \tilde{\tau}_1, \tilde{\phi}_1\right), \min_{\tilde{\phi}_1} \varepsilon\left(\tilde{\alpha}_1, \tilde{\tau}_1, \tilde{\phi}_1\right) \right) \tag{6.47}$$

The resulting envelope of ranging errors is obtained by multiplying the envelope of delay errors by the speed of light.

Figure 6.13 shows multipath ranging error envelopes for BPSK-R(1) modulation with two different precorrelation bandwidths, and BPSK-R(10), all with early-late spacing of 50 ns. For the BPSK-R(1) modulation, the wider precorrelation bandwidth, combined with the narrow early-late spacing, provides smaller error, as recognized in [18]. The BPSK-R(10) modulation provides even smaller errors.

To assess multipath performance over a range of possible delay values, define the average range error envelope as $\dfrac{1}{\tilde{\tau}_1} \displaystyle\int_0^{\tilde{\tau}_1} [\max_{\tilde{\phi}_1} \varepsilon(\tilde{\alpha}_1, u, \tilde{\phi}_1) - \min_{\tilde{\phi}_1} \varepsilon(\tilde{\alpha}_1, u, \tilde{\phi}_1)] du$. The average envelope can provide useful insights, particularly for modulations whose range error envelopes oscillate with delay, such as some BOC modulations.

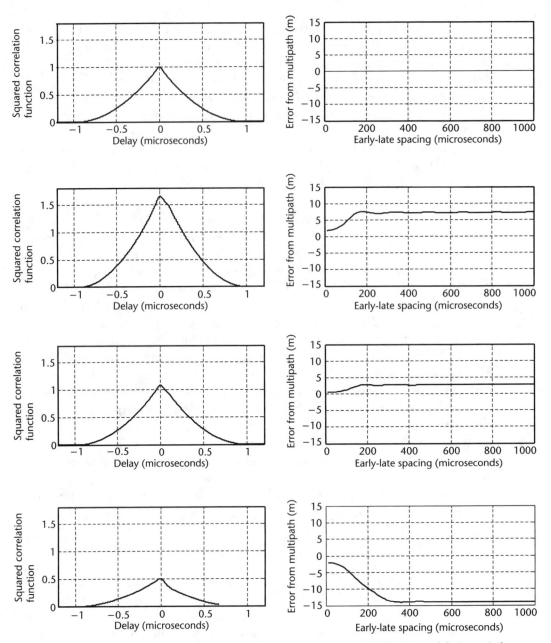

Figure 6.11 Effects of one-path multipath on pseudorange estimation, BPSK-R(1) modulation strictly bandlimited to 24 MHz. Top row shows no multipath, while in subsequent rows MDR is –10 dB and excess delay is 0.1 μs, while phase is 0°, 90°, and 180°. Left-hand column shows distorted correlation functions, while right-hand column shows dependence of range error on early-late spacing.

To assess the effect of one-path multipath on carrier phase estimation, consider further the composite correlation function obtained in (6.46) resulting from one-path multipath, $\tilde{R}_x(\tau - \tau_0) = R_x(\tau - \tau_0) + \tilde{\alpha}_1 e^{-j\tilde{\phi}_1} R_x(\tau - \tau_0 - \tilde{\tau}_1)$. It has real part $R_x(\tau - \tau_0) + \tilde{\alpha}_1 \cos\tilde{\phi}_1 R_x(\tau - \tau_0 - \tilde{\tau}_1)$ and imaginary part $\tilde{\alpha}_1 \sin\tilde{\phi}_1 R_x(\tau - \tau_0 - \tilde{\tau}_1)$. The phase angle is given by

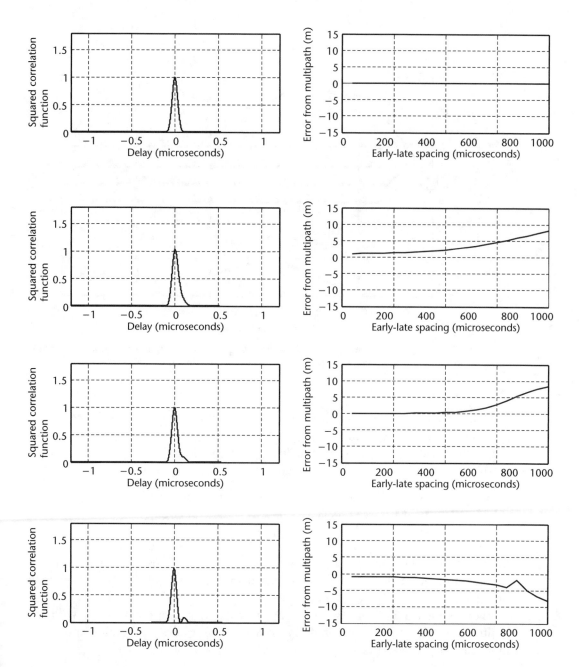

Figure 6.12 Effects of one-path multipath on pseudorange estimation, BPSK-R(10) modulation strictly bandlimited to 24 MHz. Top row shows no multipath, while in subsequent rows MDR is −10 dB and excess delay is 0.1 μs, and phase is 0°, 90°, and 180°. Left-hand column shows distorted correlation functions, while right-hand column shows dependence of range error on early-late spacing.

$$\psi = \tan^{-1}\left[\frac{\tilde{\alpha}_1 \sin\tilde{\phi}_1 R_x(\tau - \tau_0 - \tilde{\tau}_1)}{R_x(\tau - \tau_0) + \tilde{\alpha}_1 \cos\tilde{\phi}_1 R_x(\tau - \tau_0 - \tilde{\tau}_1)}\right] \tag{6.48}$$

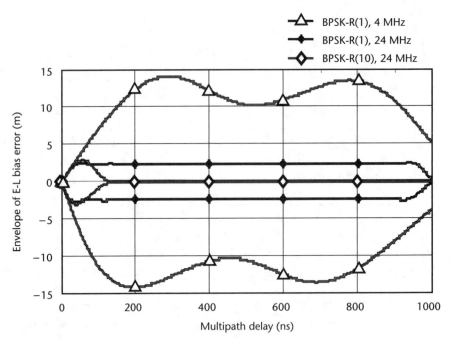

Figure 6.13 Multipath ranging error envelopes showing the maximum and minimum code tracking error for one-path multipath with MDR −10 dB, at different multipath delays.

Since the carrier phase of the direct path is defined to be zero, ψ is the carrier phase error introduced by the multipath. The carrier phase error is then a function of the multipath characteristics and the delay error.

Observe that when $\tilde{\tau}_1$ is very small, $R_x(\tau - \tau_0) \cong R_x(\tau - \tau_0 - \tilde{\tau}_1)$, and $\tan \psi \cong \dfrac{\tilde{\alpha}_1 \sin \tilde{\phi}_1}{1 + \tilde{\alpha}_1 \cos \tilde{\phi}_1}$. When the multipath power is equal to the power in the direct path, the carrier phase error is greatest when the multipath carrier phase is 90° relative to the direct path, producing a carrier phase error of 45°. As long as the MDR is less than or equal to unity, and the delay-locked loop maintains track on the correlation function of the direct path, the magnitude of the carrier phase error is less than or equal to 45°.

For a given MDR and excess delay, the carrier phase error varies with the multipath phase and the error in delay estimate. The resulting minimum and maximum carrier phase errors are given respectively by

$$
\begin{aligned}
\psi_{\min}(\tilde{\alpha}_1, \tilde{\tau}_1) &= \min_{\substack{\tilde{\phi}_1 \in (0, 2\pi] \\ \varepsilon \in \Delta\varepsilon(\tilde{\alpha}_1, \tilde{\tau}_1)}} \tan^{-1} \left[\frac{\tilde{\alpha}_1 \sin \tilde{\phi}_1 R_x(\varepsilon - \tilde{\tau}_1)}{R_x(\varepsilon) + \tilde{\alpha}_1 \cos \tilde{\phi}_1 R_x(\varepsilon - \tilde{\tau}_1)} \right] \\
\psi_{\max}(\tilde{\alpha}_1, \tilde{\tau}_1) &= \max_{\substack{\tilde{\phi}_1 \in (0, 2\pi] \\ \varepsilon \in \Delta\varepsilon(\tilde{\alpha}_1, \tilde{\tau}_1)}} \tan^{-1} \left[\frac{\tilde{\alpha}_1 \sin \phi_1 R_x(\varepsilon - \tilde{\tau}_1)}{R_x(\varepsilon) + \tilde{\alpha}_1 \cos \tilde{\phi}_1 R_x(\varepsilon - \tilde{\tau}_1)} \right]
\end{aligned}
\tag{6.49}
$$

so the resulting envelope of carrier phase error is given by $(\psi_{\max}(\tilde{\alpha}_1, \tilde{\tau}_1), \psi_{\min}(\tilde{\alpha}_1, \tilde{\tau}_1))$. Figure 6.14 shows multipath carrier phase error envelopes for the same conditions as Figure 6.13: BPSK-R(1) modulation with two different precorrelation

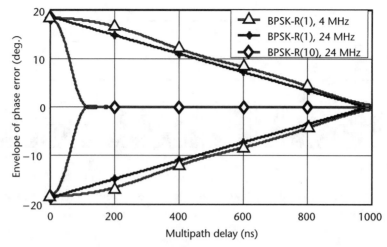

Figure 6.14 Multipath carrier phase error envelopes showing the maximum and minimum code tracking error for one-path multipath with MDR –10 dB at different multipath delays.

bandwidths and BPSK-R(10), all with early-late spacing of 50 ns. While the smaller ranging error envelope for BPSK-R(1) with wider precorrelation bandwidth translates into a somewhat smaller carrier phase error envelope, the distinctly sharper correlation function of BPSK-R(10) produces a much greater difference for this multipath model.

Since this one-path specular multipath model has limited realism (only one multipath with delay-invariant MDR and no time variation) and the processing model does not include smoothing of time varying errors by loop filters in the receiver, the quantitative results in Figure 6.10 through Figure 6.14 tend not to represent actual errors in actual multipath environments. But the qualitative reduction of multipath errors through use of small early-late spacings, wider precorrelation bandwidths, and modulations with sharper correlation function peaks is borne out in practice. Further, it is sufficient but not necessary in all situations to mitigate the errors caused by fixed multipath, since signal tracking loops integrate out some of the multipath error when the rate of multipath variation exceeds the loop bandwidth. This relatively rapid multipath variation occurs particularly when the receiver moves relative to the scatterers reflecting the multipath, so that at least the received multipath phase varies differently from the received phase of the direct path. When the receiver is stationary, however, multipaths from stationary scatterers can produce errors that vary little over typical loop filter time constants in a receiver—particularly for nearby scatterers.

As discussed in Section 6.3.1, multipath models other than the one-path static model are often more realistic and thus provide more realistic quantitative results. Figure 6.15 shows range errors computed using the diffuse multipath model [19]. These simulated results are similar to measured results and confirm the previous qualitative conclusions that wider precorrelation bandwidths are the most important way to obtain lower errors in multipath; wider bandwidth modulations also provide benefits. The corresponding RMS carrier phase error is shown in Figure 6.16. The differences are not as significant as for code tracking error.

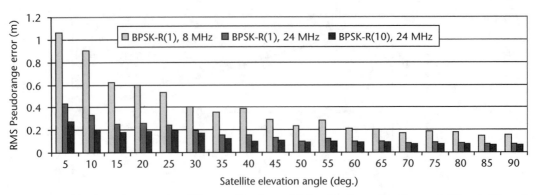

Figure 6.15 RMS ranging error for diffuse multipath model, for signals received from satellites at different elevation angles (numerical results from [19]).

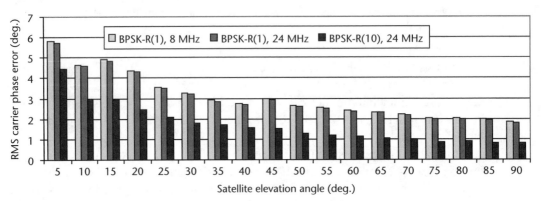

Figure 6.16 RMS carrier phase tracking error for diffuse multipath model, for signals received from satellites at different elevation angles (numerical results from [19]).

The results in this section demonstrate that smaller errors from multipath can be obtained through use of wider signal bandwidths, wider precorrelation bandwidths, and narrower early-late spacing (when used in conjunction with wider precorrelation bandwidths). The quantitative amount of improvement depends critically on the specific multipath environment, including the time variation of the multipath and smoothing of errors within the receiver processing. In some applications, shadowing of the direct path is common, and the errors that result from tracking of a multipath can be more important than the errors from multipath when the direct path is present. When wider precorrelation bandwidths and narrower early-late spacing are employed, the complexity of receiver processing increases, as discussed in Chapter 5.

6.3.3 Multipath Mitigation

The dominance of multipath-induced errors in some applications has motivated considerable investigation into development of multipath mitigation techniques that go beyond the straightforward strategies described in Section 6.3.2. Some multipath mitigation techniques have been incorporated into production receivers, while others remain research topics.

A number of considerations arise in assessing multipath mitigation techniques. Good performance in realistic multipath conditions must be provided. Robustness is also important, ensuring that performance is satisfactory over the range of environmental conditions (including noise and interference) in which the receiver must operate. Implementation complexity is also a factor, as are any restrictions on how the receiver would be employed (such as requirements for multipath characteristics to be time-invariant over long periods of time or restrictions to use by fixed receivers.) While multipath mitigation techniques remain important research topics, this section outlines some of the strategies that have been pursued and remain areas of active work.

One important group of multipath mitigation techniques attempts to reduce the reception of multipath signals, reducing the need to discriminate against these multipaths by the receiver processing. Antenna siting, and even removal or modification (e.g., coating with RF-absorptive materials) of reflective structures in the vicinity of the antenna can produce significant benefits. In benign environments, such as an open field, placing an antenna closer to the ground can decrease observed multipath errors. The reason is that with the antenna closer to the ground, the multipath reflections from the ground experience shorter excess path delays that tend to produce smaller multipath errors, as shown in Figure 6.13. Conversely, in environments with obstacles near the horizon, the opposite course of action is often beneficial—raising the antenna decreases antenna gain toward dominant reflectors that produce multipath.

Antennas can also be designed to attenuate multipath reflections, particularly multipaths that arrive at elevation angles near or below the horizon, where desired signals are not expected to arrive. Choke ring antennas have been particularly successful for mitigating multipath arrivals from the ground or low-elevation scatterers. In short-baseline differential systems, multipath errors can also be reduced through calibrations that measure multipath error based on satellite position [20].

Techniques for multipath mitigation receiver processing can be divided into nonparametric and parametric processing. Nonparametric processing employs discriminator designs that are less sensitive to multipath-induced errors, while parametric processing attempts to estimate parameters associated with the multipath and then correct for their effect on the estimate of the direct path's TOA.

Some nonparametric techniques, such as [21, 22], rely on precise prior knowledge of the signal's correlation function and employ novel receiver processing approaches that attempt to match the ideal correlation function to the observed correlation function in multipath. Nonparametric techniques in most common use, however, are based on variations of early-late processing described in Chapter 5. They go beyond the narrow correlator approach considered in Section 6.3.2, however, by either time-gating the reference signal or by computing two pairs of early and late correlations with different early-late spacings. A number of similar techniques have been developed and implemented in different brands of receivers.

An excellent overview of these modified-reference techniques, their capabilities, and their limitations is provided in [23]. One interpretation is that this processing is equivalent to generating a modified locally generated reference signal that does not replicate the desired signal, but rather approximates the derivative of the desired signal. The resulting correlation between the received signal and the modified reference has a much sharper correlation peak (along with, for some approaches, small artifacts at larger delays) than the original signal, providing better resolution of multipaths just as P(Y) code signal provides better resolution as shown in Section 6.3.2. These approaches provide little or no benefit for multipaths with very small excess delay—a few tens of nanoseconds for BPSK-R(1) modulations—but they do provide enhanced performance for multipaths with larger delays, compensating in part for the limitations of narrower bandwidth modulations (as long as the precorrelation bandwidth is wide). As discussed later in this section, however, their benefits are offset to some degree by poorer performance in noise and interference compared to use of conventional early-late processing with more capable modulations and the same precorrelation bandwidth.

Most parametric approaches rely on the discrete model of multipath defined in (6.42) or (6.43). A parametric algorithm either estimates or assumes the number of multipaths and then estimates *nuisance parameters* such as MDR, excess delay, and relative carrier phase of each multipath. Typically, these parametric approaches employ carrier-coherent processing and use very long coherent integration times (greater than 1 second), requiring the received multipath characteristics (including phase relative to the direct path) to be constant over the integration time. One such approach is the multipath estimating delay lock loop (MEDLL) [24], which applies maximum likelihood estimation theory to minimize the mean-squared error between the received signal, modeled as in (6.42), and the locally generated reference signal. Other approaches have been proposed [25] and shown to minimize mean-squared error and RMS error for specific multipath models.

Only limited evaluations have been published to describe the effect of noise and interference on performance of multipath mitigation techniques. The analysis in [23] shows that modified-reference processing degrades post-correlation SNR by large amounts. However, this degradation is easily overcome by use of a conventional prompt correlator with a locally generated reference signal matched to the transmitted signal. The results in [23] also demonstrate, however, that the code tracking accuracy of modified reference techniques in white noise is degraded relative to conventional early-late processing by an amount equivalent to reducing the signal power by 3 dB at higher input signal-to-noise conditions, and perhaps greater amounts at C/N_0 less than 35 dB-Hz. While the effect of nonwhite interference has not been evaluated, it can be expected that performance would be degraded more by interference with power concentrated away from band center, compared to conventional early-late processing. This increased sensitivity to noise and interference can be offset by use of narrower loop bandwidths, although practical considerations impose limits on narrowing loop bandwidths.

Multipath mitigation remains an area of active research interest. Designs of new GNSS signals provide opportunities for new modulation designs, and better performance in multipath can be one consideration. There are, however, many other constraints and factors that must be considered in GNSS modulation design, including issues that arise in sharing frequency bands with multiple signals. The increasing opportunity to process signals at multiple frequency bands opens up new potential for multipath mitigation processing that takes advantage of multiple carrier frequencies and multipath's frequency-selective characteristics. There are also opportunities to explore processing of multiple polarizations, although many antenna designs exhibit predominantly linear polarization response at low elevation angles of many multipath arrivals. Improved receiver processing techniques may still be developed, as may better theoretical understanding of capabilities and limitations of multipath mitigation. Most multipath mitigation techniques incur practical consequences, such as increased receiver complexity and poorer performance in noise and interference, that must be evaluated on a case-by-case basis.

6.4   Ionospheric Scintillation

Irregularities in the ionospheric layer of the Earth's atmosphere can at times lead to rapid fading in received signal power levels [26–28]. This phenomenon, referred to as ionospheric scintillation, can lead to a receiver being unable to track one or more visible satellites for short periods of time. This section describes the causes of ionospheric scintillation, characterizes the fading associated with scintillation, and details the effects of scintillation upon the performance of a receiver.

The ionosphere is a region of the Earth's atmosphere from roughly 50 km up to several Earth radii where incident solar radiation separates a small fraction of the normally neutral constituents into positively charged ions and free electrons. The maximum density of free electrons occurs at an altitude of around 350 km above the surface of the Earth in the daytime. Most of the time, the principal effect of the presence of free electrons in the ionosphere is to impart a delay on the signals (see Section 7.2.4.1). However, irregularities in the electron density occasionally arise that cause constructive and destructive interference among each signal. Such irregularities are most common and severe after sunset in the equatorial region (within +/–20° from the geomagnetic equator). High-latitude regions also experience scintillation, which is generally less severe than in the equatorial region, but may persist for long periods of time. Scintillation is also more common and severe during the peak of the 11-year solar cycle.

In the absence of scintillation, a simplified model for one particular signal as seen by a receiver is:

$$r(t) = \sqrt{2P}\,s(t)\cos(\omega t + \phi) + n(t) \tag{6.50}$$

where P is the received signal power (in watts), ω is the carrier frequency (in radians/second), $s(t)$ is the normalized transmitted signal, and $n(t)$ is noise.

Scintillation causes a perturbation to both the received signal amplitude and phase, and the received signal in the presence of scintillation may be modeled as [29]:

$$r(t) = \sqrt{2P \cdot \delta P}\; s(t)\cos(\omega t + \phi + \delta\phi) + n(t) \tag{6.51}$$

where $\sqrt{\delta P}$ is a positive, unitless parameter that characterizes amplitude fading due to scintillation, and $\delta\phi$ is a parameter with units of radians that represents phase variations due to scintillation. The power fluctuation, δP, is generally modeled as following a Nakagami-m pdf given by:

$$p(\delta P) = \frac{m^m \delta P^{m-1}}{\Gamma(m)} e^{-m\delta P}, \delta P \geq 0 \tag{6.52}$$

with mean value of one and variance of $1/m$. The strength of amplitude fading due to scintillation is characterized using a parameter referred to as the S_4 *index*, which is equal to the standard deviation of the power variation δP:

$$S_4 = \sqrt{\frac{1}{m}} \tag{6.53}$$

Due to the properties of the Nakagami-m distribution, the S_4 index cannot exceed $\sqrt{2}$.

Power fluctuations are highly correlated over short time intervals. Measured power spectral densities of scintillation-induced power fluctuations fall off with increasing frequency with a level proportional to f^{-p} with p in the range of 2.5–5.5 [25]. The spectral density of the power fluctuations also tends to fall off at extremely low frequencies (below around 0.1 Hz). Figure 6.17 shows simulated receiver power fluctuations due to strong scintillation ($S_4 = 0.9$).

Phase variations due to scintillation are most commonly modeled as following a zero-mean Gaussian distribution:

$$p(\delta\phi) = \frac{1}{\sqrt{2\pi}\sigma_\phi} e^{-\frac{\delta\phi^2}{2\sigma_\phi^2}} \tag{6.54}$$

with standard deviation σ_ϕ. Phase variations are highly correlated over short periods of time, with observed power spectral densities approximately following the form

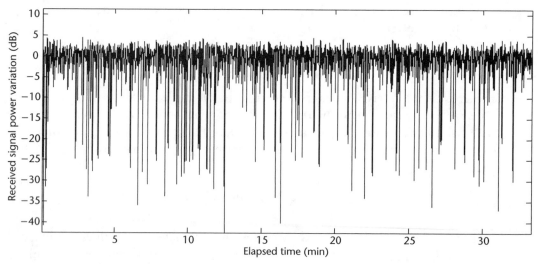

Figure 6.17   Simulated effects of strong scintillation ($S_4 = 0.9$) on received signal level.

Tf^{-p} with p in the range of 2.0–3.0 [26] and where T is a strength parameter (in units of rad^2/Hz).

Scintillation can lead to intermittent tracking outages in two different ways. First, if an amplitude fade is of sufficient depth and time duration, from a receiver perspective the desired signal is absent, and loss of lock of the code and carrier phase tracking loops is inevitable. If the desired signal is being received at a very high level, such as 50 dB-Hz, a 20-dB fade is generally tolerable, but a much deeper fade will typically cause an outage if the fade persists longer than the time constant of the tracking loops. At low SNRs, even a 5–10-dB fade can cause a disruption in tracking. Second, strong phase scintillation can cause loss of phase lock within the receiver if the phase variations introduce a level of dynamics that is greater than the phase lock loop can accommodate (see discussion in Section 5.6.1).

Fortunately, scintillation rarely occurs on all visible satellites simultaneously. The irregularities that cause scintillation are not generally present within the ionosphere at each of the points where the signals from the visible satellites intersect the ionosphere. Thus, scintillation tends to only impact one or at most a few satellites simultaneously.

Both S_4 index and phase standard deviation are a function of carrier frequency:

$$S_4 \propto \frac{1}{f^{1.5}} \tag{6.55}$$

$$\sigma_\phi \propto \frac{1}{f} \tag{6.56}$$

so that when fading due to ionospheric scintillation occurs, the observed S_4 index for a signal on L2 is approximately 1.45 times greater than the S_4 index for an L1 signal and observed σ_ϕ for L2 is approximately 1.28 times greater than for L1. The implication of this carrier frequency dependency is that scintillation would be much more likely to cause outages for GPS signals on L2 and L5 than for L1 signals, if the same signal was to be broadcast on all three frequencies at similar received power levels. Variations in signal design and power levels between the GPS signals at L1, L2, and L5 make it more difficult to make such a general statement.

References

[1] Spilker, J. J., and F. D. Natali, "Interference Effects and Mitigation Techniques," *Global Positioning System: Theory and Applications*, Vol. 1, American Institute of Aeronautics and Astronautics, Washington, D.C., Vol. 163, 1996, p. 726.

[2] Van Dierendonck, A. J., "GPS Receivers," *Global Positioning System: Theory and Applications*, Vol. 1, American Institute of Aeronautics and Astronautics, Washington, D.C., Vol. 163, 1996, pp. 354–355.

[3] Amoroso, F., "Adaptive A/D Converter to Suppress CW Interference in DSPN Spread-Spectrum Communications," *IEEE Trans. on Communications*, Vol. COM-31, No. 10, October 1983, pp. 1117–1123.

[4] Amoroso, F., and J. L. Bricker, "Performance of the Adaptive A/D Converter in Combined CW and Gaussian Interference," *IEEE Trans. on Communications*, Vol. COM-34, No. 3, March 1986, pp. 209–213.

[5]   Betz, J. W., "Effect of Narrowband Interference on GPS Code Tracking Accuracy," *Proc. of ION 2000 National Technical Meeting*, Institute of Navigation, January 2000.

[6]   Ward, P. W., "GPS Receiver RF Interference Monitoring, Mitigation, and Analysis Techniques," *NAVIGATION: Journal of The Institute of Navigation*, Vol. 41, No. 4, Winter 1994–1995, pp 367–391.

[7]   Betz, J. W., and D. B. Goldstein, "Candidate Designs for an Additional Civil Signal in GPS Spectral Bands," *Proc. of The Institute of Navigation National Technical Meeting*, San Diego, CA, January 2002.

[8]   Spilker, Jr., J. J., "GPS Signal Structure and Performance Characteristics," *NAVIGATION: Journal of The Institute of Navigation*, Vol. 25, No. 2, 1978.

[9]   Scott, H. L., "GPS Principles and Practices," The George Washington University Course 1081, Vol. I, Washington, D.C., March 1994.

[10]   Betz, J. W., and K. R. Kolodziejski, "Generalized Theory of GPS Code-Tracking Accuracy with an Early-Late Discriminator," 2000, unpublished.

[11]   Hegarty, C., et al., "Suppression of Pulsed Interference Through Blanking," *Proc. of The International Association of Institutes of Navigation 25th World Congress/The Institute of Navigation 56th Annual Meeting*, San Diego, CA, June 2000.

[12]   Proakis, J. G., *Digital Communications*, New York: McGraw-Hill, 1995.

[13]   Parsons, J. D., *The Mobile Radio Propagation Channel*, 2nd ed., New York: John Wiley and Sons, 2000.

[14]   Braasch, M., "GPS Multipath Model Validation," *Proc. of IEEE Position, Location and Navigation Symposium, PLANS 96*, Atlanta, GA, April 22–25, 1996.

[15]   Brenner, M., R. Reuter, and B. Schipper, "GPS Landing System Multipath Evaluation Techniques and Results," *Proc. of The Institute of Navigation ION GPS-98*, Nashville, TN, September 1998.

[16]   Jahn, A., H. Bischl, and G. Heiß, "Channel Characterisation for Spread Spectrum Satellite Communications," *Proc. of IEEE 4th International Symposium on Spread Spectrum Techniques and Applications (ISSSTA'96)*, Mainz, Germany, September 1996.

[17]   O'Donnell, M., et al., "A Study of Galileo Performance: GPS Interoperability and Discriminators for Urban and Indoor Environments," *Proc. of The Institute of Navigation's ION-GPS/GNSS-2002*, Portland, OR, September 2002.

[18]   Van Dierendonck, A. J., P. Fenton, and T. Ford, "Theory and Performance of Narrow Correlator Spacing in a GPS Receiver," *NAVIGATION: Journal of The Institute of Navigation*, Vol. 38, No. 3, Fall 1992, pp. 265–283.

[19]   Hegarty, C. J., et al., "Multipath Performance of the New GNSS Signals," *Proc. of The Institute of Navigation National Technical Meeting*, San Diego, CA, January 2004.

[20]   Wanninger, L., and M. May, "Carrier Phase Multipath Calibration of GPS Reference Stations," *Proc. of The Institute of Navigation ION-GPS-2000*, Salt Lake City, UT, September 2000.

[21]   Phelts, R. E., and P. Enge, "The Multipath Invariance Approach for Code Multipath Mitigation," *Proc. of The Institute of Navigation ION-GPS-2002*, Portland, OR, September 2002.

[22]   Fante, R. L., and J. J. Vaccaro, "Multipath and Reduction of Multipath-Induced Bias on GPS Time-of-Arrival," *IEEE Trans. on Aerospace and Electronic Systems*, Vol. 39, No. 3, July 2003.

[23]   McGraw, G. A., and M. S. Braasch, "GNSS Multipath Mitigation Using Gated and High Resolution Correlator Concepts," *Proc. of The Institute of Navigation ION-NTM-99*, January 1999.

[24]   Townsend, B., et al., "Performance Evaluation of the Multipath Estimating Delay Lock Loop," *Proc. of The Institute of Navigation ION GPS-94*, Salt Lake City, UT, September 1994.

[25] Weill, Lawrence R., "Multipath Mitigation Using Modernized GPS Signals: How Good
      Can It Get?" *Proc. of the Institute of Navigation ION-GPS-2002*, September 2002.

[26] Basu, S., et al., "250 MHz/GHz Scintillation Parameters in the Equatorial, Polar, and
      Auroral Environments," *IEEE Selected Areas in Communication*, Vol. SAC-5, No. 2,
      1987, pp. 102–115.

[27] Aarons, J., and S. Basu, "Ionospheric Amplitude and Phase Fluctuations at the GPS Fre-
      quencies," *Proc. of The Institute of Navigation ION GPS-94*, Salt Lake City, UT, 1994,
      pp. 1569–1578.

[28] Klobuchar, J., "Ionospheric Effects on GPS," *Global Positioning System: Theory and
      Applications*, Vol. 1, American Institute of Aeronautics and Astronautics, Washington,
      D.C. 1996, pp. 485–515.

[29] Hegarty, C., et al., "Scintillation Modeling for GPS-Wide Area Augmentation System
      Receivers," *Radio Science*, Vol. 36, No. 5, September/October 2001, pp. 1221–1231.

CHAPTER 7

Performance of Stand-Alone GPS

Rob Conley
Overlook Systems

Ronald Cosentino
Consultant

Christopher J. Hegarty, Elliott D. Kaplan, and Joseph L. Leva
The MITRE Corporation

Maarten Uijt de Haag
Ohio University

Karen Van Dyke
Volpe Center

7.1 Introduction

The accuracy with which a user receiver can determine its position or velocity, or synchronize to GPS system time, depends on a complicated interaction of various factors. In general, GPS accuracy performance depends on the quality of the pseudorange and carrier phase measurements as well as the broadcast navigation data. In addition, the fidelity of the underlying physical model that relates these parameters is relevant. For example, the accuracy to which the satellite clock offsets relative to GPS system time are known to the user, or the accuracy to which satellite-to-user propagation errors are compensated, are important. Relevant errors are induced by the control, space, and user segments.

To analyze the effect of errors on accuracy, a fundamental assumption is usually made that the error sources can be allocated to individual satellite pseudoranges and can be viewed as effectively resulting in an equivalent error in the pseudorange values. The effective accuracy of the pseudorange value is termed the user-equivalent range error (UERE). The UERE for a given satellite is considered to be the (statistical) sum of the contributions from each of the error sources associated with the satellite. Usually, the error components are considered independent, and the composite UERE for a satellite is approximated as a zero mean Gaussian random variable where its variance is determined as the sum of the variance of each of its components. UERE is usually assumed to be independent and identically distributed from satellite to satellite. However, for certain cases of interest, it is sometimes appropriate for these assumptions to be modified. For example, if one is considering the addition of geosynchronous ranging satellites (GEOs) to the GPS constellation, the UERE associated with the GEOs might be modeled with a different variance than the standard constellation satellites, depending on the design characteristics of the satellites. In other situations, it might be appropriate to model certain components of UERE as correlated among the satellites.

The accuracy of the position/time solution determined by GPS is ultimately expressed as the product of a geometry factor and a pseudorange error factor. Loosely speaking, error in the GPS solution is estimated by the formula

$$\text{(error in GPS solution)} = \text{(geometry factor)} \times \text{(pseudorange error factor)} \qquad (7.1)$$

Under appropriate assumptions, the pseudorange error factor is the satellite UERE. The geometry factor expresses the composite effect of the relative satellite/user geometry on the GPS solution error. It is generically known as the DOP associated with the satellite/user geometry.

Section 7.2 describes the major error sources in GPS and develops error budgets for the PPS and SPS pseudorange UERE. Section 7.3 presents algorithms for estimating PVT and provides a derivation of (7.1). A variety of geometry factors are defined that are used in the estimation of the various components (e.g., horizontal, vertical) of the GPS navigation solution. Sections 7.4 through 7.6 discuss, respectively, the three other important performance metrics of availability, integrity, and continuity. The final section, Section 7.7, describes typical measured GPS performance using data from operational receiver networks, including the CS.

7.2 Measurement Errors

In Chapters 2 and 5, we discussed the formulation of the pseudorange and carrier-phase measurements. There are a number of sources of error that corrupt these measurements. An examination of these error sources is presented within this section. An overview is presented in the following paragraphs.

Satellite and receiver clock offsets directly translate into pseudorange and carrier-phase errors. The PRN code component of the satellite signal experiences delays as it propagates through the atmosphere, making the pseudorange larger than it would be if the signal were propagated in a vacuum. The carrier component of the signal is delayed by the troposphere but is actually advanced by the ionosphere in a phenomenon referred to as *ionospheric divergence* that will be discussed in more detail in Section 7.2.4.1. Further, reflections (i.e., multipath) and hardware effects between the user's antenna phase center and receiver code correlation point may delay (or advance) the signal components [1]. The total time offset due to all of these effects on the PRN component of each received signal is:

$$\delta t_D = \delta t_{atm} + \delta t_{noise\&int} + \delta t_{mp} + \delta t_{hw} \qquad (7.2)$$

where:

δt_{atm} = delays due to the atmosphere

$\delta t_{noise \& int}$ = errors due to receiver noise and interference

δt_{mp} = multipath offset

δt_{hw} = receiver hardware offsets

A delay expression with the same form as (7.2) but with generally different numerical values is incurred on the RF carrier component of each signal.

Before May 2000, (7.2) included the effects of SA, an error intentionally induced by the DOD to degrade the user's navigation solution. The degradation was accomplished primarily through dithering of the satellite clock (clock error component), although the manipulation of the broadcast ephemeris data (orbital error component) was also possible but not observed [2]. On May 1, 2000 SA was officially removed [3].

The pseudorange time equivalent is the difference between the receiver clock reading when the signal (i.e., a particular code phase) was received and the satellite clock reading when the signal was sent. These timing relationships are shown in Figure 7.1, where:

Δt = geometric range time equivalent

T_s = system time at which the signal left the satellite

T_u = system time at which the signal would have reached the user receiver in the absence of errors (i.e., with δt_D equal to zero)

T'_u = system time at which the signal reached the user receiver with δt_D

δt = offset of the satellite clock from system time—advance is positive; retardation (delay) is negative

t_u = offset of the receiver clock from system time

$T_s + \delta t$ = satellite clock reading at time which the signal left the satellite

$T'_u + t_u$ = user receiver clock reading at time when the signal reached the user receiver

c = speed of light

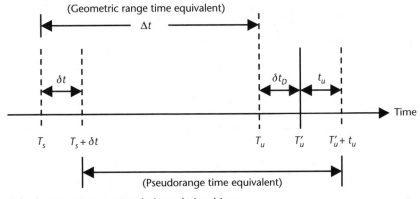

Figure 7.1   Range measurement timing relationships.

It is observed that the pseudorange ρ is:

$$\begin{aligned}
\rho &= c\big[(T'_u + t_u) - (T_s + \delta t)\big] \\
&= c(T'_u + T_s) + c(t_u - \delta t) \\
&= c(T_u + \delta t_D - T_s) + c(t_u - \delta t) \\
&= r + c(t_u - \delta t + \delta t_D)
\end{aligned}$$

where r is the geometric range, $r = c(T_u - T_S) = c\Delta t$.

A similar expression can be derived for the carrier-phase measurement when the raw measurement (see Section 5.7.3), usually computed in units of cycles, is converted to units of meters by multiplying by the carrier wavelength in meters. As noted earlier, the error terms are in general different for the carrier-phase measurement. Further, as discussed in Section 5.7.3, the carrier-phase measurement includes an ambiguity that is an integer multiple of a wavelength. Elaboration on the pseudorange and carrier-phase error sources, including relativistic effects, is provided in the following sections.

7.2.1 Satellite Clock Error

As discussed in Chapter 3, the satellites contain atomic clocks that control all onboard timing operations, including broadcast signal generation. Although these clocks are highly stable, the clock correction fields in the navigation data message are sized such that the deviation between SV time and GPS time may be as large as 1 ms [4]. (An offset of 1 ms translates to a 300-km pseudorange error.) The MCS determines and transmits clock correction parameters to the satellites for rebroadcast in the navigation message (see Section 3.1.2). These correction parameters are implemented by the receiver using the second-order polynomial [4]:

$$\delta t_{clk} = a_{f0} + a_{f1}(t - t_{oc}) + a_{f2}(t - t_{oc})^2 + \Delta t_r \tag{7.3}$$

where:

a_{f0} = clock bias (s)

a_{f1} = clock drift (s/s)

a_{f2} = frequency drift (i.e., aging) (s/s^2)

t_{oc} = clock data reference time (s)

t = current time epoch (s)

Δt_r = correction due to relativistic effects (s)

The correction Δt_r compensates for one of three GPS-related relativistic effects discussed in Section 7.2.3.

Since these parameters are computed using a curve-fit to predicted estimates of the actual satellite clock errors, some residual error remains. This residual clock error, δt, results in ranging errors that typically vary from 0.3–4m, depending on the type of satellite and age of the broadcast data. Range errors due to residual clock errors are generally the smallest following a control segment upload to a satellite, and they slowly degrade over time until the next upload (typically daily). At zero age of data (ZAOD), clock errors for a typical satellite are on the order of 0.8m [5, 6]. Errors 24 hours after an upload are generally within the range of 1–4m. User equipment that is tracking all visible satellites will observe satellites with ages of data (AODs) varying from 0 to 24 hours. It is thus appropriate, in the development of a statistical model for clock errors suitable for position or time error budgets, to average over AOD. The nominal 1-sigma clock error for the constellation in 2004 averaged over AOD was 1.1m, based on the data presented in [5, 6]. It is expected that residual clock errors will continue to decrease as newer satellites are launched with better performing clocks and as improvements are made to the control segment [7]. Average clock errors are also influenced by the frequency of uploads to each satellite, as discussed in Chapter 3.

Prior to May 2000, GPS clock errors were dominated by SA. Although SA is now discontinued, a rudimentary understanding of SA is still of importance because the presence of the SA dither component influenced the design of many fielded GPS receivers and augmentations. This intentional dithering of the satellite clock was observed to impart errors in GPS pseudorange and carrier-phase measurements with a 1-sigma value of approximately 23m [2]. Errors were observed to be statistically independent from satellite to satellite with significant correlation over time. SA errors for one satellite would typically randomly walk from a maximum positive value to a maximum negative value and back with a period of oscillation of around 2–5 minutes. Several detailed statistical models for simulating observed SA errors are presented in [2].

7.2.2   Ephemeris Error

Estimates of ephemerides for all satellites are computed and uplinked to the satellites with other navigation data message parameters for rebroadcast to the user. As in the case of the satellite clock corrections, these corrections are generated using a curve fit of the control segment's best prediction of each satellite's position at the time of upload. The residual satellite position error is a vector that is depicted in Figure 7.2, with typical magnitudes in the range of 1–6m [8]. The effective pseudorange and carrier-phase errors due to ephemeris prediction errors can be computed by projecting the satellite position error vector onto the satellite-to-user LOS vector. Ephemeris errors are generally smallest in the radial (from the satellite toward the center of the Earth) direction. The components of ephemeris errors in the along-track (the instantaneous direction of travel of the satellite) and cross-track (perpendicular to the along-track and radial) directions are much larger. Along-track and cross-track components are more difficult for the control segment to observe through its monitors on the surface of the Earth, since these components do not project significantly onto LOSs toward the Earth. Fortunately, the user does not experience large measurement errors due to the largest ephemeris error components for the same reason. The effective pseudorange or carrier-phase error due to ephemeris prediction errors is on the order of 0.8m (1σ) [6].

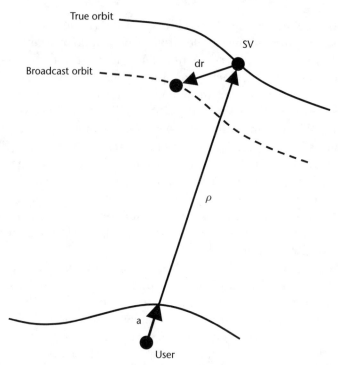

Figure 7.2 Ephemeris error. (*After:* [9].)

7.2.3 Relativistic Effects

Both Einstein's general and special theories of relativity are factors in the pseudorange and carrier-phase measurement process [10, 11]. The need for special relativity (SR) relativistic corrections arises any time the signal source (in this case, GPS satellites) or the signal receiver (GPS receiver) is moving with respect to the chosen isotropic light speed frame, which in the GPS system is the ECI frame. The need for general relativity (GR) relativistic corrections arises any time the signal source and signal receiver are located at different gravitational potentials.

The satellite clock is affected by both SR and GR. In order to compensate for both of these effects, the satellite clock frequency is adjusted to 10.22999999543 MHz prior to launch [4]. The frequency observed by the user at sea level will be 10.23 MHz; hence, the user does not have to correct for this effect.

The user does have to make a correction for another relativistic periodic effect that arises because of the slight eccentricity of the satellite orbit. Exactly half of the periodic effect is caused by the periodic change in the speed of the satellite relative to the ECI frame and half is caused by the satellite's periodic change in its gravitational potential.

When the satellite is at perigee, the satellite velocity is higher and the gravitational potential is lower—both cause the satellite clock to run more slowly. When the satellite is at apogee, the satellite velocity is lower and the gravitational potential is higher—both cause the satellite clock to run faster [10, 11]. This effect can be compensated for by [4]:

$$\Delta t_r = Fe\sqrt{a}\sin E_k \tag{7.4}$$

where:

$F = -4.442807633 \times 10^{-10}$ s/m$^{1/2}$

e = satellite orbital eccentricity

a = semimajor axis of the satellite orbit

E_k = eccentric anomaly of the satellite orbit

Reference [9] states that this relativistic effect can reach a maximum of 70 ns (21m in range). Correcting the satellite clock for this relativistic effect will result in a more accurate estimation of the time of transmission by the user.

Due to rotation of the Earth during the time of signal transmission, a relativistic error is introduced, known as the *Sagnac effect*, when computations for the satellite positions are made in an ECEF coordinate system (see Section 2.2.2). During the propagation time of the SV signal transmission, a clock on the surface of the Earth will experience a finite rotation with respect to an ECI coordinate system (see Section 2.2.1). Figure 7.3 illustrates this phenomenon. Clearly, if the user experiences a net rotation away from the SV, the propagation time will increase, and vice versa. If left uncorrected, the Sagnac effect can lead to position errors on the order of 30m [12]. Corrections for the Sagnac effect are often referred to as *Earth rotation corrections*.

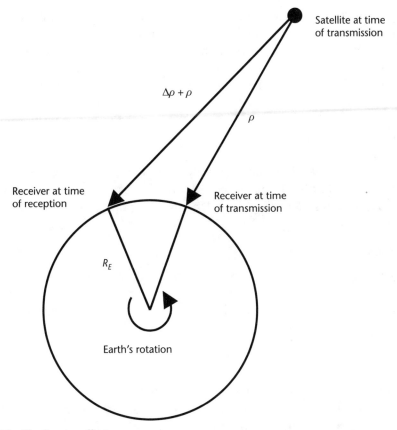

Figure 7.3   The Sagnac effect.

There are a number of approaches for correcting for the Sagnac effect. One common approach is to avoid the Sagnac effect entirely by working within an ECI coordinate system for satellite and user position computations. An ECI frame can be conveniently obtained by freezing an ECEF frame at the instant of time when pseudorange measurements are made to the set of visible satellites. The Sagnac effect does not arise in an ECI frame. Importantly, the satellite positions that are used in the standard GPS user position solution (Section 2.4) must correspond to the times of transmission, which are generally not the same. The time of transmission for each satellite, T_s, is a natural measurement of a GPS receiver, as discussed in Section 5.7.1. Users of commercial equipment can access time of transmission for each satellite by simply subtracting the pseudorange measurement (after applying the clock corrections discussed in Section 7.2.1) divided by the speed of light from the receiver's time-tag for the measurement. Next, each satellite position can be computed in terms of its ECEF coordinates (x_s, y_s, z_s) at its time of transmission using the broadcast ephemeris data described in Table 2.3. Then, each satellite position can be transformed into the common ECI frame using the rotation:

$$\begin{bmatrix} x_{eci} \\ y_{eci} \\ z_{eci} \end{bmatrix} = \begin{bmatrix} \cos \dot{\Omega}(T_u - T_s) & \sin \dot{\Omega}(T_u - T_s) & 0 \\ -\sin \dot{\Omega}(T_u - T_s) & \cos \dot{\Omega}(T_u - T_s) & 0 \\ 0 & 0 & 1 \end{bmatrix} \begin{bmatrix} x_s \\ y_s \\ z_s \end{bmatrix}$$

In this formulation, the time of reception, T_u, is initially unknown prior to the position/time estimate. It may be initially approximated as the average time of transmission among visible satellites plus 75 ms for an Earth-based user. Once the position solution is generated using the least-squares technique described in Section 2.4, the user clock correction can be applied to obtain a much better estimate of T_u, and the process can be iterated. The user's position coordinates are the same in both the ECEF and ECI frames at the signal reception time, since by definition these two frames were fixed at that instant. A number of alternative Earth rotation correction formulations, along with numerical examples, are provided in the excellent reference [12].

Finally, the GPS signal experiences space-time curvature due to the gravitational field of the Earth. The magnitude of this relativistic effect can range from 0.001 ppm in relative positioning to about 18.7 mm for point positioning [13].

7.2.4 Atmospheric Effects

The propagation speed of a wave in a medium can be expressed in terms of the index of refraction for the medium. The index of refraction is defined as the ratio of the wave's propagation speed in free space to that in the medium by the formula

$$n = \frac{c}{v} \tag{7.5}$$

where c is the speed of light equal to 299,792,458 m/s as defined within the WGS-84 system. The medium is dispersive if the propagation speed (or, equivalently, the index of refraction) is a function of the wave's frequency. In a dispersive medium, the propagation velocity v_p of the signal's carrier phase differs from the velocity v_g associated with the waves carrying the signal information. The information-carrying aspect can be thought of as a group of waves traveling at slightly different frequencies.

To clarify the concepts of group and phase velocities, consider two components, S_1 and S_2, of an electromagnetic wave with frequencies f_1 and f_2 (or ω_1 and ω_2) and phase velocities v_1 and v_2, traveling in the x-direction. The sum S of these signals is

$$S = S_1 + S_2 = \sin \omega_1 \left(t - \frac{x}{v_1}\right) + \sin \omega_2 \left(t - \frac{x}{v_2}\right)$$

Using the trigonometric identity,

$$\sin \alpha + \sin \beta = 2 \cos \frac{1}{2}(\alpha - \beta) \cdot \sin \frac{1}{2}(\alpha + \beta)$$

we find that

$$S = 2 \cos \left[\frac{1}{2}(\omega_1 - \omega_2)t - \frac{1}{2}\left(\frac{\omega_1}{v_1} - \frac{\omega_2}{v_2}\right)x\right] \times \sin\left[\frac{1}{2}(\omega_1 + \omega_2)t - \frac{1}{2}\left(\frac{\omega_1}{v_1} + \frac{\omega_2}{v_2}\right)x\right]$$

$$= 2 \cos \frac{1}{2}(\omega_1 - \omega_2)\left[t - \frac{x}{\dfrac{\frac{1}{2}(\omega_1 - \omega_2)}{\frac{1}{2}\left(\dfrac{\omega_1}{v_1} - \dfrac{\omega_2}{v_2}\right)}}\right] \times \sin\left[\frac{1}{2}(\omega_1 + \omega_2)t - \frac{1}{2}\left(\frac{\omega_1}{v_1} + \frac{\omega_2}{v_2}\right)x\right]$$

The cosine part is a wave group (the modulation imposed on the sinusoid—that part of the wave that carries the information) that moves with velocity

$$v_g = \frac{\frac{1}{2}(\omega_1 - \omega_2)}{\frac{1}{2}\left(\dfrac{\omega_1}{v_1} - \dfrac{\omega_2}{v_2}\right)} = \frac{2\pi(f_1 - f_2)}{2\pi\left(\dfrac{f_1}{v_1} - \dfrac{f_2}{v_2}\right)} = \frac{f_1 - f_2}{\dfrac{1}{\lambda_1} - \dfrac{1}{\lambda_2}} = \frac{\left(\dfrac{v_1}{\lambda_1} - \dfrac{v_2}{\lambda_2}\right)}{\left(\dfrac{1}{\lambda_1} - \dfrac{1}{\lambda_2}\right)}$$

$$= \frac{\left(\dfrac{v_1}{\lambda_1} - \dfrac{v_1}{\lambda_2} + \dfrac{v_1}{\lambda_2} - \dfrac{v_2}{\lambda_2}\right)}{\left(\dfrac{1}{\lambda_1} - \dfrac{1}{\lambda_2}\right)} = v_1 - \lambda_1 \frac{v_2 - v_1}{\lambda_2 - \lambda_1}$$

(7.6)

where λ_1 and λ_2 are the corresponding signal wavelengths.

For signals with narrow bandwidths relative to the carrier frequency, such as the GPS signals, we can replace $v_2 - v_1$ by the differential dv, $\lambda_2 - \lambda_1$ by the differential $d\lambda$, and λ_1 by λ_2, and add the subscript p to v to denote phase velocity explicitly to get

$$v_g = v_p - \lambda \frac{dv_p}{d\lambda} \tag{7.7}$$

which implies that the difference between the group velocity and phase velocity depends on both the wavelength and the rate of change of phase velocity with wavelength.

The corresponding indices of refraction are related by [13]

$$n_g = n_p + f \frac{dn_p}{df} \tag{7.8}$$

where the indices of refraction are defined by

$$n_p = \frac{c}{v_p} \qquad n_g = \frac{c}{v_g} \tag{7.9}$$

and f denotes the signal frequency. In a nondispersive medium, wave propagation is independent of frequency, and the signal phase and signal information propagate at the same speed with $v_g = v_p$ and $n_g = n_p$.

7.2.4.1 Ionospheric Effects

The ionosphere is a dispersive medium located primarily in the region of the atmosphere between about 70 km and 1,000 km above the Earth's surface. Within this region, ultraviolet rays from the sun ionize a portion of gas molecules and release free electrons. These free electrons influence electromagnetic wave propagation, including the GPS satellite signal broadcasts.

The following is based on a similar development in [13]. The index of refraction for the phase propagation in the ionosphere can be approximated as

$$n_p = 1 + \frac{c_2}{f^2} + \frac{c_3}{f^3} + \frac{c_4}{f^4} \cdots \tag{7.10}$$

where the coefficients c_2, c_3, and c_4 are frequency independent but are a function of the number of electrons (i.e., electron density) along the satellite-to-user signal propagation path. The electron density is denoted as n_e. A similar expression for n_g can be obtained by differentiating (7.10) with respect to frequency and substituting the result along with (7.10) into (7.8). This results in the following:

$$n_g = 1 - \frac{c_2}{f^2} - \frac{2c_3}{f^3} - \frac{3c_4}{f^4} \cdots$$

Neglecting higher-order terms, the following approximations are obtained:

$$n_p = 1 + \frac{c_2}{f^2} \qquad n_g = 1 - \frac{c_2}{f^2} \tag{7.11}$$

The coefficient c_2 is estimated as $c_2 = -40.3\ n_e$ Hz^2. Rewriting this yields

$$n_p = 1 - \frac{40.3n_e}{f^2} \qquad n_g = 1 + \frac{40.3n_e}{f^2} \qquad (7.12)$$

Using (7.9), the phase and group velocity are estimated as

$$v_p = \frac{c}{1 - \dfrac{40.3n_e}{f^2}} \qquad v_g = \frac{c}{1 + \dfrac{40.3n_e}{f^2}} \qquad (7.13)$$

It can be observed that the phase velocity will exceed that of the group velocity. The amount of retardation of the group velocity is equal to the advance of the carrier phase with respect to free-space propagation. In the case of GPS, this translates to the signal information (e.g., PRN code and navigation data) being delayed and the carrier phase experiencing an advance, a phenomenon referred to as *ionospheric divergence*. Importantly, the magnitude of the error on the pseudorange measurement and the error on the carrier-phase measurement (both in meters) are equal—only the sign is different. The reduction in the carrier-phase measurement value due to the presence of free electrons in the ionosphere can be intuitively explained as being due to the fact that the distance from crest to crest in the electric field of the signal is lengthened for the portion of the signal path contained within the ionosphere.

The measured range is

$$S = \int_{SV}^{User} n\ ds \qquad (7.14)$$

whereas the LOS (i.e., geometric) range is

$$l = \int_{SV}^{User} dl \qquad (7.15)$$

The path length difference due to ionospheric refraction is

$$\Delta S_{iono} = \int_{SV}^{User} n\ ds - \int_{SV}^{User} dl \qquad (7.16)$$

The delay attributed to the phase refractive index is

$$\Delta S_{iono,p} = \int_{SV}^{User}\left(1 - \frac{40.3n_e}{f^2}\right) ds - \int_{SV}^{User} dl \qquad (7.17)$$

Similarly, the delay induced by the group refractive index is

$$\Delta S_{iono,g} = \int_{SV}^{User}\left(1 + \frac{40.3n_e}{f^2}\right) ds - \int_{SV}^{User} dl \qquad (7.18)$$

Since the delay will be small compared to the satellite-to-user distance, we simplify (7.17) and (7.18) by integrating the first term along the LOS path. Thus, ds changes to dl, and we now have

$$\Delta S_{iono,p} = -\frac{40.3}{f^2} \int_{SV}^{User} n_e \, dl \qquad \Delta S_{iono,g} = \frac{40.3}{f^2} \int_{SV}^{User} n_e \, dl \qquad (7.19)$$

The electron density along the path length is referred to as the *total electron count* (TEC) and is defined as

$$TEC = \int_{SV}^{User} n_e \, dl$$

The TEC is expressed in units of electrons/m^2 or occasionally *TEC units* (TECU) where 1 TECU is defined as 10^{16} electrons/m^2. The TEC is a function of time of day, user location, satellite elevation angle, season, ionizing flux, magnetic activity, sunspot cycle, and scintillation. It nominally ranges between 10^{16} and 10^{19}, with the two extremes occurring around midnight and mid-afternoon, respectively. We can now rewrite (7.19) in terms of the TEC:

$$\Delta S_{iono,p} = \frac{-40.3TEC}{f^2} \qquad \Delta S_{iono,g} = \frac{40.3TEC}{f^2} \qquad (7.20)$$

Since the TEC is generally referenced to the vertical direction through the ionosphere, the previous expressions reflect the path delay along the vertical direction with the satellite at an elevation angle of 90° (i.e., zenith). For other elevation angles, we multiply (7.20) by an *obliquity factor*. The obliquity factor, also referred to as a *mapping function*, accounts for the increased path length that the signal will travel within the ionosphere. Various models exist for the obliquity factor. One example, from [14], is (terms are defined in Figure 7.4):

$$F_{pp} = \left[1 - \left(\frac{R_e \cos\phi}{R_e + h_I} \right)^2 \right]^{-\frac{1}{2}} \qquad (7.21)$$

The height of the maximum electron density, h_I, in this model is 350 km. With the addition of the obliquity factor, the path delay expressions from (7.20) become

$$\Delta S_{iono,p} = -F_{pp} \frac{40.3TEC}{f^2} \qquad \Delta S_{iono,g} = F_{pp} \frac{40.3TEC}{f^2}$$

Since the ionospheric delay is frequency dependent, it can be virtually eliminated by making ranging measurements with a dual-frequency receiver. Differencing pseudorange measurements made on both L1 and L2 enables the estimation of both the L1 and L2 delays (neglecting multipath and receiver noise errors). These are first-order estimates, since they are based on (7.11). An *ionospheric-free* pseudorange may be formed as [4]:

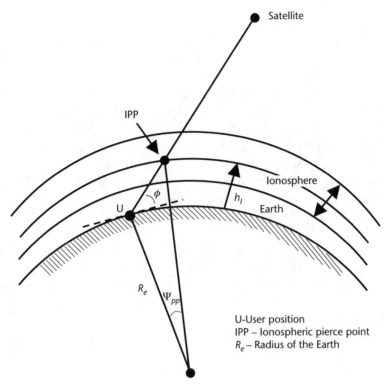

Figure 7.4   Ionospheric modeling geometry.

$$\rho_{ionospheric-free} = \frac{\rho_{L2} - \gamma\rho_{L1}}{1-\gamma} \tag{7.22}$$

where $\gamma = (f_{L1}/f_{L2})^2$. Although ionospheric delay errors are removed, this approach has the drawback that measurement errors are significantly magnified through the combination. A preferred approach is to use the L1 and L2 pseudorange measurements to estimate the ionospheric error on L1 using the following expression:

$$\Delta S_{iono,corr_{L1}} = \left(\frac{f_{L2}^2}{f_{L2}^2 - f_{L1}^2}\right)(\rho_{L1} - \rho_{L2}) \tag{7.23}$$

The path length difference on L2 can be estimated by multiplying $\Delta S_{iono,corr_{L1}}$ by

$$(f_1/f_2)^2 = (77/60)^2$$

These estimated corrections may be smoothed over time, since ionospheric delay errors typically do not change very rapidly and are subtracted from pseudorange measurements made by each frequency.

In case of a single-frequency receiver, it is obvious that (7.23) cannot be used. Consequently, models of the ionosphere are employed to correct for the ionospheric delay. One important example is the Klobuchar model, which removes (on average) about 50% of the ionospheric delay at midlatitudes through a set of coefficients included in the GPS navigation message. This model assumes that the vertical ionospheric delay can be approximated by half a cosine function of the local time during daytime and by a constant level during nighttime [15]. The original Klobuchar model was adapted by the GPS CS and the correction algorithm is provided in [4, 16].

Almost three times as much delay is incurred when viewing satellites at low elevation than at the zenith. For a signal arriving at vertical incidence, the delay ranges from about 10 ns (3m) at night to as much as 50 ns (15m) during the day. At low satellite viewing angles (0° through 10°), the delay can range from 30 ns (9m) at night up to 150 ns (45m) during the day [15]. A typical 1-sigma value for residual ionospheric delays, averaged over the globe and over elevation angles, is 7m [17].

7.2.4.2 Tropospheric Delay

The troposphere is the lower part of the atmosphere that is nondispersive for frequencies up to 15 GHz [13]. Within this medium, the phase and group velocities associated with the GPS carrier and signal information (PRN code and navigation data) on both L1 and L2 are equally delayed with respect to free-space propagation. This delay is a function of the tropospheric refractive index, which is dependent on the local temperature, pressure, and relative humidity. Left uncompensated, the range equivalent of this delay can vary from about 2.4m for a satellite at the zenith and the user at sea level to about 25m for a satellite at an elevation angle of approximately 5° [13].

From (7.16), we see that the path length difference attributed to the tropospheric delay is

$$\Delta S_{tropo} = \int_{SV}^{User} (n-1) ds$$

where the integration is along the signal path. The path length difference can also be expressed in terms of refractivity,

$$\Delta S_{tropo} = 10^{-6} \int_{SV}^{User} N ds \qquad (7.24)$$

where the refractivity, N, is defined by

$$N \equiv 10^6 (n-1)$$

The refractivity is often modeled as including both a dry (hydrostatic) and wet (nonhydrostatic) component [18]. The dry component, which arises from the dry air, gives rise to about 90% of the tropospheric delay and can be predicted very accurately. The wet component, which arises from the water vapor, is more difficult to predict due to uncertainties in the atmospheric distribution. Both components extend to different heights in the troposphere; the dry layer extends to a height of about 40 km, while the wet component extends to a height of about 10 km.

We define $N_{d,0}$ and $N_{w,0}$ as the dry and wet component refractivities, respectively, at standard sea level. To express both $N_{d,0}$ and $N_{w,0}$ in pressure and temperature, the formulas of [19] can be used:

$$N_{d,0} \approx a_1 \frac{p_0}{T_0}$$

with

p_0 = partial pressure of the dry component at standard sea level (mbar)

T_0 = absolute temperature at standard sea level (K)

a_1 = empirical constant (77.624 K/mbar)

$$N_{w,0} \approx a_2 \frac{e_0}{T_0} + a_3 \frac{e_0}{T_0^2}$$

where a_2 and a_3 are empirical constants (−12.92 K/mbar and 371,900 K^2/mbar, respectively).

Path delay also varies with the user's height, h. Thus, both the dry and wet component refractivities are dependent on the atmospheric conditions at the user's height above the reference ellipsoid. One model that takes the height into account and is successfully demonstrated in [20] combines parts of the works cited in [18, 19, 21, 22]. The dry component as a function of the height is determined by

$$N_d(h) = N_{d,0} \left[\frac{h_d - h}{h_d} \right]^{\mu} \tag{7.25}$$

and h_d, the upper extent of the dry component of the troposphere referenced to sea level, is determined from

$$h_d = 0.011385 \frac{p_0}{N_{d,0} \times 10^{-6}}$$

where μ stems from the underlying use of the ideal gas law. Hopfield [18] found that setting $\mu = 4$ gives the best results for the model.

Similarly the refractivity, $N_w(h)$, of the wet component of the troposphere is determined from

$$N_w(h) = N_{w,0} \left[\frac{h_w - h}{h_w} \right]^{\mu} \tag{7.26}$$

where h_w is the extent of the wet component of troposphere determined by

$$h_w = 0.0113851 \frac{1}{N_{w,0} \times 10^{-6}} \left[\frac{1,255}{T_0} + 0.05 \right] e_0$$

The path length difference when the satellite is at zenith and the user is at sea level is from (7.24):

$$\Delta S_{tropo} = 10^{-6} \int_{h=0}^{h_d} N_d(h)dh + 10^{-6} \int_{h=0}^{h_d} N_d(h)dh \qquad (7.27)$$

Evaluation of (7.27) using the expressions for $N_d(h)$ and $N_w(h)$ in (7.25) and (7.26) yields

$$\begin{aligned}\Delta S_{tropo} &= \frac{10^{-6}}{5}\left[N_{d,0}h_d + N_{w,0}h_w\right] \\ &= d_{dry} + d_{wet}\end{aligned} \qquad (7.28)$$

To compute the tropospheric correction in (7.28), pressure and temperature inputs are required, which can be obtained using meteorological sensors. When the satellite is not at zenith, a mapping function model is needed to determine how much greater a delay can be anticipated due to the larger path length of the signal through the troposphere. It is common to refer to the delay for a satellite at zenith as a *vertical delay* or *zenith delay* and the delay for satellites at any other arbitrary elevation angle as a *slant delay*. Mapping functions that relate slant and vertical delays will be discussed later in this section.

One accurate method for modeling the troposphere's dry and wet components at zenith without meteorological sensors was developed at the University of New Brunswick. In this model [17, 22, 23], referred to as UNB3, the dry and wet components are considered functions of height, h, in meters above mean sea level and of five meteorological parameters: pressure, p, in millibars, temperature, T, in Kelvin, water vapor pressure, e, in millibars, temperature lapse rate, β, in K/m, and water vapor lapse rate, λ (unitless). Each of the meteorological parameters is calculated by interpolating values from Tables 7.1 and 7.2. Using pressure as an example, the average pressure, $p_0(\phi)$, at latitude ϕ ($15° < \phi < 75°$) is calculated by using the two values in the p_0 column of Table 7.1 corresponding to those two values of latitude, ϕ_i and ϕ_{i+1}, that are closest to ϕ, as follows:

$$p_0(\phi) = p_0(\phi_i) + \left[p_0(\phi_{i+1}) - p_0(\phi_i)\right] \cdot \frac{(\phi - \phi_i)}{(\phi_{i+1} - \phi_i)}$$

Similarly, the seasonal variation, $\Delta p(\phi)$, is found in the same way from Table 7.2, as follows:

$$\Delta p(\phi) = \Delta p(\phi_i) + \left[\Delta p(\phi_{i+1}) - \Delta p(\phi_i)\right] \cdot \frac{(\phi - \phi_i)}{(\phi_{i+1} - \phi_i)}$$

For latitudes less than 15°, simply use the values of parameters in the first row without interpolation; for latitudes greater than 75°, use the values of parameters in the last row. Finally, the pressure, p, is determined, taking into account the day of the year, D, with the first day being January 1, as follows:

$$p = p_0(\phi) - \Delta p(\phi) \cdot \cos\left[\frac{2\pi(D - D_{min})}{365.25}\right]$$

Table 7.1   Average Meteorological Parameters for Tropospheric Delay

Parameter Averages

Latitude (deg)	p_0 (mbar)	T_0 (K)	e_0 (mbar)	β_0 (K/m)	λ_0
15° or less	1,013.25	299.65	26.31	6.30×10^{-3}	2.77
30	1,017.25	294.15	21.79	6.05×10^{-3}	3.15
45	1,015.75	283.15	11.66	5.58×10^{-3}	2.57
60	1,011.75	272.15	6.78	5.39×10^{-3}	1.81
75° or greater	1,013.00	263.65	4.11	4.53×10^{-3}	1.55

Table 7.2   Seasonal Meteorological Parameters for Tropospheric Delay

Seasonal Variation of Parameters

Latitude (°)	Δp (mbar)	ΔT (K)	Δe (mbar)	$\Delta \beta$ (K/m)	$\Delta \lambda$
15° or less	0.00	0.00	0.00	0.00×10^{-3}	0.00
30	−3.75	7.00	8.85	0.25×10^{-3}	0.33
45	−2.25	11.00	7.24	0.32×10^{-3}	0.46
60	−1.75	15.00	5.36	0.81×10^{-3}	0.74
75° or greater	−0.50	14.50	3.39	0.62×10^{-3}	0.30

where

$$D_{min} = \begin{cases} 28 & \text{in northern latitudes} \\ 211 & \text{in southern latitudes} \end{cases}$$

The difference in the values of the parameter D_{min} in the northern and southern hemispheres accounts for the difference (183 days) in seasons in these hemispheres. Once all five meteorological parameters have been calculated in exactly the same way that the pressure is calculated, the wet and dry components of the delay can be determined from the following equations for d_{dry} and d_{wet} in (7.25):

$$d_{dry} = \left(1 - \frac{\beta \cdot H}{T}\right)^{\frac{g}{R_d \beta}} \cdot \left(\frac{10^6 \, k_1 R_d \, p}{g_m}\right)$$

$$d_{wet} = \left(1 - \frac{\beta \cdot H}{T}\right)^{\frac{(\lambda+1)g}{R_d \beta}} \cdot \left(\frac{10^6 \, k_2 R_d \, p}{g_m(\lambda+1) - \beta R_d} \cdot \frac{e}{T}\right)$$

where:

$k_1 = 77.604$ K/mbar

$k_2 = 382000$ K²/mbar

$R_d = 287.054$ J/kg/K

$g_m = 9.784$ m/s²

$g = 9.80665$ m/s²

For elevation angles other than 90°, the model in (7.28) does, in general, not apply. To account for the elevation angle of the satellite, for example, so-called mapping functions may be introduced in the equation:

$$\Delta S_{tropo} = m_d \cdot d_{dry} + m_w \cdot d_{wet}$$

or   (7.29)

$$\Delta S_{tropo} = m \cdot \left(d_{dry} + d_{wet}\right)$$

where:

m_d = dry-component mapping function

m_w = wet-component mapping function

m = general mapping function

Existing mapping functions can be divided into two groups: the geodetic survey–oriented applications and the navigation-oriented applications [24]. An example of the geodetic survey–oriented group is the Niell mapping function as described in [25]. Navigation-oriented mapping functions include both analytical models and more complex forms such as the fractional form introduced by [26]. The advantage of the analytical forms is that it is not computationally intensive to determine the mapping function values. An example of analytical models is Black and Eisner's mapping function, which is a function of the satellite's elevation angle, E:

$$m(E) = \frac{1.001}{\sqrt{0.002001 + \sin^2(E)}}$$

A more accurate, but more complex, model that may be used for the mapping function has the following continued fractional form [26]:

$$m_i(E) = \frac{1 + \dfrac{a_i}{1 + \dfrac{b_i}{1 + \dfrac{c_i}{1+\ldots}}}}{\sin E + \dfrac{a_i}{\sin E + \dfrac{b_i}{\sin E + \dfrac{c_i}{\sin E+\ldots}}}}$$

where E is the elevation angle; a_i, b_i, and c_i are the mapping function parameters; and i represents either the dry or wet component. Note that the term in the numerator normalizes the mapping function with respect to zenith. The parameters a_i, b_i, and c_i can be estimated from ray-tracing delay values at various elevation angles. Examples of mapping functions that describe the troposphere delay accurately down to a satellite elevation of 2° are described in [25]. The models in [25] are a function of satellite elevation and height. Note that these models require more computation time than the analytical models. One example of a three-parameter fractional form is the UNBabc model. The a, b, and c parameters for the dry component mapping function are given by:

$$a_d = (1.18972 - 0.026855h + 0.10664\cos\phi)/1,000$$
$$b_d = 0.0035716$$
$$c_d = 0.082456$$

The a, b, and c parameters for the wet component mapping function are given by:

$$a_w = (0.61120 - 0.035348h + 0.01526\cos\phi)/1,000$$
$$b_w = 0.0018576$$
$$c_w = 0.062741$$

7.2.5   Receiver Noise and Resolution

Measurement errors are also induced by the receiver tracking loops. In terms of the DLL, dominant sources of pseudorange measurement error (excluding multipath, which will be discussed in Section 7.2.6) are thermal noise jitter and the effects of interference. The C/A code composite receiver noise and resolution error contribution will be slightly larger than that for P(Y) code because the C/A code signal has a smaller RMS bandwidth than the P(Y) code. Typical modern receiver 1σ values for the noise and resolution error are on the order of a decimeter or less in nominal conditions (i.e., without external interference) and negligible compared to errors induced by multipath.

Receiver noise and resolution errors affect carrier phase measurements made by a PLL. PLL measurements errors in nominal conditions are on the order of 1.2 mm (1σ) when tracking the C/A code and 1.6 mm (1σ) when tracking the P(Y) code. Extensive treatment of DLL and PLL errors is provided in Section 5.6. The effects of interference on DLLs and PLLs are discussed in Section 6.2.

7.2.6   Multipath and Shadowing Effects

One of the most significant errors incurred in the receiver measurement process is multipath. Multipath errors on both pseudorange and carrier-phase measurements were discussed in detail in Section 6.3. As described in that section, multipath errors vary significantly in magnitude depending on the environment within which the receiver is located, satellite elevation angle, receiver signal processing, antenna gain pattern, and signal characteristics. Within this chapter, as an example, we will use typical 1-sigma multipath levels in a relatively benign environment of 20 cm and 2 cm, respectively, for a wide bandwidth C/A code receiver's pseudorange and carrier-phase measurements.

7.2.7 Hardware Bias Errors

7.2.7.1 Satellite Biases

Upon signal transmission, the GPS signals on each carrier frequency and among frequencies are imperfectly synchronized due to the different digital and analog signal paths corresponding to each signal. The timing bias between the L1 and L2 P(Y) code signals is inconsequential for most dual-frequency users since the broadcast clock corrections compensate for this bias under the presumption that the user is combining L1 and L2 pseudorange measurements via the ionospheric-free pseudorange equation.

Single-frequency users (L1 or L2) employing the broadcast clock corrections, however, must correct for the L1-L2 timing bias by using a broadcast correction, T_{GD}, contained in word 7 of subframe 1 of the GPS navigation message. The absolute value of the uncorrected L1-L2 group delay bias is specified to be less than 15 ns with random variations about the mean less than 3 ns (2 sigma) [4]. Observed values are generally less than 8 ns in magnitude. Until 1999, broadcast T_{GD} values were derived from factory measurements. Since April 1999, the broadcast T_{GD} values have been provided to the Air Force by JPL [27, 28]. At present, the accuracy of the broadcast values is limited by a nearly 0.5-ns message quantization error.

C/A code users have an additional timing bias of the transmitted signals to account for, which is the bias between the L1 C/A code and P(Y) code signals. This bias is specified to be less than 10 ns (2 sigma) [4]. Typical observed magnitudes are less than 3 ns. Although various organizations, including JPL, routinely estimate this bias, the present GPS navigation message does not include a field for this data. Future GPS navigation messages, however, will disseminate corrections for the L1 C/A code to P(Y) code bias, as well as a number of additional group delay corrections, referred to as *intersignal corrections* (ISCs) that will be introduced on future satellites (i.e., Blocks IIR-M and beyond) that will broadcast the new L2C, M code, and L5 signals [4, 29].

7.2.7.2 User Equipment Biases

User equipment bias errors introduced by the receiver hardware are often ignored because they are relatively small in comparison to other error sources, especially when cancellation is considered. GPS signals are delayed as they travel through the antenna, analog hardware (e.g., RF and IF filters, low-noise amplifiers, and mixers) and digital processing until the point where pseudorange and carrier-phase measurements are physically made within the digital receiver channels (see Chapter 5). Although the absolute delay values for propagation from the antenna phase center until the digital channels may be quite large (over 1 μs with long antenna-receiver cable runs or when SAW filters are employed), for similar signals on the same carrier frequency the delays experienced for the set of visible signals are nearly exactly equal. The absolute delay is important for timing applications and must be calibrated out. For many applications, however, the common delay does not affect performance, since it does not influence positioning accuracy, but rather directly appears only in the least-squares estimate of receiver clock bias. The C/A code signals have measurably different power spectra due to their short PRN codes. Since GPS receiver front ends, in general, do not have constant group delay throughout the passband, very small intersatellite biases can be observed upon C/A code pseudoranges. These biases are typically on the order of a few millimeters [30].

Hardware biases between spectrally different signals on one frequency, or among signals on different carrier frequencies, are larger in magnitude. In [31], differential group delay biases between L1 GPS C/A and GALILEO Open Service signals were analyzed within a representative receiver to be on the order of several nanoseconds (~1m in range). These biases are not common to all measurements and thus would influence positioning performance if not calibrated or estimated.

Within dual-frequency receivers, a portion of electrical paths followed by the L1 and L2 signals may be physically different, resulting in sizeable differential range errors. For the positioning user, the L1-L2 bias may often be ignored since it results in a common error for every ionospheric-free pseudorange (see Section 7.2.4.1), which will drop out in the estimated receiver clock bias.

Another error that can be attributed to the receiver hardware is hardware-induced multipath [32]. This error is caused by reflections of the GPS signal that occur within the receiver hardware due to the presence of an impedance mismatch between RF components. This error can be removed or reduced by careful design of the receiver front end.

7.2.8   Pseudorange Error Budgets

Based on the earlier discussion regarding error constituents, we can develop pseudorange error budgets to aid our understanding of stand-alone GPS accuracy. These budgets are intended to serve as guidelines for position error analyses. As indicated in (7.1), position error is a function of both the pseudorange error (UERE) and user/satellite geometry (DOP). The geometry factor will be discussed in Section 7.3.1.

The total system UERE comprises components from each system segment: the space segment, the control segment, and the user segment. This budget can be made based on either the use of single-frequency measurements or the use of dual-frequency measurements to determine the ionospheric delay. The error components are root-sum-squared to form the total system UERE, which is assumed to be Gaussian distributed. The use of RSS addition of UERE components is justified under the assumption that the errors can be treated as independent random variables such that the variances add or equivalently the 1-sigma total error is the RSS of the individual 1-sigma values.

Tables 7.3 and 7.4 show estimates of typical contemporary UERE budgets based on the data presented in Sections 7.2.1–7.2.7. Table 7.3 describes a typical UERE budget for a dual-frequency P(Y) code receiver. Table 7.4 shows the UERE budget for a single-frequency C/A code receiver. For a single-frequency user, the dominant pseudorange error source is the residual ionospheric delay after applying the broadcast ionospheric delay corrections. Dual frequency users can use the technique described in Section 7.2.4.1 to nearly completely remove the error due to ionospheric delays.

Table 7.3   GPS Precise Positioning Service Typical UERE Budget

Segment Source	Error Source	1σ Error (m)
Space/control	Broadcast clock	1.1
	Broadcast ephemeris	0.8
User	Residual ionospheric delay	0.1
	Residual tropospheric delay	0.2
	Receiver noise and resolution	0.1
	Multipath	0.2
System UERE	Total (RSS)	1.4

Table 7.4   GPS Standard Positioning Service Typical UERE Budget

Segment Source	Error Source	1σ Error (m)
Space/control	Broadcast clock	1.1
	L1 P(Y)-L1 C/A group delay	0.3
	Broadcast ephemeris	0.8
User	Ionospheric delay	7.0*
	Tropospheric delay	0.2
	Receiver noise and resolution	0.1
	Multipath	0.2
System UERE	Total (RSS)	7.1*

*Note that residual ionospheric errors tend to be highly correlated among satellites resulting in position errors being far less than predicted using DOP · UERE (see discussion in Section 7.3.2).

7.3   PVT Estimation Concepts

Chapter 2 described some basic techniques for estimating the PVT of a possibly mobile GPS receiver. This section discusses a variety of additional concepts regarding PVT estimation, beginning with an expanded description of the role of geometry in GPS PVT accuracy and a number of accuracy metrics that are commonly used. This section also describes a number of advanced PVT estimation techniques including the use of WLS, additional estimated parameters (beyond the user x, y, z position coordinates and clock offset), and Kalman filtering.

7.3.1   Satellite Geometry and Dilution of Precision in GPS

As motivation for the concept of dilution of precision as it applies to GPS, consider once again the foghorn example introduced in Section 2.1.1. In this example, a user locates his or her position from ranging measurements from two foghorns. The assumptions are that the user has a synchronized time base relative to the foghorns and has knowledge of the location of the foghorns and their transmission times. The user measures the TOA of each foghorn signal and computes a propagation time that determines the user's range from each foghorn. The user locates his or her position from the intersection of the range rings determined from the TOA measurements.

In the presence of measurement errors, the range rings used to compute the user's location will be in error and result in error in the computed position. The concept of dilution of precision is the idea that the position error that results from measurement errors depends on the user/foghorn relative geometry. Graphically, these ideas are illustrated in Figure 7.5. Two geometries are indicated. In Figure 7.5(a),

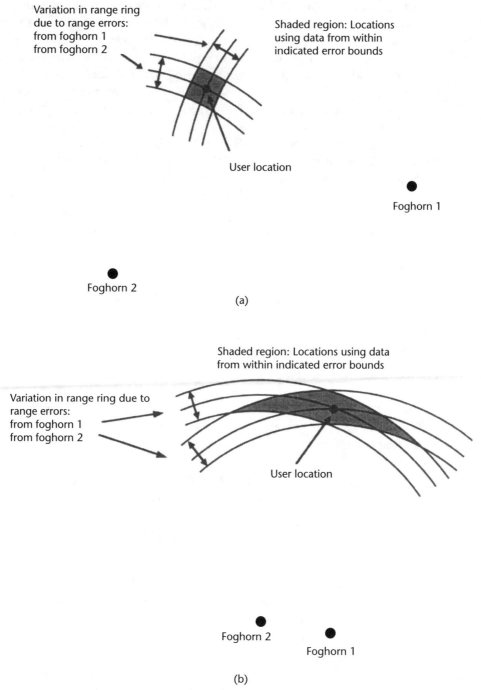

Figure 7.5   Relative geometry and dilution of precision: (a) geometry with low DOP, and (b) geometry with high DOP.

the foghorns are located approximately at right angles with respect to the user location. In Figure 7.5(b), the angle between the foghorns as viewed from the user is much smaller. In both cases, portions of the error-free range rings are indicated and intersect at the user's location. Additional ring segments that illustrate the variation in range ring position resulting from ranging errors to the foghorns are included. The error range illustrated in both figures is the same. The shaded regions indicate the set of locations that can be obtained if one uses ranging measurements within the illustrated error bounds. The accuracy of the computed location is very different for the two cases. With the same measurement error variation, geometry in Figure 7.5(b) gives considerably more error in the computed user's location than in Figure 7.5(a), as is evident from comparison of the shaded regions. Geometry in Figure 7.5(b) is said to have a larger dilution of precision than geometry in Figure 7.5(a). For comparable measurement errors, geometry in Figure 7.5(b) results in larger errors in the computed location.

A formal derivation of the DOP relations in GPS begins with the linearization of the pseudorange equations given in Section 2.4.2. The linearization is the Jacobian relating changes in the user position and time bias to changes in the pseudorange values. This relationship is inverted in accordance with the solution algorithm and is used to relate the covariance of the user position and time bias to the covariance of the pseudorange errors. The DOP parameters are defined as geometry factors that relate parameters of the user position and time bias errors to those of the pseudorange errors.

The offset $\Delta\mathbf{x}$ in the user's position and time bias relative to the linearization point is related to the offset in the error-free pseudorange values $\Delta\boldsymbol{\rho}$ by the relation

$$\mathbf{H}\Delta\mathbf{x} = \Delta\boldsymbol{\rho} \qquad (7.30)$$

The vector $\Delta\mathbf{x}$ has four components. The first three are the position offset of the user from the linearization point; the fourth is the offset of the user time bias from the bias assumed in the linearization point. $\Delta\boldsymbol{\rho}$ is the vector offset of the error-free pseudorange values corresponding to the user's actual position and the pseudorange values that correspond to the linearization point. $\mathbf{H}$ is the $n \times 4$ matrix

$$\mathbf{H} = \begin{bmatrix} a_{x1} & a_{y1} & a_{z1} & 1 \\ a_{x2} & a_{y2} & a_{z2} & 1 \\ \vdots & \vdots & \vdots & \vdots \\ a_{xn} & a_{yn} & a_{zn} & 1 \end{bmatrix} \qquad (7.31)$$

and the $\mathbf{a}_i = (a_{xi}, a_{yi}, a_{zi})$ are the unit vectors pointing from the linearization point to the location of the ith satellite. If $n = 4$ and data from just four satellites are being used, and if the linearization point is close to the user's location, the user's location and time offset are obtained by solving (7.30) for $\Delta\mathbf{x}$ (i.e., if the linearization point is close enough to the user position, iteration is not required). One obtains

$$\Delta\mathbf{x} = \mathbf{H}^{-1}\Delta\boldsymbol{\rho} \qquad (7.32)$$

and the offset of the user's position from the linearization point is expressed as a linear function of $\Delta\boldsymbol{\rho}$. In the case of $n > 4$, the method of least squares can be used to solve (7.30) for $\Delta\mathbf{x}$ (see Appendix A). The least square result can be obtained formally by multiplying both sides of (7.30) on the left by the matrix transpose of $\mathbf{H}$ obtaining $\mathbf{H}^T\mathbf{H}\Delta\mathbf{x} = \mathbf{H}^T\Delta\boldsymbol{\rho}$. The matrix combination $\mathbf{H}^T\mathbf{H}$ is a square 4×4 matrix, and one can solve for $\Delta\mathbf{x}$ by multiplying both sides by the inverse, $(\mathbf{H}^T\mathbf{H})^{-1}$. (The matrix will be invertible provided the tips of the unit vectors $\mathbf{a}_i$ do not all lie in a plane.) One obtains

$$\Delta\mathbf{x} = \left(\mathbf{H}^T\mathbf{H}\right)^{-1}\mathbf{H}^T\Delta\boldsymbol{\rho} \tag{7.33}$$

which is the least square formulation for $\Delta\mathbf{x}$ as a function of $\Delta\boldsymbol{\rho}$. We observe that if $n = 4$, $(\mathbf{H}^T\mathbf{H})^{-1} = \mathbf{H}^{-1}(\mathbf{H}^T)^{-1}$ and (7.33) reduces to (7.32).

The pseudorange measurements are not error-free and can be viewed as a linear combination of three terms,

$$\Delta\boldsymbol{\rho} = \boldsymbol{\rho}_T - \boldsymbol{\rho}_L + d\boldsymbol{\rho} \tag{7.34}$$

where $\boldsymbol{\rho}_T$ is the vector of error-free pseudorange values, $\boldsymbol{\rho}_L$ is the vector of pseudorange values computed at the linearization point, and $d\boldsymbol{\rho}$ represents the net error in the pseudorange values. Similarly, $\Delta\mathbf{x}$ can be expressed as

$$\Delta\mathbf{x} = \mathbf{x}_T - \mathbf{x}_L + d\mathbf{x} \tag{7.35}$$

where $\mathbf{x}_T$ is the error-free position and time, $\mathbf{x}_L$ is the position and time defined as the linearization point, and $d\mathbf{x}$ is the error in the position and time estimate. Substituting (7.34) and (7.35) into (7.33) and using the relation $\mathbf{x}_T - \mathbf{x}_L = (\mathbf{H}^T\mathbf{H})^{-1}\mathbf{H}^T(\boldsymbol{\rho}_T - \boldsymbol{\rho}_L)$—this follows from the relation $\mathbf{H}(\mathbf{x}_T - \mathbf{x}_L) = (\boldsymbol{\rho}_T - \boldsymbol{\rho}_L)$, which is a restatement of (7.30)—one obtains

$$d\mathbf{x} = \left[\left(\mathbf{H}^T\mathbf{H}\right)^{-1}\mathbf{H}^T\right]d\boldsymbol{\rho} = \mathbf{K}d\boldsymbol{\rho} \tag{7.36}$$

The matrix $\mathbf{K}$ is defined by the expression in brackets. Equation (7.36) gives the functional relationship between the errors in the pseudorange values and the induced errors in the computed position and time bias. It is valid provided that the linearization point is sufficiently close to the user's location and that the pseudorange errors are sufficiently small so that the error in performing the linearization can be ignored.

Equation (7.36) is the fundamental relationship between pseudorange errors and computed position and time bias errors. The matrix $(\mathbf{H}^T\mathbf{H})^{-1}\mathbf{H}^T$, which is sometimes called the least-squares solution matrix, is a $4 \times n$ matrix and depends only on the relative geometry of the user and the satellites participating in the least square solution computation. In many applications, the user/satellite geometry can be considered fixed, and (7.36) yields a linear relationship between the pseudorange errors and the induced position and time bias errors.

The pseudorange errors are considered to be random variables, and (7.36) expresses dx as a random variable functionally related to $d\rho$. The error vector $d\rho$ is usually assumed to have components that are jointly Gaussian and to be zero mean. With the geometry considered fixed, it follows that dx is also Gaussian and zero mean. The covariance of dx is obtained by forming the product $dx dx^T$ and computing an expected value. By definition, one obtains

$$\operatorname{cov}(dx) = E\left[dx dx^T \right] \tag{7.37}$$

where $\operatorname{cov}(dx) = E[dx dx^T]$ denotes the covariance of dx and E represents the expectation operator. Substituting from (7.36) and viewing the geometry as fixed, one obtains

$$\operatorname{cov}(dx) = E\left[K d\rho k \rho^T K^T \right] = E\left[\left(H^T H \right)^{-1} H^T d\rho d\rho^T H \left(H^T H \right)^{-1} \right]$$
$$= \left(H^T H \right)^{-1} H^T \operatorname{cov}(d\rho) H \left(H^T H \right)^{-1} \tag{7.38}$$

Note that in this computation, $(H^T H)^{-1}$ is symmetric. [This follows from an application of the general matrix relations $(AB)^T = B^T A^T$ and $(A^{-1})^T = (A^T)^{-1}$, which are valid whenever the indicated operations are defined.] The usual assumption is that the components of $d\rho$ are identically distributed and independent and have a variance equal to the square of the satellite UERE. With these assumptions, the covariance of $d\rho$ is a scalar multiple of the identity

$$\operatorname{cov}(d\rho) = I_{n \times n} \sigma_{UERE}^2 \tag{7.39}$$

where $I_{n \times n}$ is the $n \times n$ identity matrix. Substitution into (7.38) yields

$$\operatorname{cov}(dx) = \left(H^T H \right)^{-1} \sigma_{UERE}^2 \tag{7.40}$$

Under the stated assumptions, the covariance of the errors in the computed position and time bias is just a scalar multiple of the matrix $(H^T H)^{-1}$. The vector dx has four components, which represent the error in the computed value for the vector $x_T = (x_u, y_u, z_u, ct_b)$. The covariance of dx is a 4×4 matrix and has an expanded representation

$$\operatorname{cov}(dx) = \begin{bmatrix} \sigma_{x_u}^2 & \sigma_{x_u y_u}^2 & \sigma_{x_u z_u}^2 & \sigma_{x_u ct_b}^2 \\ \sigma_{x_u y_u}^2 & \sigma_{y_u}^2 & \sigma_{y_u z_u}^2 & \sigma_{y_u ct_b}^2 \\ \sigma_{x_u z_u}^2 & \sigma_{y_u z_u}^2 & \sigma_{z_u}^2 & \sigma_{z_u ct_b}^2 \\ \sigma_{x_u ct_b}^2 & \sigma_{y_u ct_b}^2 & \sigma_{z_u ct_b}^2 & \sigma_{ct_b}^2 \end{bmatrix} \tag{7.41}$$

The components of the matrix $(H^T H)^{-1}$ quantify how pseudorange errors translate into components of the covariance of dx.

Dilution of precision parameters in GPS are defined in terms of the ratio of combinations of the components of $\operatorname{cov}(dx)$ and σ_{UERE}. [It is implicitly assumed in the DOP definitions that the user/satellite geometry is considered fixed. It is also assumed that local user coordinates are being used in the specification of cov($d\mathbf{x}$) and $d\mathbf{x}$. The positive x-axis points east, the y-axis points north, and the z-axis points up.] The most general parameter is termed the geometric dilution of precision (GDOP) and is defined by the formula

$$\text{GDOP} = \frac{\sqrt{\sigma_{x_u}^2 + \sigma_{y_u}^2 + \sigma_{z_u}^2 + \sigma_{ct_b}^2}}{\sigma_{UERE}} \tag{7.42}$$

A relationship for GDOP is obtained in terms of the components of $(\mathbf{H}^T\mathbf{H})^{-1}$ by expressing $(\mathbf{H}^T\mathbf{H})^{-1}$ in component form

$$\left(\mathbf{H}^T\mathbf{H}\right)^{-1} = \begin{bmatrix} D_{11} & D_{12} & D_{13} & D_{14} \\ D_{21} & D_{22} & D_{23} & D_{24} \\ D_{31} & D_{32} & D_{33} & D_{34} \\ D_{41} & D_{42} & D_{43} & D_{44} \end{bmatrix} \tag{7.43}$$

and then substituting (7.43) and (7.41) into (7.40). A trace operation on (7.40) followed by a square root shows that GDOP can be computed as the square root of the trace of the $(\mathbf{H}^T\mathbf{H})^{-1}$ matrix:

$$\text{GDOP} = \sqrt{D_{11} + D_{22} + D_{33} + D_{44}} \tag{7.44}$$

Equation (7.42) can be rearranged to obtain

$$\sqrt{\sigma_{x_u}^2 + \sigma_{y_u}^2 + \sigma_{z_u}^2 + \sigma_{ct_b}^2} = \text{GDOP} \times \sigma_{UERE} \tag{7.45}$$

which has the form given in (7.1) The square root term on the left side gives an overall characterization of the error in the GPS solution. GDOP is the geometry factor. It represents the amplification of the standard deviation of the measurement errors onto the solution. From (7.44), GDOP is seen to be a function solely of the satellite/user geometry. The value σ_{UERE} is the pseudorange error factor.

Several other DOP parameters in common use are useful to characterize the accuracy of various components of the position/time solution. These are termed position dilution of precision (PDOP), horizontal dilution of precision (HDOP), vertical dilution of precision (VDOP), and time dilution of precision (TDOP). These DOP parameters are defined in terms of the satellite UERE and elements of the covariance matrix for the position/time solution as follows:

$$\sqrt{\sigma_{x_u}^2 + \sigma_{y_u}^2 + \sigma_{z_u}^2} = \text{PDOP} \times \sigma_{UERE} \tag{7.46}$$

$$\sqrt{\sigma_{x_u}^2 + \sigma_{y_u}^2} = \text{HDOP} \times \sigma_{UERE} \tag{7.47}$$

$$\sigma_{z_u} = \text{VDOP} \times \sigma_{UERE} \tag{7.48}$$

$$\sigma_{t_b} = \text{TDOP} \times \sigma_{UERE} \tag{7.49}$$

The DOP values can be expressed in terms of the components of $(\mathbf{H}^T\mathbf{H})^{-1}$ as follows:

$$PDOP = \sqrt{D_{11} + D_{22} + D_{33}} \tag{7.50}$$

$$HDOP = \sqrt{D_{11} + D_{22}} \tag{7.51}$$

$$VDOP = \sqrt{D_{33}} \tag{7.52}$$

$$TDOP = \sqrt{D_{44}}/c \tag{7.53}$$

(In some treatments of DOP, TDOP is defined by the formula $\sigma_{ct_b} = TDOP \times \sigma_{UERE}$. In this case, (7.53) takes the simpler form $TDOP = \sqrt{D_{44}}$. The variable ct_b represents a range equivalent of the time bias error, and σ_{ct_b} is its standard deviation. In the current formulation, TDOP is defined so that when multiplied by σ_{UERE}, the standard deviation of the time bias error is obtained directly. This is the more relevant formulation if actual time accuracy is of interest. The linear relationship between t_b and ct_b yields the formula $c\sigma_{t_b} = \sigma_{ct_b}$ between their standard deviations, and one can easily convert between the formulations.)

7.3.2 Accuracy Metrics

The formulas derived in Section 7.3.1 allow one to compute 1-sigma horizontal, vertical, or three-dimensional position errors as a function of satellite geometry and the 1-sigma range error. They also allow one to compute 1-sigma user clock errors. It is important to recall that these formulas were derived under the assumptions that range errors are zero mean with a Gaussian distribution and that range errors are independent from satellite to satellite. Oftentimes, other metrics besides 1-sigma position errors are used to characterize GPS accuracy performance. Some common metrics are derived and discussed in this subsection.

If pseudorange errors are Gaussian-distributed, (7.36) tells us that vertical position errors also have a Gaussian distribution:

$$dz = \sum_{m=1}^{N} K_{3,m} d\rho_m \tag{7.54}$$

where dz is the error in the vertical component of the computed position. This result is obtained by noting that a linear function of Gaussian random variables is itself a Gaussian random variable. One common measure of vertical positioning accuracy is the error magnitude that 95% of the measurements fall within, which is approximately equal to the 2-sigma value for a Gaussian random variable. Thus:

$$95\% \text{ vertical position accuracy} \approx 2\sigma_{dz} = 2 \cdot VDOP \cdot \sigma_{UERE} \tag{7.55}$$

assuming that pseudorange errors are additionally zero mean and independent among satellites. Using a global average value of 1.6 for VDOP for the nominal 24-satellite GPS constellation and the UERE values from Tables 7.3 and 7.4 yields 95% vertical position accuracy of 4.5m for the PPS and 22.7m for the SPS, respectively. The value for the PPS is reasonably consistent with observed performance, but the value for the SPS is significantly pessimistic as compared with observed performance (see Section 7.7). The reason for this discrepancy is that the dominant SPS UERE component, residual ionospheric delay error, is highly correlated among satellites. This correlation invalidates one of the assumptions used in the derivation of the DOPs. When the Klobuchar model's estimate of vertical ionospheric delay is too high (low), the slant delay estimate for each visible satellite also tends to be too high (low). A significant component of each residual ionospheric delay error is thus common to each satellite and drops out into the user clock solution.

With regard to horizontal position errors, (7.36) can be specialized to the horizontal plane yielding

$$dR = K_{2 \times n} d\rho \qquad (7.56)$$

where $dR = (dx, dy)^T$ is the vector component of the position error in the horizontal plane, $d\rho = (d\rho_1, \ldots, d\rho_n)^T$ is the pseudorange measurement errors, and n is the number of satellites being used in the position calculation. $K_{2 \times n}$ is the upper $2 \times n$ submatrix of K and consists of its first two rows. For the standard least square solution technique, $K = (H^T H)^{-1} H^T$.

For a fixed satellite geometry, (7.56) expresses the horizontal position errors as a linear function of the pseudorange measurement errors. If the pseudorange errors are zero mean and jointly Gaussian, dR also has these properties. If the pseudorange errors are also uncorrelated and identically distributed with variance σ_{UERE}^2, the covariance of the horizontal errors is given as

$$\text{cov}(dR) = \left(\left(H^T H \right)^{-1} \right)_{2 \times 2} \sigma_{UERE}^2 \qquad (7.57)$$

where the subscript notation denotes the upper left 2×2 submatrix of $(H^T H)^{-1}$. The density function for dR is

$$f_{dR}(x, y) = \frac{1}{2\pi \left[\det(\text{cov}(dR)) \right]^{\frac{1}{2}}} \exp\left(-\frac{1}{2} u^T \left[\text{cov}(dR) \right]^{-1} u \right) \qquad (7.58)$$

where $u = (x, y)^T$ and det represents the determinant of a matrix.

The density function defines a two-dimensional bell-shaped surface. Contours of constant density are obtained by setting the exponent in parenthesis to a constant. One obtains equations of the form

$$u^T \left[\text{cov}(dR) \right]^{-1} u = m^2 \qquad (7.59)$$

where the parameter m ranges over positive values. The contour curves that result form a collection of concentric ellipses when plotted in the plane. The ellipse obtained when m equals 1 is termed the 1σ ellipse and has the equation

$$u^T \left[\text{cov}(dR) \right]^{-1} u = 1 \qquad (7.60)$$

(The 1σ ellipse is defined here as a specific cut through the pdf and is not to be confused with 1σ containment. The latter curve is the locus of points, one point on each ray from the origin, where the points are at a distance of 1σ for the ray's direction. In general, the 1σ containment curve is a figure-eight-shaped curve that encloses the 1σ ellipse.) If the major and minor axis of the ellipse are aligned with the x and y axes, the equation for the ellipse reduces to $x^2 / \sigma_x^2 + y^2 / \sigma_y^2 = 1$. In general, however, the off-diagonal terms in $\mathrm{cov}(d\mathbf{R})$ are nonzero, and the elliptical contours for the density function are rotated relative to the x and y axes. Denote the major and minor axes of the 1σ ellipse by σ_L and σ_s ("long" and "short"), respectively. In general, the 1σ ellipse is contained in a box of width σ_x and height σ_y centered on the ellipse. Figure 7.6 illustrates graphically the relationship between the ellipse and the parameters σ_x, σ_y, σ_L, and σ_s.

The probability that the error lies within the elliptical contour defined for a specific value of m is $1 - e^{-m^2/2}$. In particular, the probability of being in the 1σ ellipse ($m = 1$) is 0.39; the probability of being in the 2σ ellipse ($m = 2$) is 0.86. (These values are in contrast to the one-dimensional Gaussian result that the probability of being within $\pm 1\sigma$ of the mean is 0.68.)

Several parameters are in common use that characterize the magnitude of the horizontal error. The *distance root mean square* (drms) is defined by the formula

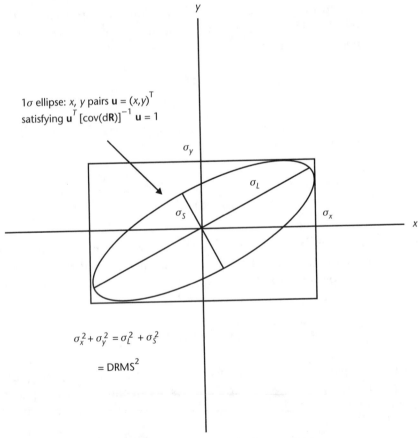

1σ ellipse: x, y pairs $\mathbf{u} = (x,y)^T$
satisfying $\mathbf{u}^T [\mathrm{cov}(d\mathbf{R})]^{-1} \mathbf{u} = 1$

$$\sigma_x^2 + \sigma_y^2 = \sigma_L^2 + \sigma_s^2$$

$$= \mathrm{DRMS}^2$$

Figure 7.6   Relationship between 1σ ellipse and distribution parameters.

$$\text{drms} = \sqrt{\sigma_x^2 + \sigma_y^2} \tag{7.61}$$

For a zero-mean random variable such as $d\mathbf{R}$, one has $\text{drms} = \sqrt{E(|d\mathbf{R}|^2)}$, and the drms corresponds to the square root of the mean value of the squared error (hence, its name). From (7.47), one immediately has

$$\text{drms} = \text{HDOP} \cdot \sigma_{UERE} \tag{7.62}$$

and the drms can be computed from the values of HDOP and σ_{UERE}. The probability that the computed location is within a circle of radius drms from the true location depends on the ratio σ_S/σ_L for the 1σ ellipse. If the two-dimensional error distribution is close to being circular ($\sigma_S/\sigma_L \approx 1$), the probability is about 0.63; for a very elongated distribution ($\sigma_S/\sigma_L \approx 0$), the probability approaches 0.69. Two times the drms is given by

$$2\,\text{drms} = 2 \cdot \text{HDOP} \cdot \sigma_{UERE} \tag{7.63}$$

and the probability that the horizontal error is within a circle of radius 2 drms ranges between 0.95 and 0.98, depending on the ratio σ_S/σ_L. The 2-drms value is commonly taken as the 95% limit for the magnitude of the horizontal error.

Another common metric for horizontal errors is *circular error probable* (CEP), defined as the radius of a circle that contains 50% of the error distributions when centered at the correct (i.e., error-free) location. Thus, the probability that the magnitude of the error is less than the CEP is precisely one-half. The CEP for a two-dimensional Gaussian random variable can be approximated by the formula

$$\text{CEP} \approx 0.59(\sigma_L + \sigma_S) \tag{7.64}$$

assuming it is zero mean. For a derivation of this and other approximations, see [33].

The CEP can also be estimated in terms of drms and, using (7.62), in terms of HDOP and σ_{UERE}. This is convenient since HDOP is widely computed in GPS applications. Figure 7.7 presents curves giving the probability that the magnitude of the error satisfies $|d\mathbf{R}| \le k$ drms as a function of k for different values of the ratio σ_S/σ_L. (The horizontal error is assumed to have a zero-mean two-dimensional Gaussian distribution.) For k equal to 0.75, one obtains a probability in the range 0.43 to 0.54. Hence, one has the approximate relation

$$\text{CEP} \approx 0.75\,\text{drms} = 0.75 \cdot \text{HDOP} \cdot \sigma_{UERE} \tag{7.65}$$

It is interesting to note that for $k = 1.23$, the probability that $|d\mathbf{R}| \le k$ drms is roughly 0.78, almost independent of σ_S/σ_L. The probabilities associated with several other values of k are summarized in Table 7.5.

As an application of these formulations, for an average global HDOP of 1.0 and with $\sigma_{UERE} = 1.4$m, estimates for the CEP, the 80% point, and the 95% point for the magnitude of the horizontal error are given as follows:

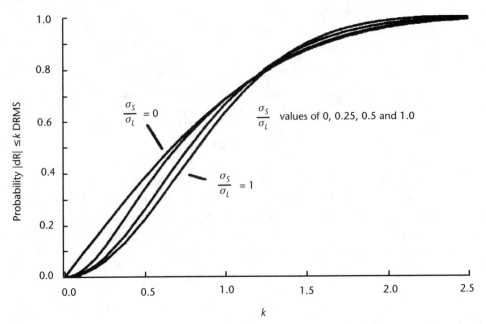

Figure 7.7 Cumulative distribution of radial error for various values of σ_s/σ_L for a two-dimensional Gaussian random variable.

Table 7.5 Approximate Formulas for the Magnitude of the Horizontal Error

Approximation Formula*	Probability Range
$\text{CEP}_{50} \approx 0.75\ \text{HDOP}\ \sigma_{\text{UERE}}$	0.43–0.54
$\text{CEP}_{80} \approx 1.28\ \text{HDOP}\ \sigma_{\text{UERE}}$	0.80–0.81
$\text{CEP}_{90} \approx 1.6\ \text{HDOP}\ \sigma_{\text{UERE}}$	0.89–0.92
$\text{CEP}_{95} \approx 2.0\ \text{HDOP}\ \sigma_{\text{UERE}}$	0.95–0.98

* CEP_{xx} is defined as the radius of the circle that when centered at the error-free location includes xx% of the error distribution. Hence, $\text{CEP}_{50} = \text{CEP}$.

$$\text{CEP}_{50} \approx 0.75 \cdot \text{HDOP} \cdot \sigma_{UERE} = 0.75 \times 1 \times 1.4 = 1.1 \text{ m}$$
$$\text{CEP}_{80} \approx 1.28 \cdot \text{HDOP} \cdot \sigma_{UERE} = 1.2875 \times 1 \times 1.4 = 1.8 \text{ m} \qquad (7.66)$$
$$\text{CEP}_{95} \approx 2.0 \cdot \text{HDOP} \cdot \sigma_{UERE} = 2.0 \times 1 \times 1.4 = 2.8 \text{ m}$$

For applications where three-dimensional error distributions are of interest, one final commonly used metric is *spherical error probable* (SEP), which is defined as the radius of a sphere centered at the true position that contains 50% of the measured positions.

7.3.3 Weighted Least Squares (WLS)

Oftentimes, the UEREs among the visible satellites are not well described as being independent and identically distributed. In such circumstances, the least-squares position estimate is not optimal. As derived in Appendix A, if the pseudorange errors are Gaussian and the covariance of UEREs for the visible satellites is given by the matrix **R**, then the optimal solution for user position is given by the WLS estimate

$$\Delta \mathbf{x} = \left(\mathbf{H}^T \mathbf{R}^{-1} \mathbf{H} \right)^{-1} \mathbf{H}^T \mathbf{R}^{-1} \Delta \boldsymbol{\rho} \tag{7.67}$$

(Note that, as with the ordinary least-squares solution, we are truly solving for a correction to an initial estimate of the user position and clock error.) Equation (7.67) collapses to (7.33) in the case when $\mathbf{R} = \sigma_{UERE}^2 \mathbf{I}$ with $\mathbf{I}$ equal to the $n \times n$ identity matrix, as expected since this case corresponds to our original independent and identically distributed assumption. For a general matrix **R**, (7.67) can be thought of as implementing an optimal weighting of pseudorange measurements based on their relative noise levels and relative importance for each estimated quantity.

As one example of an error covariance matrix, consider the single-frequency SPS user whose pseudorange measurement errors are dominated by residual ionospheric delays. As noted in the discussion in Section 7.3.2, residual ionospheric errors for single-frequency users are highly correlated. The covariance matrix of residual ionospheric errors can be approximated as

$$\mathbf{R} = \sigma_{iv}^2 \begin{bmatrix} m^2(el_1) & m(el_1)m(el_2) & \cdots & m(el_1)m(el_n) \\ m(el_1)m(el_2) & m^2(el_2) & & \\ \vdots & & \ddots & \\ m(el_1)m(el_n) & & & m^2(el_n) \end{bmatrix} \tag{7.68}$$

where σ_{iv}^2 is the residual vertical ionospheric delay variance, which could be approximated as some fraction of the Klobuchar vertical delay estimate. The ijth element of the matrix in (7.68) is the product of two ionospheric mapping functions, $m(el)$. For example, (7.21) could be used, corresponding to the elevation angles (el) for satellite i and j.

Another typical example of a covariance matrix is a diagonal matrix whose diagonal elements are obtained using an approximation for pseudorange error variance versus elevation angle, usually a monotonically increasing function as elevation angle decreases (e.g., see [14]). The use of such a covariance matrix in a WLS solution deweights low-elevation angle satellites that are expected to be noisier due to typical characteristics of multipath and residual tropospheric errors.

7.3.4   Additional State Variables

Thus far, we have focused on estimation of the user's (x, y, z) position coordinates and clock bias. The complete set of parameters that are estimated within a GPS receiver, often referred to as the *state* or *state vector*, may include a number of other variables. For instance, if in addition to pseudorange measurements, Doppler measurements (from an FLL or PLL) or differenced carrier-phase measurements are available, then velocity in each of the three coordinates $(\dot{x}, \dot{y}, \dot{z})$, and clock drift, $\dot{t}_u$, may also be estimated. The same least squares or WLS techniques used for position estimation may be used and the same DOPs apply. The only difference is that in the linearization process, satellite velocities and initial estimates of user velocity and clock drift are employed. Also, for precise velocity estimation it is important to account for the fact that satellite geometry is slowly changing with time (e.g., see [34]).

Additional state variables may also be included for vertical tropospheric delays [35] or system time offsets when using measurements from both GPS and a separate satellite navigation system [36].

7.3.5 Kalman Filtering

The least-squares and WLS solutions that were described in Chapter 2 and previously in this chapter have utilized a set of pseudorange measurements at one snapshot in time, along with initial estimates of the user position and clock, to derive an improved estimate of the user's position and clock error at that instant. In practice, the user frequently has access to an entire sequence of measurements over time. Past measurements may often be useful for obtaining a more accurate PVT estimation. For instance, a stationary user can average least-square position estimates over an hour, a day, or longer to obtain a more accurate estimate of his or her position than would be possible using just the latest set of measurements. In principle, even the most agile user can obtain some benefit from incorporating past measurements into his or her position estimator, provided that it is possible to accurately model the motion of the platform over time and to model the progression of user clock errors with time. The most common algorithm used to incorporate past measurements in GPS PVT applications is referred to as a *Kalman filter*. Kalman filters also facilitate the blending of GPS measurements with measurements from other sensors and are discussed in detail in Chapter 9.

7.4   GPS Availability

Availability of a navigation system is the percentage of time that the services of the system are usable. Availability is an indication of the ability of the system to provide a usable navigation service within a specified coverage area. Availability is a function of both the physical characteristics of the environment and the technical capabilities of the transmitter facilities [37]. In this section, GPS availability is discussed under the assumption that *usable navigation service* can be equated to GPS accuracy meeting a threshold requirement. It should be noted that some applications include additional criteria (e.g., the provision of integrity—see Section 7.5) that must be met for the system to be considered available.

As discussed in Section 7.3.1, GPS accuracy is generally expressed by

$$\sigma_p = \text{DOP} \cdot \sigma_{UERE}$$

where σ_p is the standard deviation of the positioning accuracy, and σ_{UERE} is the standard deviation of the satellite pseudorange measurement error. Representative σ_{UERE} values are provided in Tables 7.3 and 7.4 for PPS and SPS, respectively. The DOP factor could be HDOP, VDOP, PDOP, and so forth, depending on the dimension for which GPS accuracy is to be determined. The availability of the GPS navigation function to provide a given accuracy level is therefore dependent on the geometry of the satellites for a specific location and time of day.

In order to determine the availability of GPS for a specific location and time, the number of visible satellites, as well as the geometry of those satellites, must first be determined. GPS almanac data, which contains the positions of all satellites in the constellation at a reference epoch, can easily be obtained from the U.S. Coast Guard (USCG) Navigation Center (NAVCEN) Web site or as an output from some GPS receivers. Since the orbits of the GPS satellites are well known, the position of the satellites at any given point in time can be predicted. The process of determining the satellite positions at a particular point in time is not intuitive, however, and software is needed in order to perform the calculations.

7.4.1   Predicted GPS Availability Using the Nominal 24-Satellite GPS Constellation

This section examines the availability of the nominal 24-satellite GPS constellation. The nominal 24-satellite constellation is defined in Section 3.1.1. Worldwide GPS coverage is evaluated from 90°N to 90°S latitude with sample points spaced every 5° (in latitude) and for a band in longitude circling the globe spaced every 5°. This grid is sampled every 5 minutes in time over a 12-hour period.

Since the GPS constellation has approximately a 12-hour orbit, the satellite coverage will then repeat itself on the opposite side of the world during the next 12 hours. (The Earth rotates 180° in the 12-hour period, and the satellite coverage areas will be interchanged.) A total of 386,280 space/time points are evaluated in this analysis.

GPS availability also is dependent on the mask angle used by the receiver. By lowering the mask angle, more satellites are visible; hence, a higher availability can be obtained. However, there may be problems with reducing the mask angle to include very low elevation angles, which is discussed later in this section. The availability obtained by applying the following mask angles is examined: 7.5°, 5°, 2.5°, and 0°.

Figure 7.8 demonstrates GPS availability based on HDOP using an all-in-view solution. This figure provides the cumulative distribution of HDOP for each of the mask angles considered. The maximum value of HDOP is 2.55 for a mask angle less than or equal to 5°.

Figure 7.9 provides the availability of GPS based on PDOP for the same mask angles. This availability is lower than that for HDOP since unavailability in the vertical dimension is taken into consideration in the calculation of PDOP. The maximum value of PDOP for a 5° mask angle is 5.15, at 2.5° it is 4.7, and for a 0° mask angle the maximum value is 3.1.

Although these graphs demonstrate the improvement in availability that can be obtained when the mask angle is lowered, there is a danger in lowering it too far. During the mission planning process, signal blockage from buildings or other objects that extend higher than the set mask angle must be taken into consideration. There also is a greater potential for atmospheric delay and multipath problems at a lower mask angle.

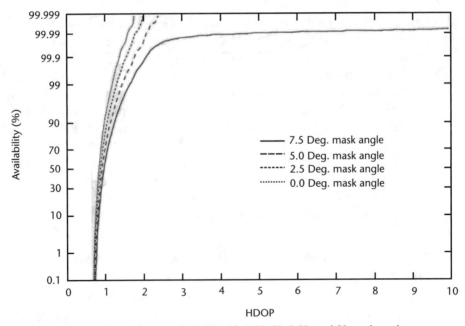

Figure 7.8   Cumulative distribution of HDOP with 7.5°, 5°, 2.5°, and 0° mask angles.

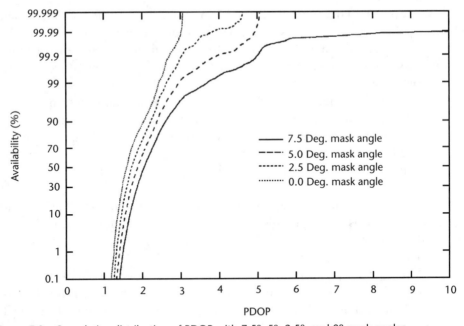

Figure 7.9   Cumulative distribution of PDOP with 7.5°, 5°, 2.5°, and 0° mask angles.

The threshold for the maximum acceptable DOP value is dependent on the desired accuracy level. The availability of GPS, therefore, will depend on the stringency of the accuracy requirement. For this analysis, availability of GPS is chosen to be defined as PDOP ≤ 6, which is commonly used as a service availability threshold in the GPS performance standards [17].

As shown in Figure 7.9, with all 24 GPS satellites operational, the value of PDOP is less than 6.0 for every location and time point analyzed at 0°, 2.5°, and 5° mask angles. Since the analysis grid is sampled every 5 minutes, there could be occurrences where PDOP is greater than 6.0 for a period of less than 5 minutes that would not be detected. Only with a 7.5° mask angle (or higher) does the GPS constellation have outages based on PDOP exceeding 6.0.

At a 7.5° mask angle, the GPS constellation provides an availability of 99.98%. Figure 7.10 displays the locations and durations of the outages that occur. The maximum outage duration is 10 minutes. The GPS constellation is designed to provide optimal worldwide coverage. As a result, when outages do occur, they are concentrated in very high and very low latitudes (above 60°N and below 60°S).

7.4.2   Effects of Satellite Outages on GPS Availability

The previous figures have demonstrated the availability of GPS when all 24 satellites are operational. However, satellites need to be taken out of service for maintenance, and unscheduled outages occur from time to time. In fact, 24 satellites may only be available 72% of the time, while 21 or more satellites are expected to be operational at least 98% of the time [17, 38].

In order to examine the effect that a reduced constellation of satellites has on the availability of GPS, the analysis is now repeated using the same worldwide grid, but removing one, two, and three satellites from the nominal 24-satellite constellation. Since a 5° mask angle is commonly used, it is the only one considered for this portion of the analysis.

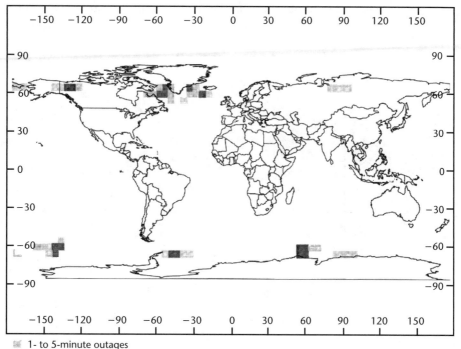

▨ 1- to 5-minute outages
■ 6- to 10-minute outages

Figure 7.10   Availability of the GPS constellation (PDOP ≤ 6) with a 7.5° mask angle.

The availability of GPS when satellites are removed from the constellation is very much dependent on which satellites, or combinations of satellites, are taken out of service. The Aerospace Corporation has performed a study that determined cases of one, two, and three satellite failures that resulted in the least, average, and greatest impact on availability [39]. The choices for satellites to be removed in this analysis were based on those satellites that caused an "average" impact on GPS availability.

The orbital positions of the GPS satellites removed from the constellation are given in the following list:

- Average one satellite—SV A3;
- Average two satellites—SVs A1 and F3;
- Average three satellites—SVs A2, E3, and F2.

(Refer to Sections 3.2.1 and 3.2.3.1 for satellite identification and orbital location information.)

Figures 7.11 and 7.12 display the cumulative distribution of HDOP and PDOP with up to three satellites removed from the constellation and applying a 5° mask angle. These plots demonstrate the increasing degradation in system performance as more satellites are removed from the constellation.

The availability of GPS, based on PDOP ≤ 6 and a 5° mask angle, is 99.969% with one satellite out of service. The locations and durations of the resulting outages are displayed in Figure 7.13. The maximum outage duration that occurs is 15 minutes.

The effects of two satellites out of service are shown in Figure 7.14. Outages now last up to 25 minutes in several locations, but there are only a couple of occur-

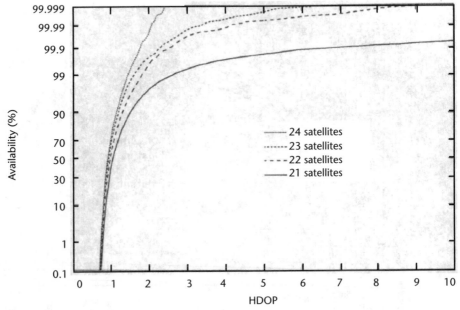

Figure 7.11 Cumulative distribution of HDOP with 5° mask angle cases of 24, 23, 22, and 21 satellites.

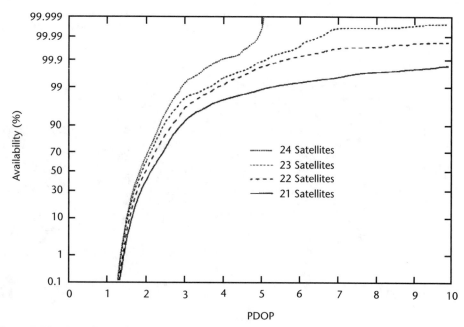

Figure 7.12 Cumulative distribution of PDOP with 5° mask angle cases of 24, 23, 22, and 21 satellites.

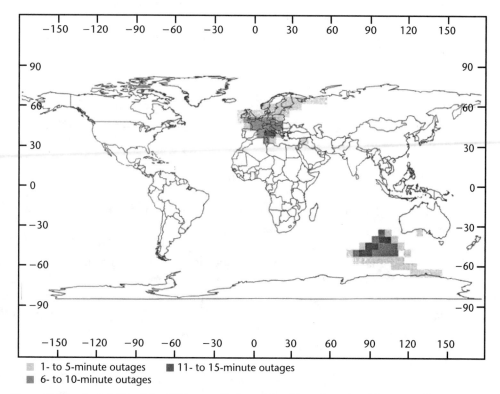

1- to 5-minute outages   11- to 15-minute outages
6- to 10-minute outages

Figure 7.13 Availability of the GPS constellation with a 5° mask angle with one satellite removed from the constellation.

rences of these during the day. The majority of the outages are 10 minutes or less. This constellation provides an availability of 99.903%.

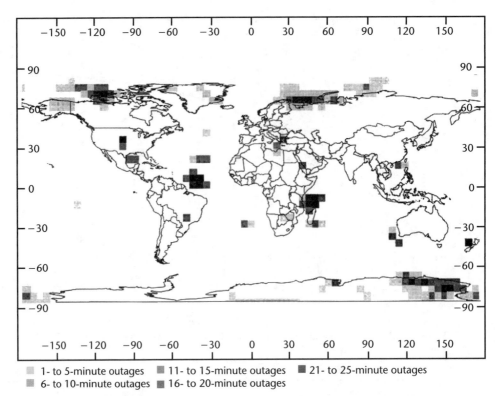

1- to 5-minute outages   11- to 15-minute outages   21- to 25-minute outages
6- to 10-minute outages   16- to 20-minute outages

Figure 7.14 Availability of the GPS constellation with a 5° mask angle with two satellites removed from the constellation.

With three satellites out of service, the overall availability of the GPS constellation drops to 99.197%. The number of outage occurrences increases dramatically and outages now last up to 65 minutes. The locations and corresponding durations of these outages are shown in Figure 7.15.

The scenario of having three satellites out of service at the same time should be a very rare occurrence. However, if it were to happen, the user could examine the predicted availability over the course of the day and plan the use of GPS accordingly.

As mentioned previously, the determination of satellite positions and the resulting GPS availability for any location and point in time is not intuitive and requires software to perform the calculations. GPS prediction software that allows a user to determine GPS coverage for a single location or for multiple locations is commercially available. Some GPS receiver manufacturers also include prediction software with the purchase of a receiver. The typical input parameters used to perform GPS availability predictions are as follows:

- *GPS almanac data:* The position of the satellites at a reference epoch may be obtained from several different sources: the USCG NAVCEN Web site or a GPS receiver that outputs almanac data.
- *Location:* Latitude, longitude, and altitude of the location(s) for which the prediction is to be performed.

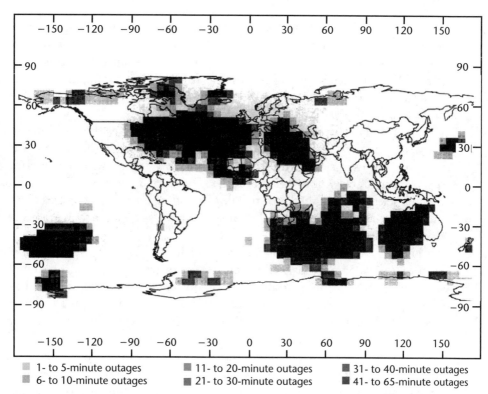

▨ 1- to 5-minute outages	▨ 11- to 20-minute outages	■ 31- to 40-minute outages
▨ 6- to 10-minute outages	▨ 21- to 30-minute outages	■ 41- to 65-minute outages

Figure 7.15 Availability of the GPS constellation with a 5° mask angle with three satellites removed from the constellation.

- *Date of prediction:* The date for which the prediction is to be performed. The GPS almanac can be used to accurately predict for approximately 7 days in the future.

- *Mask angle:* The elevation angle above the horizon at which satellites are considered visible by the GPS receiver.

- *Terrain mask:* The azimuth and elevation of terrain (buildings, mountains, and so on) that may block the satellite signal can be entered into the program to ensure an accurate prediction.

- *Satellite outages:* If any satellites are currently out of service, their status will be reflected in the almanac data. However, if satellites are scheduled for maintenance for a prediction date in the future, the software allows the user to mark those satellites unusable. This data can be obtained from the USCG NAVCEN Web site.

- *Maximum DOP:* As discussed previously, in order to determine availability, a maximum DOP threshold must be set (e.g., PDOP = 6). If the DOP exceeds that value, the software will declare GPS to be unavailable. Other applications may use criteria other than DOP as the availability threshold. This will be discussed further in Section 7.3 for aviation applications.

Once these parameters have been input into the software, the prediction can be performed. A prediction was performed for Boston (42.35°N, 71.08°W) on December 23, 1994. (This and the following predictions are still representative of performance circa 2006.) Figure 7.16 shows the location of the GPS satellites and the satellite horizon line for the selected location at a snapshot in time [12:10 UTC (USNO)]. The satellites with squares next to them (17, 23, 26, and 27) are the four used to form the navigation solution. The corresponding HDOP and PDOP for that point in time also are displayed.

Figure 7.17 is an azimuth and elevation plot that gives the position of the satellites from the perspective of looking at the sky directly overhead from the selected location. The user is at the center of the concentric circles, with the outermost circle representing 0° elevation, or the horizon. The second circle is at 7° elevation, which was the selected mask angle for this portion of the analysis. The third is at 10°, and each circle increases by 10°. The azimuth is 0° at North and increases in the clockwise direction.

Figure 7.18 displays the rise and set time for the 25 GPS satellites at the selected location over a 24-hour period. (There generally are more than the nominal 24 GPS satellites in orbit in order to maintain a constellation of 24 operational satellites.) This type of graph can be very useful for a researcher who wants to plan an experiment with a particular set of satellites and doesn't want the satellite geometry to change significantly due to a rising or setting satellite.

The solid line at the bottom of the graph indicates that GPS is available for the entire day (PDOP ≤ 6). Gaps in this line would indicate that GPS is unavailable. This unavailability is demonstrated in Figure 7.19 when satellites 16, 25, and 26 are removed (by the author) from the constellation for simulation purposes. As shown in this figure, removing three satellites from the GPS constellation would result in two outage periods during the day for Boston.

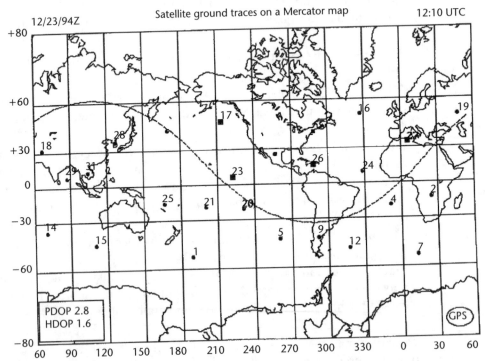

Figure 7.16 Locations of satellites worldwide.

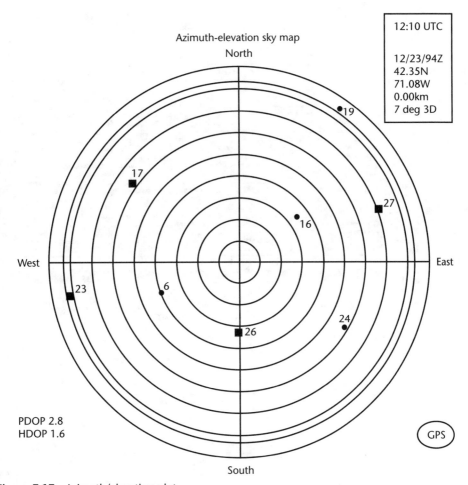

Figure 7.17 Azimuth/elevation plot.

Another feature of mission planning software involves determining the number of satellites that will be visible at a location over the course of a day. This information is useful for applications that may require the maximum number of visible satellites. Figure 7.20 displays the number of visible satellites over a 24-hour period with all of the satellites operational. As shown in this figure, the minimum number of satellites available is 6 and the maximum is 10 for this location. At lower latitudes (near the equator), it is possible to have 12 or more GPS satellites visible at a time.

Availability prediction software generally also plots DOP over the course of the day.

7.5 GPS Integrity

In addition to providing a position, navigation, and timing function, a system such as GPS must have the ability to provide timely warnings to users when the system should not be used. This capability is known as the integrity of the system. Integrity is a measure of the trust that can be placed in the correctness of the information sup-

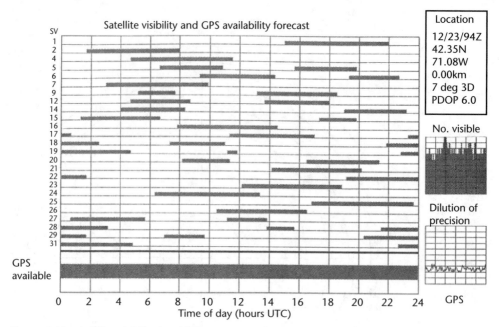

Figure 7.18 Satellite visibility/availability over a 24-hour period.

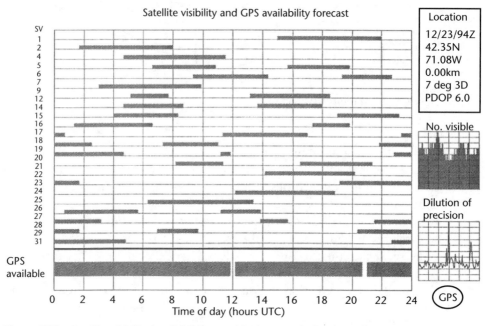

Figure 7.19 Satellite visibility/availability over a 24-hour period with satellites 16, 25, and 26 removed from the constellation.

plied by the total system. Integrity includes the ability of a system to provide valid and timely warnings to the user, known as alerts, when the system must not be used for the intended operation.

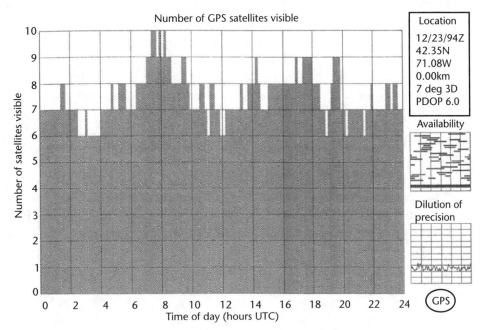

Figure 7.20   Number of visible GPS satellites over a 24-hour period.

7.5.1   Discussion of Criticality

Anomalies can occur, caused by either the satellite or the CS, which result in unpredictable range errors above the operational tolerance. These errors are different from the predictable degraded accuracy resulting from poor satellite geometry, which was discussed in the previous section. Integrity anomalies should be rare, occurring only a few times per year [17, 40], but can be critical, especially for air navigation.

7.5.2   Sources of Integrity Anomalies

There are four main sources of integrity anomalies: system-allocated signal-in-space (SIS) aberrations, space segment–allocated SIS aberrations, control segment–allocated SIS aberrations, and user segment SIS aberrations [41]. Satellite clock anomalies are due to frequency standard problems such as random phase run-off, a large frequency jump, or a combination of both. The MCS has reported clock jumps when the beam current or temperature of the frequency standard has varied greatly. Clock anomalies are the most prevalent source of space segment anomalies and the most common source of major service anomalies. These anomalies can result in thousands of meters of range error.

The first generation Block I satellites experienced many more clock anomalies than the Block II generation of satellites [40] and did not have the radiation hardening against the space environment that has been built into the Block II satellites. Consequently, Block I satellites were subject to *bit hits*, which affect the navigation message, as well as C-field tuning *word hits*. The C-field tuning register that aligns the cesium beam is affected by solar radiation. Changing the bits that account for the alignment/direction of the cesium beam has in some instances resulted in ranging errors of thousands of meters in only a few minutes.

Other types of integrity anomalies can result in smaller ranging errors. An example of this occurred on GPS SVN 19. After approximately 8 months on orbit, an anomalous condition developed on the satellite that resulted in carrier leakage on the observed L1 signal spectrum, which is normally carrier suppressed. In this case no control segment problems were observed or user equipment problems reported, so the SV was left to operate in the off-nominal mode. No incident reports or problems regarding the SVN 19 C/A code occurred until March 1993 during FAA field tests using differential navigation for aided landings. The differential navigation solution was corrupted with a 4-m bias [42].

The GPS ground-monitoring network currently does not provide coverage for all satellites 24 hours a day [40]. Therefore, if an integrity problem were to occur, it may not be detected immediately. An example of this occurred on July 28, 2001, when SVN22 experienced a clock failure over the southern Pacific Ocean region resulting in user range errors in excess of 200,000m. For about a half-hour, this was undetectable by the GPS CS because the satellite was not in view of any CS monitor stations [42].

Most MCS problems are due to hardware, software, or human error. Past problems have involved incorrect ionospheric correction database coefficients being incorporated in the navigation message of all satellites. Single frequency receivers may have experienced ranging errors of up to 16m before the problem was detected.

The MCS is continuously working to minimize integrity anomalies as much as possible by installing redundant hardware, robust software, and providing training to prevent human error. The best response time, however, may still be several minutes, which is insufficient for aviation applications. There are methods, however, by which the user is independently able to be notified of a satellite anomaly if it does occur.

7.5.3 Integrity Enhancement Techniques

The integrity problem is important for many applications, but crucial for aviation since the user is traveling at high speeds and can quickly deviate from the flight path. The integrity function becomes especially critical if GPS is to be used as a primary navigation system. RTCA Special Committee 159 (SC-159), a federal advisory committee to the FAA, has devoted much effort to developing techniques to provide integrity for airborne use of GPS. Three methods used for GPS integrity monitoring are RAIM—one element of a set of airborne GPS enhancements defined by ICAO as aircraft-based augmentation systems (ABAS)—SBAS, and GBAS.

This section primarily concentrates on RAIM, since SBAS and GBAS are differential GPS-based techniques discussed in more detail in Chapter 8.

7.5.3.1 RAIM and FDE

The use of standalone GPS or GPS in conjunction with use of ranging sources from other satellites, such as geostationary satellites, GALILEO, and GLONASS, where integrity is provided by RAIM and FDE, is referred to as an ABAS. The RAIM algorithm is contained within the receiver, hence the term *autonomous* monitoring. RAIM is a technique that uses an overdetermined solution to perform a consistency check on the satellite measurements [43].

    RAIM algorithms require a minimum of five visible satellites in order to detect the presence of an unacceptably large position error for a given mode of flight. If a failure is detected, the pilot receives a warning flag in the cockpit that indicates that GPS should not be used for navigation. Certified GPS receivers that contain FDE, an extension of RAIM that uses a minimum of six visible satellites, can not only detect the faulty satellite, but can exclude it from the navigation solution so the operation can continue without interruption.

    The inputs to the RAIM algorithm are the standard deviation of the measurement noise, the measurement geometry, and the maximum allowable probabilities for a false alert and a missed detection. The output of the algorithm is the *horizontal protection level* (HPL), which is the radius of a circle, centered at the true aircraft position that is assured to contain the indicated horizontal position with the given probability of false alert and missed detection discussed next. If the aircraft is conducting phases of flight that require vertical guidance, a *vertical protection level* (VPL) is output as well; however, VPL is generally associated with differential-based systems. This section concentrates on the generation of HPL using a *snapshot* RAIM algorithm that has been developed in support of RTCA SC-159 [43].

    The linearized GPS measurement equation is given as

$$\mathbf{y} = \mathbf{Hx} + \boldsymbol{\epsilon} \tag{7.69}$$

where $\mathbf{x}$ is the 4×1 vector whose elements are incremental deviations from the nominal state about which the linearization takes place. The first three elements are the east, north, and up position components, and the fourth element is the receiver clock bias. $\mathbf{y}$ is the $n \times 1$ vector whose elements are the differences between the noisy measured pseudoranges and the predicted ones based on the nominal position and clock bias (i.e., the linearization point). The value n is the number of visible satellites (number of measurements). $\mathbf{H}$ is the $n \times 4$ linear connection matrix between $\mathbf{x}$ and $\mathbf{y}$. It consists of three columns of direction cosines and a fourth column containing the value 1, which corresponds to the receiver clock state. $\boldsymbol{\epsilon}$ is the $n \times 1$ measurement error vector. It may contain both random and deterministic (bias) terms.

    GPS RAIM is based on the self-consistency of measurements, where the number of measurements, n, is greater than or equal to 5. One measure of consistency is to work out the least squares estimate for $\mathbf{x}$, substitute it into the right-hand side of (7.69), and then compare the result with the empirical measurements in $\mathbf{y}$. The difference between them is called the range residual vector, $\mathbf{w}$. In mathematical terms,

$$
\begin{aligned}
\hat{\mathbf{x}}_{LS} &= \left(\mathbf{H}^T\mathbf{H}\right)^{-1}\mathbf{H}^T\mathbf{y} \quad \text{(least square estimate)} \\
\hat{\mathbf{y}}_{LS} &= \mathbf{H}\hat{\mathbf{x}}_{LS} \\
\mathbf{w} &= \mathbf{y} - \hat{\mathbf{y}}_{LS} = \mathbf{y} - \mathbf{H}\left(\mathbf{H}^T\mathbf{H}\right)^{-1}\mathbf{H}^T\mathbf{y} = \left[\mathbf{I}_n - \mathbf{H}\left(\mathbf{H}^T\mathbf{H}\right)^{-1}\mathbf{H}^T\right]\mathbf{y} \\
&= \left[\mathbf{I}_n - \mathbf{H}\left(\mathbf{H}^T\mathbf{H}\right)^{-1}\mathbf{H}^T\right](\mathbf{Hx} + \boldsymbol{\epsilon}) = \left[\mathbf{I}_n - \mathbf{H}\left(\mathbf{H}^T\mathbf{H}\right)^{-1}\mathbf{H}^T\right]\boldsymbol{\epsilon}
\end{aligned}
\tag{7.70}
$$

Since $\boldsymbol{\epsilon}$ is not known to the user aircraft, (7.70) is only used in simulations.

    Let

$$S \equiv I_n - H(H^T H)^{-1} H^T \qquad (7.71)$$

where I_n is the $n \times n$ unit matrix. Then, the $n \times 1$ range residual vector, $\mathbf{w}$, is given as $\mathbf{w} = S\mathbf{y}$ (used in practice) or $\mathbf{w} = S\varepsilon$ (used in the simulations). The range residual vector, $\mathbf{w}$, could be used as a measure of consistency. This is not ideal, however, because there are four constraints (associated with the four unknown components of the vector $\mathbf{x}$) among the n elements of $\mathbf{w}$, which obscure some of the aspects of the inconsistency that are of interest. Therefore, it is useful to perform a transformation that eliminates the constraints and transforms the information contained in $\mathbf{w}$ into another vector known as the parity vector, $\mathbf{p}$.

Performing a transformation on $\mathbf{y}$, $\mathbf{p} = P\mathbf{y}$, where the parity transformation matrix P is defined as an $(n - 4) \times n$ matrix, which can be obtained by QR factorization of the H matrix [44]. The rows of P are mutually orthogonal, unity in magnitude, and mutually orthogonal to the columns of H. Due to these defining properties, the resultant $\mathbf{p}$ has special properties, especially with respect to the noise [43]. If ε has independent random elements that are all $N(0, \sigma^2)$, then

$$\mathbf{p} = P\mathbf{w} \qquad (7.72a)$$

$$\mathbf{p} = P\varepsilon \qquad (7.72b)$$

$$\mathbf{p}^T \mathbf{p} = \mathbf{w}^T \mathbf{w} \qquad (7.72c)$$

These equations state that the same transformation matrix P that takes $\mathbf{y}$ into the parity vector, $\mathbf{p}$, also takes either $\mathbf{w}$ or ε into $\mathbf{p}$. The sum of the squared residuals is the same in both range space and parity space. In performing failure detection, it is much easier to work with $\mathbf{p}$ than with $\mathbf{w}$.

Using a case of six visible satellites as an example, the following analysis demonstrates how the parity transformation affects a deterministic error in one of the range measurements. Suppose there is a range bias error, b, in satellite 3. From (7.72b),

$$\mathbf{p} = \begin{bmatrix} P_{11} & P_{12} & P_{13} & \cdots & P_{16} \\ P_{21} & P_{22} & P_{23} & \cdots & P_{26} \end{bmatrix} \begin{bmatrix} 0 \\ 0 \\ b \\ 0 \\ 0 \\ 0 \end{bmatrix} \quad \text{or}$$

$$\mathbf{p} = b \times (3\text{rd column of } P)$$

The third column of P defines a line in parity space called the characteristic bias line associated with satellite 3. Each satellite has its own characteristic bias line. The magnitude of the parity bias vector induced by the range bias b is given by

|parity bias vector| $= b \cdot$ norm $|[P_{13} \; P_{23}]^T|$, (bias on satellite 3, assuming $b > 0$)

where $|[P_{13} \ P_{23}]^T| = \sqrt{P_{13}^2 + P_{23}^2}$.

In general,

(range bias b on ith satellite) = (norm of parity bias vector)/(norm of ith column of **P**)

The position error vector **e** is defined as: $\mathbf{e} = \hat{\mathbf{x}}_{LS} - \mathbf{x}$

$$\mathbf{e} = \left(\mathbf{H}^T\mathbf{H}\right)^{-1}\mathbf{H}^T\mathbf{y} - \mathbf{x}$$

$$= \left(\mathbf{H}^T\mathbf{H}\right)^{-1}\mathbf{H}^T\left(\mathbf{Hx} + \boldsymbol{\epsilon}\right) - \mathbf{x}$$

$$= \left(\mathbf{H}^T\mathbf{H}\right)^{-1}\mathbf{H}^T\boldsymbol{\epsilon} \quad \text{(Vector position error)}$$

which, for a bias b in the ith satellite, can be written as

$$\text{(position error vector)} = \left(\mathbf{H}^T\mathbf{H}\right)^{-1}\mathbf{H}^T \cdot \begin{bmatrix} 0 \\ \cdot \\ b \\ \cdot \\ \cdot \\ 0 \end{bmatrix}$$

These equations provide a means of getting back and forth from a bias in parity space to the corresponding bias in range space, and finally to the corresponding position error. The norm of the first two components of the position error vector provides the horizontal radial position error.

The objective is to protect against excessive horizontal position error. The RAIM algorithm must detect whether the horizontal error goes beyond a certain threshold within a specified level of confidence. Since the position error cannot be observed directly, something must be inferred from the quantity that can be observed, which in this case is the parity vector.

The magnitude of the parity vector is used as the test statistic (mathematical indicator) for detection of a satellite failure. The inputs to the parity space algorithm are the standard deviation of the measurement noise, the measurement geometry, and the maximum allowable probabilities for a false alert and a missed detection. The output of the algorithm is the HPL, which defines the smallest horizontal radial position error that can be detected for the specified false alert and missed detection probabilities.

A false alert is an indication of a positioning failure to the pilot when a positioning failure has not occurred, as the result of a false detection. The detection threshold for the RAIM and FDE algorithms is determined by integrating the pdf from the detection threshold to infinity so that the area under the curve is equal to the probability of a false alert, P_{FA}.

The parity space method is based on modeling the test statistic using a chi distribution with $n - 4$ degrees of freedom for six or more visible satellites. The sum of the squared measurement residuals has a chi-square distribution. A Gaussian distribution is used for the case where five satellites are in view. The general formulas for the chi-square density functions are provided next.

For a central chi-square,

$$fcent(x) = \left[x^{((k/2)-1)} e^{-x/2} \right] \big/ \left[2^{k/2} \Gamma(k/2) \right], \quad x > 0,$$
$$= 0, \quad x \leq 0$$

where Γ is the gamma function.

For the probability of missed detection, the noncentral chi-square density function is integrated from 0 to the chi-square detection threshold to determine λ, the noncentrality parameter that provides the desired P_{md}. The minimum detectable bias based on the selected probabilities of false alert and missed detection is denoted as pbias, where pbias $= \sigma_{UERE} \sqrt{\lambda}$.

For a noncentral chi-square,

$$f_{N.C.}(x) = \left[e^{-(x+\lambda)/2} \big/ 2^{k/2} \right] \sum_{j=0}^{\infty} \left\{ \lambda^j x^{(k/2)+j-1} \big/ \left[\Gamma((k/2)+j) \cdot 2^{2j} \cdot j! \right] \right\}, \quad x > 0$$
$$= 0, \quad x \leq 0$$

where λ is the noncentrality parameter. It is defined in terms of the normalized mean m and the number of degrees of freedom k, as $\lambda = km^2$.

The chi-square density functions for a case of six visible satellites (2 degrees of freedom) are shown in Figure 7.21. These density functions are used to define the detection threshold to satisfy the false alarm and missed detection probabilities. For supplemental navigation, the maximum allowable false alarm rate is one alarm per 15,000 samples or 0.002/hour. One sample was considered a 2-minute interval based on the correlation time of SA. The maximum false alarm rate for GPS primary means navigation is 0.333×10^{-6} per sample. The minimum detection probability for both supplemental and primary means of navigation is 0.999, or a missed detection rate of 10^{-3} [45].

Figure 7.22 displays a linear no-noise model of the estimated horizontal position error versus the test statistic, forming a characteristic slope line for each visible satellite. These slopes are a function of the linear connection, or geometry matrix, $\mathbf{H}$, and vary slowly with time as the satellites move about their orbits. The slope associated with each satellite is given by

$$\mathrm{SLOPE}(i) = \sqrt{A_{1i}^2 + A_{2i}^2} \big/ \sqrt{S_{ii}}, \quad i = 1, 2, \cdots n$$

where

$$\mathbf{A} \equiv \left(\mathbf{H}^{\mathrm{T}} \mathbf{H} \right)^{-1} \mathbf{H}^{\mathrm{T}}$$

and $\mathbf{S}$ was defined previously in (7.71), but also can be computed directly from $\mathbf{P}$ as

$$\mathbf{S} = \mathbf{P}^{\mathrm{T}} \mathbf{P}$$

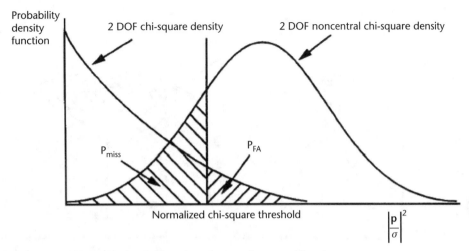

Figure 7.21   Chi-square density functions for two degrees of freedom.

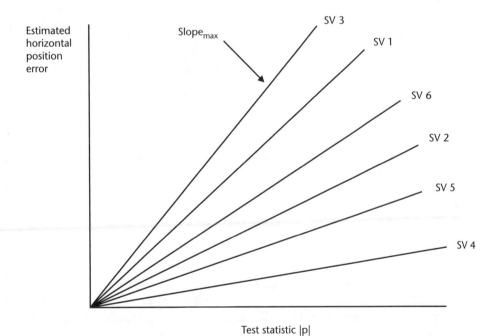

Figure 7.22   Characteristic slopes for six visible satellites.

For a given position error, the satellite with the largest slope has the smallest test statistic and will be the most difficult to detect. Therefore, there is a poor coupling between the position error to be protected and the magnitude of the parity vector that can be observed when a bias actually occurs in the satellite with the maximum slope.

The oval-shaped *cloud of data* shown in Figure 7.23 is a depiction of the scatter that would occur if there were a bias on the satellite with the maximum slope. This bias is such that the fraction of data to the left of the detection threshold is equal to the missed detection rate. Any bias smaller than this value will move the data cloud

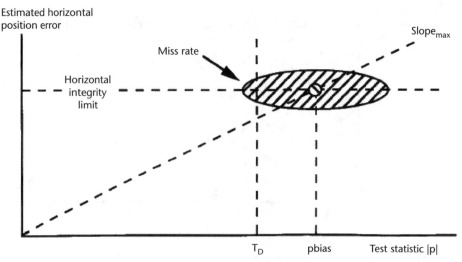

Figure 7.23   Scatter plot with critical bias on Slope$_{max}$ satellite.

to the left, increasing the missed detection rate beyond the allowable limit. This critical bias value in parity space is denoted as pbias. The pbias term is completely deterministic, but it is dependent on the number of visible satellites [43]:

$$\text{pbias} = \sigma_{UERE} \sqrt{\lambda}$$

where λ is the noncentrality parameter of the noncentral chi-square density function, and σ_{UERE} is the standard deviation of the satellite pseudorange measurement error.

The HPL is determined by

$$\text{HPL} = \text{Slope}_{max} \times \text{pbias}$$

When SA was the dominant error source, other error terms that depend heavily on the elevation angle were negligible. For this reason, pre-2000 RAIM and FDE availability analyses typically assumed a fixed σ_{UERE} value of 33.3m for all satellites, regardless of the satellite elevation angles. Now that SA has been discontinued, errors that depend on the elevation angles make σ_{UERE} values for each satellite significantly different.

Accounting for elevation-dependent errors is accomplished through weighting (or deweighting) of individual satellite range measurements [46]. The only difference between the weighted solution RAIM and the nonweighted solution RAIM is the formula for the maximum horizontal slope, which is shown next.

The threshold and pbias values are the same as with SA on. This is because the maximum false alarm rate is set at 0.333×10^{-6}/sample, which is consistent with the guidance in [14] for SA off.

$$\text{SLOPE}(i) = \sqrt{A_{1i}^{2} + A_{2i}^{2}}\, \sigma_i \Big/ \sqrt{S_{ii}}$$

where:

$$A \equiv \left(H^T WH \right)^{-1} H^T W$$

$$S \equiv I_n - H\left(H^T WH \right)^{-1} H^T W$$

$$W^{-1} = \begin{bmatrix} \sigma_1^2 & 0 & \cdot\cdot & 0 \\ 0 & \sigma_2^2 & \cdot\cdot & 0 \\ \cdot\cdot & \cdot\cdot & \cdot\cdot & \cdot\cdot \\ 0 & 0 & \cdot\cdot & \sigma_n^2 \end{bmatrix}$$

$$\sigma_i^2 = \sigma_{i,URA}{}^2 + \sigma_{i,uire}{}^2 + \sigma_{i,tropo}{}^2 + \sigma_{i,mp}{}^2 + \sigma_{i,revr}{}^2 \tag{7.73}$$

where the error components are user range accuracy (clock and ephemeris error), user ionospheric range error, tropospheric error, multipath, and receiver noise.

The HPL is formed by the same method as nonweighted RAIM.

$$HPL = Slope_{max} \times normalized\ pbias = Slope_{max} \times \sqrt{\lambda}$$

Availability of RAIM

Availability of RAIM is determined by comparing the HPL to the maximum alert limit for the intended operation. RAIM was developed and primarily has been used to support aviation applications. Therefore, the focus of the availability analysis in this section will be on aviation applications. The *horizontal alert limits* for various phases of flight are shown in Table 7.6.

If the HPL is below the alert limit, RAIM is said to be available for that phase of flight. Since the HPL is dependent on the satellite geometry, it must be computed for each location and point in time. Since RAIM requires a minimum of five visible satellites in order to perform fault detection and a minimum of six for fault detection and exclusion, RAIM and FDE will have a lower availability than the navigation function. An analysis of the nominal 24-satellite constellation has been performed to evaluate the availability of RAIM [47–51].

Although a 7.5° mask angle is specified in FAA TSO C129, a 5° mask angle is specified for FAA TSO C146 receivers, and most receivers use a 5° mask angle or lower. A 5° mask angle is applied to this analysis, and availability is evaluated over a worldwide grid of points at 5-minute samples over a 24-hour period.

Table 7.6 GPS Integrity Performance Requirements

Phase of Flight	Horizontal Alert Limit
En route	2 nmi
Terminal	1 nmi
NPA	0.3 nmi

Source: [45].

The analysis considers both SA on and off cases. Although SA was turned off in May 2000, TSO C129 receivers have the SA on pseudorange error hard coded into the software. The availability results shown with SA on in Tables 7.7 and 7.8 still apply to those receivers.

The availability of RAIM fault detection is well above 99% for the en route and terminal phases of flight and 97.3% for nonprecision approaches. In order to improve availability, the barometric altimeter can be included as an additional measurement in the RAIM solution. With baro aiding, availability improves to 100% for en route navigation with 99.99% availability for the terminal phase of flight and 99.9% for nonprecision approach. The maximum outage duration over the course of the day decreases from over half an hour to 15 minutes for nonprecision approach.

The availability of fault detection and exclusion with baro aiding ranges from 81.4% during nonprecision approaches to 98.16% for en route navigation (FDE without baro aiding isn't considered in this analysis due to its low availability). For a nonprecision approach, FDE outages can last for more than 1.5 hours at a location. These results are summarized in Tables 7.7 and 7.8.

The availability of RAIM and FDE with SA off applying a 5° mask angle are shown in Tables 7.9 and 7.10. As shown in Table 7.9, availability of the RAIM fault detection function has nearly 100% availability with SA turned off and the use of baro aiding. The removal of the SA noise allows better detection of a bias present on a satellite.

The availability of FDE also improves substantially with SA off such that greater than 99% availability can be achieved for en route navigation through nonprecision approach. However, the outage duration for nonprecision approach can still be substantial, with outages lasting on the order of an hour.

Table 7.7   RAIM/FDE Availability with a 5° Mask Angle and SA On

RAIM/FDE Function	En Route	Terminal	Nonprecision Approach
Fault detection	99.98%	99.94%	97.26%
Fault detection with baro aiding	100%	99.99%	99.92%
Fault detection and exclusion with baro aiding	99.73%	97.11%	81.40%

Table 7.8   Maximum Duration of RAIM/FDE Outages with 5° Mask Angle and SA On

RAIM/FDE Function	En Route	Terminal	Nonprecision Approach
Fault detection	5 minutes	10 minutes	35 minutes
Fault detection with baro aiding	0 minutes	5 minutes	15 minutes
Fault detection and exclusion with baro aiding	25 minutes	55 minutes	100 minutes

Table 7.9   RAIM/FDE Availability with a 5° Mask Angle and SA Off

RAIM/FDE Function	En Route	Terminal	Nonprecision Approach
Fault detection	99.998%	99.990%	99.903%
Fault detection with baro aiding	100%	100%	99.998%
Fault detection and exclusion with baro aiding	99.923%	99.643%	99.100%

Table 7.10   Maximum Duration of RAIM/FDE Outages with 5° Mask Angle and SA Off

RAIM/FDE Function	En Route	Terminal	Nonprecision Approach
Fault detection	5 minutes	10 minutes	30 minutes
Fault detection with baro aiding	0 minutes	0 minutes	5 minutes
Fault detection and exclusion with baro aiding	10 minutes	35 minutes	60 minutes

As shown in Figure 7.24, outages can last up to 60 minutes in several locations, but there is virtually 100% coverage near the equator. This high availability of FDE near the equator is due to the increased number of visible satellites.

Another method for improving availability of RAIM and FDE is to lower the mask angle so that more satellites are visible to the user equipment. However, as mentioned previously, low elevation satellites will have higher atmospheric errors. These satellites are deweighted in the solution according to (7.73). As demonstrated in Tables 7.11 and 7.12, availability of the fault detection function is very high, even without baro aiding. For FDE with baro aiding, outages remain, but the number of occurrences and duration is shortened.

Satellite-Based Augmentation Systems

As discussed in the previous section, one of the limitations of the RAIM and FDE algorithms is that they do not always have enough ranging sources with sufficient geometry to meet availability requirements. Even with the availability improvement obtained with SA off and employing a 2° mask angle, outages of up to 30 minutes can occur for the nonprecision approach phase of flight with all 24 satellites operational. Satellites occasionally are taken out of service for maintenance, further reducing the availability of RAIM and FDE.

Therefore, aviation authorities are developing augmentation systems to GPS. One such augmentation is the SBAS. The U.S. version of SBAS is known as the WAAS. Other SBAS systems under development are the EGNOS, the Japanese MSAS, and the Indian GAGAN system.

SBAS systems consist of widely dispersed reference stations that monitor and gather data on the GPS satellites. These data are forwarded to the SBAS master stations for processing to determine the integrity and differential corrections for each monitored satellite. The integrity information and differential corrections are then

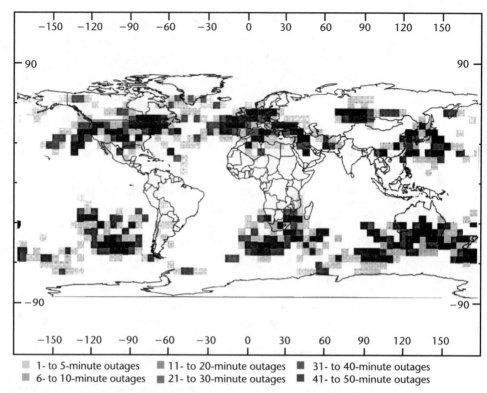

Figure 7.24 FDE availability for NPA with baro aiding with a 5° mask angle.

Table 7.11 RAIM/FDE Availability with 2° Mask Angle and SA Off

RAIM/FDE Function	En Route	Terminal	Nonprecision Approach
Fault detection	100%	100%	99.988%
Fault detection with baro aiding	100%	100%	100%
Fault detection and exclusion with baro aiding	99.981%	99.904%	99.854%

Table 7.12 Maximum Duration of RAIM/FDE Outages with 2° Mask Angle and SA Off

RAIM/FDE Function	En Route	Terminal	Nonprecision Approach
Fault detection	0 minutes	0 minutes	5 minutes
Fault detection with baro aiding	0 minutes	0 minutes	0 minutes
Fault detection and exclusion with baro aiding	10 minutes	15 minutes	30 minutes

sent to a ground Earth station and uplinked to a geostationary satellite, along with the geostationary satellite navigation message.

The geostationary satellites downlink the integrity and differential corrections for each monitored satellite using the GPS L1 frequency with a modulation similar to that used by GPS. Therefore, the geostationary satellite also can serve as an additional GPS ranging signal. Based on this information, the user receiver forms horizontal and vertical protection levels based on a weighted solution. The initial phase of the U.S. WAAS system consists of two geostationary satellites, Atlantic Ocean Region West (AORW) and Pacific Ocean Region (POR), provided by Inmarsat. SBAS systems are discussed in much greater detail in Chapter 8.

The initial four INMARSAT satellites that broadcast the SBAS signal as an augmentation to GPS can be included in a similar analysis to that performed in Section 7.2 to determine the distribution of HDOP and PDOP. The same analysis was performed as before with a 5° mask angle and up to three satellites removed from the constellation in order to investigate the overall improvement in the availability of GPS. The locations of the ranging geostationary satellites are POR at 179.5°E, Indian Ocean region (IOR) at 64.5°E, AORW at 55.5°W, and Atlantic Ocean Region East (AORE) at 15.5°W.

The cumulative distributions of HDOP and PDOP augmented with the four geostationary satellites are displayed in Figures 7.25 and 7.26, respectively. Again applying a PDOP threshold of 6.0 to determine the availability of these satellite constellations, it can be seen that both the 24- and 23-satellite constellations provide coverage 100% of the time. With two satellites removed from the constellation, the availability is 99.97%, and with 21 satellites the constellation provides an availability of 99.65%. This is an improvement from an availability of 99.9% and 99.2% that the 22 and 21 satellite constellations respectively provided without the aiding of the geostationary satellites.

Next, the improvement in the availability of RAIM and FDE over the conterminous United States (CONUS) is examined when the constellation is augmented

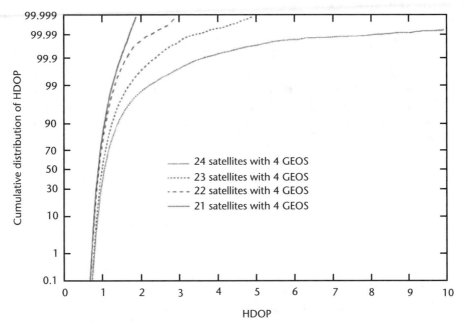

Figure 7.25 Cumulative distribution of HDOP with four geostationary satellites.

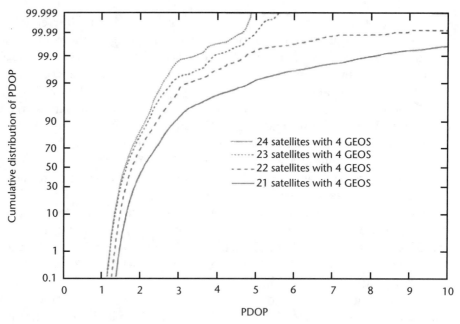

Figure 7.26   Cumulative distribution of PDOP with four geostationary satellites.

by geostationary satellites. RAIM and FDE would be employed for integrity monitoring if the WAAS signal was unavailable from the geostationary or the user is outside of the WAAS service area but within the footprint of the WAAS geostationary satellite. The three geostationary satellites visible from CONUS (POR, AORW, and AORE) are used to augment the constellation. The analysis is again conducted for SA on and SA off conditions. As shown in Tables 7.13 and 7.14, there is a significant improvement in availability when the geostationary satellites are used to augment the constellation even with SA on.

There is 100% availability of fault detection for the en route and terminal phases of flight even without baro aiding. The availability for a nonprecision approach increases to 99.88% with a maximum outage duration of 15 minutes. Availability with baro aiding is 100% for all phases of flight and is not presented here. Since the availability of FDE is much higher with use of geostationary satellites, availability of FDE without baro aiding is evaluated; however, the outages are fairly substantial for nonprecision approach, lasting up to 2 hours in duration.

Table 7.13   RAIM/FDE Availability over CONUS with a 5° Mask Angle and Three Geostationary Satellites with SA On

RAIM/FDE Function	En Route	Terminal	Nonprecision Approach
Fault detection	100%	100%	99.88%
Fault detection and exclusion	99.90%	99.52%	89.37%
Fault detection and exclusion with baro aiding	100%	99.91%	98.13%

Table 7.14 Maximum Duration of RAIM/FDE Outages over CONUS with a 5° Mask Angle and Three Geostationary Satellites with SA On

RAIM/FDE Function	En Route	Terminal	Nonprecision Approach
Fault detection	0 minutes	0 minutes	15 minutes
Fault detection and exclusion	10 minutes	30 minutes	120 minutes
Fault detection and exclusion with baro aiding	0 minutes	15 minutes	45 minutes

There is 100% availability of FDE for en route navigation when baro aiding is applied in conjunction with the geostationary satellites. Outage durations also are significantly reduced for all phases of flight.

Tables 7.15 and 7.16 provide RAIM/FDE availability results when the geostationary satellites are used to augment the constellation with SA off. There is 100% availability of the fault detection function without baro aiding. Availability of FDE for nonprecision approach without baro aiding improves to 99.99% for en route, 99.9% for terminal, and 99% for nonprecision approach. With baro aiding, the duration of FDE outages decreases from over an hour to 35 minutes for nonprecision approach.

GBASs

GBASs are designed to be specific to an airfield in order to support precision approach and perhaps terminal area and surface navigation. GBAS systems, such as the Local Area Augmentation System (LAAS) under development by the FAA, utilize multiple GPS reference receivers. Data from the reference receivers are processed using an averaging technique to determine integrity and develop differential corrections.

The LAAS integrity algorithm involves placing an upper confidence bound on the lateral and vertical position error by computing lateral protection level (LPL) and VPL using an assumed fault hypothesis. There are two fault hypotheses for LAAS: H_0 and H_1. The H_0 hypothesis refers to normal measurement conditions (i.e., no faults) in all reference receivers and on all ranging sources (satellites and airport pseudolites). The H_1 hypothesis represents a latent fault associated with one reference receiver. A latent fault includes any erroneous measurement(s) that are not

Table 7.15 RAIM/FDE Availability over CONUS with a 5° Mask Angle and Three Geostationary Satellites with SA Off

RAIM/FDE Function	En Route	Terminal	Nonprecision Approach
Fault detection	100%	100%	100%
Fault detection and exclusion	99.991%	99.952%	99.463%
Fault detection and exclusion with baro aiding	100%	99.997%	99.893%

Table 7.16 Maximum Duration of RAIM/FDE Outages over CONUS with a 5° Mask Angle and Three Geostationary Satellites with SA Off

RAIM/FDE Function	En Route	Terminal	Nonprecision Approach
Fault detection	0 minutes	0 minutes	0 minutes
Fault detection and exclusion	5 minutes	15 minutes	65 minutes
Fault detection and exclusion with baro aiding	0 minutes	5 minutes	35 minutes

immediately detected by the ground subsystem, such that the broadcast data are affected and there is an induced position error in the airborne subsystem. The differential corrections and integrity parameters for each monitored satellite are broadcast to the aircraft via a VHF datalink. GBAS systems are discussed in detail in Chapter 8.

7.6 Continuity

Continuity, as defined in [37], is "the probability that the specified system performance will be maintained for the duration of a phase of operation, presuming that the system was available at the beginning of that phase of operation." The level of continuity provided by GPS thus varies with the specific performance requirements for any given application. For example, the level of continuity of GPS for a low-accuracy time-transfer application will be much higher than the level of GPS continuity for an aircraft nonprecision approach. The former application only requires a single visible GPS satellite, whereas the latter requires at least five visible satellites with good geometry to support RAIM.

Some useful information regarding the continuity of the GPS satellites, based upon observed performance from January 1994 to July 2000, is provided in [17]. During this timespan, on average, each in-orbit GPS satellite ceased functioning 2.7 times per year and was out of service for a total downtime of 58 hours. The majority of these instances (referred to as *downing events*) were related to scheduled maintenance—accounting for 1.9 downing events per year and an average total downtime of 18.7 hours. The remaining 0.9[1] downing events per year per satellite were unscheduled and accounted for a total average downtime of 39.3 hours. Causes of unscheduled outages include failures of one or more satellite subsystems that resulted in a loss of service.

For many applications, only unscheduled downing events are of concern. Scheduled maintenance activities are generally announced well in advance and can often be planned around. For such applications, the probability that any given GPS satellite will fail over a 1-hour time interval is approximately 0.0001. This value is computed by dividing the average of 0.9 unscheduled downing events per year by the number of hours in a year, 8,760.

---

1. Note that the component values provided in [17] of 0.9 and 1.9 do not add to the total of 2.7, also in [17]. This is presumably due to rounding errors.

7.7 Measured Performance

The purpose of this section is to discuss assessments of GPS accuracy, to include but not be limited to direct measurements. This is a complex topic due to the global nature of GPS, the wide variety of receivers and how they are employed by their users, and the complex environment in which the receivers must receive GPS signals. The discussion in this section leads the reader through an overview of the factors that affect GPS performance measurements. Techniques to combine measurement and estimation to generate regional and even global assessments of GPS performance are discussed, and performance trends resulting from such techniques are provided. The section ends with a description of the range of typical performance users can expect from a cross-section of receivers in use today, given current GPS constellation performance.

Long-term accuracy measurements provide an indication of the stability and consistency of GPS, as evidenced in the following plot. The data provided in Figure 7.27 was collected from the U.S. FAA National Satellite Test Bed (NSTB) [52]. Horizontal position errors (HPE) and vertical position errors (VPE) were computed at the 95% and 99.99% levels at each NSTB site, and averaged to generate the figure. The network in 1999 consisted of eight sites:

- Bangor, Maine;
- Dayton, Ohio;
- Elko, Nevada;
- Gander, Newfoundland;
- Honolulu, Hawaii;
- Seattle, Washington;

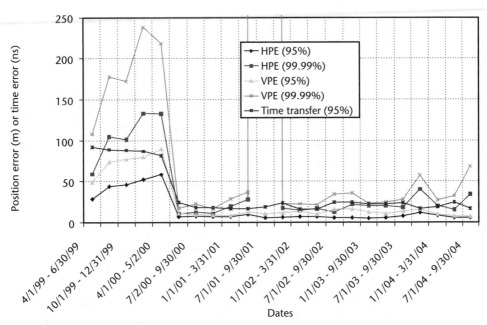

Figure 7.27 GPS SPS performance as observed within the United States from 1999–2004. (*After:* [52].)

- Sitka, Alaska;
- Winnipeg, Manitoba.

By 2004, the network had evolved into 20 sites:

- Billings, Montana;
- Cold Bay, Alaska;
- Juneau, Alaska;
- Albuquerque, New Mexico;
- Anchorage, Alaska;
- Boston, Massachusetts;
- Washington, D.C.;
- Honolulu, Hawaii;
- Houston, Texas;
- Mauna Loa, Hawaii;
- Kansas City, Kansas;
- Los Angeles, California;
- Salt Lake City, Utah;
- Miami, Florida;
- Minneapolis, Minnesota;
- Oakland, California;
- Cleveland, Ohio;
- Seattle, Washington;
- San Juan, Puerto Rico;
- Atlanta, Georgia.

Until May 2000, when SA was discontinued, observed 95% HPE and VPE were on the order of 50m and 75m, respectively. Since SA has been discontinued, the average values of the 95% HPE and VPE levels have been 7.1m and 11.4m, respectively. The 99.99% HPE and VPE values, since SA discontinuance, have generally been below 50m with a few notable exceptions. In July 2001, for instance, a failure of one GPS satellite (PRN 22) caused instantaneous GPS position errors to exceed well over 100 km over a significant portion of the western hemisphere. This event is noted for its magnitude, but also for the rarity of occurrence for such an event. In general, the GPS constellation has provided stable and consistent service since GPS was declared operational.

Saying that GPS is generally stable and consistent should not be taken to mean that all users view the performance they achieve using GPS in the same manner. Difficulties arise when we try to ascertain exactly what is meant when we refer to GPS operational performance and what conclusions we can draw from its measurement. These difficulties are based on the large number of possible GPS receiver configurations and integrations, operating within a wide range of environmental conditions.

Figure 7.28 represents a detailed report of performance from the NSTB's Hawaii reference station for July 19, 2004. The dual-frequency SPS (i.e., commer-

Honolulu, Hawaii Reference Station
July 19, 2004
Best 4 satellite position solution, 5-degree mask
Dual-frequency SPS measurements sampled every minute

Daily range domain report

	Range	Rate	Accel	Iono	Tropo
Average	1.19	-0.003	0.00002	10.03	-5.36
RMS	1.79	0.061	0.00038	9.58	5.48
Max	10.34	0.142	0.00180	36.48	0.00
Min	-12.85	-0.129	-0.00232	0.00	-14.32
95%	4.01	0.106	0.00089	17.25	11.41

Daily position error report

	East	North	Vert	Horiz	Pos
Average	0.26	0.29	0.24	2.26	4.18
RMS	1.84	1.88	3.97	2.63	4.76
Max	9.72	8.91	18.02	10.88	18.08
Min	-6.99	-7.67	-11.51		
50%			2.46	2.02	3.59
95%	3.71	3.74	7.54	4.65	8.23

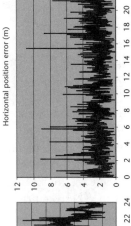

Daily GPS navigation performance report

Total Position Error (m)

East position error (m)

North position error (m)

Horizontal position error (m)

Vertical position error (m)

Figure 7.28 Daily navigation performance report from Honolulu, Hawaii, NSTB reference station.

cial receivers tracking L1 C/A code plus L2 Y code using semicodeless processing—see Section 5.14) pseudorange measurements were all processed in accordance with the algorithms in [4], with no filtering to reduce measurement noise. The measurements from the best four satellites (based on a minimum PDOP criterion) were then used to generate an instantaneous position solution relative to the reference station's surveyed location. The resulting instantaneous position errors indicated in Figure 7.28 are predictably noisy but provide performance in line with the trends shown in Figure 7.27.

The position error behavior in Figure 7.28 is contrasted with other perspectives in Figure 7.29. The GPS CS computes smoothed UREs called observed range deviations (ORDs) every 15 minutes for each CS monitor station. In Figure 7.29, we compare position solution errors using interpolated ORDs from the CS Hawaii monitor station located at Kaena Point with the three-dimensional position errors from Figure 7.28. The primary distinction between the two sets of data is the relative smoothness of the position error for the CS Hawaii monitor station. If we filter the data from the NSTB Hawaii reference station, we see that it is reasonably consistent with the CS Hawaii monitor station solution error using ORD values. Most of the divergence between the filtered NSTB solution and the CS ORD-based solution lies in the fact that optimum satellite selection varied slightly due to the approximately 43 km between the two locations.

One final element of Figure 7.29 is the line representing an all-in-view (AIV) position solution error using interpolated CS ORD values. Over the 24 hours of data presented, the AIV position solution provided a 29% improvement in performance using the same basic measurements. The current constellation's geometry provides an overall 27% improvement across the globe when using an AIV position solution instead of one based on a best four-satellite selection algorithm.

The point we focus on here is the fact that we used four different ways to measure GPS accuracy at two locations very close together and witnessed a 40% spread in our resulting statistics. If we can see such divergence resulting from vary similar measurement processing techniques, how much variation can we expect with the wider range of possible GPS measurement techniques and environments?

Before answering that question, we need to step back and examine briefly the major factors that affect measured GPS performance. Figure 7.30 provides an overview of these factors. Figure 7.30 also illustrates an approach for breaking the problem into different levels of abstraction based on the scope and fidelity required by any given group for their GPS performance assessment.

Note that we have begun to use the term *assessment* as opposed to *measurement*. This change in term is due to the fact that any but the most basic of GPS performance assessments sometimes require complementing measurements with estimates or predictive statistics. Situations where direct measurement of all necessary information to assess performance is not practical include global performance monitoring for GPS CS constellation management purposes, and near-real-time monitoring of aircraft accuracy inside a national airspace.

Figure 7.30 establishes a framework for developing application-appropriate methods for assessing GPS performance. All of the performance assessments provided in this section were generated using this framework. In the figure, we establish three related paradigms for performance assessment. The three paradigms are:

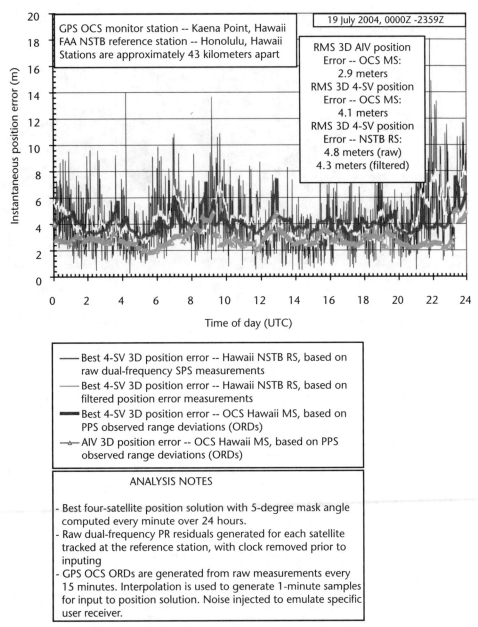

Figure 7.29 Contrast between performance measurements from the FAA NSTB Hawaii reference station and the GPS CS Hawaii monitor station.

- *Core performance paradigm*: global in nature, includes all of the parameters associated with the design of the core GPS program, lowest correlation with individual user performance, provides the mechanisms for effects-based sustainment and operations of the GPS constellation;

- *Regional performance paradigm*: tailored to a specified user category for any area of interest, supports performance monitoring for a specific application within a region such as general aviation across the U.S. national airspace, often used to support performance predictions for military planning;

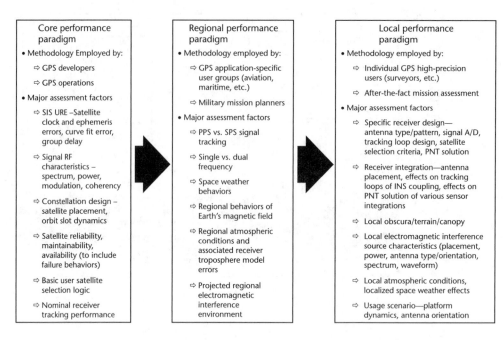

Figure 7.30   Framework for establishing application-specific methods to assess GPS performance.

- *Local performance paradigm:* focused on an individual user application and usage scenario within a local environment, provides the highest correlation to individual user performance.

The techniques and procedures for assessing GPS performance on a global basis cover an extensive list of topics. We discuss here two specific topics that are key in the support of the performance assessment framework and can provide the reader with a perspective on the assessment process:

- Compensating for a relatively low density of global performance measurements;
- Estimating the effect of global ionosphere effects on single frequency performance.

The method for complementing direct performance measurements for global performance assessments requires the generation of PPS estimated range deviations (ERDs), the CS term for estimated SIS UREs. ERDs are very flexible in that they may be computed for any location within view of the GPS satellite of interest. ERDs are limited in that they are based on the difference between the CS Kalman Filter's current state estimate and the predicted state at the time of upload. CS ERDs tend to be optimistic in their representation of the PPS SIS URE, because they do not include curve fit error, and a portion of the ephemeris error tends to be unobservable within the current CS architecture. These limitations in the ERD computation result in an estimate that is generally 10% to 20% below the "true" SIS PPS URE within the current GPS program. This optimism is mitigated somewhat in practice by comparing

CS monitor station ORDs and ERDs against a difference threshold, and rejecting ERDs that vary too much relative to the measured SIS URE.

The following computation supports generation of ERDs for any arbitrary location. The error in satellite position is computed by subtracting the current state position estimate from the predicted position based (nominally) on the navigation message. The error in satellite clock is computed by subtracting the current state clock estimate from the predicted clock from the navigation message. Examples of ERD computation results and a comparison with ORD values are provided in Figure 7.31.

$$EPH\_ERD(SV_j, Site_m, t_k) = \Delta\bar{\mathbf{r}}_{sv}^{ecef}(SV_j, t_k) \cdot \frac{\left[\bar{\mathbf{r}}_{sv}^{predicted}(SV_j, t_k) - \bar{\mathbf{r}}_{site}(Site_m)\right]}{\left\|\bar{\mathbf{r}}_{sv}^{predicted}(SV_j, t_k) - \bar{\mathbf{r}}_{site}(Site_m)\right\|} \quad (m)$$

$$ERD(SV_j, Site_m, t_k) = EPH\_ERD(SV_j, Site_m, t_k) - CLOCK\_ERD(SV_j, t_k) \quad (m)$$

where:

$t_k = k$th time corresponding to the estimated signal reception times for all satellites in view

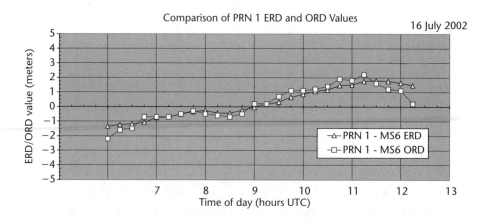

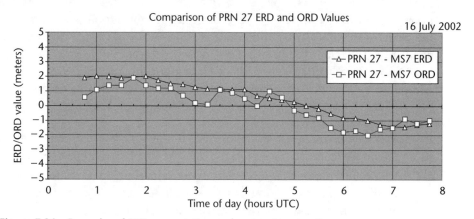

Figure 7.31 Examples of ERD computation and comparison results.

$\Delta \bar{\mathbf{r}}_{sv}^{ecef}(SV_j,t_k)$ = error in satellite position computation using navigation message, in ECEF coordinates

$EPH\_ERD(SV_j, Site_m, t_k)$ = satellite position error mapped into LOS to the mth user location

$CLOCK\_ERD (SV_j, t_k)$ = error in the navigation message representation of each satellite's clock phase

Once ERDs are available for a given location, they can be used in a straightforward position error computation. First, compute the position solution geometry matrix ($\mathbf{G}$) and rotate it into local coordinates. Then, compute the inverse direction cosine matrix ($\mathbf{K}$) for each time t_k. Several algorithms are available for computing the inverse of a nonsquare matrix, such as the $\mathbf{K}$-matrix for an overdetermined, AIV solution. Once the $\mathbf{K}$-matrix is available, the SIS instantaneous positioning, navigation, and timing (PNT) error vector ($\Delta \bar{\mathbf{x}}_{sis}$) for each time t_k can then be computed.

$$\Delta \bar{\mathbf{x}}_{sis}(Site_m,t_k) = \left[\mathbf{G}_{enu}^{allsys} \right]^+ \Delta \bar{\mathbf{r}}_{sis}(Site_m,t_k) = \mathbf{K}_{enu}^{allsys} \Delta \bar{\mathbf{r}}_{sis}(Site_m,t_k) \quad \text{or}$$

$$\begin{bmatrix} \Delta e_{sis}(Site_m,t_k) \\ \Delta n_{sis}(Site_m,t_k) \\ \Delta u_{sis}(Site_m,t_k) \\ \Delta t_{sis}(Site_m,t_k) \end{bmatrix} = \begin{bmatrix} K_{11} & \bullet & \bullet & K_{1n} \\ K_{21} & \bullet & \bullet & K_{2n} \\ K_{31} & \bullet & \bullet & K_{3n} \\ K_{41} & \bullet & \bullet & K_{4n} \end{bmatrix} \begin{bmatrix} ERD(SV_1, Site_m,t_k) \\ \bullet \\ \bullet \\ ERD(SV_n, Site_m,t_k) \end{bmatrix} \quad \text{(m)}$$

where:

$\Delta \bar{\mathbf{x}}_{sis}(Site_m,t_k)$ = SIS position solution error vector in local coordinates (east, north, up, and time) at the kth solution time for the mth site

$\Delta \bar{\mathbf{r}}_{sis}(Site_m,t_k)$ = ERD(SV_j, $Site_m$, t_k) values from step 1, for all satellites used in the kth position solution at the mth site

The resulting SIS PNT error vector can be injected with an estimate of a given receiver's noise contribution to pseudorange measurement. This noise is mapped through the position solution geometry and RSS into the individual PNT error components to form an estimate of the receiver in question's total error vector. An example result of this PNT error computation is presented in Figure 7.32 and contrasted against the ORD-derived position errors first presented in Figure 7.29.

One of the advantages of the PNT error algorithm just discussed is that it can be computed for any location at any desired time step. An example of initial conditions for conducting such a core performance analysis on a global basis is provided next:

- *Receiver characteristics:* AIV, dual-frequency, keyed PPS, 5° mask angle, 80-cm RMS thermal noise in the dual-frequency pseudorange measurement;
- *Noise environment characteristics:* noise level below threshold for impacting satellite signal acquisition or tracking and consistent with maintaining tracking performance within the receiver thermal noise assumption;

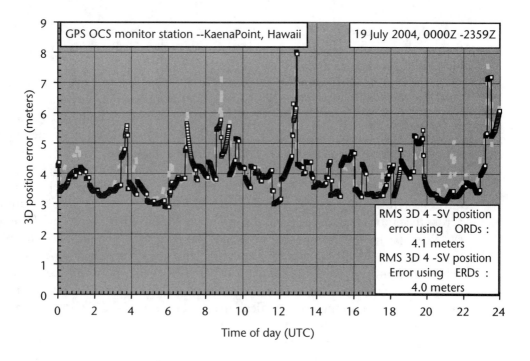

Figure 7.32 Comparison of position errors derived from CS ERDs and ORDs.

- *Physical environment characteristics:* no terrain above the mask angle and no multipath;
- *Sampling requirements:* once per minute over a 24-hour interval, across a 1° × 1° equidistantly spaced global grid.

We chose an all-satellite-in-view solution because most receivers built today employ some form of overdetermined solution that uses more than four satellites if they are available. A nonaugmented GPS position solution requires a minimum of four satellites. Since the GPS constellation (as of 2006) provides an average of eight or more satellites in view at any time, most of the time an AIV receiver will have more than four satellites in the position solution. We note here that most receivers that employ an overdetermined solution do not truly use all satellites in view; they limit their tracking generally to no more than eight.

From a system management point of view, the core performance metric just discussed provides a reasonable way to evaluate global performance on a daily basis. Still, every user group has its own unique needs and ways to employ GPS, under a wide variety of physical and environmental conditions. The effect of making one simple change to the accuracy metric (e.g., a switch from a dual- to a single-frequency receiver) can have a profound effect on the results of the metric. An example of such a contrast may be seen by examining data from June 3, 2000. Dual-frequency performance for the selected day was nominal and reasonably uniform across the globe [53]. The selected day, however, occurred at the height of the solar cycle, and performance for single-frequency receivers varied considerably from that experienced by dual-frequency receivers. Single-frequency accuracy across the globe exhibited significant variation compared to dual-frequency performance, with vertical 95% errors sampled over 24 hours reaching as high as 55m. Contrast this performance with a maximum 95% vertical error over 24 hours of slightly greater than 8m for the same day.

GPS error distributions are driven by several factors. For a dual-frequency position solution, the geometry of the position solution is generally the primary factor in determining how errors are distributed. For a single-frequency position solution, however, URE has a significant correlation with elevation angle and tends to correlate across all satellites in view as the elevation angle increases. This correlation is driven by the error in the ionosphere single-frequency model. The result is to increase the ratio of local vertical to horizontal error in the position solution. One important result of this behavior is that performance predictions of three-dimensional position error computed by multiplying URE and the PDOP will not give a valid result for single-frequency position solutions. An example of a global comparison of vertical/horizontal error ratios for single- and dual-frequency receivers is presented in Figure 7.33.

Regardless of the metric employed, GPS has continued to exceed expectations based on original specifications since it began operations. Several factors contribute to the long-term trend of excellent GPS performance. These factors are:

- *On-orbit frequency standard performance:* Clocks are approaching an order-of-magnitude improvement in frequency stability compared to original performance specifications.

- *Constellation size:* Original satellite life expectancy was conservative, yielding a constellation that has averaged 25–29 satellites over the past decade.

- *Satellite availability:* The majority of operational satellites have proven more reliable than their original specifications, resulting in an average of more than 25 healthy satellites being available at any time over the past decade.

- *Consistent constellation operations:* U.S. Air Force Space Command has maintained a long-term degree of consistency in its conduct of constellation navigation uploads and satellite maintenance, and has gradually tuned the GPS MCS to take full advantage of improving satellite performance.

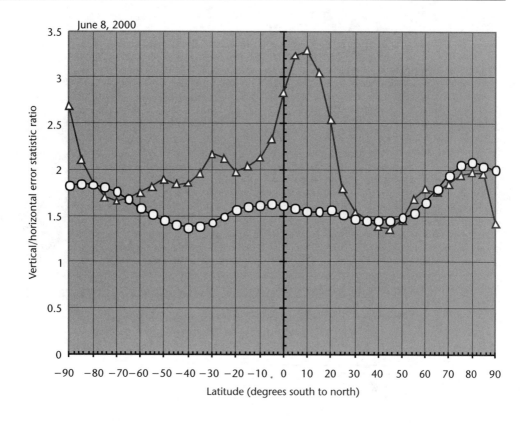

Figure 7.33 Comparison of vertical/horizontal error ratios for single- and dual-frequency receivers.

A 2-year trend of dual-frequency PPS three-dimensional position error across the globe is presented in Figure 7.34.[2] The demonstrated performance is consistent, with global median 95% position errors trending to well below 5m over a 24-hour

2. Derived from GPS performance data posted daily on the DoD GPS Support Center's Web site (http://www. schriever.af.mil/GPSSupportCenter).

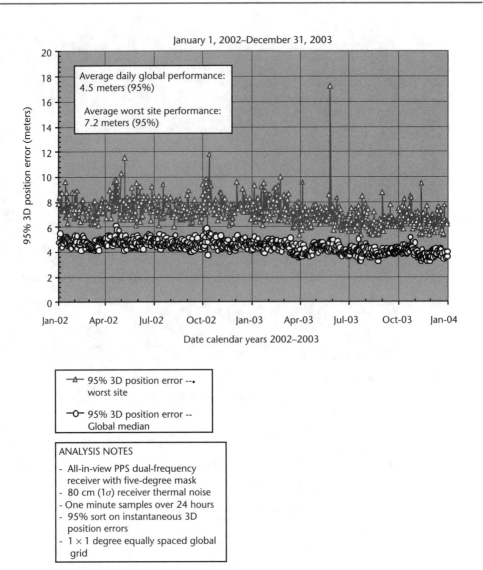

Figure 7.34   Global trend in GPS three-dimensional position error performance.

sample interval (1-minute samples). Worst-site performance understandably demonstrates more variance but still trends to below 8m (95%).

Since GPS is a PNT system, it is appropriate to include time transfer performance in our discussion. We consider time transfer performance from two perspectives: dynamic and static. Dynamic time transfer is based on the time portion of the navigation receiver's position solution. Static time transfer is the direct solution for time, bypassing the position solution geometry, using a time transfer receiver from a surveyed location. Figure 7.35 provides a 1-year trend of dynamic time transfer performance, while Figure 7.36 provides a 1-year trend for static time transfer performance. Note that static time transfer performance is generally better and more consistent than dynamic time transfer. Static time transfer is computed from an

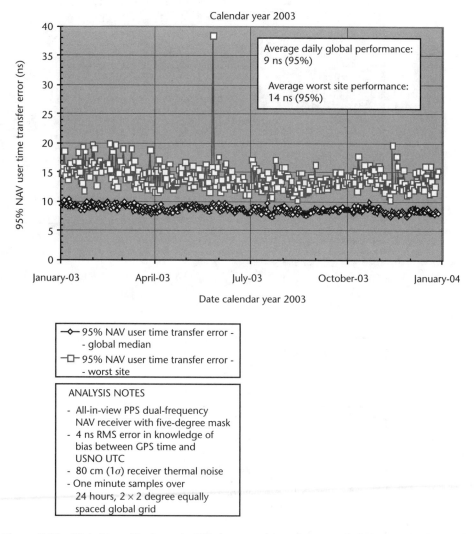

Figure 7.35   Global trend in dynamic GPS time transfer performance [relative to UTC (USNO)].

ensemble average of pseudorange residuals from all satellites in view, so it is independent of the position solution geometry.

We have seen throughout the discussion in this section that GPS provides a global PNT capability that provides predictable and consistent performance. We have also seen that GPS performance can vary widely across users and their operating environment. Measuring performance under such a varied set of conditions and on such a scale is impractical, so we established a framework that supports assessments using a combination of measurements and estimates. To close the discussion, Table 7.17 summarizes the range of typical performance for a variety of receiver types under current GPS operational conditions. Analysis notes are included after the table to provide some context to the representative performance values.

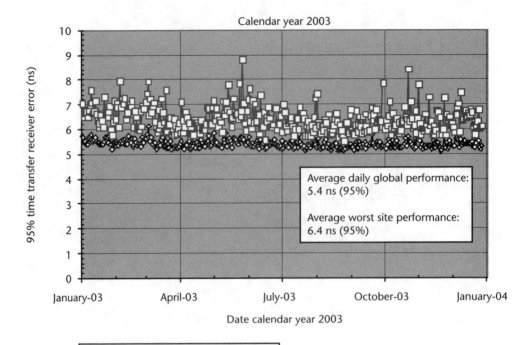

Figure 7.36   Global trend in static GPS time transfer receiver performance [relative to UTC (USNO)].

Table 7.17 Comparison of Typical Performance Range Across Various Receivers

Comparative 95% Three-Dimensional Position/Time Error Across Various Receivers	SPS			PPS		
	Best Location	Median Location	Worst Location	Best Location	Median Location	Worst Location
Handheld (best 4-SV solution)	16m	32m	72m	10m	30m	71m
Handheld (AIV solution)	11m	25m	54m	8m	23m	53m
Mobile (land/marine vehicle)	7m	23m	53m	N/A	N/A	N/A
Aviation receiver (AIV, RAIM, tightly coupled with INS)	7m	24m	55m	4m	5m	6m
Survey receiver (dual-frequency, real-time performance)	3m	4m	5m	3m	4m	5m
Aviation receiver dynamic time transfer performance	14 ns	45 ns	105 ns	12 ns	13 ns	14 ns
Time transfer receiver static time transfer performance	10 ns	19 ns	35 ns	10 ns	10 ns	11 ns

Analysis notes:

- Performance reported in the table is based on a 24-hour assessment period, using the full operational GPS constellation as of July 2004. Performance variations increase as satellites are removed from the constellation or environmental conditions degrade from the assumptions used to generate the table.
- The distinction between SPS and PPS is the use of C/A versus P(Y) code. For dual-frequency receivers, the distinction is the ability to code track on L2 for PPS receivers versus the use of semicodeless L2 tracking techniques for SPS.
- Ionosphere conditions and associated single-frequency model errors are based on a "typical" day. No scintillation effects are included.
- Each receiver antenna is assumed to be oriented with its bore sight aligned with local vertical.
- A nominal noise environment and no overhead canopy or other shielding is assumed. The effect of these assumptions is to maximize C/N_0 for each receiver/satellite link.
- Note that SPS aviation receiver performance is represented without augmentation (such as the WAAS in the United States). WAAS (and other similar international systems) provides significant accuracy improvement for its area of operations.
- Aviation receiver performance assumes the use of a RAIM algorithm, tightly coupled with an INS.
- No terrain above the receiver-specific mask angle was included in this analysis.
- The survey receiver's tracking loop noise contribution to URE was based on carrier, not code. The dominant survey receiver error in the absence of environmental noise is signal-in-space URE.
- Representing survey receiver performance as a 95th percentile can be misleading, since the very high accuracies achieved by survey receivers comes from averaging measurements over a user-specified time interval. Survey receiver performance is presented earlier as a 95th percentile statistic only to illustrate the range of possible receiver performance.
- Time transfer performance numbers for either a positioning or time transfer receiver represent the accuracy of internal receiver computations and presentations to the user. They do not include errors associated with generating a time mark pulse for use by other equipment outside the receiver. Depending on the receiver, this error can be significantly greater than the error of the PNT solution itself.

References

[1]   Ward, P., "An Inside View of Pseudorange and Delta Pseudorange Measurements in a Digital NAVSTAR GPS Receiver," International Telemetering Conference, GPS-Military and Civil Applications, San Diego, CA, October 14, 1981, pp. 63–69.

[2]   van Graas, F., and M. Braasch, "Selective Availability," in *Global Positioning System: Theory and Applications, Volume I*, B. Parkinson, and J. J. Spilker, Jr., (eds.), American Institute of Aeronautics and Astronautics, Washington, D.C., 1996.

[3]   The White House, Office of the Press Secretary, "Statement by the President Regarding the United States' Decision to Stop Degrading Global Positioning System Accuracy," White House Press Announcement, May 1, 2000.

[4]   ARINC Research Corporation, *NAVSTAR GPS Space Segment/Navigation User Interfaces*, Interface Specification, IS-GPS-200D (Public Release Version), ARINC Research Corporation, Fountain Valley, CA, 2004.

[5]   Dieter, G. L., G. E. Hatten, and J. Taylor, "MCS Zero Age of Data Measurement Techniques," *Proc. of 35th Annual Precise Time and Time Interval (PTTI) Meeting*, Washington, D.C., December 2003.

[6]   Taylor, J., and E. Barnes, "GPS Current Signal-in-Space Navigation Performance," *Proc. of The Institute of Navigation National Technical Meeting,* San Diego, CA, January 2005.

[7]   Yinger, C. H., et al., "GPS Accuracy Versus Number of NIMA Stations," *Proc. of ION GPS/GNSS 2003,* Portland, OR, September 9–12, 2003.

[8]   Warren, D. L. M., and J. F. Raquet, "Broadcast vs. Precise GPS Ephemerides: A Historical Perspective," *Proc. of ION National Technical Meeting,* San Diego, CA, January 28–30, 2002.

[9]   Seeber, G., *Satellite Geodesy,* Berlin, Germany: Walter de Gruyter, 1993.

[10] Hatch, R., "Relativity and GPS-I," *Galilean Electrodynamics,* Vol. 6, No. 3, May–June 1995, pp. 52–57.

[11] Ashby, N., and J. J. Spilker, Jr., "Introduction to Relativity Effects on the Global Positioning System," in *Global Positioning System: Theory and Applications,* Volume II, B. Parkinson and J. J. Spilker, Jr., (eds.), Washington, D.C.: American Institute of Aeronautics and Astronautics, 1996.

[12] Ashby, N., and M. Weiss, *Global Positioning System Receivers and Relativity,* National Institute of Standards and Technology (NIST) Technical Note 1385, Boulder, CO, March 1999.

[13] Hofmann-Wellenhof, B., H. Lichtenegger, and J. Collins, *GPS Theory and Practice,* New York: Springer-Verlag, 1993.

[14] Special Committee 159, "Minimum Operational Performance Standards for Global Positioning System/Wide Area Augmentation System Airborne Equipment," *Document DO-229C,* Washington, D.C.: RTCA, 2001.

[15] Jorgensen, P. S., "An Assessment of Ionospheric Effects on the User," *NAVIGATION: Journal of the Institute of Navigation,* Vol. 36, No. 2, Summer 1989.

[16] Uijt de Haag, M., and M. S. Braasch, *DGPS Signal Model, Vol. I, Reference: DGPS And Its Error Sources,* Athens: Ohio University/Delft University of Technology, 1994.

[17] *Global Positioning System Standard Positioning Service Performance Standard,* Washington, D.C.: U.S. Department of Defense, October 2001.

[18] Hopfield, H., "Two-Quartic Tropospheric Refractivity Profile for Correcting Satellite Data," *Journal of Geophysical Research,* Vol. 74, No. 18, 1969.

[19] Smith, E., Jr., and S. Weintraub, "The Constants in the Equation for Atmospheric Refractive Index at Radio Frequencies," *Proc. of Institute of Radio Engineers,* No. 41, 1953.

[20] Remondi, B., "Using the Global Positioning System (GPS) Phase Observable for Relative Geodesy: Modeling, Processing, and Results," Ph.D. Dissertation, Center for Space Research, University of Austin, Austin, TX, 1984.

[21] Goad, C., and L. Goodman, "A Modified Hopfield Tropospheric Refraction Correction Model," *Proc. of Fall Annual Meeting of the American Geophysical Union,* San Francisco, CA, 1974.

[22] Saastomoinen, J., "Atmospheric Correction for the Troposphere and Stratosphere in Radio Ranging of Satellites," *Use of Artificial Satellites for Geodesy,* Geophysical Monograph 15, American Geophysical Union, Washington, D.C., 1972.

[22] Collins, P., R. Langley, and J. LaMance, "Limiting Factors in Tropospheric Propagation Delay Error Modelling for GPS Airborne Navigation," *Proc. of The Institute of Navigation Annual Meeting,* Cambridge, MA, June 1996.

[23] Collins, J. P., *Assessment and Development of a Tropospheric Delay Model for Aircraft Users of the Global Positioning System,* M.Sc.E. thesis, Department of Geodesy and Geomatics Engineering, Technical Report No. 203, University of New Brunswick, Fredericton, Canada, 1999.

[24] Guo, J., and R. B. Langley, "A New Tropospheric Propagation Delay Mapping Function for Elevation Angles Down to 2°," *Proc. of The Institute of Navigation ION GPS/GNSS 2003,* Portland, OR, September 9–12, 2003.

[25] Niell, A. E., "Global Mapping Functions for the Atmosphere Delay at Radio Wavelengths," *Journal of Geophysical Research*, Vol. 101, No. B2, 1996, pp. 3227–3246.

[26] Marini, J. W., "Correction of Satellite Tracking Data for an Arbitrary Tropospheric Profile," *Radio Science*, Vol. 7, No. 2, 1972, pp. 223–231.

[27] Yinger, C., et al., "GPS Satellite Interfrequency Biases," *Proc. of The Institute of Navigation Annual Meeting*, Cambridge, MA, June 1999.

[28] Rivers, M., "The 2 SOPS User Range Accuracy (URA) Improvement and Broadcast Inter-Frequency Bias (TGD) Updates," *Proc. of The Institute of Navigation ION GPS 2000*, Salt Lake City, UT, September 2000.

[29] ARINC, *NAVSTAR GPS Space Segment/Navigation User Interfaces, Interface Specification, IS-GPS-705*, ARINC Engineering Services LLC, El Segundo, CA, December 2004.

[30] Johnson, G., and T. Zaugg, "Measuring Interchannel Bias in GPS Receiver," *Proc. of ION 57th Annual Meeting and the CIGTF 20th Biennial Guidance Test Symposium*, Albuquerque, NM, June 11–13, 2001.

[31] Hegarty, C., E. Powers, and B. Fonville, "Accounting for Timing Biases Between GPS, Modernized GPS, and Galileo Signals," *Proc. of 36th Annual Precise Time and Time Interval (PTTI) Meeting*, Washington, D.C., December 2004.

[32] Keith, J. P., "Multipath Errors Induced by Electronic Components in Receiver Hardware," M.S.E.E. thesis, Ohio University, Athens, OH, November 2002.

[33] Nelson, W., *Use of Circular Error Probability in Target Detection*, United States Air Force, ESD-TR-88-109, Hanscom Air Force Base, Bedford, MA, May 1988.

[34] van Graas, F., and A. Soloviev, "Precise Velocity Estimation Using a Stand-Alone GPS Receiver," *NAVIGATION: Journal of The Institute of Navigation*, Winter 2004–2005.

[35] Kouba, J., and P. Héroux, "GPS Precise Point Positioning Using IGS Orbit Products," *GPS Solutions*, Vol. 5, No. 2, Fall 2000, pp. 12–28.

[36] Moudrak, A., et al., "GPS Galileo Time Offset: How It Affects Positioning Accuracy and How to Cope with It," *Proc. of The Institute of Navigation ION GNSS 2004*, Long Beach, CA, September 2004.

[37] DOD/DOT, *2001 Federal Radionavigation Plan*, DOT-VNTSC-RSPA-01-3.1/DOD-4650.5, March 2002.

[38] RTCA, "Minimum Aviation System Performance Standards for the Local Area Augmentation System (LAAS)," Document No. RTCA/DO-245, Prepared by SC-159, September 28, 1998.

[39] Sotolongo, G. L., "Proposed Analysis Requirements for the Statistical Characterization of the Performance of the GPSSU RAIM Algorithm for Appendix A of the MOPS," RTCA 308-94/SC159-544, July 20, 1994.

[40] Shank, C., and J. Lavrakas, "GPS Integrity: An MCS Perspective," *Proc. of ION GPS-93, 6th International Technical Meeting of the Satellite Division of the Institute of Navigation*, Salt Lake City, UT, September 22–24, 1993, pp. 465–474.

[41] RTCA, "Aberration Characterization Sheet (ACS)," RTCA Paper No. 034-01/SC-159-867, July 1998.

[42] Van Dyke, K., et al., "GPS Integrity Failure Modes and Effects Analysis (IFMEA)," *Proc. of The Institute of Navigation National Technical Meeting*, Anaheim, CA, January 2003.

[43] Brown, R. G., "GPS RAIM: Calculation of Thresholds and Protection Radius Using Chi-Square Methods—A Geometric Approach," *Navigation* ION Red Book Series, Vol. 5, 1998.

[44] van Graas, F., and P. A. Kline, "Hybrid GPS/LORAN-C," Ohio University technical memorandum OU/AEC923TM00006/46+46A-1, Athens, OH, July 1992.

[45] RTCA, "Minimum Operational Performance Standards for Airborne Supplemental Navigation Equipment Using Global Positioning System (GPS)," Document No. RTCA/DO-208, SC-159, July 1991.

[46] RTCA SC-159, "Response to the JHU/APL Recommendation Regarding Receiver Autonomous Integrity Monitoring," July 19, 2002.

[47] Van Dyke, K. L., "Analysis of Worldwide RAIM Availability for Supplemental GPS Navigation," DOT-VNTSC-FA360-PM-93-4, May 1993.

[48] Brown, R. G., et al., "ARP Fault Detection and Isolation: Method and Results," DOT-VNTSC-FA460-PM-93-21, December 1993.

[49] Van Dyke, K. L., "RAIM Availability for Supplemental GPS Navigation," *NAVIGATION: Journal of The Institute of Navigation*, Vol. 39: No. 4, Winter 1992–1993, pp. 429–443.

[50] Van Dyke, K. L., "Fault Detection and Exclusion Performance Using GPS and GLONASS," *Proc. of the ION National Technical Meeting*, Anaheim, CA, January 18–20, 1995, pp. 241–250.

[51] Van Dyke, K. L., "World After SA: Improvements in RAIM/FDE Availability," *IEEE PLANS Symposium*, April 2000.

[52] National Satellite Test Bed/Wide Area Augmentation System Test and Evaluation (T&E) Team, "Global Positioning System (GPS) Standard Positioning Service (SPS) Performance Analysis Report," Federal Aviation Administration William J. Hughes Technical Center, Atlantic City International Airport, NJ, Quarterly Reports, 1999–2004, http://www.nstb.tc.faa.gov.

[53] Headquarters U.S. Air Force/XOS, "Assessment of Single-Frequency Model Error Contributions to GPS Performance," a presentation included in minutes from meetings of the U.S. DoD/DOT SPS Performance Standard Working Group, April 25, 2001.

CHAPTER 8

Differential GPS

Ronald J. Cosentino
Consultant

David W. Diggle and Maarten Uijt de Haag
Ohio University

Christopher J. Hegarty
The MITRE Corporation

Dennis Milbert
NOAA (retired)

Jim Nagle
ICAO

8.1 Introduction

As discussed in Chapter 7, a single-frequency SPS GPS user can often attain better than 10m, 95% positioning and 20-ns, 95% timing accuracy worldwide. There are many applications, however, that demand levels of accuracy, integrity, availability, and continuity beyond even what a GPS PPS receiver can deliver. For such applications, augmentation is required. There are two general classes of augmentation: differential GPS (DGPS) and external sensors/systems. This chapter introduces DGPS. Chapter 9 will discuss various external sensors/systems and their integration with GPS.

DGPS is a method to improve the positioning or timing performance of GPS using one or more reference stations at known locations, each equipped with at least one GPS receiver. The reference station(s) provides information to the end user via a data link that may include:

- Corrections to the raw end user's pseudorange measurements, corrections to GPS satellite-provided clock and ephemeris data, or data to replace the broadcast clock and ephemeris information;
- Raw reference station measurements (e.g., pseudorange and carrier phase);
- Integrity data (e.g., "use" or "don't use" indications for each visible satellite, or statistical indicators of the accuracy of provided corrections);
- Auxiliary data including the location, health, and meteorological data of the reference station(s).

Many types of data links may be used, such as radio links at frequencies ranging from low frequencies below 300 kHz to L-band (1,000–2,000 MHz) and beyond to the Internet, and importantly, the link may not be real time. For instance, it is possible to implement DGPS methods using two GPS receivers that each simply log data to a hard drive or other storage device.

DGPS techniques may be categorized in different ways: as *absolute* or *relative* differential positioning; as *local area*, *regional area*, or *wide area*; and as *code based* or *carrier based*.

Absolute differential positioning is the determination of the user's position with respect to an ECEF coordinate system (see Section 2.2.2). This is the most common goal of DGPS systems. For absolute differential positioning, each reference station's position must be accurately known with respect to the same ECEF coordinate system in which the user position is desired. Aircraft use this type of positioning as an aid for remaining within certain bounds of the desired flight path; ships use it as an aid for remaining within a harbor channel.

Relative differential positioning is the determination of the user's position with respect to a coordinate system attached to the reference station(s), whose absolute ECEF position(s) may not be perfectly known. For instance, if DGPS is implemented to land aircraft on an aircraft carrier, the ECEF positions of the reference stations may be imperfectly known and time varying. In this case, only the position of the plane with respect to the aircraft carrier is required.

DGPS systems may also be categorized in terms of the geographic area that is to be served. The simplest DGPS systems are designed to function only over a very small geographic area (i.e., with the user separated by less than 10–100 km from a single reference station). To effectively cover larger geographic regions, multiple reference stations and different algorithms are typically employed. The terms *regional area* and *wide area* are frequently used in the literature to describe DGPS systems covering larger geographic regions with regional-area systems generally covering areas up to around 1,000 km and wide-area systems covering yet larger regions. There are not, however, universally agreed-upon demarcations in terms of distance for the applicability of each term.

One final categorization of DGPS systems is between so-called code-based or carrier-based techniques. Code-based DGPS systems rely primarily on GPS code (i.e., pseudorange) measurements, whereas carrier-based DGPS systems ultimately rely primarily on carrier-phase measurements.[1] As discussed in Chapter 5, carrier-phase measurements are much more precise than pseudorange measurements, but they contain unknown integer wavelength components that must be resolved. Code-based differential systems can provide decimeter-level position accuracies, whereas state-of-the-art carrier-based systems can provide millimeter-level performance.

This chapter describes the underlying concepts of DGPS and details a number of operational and planned DGPS systems. Section 8.2 provides a discussion of the spatial and time correlation characteristics of GPS errors (i.e., how GPS errors vary from location to location and how they change over time). These characteristics are

---

1.   It should be noted that virtually all DGPS systems employ both pseudorange and carrier-phase measurements, so the distinction between code-based and carrier-based techniques is a matter of degree of reliance on the respective measurement type.

extremely important, since they directly influence the performance achievable for any type of DGPS system. The underlying algorithms and performance of code- and carrier-based DGPS systems are presented in Sections 8.3 and 8.4, respectively. Some important DGPS message standards are introduced in Section 8.5. The final section, Section 8.6, details a number of operational and planned DGPS systems.

8.2   Spatial and Time Correlation Characteristics of GPS Errors

Many of the GPS error sources discussed in Chapter 7 are highly correlated over space and time. All DGPS systems exploit these correlations to improve overall system performance. For instance, in a simple local-area DGPS system with a single reference station (see Figure 8.1), the errors in the reference station's pseudorange and carrier-phase measurements for visible satellites are expected to be very similar to those experienced by a nearby user. If the reference station estimates the errors by leveraging its known surveyed position and provides this information in the form of corrections to the user, it is expected that the user's position accuracy will be improved as a result. This section quantifies the correlation of GPS errors between receivers separated over some distance (often referred to as the *baseline*, which may be interpreted as a vector) and over time. Time correlations (i.e., how rapidly the errors change with time), are also of interest, because in general DGPS systems cannot instantaneously provide data to the end user—even with a high-speed radio link there is some finite delay associated with the generation, transmission, reception, and application of the data.

8.2.1   Satellite Clock Errors

Satellite clock errors are one of the simplest GPS errors to correct. This is because a satellite clock error causes the same effect on pseudorange and carrier-phase measurements, regardless of the location of the user. For instance, if the satellite clock

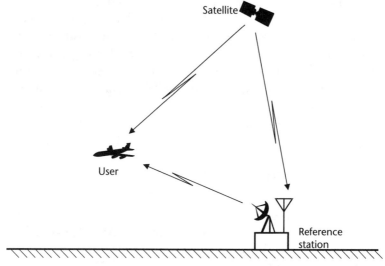

Figure 8.1   Local-area DGPS concept.

(after application of the broadcast navigation data corrections) is in error by 10 ns, it will result in a 3m pseudorange and carrier-phase measurement error for a user at any location.

Since SA was discontinued in May 2000, satellite clock errors have varied extremely slowly with time. Over short intervals (e.g., 1–60 seconds), a 1–2 mm/s rate of change is typical [1], corresponding to a satellite Allan deviation of around 3×10^{-12} to 6×10^{-12} s/s (see Appendix B for the definition of the Allan deviation). Before SA was discontinued, satellite clock rate of change was limited by a U.S. government commitment not to exceed 2 m/s in rate with a maximum acceleration of 19 mm/s^2 [2]. The extremely rapid changes of SA-induced clock errors had a very important influence on the operational DGPS systems that were developed prior to 2000. As will be discussed in more detail in Section 8.3, many DGPS systems provide estimates of first derivatives of pseudorange errors. This feature was driven mostly by SA. Residual pseudorange errors (in meters) after applying pseudorange rate corrections are on the order of $1/2\ at^2$, where a is the acceleration of the error (in m/s^2) and t is the latency of the correction (in seconds). For instance, with SA on (i.e., $a = 0.019$ m/s^2), pseudorange corrections had to be sent once per 10 seconds to keep range errors due to latency less than 1m. This observation directly influenced the DGPS data link requirements for many of the operating systems discussed in Section 8.6.

8.2.2 Ephemeris Errors

As discussed in Section 7.2.2, errors in the broadcast satellite positions lead to pseudorange and carrier-phase errors. Since the magnitude of ephemeris-induced pseudorange or carrier-phase errors are dependent on the LOS between the user and the satellite, these errors change with user location. However, the difference in pseudorange or carrier-phase errors as seen by receivers in close proximity is very small, since their respective LOSs to each satellite are very similar. To quantify the amount of change, let the separation between a user U and reference station M be denoted as p (see Figure 8.2). We will refer to the actual orbital satellite position as the true position. The error in the estimated satellite position (i.e., the broadcast ephemeris) is represented as ε_S. Let d_m and d'_m be the true and estimated distances, respectively, of the reference station to the satellite, and let d_u and d'_u be the corresponding distances of the user to the satellite. Let ϕ_m be the angle formed by the directions of the reference station to the user and to the actual satellite position. Let α be the angle formed by the directions of the reference station to the actual and estimated positions of the satellite, S and S', respectively. The law of cosines gives us the following two relationships:

$$d_u'^2 = d_m'^2 + p^2 - 2pd_m \cos(\phi_m - \alpha')$$
$$d_u^2 = d_m^2 + p^2 - 2pd_m \cos\phi_m$$

where α' is the difference $\phi_m - \phi'_m$ in elevation angles between the actual and estimated satellite positions from the monitor station. (The absolute value of α' is less than or equal to the absolute value of α, and the two are equal when the two triangles lie in the same plane.)

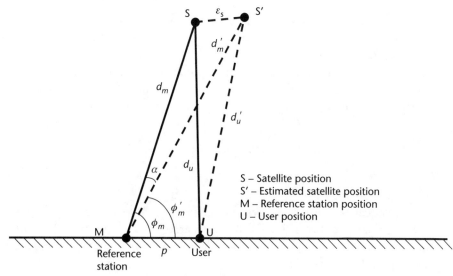

Figure 8.2 Variation of broadcast ephemeris errors with viewing angle.

Solving the first equation for $d'_m - d'_u$ and the second for $d_u - d_m$, and neglecting the higher order terms in the binomial expansion of the square root in each of these equations, we obtain

$$d'_m - d'_u \approx -\frac{1}{2} \cdot \left(\frac{p}{d'_m}\right) \cdot p + p \cdot \cos \phi_m + \alpha' \cdot p \cdot \sin \phi_m + \frac{1}{2} \cdot \alpha'^2 \cdot p \cdot \cos \phi_m$$

$$d_u - d_m \approx +\frac{1}{2} \cdot \left(\frac{p}{d'_m}\right) \cdot p - p \cdot \cos \phi_m$$

Adding these two equations, we find that the difference between the errors, $\varepsilon_u = d'_u - d_u$ and $\varepsilon_m = d'_m - d_m$, is

$$\varepsilon_m - \varepsilon_u = \left(d'_u - d'_m\right) + \left(d_m - d_u\right) = \alpha' \cdot p \cdot \sin \phi_m + \frac{1}{2} \cdot \alpha'^2 \cdot p \cdot \cos \phi_m$$

or

$$\left|\varepsilon_m - \varepsilon_u\right| = \left|\left(d'_u - d'_m\right) + \left(d_m - d_u\right)\right| \leq \alpha \cdot p \cdot \sin \phi_m + \frac{1}{2} \cdot \alpha^2 \cdot p \cdot \cos \phi_m$$

where the equality holds if the estimated satellite position lies in the plane defined by the user position, reference station position, and true satellite position.

The difference $\varepsilon_m - \varepsilon_u$ is the error introduced by the pseudorange correction at the user. To simplify the expression, assume that the angle ϕ_m is greater than 5°, that the separation between the user and reference station is less than 1,000 km, and that the direction $\overline{SS'}$ is parallel to the direction $\overline{MU}$. Then

$$\varepsilon_m - \varepsilon_u \leq \alpha \cdot p \cdot \sin \phi_m \approx \left(\frac{\varepsilon_S \cdot \sin \phi_m}{d_m}\right) \cdot p \cdot \sin \phi_m = \left(\frac{\varepsilon_S}{d_m}\right) \cdot p \cdot \sin^2 \phi_m \qquad (8.1)$$

where ε_s is the error in the satellite's estimated position.

Equation (8.1) implies that the error increases directly with the separation between the reference station measuring the error and the user receiver employing the correction. Suppose, for example, that the error in the satellite's estimated position is 5m and suppose the user is 100 km from the reference station. Then the error in the correction due to that separation is less than

$$\left(\frac{5\,\text{m}}{2\times10^4\,\text{km}}\right)\times100\ \text{km} = 2.5\,\text{cm}$$

for elevation angles > 5°.

Broadcast ephemeris errors change very slowly over time, with typical growth rates of the three-dimensional ephemeris error of 2–6 cm/min [1]. Error growth has been observed to be approximately linearly proportional to elapsed time for intervals up to 30 minutes [1].

8.2.3 Tropospheric Errors

As discussed in Section 7.2.4.2, the speed of electromagnetic radiation varies, depending on temperature, pressure, and relative humidity, as it passes through the troposphere. Considerations of the physics behind tropospheric delays are provided in Section 7. 2.4.2. In this section, we obtain an estimate of the kind of delay difference we can expect from the signal traveling through the troposphere and choose a model described in [3], which expresses the tropospheric delay of a signal from a GPS satellite to a user at the Earth's surface, as follows:

$$\varepsilon_u^{Tropo} = \csc\phi\cdot(1.4588+0.0029611\cdot N_s)$$
$$-0.3048\cdot\left[0.00586\cdot(N_s-360)^2+294\right]\cdot\phi^{-2.30}$$
(8.2)

where:

ε_u^{Tropo} = tropospheric delay experienced by the user in meters,

ϕ = elevation angle from the user to the satellite in degrees

N_s = surface refractivity

If we denote the elevation angle of the satellite from the reference station by ϕ_m, then from Figure 8.3 we can determine the difference $\csc\phi-\csc\phi_m$ in terms of the horizontal distance p between the user and reference station and the height d_s of the satellite, as follows:

$$|\csc\phi-\csc\phi_m| = \left|\frac{d_u}{d_s}-\frac{d_m}{d_s}\right| = \left|\frac{d_u-d_m}{d_s}\right| \le p\cdot\frac{\cos\phi_m}{d_s}$$

where d_m is the distance from the monitoring station to the satellite and d_u is the distance from the user receiver to the satellite. (The inequality sign may be dropped if

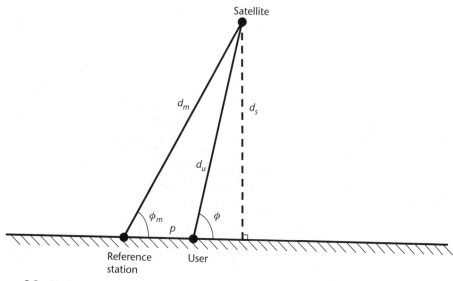

Figure 8.3 Horizontal tropospheric delay difference.

the triangle lies in a vertical plane.) This yields the following equation for the delay difference where, for the moment, we hold N_s constant:

$$\left|\varepsilon_u^{Tropo} - \varepsilon_m^{Tropo}\right| \le p \cdot \frac{\csc\phi_m}{d_s} \cdot \left(1.4588 + 0.0029611 \cdot N_s\right)$$
$$-0.3048 \cdot \left[0.00586 \cdot \left(N_s - 360\right)^2 + 294\right] \cdot \left(\phi^{-2.30} - \phi_m^{-2.30}\right)$$

(8.3)

The second term of the right-hand side of (8.3) was added to fit data at low elevation angles—about 10° or less—and is negligible for higher GPS elevation angles (i.e., greater than 10°). For higher elevation angles, the difference in tropospheric delay error is proportional to the separation between the user and reference station.

Suppose, for example, that the elevation angle is 45° and $p = 100$ km. Then, if we use a midrange value for N_s of 360, we find from the model that the deviation of the tropospheric correction at the user position differs from that at the reference station position by an amount

$$\left|\varepsilon_u^{Tropo} - \varepsilon_m^{Tropo}\right| \le p \cdot \frac{\csc\phi_m}{d_s} \cdot \left(1.4588 + 0.0029611 \cdot N_S\right)$$

$$= \left(100 \text{ km}\right) \cdot \frac{\csc 45°}{2 \times 10^4 \text{ km}} \times \left(1.4588 + 0.0029611 \times 360\right)$$

$$\approx 0.02 \text{m}$$

Thus, the error is on the order of 2 cm. The variation of the deviation as a function of separation due to elevation angle differences is shown in Figure 8.4. Note that over the entire 100-km separation, the variation of delay difference due to variation in the surface refractivity is less than 1.5 mm for this tropospheric model, an order of magnitude smaller than that due to a variation in elevation angle from 10° to 90°. Thus, allowing N_s to vary in the derivation of (8.3) would have produced a

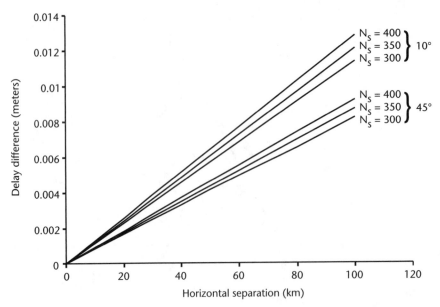

Figure 8.4 Variation in tropospheric delay difference due to elevation angle.

small, negligible additional term in (8.3). However, the total delay difference is also small. Even for extreme values of refractivity (400) and low angles (10°), the differences in delays are not much more than 2 cm.

Real-world data suggests that tropospheric delays vary more rapidly with distance than can be attributed solely to differences in viewing angle. Much larger differences in tropospheric delay from location to location arise in reality because the troposphere often differs significantly from the model, especially at an interface between land and water or where the user and reference station are separated by a weather front. In a study described in [4], differences in tropospheric delays as large as 40 cm were observed over a 25-km baseline for satellites above 5°. This suggests a vertical tropospheric delay difference on the order of 4 cm over this baseline—leading to much larger slant differences than could be attributed to differences in viewing angle alone. The smallest difference in tropospheric error observed in [4] over a 25-km baseline was 10 cm.

A difference in heights between the user receiver and the reference station has a greater effect than a horizontal displacement. Reference [3] develops the following relationship between the tropospheric delay, ε_m^{Tropo} meters, experienced by the reference station and delay, ε_h^{Tropo} meters, experienced by a user at a height h kilometers above the station (Figure 8.5):

$$\varepsilon_h^{Tropo} = \varepsilon_m^{Tropo} \cdot e^{-\left[(0.0002\,N_S + 0.07)\cdot h + \left(\frac{0.83}{N_S} - 0.0017\right)\cdot h^2\right]}$$

At an altitude of 1 km above the reference station, the user experiences a delay of

$$\varepsilon_h^{Tropo} = \varepsilon_m^{Tropo} \cdot e^{-\left[(0.0002 \times 360 + 0.07)\cdot 1 + \left(\frac{0.83}{360} - 0.0017\right)\cdot 1^2\right]}$$

$$= 0.45 \times \varepsilon_m^{Tropo} = 0.45 \times 3.6\text{m} = 1.6\text{m}$$

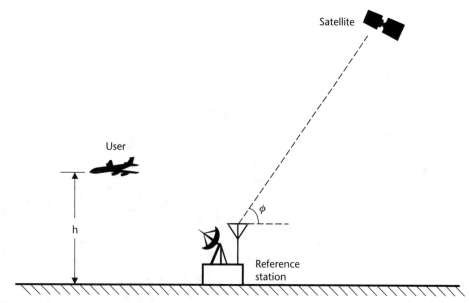

Figure 8.5   Vertical tropospheric delay difference.

and the difference in delays is

$$\varepsilon_{h}^{Tropo} - \varepsilon_{m}^{Tropo} = 3.6m - 1.6m = 2m$$

That is, assuming $N_s = 360$ and that the elevation angle is 45°, the delay at a height of 1 km is only 45% of the 3.6-m delay, calculated from (8.2) at the reference station, or 1.6m. The difference is 2m.

The variation in the difference in tropospheric delays between a signal reaching the ground having a refractivity of N_s and the signal at an altitude h above the ground is shown in Figure 8.6 for two different elevation angles of the satellite.

Although vertical tropospheric delays do not change very rapidly with time for a stationary receiver, slant tropospheric delays can change due to the rate of change of elevation angle. For stationary users, the elevation angle to a GPS satellite can vary at a rate up to 0.5°/min due just to the motion of the satellite. For a satellite at 5°, this can lead to tropospheric delay changing at a rate of up to 2 m/min. For satellites above 10°, the maximum rate of change is around 0.64 m/min. A receiver on a moving platform that is rapidly changing altitude can experience an even higher rate of change in tropospheric error due to the altitude dependence discussed earlier.

8.2.4   Ionospheric Errors

As given in Section 7.2.4.1, we have the following relationship between the delay, ε^{Iono}, expressed in units of length, due to the ionosphere, the frequency, f, of the signal, the elevation angle, ϕ', at the ionospheric pierce point, and the total electron content, TEC, along the path of the signal:

$$\varepsilon^{Iono} = \frac{1}{\sin\phi'} \cdot \frac{40.3}{f^2} \cdot TEC$$

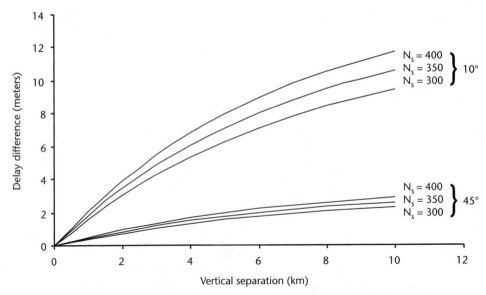

Figure 8.6   Variation in the vertical delay difference with refractivity and elevation angle.

The sin ϕ' term accounts for the additional path length in the ionosphere when the direction of the satellite is off the vertical. The *ionospheric pierce point* is that point on the displacement vector from the user position to the satellite position midway through the ionosphere, typically taken to be 300 km to 400 km in altitude [5] (see Figure 8.7).

The difference in delay due to the difference in elevation angles for a horizontal separation of user and reference station is

$$\left| \varepsilon_u^{Iono} - \varepsilon_m^{Iono} \right| = \frac{1}{\sin \phi'} \cdot \frac{40.3}{f^2} \cdot TEC - \frac{1}{\sin \phi'_m} \cdot \frac{40.3}{f^2} \cdot TEC$$

$$= \left| \frac{1}{\sin \phi'} - \frac{1}{\sin \phi'_m} \right| \cdot \frac{40.3}{f^2} \cdot TEC \qquad (8.4)$$

$$\frac{p}{d_m} \cdot \left| \frac{p}{d_m} - \cos \phi'_m \right| \cdot \frac{40.3}{f^2} \cdot TEC$$

where:

  p = distance between the user and the reference station

  ϕ_m = elevation angle of the satellite from the reference station

  ϕ'_m = elevation angle at the reference station's ionospheric pierce point

The *TEC* usually lies in the range 10^{16} to 10^{18} electrons/m^2, with 50×10^{16} electrons/m^2 typical in the temperate zones, so that the difference in delays experienced by the reference station and the user 100 km away due to the difference in elevation angle is typically

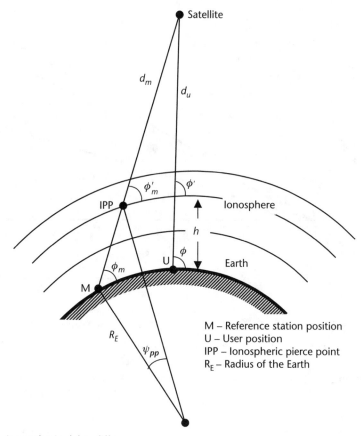

Figure 8.7   Ionospheric delay difference.

$$\left| \varepsilon_u^{Iono} - \varepsilon_m^{Iono} \right| = \left| \frac{p}{d_m} \cdot \left(\frac{p}{d_m} - \cos \phi'_m \right) \cdot \frac{40.3}{f^2} \cdot TEC \right|$$

$$\approx \left| -\frac{100 \text{ km}}{2 \times 10^4 \text{ km}} \cdot \cos 45° \cdot \frac{40.3}{\left(1.575 \times 10^9 \right)^2} \cdot 50 \times 10^{16} \right|$$

$$= 0.03 \text{m}$$

The variation of the ionospheric delay difference due to differences in elevation angle as a function of separation is shown in Figure 8.8 for three values of satellite elevation angle and a TEC of 50×10^{16} electrons/m^2.

Spatial variations in TEC within the ionosphere typically lead to much greater differences in ionospheric delay than those attributable to elevation angle. The difference in vertical ionospheric delays (i.e., delays observed for a satellite that is directly overhead) due to TEC gradients is typically in the range of 0.2–0.5m over 100 km when the ionosphere is undisturbed, but it can be greater than 4m over 100 km when the ionosphere is disturbed [6, 7]. Slant range delays during daylight hours were evaluated in [8] for a network of GPS receivers over a 1-year time frame. The conclusions from [8] were that the difference in ionospheric delays seen by two receivers separated by 400 km in a midlatitude region is expected to be less than 2m

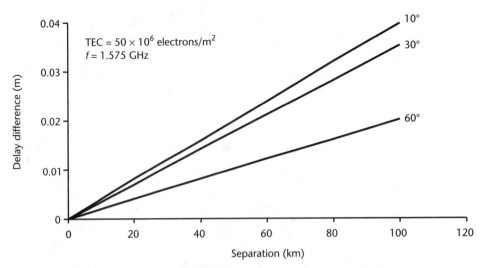

Figure 8.8 Variation of ionospheric delay difference due to elevation angle differences.

in magnitude 95% of the time, even during the peak of the 11-year solar cycle. Various physical phenomena, including *traveling ionospheric disturbances* (TIDs), which are small-scale irregularities in the ionosphere, can cause steep spatial gradients in TEC over distances as short as 10 km.

Ionospheric delays typically change very slowly with time, normally following a daily cycle of very low values at local nighttime, followed by a ramping up to a maximal delay in the early local afternoon, and then a decline back to the steady night value again. In midlatitude regions, the time rate of change of vertical ionospheric delays rarely exceeds 8 cm/min [9]. In other regions of the world, rates of up to 65 cm/min have been observed [9]. Some recent studies have indicated that rates of over 3 m/min may occur on rare occasions. These observed rates include both the effect of changing elevation angles and TEC.

8.2.5 Receiver Noise and Multipath

Unlike the other error sources considered thus far, receiver noise and multipath result in pseudorange and carrier-phase errors that are uncorrelated between receivers separated by even very short baselines. Multipath, in particular, often dominates error budgets for short-baseline code- and carrier-based DGPS systems for two reasons. First, it causes pseudorange and carrier-phase errors that are generally statistically larger than those caused by receiver noise. Second, the fact that multipath errors are uncorrelated from receiver to receiver means that the difference in measurement error caused by multipath between two receivers has a variance described as the sum of the multipath error variance attributable to each alone. As discussed in Section 6.3, the magnitude of multipath errors varies significantly depending on the type of receiver and environment. In this section, we will assume a 1-sigma pseudorange multipath error of 0.2m for each receiver, which is consistent with the performance of a high-end C/A code receiver in a relatively benign multipath environment.

Both receiver noise and multipath errors can change very rapidly. Since these errors are not common between the user and reference station in a DGPS scenario, the rates of change of these errors are only important in that averaging of some form within the user equipment can often be employed to reduce their consequence.

8.3 Code-Based Techniques

Many code-based DGPS techniques have been proposed to provide improvements in performance over stand-alone GPS. These techniques vary in sophistication and complexity from a single reference station that calculates the errors at its position for use with nearby GPS receivers to worldwide networks that provide data for estimating errors from detailed error models at any position near the Earth's surface. As discussed in Section 8.1, they may be sorted into three categories, local-area, regional area, and wide area, depending on the geographic area that they are intended to serve. This section discusses code-based techniques for each of these categories.

8.3.1 Local-Area DGPS

A local-area DGPS (LADGPS) system improves on the accuracy of stand-alone GPS by estimating errors corrupting the stand-alone GPS position solution and transmitting these estimates to nearby users.

8.3.1.1 Position Domain Corrections

Conceptually, the simplest way to implement LADGPS is to place a single GPS reference receiver at a surveyed location, compute the coordinate differences (in latitude, longitude, and geodetic height) between that surveyed position and the position estimate derived from GPS measurements, and transmit these latitude, longitude, and height differences to nearby users. For the most part, the coordinate differences represent the common errors in the reference and user receiver GPS position solutions at the measurement time. The user receivers can use these coordinate differences to correct their own GPS position solutions.

Although extremely simple, this technique has a number of significant deficiencies. First, it requires that all receivers make pseudorange measurements to the same set of satellites to ensure that common errors are experienced. Therefore, the user receivers must coordinate their choice of satellites with the reference station; or the reference station may determine and transmit position corrections for all combinations of visible satellites. When eight or more satellites are visible, the number of combinations becomes impractically large (80 or more combinations of four satellites). A second problem may also arise if the user and reference station receivers employ different position solution techniques. Unless both receivers employ the same technique, (e.g., least-squares, WLS, or Kalman filters), with equivalent smoothing time constants, filter tunings, and so forth, position domain corrections may yield erratic results. For these reasons, position domain corrections are seldom, if ever, employed in operational DGPS systems.

8.3.1.2   Pseudorange Domain Corrections

In most operational LADGPS systems, instead of determining position coordinate errors, the reference station determines and disseminates pseudorange corrections for each visible satellite. The process is explained in the following mathematical treatment.

In order for the user receiver to determine its position accurately with respect to the Earth (i.e., for absolute DGPS applications), the reference station must have accurate knowledge of its own position in ECEF coordinates. Given that the reported position of the ith satellite is (x_i, y_i, z_i) and the position of the reference station is known through a survey to be at position (x_m, y_m, z_m), the computed geometric distance, R_m^i, from the reference station to the satellite is

$$R_m^i \sqrt{\left(x_i - x_m\right)^2 + \left(y_i - y_m\right)^2 + \left(z_i - z_m\right)^2}$$

The reference station then makes a pseudorange measurement, ρ_m^i, to the ith satellite. This measurement contains the range to the satellite, along with the errors discussed in Chapter 7 and Section 8.2:

$$\rho_m^i = R_m^i + c\delta t_m + \varepsilon_m \tag{8.5}$$

where ε_m are the pseudorange errors and $c\delta t_m$ represents the reference station clock offset from GPS time.

The reference station differences the computed geometric range, R_m^i, with the pseudorange measurement to form the differential correction

$$\Delta\rho_m^i = R_m^i - \rho_m^i = -c\delta t_m - \varepsilon_m$$

This correction, which may be a positive or negative quantity, is broadcast to the user receiver, where it is added to the user receiver's pseudorange measurement to the same satellite

$$\rho_u^i + \Delta\rho_m^i = R_u^i + c\delta t_u + \varepsilon_u$$
$$+ \left(-c\delta t_m - \varepsilon_m\right)$$

To a significant extent, the user receiver's pseudorange error components will be common to those experienced by the reference station with the exception of multipath and receiver noise. The corrected pseudorange can be expressed as

$$\rho_{u,cor}^i = R_u^i + \varepsilon_{um} + c\delta t_m \tag{8.6}$$

where $\varepsilon_{um} = \varepsilon_u - \varepsilon_m$ represents residual pseudorange errors and δt_{um} is the difference in user and reference station clock offsets, $\delta t_u - \delta t_m$.

In Cartesian coordinates (8.6) becomes

$$\rho_{u,cor}^i = \sqrt{\left(x_i - x_u\right)^2 + \left(y_i - y_u\right)^2 + \left(z_i - z_u\right)^2} + \varepsilon_{um} + c\delta t_{um} \tag{8.7}$$

By making pseudorange measurements to four or more satellites, the user receiver can compute its position by using one of the position determination techniques discussed in Chapter 2. Since the residual pseudorange error, ε_{um}, is generally smaller statistically than the error of the uncorrected pseudorange, a more accurate position solution is generally attained. Importantly, when pseudorange corrections are applied, the clock offset produced by the position solution is the difference between the user's clock error and the reference station clock error. For applications where the user requires accurate time, the reference station clock offset may be estimated using the standard position solution technique and removed from the pseudorange corrections. Removal of the reference station clock offset is generally desirable, even when the user does not require accurate time, since a large reference station clock bias could result in excessively large pseudorange corrections (e.g., to fit within a fixed-size data field in a digital message).

Because pseudorange errors vary with time, as discussed in Section 8.2, the transmitted pseudorange correction,

$$\Delta\rho^i_m(t_m) = \left[R^i_m(t_m) - \rho^i_m(t_m) \right]$$

which is an estimate of the pseudorange error with the sign inverted, is most accurate at the instant of time t_m, for which the correction was calculated. To enable the user receiver to compensate for pseudorange error rate, the station may also transmit a pseudorange rate correction, $\Delta\dot{\rho}^i_m(t_m)$. The user receiver then adjusts the pseudorange correction to correspond to the time of its own pseudorange measurement, t, as follows:

$$\Delta\rho^i_m(t) = \Delta\rho^i_m(t_m) + \Delta\dot{\rho}^i_m(t_m)(t - t_m)$$

The corrected user receiver pseudorange, $\rho^i_{cor}(t)$, for time t is then calculated from

$$\rho^i_{u,corr}(t) = \rho^i(t) + \Delta\rho^i_m(t)$$

8.3.1.3 Performance of Code-Based LADGPS

Using the information presented in Section 8.2 on the spatial and time correlation characteristics of GPS errors, Table 8.1 presents an error budget for a LADGPS system in which the reference station and the user rely only on the GPS SPS (i.e., L1 C/A code only). The values in the table assume that latency errors are negligible (e.g., that the pseudorange corrections are transmitted over a high-speed data link). It is also assumed that the reference station and user are either at the same altitude or that a tropospheric height difference correction is employed. Note that multipath is the dominant error component over short baselines. For longer baselines, the residual ionospheric or tropospheric errors may dominate. Over very long baselines, performance may be improved by applying a local tropospheric error model at both the reference station and user locations, rather than the conventional short-baseline design in which neither side applies a model.

Table 8.1 Pseudorange Error Budget for GPS SPS With and Without LADGPS Corrections

Segment Source	Error Source	1σ Error (m)	
		GPS Only	with LADGPS
Space/control	Broadcast clock	1.1	0.0
	L1 P(Y)-L1 C/A group delay	0.3	0.0
	Broadcast ephemeris	0.8	0.1–0.6 mm/km × baseline in km
User	Ionospheric delay	7.0	0.2–4 cm/km × baseline in km
	Tropospheric delay	0.2	1–4 cm/km × baseline in km
	Receiver noise and resolution	0.1	0.1
	Multipath	0.2	0.3
System UERE	Total (RSS)	7.1	0.3m + 1–6 cm/km × baseline in km

8.3.2 Regional-Area DGPS

To extend the region over which LADGPS corrections can be used without the decorrelation of errors that accompanies the separation of the user from the station, three or more reference stations may be distributed along the perimeter of the region of coverage in a concept referred to as regional-area DGPS. The user receiver can then obtain a more accurate position solution by employing a weighted average of pseudorange corrections from the stations. Because the error in the broadcast corrections grows with distance from each station, the weights may be determined by geometric considerations alone to give the largest weight to the closest station, such as by choosing those weights that describe the user position as the weighted sum of the station positions [10]. For example, with three stations at locations denoted by latitude ϕ and longitude λ, the three weights, w_1, w_2, and w_3, of stations $M_1(\phi_1, \lambda_1)$, $M_2(\phi_2, \lambda_2)$, and $M_3(\phi_3, \lambda_3)$ for user $U(\phi, \lambda)$ may be determined by the following set of three equations (Figure 8.9):

$$\phi = w_1\phi_1 + w_2\phi_2 + w_3\phi_3$$
$$\lambda = w_1\lambda_1 + w_2\lambda_2 + w_3\lambda_3$$
$$(w_1 + w_2 + w_3) = 1$$

A two-step approach to using multiple monitoring stations to improve the accuracy of the user's position estimate is described in [10]. In the first step, the pseudorange corrections from each monitor are used to determine the position of the user individually. The second step entails computing a weighted average of the individual position estimates to provide a more accurate estimate. Each weight is formed from the inverse of the product of the distance of the monitor from the user and the standard deviation from the average of the estimates from that station, normalized by the sum of the weights. The error introduced by each monitor receiver is thus diluted by its weight, so that if, for example, the weights were all equal, then each monitor receiver error would be diluted by a factor of $1/n$. But since the errors are uncorrelated, the standard deviation of their sum is $1/\sqrt{n}$; thus, the standard

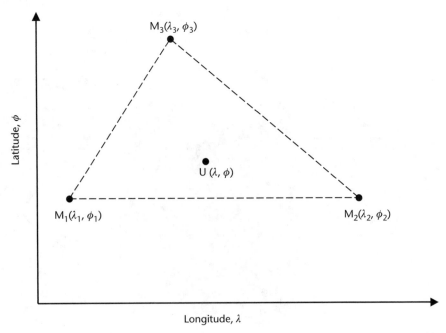

Figure 8.9 Calculating the correction weights.

deviation of the total error due to the monitors is decreased by a factor of $\sqrt{n}$ from that of one monitor.

8.3.3   Wide-Area DGPS

Wide-area DGPS (WADGPS) attempts to attain meter-level accuracy over a large region while using a fraction of the number of reference stations that LADGPS would require to attain the same accuracy within the same coverage region. The general approach (e.g., see [11–13])—in contrast to that of LADGPS—is to break out the total pseudorange error into its components and to estimate the variation of each component over the entire region, rather than just at the station positions. The accuracy, then, does not depend on the proximity of the user to a single reference station.

The WADGPS concept, illustrated in Figure 8.10, includes a network of reference stations, one or more central processing sites, and a data link to provide corrections to users. Each reference station includes one or more GPS receivers that measure pseudorange and carrier phase for the broadcast signals from all visible satellites. This data is provided to the central processing site(s), which process the raw data to develop estimates of the broadcast ephemeris and broadcast clock errors for each satellite. Single-frequency WADGPS systems also estimate ionospheric errors throughout the service volume. Tropospheric delays are typically addressed through the use of models employed by the reference stations and by the user.

8.3.3.1   Satellite Ephemeris and Clock Errors

Using pseudorange and carrier-phase data from the entire network of reference stations, each central processing site can develop precise estimates of the true locations

Figure 8.10   WADGPS concept.

and clock errors of the GPS satellites that are visible to the network. For each satellite, the three-dimensional position error (e.g., in an ECEF coordinate system) between the WADGPS position estimate and the broadcast position is provided to the user. The user then maps this satellite position correction into a pseudorange correction by projecting the position error onto the LOS direction to the satellite. A separate clock correction is also broadcast to the user that can be directly applied as an additional pseudorange correction.

The central processing site can estimate the true GPS satellite positions and clocks by reversing the basic GPS algorithm. Here four or more widely separated ground stations whose positions are accurately known each calculate the pseudorange to a given satellite, after estimating and removing the atmospheric delays [11, 12]. Synchronization of the reference station clocks is required, which may be accomplished using GPS. In practice, extremely accurate position and clock estimates can be achieved by combining the concept of a reverse-GPS solution with sophisticated models to describe the motion of the GPS satellites over time. Such modeling is a standard method used for orbit determination for many satellite systems. An excellent introduction to the methods of satellite orbit determination may be found in [14].

8.3.3.2 Determining Ionospheric Propagation Delays

Ionospheric delays can be addressed in various ways within a WADGPS system. The simplest approach is for the user to directly measure ionospheric delays using a dual-frequency receiver. This option is currently available to authorized PPS users or to civilian users using semicodeless methods (see Section 5.14) to track the L2 P(Y) code. Because of the fragility of semicodeless L2 P(Y) code tracking, some important operational WADGPS systems discussed in Section 8.6 are designed to support users with single-frequency L1 C/A code receivers. These systems estimate ionospheric delays throughout their service volumes using dual-frequency semicodeless receivers in their reference stations. The slant ionospheric delays measured by the reference stations are used by the central processing site, along with models of the ionosphere, to develop estimates of vertical ionospheric delays for discrete latitude/longitude points across the coverage volume. These vertical delay estimates are broadcast to the user. The user equipment then interpolates among these points to develop a vertical ionospheric delay correction for each visible GPS signal. The vertical delay correction is mapped into an appropriate slant delay correction based on the elevation angle for each visible satellite. The vertical delay corrections for the visible satellites are generally not the same, since the points of intersection between the signal paths and the ionosphere are not collocated.

8.4 Carrier-Based Techniques

The constant motion of the GPS satellite constellation requires that the GPS receiver, in general, be capable of accounting for the changing Doppler frequency shift on L1. Where dual-frequency receivers are used, both L1 and L2 are tracked. The shift in frequency arises due to the relative motion between the satellites and the receiver(s). Typical satellite motion with respect to an Earth-fixed observer can result in a maximum range of Doppler frequencies of ±4,000 Hz with respect to the L1 and L2 carriers. Integration of the Doppler frequency offset results in an extremely accurate measurement of the advance in signal carrier phase between time epochs (see Section 5.7.3). Interferometric techniques can take advantage of these precise phase measurements and, assuming sources of error can be mitigated, real-time positional accuracies in the centimeter range are achievable. While changes in signal phase from epoch to epoch can be measured with extreme accuracy, the number of whole carrier cycles along the propagation path from satellite to receiver remains ambiguous. Determining the number of whole carrier cycles in the propagation path is known as *carrier-cycle integer ambiguity resolution* and remains an active area of investigation in the field of kinematic DGPS research. Remondi [15] has made extensive use of the *ambiguity function* for resolving these unknown integer wavelength multiples, but the pioneering work in this area arose from the efforts of Counselman and Gourevitch [16] and Greenspan et al. [17]. As a rule, the ambiguity function approach is successful for postprocessing applications arising in land surveying, where one has the luxury of time. More recently, for applications where the user is moving with respect to the fixed reference station and real-time positioning is required (i.e., a kinematic environment), rapid resolution of carrier-cycle integer ambiguities is highly desirable and an absolute must if centimeter-level accuracies are to be achieved. The ambiguity function technique is thus no longer used in most current systems.

Advantage can be taken by combining the L1 and L2 frequencies to speed the ambiguity resolution process, and this approach has been the subject of a number of articles in the literature (e.g., Hatch [18]). After the P code was encrypted (becoming the Y code) by the DOD, a number of receiver manufacturers were successful in recovering the full carrier phase and pseudorange Y code observables. This has allowed the continued use of the dual-frequency property of the GPS signal structure. These dual-frequency receiver measurements can be combined to produce the sum and difference of the L1 and L2 frequencies. The result is sum and difference wavelengths of 10.7 cm and 86.25 cm, respectively. Using the difference wavelength (known as the wide lane) makes the integer ambiguity search more efficient. A change of one wide-lane wavelength results in virtually a fourfold increase in distance over that of one wavelength at either the L1 and L2 frequencies alone. Obviously, the search for the proper combination of integer ambiguities progresses more quickly using wide-lane observables, but the requirements on the receiver for simultaneous dual-frequency tracking—here, the P(Y) code is generally used—are more stringent. In particular, the noise factor for the wide-lane processing goes up by a factor of nearly six [19]. These matters aside, wide-lane techniques offer great advantage for obtaining rapid, *on-the-fly*, integer ambiguity resolution, and the methodology will be presented later in this chapter.

8.4.1 Precise Baseline Determination in Real Time

Determination of the carrier-cycle ambiguities on the fly is key to any application where precise positioning at the centimeter level, in real time, is required. Such techniques have been successfully applied to aircraft precision approach and automatic landing for approach baselines extending to 50 km in some instances [20–23]. They are equally applicable, however, to land-based or land-sea applications (e.g., precise desert navigation or off-shore oil exploration). In contrast, land-surveying applications and the like, often involving long baselines, have had the luxury of the postprocessing environment and, as a result, accuracies at the millimeter level are commonplace today. Techniques applied in such instances involve resolution of carrier cycle ambiguities on the data sets collected over long periods of time (generally an hour or more). In addition, postprocessing of the data lends itself to recognition and repair of receiver cycle slips. Precision can be further enhanced by use of precise satellite ephemerides. These topics, while of interest, are beyond the scope of this book. Texts such as [24] ably cover these applications.

The following discussion focuses on an integer ambiguity resolution technique first proposed in [25], which capitalizes on some concepts from [26] to resolve the inconsistencies between redundant measurements. The latter work maintains that "all information about the 'inconsistencies' resides in a set of linear relationships known as *parity equations*." While these techniques were originally applied to inertial systems and their associated instruments (e.g., accelerometers and gyros), there is similar applicability to GPS measurement inconsistencies that manifest themselves, in this instance, in the integer wavelength ambiguities inherent in the carrier-phase observables. In [27], it has been shown that a similar approach using a technique that minimizes least square residuals has application to the rapid resolution of the ambiguities, albeit in a static, nonkinematic environment. This reference also suggests the use of the wide-lane measurements to reduce computational overhead, thus speeding up the ambiguity-resolution process.

8.4.1.1   Combining Receiver Measurements

As mentioned in Chapter 3, two distinct measurements are provided by a GPS SPS receiver: the L1 C/A code pseudorange measurement, also referred to as the code measurement, and the L1 carrier-phase measurement. Code and carrier-phase measurements are available from each satellite vehicle tracked by the receiver. Dual-frequency GPS receivers, which are capable of recovering the P(Y) code observables, provide such measurements for both the L1 and L2 frequencies, as well as the C/A code observables. Unfortunately, these measurements are subject to some detrimental effects. Inherent in the GPS signal is a variety of errors—errors due to signal propagation through the ionosphere and troposphere, satellite ephemeris errors and clock errors, and of course noise. GPS receivers have their own set of problems—clock instability, signal multipath, and also noise. Fortunately, the term DGPS implies that we have similar sets of measurements from at least two GPS receivers separated by some fixed distance called a baseline. By forming linear combinations (differences) of like measurements from two receivers, it becomes possible to eliminate errors that are common to both receivers. Such a combination is referred to as a *single difference* (SD). By differencing two SD measurements from the same satellite vehicle, we form what is called the *double difference* (DD). The result is that by using DD processing techniques on the C/A or P(Y) code and carrier-phase observables, most of the error sources are removed [15]. One major exception remains, however, and that is multipath—it can be mitigated but not eliminated. Note that receiver noise is still present, but its contribution is generally much less than that of multipath.

8.4.1.2   Carrier-Phase Measurement

Once the receiver locks on to a particular satellite, it not only makes C/A and/or P(Y) code pseudorange measurements on L1 and L2 (if L2-capable), it also keeps a running cycle count based on the Doppler frequency shift present on the L1 and L2 carrier frequencies (one cycle represents an advance of 2π radians of carrier phase or one wavelength). For each epoch, this running cycle count (the value from the previous epoch plus the advance in phase during the present epoch) is available from the receiver. More specifically, the advance in carrier phase during an epoch is determined by integrating the carrier Doppler frequency offset (f_D) over the interval of the epoch. Frequency f_D is the time rate of change of the carrier phase; hence, integration over an epoch yields the carrier phase advance (or recession) during the epoch. Then, at the conclusion of each epoch, a fractional phase measurement is made by the receiver. This measurement is derived from the carrier-phase tracking loop of the receiver. Mathematically, the relationship is as follows:

$$\phi_{l1_n} = \phi_{l1_{n-1}} + \int_{t_{n-1}}^{t_n} f_{D_{l1}}(\tau)d\tau + \phi_{r_{l1_n}} \quad \text{where } \phi_{l1_0} = A_{l1}$$

(8.8)

$$\phi_{l2_n} = \phi_{l2_{n-1}} + \int_{t_{n-1}}^{t_n} f_{D_{l2}}(\tau)d\tau + \phi_{r_{l2_n}} \quad \text{where } \phi_{l2_0} = A_{l2}$$

where:

ϕ is the accumulated phase at the epoch shown

$l1$ and $l2$ are the link 1 and link 2 frequencies

n and $n-1$ are the current and immediately past epochs

f_D is the Doppler frequency as a function of time

ϕ_r is the fractional phase measured at the epoch shown

A_{l1}, A_{l2} are whole plus fractional cycle count (arbitrary) at receiver acquisition

Even though the receiver carrier-phase measurement can be made with some precision (better than 0.01 cycle for receivers in the marketplace) and any advance in carrier cycles since satellite acquisition by the receiver can be accurately counted, the overall phase measurement contains an unknown number of carrier-cycles. This is called the carrier-cycle integer ambiguity (N). This ambiguity exists because the receiver merely begins counting carrier cycles from the time a satellite is placed in active track. If it was possible to relate N to the problem geometry, the length of the path between the satellite and the user receiver, in terms of carrier cycles or wavelengths, could be determined with the excellent precision mentioned earlier.

Figure 8.11 depicts such a situation and also illustrates the effect of the calculated carrier-phase advance as a function of time (e.g., ϕ_1 or ϕ_2). Clearly, determining N for each satellite used to generate the user position is of paramount concern when interferometric techniques are used. As the term interferometry implies, phase measurements taken at two or more locations are combined. Normally, the baseline(s) between the antennas are known, and the problem becomes one of reducing the combined phase differences to determine the precise location of the source of the signal. In the case of relative DGPS, the baseline is unknown but the location of the signal sources (the GPS satellites sometimes referred to as SVs) can be precisely determined using ephemerides available from the navigation data in the satellite transmission.

8.4.1.3 Double Difference Formation

Generation of both carrier-phase and pseudorange (code) double differences (DDs) is key to determining the baseline vector between the ground and airborne platform antennas. In so doing, satellite ephemerides must be properly manipulated to ensure that the carrier-phase and code measurements made at the two receiver locations are adjusted to a common measurement time base with respect to GPS system time.

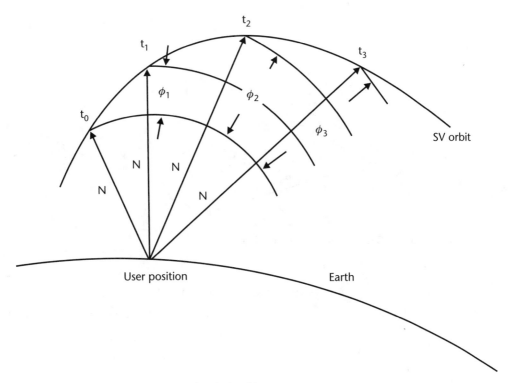

Figure 8.11 Carrier-phase geometric relationships.

Formation of the DD offers tremendous advantage because of the ultimate cancellation of receiver and satellite clock biases, as well as most of the ionospheric propagation delay. If the two antennas are located at the same elevation, the tropospheric propagation delay will largely cancel as well. This is not the case if one of the antennas is on an airborne platform, and thus the path delay due to the troposphere experienced at the two antenna locations differs based upon their altitude differential.

Carrier-Phase Double Difference
Figure 8.12 schematically depicts a simple GPS interferometer interacting with a single satellite. The phase centers of two antennas are located at k and m, and **b** represents the unknown baseline between them. SV p is in orbit at a mean distance of 20,200 km, and we assume the paths of propagation between the satellite and the two antennas are parallel. The lengths of the propagation path between SV p and k (Φ_k^p) or SV p and m (Φ_k^p), in terms of fractional and integer carrier cycles, are as follows:

$$\Phi_k^p(t) = \phi_k^p(t) - \phi^p(t) + N_k^p + S_k + f\tau_p + f\tau_k - \beta_{iono} + \delta_{tropo}$$
$$\Phi_m^p(t) = \phi_m^p(t) - \phi^p(t) + N_m^p + S_m + f\tau_p + f\tau_m - \beta_{iono} + \delta_{tropo} \qquad (8.9)$$

where:

    k and m refer to the receiver/receiver antennas phase centers

    p is the satellite signal source

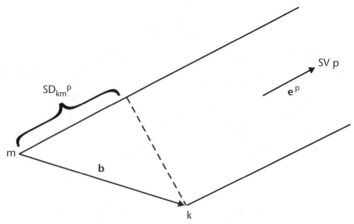

Figure 8.12 GPS interferometer—one satellite.

ϕ^p is the transmitted satellite signal phase as a function of time

$\phi_k^p(t)$ and $\phi_m^p(t)$ are the receiver-measured satellite signal phase as a function of time

N is the unknown integer number of carrier cycles from SV p to k or SV p to m

S is phase noise due to all sources (e.g., receiver, multipath)

f is the carrier frequency

τ is the associated satellite or receiver clock bias

β_{iono} is the advance of the carrier (cycles) due to the ionosphere

δ_{tropo} is the delay of the carrier (cycles) due to the troposphere

The minus sign associated with the ionospheric effects will be discussed later in this section.

The interferometric variable, the SD, is now created by differencing the carrier-cycle propagation path lengths (SV p to k and SV p to m):

$$SD_{km}^p = \phi_{km}^p + N_{km}^p + S_{km}^p + f\tau_{km} \tag{8.10}$$

The nomenclature remains the same as in (8.9) but certain advantages accrue in forming the SD metric. Prime among these are the cancellation of the transmitted satellite signal phase and clock biases, and the formation of a combined integer ambiguity term that represents the integer number of carrier cycles along the path from m to the projection of k onto the mp LOS. A combined phase-noise value has been created, as well as a combined receiver clock-bias term. With regard to the ionosphere and troposphere, these effects cancel, too, if the receivers are coaltitude and closely spaced (baselines less than 50 km). This condition will be assumed to exist for purposes of the discussion. (See Sections 8.2.3 and 8.2.4 for a discussion of differential ionospheric and tropospheric error characteristics.) Errors in satellite ephemerides (see Section 8.2.2) have not been considered but are usually very small (ranging from 5m to 10m). Since they are a common term, like the satellite clock bias, they cancel when the SD is formed.

Figure 8.13 extends the GPS interferometer to two satellites. For q, the additional SV, a second SD metric can be formed:

$$SD_{km}^q = \phi_{km}^q + N_{km}^q + S_{km}^q + f\tau_{km} \tag{8.11}$$

As with (8.6), the expected cancellation of SV transmitted signal phase and clock bias occurs, and a short baseline will be assumed such that ionospheric and tropospheric propagation delays cancel as well.

The interferometric DD is now formed using the two SDs. Involved in this metric are two separate satellites and the two receivers, one at either end of the baseline, **b**. Differencing (8.10) and (8.11) yields the following:

$$DD_{km}^{pq} = \phi_{km}^{pq} + N_{km}^{pq} + S_{km}^{pq} \tag{8.12}$$

where the superscripts p and q refer to the individual satellites, and k and m are the individual antennas. With the formation of the DD, the receiver clock-bias terms now cancel. Remaining is a phase term representing the combined carrier-phase measurements made at k and m by the receivers using SVs p and q, an integer term made up of the combined unknown integer ambiguities, and a system phase-noise term consisting primarily of combined multipath and receiver effects [27]. It now remains to relate the DD to the unknown baseline **b**, which exists between the two receiver antennas.

Referring again to Figure 8.13, it is evident that the projection of **b** onto the LOS between p and m can be written as the inner (dot) product of **b** with a unit vector e^p in the direction of SV p. This projection of **b** (if converted to wavelengths by dividing by λ) is SD_{km}^p. Similarly, the dot product of **b** with a unit vector e^q in the direction of SV q would result in SD_{km}^q. Rewriting SD (8.10) and (8.11) with this substitution yields:

$$
\begin{aligned}
SD_{km}^p = \left(\mathbf{b}\cdot e^p\right)\lambda^{-1} = \phi_{km}^p + N_{km}^p + S_{km}^p + f\tau_{km} \\
SD_{km}^q = \left(\mathbf{b}\cdot e^q\right)\lambda^{-1} = \phi_{km}^q + N_{km}^q + S_{km}^q + f\tau_{km}
\end{aligned} \tag{8.13}
$$

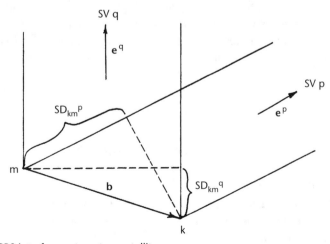

Figure 8.13   GPS interferometer—two satellites.

Clearly, we can incorporate this result into the DD as well:

$$DD_{km}^{pq} = \left(\mathbf{b} \cdot \mathbf{e}^{pq} \right)\lambda^{-1} = \phi_{km}^{pq} + N_{km}^{pq} + S_{km}^{pq} \qquad (8.14)$$

where $\mathbf{b} \cdot \mathbf{e}^{pq}$ is the inner product between the unknown baseline vector and the difference of the unit vectors to SVs p and q. Since determining the unknown baseline between the antennas is at the heart of the matter, it is this second formulation for the DDs, (8.14), that will serve as the basis for further derivation.

Of the variables shown in (8.14), only one can be precisely measured by the receiver—the carrier phase. In actuality, then, it is the carrier-phase measurements of the receivers that are combined to produce the DDs. The term DD_{cp} is adopted to represent this, and implicit in its formulation is conversion to meters. The noise term will be dropped to simplify the expression. In the end, as the carrier-cycle ambiguity search progresses, the noise sources tend to cancel. There remains to be determined the baseline vector ($\mathbf{b}$), which has three components (b_x, b_y, b_z), plus an unknown integer carrier-cycle ambiguity (N) associated with each of the DD_{cp} terms. Toward this end, four DDs will be used. While additional DDs could be formed depending on the number of satellites in track by the receiver, this is a sufficient number and minimizes the computational requirements of the carrier-cycle ambiguity-search algorithm. In terms of satellites, two satellites are required to form each DD. Thus, in order to form four DD equations, a minimum of five satellites is necessary. The transfiguration and extension of (8.14) to four DDs appears as follows:

$$\begin{bmatrix} DD_{cp1} \\ DD_{cp2} \\ DD_{cp3} \\ DD_{cp4} \end{bmatrix} = \begin{bmatrix} e_{12x} & e_{12y} & e_{12z} \\ e_{13x} & e_{13y} & e_{13z} \\ e_{14x} & e_{14y} & e_{14z} \\ e_{15x} & e_{15y} & e_{15z} \end{bmatrix} \begin{bmatrix} b_x \\ b_y \\ b_z \end{bmatrix} + \begin{bmatrix} N_1 \\ N_2 \\ N_3 \\ N_4 \end{bmatrix} \lambda \qquad (8.15)$$

where DD_{cp1}, for example, is the first of four DDs, $\mathbf{e}_{12}$ represents the differenced unit vector between the two satellites under consideration, $\mathbf{b}$ is the baseline vector, N_1 is the associated integer carrier-cycle ambiguity, and λ is the applicable wavelength. The wavelength is introduced at this point to provide consistency with DD_{cp} and $\mathbf{b}$, which are now in meters. During this and subsequent discussion, all DD formulations will be in units of length. Using matrix notation, (8.15) takes the following form:

$$\mathbf{DD}_{cp} = \mathbf{Hb} + \mathbf{N}\lambda \qquad (8.16)$$

where $\mathbf{DD}_{cp}$ is a 4×1 column matrix of carrier-phase DDs, $\mathbf{H}$ is a 4×3 data matrix containing the differenced unit vectors between the two satellites represented in the corresponding DD, $\mathbf{b}$ is a 3×1 column matrix of the baseline coordinates, and $\mathbf{N}$ is a 4×1 column matrix of integer ambiguities. Once the carrier-phase DDs are formed, a similar set of DDs is determined using the pseudoranges between each antenna and the same set of satellites.

Pseudorange (Code) Double Difference

As in the case of the carrier-phase measurement, the receiver makes a pseudorange measurement for each epoch for all satellites being actively tracked. The pseudorange suffers from similar propagation and timing effects as is the case for the carrier phase. The only basic difference is that where the ionosphere advances the carrier phase, the pseudorange information experiences a group delay. In considering the propagation of electromagnetic waves through a plasma, of which the ionosphere is an example, the propagation velocity (v_g) of the modulation on a carrier is retarded, while the phase velocity (v_p) of the carrier itself is advanced [28] (see Section 7.2.4.1). The following relationship holds:

$$v_g v_p = c^2 \tag{8.17}$$

where c is the speed of light. Thus, when the code DD is formed, the effects of the ionospheric delay are additive. Formulation of the code DD begins with the pseudorange equation as follows:

$$P_k^p(t) = t_k^p(t) - t^p(t) + Q_k + \tau_p + \tau_k + \gamma_{iono} + \delta_{tropo}$$
$$P_m^p(t) = t_m^p(t) - t^p(t) + Q_m + \tau_p + \tau_m + \gamma_{iono} + \delta_{tropo} \tag{8.18}$$

where:

P is the receiver-measured pseudorange as a function of time in seconds

k, m refer to receiver/receiver antennas phase centers

p is the satellite-signal source

t_k^p or t_m^p is signal-reception time as measured by the receiver clocks

t^p is signal-transmission time as determined from the SV clock

Q is noise (timing jitter) due to all sources (e.g., receiver, multipath)

τ is the associated satellite or receiver clock bias

γ_{iono} represents group delay (seconds) of the modulation due to the ionosphere

δ_{tropo} represents the delay (seconds) of the modulation due to the troposphere

Note the absence of the integer carrier-cycle ambiguity N—the pseudorange measurement is unambiguous. In other words, code DD observables formed from the pseudoranges measured by the receivers contain no carrier-cycle ambiguities. Unfortunately, pseudorange cannot be measured as precisely as the carrier phase, so it is noisier. Also of note is the change in the sign for the ionospheric effects from that in (8.9) due to the group delay. The unambiguous nature of the code DD will serve as the basis for code/carrier smoothing to be described in the next section.

Pseudorange SDs are now formed:

$$SD_{km}^p = t_{km}^p + Q_{km}^p + \tau_{km}$$
$$SD_{km}^q = t_{km}^q + Q_{km}^p + \tau_{km} \tag{8.19}$$

Finally, the pseudorange DD, in meters, is formed:

$$DD_{km}^{pq} = t_{km}^{pq} + Q_{km}^{pq} \tag{8.20}$$

Paralleling the development of the carrier phase DDs, the same five satellites are used to form four code DDs. Figure 8.14 is similar to Figure 8.12 with the exception that it has been labeled in terms of pseudoranges. It is evident that the inner product of the baseline **b** and the unit vector to satellite p can be expressed as the difference of two pseudoranges to the SV, one measured at receiver antenna k, the other at m. Recasting the baseline vector **b** in terms of the code SDs and DDs is virtually identical to that previously done with the carrier-phase SD and DD formulations. There is one very important difference, however—there are no ambiguities when code measurements are used. Further, the DDs are converted to units of length by multiplying by the speed of light, and, for simplicity, the noise term is dropped. The pseudorange-based equivalent of (8.15) is depicted next:

$$\begin{bmatrix} DD_{pr1} \\ DD_{pr2} \\ DD_{pr3} \\ DD_{pr4} \end{bmatrix} = \begin{bmatrix} e_{12x} & e_{12y} & e_{12z} \\ e_{13x} & e_{13y} & e_{13z} \\ e_{14x} & e_{14y} & e_{14z} \\ e_{15x} & e_{15y} & e_{15z} \end{bmatrix} \begin{bmatrix} b_x \\ b_y \\ b_z \end{bmatrix} \tag{8.21}$$

Once again, the integer ambiguities N, as appear in (8.11), are absent because the pseudorange is unambiguous. Using matrix notation to express (8.21) yields the following, which is the code DD counterpart of (8.16):

$$\mathbf{DD}_{pr} = \mathbf{Hb} \tag{8.22}$$

where $\mathbf{DD}_{pr}$ is the 4×1 column matrix of pseudorange (code) double differences, **H** is a 4×3 data matrix containing the differenced unit vectors between the two satellites represented in the corresponding DD, and **b** is a 3×1 column matrix of the baseline coordinates.

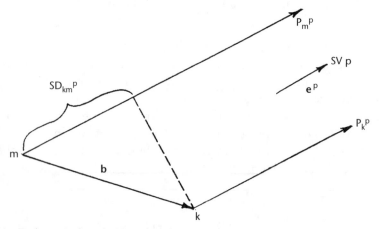

Figure 8.14 Code-equivalent GPS interferometer.

8.4.1.4 Pseudorange (Code) Smoothing

Thus far in this description of GPS interferometry, two distinct sets of DDs have been created. The first is based on differencing the low noise (less than 1 cm) but ambiguous carrier phase measurements; the second set is formed from the unambiguous but noisier (1–2m) pseudorange (code) measurements. The two sets of measurements can be combined using a variety of techniques to produce a smoothed-code DD measurement. This is extremely important since the baseline vector **b** determined from the smoothed-code DDs provides an initial solution estimate for resolving the carrier-cycle integer ambiguities. Based on [25], a complementary Kalman filter is used to combine the two measurement sets. The technique uses the average of the noisier code DDs to center the quieter carrier-phase DDs, thereby placing a known limit on the size of the integer ambiguity.

The filter equations are as follows:

$$
\begin{aligned}
DD^-_{s_n} &= DD^+_{s_{n-1}} + \left(DD_{cp_n} - DD_{cp_{n-1}}\right) \\
p^-_n &= p^+_{n-1} + q \\
k_n &= p^-_n \left(p^-_n + r\right)^{-1} \\
DD^+_{s_n} &= DD^-_{s_n} + k_n \left(DD_{pr_n} - DD^-_{s_n}\right) \\
p^+_n &= \left(1 - k_n\right) p^-_n
\end{aligned}
\tag{8.23}
$$

The first line of (8.23) propagates the smoothed-code DD to the current time epoch (n) using the estimate of the smoothed-code DD from the previous epoch ($n-1$) and the difference of the carrier-phase DD across the current and past epochs. The estimate (DD^+_s), which is based on averaging the DD_{pr} (code) difference, centers the calculation; the DD_{cp} (carrier-phase) difference adds the latest low-noise information. Note that differencing two carrier-phase DDs across an epoch removes the integer ambiguity; hence, the propagated smoothed-code DD (DD^-_s) remains unambiguous. The estimation-error variance (p^-_n) is brought forward (line two) using its previously estimated value plus the variance of the carrier-phase DD measurement q. The Kalman gain is next calculated in preparation for weighting the effect of the current code DD measurement. Line three shows that as the variance on the code DD r approaches zero, the Kalman gain tends to unity. This is not surprising since the higher the accuracy of a measurement (the smaller the variance), the greater is its effect on the outcome of the process. Lines four and five of (8.23) propagate the estimate of the smoothed-code DD (DD^+) and estimation-error variance to the current epoch (n) in preparation for repeating the process in the next epoch ($n+1$). DD^+ (to be used in the next epoch) involves the sum of the current value of the smoothed-code DD (just predicted) and its difference from the current code DD (just measured) weighted by the Kalman gain. Intuitively, if the prediction is accurate, then there is little need to update it with the current measurement. Finally, the estimation-error variance p is updated. The update maintains a careful balance between the "goodness" of the code and that of the carrier-phase DDs based on whether the Kalman gain approaches unity or zero or lies somewhere in between.

Equation (8.23) represents a set of scalar complementary Kalman filter equations that can operate on each of the requisite DD measurement pairs (code and carrier-phase) in turn. Alternatively, these equations can be set up in matrix form and accomplish the same end once all DD measurements for a given epoch are calculated and collected together in respective arrays. Either approach is satisfactory, but, for ease of programming, the scalar formulation is used here.

Figure 8.15 shows actual carrier phase (top line) and code (bottom line) DD measurements collected over a period of 20 minutes during a flight test [25]. The offset between the two plots is arbitrary but can be thought of in terms of some unknown ambiguity included in the carrier-phase DD measurements. It is apparent that the two sets of data are quite similar with the exception of apparent noise on the code DDs.

Figure 8.16 shows the output of the complementary Kalman filter (i.e., the smoothed-code DDs, bottom, and the original carrier phase DDs, top, over the same 20-minute interval). With the exception of the first few epochs (nominally about 10), the smoothed-code DD virtually mirrors the carrier-phase DD. It has the added advantage that it is centered about the original code DD measurements and is thus unambiguous.

Depending upon the multipath in the local environment, the smoothed-code DD, once the complementary Kalman filter is initialized, is generally within ±1–2m. In terms of carrier wavelengths, this represents approximately ±5–10λ at L1.

Figure 8.17 shows the difference between the carrier-phase and smooth-code DDs of Figure 8.16 with the nominal offset removed from the former. For this particular set of data, the difference is well within ±1m and is indicative of low multipath at both the ground and airborne antennas. Again, the behavior prior to completing the initialization of the complementary Kalman filter is clearly evident during the first few epochs, but, once initialized, the difference is very well behaved.

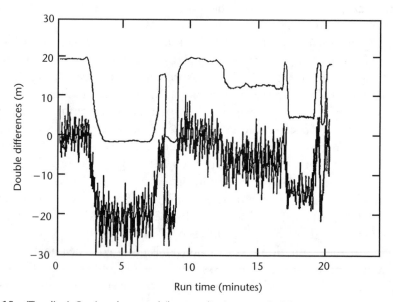

Figure 8.15   (Top line) Carrier-phase and (bottom line) raw-code DDs.

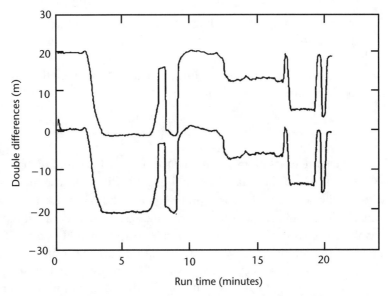

Figure 8.16 (Top line) Carrier-phase and (bottom line) smoothed-code DDs.

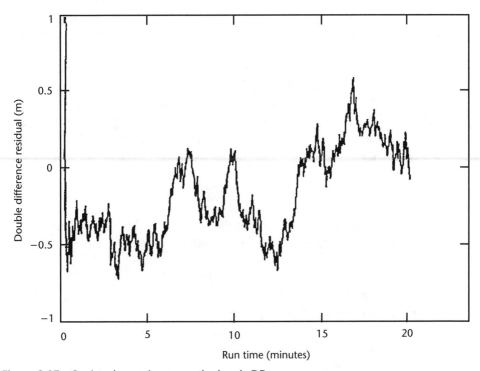

Figure 8.17 Carrier-phase minus smoothed-code DDs.

8.4.1.5 Initial Baseline Determination (Floating Solution)

The smoothed-code DD from the complementary Kalman filter, once the filter is initialized, is key to determining the floating solution. The floating baseline solution is a least squares fit yielding an estimate of the baseline vector $\mathbf{b}$, accurate to within a few integer wavelengths depending on the effects of satellite geometry and the severity of the multipath environment surrounding the antenna at either end of the baseline.

Using the vector notation introduced with (8.19), the DD baseline equation for the smoothed-code DDs is as follows:

$$\mathbf{DD}_s = \mathbf{Hb}_{float} \tag{8.24}$$

In a general least-squares sense, $\mathbf{DD}_s$ is an $m \times 1$ column matrix of DDs for $m + 1$ SVs, $\mathbf{H}$ is an $m \times 3$ data matrix containing the differenced unit vectors between the two SVs represented in the corresponding DD, and $\mathbf{b}$ is a 3×1 column matrix of the estimated floating baseline solution coordinates. Were the least squares solution for $\mathbf{b}$ the only desired result, the generalized inverse approach $\mathbf{H}^T\mathbf{H}$ could be applied immediately. In this situation, however, the floating baseline solution represents an intermediate step along the way to the desired final result, which is an integer-ambiguity resolution or the fixed baseline solution. With this end in mind, some matrix conditioning is performed on the elements of (8.24) prior to determining the floating baseline solution. The $\mathbf{H}$ matrix is decomposed using QR *factorization*, where $\mathbf{Q}$ is a real, orthonormal matrix (thus $\mathbf{Q}^T\mathbf{Q} = \mathbf{I}$) and $\mathbf{R}$ is an upper triangular matrix [29]. QR factorization allows the least squares residual vector to be obtained by projecting the DDs onto a measurement space that is orthogonal to the least-squares solution space spanned by the columns of $\mathbf{H}$. Hence, the least-squares residual vector is projected onto the left null space of $\mathbf{H}$, called *parity space*, while the least-squares solution is mapped onto the column space of $\mathbf{H}$, known as the *estimation space* [26]. Since the parity space and the estimation space are orthogonal, the residuals therein are independent of the estimate. This will be used to an advantage to isolate the carrier-cycle integer ambiguities and subsequently adjust the smoothed-code DDs. Incorporating the properties of the QR factorization into (8.24) yields:

$$\mathbf{DD}_s = \mathbf{QRb}_{float} \tag{8.25}$$

Capitalizing on the property of the orthonormal matrix, where the inverse and transpose are equivalent, and then rearranging gives:

$$\mathbf{Rb}_{float} = \mathbf{Q}^T\mathbf{DD}_s \tag{8.26}$$

Expanding the matrices for clarity yields:

$$\begin{bmatrix} R_{11} & R_{12} & R_{13} \\ 0 & R_{22} & R_{23} \\ 0 & 0 & R_{33} \\ 0 & 0 & 0 \end{bmatrix} \begin{bmatrix} b_x \\ b_y \\ b_z \end{bmatrix} = \begin{bmatrix} Q_{11}^T & Q_{12}^T & Q_{13}^T & Q_{14}^T \\ Q_{21}^T & Q_{22}^T & Q_{23}^T & Q_{24}^T \\ Q_{31}^T & Q_{32}^T & Q_{33}^T & Q_{34}^T \\ q_1 & q_2 & q_3 & q_4 \end{bmatrix} \begin{bmatrix} DD_{s_1} \\ DD_{s_2} \\ DD_{s_3} \\ DD_{s_4} \end{bmatrix} \tag{8.27}$$

Equation (8.27) lends itself readily to horizontal partitioning, and elements of the $\mathbf{Q}^T$ matrix have been labeled with capital $\mathbf{Q}$ to show the portion that corresponds to the least-squares solution (estimation space) and with small $\mathbf{q}$ to indicate the elements making up the least-squares residual vector (parity space). The partitioning of (8.27) is:

$$\mathbf{R}_u \mathbf{b}_{float} = \mathbf{Q}_u^T \mathbf{DD}_s \qquad (8.28)$$

$$0 = \mathbf{q}\mathbf{DD}_s \qquad (8.29)$$

Solving (8.28) gives the floating baseline solution:

$$\mathbf{b}_{float} = \mathbf{R}_u^{-1} \mathbf{Q}_u^T \mathbf{DD}_s \qquad (8.30)$$

Equation (8.29), while ideally equal to zero, is the least-squares residual vector and can be exploited to provide the means for resolving the carrier-cycle integer ambiguities, a discussion of which follows in the next section. The floating baseline solution is freshly calculated for each epoch and serves as a temporal benchmark during the ambiguity resolution process while the fixed baseline solution is being pursued. Once the fixed baseline solution is in hand, the floating solution subsequently serves as a cross-check to ensure the continued integrity of the former. Recall that this is a dynamic process—one end of the baseline is usually in motion (e.g., airborne)—thus, both the fixed and floating baseline solutions will vary from epoch to epoch and must be constantly monitored. On the other hand, the carrier-cycle integer ambiguities, once resolved, remain fixed in the solution since the receivers dynamically track the change (i.e., growth or contraction) in the number of carrier cycles between the baseline antennas and the respective SVs used in the solution for the baseline. This holds true as long as all SVs remain in constant track by the receivers with no cycle slips occurring.

8.4.1.6   Carrier-Cycle Ambiguity Resolution

Using the complementary Kalman filter to produce the smoothed-code DDs insures that each of the DD measurements contributes to a solution whose accuracy is within 1–2m, as previously stated. In terms of integer wavelengths at L1, for example, the DDs values are each within about ± 5–10λ. Intuitively, it would seem possible to iterate each DD through this range of carrier wavelengths, recalculate the least squares solution for each iteration, and then examine the residuals. Residuals "near" to zero, since there is noise in the process, would be identified, and the number of integer wavelengths added to each of the DDs would be kept as a candidate integer ambiguity set for the particular trial. This could be done on an epoch-by-epoch basis, and those sets of integer ambiguities that continued to remain valid would be marked and tallied. The list would diminish over time, and eventually one set of integer ambiguities would emerge victorious. The approach just described would take place in parity space, since we would be adjusting the DDs measurements (iteratively) and subsequently examining the new set of least-squares residuals that resulted. To search the uncertainty volume about the floating baseline solution would be computational inefficiency at its extreme. For example, an uncertainty of $\pm 11\lambda$ would require initially that 23^4 least-square solutions be generated each epoch and the residuals for each examined. Even though the number would diminish over time, the technique would in general remain computationally inefficient. A far better approach is to screen candidate integer ambiguity sets/test points using predetermined criteria, and then test only those sets that meet that criteria. Examples of the most prominent techniques currently in use are summarized in [30]. These include the fast ambiguity resolution approach (FARA) [31], the least squares ambiguity search technique (LSAST) [32], and the ambiguity function method (AFM) [16] (later refined in [15]). The applications cited in [30] for these techniques are directed more toward the static surveying environment rather than the kinematic DGPS regime. However, [30] provides insight into these methods, and all could find application in more dynamic situations where real-time applications are involved.

To generalize the foregoing, an initial solution is obtained, a search domain about the solution is established, and some methodology is used to preselect candidate test points/ambiguity sets within the domain, which are subsequently used to generate candidate fixed baseline solutions. Finally, using a given selection criteria, the candidate fixed baseline solutions are accepted or rejected until ultimately only one remains. AFM and LSAST can potentially accomplish this in a single period of several minutes; FARA generally requires two to three such periods. Reference [30] goes on to point out that caution must be exercised when relying upon least-squares covariance information for ambiguity resolution because of the possibility of correlations among the observations. It was subsequently pointed out in [33] that DDs are usually highly correlated and subject to poor precision. This leads to the possibility that the search space, while centered on the floating baseline solution, may not in fact even contain the carrier-cycle ambiguities. Toward this end, the least-squares ambiguity decorrelation adjustment (LAMBDA) method uses an ambiguity transformation that decorrelates the ambiguities and reshapes the search space. For example, a highly elongated ellipse in a two-dimensional ambiguity example becomes near circular in the transformed domain. The new ambiguity-search space is constructed to be integer in nature and volume preserving. Further, the search space can be appropriately scaled and all but guarantees that the proper set of integer ambiguities resides within.

Thus far in the development of the parity-space methodology used for resolving the carrier-cycle integer ambiguities, the steps necessary to develop the initial solution have been covered in detail. These include the formation of both carrier-phase and pseudorange (code) DDs, the creation of the smoothed-code DDs, the formulation of the DD baseline equations, and the separation of these equations into a least-squares (floating) baseline solution and a least-squares residual vector. A search volume has been established based upon the accuracy inherent in the smoothed-code DDs—nominally ±1–2m. It remains to formulate the DDs in a manner such that they can be selectively examined over the search volume as a function of integer carrier-cycle ambiguities. Once this is accomplished, candidate ambiguity sets can be isolated, thresholded, and eventually retained or eliminated. From those few remaining sets, fixed baseline solutions are determined. These solutions are then subjected to additional checks (e.g., comparison with the floating solution, among others), until the ultimate fixed baseline solution emerges.

The QR factorization is a powerful technique that allows the least-squares residuals to be isolated from the least-squares solution space without the necessity of performing the least-squares solution itself. Application of the residuals to the process of sorting out the integer ambiguities is the next area of interest. To do so requires that the carrier-phase DD measurement be examined in light of its constituent parts. The following equation so illustrates:

$$DD_{cp} = \left(\phi_{DD} + \hat{n} + R_b + S\right)\lambda \tag{8.31}$$

where ϕ_{DD} is the DD fractional phase from the receiver measurements, $\hat{n}$ is the unknown DD ambiguity, R_b is the inherent receiver channel bias plus residual propagation delays, S is the noise due to all sources (e.g., receiver, multipath), and the use of λ converts the DD to units of length. Strictly speaking, multipath is not noise. It does, however, add a noise-like uncertainty to the DD measurement, which, unfortunately, cannot be uniquely separated at a given instant in time from other noise sources. To solve this dilemma, multipath is simply included with the noise.

Equation (8.31) can be reexpressed using the smoothed-code DDs and with the knowledge that the uncertainty in the sources on the right-hand side of the equation is bounded. The terms ϕ_{DD} and $\hat{n}$ are replaced with ρ_{DD} and $\tilde{n}$. This follows from the knowledge that the smoothed-code DDs are accurate to within 1–2m, their inherent noise level. This noise level is equivalent to ±11 wavelengths at L1 and allows the integer ambiguity to be bounded; hence $-11 \leq \tilde{n} \leq +11$. The term ρ_{DD}, then, represents the geometric distance (in carrier-cycles) of the smoothed-code DD within the noise bound. The equation now appears as follows:

$$DD_s = \left(\rho_{DD} + \tilde{n} + R_b + S\right)\lambda \tag{8.32}$$

The resolution of $\tilde{n}$ can now be attacked using the residuals from the least-squares solution developed as (8.28). This equation is expanded and shown next:

$$\mathbf{qDD}_s = \left[q_1\left(\rho_{DD_1} + \tilde{n}_1 + R_{b_1} + S_1\right) + q_2\left(\rho_{DD_2} + \tilde{n}_2 + R_{b_1} + S_2\right)\right.$$
$$\left. + q_3\left(\rho_{DD_3} + \tilde{n}_3 + R_{b_3} + S_3\right) + q_4\left(\rho_{DD_4} + \tilde{n}_4 + R_{b_4} + S_4\right)\right]\lambda = \eta \tag{8.33}$$

where the q_r are the elements of the least-squares residual vector and $\tilde{n}_r$ represents a wavelength ambiguity number associated with the applicable DD. Ideally, the value of η, the measurement inconsistency, would be zero, but this could only be true in the presence of noiseless measurements and resolved carrier-cycle integer ambiguities.

In any particular epoch, the values for q remain constant—the residual of the least squares solution does not change until another set of measurements is taken, the DDs are computed and smoothed, and the QR factorization is completed. In modern receivers, great effort is expended to minimize interchannel biases; the same holds true for receiver noise. This leaves multipath as the major component of noise. Fortunately, code multipath, over time, behaves in a noise-like fashion, although not necessarily tending to a zero mean [34]. It is worthwhile, then, to consider (8.33) with emphasis on the component that is constant from epoch to epoch, knowing that the other sources of error will be mostly random or small over an extended period of time. This component is the unknown carrier-cycle integer ambiguity in each of the smoothed-code DDs. If the ambiguity can be removed from the DD, then the only remaining error sources are noiselike and will approach zero or, in the case of multipath, some mean value. Equation (8.33) is rewritten next in light of these ideas:

$$q_1 \left[DD_{s1} - \tilde{n}_1 \lambda \right] + q_2 \left[DD_{s2} - \tilde{n}_2 \lambda \right]$$
$$+ q_3 \left[DD_{s3} - \tilde{n}_3 \lambda \right] + q_4 \left[DD_{s4} - \tilde{n}_4 \lambda \right] = \gamma \tag{8.34}$$

Once again it is noted that the smoothed-code DDs are bounded within ±1–2m, depending on the multipath environment. With this in mind, the values for $\tilde{n}$ in (8.34) can be adjusted such that the result is near to zero—at least within some pre-determined threshold (γ). Assuming that the receiver noise and interchannel biases can be kept to below $\lambda/2$ (which is generally the case), it becomes possible to use (8.34) to resolve the carrier-cycle ambiguities. Putting (8.34) into matrix form:

$$\mathbf{q}[\mathbf{DD}_s - \mathbf{N}\lambda] = \gamma \tag{8.35}$$

where $\mathbf{N} = [\tilde{n}_1 \ \tilde{n}_2 \ \tilde{n}_3 \ \tilde{n}_4]$ and represents a set of integer values that, when substituted into the equation, satisfy the threshold constraint (i.e., γ). The question now becomes one of how to find the $\mathbf{N}$ vectors that produce such a result.

Since there are only four multiplication operations and three additions required to examine each case, one answer to such a question is to use an exhaustive search. With a ±1–2m bound on the accuracy using the smoothed-code DDs, such a search requires that components of $\mathbf{N}$ contain iterations covering ±11λ at L1, where the wavelength is 19.03 cm. There are 23^4, slightly less than 300,000, possible candidates for the first epoch, which is not an unreasonable number. If necessary, more efficient search strategies could be implemented; however, when the wide-lane wavelength is examined at the end of this chapter, the number of candidates will drop to less than 3,000, which then makes the exhaustive search almost trivial. In any event, as the integer values are cycled from [–11 –11 –11 –11] to [+11 +11 +11 +11], those integer sets that are within the threshold are retained and become candidates for the fixed baseline solution.

8.4.1.7   Final Baseline Determination (Fixed Solution)

For each epoch, the various $\mathbf{N}$ sets that meet the γ threshold constraint of (8.35) are stored, or, if stored previously, a counter (j) is incremented to indicate persistence of the particular ambiguity set. For those sets that persist, a sample mean (η_{avg}) is calculated based on the first 10 values of the residual. The variance (η_{σ^2}) about the sample mean is determined as well. These calculations are as follows:

$$\eta_{avg_j} = \frac{\left[\eta_{avg_{j-1}} (j-1) + \eta_j \right]}{j} \quad j \leq 10 \text{ and } \eta_{avg_0} = 0 \tag{8.36}$$

$$\eta_{\sigma_j^2} = \eta_{\sigma_{j-1}^2} + \left(\eta_{avg_j} - \eta_j \right)^2 \quad j = 1,2$$

$$\eta_{\sigma_j^2} = \frac{\left[(j-2)\eta_{\sigma_{j-1}^2} + \left(\eta_{avg_j} - \eta_j \right) \right]^2}{(j-1)} \quad j > 2 \tag{8.37}$$

Those ambiguity sets with the smallest variance (usually about 10 in number) are then ranked in ascending order. Persistence is defined as a minimum of 10 epochs (seconds for the research upon which this discussion is based) and has been determined experimentally. For a particular ambiguity set to be selected for the fixed solution, one additional requirement must now be met. The ratio of the residual calculated for the ambiguity set with the smallest and next smallest variances must exceed a minimum value. This value has also been determined experimentally and set to 0.5.

Upon selection of an ambiguity set, the $\tilde{n}$ values of the $\mathbf{N}$ vector multiplied by λ become literally the amount of path length used to adjust the current smoothed-code DD to create the exact (resolved) DD path length. To complete the process, the smoothed-code DDs are recomputed using the ambiguity set(s) that were generated during the search/selection process. The following relationship is used:

$$\mathbf{DD}_r = \mathbf{DD}_s - \mathbf{N}\lambda \tag{8.38}$$

The resolved smoothed-code double differences ($\mathbf{DD}_r$) are then used to calculate the fixed baseline solution using (8.30) as modified here:

$$\mathbf{b}_{fixed} = \mathbf{R}_u^{-1}\mathbf{Q}_u^T\mathbf{DD}_r \tag{8.39}$$

The RMS of the difference between the floating and fixed baseline solution is calculated for the current and subsequent epochs and monitored for consistency. Should the difference begin to diverge, the fixed baseline solution is discarded and a new search for integer ambiguities begins. Recall that the receivers, once acquisition of a given SV is established, keep track of advances or retreats in the receiver-to-satellite path length. Hence, a valid integer-ambiguity set in one epoch remains equally valid in the next and subsequent epochs. This being the case, the fixed baseline solution can be recalculated each epoch by adjusting the current set of smoothed-code DDs with the resolved ambiguity set ($\mathbf{N}$), followed by an updated least squares solution, or successive application of (8.38) and (8.39). Particularly noteworthy is that during the entire carrier-cycle ambiguity resolution process, it is unnecessary to generate the least-squares solution. All calculations remain in the measurement (parity) space using the least-squares residual vector obtained during the QR factorization. It is only after the proper consistency among the measurements (DDs) emerges (i.e., the emergence of a final resolved integer-ambiguity set) that the fixed baseline solution is calculated. True, the floating baseline solution is calculated each epoch, but this is more for monitoring than mathematical necessity. Remaining in the measurement space minimizes computational overhead and speeds the process as a result.

Two separate phenomena work to accelerate the process, which nominally takes three to four minutes before the carrier-cycle integer ambiguities are determined with sufficient confidence. First, the GPS constellation is dynamic. Its movement in relationship to the ground and user receiver antennas provides an overall change in geometry that has a very positive influence when interferometric techniques are used.

Second, under most conditions, the user platform is also in motion. This movement provides additional, though less significant, changes in geometry. Furthemore, if the user is airborne, there is a substantial averaging effect on the multipath seen by the airborne antenna. In fact, with kinematic GPS implementations, multipath from the ground site is the single biggest contributor to error in the overall airborne system.

As a further aid to resolving the ambiguities, SVs in track by the receiver, beyond the minimum five required, can be used for cross-checking, thereby accelerating the ambiguity-resolution process. With six SVs, for example, two sets of four DDs can be generated. This provides a second floating baseline solution and a corresponding least-squares residual vector that can be searched. DD measurements that are common between the two floating baseline solutions will produce associated integer ambiguities, which can be compared for consistency. Such redundancy usually leads to faster isolation of the proper ambiguity set.

8.4.1.8 Wide-Lane Considerations

With some receivers, it is possible to track SVs in the GPS constellation on both L1 and L2 simultaneously. With dual-frequency tracking, the P(Y) code must be used, because the C/A code is not modulated on both L1 and L2 carrier frequencies. Use of dual-frequency techniques permits the ionospheric path delay to be precisely determined and, in some cases, eliminated. Additionally, there are advantages to using the P(Y) code due to its higher chipping rate—10 times that of the C/A code. The advantages include increased pseudorange accuracies (since receiver correlation of the signal with added precision is possible) and reduced multipath errors. These positive aspects aside, great utility in isolating the carrier-cycle integer ambiguities can be obtained by combining the two frequencies to produce a wide-lane metric, the wavelength of which is roughly 86 cm. This is almost five times greater than the L1 wavelength. The wide-lane wavelength results from the beat frequency of the L1 and L2 carriers:

$$f_{wl} = 1{,}575.42 - 1{,}227.6 = 347.82 \text{ MHz}$$
$$\lambda_{wl} = 86.25 \text{ cm}$$

When applied to searching the uncertainties of smoothed-code DD measurements, the bound of ±1–2m on the search volume can be spanned in theory with $\pm 3\lambda_{wl}$ instead of $\pm 11\lambda$ at L1. This results in a hundredfold decrease in the number of integer-ambiguity set residuals that must be computed and examined during a given epoch. The penalty for using the wide-lane wavelength is an increased noise level noise level (S_{wl}) as shown next:

$$S_{wl} = \lambda_{wl} \sqrt{\left(\frac{S_{L1}}{\lambda_1}\right)^2 + \left(\frac{S_{L2}}{\lambda_2}\right)^2} \qquad (8.40)$$

Current receiver technology, however, can readily cope with this increase in noise and, assuming the magnitude of the noise level on each carrier is approximately equal, the equation reduces to 5.7 times either S_{L1} or S_{L2}, the L1 or L2 noise levels, respectively. Considering the increase in noise that will tend to expand the search volume, in practice it may be become necessary to search beyond $\pm 3\lambda_{wl}$.

The creation of the wide-lane carrier phase (ϕ_{wl}) is straightforward:

$$\phi_{wl} = \phi_{L1} - \phi_{L2}$$

Just as there exists a combination (the difference) of L1 and L2 that yields a wide-lane metric, there exists an alternative combination (the sum) that yields a narrow lane. It can be shown that frequency-independent errors (e.g., clock, troposphere, and ephemeris errors) are unchanged in either the wide-lane or narrow-lane observations from their L1 and L2 values [19]. Such is not the case with frequency-dependent effects (e.g., ionospheric, multipath, and noise effects), so wide-lane carrier phase observables must be paired with narrow-lane pseudorange observables to realize the same frequency-dependent effects. A detailed explanation can be found in [35]. The narrow-lane pseudorange relationship (P_{nl}) is presented without further elaboration:

$$P_{nl} = \frac{f_{l1} \cdot P_{l1} + f_{l2} \cdot P_{l2}}{f_{l1} + f_{l2}} \tag{8.41}$$

There is no change in the formation of either the carrier-phase or the pseudorange (code) DDs once the wide-lane carrier phase and narrow-lane pseudorange observables are formed, and the methodology previously described in terms of the L1 carrier and code measurements is directly applicable. The prime advantage accrues from the fact that the search volume can be canvassed far more efficiently since fewer wide-lane wavelengths need to be searched. As mentioned earlier, to search the same $\pm 11\lambda$ at L1 could be done, in theory, with $\pm 3\lambda_{wl}$. In terms of **N**, the iterations would range from [−3 −3 −3 −3] to [+3 +3 +3 +3]. The integers in the ambiguity sets that result from the search represent a greater physical span, but, other than that, the procedure for isolating the proper set of carrier-cycle integer ambiguity values is unchanged.

Once the proper wide-lane integer ambiguity set is determined, it is most advantageous to revert to single-frequency tracking: The signal strength of L1 C/A code is 6 dB greater than that of the P(Y) code on L2, and there is an almost sixfold reduction in noise when using single-frequency observables over their dual-frequency counterparts. In essence, such a move significantly improves system robustness. While the transformation is quite straightforward, it is not without pitfalls. A close look at the formation of the wide-lane carrier phase DD shows the following:

$$\mathbf{DD}_{cp_{wl}} = \mathbf{DD}_{cp_{l1}} - \mathbf{DD}_{cp_{l2}} \tag{8.42}$$

This being the case, the integer ambiguity set for L1 can be determined by expanding and rearranging (8.22) as shown next:

$$\mathbf{DD}_{cp_{l1}} - \mathbf{N}_{l1}\lambda_{l1} = \mathbf{Hb} = \mathbf{DD}_{cp_{wl}} - \mathbf{N}_{wl}\lambda_{wl} \tag{8.43}$$

Combining (8.42) and (8.43) allows the recovery of the L1 integer ambiguity set:

$$\mathbf{N}_{l1} = \frac{\mathbf{N}_{wl}\lambda_{wl} - \mathbf{DD}_{cp_{l2}}}{\lambda_{l1}} \qquad (8.44)$$

Care must be taken at this point, since the calculation of the L1 ambiguity set will occasionally be incorrect. Referring to (8.14), it is shown that the carrier phase DD also contains an amount of noise; ultimately, this noise is swept into the resolved ambiguities. An intuitive glance at (8.44) leads to the conclusion that conversion to the L1 ambiguity set seldom if ever produces integer values. Generally speaking, the results are very close to integers, and the proper set can usually be realized by picking the nearest integer values. Occasionally, however, there is enough noise on one or more of the wide-lane measurements to cause the next higher or lower integer ambiguity value to emerge from the conversion process. Reference [20] uses wide-lane techniques with subsequent conversion to the L1 wavelength for ambiguity resolution and points out that a phase error as small as 1.2 cm can produce a conversion error of 9.72 cm ($\lambda/2$ at L1), which results in the selection of the wrong ambiguity if the nearest integer is chosen. The conclusion is that, while reversion to single-frequency tracking adds robustness, the conversion process must be done with care. The L1 integer-ambiguity values that are generated by rounding the results from (8.44) must be near integer values to begin with or the operation potentially becomes suspect. One approach to solving this problem would be to follow (8.44) with a limited search around the L1 ambiguities.

As a final note, starting in 2007, GPS satellites will incorporate an L5 signal at 1,176.45 MHz. This signal will permit the construction of an extra-wide-lane metric from the difference between L2 and L5. The resulting wavelength will be 5.861m, and extremely rapid ambiguity searches will result. With the reliability of the current GPS constellation, full operational capability for use of the L5 signal will probably not occur before 2015.

8.4.2 Static Application

While land surveying is probably the most common of static applications, many other near-static applications are taking advantage of interferometric techniques. Among these could be counted precise dredging requirements for harbors and inland waterways, accurate leveling of land for highway construction and agricultural needs (especially land under irrigation), trackage surveys done to exacting standards for high-speed rail service, and a whole host of others. Generally, the driving factor in near-static or low-dynamic applications is the necessity for centimeter-level accuracy in the vertical dimension. For land surveying, requirements for accuracies in the millimeter regime in three dimensions are not uncommon. The classical approach, used initially in [16], demanded occupation times of up to several hours with simultaneous collection of GPS pseudorange and phase data at both ends of a prescribed baseline. This classic paper reported that "analyses of data from different observation periods yielded baseline determinations consistent within less than 1 cm in all vector components." That was in December 1980, the baseline was 92.07m, and the occupation time was a minimum of 1 hour. The survey data was processed after the fact, as remains typical today. The requirement for the occupation time of at least 1 hour was driven by the need to have sufficient movement in the GPS satellite constellation to allow the carrier-cycle integer ambiguities to be resolved. Another key consideration was the overall lack of GPS satellites, which eliminated the use of redundant measurements for resolving the carrier-cycle ambiguities. In this pioneering work, the ambiguity function method was used for determining the integer-cycle ambiguities.

Once the level of accuracy using GPS interferometric techniques was established, it became a natural desire to improve the efficiency of their application. The technique of kinematic surveying came into being as a result. Here, through use of a known survey point and an existing baseline, the carrier-cycle ambiguities are first determined. One technique that can be used to do this quickly is an antenna swap, wherein GPS data is collected for several minutes at each end of the baseline, the receivers/antennas are then exchanged without losing SV lock, and another period of GPS data is collected. Several minutes of GPS data, with epoch times on the order of 10 seconds, are required during each occupation period to collect sufficient data to resolve the ambiguities. Four (and preferably more) SVs yielding improved satellite geometry are required to accomplish this. Subsequent to the *antenna swap*, one receiver/antenna is moved to each of the points making up the survey. Generally, the receiver/antenna at the known survey point becomes the control point (base station) for the survey and the other becomes the rover. Following a 1- to 2-minute occupation of each survey point, the rover is returned to its initial starting location to provide data for closure of the overall survey. In all instances, it remains necessary to have continuous track on a minimum of the same four (but preferably more) GPS satellites. The GPS data is postprocessed, and the survey results are calculated. For baselines of up to 10 km, the effects of the ionosphere are minimal and centimeter-level accuracies can be expected. There are variations on the static and kinematic surveying methods, but generally the resulting accuracies remain at or near the centimeter level. Furthermore, it is the kinematic method that allows for the extension of GPS interferometric techniques to the near-static or low-dynamic environment mentioned previously.

Nowadays, with a complete GPS constellation of 24 SVs and the availability of low-noise receivers that can track both the L1 and L2 P(Y) codes, it has become possible to resolve the carrier-cycle ambiguities without the need for either the presurveyed baseline or an initial period of GPS data collection (e.g., the antenna swap procedure). The term applied to this technique is *on the fly*. Implicit in this approach is differential, carrier-phase integer-cycle ambiguity resolution. As a rule, the base station broadcasts either differential corrections or raw measurement data over a datalink, and the rover computes its position relative to the base station by combining its own measurements with the information received over the datalink. Such an implementation reduces the dependence on postprocessing and permits the user to know immediately whether or not the survey is progressing in a successful manner. In most instances, the base station is located at a precisely known surveyed point; thus, the rover can determine its absolute position (i.e., latitude, longitude, and elevation), since it has calculated the baseline vector between it and the base station. Accuracies on the order of 10 cm ($\lambda/2$ at L1) are achievable in near real time with the rover in motion. With longer occupation times, the accuracy will increase as multipath tends to average out.

8.4.3 Airborne Application

Flight reference systems (FRSs) using carrier phase or interferometric GPS (IGPS) techniques have been implemented and flight-tested on transport-category aircraft. The underlying principle of operation is similar to that used for kinematic surveying and is also referred to as differential carrier-phase tracking. Figure 8.18 depicts such a system where differential techniques are employed. In this case, raw observables from all SVs in view are transmitted from a ground subsystem via datalink. The carrier-cycle ambiguity resolution is done on the fly aboard the aircraft. Onboard the aircraft, position relative to the runway touchdown point is calculated in near real time and provided to the aircraft autoland system [21]. The objectives of this IGPS FRS included such things as 0.1-m accuracy RMS (each axis), one or more updates per second, UTC (USNO) time synchronization better than 0.1 ms real time, all-weather operation, and repeatable flight paths. The latter requirement calls for full aircraft integration and coupled flight. Specific applications for such systems include evaluation of approach/landing systems [such as instrument landing system (ILS), microwave landing system (MLS), and transponder landing system (TLS)], and test range instrumentation calibration (e.g., all manner of tracking systems: laser, infrared, optical, and radar). Precision instrumentation of test ranges themselves can be accomplished with special GPS receiver/datalink equipment aboard aircraft using the test range. Such a system would perform the ambiguity resolution at an appropriate ground site for each vehicle using the test range and provide position data to designated test range tracking facilities. In addition, feasibility studies in the areas of precision landing/autoland, low-visibility surface operations (taxiing, docking), high-speed turn-off, parallel runway operations, input to electronic charts, and four-dimensional navigation can also be supported.

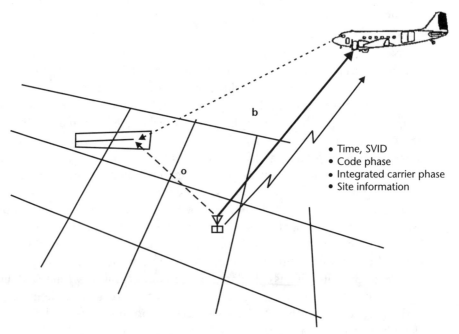

Figure 8.18 Interferometric GPS flight reference system.

8.4.3.1 Stand-Alone Ambiguity Resolution

Using the approach outlined in Section 8.4.1, approximately 2 to 5 minutes are required to resolve the carrier-phase integer-cycle ambiguities. The time required depends on a sufficiency of satellites—six or more are generally needed. Good satellite geometry is also beneficial, as is motion of the airborne platform (though not necessarily required). The latter supplements the normal motion of the GPS constellation and reduces carrier-phase and code multipath. Motion of the constellation is vital to the resolution of the carrier-cycle ambiguities. As the various candidate ambiguity sets are identified and evaluated over time, only one set can persist given the dynamics of the constellation and, to a lesser degree, the added motion of the platform. Simply stated, without motion, the technique presented would not work.

8.4.3.2 Pseudolite Ambiguity Resolution

During the initial feasibility studies for the FAA LAAS, integrity beacons (a form of pseudolite) were used for rapid carrier-cycle integer-ambiguity resolution. These devices are low-power transmitters, two of which are placed within several miles of a runway threshold along the nominal approach path. These transmitters typically operate at L1 and are modulated with an unused PRN code such that they are not mistaken for an SV. The several minutes of time required to resolve the carrier-cycle ambiguities as described earlier are reduced to seconds with this method due to the rapid change in geometry as the aircraft passes through the signal "bubble" created above the pseudolites. A second GPS antenna mounted on the belly of the aircraft is used to acquire the pseudolite signals. The presence of the two pseudolites also reduces the requirement of visible SVs to four and ensures that as the aircraft exits the bubble, the carrier-phase integer-cycle ambiguities are resolved. Centimeter-level positioning accuracy is thus ensured from this point to touchdown and rollout. Both the real-time cycle ambiguity resolution and the centimeter-level positioning accuracy have been demonstrated in flight testing with transport category aircraft [22, 23]. More recently, pseudolites have been investigated as a means of improving local GPS satellite availability [36].

8.4.3.3 Accuracy

Once the carrier-phase ambiguities are resolved, the accuracy of the DD measurement is determined by the carrier-phase measurement. In this case, multipath is the dominant error source. If the reflected signal is weaker than the direct signal, the phase measurement can be in error by up to 0.25λ. If the reflected signal is stronger than the direct signal, cycle slips are likely to occur. Typical wide-lane DD measurement errors are on the order of 2 to 10 cm (2σ). Due to geometry, vertical positioning errors are between 1.5 to 2 times the DD measurement error, resulting in up to 20 cm (2σ) vertical positioning errors. Horizontal positioning errors are generally less than 20 cm (2σ). If both the ground and the airborne antennas are placed in a rich multipath environment, vertical positioning error further degrades to approximately 40 cm. However, as soon as the aircraft is in motion, airborne multipath is mitigated due to the rapid changing path length difference between the direct and reflected signals, which tends to average the multipath error.

The use of dual-frequency measurements can be very important for an IGPS FRS in some applications since it allows for the mitigation of ionospheric errors, particularly for longer baselines. Once the ambiguities are resolved, the system could revert back to a single-frequency system. Because of the shorter wavelength of the L1 signal, multipath error would be reduced by approximately a factor of 4.5.

SA was turned off in May 2000. The following discussion has been retained for a historical perspective. The effect of SA is negligible for most differential systems because the ground and airborne GPS receiver measurements are usually synchronized with GPS time, some to within 2 ms. A constant SA velocity error is removed through a simple linear extrapolation. SA acceleration error growth is limited due to the 2-ms synchronization. Typically, SA acceleration is on the order of a few mm/s^2. After 1 second, the unknown SA acceleration cannot introduce more than 1 cm of error ($1/2at^2$). Even in the worst imaginable case of an SA acceleration of 100 m/s^2 (10.2g), the SA error growth during the 2-ms interval would only amount to 0.2 mm. Tracking loop error would likely be a much larger concern under these circumstances. It is noted, however, that the airborne position can only be calculated to the centimeter-level accuracy after the measurements from the reference receiver are received. This can introduce data latencies of 1–2 seconds. During this time, the aircraft position must be propagated to maintain the desired flight path. During periods of time with normal SA levels, the airborne integrated carrier phase measurements, corrected for SA velocity error, can be used to propagate the aircraft position with centimeter-level accuracy. During times of exceptionally large SA accelerations, the aircraft inertial velocities could be used to propagate the aircraft position.

8.4.3.4 Carrier Cycle Slips

The carrier-phase observable must be tracked continuously by the receiver, or the agreement between the fixed and floating baseline solutions will diverge rapidly. Loss of signal can occur due to the setting of a satellite, excessive maneuvering of the user (a large bank angle in the case of an airborne user during approach or take-off), or an obstructed view of the sky in the direction of the satellite. In any event, a loss of signal continuity, no matter how brief, results in an unknown signal loss or gain of carrier cycles when the signal is reacquired by the receiver. In a kinematic environment, detection of cycle slips is vital, since allowing corrupted carrier-phase measurements to propagate forward usually causes immediate loss of the fixed solution. As such, identification of the cycle slip becomes paramount, and, rather than attempt repair, the offending SV is "ignored" for a predetermined number of epochs with the assumption that the signal will quickly return to normal. At the conclusion of this time-out period, the data from the offending SV is once again accepted, and the carrier-cycle integer ambiguity resolution process restarts for the SV. In the interim, if a minimum of four SVs (not including the offending SV) had their ambiguities resolved at the time of cycle-slip detection, the fixed baseline solution is maintained. Otherwise, at best only a floating baseline solution can be provided.

8.4.4   Attitude Determination

An additional application of the interferometric techniques described earlier in this section is *attitude determination*. If antennas are placed on a rigid body, such as an aircraft, then the baseline vectors between each pair of antennas are known quantities within the body-frame coordinate frame defined in Figure 8.19. The x-axis extends through the nose of the vehicle, the z-axis points downward, and the y-axis is mutually perpendicular to the x- and z-axes to form a right-handed coordinate system (e.g., through the right wing as viewed by the pilot for an aircraft). Typically, the nominal center of mass of the platform is chosen as the origin.

If carrier-phase measurements are taken from each of the antennas, the integer ambiguities may be resolved, as discussed earlier, to determine the baseline vectors within the local north, east, down (NED) coordinate frame. This may be mechanized by first solving for these quantities in an ECEF coordinate frame (e.g., WGS-84) and then applying the appropriate transformation (see Chapter 2). At any given time, the relationship between the coordinates of three antennas expressed in the body frame (known from the installation) and expressed in the NED frame (computed from GPS carrier-phase measurements) may be written as [25]:

$$\mathbf{R}_{ned} = \mathbf{T}\mathbf{R}_{body} \tag{8.45}$$

where $\mathbf{R}_{ned}$ is the matrix of antenna coordinates in the NED frame, $\mathbf{R}_{body}$ is the matrix of antenna coordinates in the body frame, and $\mathbf{T}$ is the 3×3 transformation matrix:

$$\mathbf{T} = \begin{bmatrix} \cos\psi\cos\theta & -\sin\psi\cos\phi + \cos\psi\sin\theta\sin\phi & \sin\psi\sin\phi + \cos\psi\sin\theta\cos\phi \\ \sin\psi\cos\theta & \cos\psi\cos\phi + \sin\psi\sin\theta\sin\phi & -\cos\psi\sin\phi + \sin\psi\sin\theta\cos\phi \\ -\sin\theta & \cos\theta\sin\phi & \cos\theta\cos\phi \end{bmatrix} \tag{8.46}$$

The desired end quantities are the *Euler angles* (ψ, θ, ϕ) that represent *heading*, *pitch*, and *roll* (more formally heading, *elevation*, and *bank angle* [37]), respec-

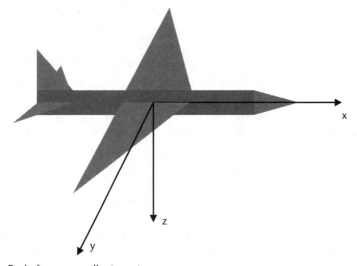

Figure 8.19   Body-frame coordinate system.

tively. Following [25], the Euler angles may be found by first determining a least-squares estimate of **T**:

$$\mathbf{T} = \mathbf{R}_{ned}\mathbf{R}_{body}^{T}\left(\mathbf{R}_{body}\mathbf{R}_{ned}^{T}\right)^{-1} \tag{8.47}$$

followed by a solution of (8.46):

$$\theta = \sin^{-1}\left(-T_{31}\right); \phi = \sin^{-1}\left(\frac{T_{32}}{\cos\theta}\right); \psi = \sin^{-1}\left(\frac{T_{21}}{\cos\theta}\right) \tag{8.48}$$

where T_{ij} refers to the (i,j)th element of the matrix **T**.

From inspection of (8.48), it is apparent that this approach is not stable for pitch angles approaching ±90°. Nonetheless, the method outlined here is practical for a number of applications where such an attitude is not encountered. The preferred mechanization for platforms that may experience any attitude is the use of *quaternions*. A quaternion is a mathematical construct that essentially extends the notion of a complex number to four dimensions. Whereas a complex number can be viewed as a mapping from a 2-vector (a,b) to a complex number $a + ib$, a four-vector (a,b,c,d) can be mapped into a quaternion $a + ib + jc + kd$ (referred to as a *pure quaternion* if $a = 0$), which has its own associated set of mathematical rules. An excellent introduction to quaternions is provided in [37].

GPS attitude determination systems are often implemented with four antennas or more, even though all three Euler angles can be determined with only three. Additional antennas provide redundancy. They are especially important for all-attitude platforms that can rotate such that they block visibility of one or more of the antennas to the visible GPS satellites. Whereas four satellites are normally required for carrier-phase positioning, only two satellites are needed for attitude determination, provided that a common receiver is utilized for phase measurements for each antenna and that the baseline lengths between the antennas are precisely known [38]. The common receiver results in cancellation of the receiver clock bias when single differences of carrier-phase measurements between antennas are formed. Although each antenna has a different analog path to the receiver, which results from differing electrical path lengths, these *line biases* can be mostly removed through calibration procedures.

Multipath is the error source that limits performance for most GPS attitude determination systems. Typical 1-sigma accuracy for each Euler angle in radians is the 1-sigma single-difference carrier phase multipath error divided by the antenna baseline length (with both the 1-sigma multipath error and the baseline length in the same units of length) [38]. Additional error sources that may be significant for GPS attitude determination applications that have not been previously discussed include structural flexing and tropospheric refraction. Structural flexing is the bending of the platform on which the multiple GPS antennas are installed due to applied forces or temperature changes. If flexing is nonnegligible, its effects can be mitigated through estimation or modeling. Tropospheric refraction is the bending of GPS signals as they pass through the troposphere. The very slight bending of each GPS signal path does not significantly alter pseudorange and carrier-phase measurements but may introduce unacceptable Euler angle errors for some applications. Tropospheric refraction effects can be mitigated through modeling (e.g., the use of Snell's law in conjunction with a slab model for the troposphere [38]). More comprehensive treatments of GPS attitude determination concepts may be found in [38, 39].

8.5   Message Formats

Many messaging protocols have been developed throughout the industry for the dissemination of code- and carrier-based DGPS data between reference stations and users. This section will present, as an important example, DGPS messages developed by the RTCM Study Committee 104 (SC-104). Although originally developed for maritime applications, RTCM SC-104 messages are now supported by the vast majority of commercial GPS receivers, including low-cost recreational devices.

Until recently, there was only one set of SC-104 messages to support both code- and carrier-based LADGPS services. This message set has evolved over time with version 2.3 published in August 2001 [40] being the most recent version. In February 2004, RTCM published guidelines for a new set of messages that use a more efficient protocol [41]. This later protocol, referred to as version 3.0, is currently focused on carrier-phase DGPS, although expansion for other applications is envisioned. Both protocols (version 2.3 and 3.0) describe digital message formats that can be broadcast from a reference station to a user using any arbitrary data link.

8.5.1   Version 2.3

Figure 8.20 shows the basic frame format of version 2.3, which consists of a variable number of 30-bit words. The last 6 bits in every word are parity, and the 30-bit word format is derived from the GPS navigation message. The first two words of each frame are referred to as the *header*. The content of the header is shown in Figure 8.21. The first word of the header contains an 8-bit preamble, consisting of the fixed sequence 01100110, followed by the 6-bit *frame ID*, which identifies 1 of 64 possible message types (see Table 8.2). Next, a 10-bit *station ID* identifies the reference station. The first 13 bits of the second word in the header, the *modified Z-count*, comprise the time reference for the message. The following three bits form the *sequence number*, which increments on each frame and is used to verify frame synchronization. The frame length is needed to identify the beginning of the next frame, since the length of the frame is variable, depending on the message type and the number of visible satellites. The 3-bit *station health* indicates whether or not the reference station is functioning properly and whether the reference station transmissions are unmonitored. Six of the possible eight patterns of the 3-bit station health

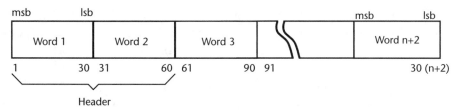

Figure 8.20   RTCM SC-104 version 2 message frame.

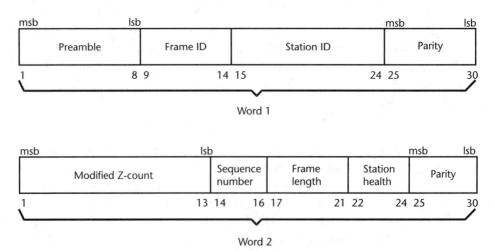

Figure 8.21   RTCM SC-104 version 2.3 message header.

are used to provide a scale factor for a field that appears in various message types referred to as *user differential range error* (UDRE) that will be described later.

For code-based DGPS systems, message types 1 and 9 are among the most important messages. The content of message type 1 is shown in Figure 8.22 (note that the two-word header that is appended at the beginning of every message type is not explicitly shown). For every visible satellite, the type 1 message includes the following parameters:

- *Scale factor:* 1 bit to indicate the resolution of the pseudorange and range-rate corrections to follow. If unset (set), resolutions of 0.02m (0.32m) and 0.002 m/s (0.032 m/s) apply for the pseudorange and range-rate corrections, respectively.

- *UDRE:* 2 bits that indicate ranges of expected 1-sigma errors of the pseudorange corrections. As mentioned earlier, 6-bit patterns in the station health field of the header are used to provide a scale factor for UDRE. UDRE values ranging from ≤ 0.1m to > 8m are possible with the scale factor applied.

- *Satellite ID:* 5 bits to indicate the satellite number for which DGPS corrections are being provided.

- *Pseudorange correction:* 16-bit correction $\Delta\rho^i_m(t_0)$ for the indicated satellite, applicable at the time t_0 provided by the Z-count in the header.

- *Range-rate correction:* 8-bit rate correction $\Delta\dot{\rho}^i_m(t_0)$ (see discussion in Section 8.3.1.2).

- *Issue of data (IOD):* The IOD indicates the specific set of GPS navigation data that was used in generating the corrections. As noted in Chapter 4, approximately every 2 hours, the broadcast clock and ephemeris data from each GPS satellite is changed. The GPS navigation message tags each set of clock and ephemeris data with IOD values referred to as IODC and IODE. IODC is a 10-bit parameter, and IODE is an 8-bit parameter (the 8 LSBs of IODC). IOD in the SC-104 messages are equal to IODE in the GPS broadcast message.

Table 8.2   RTCM SC-104 Version 2.3 Message Types

Message Type	Status	Use
1	Fixed	DGPS corrections
2	Fixed	Delta DGPS corrections
3	Fixed	GPS reference station parameters
4	Tentative	Reference station datum
5	Fixed	GPS constellation health
6	Fixed	GPS null frame
7	Fixed	DGPS radiobeacon almanac
8	Tentative	Pseudolite almanac
9	Fixed	GPS partial correction set
10	Reserved	P code differential corrections
11	Reserved	C/A code L1, L2 delta corrections
12	Reserved	Pseudolite station parameters
13	Tentative	Ground transmitter parameters
14	Fixed	GPS time of week
15	Fixed	Ionosphere delay message
16	Fixed	GPS special message
17	Fixed	GPS ephemerides
18	Fixed	RTK uncorrected carrier phases
19	Fixed	RTK uncorrected pseudoranges
20	Fixed	RTK carrier-phase corrections
21	Fixed	RTK/high-accuracy pseudorange corrections
22	Tentative	Extended reference station parameters
23	Tentative	Antenna type definition record
24	Tentative	Antenna reference point (ARP)
25–26	—	Undefined
27	Tentative	Extended radiobeacon almanac
28–30	—	Undefined
31–36	Tentative	GLONASS messages
37	Tentative	GNSS system time offset
38–58	—	Undefined
59	Fixed	Proprietary message
60–63	Reserved	Multipurpose messages

Message type 1 repeats these fields for every visible satellite. Message type 9 uses the same format, except that it only allows up to three satellites per message. The use of message type 9 requires a more stable clock in the reference station, since pseudorange corrections for all visible satellites must be broadcast with different reference times.

For carrier-phase DGPS, message types 18–21 are used. Message types 18 and 19 convey the reference station's raw (i.e., uncorrected with the broadcast GPS ephemerides) carrier-phase and pseudorange measurements, respectively, so that the user can compute the DDs described in Section 8.4. Message types 20 and 21 are

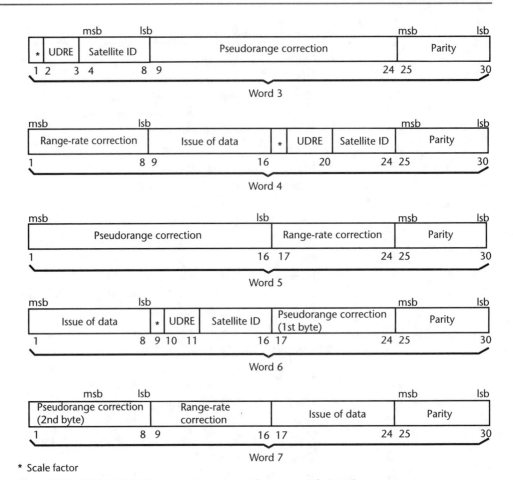

Figure 8.22 RTCM SC-104 version 2 message 1 format: words 3 to 7.

similar, but they convey carrier-phase and pseudorange measurements, respectively, that have been corrected using the GPS broadcast ephemerides.

8.5.2 Version 3.0

The development of the SC-104 version 3.0 standard [41, 42] was driven primarily by a need to treat RTK carrier-phase operations. The format is radically different from version 2.3, in part to provide a more efficient parity scheme designed to protect against bursts errors as well as random bit errors and in part to overcome limitations of the version 2.3 format, including an increased efficiency that will allow more timely broadcasts for RTK operations.

Version 3.0 messages are broadcast in variable length frames shown in Figure 8.23. Each frame begins with an 8-bit preamble, followed by 6 reserved bits and a 10-bit message length field. The data message, ranging from 0 to 1,023 bytes, is then broadcast followed by 24 bits of parity for error detection referred to as a cyclic redundancy check (CRC) code. This message format is much more efficient than version 2.3, which devotes more than 20% of the data link throughput to overhead (e.g., parity). Furthermore, the version 3.0 parity scheme is much stronger than that used for version 2.3.

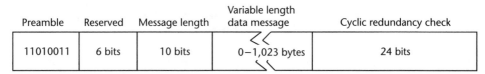

Preamble	Reserved	Message length	Variable length data message	Cyclic redundancy check
11010011	6 bits	10 bits	0–1,023 bytes	24 bits

Figure 8.23   RTCM SC-104 version 3.0 message frame.

The initial release of version 3.0 includes 13 message types, designed primarily to support RTK applications using GPS or GLONASS. These message types provide the reference station's pseudorange and carrier-phase measurements for L1 or L1/L2, as well as a wealth of auxiliary information including precise station coordinates, receiver configuration, and antenna characteristics. Later versions will include a number of new message types, at least eight of which have been proposed, as well as a number of legacy message types to support both RTK and conventional differential GNSS.

8.6   Examples

8.6.1   Code Based

8.6.1.1   MDGPS/NDGPS

In the late 1980s, the USCG began the development of a MDGPS system to satisfy maritime navigation requirements in the United States. In 1989, a radiobeacon located on Montauk Point, New York, was modified to broadcast DGPS corrections in the RTCM SC-104 message format. By February 1997, 54 radiobeacons had been modified to provide DGPS correction coverage for most U.S. coastal areas and inland waterways, and the MDGPS service was declared to have achieved full operational capability. That same year, a decision was made to expand radiobeacon DGPS coverage throughout the United States. This program, referred to as Nationwide DGPS (NDGPS), is supported by a partnership of U.S. agencies including the USCG, the U.S. Air Force Air Combat Command, the Federal Railroad Administration, the Federal Highway Administration, the National Oceanic and Atmospheric Administration (NOAA), the U.S. Army Corps of Engineers, and the Office of the Secretary of Transportation [43]. At the time of this writing, 84 of 136 proposed sites were operational, providing nearly complete coverage over the United States with two or more sites visible to users in many locations. This section provides a short description of the MDGPS/NDGPS systems.

Network Design
The network architecture for MDGPS/NDGPS is shown in Figure 8.24 [44]. These systems essentially utilize the code-based LADGPS techniques described in Section 8.3.1. The network includes reference stations (RSs) to monitor GPS and generate differential corrections. Each reference station consists of two GPS receivers for redundancy. Integrity monitors (IMs) are collocated with the RSs. All of the equipment is generally installed in unmanned equipment sheds with a backup power source (e.g., batteries or a generator). Each IM includes another pair of GPS receivers and radiobeacon receivers to monitor the corrections that the site is itself broad-

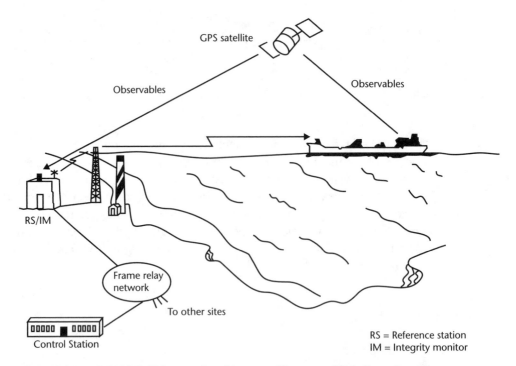

Figure 8.24   MDGPS/NDGPS network architecture. (Courtesy of U.S. Coast Guard.)

casting. The IMs compute their positions using GPS and the differential corrections and compare their computed positions with their known (surveyed) positions. If the position exceeds a preset tolerance, problem satellites are expunged from the differential correction calculation and the user is notified that the satellite is "unhealthy" or the site is shut down to guarantee accurate and reliable information.

A frame relay network is used so that two central control stations, which are manned 24 hours a day, 7 days a week, can monitor the status of all the sites. One control station is in Alexandria, Virginia; the other is in Petaluma, California. Personnel at the control stations, upon observing an equipment failure, can switch in redundant hardware or dispatch a maintenance crew if necessary.

Data Link

Each RS/IM broadcasts digital DGPS corrections in the RTCM SC-104 message format. Version 2.1 message types 3, 5, 6, 7, 9, and 16 are currently supported [45]. These message types are retained in the later RTCM SC-104 version 2.3 standard, described in Section 8.5.1. The digital data is broadcast in the 285–325-kHz medium frequency (MF) band, which is allocated internationally for radiobeacons. A digital modulation technique referred to as minimum shift keying (MSK) (e.g., see [46]) is employed either directly on the radiobeacon center frequencies or on a subcarrier. The use of a subcarrier was originally motivated by the desire to not interfere with direction-finding receivers that employed existing radiobeacon signals [47]. At present, all marine radiobeacons in the United States that are not used for MDGPS have been decommissioned, so backwards compatibility is no longer an issue. Impulsive noise due, for example, to lightning strikes, is prevalent in the MF band at sea because of the excellent conductivity of salt water. This led to a decision to use type 9 SC-104 messages rather than type 1 to broadcast pseudorange and range-rate corrections. The use of type 9 messages provides more frequent preambles for user equipment to resynchronize following a strong impulse. The standards for MDGPS/NDGPS support data rates of 50, 100, or 200 bps.

A large antenna is required to broadcast efficiently at MF because of the large wavelength (1 km). Most of the MDGPS sites use converted radiobeacon broadcast towers with heights ranging from 90–150 feet. The NDGPS expansion began with the conversion of 47 obsolete U.S. Air Force low-frequency ground wave emergency network (GWEN) sites in one of the largest military-to-civilian reutilization projects. The GWEN sites were already equipped with 299-foot antennas. A minimum field strength of 75 μV/m for a 100-bps transmission is specified within each transmitter's coverage volume [45], which is typically on the order of 250 nmi.

Performance

The specified accuracy of the MDGPS/NDGPS systems is 10m, 2 drms, within coverage areas [44]. Typical accuracies are much better, typically 1–3m. An often-used general rule is 1-m accuracy at the base of a transmitter with errors growing by 1m per 150 km of separation [43]. The specified availability is 99.9% for dual-coverage areas and 99.7% for areas with single coverage, based on a 1-month average per site and discounting GPS anomalies [44]. Current coverage is shown in Figure 8.25.

International Harmonization

International standards for maritime DGPS systems, fully compatible with MDGPS and NDGPS, have been developed by the International Maritime Organization. At the time of this writing, radiobeacon-based DGPS services had been deployed in over 30 nations.

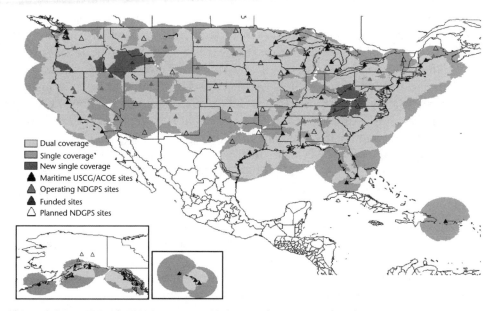

Figure 8.25 MDGPS/NDGPS coverage. (Courtesy of U.S. Coast Guard.)

8.6.1.2 SBAS

ICAO has developed standards [48] for two types of code-based DGPS systems for civil aircraft navigation applications. This section will describe SBAS systems, and the following section will describe GBAS systems.

An SBAS is a WADGPS system that provides differential GPS corrections and integrity data using GEOs as the communications path. A unique feature of SBASs is that they provide DGPS data, using a signal broadcast directly at the GPS L1 frequency, that can be used for ranging. The goal of SBASs is to meet navigation system requirements for civil aviation from the en-route phase of flight through vertically guided precision approach. A number of SBASs had been implemented or were planned at the time of this writing [49]. These include the WAAS within the United States, the EGNOS within Europe, the Multifunctional Transport Satellite (MTSAT)–based MSAS within Japan and Southeast Asia, and the GPS and GEO Augmented Navigation (GAGAN) system in India.

History

As discussed in Chapter 7, RAIM or DGPS are required to provide the necessary levels of integrity to GNSS to support air navigation. In the early 1980s, a concept of providing integrity data for GPS over a GEO communications link using a signal on the GPS L1 frequency emerged. This concept was referred to as a GPS integrity channel (GIC) [50]. In 1989, Inmarsat began test transmissions of GPS-like spread spectrum signals through a geostationary satellite over the Atlantic Ocean to prove the feasibility of using a navigation repeater to transmit pseudorandom-coded spread spectrum ranging signals. The test results indicated that transmitting these signals through geostationary satellites was possible [51]. In the same time frame, organizations including Inmarsat and RTCA's Special Committee 159 (SC-159) began establishing a signal format for GIC, which later evolved into SBAS. In the 1990s, SBAS programs were well underway within the United States, Europe, and Japan. Inmarsat on their own initiative included navigation transponders on the five Inmarsat-3 satellites that were launched from April 1996–February 1998. In November 1999, Japan attempted to launch its own SBAS GEO for MSAS, but experienced a setback when the satellite, MTSAT-1, had to be destroyed following a launch failure. In August 2000, the U.S. FAA's WAAS system, using two of the Inmarsat-3 satellites—AORW and POR—was declared to be continually available for nonsafety applications. In July 2003, WAAS was commissioned for safety of life services. At the time of this writing, the EGNOS system was operational with three GEOs and anticipating commissioning for safety of life operations; the MSAS ground segment was complete, the replacement satellite, MTSAT-1R, was successfully launched in February 2005; and GAGAN was in an advanced stage of development with operations expected to commence within the next several years.

SBAS Requirements

ICAO requirements for SBAS and GBAS for en-route through category I precision approach operations are shown in Table 8.3 [48]. Most researchers believe that category I requirements cannot be met by SBAS in the near term (before the population of the GPS constellation with L5-capable satellites). New classes of less stringent vertically guided approaches, referred to as GNSS approach and operations with

Table 8.3 ICAO GNSS Signal-in-Space Performance Requirements

Operation	Horizontal/ Vertical Accuracy (95%)	Integrity Level	Horizontal/ Vertical Alert Limit	Time to Alert	Continuity	Availability
En-route	3.7 km N/A	$1-1\times10^{-7}$/hour	3.7–7.4 km N/A	5 minutes	$1-1\times10^{-4}$/hour to $1-1\times10^{-8}$/hour	0.99 to 0.99999
Terminal	0.74 km N/A	$1-1\times10^{-7}$/hour	1.85 km N/A	15 seconds	$1-1\times10^{-4}$/hour to $1-1\times10^{-8}$/hour	0.999 to 0.99999
Nonprecision approach	220m N/A	$1-1\times10^{-7}$/hour	556m N/A	10 seconds	$1-1\times10^{-4}$/hour to $1-1\times10^{-8}$/hour	0.99 to 0.99999
APV-I	16m 20m	$1-2\times10^{-7}$/approach	40m 50m	10 seconds	$1-8\times10^{-6}$ in any 15 seconds	0.99 to 0.99999
APV-II	16m 8m	$1-2\times10^{-7}$/approach	40m 20m	6 seconds	$1-8\times10^{-6}$ in any 15 seconds	0.99 to 0.99999
Category I	16m 4–6m	$1-2\times10^{-7}$/approach	40m 10–15m	6 seconds	$1-8\times10^{-6}$ in any 15 seconds	0.99 to 0.99999

Source: [48].

vertical guidance (APV)-I and vertical guidance (APV)-II have been defined to enable the full utility of the performance that near-term SBASs can provide.

SBAS Architecture and Functionality

All SBAS systems are comprised of four subelements: monitoring receivers, central processing facilities, satellite uplink facilities, and one or more geostationary satellites. Unfortunately, the terminology for these subelements is not consistent among the specific implementations. Within the U.S. WAAS, the monitors are referred to as wide-area reference stations (WRSs), the central processing facilities are known as wide area master stations (WMSs), and the uplink facilities as ground Earth stations (GESs) (see Figure 8.26). Within EGNOS, these elements are referred to as ranging and integrity monitoring stations (RIMS), mission control centers (MCCs), and navigation land Earth stations (NLES), respectively (see Figure 8.27). Within MSAS, the respective terms are ground monitoring stations (GMSs), MCSs, and GESs. MSAS also includes additional elements referred to as monitor and ranging stations (MRSs) that are similar to GMSs but are specifically dedicated to orbit determination. MSAS will be implemented in two phases. The initial MSAS contains 4 GMSs, 2 MRSs, and 2 MCSs (see Figure 8.28). For GAGAN, the terms Indian Reference Station (INRES), Indian Master Control Centre (INMCC) and Indian Land Uplink Station (INLUS) are used (see Figure 8.29).

The functionality provided by the SBAS subelements is summarized in Figure 8.30. As observed in Figure 8.30, users receive navigation signals transmitted from GPS and, in some instances, GLONASS satellites. These signals are also received by monitoring networks operated by the SBAS service providers. Each site within the monitoring networks generally includes a number of GNSS receivers (for redundancy) that provide L1 C/A code and L2 P(Y) code pseudorange and carrier-phase data (using semicodeless processing techniques for the L2 measurements—see Section 5.14) to the central processing facilities. At each central processing facility, the

Figure 8.26 WAAS ground network.

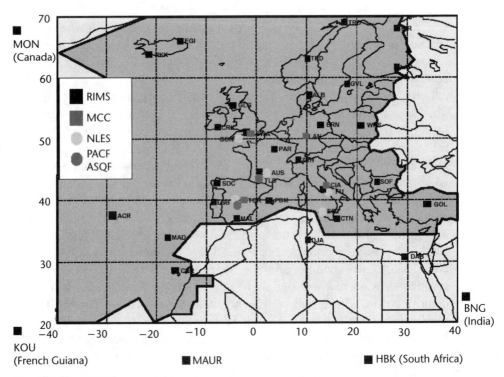

Figure 8.27 EGNOS ground network.

data from the entire network are processed to develop estimates of each GPS satellite's true position and clock error, corrections based on the differences between the network's estimates of these parameters and the values in the broadcast GPS navigation data, and an estimate of the vertical ionospheric delay error across the service area. Each central processing facility also checks for "problem" satellites (e.g., those

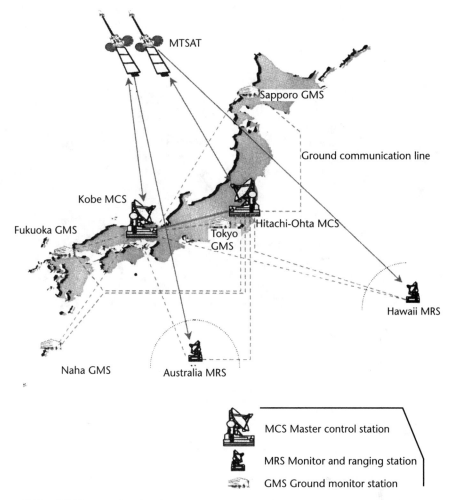

Figure 8.28 MSAS ground network.

whose signals are distorted or whose clocks are running erratically, in case of which the SBAS user may be sent the warning: "do not use"). These estimates and integrity information are used to form wide-area differential corrections and integrity messages that are then forwarded to the satellite uplink facilities. At the uplink facilities, the spread spectrum navigation signal is generated and precisely synchronized to a reference time and modulated with the SBAS data. This composite signal is continuously transmitted to a geostationary satellite. On board the satellite, this navigation signal is frequency translated within the navigation payload and transmitted to the user on the GPS L1 frequency. The timing of the signal is done in a very precise manner in order that the signal appears as though it was generated on board the satellite as a GPS ranging signal. Redundant central processing and uplink facilities may be used to provide *hot standbys* in the event of a failure at the primary facility.

SBAS Signal Structure

The signal broadcast via the SBAS geostationary satellite to the SBAS users [52] is designed to minimize standard GPS receiver hardware modifications. The GPS L1

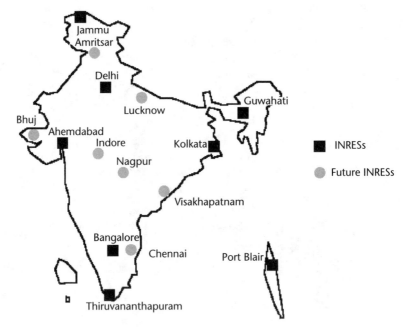

Figure 8.29 GAGAN ground network.

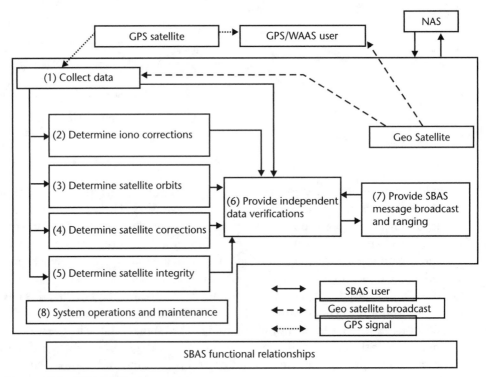

Figure 8.30 SBAS functional overview.

frequency and GPS C/A code type of modulation, including the use of length-1,023 Gold codes at a 1.023-MHz chip rate, are used. In addition, the code phase timing is synchronized to GPS system time to emulate a GPS satellite and provide a ranging capability. A data rate of 250 bps is used. The data is convolutionally encoded using a rate half constraint length 7 encoder to generate an overall symbol rate of 500 symbols/s. The SBAS data symbols are synchronized with the 1-kHz GPS C/A code epochs.

The C/A codes used by SBAS belong to the same family of 1,023-bit Gold codes as the 37 PRN codes reserved by the GPS system described in Chapter 4. The SBAS C/A codes were specifically selected to not adversely interfere with GPS signals (e.g., see [53]). The 39 current SBAS C/A codes and the associated geostationary satellites are shown in Table 8.4. The listing of PRN code assignments is maintained by the GPS Joint Program Office at http://gps.losangeles.af.mil. The SBAS C/A codes are identified by the PRN number, the G2 delay in chips, and the initial G2 state. The definition of either the G2 delay or initial G2 setting is required for implementation of the generation of the SBAS C/A codes. Like the GPS C/A codes, the PRN number is arbitrary, but they start with 120 instead of 1. The actual codes are defined by either the G2 delay or the initial G2 register setting. The codes are ranked by the average number of cross-correlation peaks when correlating these codes with the 36

Table 8.4   SBAS Ranging C/A Codes

PRN	G2 Delay (Chips)	Initial G2 Setting (Octal)	First 10 SBAS Chips (Octal)	Geostationary Satellite PRN Allocations	Orbital Slot
120	145	1106	0671	INMARSAT 3F2, AOR-E	15.5°W
121	175	1241	0536	INMARSAT 4F2	53°W
122	52	0267	1510	INMARSAT 3F4, AOR-W	54°W
123	21	0232	1545	Unallocated	
124	237	1617	0160	ARTEMIS	21.5°E
125	235	1076	0701	Unallocated	
126	886	1764	0013	INMARSAT 3F5, IND-W	25°E
127	657	0717	1060	GAGAN-1	TBD[1]
128	634	1532	0245	GAGAN-2	TBD[1]
129	762	1250	0527	MTSAT-1R (or MTSAT-2)[2]	TBD
130	355	0341	1436	INMARSAT 4F1	63°E
131	1012	0551	1226	INMARSAT 3F1, IOR	64°E
132	176	0520	1257	Unallocated	
133	603	1731	0046	INMARSAT 4F3	N/A
134	130	0706	1071	INMARSAT 3F3, POR	178°E
135	359	1216	0561	Unallocated	
136	595	0740	1037	INMARSAT Reserved	8°E
137	68	1007	0770	MTSAT-2 (or MTSAT-1R)[2]	TBD
138	386	0450	1327	Unallocated	

1. The proposed GAGAN geostationary orbital longitudes are 55°E, 74°E, and 93.5°E.
2. When MTSAT-2 is unavailable, MTSAT-1R will broadcast two PRN signals—each of which is received from an independent uplink station—in order to maintain continuity in case of uplink signal attenuation or equipment failure at either uplink station. Similarly, MTSAT-2 will broadcast two PRN signals when MTSAT-1R is unavailable. When MTSAT-1R and MTSAT-2 are available, MTSAT-1R will broadcast PRN 129 signal only and MTSAT-2 will broadcast PRN 137 signal only.

GPS codes that have zero Doppler difference. In the octal notation for the first 10 chips of the SBAS code as shown in the table, the first digit on the left represents a "0" or "1" for the first chip. The last three digits are the octal representation of the remaining 9 chips. For example, the initial G2 setting for PRN 120 is 1001000110. Note that the first 10 SBAS chips are simply the octal inverse of the initial G2 setting.

Some future SBAS satellites will also be capable of transmitting a signal on the GPS L5 frequency. Such signals will likely use PRN codes from the same family as the GPS L5 signals (see Section 4.5.2), but they may not include a dataless component. A baseline data rate of 250 bps is anticipated, convolutionally encoded into a 500-symbol/s stream.

SBAS Message Format and Contents

The 250-bps data from each SBAS GEO is packed into 1-second blocks of 250 bits, as shown in Figure 8.31. Each block includes an 8-bit preamble (one of three parts of a 24-bit unique word, 01010011 10011010 11000110, that is distributed over three blocks), a 6-bit message-type field (allowing for up to 64 message types), a 212-bit payload with unique meaning specifically defined for each message type, and 24 bits of CRC parity for error detection, as shown in Figure 8.31. The start of every other 24-bit preamble is synchronous with a 6-second GPS subframe epoch. The preambles and timing information provided in the messages facilitate data acquisition. They also aid the user receiver to perform time synchronization during initial acquisition before GPS satellites are acquired, thus aiding the receiver in subsequent GPS satellite acquisitions.

Table 8.5 lists the message types that have been defined thus far for SBAS. These message types support the basic wide area GPS concepts discussed in Section 8.3.3. Message types 2–5 provide broadcast clock corrections. Message type 25 provides broadcast orbit corrections. Message type 26 provides the L1-only user with vertical ionospheric delay values over a grid of locations with predefined latitude and longitude values. Each user receiver calculates the latitude and longitude of the intersection points between each GPS signal and the ionosphere, which is modeled as a thin shell at 350-km altitude above the surface of the Earth. The vertical ionospheric delays at these intersection points, referred to as *ionospheric pierce points* (IPPs), are determined for each visible satellite by interpolating the delays from the three or four nearest grid points, as discussed later in this section. The reader is referred to [52] for a complete description of the messages and their applications.

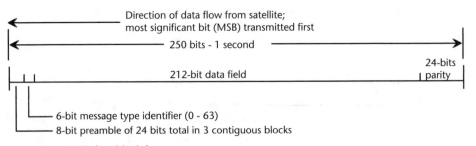

Figure 8.31   SBAS data block format.

Table 8.5 SBAS Message Types

Type	Contents
0	Don't use for safety applications (for SBAS testing)
1	PRN mask assignments, set up to 51 of 210 bits
2–5	Fast corrections
6	Integrity information
7	Fast correction degradation factor
8	Reserved for future messages
9	GEO navigation message (X, Y, Z, time)
10	Degradation parameters
11	Reserved for future messages
12	SBAS network time/UTC offset parameters
13–16	Reserved for future messages
17	GEO satellite almanacs
18	Ionospheric grid point masks
19–23	Reserved for future messages
24	Mixed fast corrections/long-term satellite error corrections
25	Long-term satellite error corrections
26	Ionospheric delay corrections
27	SBAS service message
28	Clock-ephemeris covariance matrix message
29–61	Reserved for future messages
62	Internal test message
63	Null message

User Algorithms

SBAS user equipment are modified GPS L1 C/A code receivers. The equipment must be modified to be able to generate and track the SBAS PRN codes described earlier; demodulate the higher rate (250 bps), convolutionally encoded data; and include modified software to apply the corrections and integrity data.

Application of the clock and ephemeris corrections is straightforward. Message types 2–5 provide range domain clock corrections that are simply added to the receiver's raw pseudorange measurements for all visible satellites. The SBAS data does not include range rate corrections. These are generated within the user equipment itself by differencing successive clock corrections [52, 54]. Message type 25 provides broadcast satellite position corrections in ECEF x, y, z coordinates. Satellite broadcast position error rate terms and a clock bias term can also be provided, if necessary, in message type 25 using a 1-bit *velocity code* flag.

As mentioned earlier, SBAS users are expected to be L1-only. Ionospheric corrections for visible satellites are determined with an interpolation algorithm using SBAS broadcast vertical ionospheric delay values. Applying the law of sines to Figure 8.32, the user first calculates the angle ψ_{pp}, the Earth's central angle between the user position and pierce point:

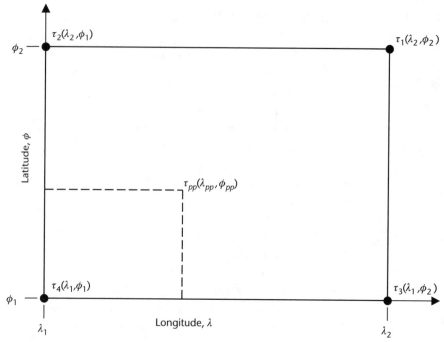

Figure 8.32 Finding the relative IPP position.

$$\psi_{pp} = \frac{\pi}{2} - E - \sin^{-1}\left(\frac{R_E}{R_E + h} \cdot \cos E\right)$$

where R_E is the radius of the Earth, h is the altitude of the IPP, and E is the elevation angle of the satellite from the user position. The user then calculates the latitude, ϕ_{pp}, and longitude, λ_{pp}, of the IPP, as follows:

$$\phi_{pp} = \sin^{-1}\left(\sin\phi_u \cdot \cos\psi_{pp} + \cos\phi_u \cdot \sin\psi_{pp} \cdot \cos A\right)$$

$$\lambda_{pp} = \lambda_u + \pi - \sin^{-1}\left(\frac{\sin\psi_{pp} \cdot \sin A}{\cos\phi_{pp}}\right)$$

$$\text{if } \phi_u > 70°, \text{ and } \tan\psi_{pp}\cos A > \tan\left(\frac{\pi}{2} - \phi_u\right)$$

$$\text{or if } \phi_u < -70°, \text{ and } \tan\psi_{pp}\cos A < \tan\left(\frac{\pi}{2} - \phi_u\right)$$

$$\lambda_{pp} = \lambda_u + \sin^{-1}\left(\frac{\sin\psi_{pp} \cdot \sin A}{\cos\phi_{pp}}\right), \text{ otherwise}$$

where the angles λ_u and ϕ_u are the azimuth and elevation angles, respectively, of the satellite from the user's position. Then the receiver determines the most suitable set of predefined grid points in the proximity of the IPP for each visible satellite. If no suitable set is available, then an ionospheric correction is unavailable for that particular satellite. If four suitable surrounding grid points are found, the receiver determines the IPP position relative to those four points, using Figure 8.18, from the following equations:

$$x_{pp} = \frac{\lambda_{pp} - \lambda_1}{\lambda_2 - \lambda_1} \qquad y_{pp} = \frac{\phi_{pp} - \phi_1}{\phi_2 - \phi_1} \text{ for IPPs between } 85°\text{N and } 85°\text{S}$$

$$\left.\begin{array}{l} y_{pp} = \dfrac{|\phi_{pp}| - 85°}{10°} \\[4mm] x_{pp} = \dfrac{\lambda_{pp} - \lambda_1}{90°} \cdot (1 - 2y_{pp}) + y_{pp} \end{array}\right\} \text{ for IPPs above } 85°\text{N and below } 85°\text{S}$$

The interpolation is weighted, with greater weights given to the nearer grid points. The weights are given by

$$\begin{aligned} W_1 &= x_{pp} \cdot y_{pp} \\ W_2 &= (1 - x_{pp}) \cdot y_{pp} \\ W_3 &= (1 - x_{pp}) \cdot (1 - y_{pp}) \\ W_4 &= x_{pp} \cdot (1 - y_{pp}) \end{aligned}$$

Finally, the vertical delay, τ_{pp}, at the IPP is determined by

$$\tau_{pp}(\lambda_{pp}, \phi_{pp}) = \sum_{i=1}^{4} W_i \cdot \tau_i \qquad (8.49)$$

where the τ_i are the vertical delays at the four grid points provided in the ionospheric delay corrections message (message type 26).

If only three of the four suitable surrounding grid points are available, the calculation of the weights is modified slightly, as follows:

$$\begin{aligned} W_1 &= y_{pp} \\ W_2 &= 1 - x_{pp} - y_{pp} \\ W_3 &= x_{pp} \end{aligned}$$

The same delay formula (8.49) is used, except that the sum is over three weightings. The remaining ionospheric delay calculation accounts for a difference in delay from the vertical and is a function of the elevation angle to the satellite. To obtain the ionospheric correction, which is added to the pseudorange measurement, the vertical delay $\tau_{pp}(\lambda_{pp}, \phi_{pp})$ is multiplied by the *obliquity factor, F*, where

$$F = \left[1 - \left(\frac{R_E \cos E}{R_E + h}\right)^2\right]^{-\frac{1}{2}}$$

To account for tropospheric delays, the user equipment is required to apply a tropospheric delay correction to each raw pseudorange measurement. The UNB3 algorithm presented in Section 7.2.4.2 is employed. After applying all specified corrections, SBAS user equipment computes user position using a WLS algorithm.

In addition to application of the SBAS differential corrections, user equipment for safety applications must also compute position error bounds, referred to as the HPL or VPL in the local horizontal and vertical directions, respectively. These levels represent the user position errors that will not be exceeded without a timely warning with the associated probability levels and time to alerts listed in Table 8.3. The HPLs and VPLs are continually compared to the applicable *horizontal alert limit* (HAL) and *vertical alert limit* (VAL) for the current phase of flight, and a warning is issued to the pilot if HPL > HAL or VPL > VAL pertaining to that operation. For instance, for APV-I approaches, VAL = 50m, HAL = 40m, and the time to alert is 10 seconds. An SBAS system is designed so that the probability is less than 2×10^{-7} per approach that an aircraft conducting an APV-I approach computes VPL < 50m and HPL < 40m when the true vertical or horizontal position errors are greater than these levels for longer than 10 seconds without a warning being issued.

The user equipment computes HPL and VPL using variances that are broadcast in message types 2–6 for the SBAS fast and long-term corrections and in message type 26 for the SBAS ionospheric corrections. A set of complicated rules is also applied to adjust these variances for latency, missed messages, and other factors [52]. Variances for receiver noise, multipath, and residual tropospheric errors are computed based upon the elevation angles of the visible satellites. The individual error variances are summed to form overall residual pseudorange error variances for the visible satellite. Finally, the geometry matrix and known weighting matrix for the WLS solution are used to bound the standard deviation of horizontal and vertical position errors. Under the assumption that all errors are Gaussian, multipliers for the horizontal and vertical position error standard deviations are applied to determine HPL and VPL. Although it is well known that the true residual errors are not Gaussian, the variances in the broadcast message and the variances for receiver noise, multipath, and tropospheric errors are inflated by design to represent Gaussian distributions that *overbound* the true errors for the probabilities of interest (e.g., see [55]).

SBAS GEOs

The current SBAS geostationary constellation consists of the five Inmarsat-3 satellites, the European Space Agency (ESA) Artemis satellite, and the MTSAT-1R satellite. The four primary Inmarsat-3 satellites are located at approximately the following longitudes in a geostationary orbit: 178°E for the POR, 64.5°E for the IOR, 55.5°W for the AORW), and 15.5°W for the AORE. The fifth Inmarsat-3 satellite was launched to location 25°E as an in-orbit spare. The ESA Artemis satellite is located at 21.5°E, and the MTSAT-1R satellite is at 140°E.

At present, the U.S. WAAS uses the Inmarsat-3 AORW and POR satellites with coverage as shown in Figure 8.33. In the near future, AORW is anticipated to be moved to 98°W. Additionally, the FAA is leasing transponders on two GEOs that will be launched in the near future. These include Telesat Canada's Anik F1R satellite, which will be located at 107°W and PanAmSat's Galaxy XV satellite to be located at 133°W (see Figure 8.34).

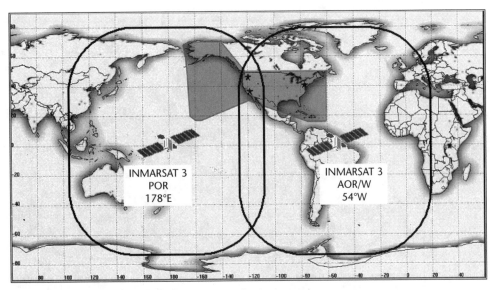

Figure 8.33   Current WAAS space segment and primary service area.

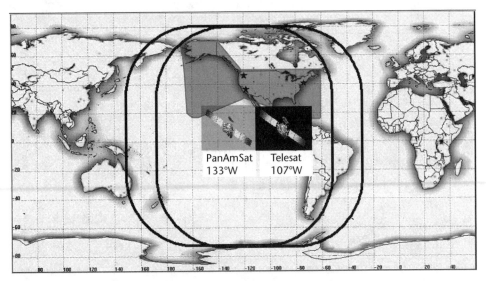

Figure 8.34   Location of additional WAAS GEOs.

The current EGNOS space segment is composed of three GEO navigation transponders payload hosts, Inmarsat-3 AORE and IOR, and the ESA ARTEMIS navigation satellite, as shown in Figure 8.35. EGNOS will likely use one or more of the Inmarsat 4 GEOs that will be launched into orbit around 2005. The Inmarsat 4s will host a navigation payload capable of transmitting SBAS information on both the GPS L1 and L5 frequencies [56]. A functional schematic of the Inmarsat-4 satellite is shown in Figure 8.36.

As mentioned earlier in this section, the first GEO planned for MSAS, MTSAT-1, was destroyed following a launch failure in 1999. A replacement, MTSAT-1R, was launched in February 2005 and is located at 140°E. A second

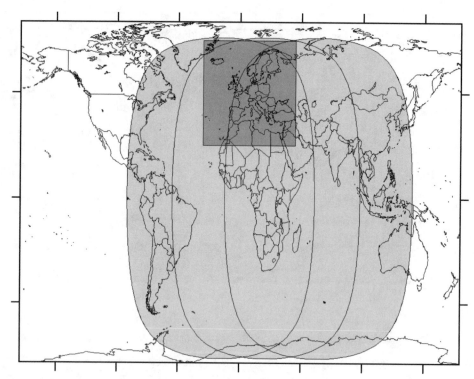

Figure 8.35 Current EGNOS space segment and primary service area.

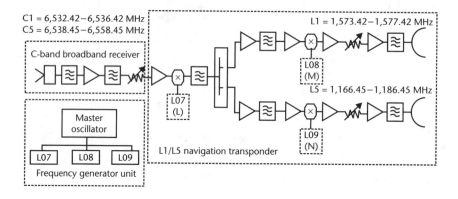

C1 = 6,532.42–6,536.42 MHz
C5 = 6,538.45–6,558.45 MHz

C-band broadband receiver

L1 = 1,573.42–1,577.42 MHz

L08
(M)

L07
(L)

Master oscillator

L5 = 1,166.45–1,186.45 MHz

L1/L5 navigation transponder

L09
(N)

L07 L08 L09

Frequency generator unit

Figure 8.36 Inmarsat 4 navigation payload.

GEO, MTSAT-2, will be launched later in the decade at a similar location. The coverage of MTSAT-1R and the MSAS primary service area are shown in Figure 8.37.

The GAGAN footprints for three potential orbital locations are shown in Figure 8.38.

Utilization by Nonaviation Users
Although the SBAS signal format in this chapter has been developed to support aeronautical requirements, the signal may also be used by nonaviation users with a suit-

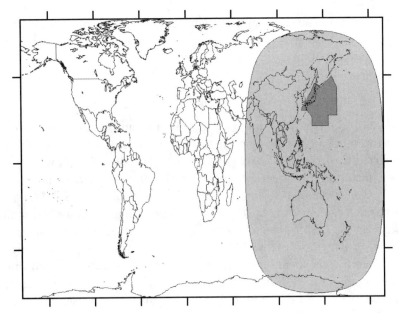

Figure 8.37   Proposed MSAS geostationary space segment and primary service area.

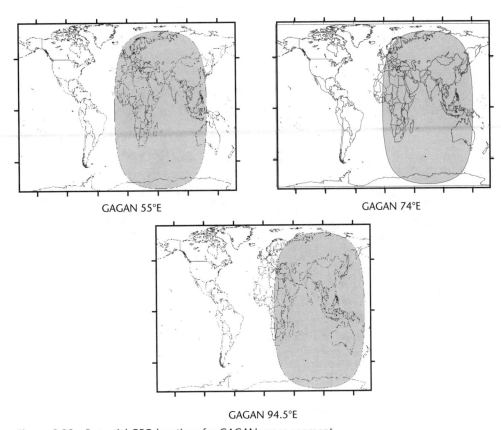

GAGAN 55°E   GAGAN 74°E

GAGAN 94.5°E

Figure 8.38   Potential GEO locations for GAGAN space segment.

able receiver. The vast majority of current SBAS users are not involved with aviation applications—many low-cost, handheld recreational receivers include an SBAS reception capability.

8.6.1.3 GBAS

In a GBAS, GPS SPS is augmented with a ground reference station to improve the performance of the navigation services in a local area. The U.S. FAA's GBAS is referred to as the LAAS and can support all phases of flight within its area of coverage, including the precision approach, landing, departure, and surface movement [57]. The remainder of this section will focus on the LAAS. LAAS is split up in three separate segments: the space segment, consisting of the GPS satellites; the ground segment or LAAS ground facility (LGF); and the airborne segment. Figure 8.39 shows a depiction of the LGF. Pseudorange corrections and correction rates are computed at the local reference station and broadcast to the airborne GBAS receiver via a communication link. In the aircraft, the corrections and correction rates are applied to the local pseudorange measurements and used to obtain an improved position estimate.

The various LAAS segments are reflected in the LAAS development efforts [58]. RTCA has published Minimum Aviation System Performance Standards (RTCA DO-245) [59] describing the requirements allocation between ground facility and airborne avionics and Minimum Operational Performance Standards (RTCA DO-253A) [60] focusing on the airborne equipment requirements. Finally, the FAA has published LGF specifications in [61].

Pseudorange Correction Computation
Originally, three LAAS position estimation approaches were investigated [62]: single frequency (L1) carrier-smoothed code-phase DGPS [63, 64], kinematic dual-

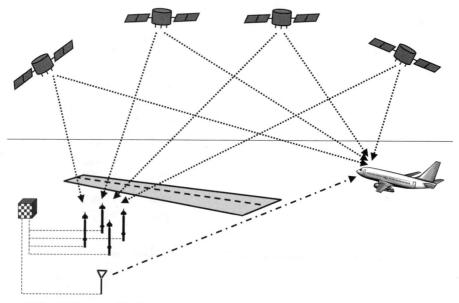

Figure 8.39 LAAS ground facility.

frequency carrier-phase GPS [65], and kinematic single-frequency carrier-phase with integrity beacons [66]. Eventually, carrier-smoothed code-phase DGPS was selected and specified in [60, 61]. The LGF in the specified architecture reduces the noise component on the pseudoranges at each reference receiver (RR) by carrier smoothing the code pseudorange measurements for each satellite. An example of carrier smoothing is

$$\rho_{smooth}(k) = \frac{N-1}{N}\left[\rho_{smooth}(k-1) + \phi(k) - \phi(k-1)\right] + \frac{1}{N}\rho_{meas}(k) \qquad (8.50)$$

where:

k = the time epoch

ϕ = the carrier-phase measurement

N = the number of measurements used for smoothing purposes

The carrier-smoothed pseudoranges are used to compute the pseudorange correction:

$$\Delta\rho_{sc,n,m} = R_{n,m} - \rho_{smooth,n,m} - t_{sv\_gps,n} \qquad (8.51)$$

where:

R = predicted range

n = satellite index

m = RR index

t_{sv_gps} = correction due to the satellite clock from the decoded GPS navigation data

The broadcast correction can be computed from (8.51) following the specifications given in [61]:

$$\Delta\rho_{corr,n} = \frac{1}{M_n}\sum_{m\in S_n}\left[\Delta\rho_{smooth,n,m} - \frac{1}{N_c}\sum_{n\in S_c}\Delta\rho_{smooth,n,m}\right]$$

where:

M_n = number of elements in set S_n

S_n = set of RRs with valid measurements for satellite n

N_c = number of elements in set S_c

S_c = set of valid ranging sources tracked by all RRs

After reception and application of the broadcast LGF corrections, the three-dimensional aircraft position is calculated using a WLS or equivalent algorithm [63].

Performance Requirements

The LAAS performance requirements are described in [59] and define navigation performance parameters such as accuracy, integrity, continuity, and availability. Furthermore, [59, 61] define the coverage area within which the LAAS service should be available. Table 8.6, based on [59, 61], assigns values to the navigation performance parameters of accuracy and integrity. Table 8.6 identifies three LAAS performance types that correspond to the three categories of precision approach and landings: CAT I, CAT II, CAT IIIa, and CAT IIIb. Each of these landing categories is defined by the decision height (DH) at which the pilot or aircraft must make the decision to either continue or abort the landing. This decision depends on the runway visual range (RVR) at the corresponding decision height. Table 8.7 shows the DH and RVR for each of the categories.

Integrity Monitoring

LAAS includes an integrity monitoring function that determines, with a certain level of probability, that the code and carrier phase corrections do not contain misleading information. The integrity monitor function can be subdivided into multiple monitors: a signal quality monitor (SQM) to detect anomalous behavior in the satellite and pseudolite signals, a data quality monitor (DQM) to check if the satellite navi-

Table 8.6 LAAS Performance Requirements

		Performance Type		
		1	2	3
Accuracy	Category supported	CAT I	CAT II/IIIa	CAT IIIb
	Decision Height*	>200 ft	>100/50 ft	>50 ft
	Vertical position Accuracy, 95%	4.4m (NSE)	2.0/2.0m (NSE)	2.0m (NSE)
	Lateral position accuracy, 95%	16.0m (NSE)	6.9/6.2m (NSE)	6.2m (NSE)
Integrity (SIS)	Vertical alert limit (VAL)	10m (200-ft HAT*)	5.3m (100-ft HAT)	5.3m (100-ft HAT)
	Lateral alert limit (LAL)	40m (200-ft HAT)	17.3 (100-ft HAT)	15.5m (100-ft HAT)
	Time to alert	2 seconds	1 second	1 second
	Exposure time	150 seconds	15 seconds	Lateral: 15 seconds Vertical: 30 seconds
	Allowable integrity risk	2×10^{-7}/approach	10^{-9}/approach	10^{-9}/approach

Table 8.7 DH and RVR for LAAS

	DH	RVR
CAT I	200 ft HAT	> 2,400 ft
CAT II	100 ft HAT	> 1,200 ft
CAT IIIa	< 100 ft HAT	> 700 ft
CAT IIIb	< 50 ft HAT	> 150m

gation data contains anomalies, a measurement quality monitor (MQM) to detect anomalies in the measurements such as pseudorange steps, a multiple reference consistency check (MRCC) to check the consistency of the corrections among the LGF RRs, and a sigma monitor (SM) to check the nominal error characteristics of the LGF.

LGF Antennas, Airport Pseudolites, and Data Broadcast

The presence of ground multipath at the LGF could introduce large errors in the airborne position and velocity computations. To mitigate the error due to ground multipath, antennas can be designed that limit the multipath error. One example is the integrated multipath limiting antennas [67]. To increase the availability of LAAS, ranging sources may be added to the LGF such as airport pseudolites (APLs) [68]. APLs transmit a GPS-like signal that can be processed by the RRs and aircraft avionics in a similar fashion as the GPS signals [68]. Having a ranging source at the ground significantly improves the geometry and therefore vertical accuracy. The communications link used to transmit corrections from the LGF to the LAAS avionics is a very high frequency data broadcast (VDB).

8.6.1.4 Precise Point Positioning

A technique referred to as precise point positioning (PPP) has emerged in the last decade that provides decimeter-level position accuracies over very broad geographic regions. In PPP systems, the user's receiver does not use the clock and empheris data broadcast by the GPS satellites. Instead, the user employs precise clock and satellite position estimates computed and provided by an external network such as the one organized by the International GPS Service (see Section 8.6.2.2). Here, we characterize PPP techniques as wide-area code-based DGPS, although others have classified PPP techniques in its category apart from stand-alone and differential GPS.

A typical implementation of PPP is described in [69]. IGS clock and orbit data (see Section 8.6.2.2) is used by a single semicodeless, dual-frequency GPS receiver at an arbitrary location. In addition to estimating its three-dimensional position in ECEF coordinates and clock bias (e.g., the standard four estimated parameters—see discussion in Section 2.4.2), the receiver also estimates the zenith tropospheric path delay (assumed to be the same for all visible satellites) and the bias between the pseudorange and carrier-phase measurement for each visible satellite (modeled as arbitrary real numbers). A sequential filter (e.g., a Kalman filter) is employed to estimate these parameters iteratively as new measurements are obtained. To obtain decimeter-level positioning results, the user equipment must account for a number of error sources that are negligible for most other stand-alone or differential GPS applications. These error sources include:

- *Satellite antenna lever-arm:* Most often, in orbit determination, it is the location of the satellite center of mass that is estimated, not the satellite's antenna phase center. The satellite antenna lever arm is the vector difference between these two locations. The lever arm is over 1m in magnitude for the GPS Block II/IIA satellites.

- *Phase wind-up:* Relative rotation between a GPS satellite and the user antenna can cause carrier-phase measurements to change by up to one cycle. This effect is referred to as phase wind-up. A correction for this effect is provided in [70].

- *Solid Earth tides and ocean loading:* The Earth's surface is not rigid, but rather somewhat pliable. Its shape varies with time, dominated by diurnal and semidiurnal components, in response to gravitational forces. These Earth surface movements are referred to as solid Earth tides. Additional motion of the Earth's surface, especially in coastal locations, due to ocean tides is referred to as ocean loading. Solid Earth tides and ocean loading site displacements can be as large as 30 cm and a few centimeters, respectively. By convention, ECEF coordinate systems such as ITRF are explicitly defined to not include solid Earth tides and ocean loading effects. Thus, these effects should be removed for applications where the user position in ECEF coordinates are desired. Accurate models for the Earth's deformation due to solid Earth tides and ocean loading can be found in [71].

Using these techniques and models, the positions of a number of sites were determined in [69] with an accuracy often better than 5 cm in each coordinate. Approximately 30 minutes of data were required to be processed before the obtained accuracy converged to these levels.

An important example of an operational PPP system is the JPL's Internet-Based Global DGPS (IGDG) system [72], which provides clock and ephemeris data over the Internet using dedicated frame relay lines. In collaboration with JPL, NavCom Technology (a subsidiary of John Deere) also distributes the data globally via L-band (1,525–1,565 MHz) geostationary satellite links as part of their StarFire network DGPS service [73].

8.6.2 Carrier Based

In the past, geodetic positioning required LOS connections to a network of monumented points in the ground. This geodetic network defined a consistent reference frame and helped control measurement error. Now, a network of continuously operating GPS receivers may replace the traditional geodetic network of monumented points. The network of receivers has an authoritative set of coordinates and supplies base station carrier-phase and code range data for accurate differential processing. Continuously operating networks are popular, and numerous examples exist. We shall focus on two, the U.S. Continuously Operating Reference Stations (CORS) and the global IGS system.

8.6.2.1 CORS

The National Geodetic Survey (NGS) of the NOAA manages a CORS system to support nonnavigation, post-processing applications of GPS. GPS receiver data are collected throughout the country and are archived at the main site in Silver Spring, Maryland, and at a parallel facility in Boulder, Colorado. The U.S. CORS system provides code range and carrier-phase data from a nationwide network of GPS stations through the Internet. The CORS Web site is http://www.ngs.noaa.gov/CORS.

The NGS makes use of stations established by other groups rather than building an independent network of reference stations. The backbone of the CORS network is the MDGPS/NDGPS and WAAS stations. A listing of CORS contributors can be found at http://www.ngs.noaa.gov/CORS/Organizations/Organizations.html. Figure 8.40 shows a breakdown of the CORS network partners affiliations.

The diverse character of the CORS partners has lead to a grouping of CORS stations into two major categories, National CORS and Cooperative CORS. The fundamental distinction is that NGS archives and disseminates the data from National CORS, and does not archive and disseminate data from Cooperative CORS. National CORS are expected to operate 24 hours/day, 7 days/week. The site, http://www.ngs.noaa.gov/CORS/Becoming_a_CORS.html, shows other distinguishing characteristics. Cooperative CORS provide a supplement to the National CORS by providing more local base stations, shorter baselines, and a variety of data rates. As of August 2005, over 660 National CORS sites and over 140 Cooperative CORS sites were operating.

The fundamental data of National CORS are *receiver independent exchange* (RINEX) format (version 2.10) files containing dual-frequency carrier-phase and pseudorange measurements. For many sites, Doppler data are also available. If supported by a receiver, the L1 pseudoranges derived from both C/A code (the C1 pseudorange) and the P(Y) code (the P1 pseudorange) are provided. The principal translation package that converts the varieties of manufacturers' binary data into RINEX is the program TEQC, maintained by UNAVCO. TECQ is documented at http://www.unavco.org/facility/software/teqc/teqc.html.

CORS positional coordinates and velocities are key values needed to use CORS as base stations for carrier-based differential GPS applications. CORS coordinates and velocities are provided in two distinct reference frames, NAD 83 and ITRF00. The formal datum label for the National CORS is NAD83 (CORS96), and they are realized with an epoch of 2002.00. Stations in the Pacific are an exception, since

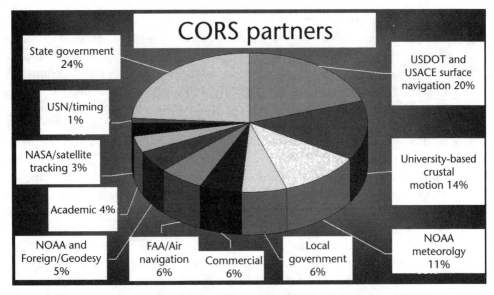

Figure 8.40   Partners in the CORS system. (*Source:* National Geodetic Survey, NOAA.)

they are on differing tectonic plates. These CORS will be in the NAD 83 (PACP00) or the NAD 83 (MARP00) frames. Also, CORS in Alaska are computed in NAD83 (CORS96), but with an epoch date of 2003.00, to accommodate the Denali earthquake activity. All published ITRF00 positions and velocities carry a common datum tag ITRF00 (1997.00) and are realized with the epoch date of 1997.00. Of course, the price of such ITRF uniformity is that tectonic plate motion, as well as local motion, is expressed in the velocity values and is seldom negligible for precision applications. More detail on the computation of CORS coordinates can be found at http://www.ngs.noaa.gov/CORS/Coords.html. A conversion utility (horizontal time-dependent positioning) between these reference frames is located at http://www.ngs.noaa.gov/TOOLS/Htdp/Htdp.html. It should be noted that, while the International GNSS Service (IGS) Analysis Centers provide GPS orbits in a reference frame denoted IGb00, users may treat IGb00 and ITRF00 as equivalent.

Coordinate locations for a CORS antenna are referred to two different station reference points, the ARP and the L1 phase center (L1 PC). The ARP is defined as the center of the bottom-most, permanently attached surface of the antenna. The L1 PC is a notional, electrical location for receipt of the L1 signal. Under most antenna designs, the L1 (and L2) phase center varies with the elevation angle to a given GPS satellite. Thus, establishment of an L1 PC origin is done in conjunction with a companion model of the L1 PC variation (http://www.ngs.noaa.gov/ANTCAL). Due to the abstract character of the L1 PC and its dependence on specific calibration models, NGS considers the ARP the definitive location for a CORS site.

Extensive metadata are also available for stations in National CORS. This includes availability profiles, detailed data sheets and site logs, maps, photos, and time series of daily coordinate solutions. These metadata answer many questions on stability and reliability.

Other data that are not RINEX receiver data or metadata are available at the CORS site. In particular, both broadcast and precise GPS orbits can be obtained. The broadcast orbits are collected from the IGS global tracking network and do not show the satellite dropouts common to single-site collections. Both IGS and NGS precise orbits are available. The IGS orbits are combined products and include the NGS contributions. Further discussion on IGS orbits is continued in the next section. For CORS sites that have a weather sensor, RINEX meteorological files are produced. And, as described earlier, users may obtain files and diagrams describing receiver antenna phase center offsets and phase center variation.

CORS RINEX data are stored in standardized directory locations. Users may access these files though the "Standard" method, or through "User Friendly CORS—UFCORS." Standard access is most readily obtained by clicking on the coverage map found on the CORS home page (http://www.ngs.noaa.gov/CORS). Successive clicks on a location of interest will enable a user to zoom down to a specific site with a unique 4-character ID (e.g., GAIT). A menu to the left will enable a user to select RINEX data or other metadata. A request for RINEX data will transfer the user from the map interface to the standard download interface. One must then again select the station of interest, the request for RINEX data, and then add the year, month, and day of interest. This will lead the user to the directory holding the RINEX data.

The standard method is convenient for access of the various metadata. But, if one is interested solely in RINEX data, it can be obtained by direct file transfer protocol (FTP) access though a Web browser at ftp://cors.ngs.noaa.gov/cors/rinex/ 2004 (for example). Multiple years are stored under the *rinex* directory; multiple days are stored under the *year* directory; the various site IDs are stored under the *day* directories; and the RINEX files are stored under the *site id* directories. A schematic of the FTP directory structure can be found at: ftp://cors.ngs.noaa.gov/cors/ readme.txt. Note that the FTP structure is most convenient for those software products that automatically download data for local processing.

In contrast to the standard access method, the UFCORS interface provides a customized file collection that is automatically compressed and downloaded to a user's computer (http://www.ngs.noaa.gov/CORS-Proxy/UFCORS/). The user fills in a two-page menu, indicating the desired block of time and the CORS site. Other options include receipt of the data sheet, IGS precise orbits, compression options, and alternative data rates. When selecting an alternative data rate, the collected data will be decimated or interpolated to accommodate the desired target rate. The UFCORS interface frees the user from knowing specifics about the RINEX file storage system.

This section cannot be closed without addressing some of the support tools available from the CORS and NGS site. Earlier in this section, HTDP was discussed as a utility for conversion of coordinates between reference frames and epochs. A dynamic map utility linked at the home page allows one to build customized views of CORS coverage. Various RINEX file manipulation utilities (e.g., interpolate and decimate) can be reached from http://www.ngs.noaa.gov/CORS/utilities.html. A multifeatured Geodetic Toolkit at http://www.ngs.noaa.gov/TOOLS supports numerous online computations and coordinate conversions.

Special remarks must be made about the Online Positioning User Service (OPUS) tool found at http://www.ngs.noaa.gov/OPUS. This service allows users to upload 2 or more hours of dual-frequency RINEX data from a stationary antenna for automated, remote processing at NGS. Single baselines are computed and merged from three nearby CORS stations, and the results are e-mailed back to the user. Turnaround is typically just a few minutes. At its heart, OPUS uses the CORS as a subsystem in computation of the user's coordinates. This is suggestive of new directions and roles that continuously operating reference stations can take in the future.

8.6.2.2   International GNSS Service (IGS)

The International Association of Geodesy established the IGS in 1993 to support geodetic and geophysical research activities by providing GPS data and products. The IGS serves a coordination role, sets standards and specifications, and encourages international adherence to its conventions. The IGS operates through a governing board and a central bureau (its executive arm), and functions through the cooperation of international groups of GPS satellite tracking networks, data centers, analysis centers, and various working groups. The IGS Web site is http://igscb.jpl.nasa.gov.

IGS is known foremost as the source of precise GPS orbits. However, IGS also produces GPS satellite clock and ground receiver clock solutions, and Earth orientation parameter (EOP) products (polar motion, polar motion rate, and length of day). The IGS solutions are combined products that integrate the solutions generated by the individual analysis centers.

IGS products come in three varieties, with progressively greater latencies and accuracies. The ultrarapid products are 48 hours in length. The first 24 hours are observed, and the remaining 24 hours are predicted. Ultrarapid products are produced twice a day, so that one can always utilize the early part of the prediction interval. Accuracies range from 5 to 10 cm (orbit) and 0.2 to 5 ns (clock). The rapid products have 17-hour latency and have better than 5-cm orbit accuracy with 0.1-ns clock accuracy. The final combination products have an approximate 13-day latency with slightly better orbit and clock accuracies.

The IGS products are organized by GPS week number and are available for FTP access through any browser. For example, ftp://igscb.jpl.nasa.gov/igscb/product/1261 contains precise orbit, clock, and EOP products for the week of March 7, 2004 (GPS week 1261). The nomenclature is described at http://igscb.jpl.nasa.gov/components/dcnav/igscb_product_wwww.html. So, for example, "igr12610.sp3.Z" refers to the Rapid product, week 1,261, day 0 (Sunday, March 7, 2004) orbit in the SP3 format, compressed with a UNIX-compatible algorithm. Note that slightly different directory trees are used at the four sites that archive IGS products.

IGS also archives and disseminates GPS CORS data globally. The master index, http://igscb.jpl.nasa.gov/components/data.html, shows CORS data grouped by update intervals and archive sites. Directory paths vary between archive sites. For example, SOPAC data are mapped at http://igscb.jpl.nasa.gov/components/dcnav/sopac_rinex.html. Continuing the example, GPS observation CORS data for Sunday, March 7, 2004, can be found at ftp://garner.ucsd.edu/pub/rinex/2004/067. The "2004" refers to the year; the "067" refers to the day number for March 7. The file name, "ajac0670.04o.Z," refers to AJAC, a site in Corsica, day number 067, a daily (not hourly) file, year 2004, GPS receiver data, compressed with a UNIX-compatible algorithm. Not all CORS sites are found at all the IGS servers.

An overview map of the IGS international cooperative GPS tracking network is found at http://igscb.jpl.nasa.gov/network/maps/allmaps.html. One can immediately note the global distribution of the sites. Some sites upload their data hourly, while others do so daily. The Web page at http://itrf.ensg.ign.fr/ITRF_solutions/2000/ITRF2000.php contains authoritative ITRF00 Cartesian coordinates and velocities for the IGS sites. Weekly network solutions are also available.

The IGS site has a rich set of resources, as would be expected from an international scientific operation. In addition to the items already mentioned, one may also find products for tropospheric zenith path delay and global grids of ionospheric TEC. Data are available from GPS sensors in LEO satellites. Publications are at http://igscb.jpl.nasa.gov/overview/pubs.html; mail archives are at http://igscb.jpl.nasa.gov/mail/mailindex.html; and analysis conventions are at http://maia.usno.navy.mil/conv2003.html.

References

[1]   Olynik, M., et al., "Temporal Variability of GPS Error Sources and Their Effect on Relative Positioning Accuracy," *Proc. of The Institute of Navigation National Technical Meeting*, January 2002.

[2]   Department of Defense, *Global Positioning System Standard Positioning Service Signal Specification*, 2nd ed., U.S. Department of Defense, Washington, D.C., June 2, 1995.

[3] Altshuler, E. E., *Corrections for Tropospheric Range Error*, Report AFCRL-71-0419, Air Force Cambridge Research Laboratory, Hanscom Field, Bedford, MA, July 27, 1971.

[4] Coster, A. J., et al., "Characterization of Atmospheric Propagation Errors for DGPS," *Proc. of The Institute of Navigation's Annual Meeting*, Denver, CO, June 1998.

[5] Hofmann-Wellenhof, B., H. Lichtenegger, and J. Collins, *GPS Theory and Practice*, Wien, Germany: Springer-Verlag, 1992.

[6] Komjathy, A., et al., "The Ionospheric Impact of the October 2003 Storm Event on WAAS," *Proc. of The Institute of Navigation ION GNSS 2004*, Long Beach, CA, September 2004.

[7] Wanninger, L., "Effects of the Equatorial Ionosphere on GPS," *GPS World*, July 1993.

[8] Klobuchar, J., P. Doherty, and M. B. El-Arini, "Potential Ionospheric Limitations to GPS Wide-Area Augmentation System," *NAVIGATION: Journal of The Institute of Navigation*, Vol. 42, No. 2, Summer 1995.

[9] Doherty, P., et al., "Statistics of Time Rate of Change of Ionospheric Range Delay," *Proc. of The Institute of Navigation ION GPS-94*, Salt Lake City, UT, September 1994.

[10] Lapucha, D., and M. Huff, "Multi-Site Real-Time DGPS System Using Starfix Link: Operational Results," *ION GPS-92*, Albuquerque, NM, September 16–18, 1992.

[11] Brown, A., "Extended Differential GPS," *NAVIGATION: Journal of The Institute of Navigation*, Vol. 36, No. 3, Fall 1989.

[12] Kee, C., B. W. Parkinson, and P. Axelrad, "Wide Area Differential GPS," *NAVIGATION: Journal of The Institute of Navigation*, Vol. 38, No. 2, Summer 1991, pp. 123–145.

[13] Ashkenazi, V., C. J. Hill, and J. Nagle, "Wide Area Differential GPS: A Performance Study," *Proc. of the Fifth International Technical Meeting of the Satellite Division of The Institute of Navigation (ION GPS-92)*, Albuquerque, NM, September 16–18, 1992, pp. 589–598.

[14] Montenbruck, O., and E. Gill, *Satellite Orbits: Models, Methods, Applications*, Berlin, Germany: Springer-Verlag, 2000.

[15] Remondi, B., "Using the Global Positioning System (GPS) Phase Observable for Relative Geodesy: *Differential GPS* 383 Modeling, Processing, and Results," Ph.D. Dissertation, Center for Space Research, University of Austin, Austin, TX, 1984.

[16] Counselman, C., and S. Gourevitch, "Miniature Interferometer Terminals for Earth Surveying: Ambiguity and Multipath with Global Positioning System," *IEEE Trans. on Geoscience and Remote Sensing*, Vol. GE-19, No. 4, October 1981.

[17] Greenspan, R. L., et al., "Accuracy of Relative Positioning by Interferometry with Reconstructed Carrier, GPS Experimental Results," *Proc. of 3rd International Geodetic Symposium on Satellite Doppler Positioning*, Las Cruces, NM, February 1982.

[18] Hatch, R., "The Synergism of GPS Code and Carrier Measurements," *Proc. of the Third International Symposium on Satellite Doppler Positioning*, Vol. 2, New Mexico State University, February 1982.

[19] Abidin, H., "Extrawidelaning for 'On the Fly' Ambiguity Resolution: Simulation of Multipath Effects," *Proc. of the ION Satellite Division's 3rd International Meeting*, ION GPS-90, Colorado Springs, CO, September 1990.

[20] Paielli, R. A., et al., "Carrier Phase Differential GPS for Approach and Landing: Algorithms and Preliminary Results," *Proc. of the 6th International Technical Meeting*, ION GPS-93, Salt Lake City, UT, September 1993, pp. 831–840.

[21] van Graas, F., D. W. Diggle, and R. M. Hueschen, "Interferometric GPS Flight Reference/Autoland System: Flight Test Results," *NAVIGATION: Journal of The Institute of Navigation*, Vol. 41, No. 1, Spring 1994, pp. 57–81.

[22] Cohen, C. E., et al., "Real-Time Flight Testing Using Integrity Beacons for GPS Category III Precision Landing," *NAVIGATION: Journal of The Institute of Navigation*, Vol. 41, No. 2, Summer 1994.

[23] Cohen, C. E., et al., "Flight Test Results of Autocoupled Approaches Using GPS and Integrity Beacons," *Proc. of the ION Satellite Division's 7th International Technical Meeting*, Salt Lake City, UT, September 1994, pp. 1145–1153.

[24] Leick, A., *GPS Satellite Surveying*, New York: John Wiley & Sons, 1990.

[25] van Graas, F., and M. Braasch, "GPS Interferometric Attitude and Heading Determination: Initial Flight Test Results," *NAVIGATION: Journal of The Institute of Navigation*, Vol. 38, No. 4, Winter 1991–1992, pp. 297–316.

[26] Potter, J., and M. Suman, "Thresholdless Redundancy Management with Arrays of Skewed Instruments," *AGARD Monograph*, No. 224, NATO, Neuilly sur Seine, France, 1979.

[27] Walsh, D., "Real-Time Ambiguity Resolution While on the Move," *Proc. of the ION Satellite Division's 5th International Meeting*, ION GPS-92, Albuquerque, NM, September 1992, pp. 473–481.

[28] Chen, H. C., *Theory of Electromagnetic Waves: A Coordinate-Free Approach*, New York: McGraw-Hill, 1983.

[29] Golub, G. H., and C. F. Van Loan, *Matrix Computations*, 2nd ed., Baltimore, MD: The Johns Hopkins University Press, 1989.

[30] Erickson, C., "An Analysis of Ambiguity Resolution Techniques for Rapid Static GPS Surveys Using Single Frequency Data," *Proc. of the ION Satellite Division's 5th International Meeting*, Albuquerque, NM, September 1992, pp. 453–462.

[31] Frei, E., and G. Beutler, "Rapid Static Positioning Based on the Fast Ambiguity Resolution Approach 'FARA': Theory and First Results," *Manuscript Geodaetica*, Vol. 15, 1990.

[32] Hatch, R., "Instantaneous Ambiguity Resolution," *Proc. of the IAG International Symposium 107 on Kinematic Systems in Geodesy, Surveying and Sensing*, New York, September 10–13, 1990.

[33] Teunissen, P. J. G., P. J. De Jonge, and C. C. J. M. Tiberius, "Performance of the LAMDA Method for Fast GPS Ambiguity Resolution," *NAVIGATION: Journal of The Institute of Navigation*, Vol. 44, No. 3, Fall 1997, pp. 373–383.

[34] Braasch, M. S., "On the Characterization of Multipath Errors in Satellite-Based Precision Approach and Landing Systems," Ph.D. Dissertation, Department of Electrical and Computer Engineering (Avionics Engineering Center), Ohio University, Athens, OH, 1992.

[35] Wuebbena, G., "The GPS Adjustment Software Package GEONAP—Concepts and Models," *Proc. of the 5th International Geodetic Symposium on Satellite Positioning*, Las Cruces, NM, March 1989.

[36] Kiran, S., "A Wideband Airport Pseudolite Architecture for the Local Area Augmentation System," Ph.D. Dissertation, School of Electrical and Computer Engineering (Avionics Engineering Center), Ohio University, Athens, OH, 2003.

[37] Kuipers, J., *Quaternions and Rotation Sequences*, Princeton, NJ: Princeton University Press, 2002.

[38] Cohen, C. E., "Attitude Determination Using GPS: Development of an All Solid-State Guidance, Navigation, and Control Sensor for Air and Space Vehicles Based on the Global Positioning System," Ph. D. thesis, Stanford University, Stanford, CA, December 1992.

[39] Cohen, C. E., "Attitude Determination," in *Global Positioning System: Theory and Applications*, Volume II, B. Parkinson and J. J. Spilker, Jr., (eds.), Washington, D.C.: American Institute of Astronautics and Aeronautics, 1996.

[40] Special Committee 104, *RTCM Recommended Standards for Differential GNSS (Global Navigation Satellite Systems) Service*, Version 2.3, Radio Technical Commission for Maritime Services, Alexandria, VA, August 20, 2001.

[41] Special Committee 104, *RTCM Recommended Standards for Differential GNSS (Global Navigation Satellite Systems) Service*, Version 3.0, Radio Technical Commission for Maritime Services, Alexandria, VA, February 10, 2004.

[42] Kalafus, R., "The New RTCM SC-104 Standard for Differential and RTK GNSS Broadcasts," *Proc. of The Institute of Navigation ION GPS/GNSS 2003*, Portland, OR, September 2003, pp. 741–747.

[43] Chop, J., et al., "Local Corrections, Disparate Uses: Cooperation Spawns National Differential GPS," *GPS World*, April 2002.

[44] *Federal Radionavigation Systems*, U.S. Department of Defense and Department of Transportation, Washington, D.C., 2001.

[45] *Broadcast Standard for the USCG DGPS Navigation Service*, COMDTINST M16577.1, United States Coast Guard, Washington, D.C., April 1993.

[46] Proakis, J., *Digital Communications*, 4th ed., New York: McGraw-Hill, 2001.

[47] Enge, P., and K. Olson, "Medium Frequency Broadcast of Differential GPS Data," *IEEE Trans. on Aerospace and Electronic Systems*, July 1990.

[48] Navigation Systems Panel, *Amendment 79 to the International Standards and Recommended Practices, Aeronautical Telecommunications (Annex 10 to the Convention on International Civil Aviation)*, International Civil Aviation Organization, Montreal, Canada, February 23, 2004.

[49] Walter, T., and M. B. El-Arini, (eds.), *Global Positioning System: Papers Published in Navigation*, Volume VI (SBAS), Institute of Navigation, Fairfax, VA, 1999.

[50] Braff, R., and C. Shively, "GPS Integrity Channel," *NAVIGATION: Journal of The Institute of Navigation*, Vol. 32, No. 4, Winter 1985–1986.

[51] Kinal, G., and O. Razumovsky, "Upgrades to the Inmarsat PN Transmission Test Bed," *Proc. of The Institute of Navigation ION GPS '90*, Colorado Springs, CO, September 1990, pp. 315–322.

[52] RTCA Special Committee SC-159, *Recommended Operational Performance Standards for Global Positioning System/Wide Area Augmentation System Airborne Equipment*, RTCA/DO-229C, Washington, D.C.: RTCA, November 28, 2001.

[53] Nagle, J., A. J. Van Dierendonck, and Q. Hua, "Inmarsat-3 Navigation Signal C/A-Code Selection and Interference Analysis," *NAVIGATION: Journal of The Institute of Navigation*, Vol. 39, No. 4, Winter 1992-1993.

[54] Hegarty, C., "Optimizing Differential GPS for a Data Rate Constrained Broadcast Channel," *Proc. of The Institute of Navigation ION GPS '93*, Salt Lake City, UT, September 1993.

[55] DeCleene, B., "Defining Pseudorange Integrity—Overbounding," *Proc. of The Institute of Navigation ION GPS 2000*, September 2000.

[56] Soddu, C., and O. Razumovsky, "Inmarsat's New Navigation Payload," *GPS World*, November 1, 2001.

[57] Braff, R., "Description of the FAA's Local Area Augmentation System (LAAS)," *NAVIGATION: Journal of The Institute of Navigation*, Vol. 44, No. 4, Winter 1997–1998.

[58] "Local Area Augmentation System—LAAS," September 2004, FAA Web site, http://gps.faa.gov.

[59] Minimum Aviation System Performance Standards for Local Area Augmentation System (LAAS), RTCA DO-245, September 1998.

[60] Minimum Operational Performance Standards for GPS Local Area Augmentation System Airborne Equipment, RTCA DO-253A, November 2001.

[61] "Specification FAA-E-2937A—Category I Local Area Augmentation System Ground Facility," United States Department of Transportation Federal Aviation Administration, FAA-E-2937A, April 17, 2002.

[62] van Graas, F., "GNSS Augmentation for High Precision Navigation Services," AGARD Lecture Series 207, System Implications and Innovative Applications of Satellite Navigation, June 1996.

[63] van Graas, F., et al., "Ohio University/FAA Flight Test Demonstartion of Local Area Augmentation System (LAAS)," *NAVIGATION: Journal of The Institute of Navigation*, Vol. 45, No. 2, Summer 1998.

[64] Hundley, W., et al., "FAA-Wilcox Electric Category IIIB Feasibility Demonstration Program—Flight Test Results," *Proc. of The Institute of Navigation GPS-95*, September 12–14, 1995.

[65] Kaufmann, D., "Flight Test Evaluation of the E-Systems Differential GPS Category IIII Automatic Landing System," NASA Ames Research Center, Moffett Field, CA, 1995.

[66] Cohen, C., et al., "Autolanding a 737 Using GPS Integrity Beacons," *NAVIGATION: Journal of The Institute of Navigation*, Vol. 42, No. 3, Fall 1995.

[67] Thornberg, D. B., et al., "LAAS Integrated Multipath-Limiting Antenna," *NAVIGATION: Journal of The Institute of Navigation*, Vol. 50, No. 2, Summer 2003.

[68] Bartone, C., and F. van Graas, "Ranging Airport Pseudolite for Local Area Augmentation," *IEEE Trans. on Aerospace and Electronic Systems*, Vol. 36, No. 1, January 2000.

[69] Kouba, J., and P. Héroux, "GPS Precise Point Positioning Using IGS Orbit Products," *GPS Solutions*, Vol. 5, No. 2, Fall 2000, pp. 12–28.

[70] Wu, J. T., et al., "Effects of Antenna Orientation on GPS Carrier Phase," *Manuscripta Geodetica*, Vol. 18, 1993, pp. 91–98.

[71] McCarthy, D. D., and G. Petit, (eds.), *IERS Conventions (2003)*, International Earth Rotation and Reference Systems Service Technical Note No. 32, Frankfurt, Germany, 2004.

[72] Armatys, M., et al., "Demonstration of Decimeter-Level Real-Time Positioning of an Airborne Platform," *Proc. of The Institute of Navigation National Technical Meeting*, Anaheim, CA, January 2003.

[73] Hatch, R., T. Sharpe, and P. Galyean, "StarFire: A Global, High-Accuracy, Differential GPS System," *Proc. of The Institute of Navigation National Technical Meeting*, Anaheim, CA, January 2003.

CHAPTER 9

Integration of GPS with Other Sensors and Network Assistance

J. Blake Bullock
Motorola

Michael Foss
Vehicle Guidance

G. Jeffrey Geier
Motorola

Michael King
General Dynamics

9.1 Overview

In the previous chapters, we have observed that GPS receivers can be thought of as discrete-time position/velocity sensors with sampling intervals of approximately 1 second. The need to provide continuous navigation between the update periods of the GPS receiver, during periods of shading of the GPS receiver's antenna, and through periods of interference is the impetus for integrating GPS with various additional sensors. The most popular are inertial sensors, but the list also includes dopplerometers (Doppler velocity/altimeters), altimeters, speedometers, and odometers, to name a few. The method most widely used for this integration is the Kalman filter. The Kalman filter is an estimator. It estimates the instantaneous state of a linear system perturbed by Gaussian white noise. One of the key attributes of the Kalman filter is that it provides a means of inferring information by the use of indirect measurements. It does not have to read control variable(s) directly, but it can read an indirect measurement (including associated noise) and estimate the control variable(s). In GPS applications, the control variables, as we will see later in this chapter, are position, velocity, and possible attitude errors. The indirect measurements are GPS measurements.

In addition to integration with other sensors, it can also be extremely beneficial to integrate a GPS sensor within a communications network. For example, many cellular handsets now include embedded GPS engines to locate the user in the event of an emergency or to support a wide variety of location-based services. These handsets are often used indoors or in other areas where the GPS signals are so highly attenuated that demodulation of the GPS navigation data by the handset is not possible. With network assistance, however, it is possible to determine the location of the handset. The network can obtain the requisite GPS navigation data from other GPS receivers with clear sky view or other sources. Further, the network can assist the handset in a number of other ways, such as the provision of timing and a coarse position estimate. Such assistance can greatly increase the sensitivity of the GPS sensor embedded in the handset.

This chapter consists of three major sections beyond this overview. In Section 9.2, we discuss integration of GPS with inertial sensors. The motivations for GPS/inertial integration are detailed. The Kalman filter is described, as well as an example of an elementary Kalman filter implementation. Various classes of GPS/inertial integrations are introduced and discussed.

Section 9.3 addresses sensor integration for land vehicles. The implementation issues related to a GPS/inertial integration as a navigator for land vehicle applications are presented. A description of the sensors, their integration with the Kalman filter, and test data taken during field testing of a practical multisensor system are presented.

Section 9.4 discusses methods of enhancing GPS performance using network assistance. This section includes discussions of network assistance techniques, performance, and emerging standards.

9.2 GPS/Inertial Integration

Navigation employing GPS and inertial sensors is a synergistic relationship. The integration of these two types of sensors not only overcomes performance issues found in each individual sensor, but also produces a system whose performance exceeds that of the individual sensors. GPS provides bounded accuracy, while inertial system accuracy degrades with time. Not only does the GPS sensor bound the navigation errors, but the GPS sensor calibrates the inertial sensor. In navigation systems, GPS receiver performance issues include susceptibility to interference from external sources, time to first fix (i.e., first position solution), interruption of the satellite signal due to blockage, integrity, and signal reacquisition capability. The issues related to inertial sensors are their poor long-term accuracy without calibration and cost.

This section first discusses in more detail the relative weaknesses of GPS (Section 9.2.1) and inertial sensors (Section 9.2.2) as outlined previously. Next, an introduction to Kalman filtering is provided (Section 9.2.3), followed by a description of a variety of practical GPS/inertial integrations and their performance features (Sections 9.2.4–9.2.6).

9.2.1 GPS Receiver Performance Issues

One primary concern with using GPS as a stand-alone source for navigation is signal interruption. Signal interruption can be caused by shading of the GPS antenna by terrain or manmade structures (e.g., buildings, vehicle structure, and tunnels) or by interference from an external source. An example of signal interruption is shown in Figure 9.1. Each vertical line in this figure indicates a period of shading while driving

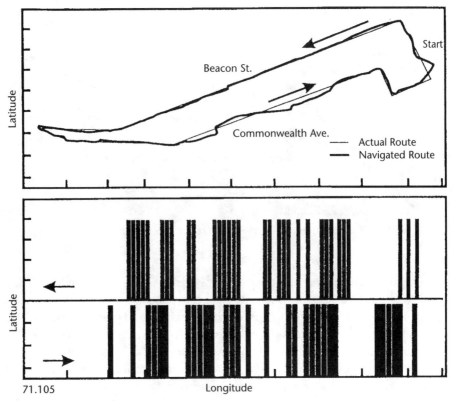

Figure 9.1   Effects of signal blockage on GPS receiver operation.

in an urban environment. The periods of shading (i.e., less than three-satellite avail-ability) are caused by buildings and are denoted by the black lines in the lower por-tion of Figure 9.1. (This experiment was conducted when five to six satellites above a 5° mask angle were available for ranging.) When only three usable satellite signals are available, most receivers revert to a two-dimensional navigation mode by utiliz-ing either the last known height or a height obtained from an external source. If the number of usable satellites is less than three, some receivers have the option of not producing a solution or extrapolating the last position and velocity solution for-ward in what is called *dead-reckoning* (DR) navigation. Inertial navigation systems (INSs) can be used as a flywheel to provide navigation during shading outages.

The discrete-time nature of the GPS solution in some equipment is also of con-cern in real-time applications, especially those related to vehicle control. As shown in Figure 9.2, if a vehicle's path changes between updates, the extrapolation of the last GPS measurement produces an error in the estimated and true position. This is particularly true for high-dynamic platforms, such as fighter aircraft. In applica-tions where continuous precision navigation is required, inertial sensors can be employed. An alternative solution is the use of a GPS receiver that provides higher rate measurement outputs. In principle, rates on the order of 100 Hz are possible.

In addition to providing navigation continuity during short GPS shading out-ages and between GPS sensor position outputs, an INS, when calibrated using a Kalman filter (see Section 9.2.3), can be used to improve the GPS receiver perfor-mance in two other ways. First, the information that is maintained by the integra-

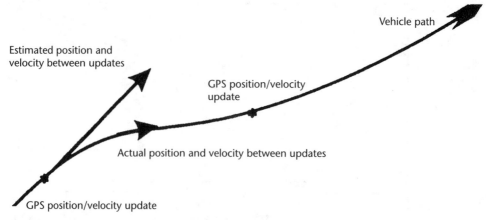

Figure 9.2 Extrapolation of GPS navigation solution in a dynamic environment.

tion filter can be used to reduce the time to reacquire GPS signals that have been lost through interference or obscuration; second, the integration filter can be used to aid the receiver's tracking loops, extending the thresholds for signal tracking. Both techniques have been used since the very first GPS sets were designed [1]. The first enhancement, often referred to as *prepositioning*, computes an a priori estimate of a signal's code phase and Doppler using the integration filter's estimates of position and velocity, and time and frequency error. If the combined position and timing errors are less than one-half a chip (roughly 150m for the C/A code, and 15m for the P(Y) code), then nearly instantaneous reacquisition of a lost signal is possible, since the prepositioning limits the tracking error to the linear range of the loop's error detector (see Section 5.4). Similarly, Doppler on the signal to be reacquired can be predicted from the integration filter's estimates of velocity and signal frequency, and if those estimates are within the linear range of the frequency error detector (see Section 5.3.3), nearly instantaneous signal acquisition may be possible. For example, if using an arctangent error detector with a 5-ms predetection integration interval (PDI), the combined frequency error can be as large as 50 Hz, which translates to a velocity accuracy of 10 m/s, which is readily achievable using a navigation grade IMU and potentially achievable with tactical grades [2]. Generally speaking, if the navigation filter is a "robust design" (i.e., its covariance matrix is consistent with the error in its navigation solution), then the uncertainty associated with the predicted code phase and Doppler is best determined from the covariance matrix. For example, if $\mathbf{P}_4$ represents the 4×4 partition of the filter's covariance matrix corresponding to position and time error, then the error variance associated with a predicted code phase can be computed using:

$$\sigma_{cp}^{\ 2} = \mathbf{h}^T \mathbf{P}_4 \mathbf{h} \tag{9.1}$$

In (9.1), $\mathbf{h}$ is the filter's measurement gradient vector to the satellite of interest, comprised of the LOS unit vector to the satellite of interest (first three elements) and the sensitivity of the user's clock phase error (fourth element). Generally, the elements of the covariance matrix $\mathbf{P}_4$ in (9.1) are expressed in units of m^2. In this case, the code phase error variance $\sigma_{cp}^{\ 2}$ will also be expressed in m^2. Given the error variance predicted by (9.1), suitable search ranges can be determined about the predicted code phase. Often, the search region is selected as *3 sigma*, corresponding to $\pm 3\sigma_{cp}$. This ensures a high probability (roughly 99% under a jointly Gaussian assumption for the probability distribution) that the signal is within the selected search region. Figure 9.3 illustrates the two-dimensional nature of the search region for a full code phase search. Prepositioning, as just described, offers the potential for drastically reducing the search space by collapsing both dimensions. If the number of cells remaining (i.e., subsets of the two-dimensional search region one-half chip by the chosen Doppler bin size) are less than or equal to the available number of receiver correlators, then parallel searching can be performed to reacquire the signal. This technique can also be used for initial acquisition of the GPS signals using an INS that has been calibrated by other means.

As mentioned earlier in this section, the use of INS velocity outputs, corrected by the Kalman filter, can be used to extend signal tracking in adverse signal conditions. Fundamentally, any tracking loop performs three functions: attenuation of the noise in the observables that are passed to the Kalman filter; tracking of the dynamics of the host vehicle in which the receiver is installed; and, finally, tracking of the dynamics of the receiver's oscillator. Use of INS aiding effectively removes the second requirement, enabling significant reduction of the tracking loop bandwidths, thus enabling tracking at lower SNRs. It is, in general, the requirement to track the dynamics of the receiver's oscillator that sets a floor on the bandwidth reduction and track extension. As discussed in Section 9.2.4, tracking loop aiding can be performed for both code and carrier tracking. The ability to extend code track can exceed 25 dB.

An area of concern in the use of GPS, especially in commercial aircraft applications, is integrity (see Section 7.5). An anomalous GPS satellite signal most likely will result in the calculation of an erroneous position. The use of inertial components allows the GPS pseudorange measurement to be compared against statistical limits (typically 6-sigma deviation) and rejection of those measurements that are beyond the limits. The components of the INS (i.e., gyros and accelerometers) can fail as well. Historically, the use of redundant INS or gyros and accelerometers has been

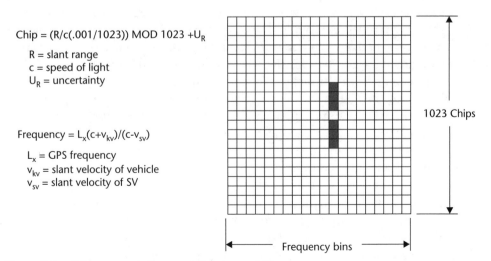

Chip = (R/c(.001/1023)) MOD 1023 +U_R

R = slant range
c = speed of light
U_R = uncertainty

Frequency = $L_x(c+v_{kv})/(c-v_{sv})$

L_x = GPS frequency
v_{kv} = slant velocity of vehicle
v_{sv} = slant velocity of SV

1023 Chips

Frequency bins

Figure 9.3 Aiding supports the acquisition/reacquisition process.

used to increase reliability. In fact, the use of redundant inertial components for failure detection and isolation predates GPS RAIM work by nearly two decades [3].

9.2.2 Inertial Sensor Performance Issues

Before addressing the sensors utilized in all inertial systems, a few remarks about the distinction between the two essential types of inertial systems are needed. INSs can be broadly classified as either *gimbaled* or *strapdown* [4]. The basic distinction between the two lies in the method by which the coordinate frame utilized for navigation is maintained: In gimbaled systems, the frame is mechanized physically by preserving a platform that is generally either the navigation frame itself or a frame related to the navigation frame by a known transformation (e.g., the azimuth in a *wander azimuth* mechanization of a gimbaled system). The platform is usually kept *locally level* (i.e., level with respect to the horizon), where the accelerometers are able to directly sense the horizontal components of host vehicle acceleration. However, use of a so-called *space stable* gimbaled orientation (e.g., as was used for the Space Shuttle's inertial system) is an example of a gimbaled system that is not locally level. To summarize, in a gimbaled inertial system, the sensors are maintained in a preferred orientation and generally isolated from the vehicle's changes in attitude. In a strapdown mechanization, on the other hand, the instruments are fixed in the vehicle (e.g., along the nose of an aircraft, out the left wing, and with third axis completing the set). The navigation frame is maintained mathematically, not physically, by the calculation of a transformation between the vehicle's body frame (where the instruments reside) and the navigation frame. This transformation is most commonly referred to as a direction cosine matrix, but its mechanization is usually as a quaternion or rotation vector [4] for improved efficiency.

The relative advantages and disadvantages of the two types of systems are fairly well known. The gimbaled systems tend to be more expensive, due to the additional hardware required for maintaining the physical platform, while the computational requirements for the strapdown system (largely for maintenance of the direction cosine matrix) are higher. Historically speaking, gimbaled systems were used almost exclusively over the last several decades in navigation systems where accuracy was a significant driver, while strapdown systems were relegated to applications with very short flight times (e.g., a missile interceptor problem). However, advances in microprocessor and inertial sensor technology have changed this trend, making strapdown inertial systems the selection in most applications except those with the most demanding requirements (e.g., submarine use). Microprocessor improvements have made the high-rate computation of the direction cosine matrix relatively easy, and the advent of optical gyros (i.e., ring laser and fiber optic) has produced designs without the significant acceleration sensitivity of their mechanical counterparts. This is quite important since the strapdown sensors see the full vehicle dynamics, which leads to additional errors relative to their gimbaled counterparts in high-dynamic applications.

Returning now to the inertial sensors, there are two types, *gyroscopes* and *accelerometers*. The output of a gyroscope is a signal proportional to angular movement about its input axis ($\Delta\theta$), and the output of an accelerometer is a signal proportional to the change in velocity sensed along its input axis (Δv). A three-axis IMU would then require three gyroscopes and three accelerometers to inertially determine its position and velocity in free space.

One of the significant factors related to the quality of an inertial system is the drift of the gyroscopes, measured in degrees/hour. The drift of a gyro is a false output signal caused by deficiencies during the manufacturing of the sensor. In inertial sensors, these are caused by mass unbalances in a gyroscope's rotating mass and by nonlinearities in the pickoff circuits, as is seen in fiber-optic gyroscopes (FOGs). This false signal is in effect telling the navigation system that the vehicle is moving when it is actually stationary. The manufacturing of gyros with low drift is very costly. A gyroscope with drifts of greater than 100°/hour would cost less than $1,000 (all costs are in 2005 U.S. dollars). Inertial units with drift from 1 to 100°/hour are currently priced from $1,000 to $10,000. Accuracies of less than 1 degree/hour are available at prices ranging from $10,000 to $100,000. The quality of the inertial sensors has a large role in the cost effectiveness of a navigation system. If 0.0001°/hour gyroscopes were to cost less than $100, GPS may not be needed today. But in actuality, inertial sensors are expensive, and a significant result of the integration of GPS with inertial sensors is the ability to use lower performing, more cost-effective sensors. This is shown in Figure 9.4, where the upper curves show the performance of three classes of inertial sensors. (Note that CEP is an indicator of delivery accuracy. It is the radius of a circle in which 50% of the projectiles are expected to fall within the given radius—see Section 7.3.2.) When these systems are integrated with GPS, the lower curve dictates the performance of the integrated GPS/inertial (GPSI) system. Therefore, during operation of a navigation system when both GPS and inertial components are operational, the inertial navigation errors are bounded by the accuracy of the GPS solution.

One significant contribution the GPS receiver makes to the operation of the inertial subsystem is the calibration of the inertial sensors (see Figure 9.5). Note that mean radial error (MRE) is another indicator of delivery accuracy. (MRE is the mean of the miss distance of all projectiles.) Inertial instruments are specified to meet a turn-on to turn-on drift requirement. (Each time a gyro is powered up, its ini-

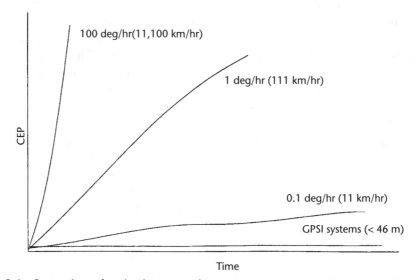

Figure 9.4 Comparison of navigation accuracies.

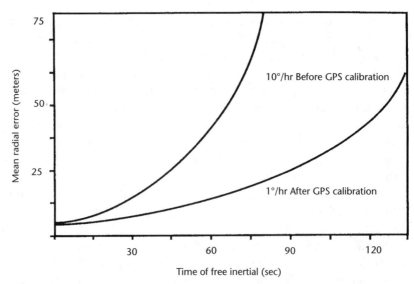

Figure 9.5   Inertial navigation before and after GPS calibration.

tial drift rate differs.) The major errors are the gyro bias and accelerometer bias, which are typically six of the states within an inertial or GPSI Kalman filter. During the operation of a GPSI system, the Kalman filter will produce an estimate of these biases as derived from the velocity data received from the GPS receiver. GPS receiver velocity accuracy is nominally 0.2 m/s, 95%.

9.2.3   The Kalman Filter

The integration of GPS and inertial sensors is typically accomplished through use of a Kalman filter [5]. Kalman filtering, introduced in 1960 by Dr. R. E. Kalman [6], is a statistical technique that combines knowledge of the statistical nature of system errors with knowledge of system dynamics, as represented as a state space model, to arrive at an estimate of the state of a system. The state space model can include any number of unknowns. In a navigation system, we are usually concerned with position and velocity, as a minimum, but it is not unusual to see filters for system models with state vector dimensions ranging from 6 to 60. The state estimate utilizes a weighting function, called the Kalman gain, which is optimized to produce a minimum error variance. For this reason, the Kalman filter is called an optimal filter. For linear system models, the Kalman filter is structured to produce an unbiased estimate.

Let us first look at a simplified filter for estimating a constant but unknown scalar quantity, x. Assume a measurement model in which at each measurement time, t_n, noise is added to x, producing an observation $y(t_n)$ of the form

$$y(t_n) = x + \varepsilon_m(t_n)$$

The measurement noise sequence $\{\varepsilon_m(t_n)\}$ is assumed to be zero mean Gaussian with variance σ_m^2 [i.e., $N(0, \sigma_m^2)$] and white [i.e., successive values of $\varepsilon_m(t_n)$ are statistically independent of each other]. The sequence $\{\varepsilon_m(t_n)\}$ is not necessarily stationary.

The Kalman filter for estimating x produces an estimate of x, incorporating the current measurement $y(t_n)$ and the estimate of x just prior to the measurement, denoted as $\hat{x}(t_n^-)$. Since x is a constant, there is no difference between $\hat{x}(t_{n-1}^+)$, the estimate just after incorporating the previous measurement, and $\hat{x}(t_n^-)$. This is not true for more general system models, as we shall see when we discuss real-world applications in this section. The measurement update equation is given by:

$$\hat{x}(t_n^+) = \hat{x}(t_n^-) + k(t_n)\left[y(t_n) - \hat{x}(t_n^-)\right] \tag{9.2}$$

In this equation, the prior estimate $\hat{x}(t_n^-)$ is corrected by addition of new information contained in the measurement. The estimation error $\tilde{x}(t_n^+)$ is given by

$$\tilde{x}(t_n^+) = x - \hat{x}(t_n^+)$$

Due to the simple measurement model and the zero mean nature of $\varepsilon_m(t_n)$, $\hat{x}(t_n^-)$ is effectively an estimate of measurement $y(t_n)$ [i.e., $\hat{x}(t_n^-) = \hat{y}(t_n)$]. The difference sequence $y(t_n) - \hat{y}(t_n)$ is called the *innovation process* and contains the new information obtained by the measurements. The parameter $k(t_n)$ in (9.2) is the Kalman gain and contains the statistical parameters required to form the combination of the prior estimate and new data resulting in a minimum error variance estimate. The quality of the estimate is characterized by the error variance, but since the estimate is unbiased, the error variance equals the estimate variance $\sigma_{\hat{x}}^2(t_n)$, and its value is different before and after updating the estimate by incorporating the measurement. The Kalman gain is computed as follows:

$$k(t_n) = \frac{\sigma_{\hat{x}}^2(t_n^-)}{\sigma_{\hat{x}}^2(t_n^-) + \sigma_m^2} \tag{9.3}$$

Note that if the measurement is less accurate (i.e., σ_m^2 is large), the weighting given to the new data is reduced because σ_m^2 appears in the denominator. After the measurement update, the error covariance is reduced according to

$$\sigma_{\hat{x}}^2(t_n^+) = \left[1 - k(t_n)\right]\sigma_{\hat{x}}^2(t_n^-) \tag{9.4}$$

If we further assume that the measurement noise variance is constant, then it is easy to show that the error variance is given by $\sigma_{\hat{x}}^2(t_n^+) = \sigma_m^2 / n$ and thus asymptotically approaches zero as more data is obtained. This property makes the estimate a consistent estimate. Thus, (9.2) to (9.4) provide a data processing scheme that recursively combines our previous state estimate with new measurement data in a way that is statistically optimal. A block diagram of the basic filter structure is shown in Figure 9.6.

In real-world applications, the state vector contains several components that are not constant but evolve dynamically, such as position and velocity. Also, the system state model includes plant noise, which expresses modeling errors as well as actual noise and system disturbances. Since, in general, the system state varies dynamically between measurements, the estimate just after the measurement update $\hat{x}(t_n^+)$ must

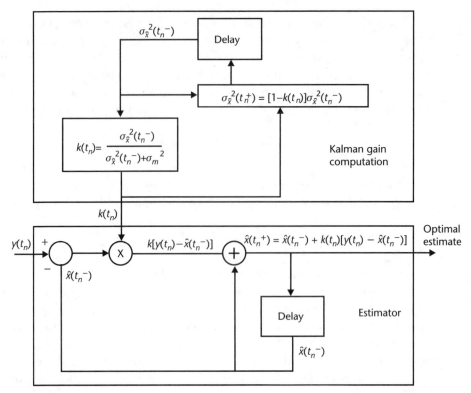

Figure 9.6   Basic Kalman filter.

be extrapolated to the next measurement time according to the system state model to compute $\hat{x}(t_{n+1}^-)$. Also, in the more general vector case, the performance of the Kalman filter estimate is characterized by an error covariance matrix denoted as $\mathbf{P}(t_n)$ and defined by

$$\mathbf{P}(t_n) = E\left[\left(\mathbf{x}(t_n) - \hat{\mathbf{x}}(t_n)\right)\left(\mathbf{x}(t_n) - \hat{\mathbf{x}}(t_n)\right)^T \right]$$

Here we summarize the Kalman filter equations for the general case. The state system model is given by

$$\mathbf{x}(t_n) = \mathbf{\Phi}(t_n, t_{n-1})\mathbf{x}(t_{n-1}) + \mathbf{u}(t_n)$$

where $\mathbf{\Phi}(t_n, t_{n-1})$ denotes the system one-step transition matrix, and $\mathbf{u}(t_n)$ is the plant or process noise vector that is assumed to be white, zero mean, and distributed normally. This is represented by the function $N(0, \mathbf{Q}(t_n))$ with covariance matrix $\mathbf{Q}(t_n)$. The measurement model is

$$\mathbf{y}(t_n) = \mathbf{H}(t_n)\mathbf{x}(t_n) + \boldsymbol{\epsilon}_m(t_n)$$

where $\mathbf{y}(t_n)$ is a vector, and the measurement matrix $\mathbf{H}(t_n)$ characterizes the sensitivity of the measurements to each of the state components. Vector $\boldsymbol{\epsilon}_m(t_n)$ is the measurement noise and is a white random process distributed normally as $N(0, \mathbf{R}(t_n))$

with covariance matrix $\mathbf{R}(t_n)$. The Kalman filter, once processing is initiated, alternates between two sets of equations describing: (1) the extrapolation of estimate and error covariance between measurements, and (2) the incorporation of the new measurements into the estimate. The state estimate extrapolation is given by

$$\hat{\mathbf{x}}(t_n^-) = \boldsymbol{\Phi}(t_n, t_{n-1})\hat{\mathbf{x}}(t_{n-1}^+)$$

and the error covariance extrapolation is given by

$$\mathbf{P}(t_n^-) = \boldsymbol{\Phi}(t_n, t_{n-1})\mathbf{P}(t_{n-1}^+)\boldsymbol{\Phi}^T(t_n, t_{n-1}) + \mathbf{Q}(t_{n-1})$$

The state estimate measurement update is given by

$$\hat{\mathbf{x}}(t_n^+) = \hat{\mathbf{x}}(t_n^-) + \mathbf{K}(t_n)\left[\mathbf{y}(t_n) - \mathbf{H}(t_n)\hat{\mathbf{x}}(t_n^-)\right]$$

where $\mathbf{K}(t_n)$ is the Kalman gain matrix and is computed by

$$\mathbf{K}(t_n) = \mathbf{P}(t_n^-)\mathbf{H}^T(t_n)\left[\mathbf{H}(t_n)\mathbf{P}(t_n^-)\mathbf{H}^T(t_n) + \mathbf{R}(t_n)\right]^{-1}$$

The error covariance update is

$$\mathbf{P}(t_n^+) = \left[\mathbf{I} - \mathbf{K}(t_n)\mathbf{H}(t_n)\right]\mathbf{P}(t_n^-)$$

Figure 9.7 shows the Kalman filter processing scheme.

In practice, one is concerned with the computational issues arising from the use of finite precision in computers. If care is not taken, the filter can become unstable, and the solution diverges from the correct values. In inertial navigation systems, where a full model may require up to 60 states, much analysis is placed on proper selection of the critical states to produce what is called a suboptimal Kalman filter, which is computationally well behaved. Also of concern are wraparound errors (i.e., in 16-bit systems $32,767 + 1 = -32,768$), which may cause a complete reversal on signs and round off errors [7, 8]. One modification seen in filters used with inertial systems is the use of the filter to determine the error in the state. By setting the initial estimate of the state to zero and inputting the observed error in the state for

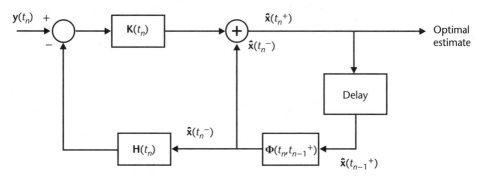

Figure 9.7   Kalman filter processing scheme.

$y(t_n)$ in place of the observed state, our state vector has become the estimated error of the state, more commonly known as the error state vector, instead of the estimated state. One can then periodically (usually every filter cycle) apply the estimated correction to the output data and reset the filter error states to zero. By doing this, the magnitude of the variables used in the filter are small, minimizing round off and nonlinearity errors. This also minimizes some of the computation errors by setting many of the elements in our matrices operation to zero. This method allows the measurement processing and Kalman filtering to execute at different frequencies. For example, one can process measurements at 100 Hz and run the filter at 1 Hz. Before outputting the data, the latest correction from the filter is applied to the data.

9.2.4 GPSI Integration Methods

Integration of GPS and inertial navigation systems was initiated in the early 1980s [5, 9] with a configuration that later came to be known as a *loosely integrated* or *loosely coupled* configuration. This configuration typically includes a GPS receiver with an 8-state Kalman filter, an IMU, a navigation processor that contains a 15- to 18-state Kalman filter, navigation equations to convert the $\Delta\theta$s and Δvs from the IMU to platform attitude, position, and velocity, as well as other functions that we will discuss later in Sections 9.2.4.1 through 9.2.4.3. The configuration, as shown in Figure 9.8, accepts GPS position from the GPS receiver, and $\Delta\theta$s and Δvs from the inertial unit. Although used in many initial applications, this system has a feed forward loop from the navigation processor and two separate filters that open the possibility of instability caused by mutual feedback. Mission scenarios for this configuration must be thoroughly simulated to ensure the stability of the filter. In situations where instability occurs, the gains in the filter are reduced, which may result in sluggish system operation. Today, most GPSI systems are *tightly integrated*, as shown in Figure 9.9. This configuration is also referred to as *tightly coupled*. In tightly integrated systems, the Kalman filter in the GPS receiver is eliminated, and pseudorange and pseudorange rate data from the GPS channel processor is sent

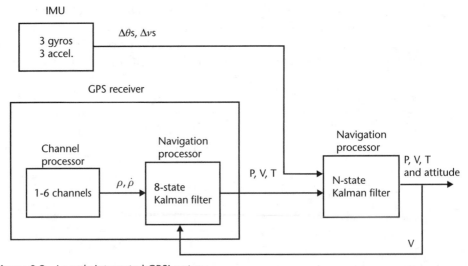

Figure 9.8 Loosely integrated GPSI system.

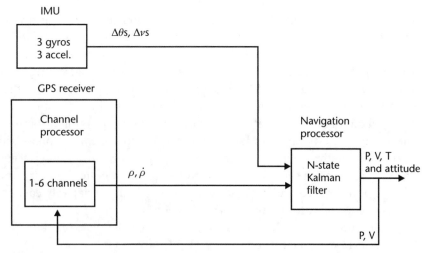

Figure 9.9   Tight integration of a GPSI system.

directly to the navigation processor. In this configuration, unmodeled errors resulting from the GPS receiver's Kalman filter are eliminated and the system designer is
allowed to set gains as tight as possible.

In the tight integration of a GPSI system, as in most inertial systems, we utilize
the Kalman filter to estimate the error in our state, not the state itself, and use the
estimated error state vector $\hat{x}$ to correct the output of the navigation equations, as
shown in Figure 9.10. Also typical in the so-called tight integration of a GPSI, especially in applications where antijam enhancement of the GPS receiver is needed, is
some form of tracking loop aiding. As introduced in Section 9.2.1, this aiding can
occur at both carrier and code loop levels. Aiding the code loop is most commonly
implemented. Aiding the phase lock loop within the receiver is much more difficult.
The difficulty is obviously driven by the relatively tight requirements, from a navigation perspective, for maintaining phase lock on the carrier. Phase lock generally
requires that tracking loop error is less than a fraction of the carrier cycle. For

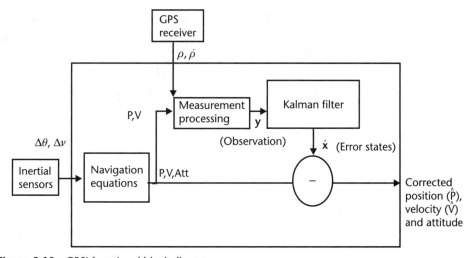

Figure 9.10   GPSI functional block diagram.

example, allowance of 90° of phase error (one quarter cycle) translates to roughly 5 cm of navigation error. Analysis performed in Section 9.2.4.6 indicates that this translates to a very tight GPS/INS velocity accuracy requirement. This requirement can be attained, but only with very careful estimation and control of certain IMU error sources, along with IMU data extrapolation to achieve the needed update rate for phase lock. In addition, special care is necessary in the installation of the GPS antenna on the vehicle, relative to the IMU, to avoid contamination by flexible body motion between the two. In fact, for best operation of carrier-phase aiding, consideration should be given to minimizing the physical separation between the INS and the GPS antenna in the host vehicle. Notwithstanding the difficulty of aiding phase lock within the GPS receiver, aiding frequency lock is relatively easy to do. Further discussion of this alternative appears in Section 9.2.4.6.

Since aiding the code loop is commonly done, let us explain its nature at a conceptual level with reference to Figure 9.11. Note that the code loop nonlinearity is neglected in this simplified model (the detector is represented by a gain of unity), and the NCO within the receiver is represented as an integrator. Also note that the code loop filter is represented simply as a gain, K_c, and a continuous time model is shown. First, to explain the action of an aided code loop with reference to Figure 9.11, the range delay, ρ, minus the loop's estimate, ρ_{est}, measures the range delay tracking error $\delta\rho$, which is computed perfectly by the detector with an additive noise error, n. The loop bandwidth is proportional to the code loop gain K_c. The INS velocity is subtracted from the satellite's velocity (in a common coordinate frame) and then projected along the LOS to the satellite that is tracked by the loop to construct $d\rho/dt^{INS}$. The INS aiding signal is added to the output from the code loop filter to drive the NCO. As mentioned previously, oscillator imperfections lead to a frequency error, δf, which also drives the NCO, in addition to an additive clock phase error $\delta\varphi$. The very simple form for this model makes certain observations intuitive. Lowering the bandwidth (reducing K_c) reduces the effect of noise, n, or interference on the loop, and places more weight on the INS aiding. As a limiting case, setting K_c to zero drives the range delay estimate entirely with inertial aiding. Even in the case of perfect INS information, this is unwise, since the frequency error of the local oscillator will integrate to a range delay error, which cannot be removed by the zero-bandwidth loop. This range delay error will grow without any corrective

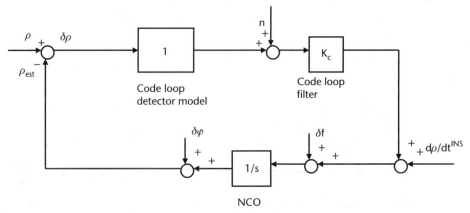

Figure 9.11   Simplified (linear) model for aided code loop.

action by the loop and, eventually, force the loop to lose lock. Thus, the clock insta-bility sets a floor for the aided bandwidth. One additional observation can be made using this simple model. If the INS aiding signal is expressed as the sum of the true range rate plus a range rate error induced by INS velocity error, it can be shown that the tracking loop error $\delta\rho$ is a function only of the INS errors. Thus, the aiding makes the loop's performance insensitive to the actual motion (i.e., velocity and acceleration) of the host, replacing it with the dynamics of the INS errors.

To demonstrate what we have described, we will implement a simplified GPSI system with a single gyro and a single-channel GPS receiver whose antenna is collo-cated with the IMU, eliminating the need for lever-arm compensation. (Lever-arm compensation is required when the GPS receiver antenna and IMU do not share the same origin in a 3-axis right-handed coordinate system.) The inertial components that have been purchased for this system have an uncompensated drift uncertainty of 10°/hour. A single channel receiver refers to a GPS receiver with the capability to measure pseudorange and pseudorange rate from only one satellite at a time. In addition to providing pseudorange and pseudorange rate, the receiver also forwards the position of the current satellite, the velocity of the current satellite, the time of the GPS measurement, and the deviations σ_ρ and $\sigma_{\dot{\rho}}$ of both the pseudorange and pseudorange rate. Ionospheric, relativistic, satellite clock, and tropospheric correc-tions are applied to the pseudorange data within the receiver prior to its forwarding to the navigation processor. We will denote corrected pseudorange and pseudorange rate as ρ_{cor} and $\dot{\rho}_{cor}$, respectively. In order to implement this system, we must first formulate the states, the observation models, and the noise model sta-tistics, and initialize our error covariance matrix $\mathbf{P}_0$ and the estimated error state vector $\hat{\mathbf{x}}_0$. We ignore, for simplicity, implementation issues related to numerical sta-bility that would often motivate more complicated forms of the filter in practice.

9.2.4.1   States

The states selected are position error (x direction, δx), velocity error (x direction, $\delta\dot{x}$), GPS receiver clock bias (t_u), and clock drift ($\dot{t}_u$). This minimum set has been selected to minimize the number of mathematical calculations that have to be per-formed. Receiver clock bias and drift are required because they will eventually be subtracted from the corrected pseudorange and pseudorange rate measurements, respectively, to form the measurement-based satellite-to-user range r_m and range rate $\dot{r}_m$. In this example, we have chosen position and velocity along our x-axis as our system outputs. Therefore, the error state vector is

$$\mathbf{x} = \begin{bmatrix} \delta x \\ \delta \dot{x} \\ \delta t \\ \delta \dot{t} \end{bmatrix}$$

Units for the states consists of kilometers for position, meters/second for veloc-ity, meters for clock bias, and meters/second for clock drift. All data is referenced to an ECEF reference frame.

9.2.4.2 Transition Matrix

To formulate the state transition matrix, one can write down the transition equations for position, velocity, clock bias, and clock drift as follows:

$$\delta x_n = \delta x_{n-1} + \delta \dot{x}_{n-1} \Delta t$$
$$\delta \dot{x}_n = \delta \dot{x}_{n-1}$$
$$\delta t_{u_n} = \delta t_{u_{n-1}} + \delta \dot{t}_{u_{n-1}} \Delta t$$
$$\delta \dot{t}_{u_n} = \delta \dot{t}_{u_{n-1}}$$

From these equations, the state transition matrix can be formulated as

$$\Phi\left(t_n, t_{n-1}\right) = \Phi\left(t_1, t_0\right) = \begin{bmatrix} 1 & \Delta t & 0 & 0 \\ 0 & 1 & 0 & 0 \\ 0 & 0 & 1 & \Delta t \\ 0 & 0 & 0 & 1 \end{bmatrix}$$

For this example, we will denote $\Phi(t_1, t_0)$ as Φ.

9.2.4.3 Measurement Matrix

The elements in the measurement matrix $\mathbf{H}(t_1)$ relate observations—in this case, range error and range rate error—to the state vector. To accomplish this, as each measurement is received, we create a LOS unit vector from the user's inertial-based position to the satellite's position. This unit vector is then placed in the measurement matrix to decompose the range error and range rate error into its x-dimension component. The navigation processor computes the unit vector from the user to the satellite by subtracting the user's inertial position (x_{ui}, y_{ui}, z_{ui}) from the satellite position (x_j, y_j, z_j) (where j denotes the jth satellite), generating an estimated range vector to the satellite. This is then normalized to a unit vector by dividing the range vector by its scalar range. Normally each element of the unit vector is placed in the measurement matrix to convert the range error and range rate error, but in our case we only need to incorporate the x-axis component of its xyz components. The errors in the clock bias and drift states are simply set to 1, since the LOS pseudorange and pseudorange rate errors directly map into the clock bias and clock drift states.

Let

$$\tilde{r}_x = x_j - x_{ui}$$
$$\tilde{r}_y = y_j - y_{ui}$$
$$\tilde{r}_z = z_j - z_{ui} \tag{9.5}$$
$$\tilde{r} = \sqrt{\tilde{r}_x^2 + \tilde{r}_y^2 + \tilde{r}_z^2}$$

$$\mathbf{H}(t_1) = \begin{bmatrix} \dfrac{\tilde{r}_x}{\tilde{r}} & 0 & 1 & 0 \\ 0 & \dfrac{\tilde{r}_x}{\tilde{r}} & 0 & 1 \end{bmatrix}$$

9.2.4.4   Initialization

Both $\mathbf{P}_0$ and $\hat{\mathbf{x}}_0$ are initialized from known data. This data is obtained from specifications on the GPS receiver for clock bias and drift, as well as the inertial specification for gyro bias. The initial position and velocity are obtained from the mission scenario. For example, an aircraft may be parked (velocity = 0.0) at a specific location at the time the navigation processor is initialized. In our example, we will assume the parameter values in Table 9.1.

From this data, we can formulate

$$\mathbf{P}_0 = \begin{bmatrix} 400 & 0 & 0 & 0 \\ 0 & 100 & 0 & 0 \\ 0 & 0 & 10^{10} & 0 \\ 0 & 0 & 0 & 10^4 \end{bmatrix}$$

$$\hat{\mathbf{x}}_0 = \begin{bmatrix} 0 \\ 0 \\ 0 \\ 0 \end{bmatrix}$$

We must also set our process noise covariance matrix $\mathbf{Q}(t_0)$ and our measurement noise covariance matrix $\mathbf{R}(t_1)$. The position and velocity elements of $\mathbf{Q}(t_0)$ are computed from the unmodeled acceleration variance, and the clock bias and drift elements are computed from the unmodeled clock variance. The measurement noise covariance matrix is a 2×2 diagonal matrix whose elements represent the noise variances in the pseudorange and pseudorange rate measurements. This is easily computed by the GPS receiver, which integrates 1-ms samples to form 1-second GPS measurements. In our example, the noise for the GPS receiver we are using is 1m for pseudorange measurements and 0.1 m/s for pseudorange rate measurements. For the sake of simplicity, we will use the following $\mathbf{Q}(t_0)$ from a commercial-grade C/A code receiver integrated with tactical-grade sensors:

$$\mathbf{Q}(t_0) = \begin{bmatrix} 0.01 & 0 & 0 & 0 \\ 0 & 1E-5 & 0 & 0 \\ 0 & 0 & 1.1E-3 & 0 \\ 0 & 0 & 0 & 1.0E-4 \end{bmatrix}$$

Table 9.1   Initial Assumptions

Parameter	One Sigma Value	Variance	Comment
Position	20m	400 m^2	Accuracy of external source
Velocity	10 m/s	100 m^2/s^2	Accuracy of external source
Clock bias	10^5 m	10^{10} m^2	Time uncertainty
Clock drift	100 m/s	10^4 m^2/s^2	Characteristic of user clock

The measurement noise is received with the pseudorange and pseudorange rate measurement. When we process the measurement and form the observation, we will set the $\mathbf{R}(t_1)$ matrix, where

$$\mathbf{R}(t_1) = \begin{bmatrix} \sigma_\rho^2 & 0 \\ 0 & \sigma_{\dot{\rho}}^2 \end{bmatrix}$$

9.2.4.5 Data Synchronization

One issue that we must deal with is that of data synchronization. The Kalman filter, being a sampled state system, assumes the time of the GPS measurement and that of the inertial measurement are identical. Failure to synchronize the measurement data results in unmodeled errors and requires the user to increase the process noise variances to compensate for this error. To accomplish this, two issues must be addressed. The first is the timing of inertial data with the GPS receiver time. The second is the buffering of inertial data to allow synchronization of the inertial data with the GPS data.

Timing of the inertial data is accomplished by having the GPS receiver transmit a 1-second timing pulse to the navigation processor. This signal, tied to a high-level interrupt, forces the inertial clock to the next second. The inertial clock is a software clock that is incremented by each inertial measurement received by the navigation processor (typically at a rate of 100 Hz to 800 Hz). The inertial clock is thus resynchronized to GPS receiver clock time once per second. To initialize the inertial clock, the GPS receiver must implement a specific message that will inform the navigation processor of the GPS receiver time at the next interrupt. This must be accomplished well before the receipt of the interrupt to give the navigation processor time to respond to the interrupt and the message, and prepare to set the inertial clock before the next interrupt is received.

Since the GPS receiver and the inertial are asynchronous, a circular queue—called a history queue—contains 1 or 2 seconds of inertial position data. By examining the time of the GPS measurement, the latest inertial position whose time tag is less than that of the GPS measurement can be extracted from the queue. Using the next queue entry, the data is then interpolated to the time of the GPS measurement. Using raw data taken from the GPS satellite measurements given in Table 9.2, we can start to see how our system will respond. In our system, the user inputs the estimated initial position as 42.1° latitude, −71.2° longitude and zero altitude. This, in ECEF coordinates, is: (1,527,397; −4,486,699; 4,253,850). When the GPS measurement data is received by the navigation processor, the measurement matrix (9.5) is formulated.

To do this, we utilize the position of the satellite x_{sv}, y_{sv}, z_{sv} and subtract the user's inertial-based position at the time of the GPS measurement x_{ui}, y_{ui}, z_{ui}. To obtain the user's inertial-derived position at the time of the GPS measurement, we utilize the previously mentioned history buffer. By obtaining this inertial position in ECEF coordinates just before the time of the GPS measurement and using the next history buffer entry, the data is interpolated to give an accurate inertial user position at the

Table 9.2 Data Received from a GPS Measurement

Parameter	Value
Time	250,812.171875 seconds
Satellite position (ECEF)	
x	−11,095,241m
y	−3,414,814m
z	23,488,864m
Satellite velocity	
$\dot{x}$	91.63 m/s
$\dot{y}$	−294.00 m/s
$\dot{z}$	3.70 m/s
Pseudorange measurement	23,049,952m
Pseudorange rate measurement	16.952 m/s
Pseudorange deviation	7m
Pseudorange rate deviation	0.05 m/s

time of the GPS measurement. In our example, the history buffer contains the value (1,527,397; −4,486,699; 4,253,850) for the position before and after the GPS measurement time because the vehicle was parked during the initialization. Thus, the interpolated value will be (1,527,397; −4,486,699; 4,253,850). Using (9.5), the measurement matrix is formulated as shown here:

$$\tilde{r}_x = x_{sv} - x_{ui} = -11,095,241 - 1,527,397 = -12,622,638$$
$$\tilde{r}_y = y_{sv} - y_{ui} = -3,414,814 - (-4,486,699) = 1,071,885$$
$$\tilde{r}_z = z_{sv} - z_{ui} = 23,488,864 - 4,253,850 = 19,235,014$$
$$\tilde{r} = \sqrt{\tilde{r}_x^2 + \tilde{r}_y^2 + \tilde{r}_z^2} = 23,031,841$$

$$\mathbf{H}(t_1) = \begin{bmatrix} \dfrac{\tilde{r}_x}{\tilde{r}} & 0 & 1 & 0 \\ 0 & \dfrac{\tilde{r}_x}{\tilde{r}} & 0 & 1 \end{bmatrix}$$

$$= \begin{bmatrix} -\dfrac{12,622,638}{23,031,841} & 0 & 1 & 0 \\ 0 & -\dfrac{12,622,638}{23,031,841} & 0 & 1 \end{bmatrix}$$

$$= \begin{bmatrix} -0.548 & 0 & 1 & 0 \\ 0 & -0.548 & 0 & 1 \end{bmatrix}$$

Extrapolate the Error Covariance Matrix and Add in the Process Noise
It can be shown that with a $\Delta t = 1$ second and using the 1-step state transition matrix $\mathbf{\Phi}$, the first extrapolated covariance $\mathbf{P}(t_1^-)$ can be calculated as follows:

$$\mathbf{\Phi P}_0 = \begin{bmatrix} 1 & 1 & 0 & 0 \\ 0 & 1 & 0 & 0 \\ 0 & 0 & 1 & 1 \\ 0 & 0 & 0 & 1 \end{bmatrix} \begin{bmatrix} 400 & 0 & 0 & 0 \\ 0 & 100 & 0 & 0 \\ 0 & 0 & 10^{10} & 0 \\ 0 & 0 & 0 & 10^{4} \end{bmatrix}$$

$$= \begin{bmatrix} 400 & 100 & 0 & 0 \\ 0 & 100 & 0 & 0 \\ 0 & 0 & 1.1\text{E}10 & 1.0\text{E}4 \\ 0 & 0 & 0 & 1.0\text{E}4 \end{bmatrix}$$

$\mathbf{\Phi P}_0 \mathbf{\Phi}^T$ computes to

$$\mathbf{\Phi P}_0 \mathbf{\Phi}^T = \begin{bmatrix} 500 & 100 & 0 & 0 \\ 100 & 100 & 0 & 0 \\ 0 & 0 & 1.1\text{E}10 & 1.0\text{E}4 \\ 0 & 0 & 1.0\text{E}4 & 1.0\text{E}4 \end{bmatrix}$$

The extrapolated covariance, $P(t_1^-) = \mathbf{\Phi P}_0 \mathbf{\Phi}^T + Q(t_0)$ computes to

$$\mathbf{\Phi P}_0 \mathbf{\Phi}^T + Q(t_0) = \begin{bmatrix} 500 & 100 & 0 & 0 \\ 100 & 100 & 0 & 0 \\ 0 & 0 & 1.1\text{E}10 & 1.0\text{E}4 \\ 0 & 0 & 1.0\text{E}4 & 1.0\text{E}4 \end{bmatrix}$$

*Compute the Kalman Gain Matrix **K***
The Kalman gain matrix **K** is computed where

$$\mathbf{K}(t_1^-) = P(t_1^-)\mathbf{H}^T(t_1)\left[\mathbf{H}(t_1)P(t_1^-)\mathbf{H}^T(t_1) + \mathbf{R}(t_1) \right]^{-1}$$

First compute $P(t_1^-)\mathbf{H}^T(t_1)$:

$$P(t_1^-)\mathbf{H}^T(t_1) = \begin{bmatrix} 500 & 100 & 0 & 0 \\ 100 & 100 & 0 & 0 \\ 0 & 0 & 1.1\text{E}10 & 1.0\text{E}4 \\ 0 & 0 & 1.0\text{E}4 & 1.0\text{E}4 \end{bmatrix} \begin{bmatrix} -0.548 & 0 \\ 0 & -0.548 \\ 1 & 0 \\ 0 & 1 \end{bmatrix}$$

$$= \begin{bmatrix} -274.6 & -54.8 \\ -54.8 & -54.8 \\ 1.1\text{E}10 & 1.0\text{E}4 \\ 1.0\text{E}4 & 1.0\text{E}4 \end{bmatrix}$$

$\mathbf{H}(t_1)P(t_1^-)\mathbf{H}^T(t_1)$ can then be computed, resulting in a 2×2 matrix as shown:

$$\mathbf{H}(t_1)P(t_1^-)\mathbf{H}^T(t_1) = \begin{bmatrix} 1.1\text{E}10 & 1.0\text{E}4 \\ 1.0\text{E}4 & 1.0\text{E}4 \end{bmatrix}$$

Measurement noise covariance matrix $\mathbf{R}(t_1)$ is added:

$$\mathbf{H}(t_1)\mathbf{P}(t_1^-)\mathbf{H}^T(t_1) + \mathbf{R}(t_1) = \begin{bmatrix} 1.1\text{E}10 & 10{,}436 \\ 10{,}436 & 10{,}436 \end{bmatrix} + \begin{bmatrix} 1 & 0 \\ 0 & 0.01 \end{bmatrix} = \begin{bmatrix} 1.1\text{E}10 & 10{,}436 \\ 10{,}436 & 10{,}436 \end{bmatrix}$$

and $[\mathbf{H}(t_1)\mathbf{P}(t_1^-)\mathbf{H}^T(t_1) + \mathbf{R}(t_1)]^{-1}$ equals

$$\left[\mathbf{H}(t_1)\mathbf{P}(t_1^-)\mathbf{H}^T(t_1) + \mathbf{R}(t_1)\right]^{-1} = \begin{bmatrix} 9.05\text{E} - 11 & -9.05\text{E} - 11 \\ -9.05\text{E} - 11 & 9.58\text{E} - 5 \end{bmatrix}$$

As required earlier, the gain matrix $\mathbf{K}(t_1)$ is computed as follows:

$$\mathbf{K}(t_1^-) = \mathbf{P}(t_1^-)\mathbf{H}^T(t_1)\left[\mathbf{H}(t_1)\mathbf{P}(t_1^-)\mathbf{H}^T(t_1) + \mathbf{R}(t_1)\right]^{-1}$$

$$= \begin{bmatrix} -1.990\text{E} - 8 & -5.251\text{E} - 3 \\ 4.900\text{E} - 13 & -5.251\text{E} - 3 \\ 9.999\text{E} - 1 & -2.878\text{E} - 3 \\ 1.174\text{E} - 12 & 9.971\text{E} - 1 \end{bmatrix}$$

Extrapolate the Current State $\mathbf{\Phi}\hat{\mathbf{x}}_0$
To extrapolate the error state $\hat{\mathbf{x}}(t_1^-) = \mathbf{\Phi}\hat{\mathbf{x}}_0$ results in the following:

$$\hat{\mathbf{x}}(t_1^-) = \mathbf{\Phi}\hat{\mathbf{x}}_0 = \begin{bmatrix} 1 & 1 & 0 & 0 \\ 0 & 1 & 0 & 0 \\ 0 & 0 & 1 & 1 \\ 0 & 0 & 0 & 1 \end{bmatrix}\begin{bmatrix} 0 \\ 0 \\ 0 \\ 0 \end{bmatrix} = \begin{bmatrix} 0 \\ 0 \\ 0 \\ 0 \end{bmatrix}$$

Compute the Observation Vector $\mathbf{y}(t_1)$ and the Predicted Observation $\mathbf{H}(t_1)\hat{\mathbf{x}}(t_1^-)$

The range observation is the difference between the estimated satellite-to-user range $\tilde{r}$, and the measurement-based range r_m. To compute the observation, $\tilde{r}$ must first be computed. To do this, we utilize the ECEF position of the satellite forwarded from the GPS receiver with the measurement data and subtract the user's inertial-based position at the time of the GPS measurement. The user's position at the time of the GPS measurement is extracted from the history buffer and interpolated to give an accurate user position. The estimated satellite-to-user range is then calculated as follows:

$$\tilde{r} = \left[(x_{sv} - x_{ui})^2 + (y_{sv} - y_{ui})^2 + (z_{sv} - z_{ui})^2\right]^{\frac{1}{2}}$$

$$= \left[\begin{array}{l} (-11{,}095{,}241 - 1{,}527{,}397)^2 + (-3{,}414{,}814 - (-4{,}486{,}699))^2 \\ + (23{,}488{,}864 - 4{,}253{,}850)^2 \end{array}\right]^{\frac{1}{2}}$$

$$= 23{,}031{,}841$$

The current clock bias (t_u) can be calculated by using the initial clock bias of 0 and adding the clock drift for 1 second. Assuming an equivalent drift rate, $c\dot{t}_u$, of 10 m/s, the clock bias at this first iteration is $ct_u + c\dot{t}_u\Delta t = 0 + 10 = 10$. Thus, the range observation is

$$OBS(r) = \tilde{r} - r_m$$
$$= \tilde{r} - \rho_{cor} + ct_u$$
$$= 23{,}031{,}841 - 23{,}049{,}952 + 10$$
$$= -18{,}101$$

Next, we compute the observed range rate, which is the LOS component of the satellite's range rate minus the user's range rate. To determine the LOS component, a LOS vector is formulated as follows:

$$LOS_x = \frac{x_{sv} - x_{ui}}{\tilde{r}} = \frac{-11{,}095{,}241 - 1{,}527{,}397}{23{,}031{,}841} = -0.548$$

$$LOS_y = \frac{y_{sv} - y_{ui}}{\tilde{r}} = \frac{-3{,}414{,}814 - (-4{,}486{,}699)}{23{,}031{,}841} = -0.0465$$

$$LOS_z = \frac{z_{sv} - z_{ui}}{\tilde{r}} = \frac{23{,}488{,}864 - 4{,}253{,}850}{23{,}031{,}841} = 0.835$$

The estimated range rate, $\dot{\tilde{r}}$, is

$$\dot{\tilde{r}} = LOS_x(\dot{x}_{sv} - \dot{x}_{ui}) + LOS_y(\dot{y}_{sv} - \dot{y}_{ui}) + LOS_z(\dot{z}_{sv} - \dot{z}_{ui})$$
$$= -0.548(91.63 - 0.0) + 0.0465(-294.01 - 0.0) - 0.835(3.70 - 0.0)$$
$$= -60.81 \text{ m/s}$$

The observed error of range rate is

$$OBS(\dot{r}) = \dot{\tilde{r}} - \dot{r}_m$$
$$= \dot{\tilde{r}} - (\dot{\rho}_{cor} - c\dot{t}_u)$$
$$= -60.8 - (-552 - 10)$$
$$= 501.2$$

and the observation vector is thus

$$y(t_1) = \begin{bmatrix} -18{,}101 \\ 501.2 \end{bmatrix}$$

The predicted observation, $H(t_1)\hat{x}(t_1^-)$, is calculated to be zero since the current estimate of the error state is zero.

$$H(t_1)\hat{x}(t_1^-) = \begin{bmatrix} 0.0 \\ 0.0 \end{bmatrix}$$

Compute the Error State Estimate
The error state vector is $\hat{\mathbf{x}}(t_1^+)$

$$\hat{\mathbf{x}}(t_1^+) = \hat{\mathbf{x}}(t_1^-) + \mathbf{K}(t_1)\left[\mathbf{y}(t_1) - \mathbf{H}(t_1)\hat{\mathbf{x}}(t_1^-)\right]$$

computes to

$$\mathbf{y}(t_1) - \mathbf{H}(t_1)\hat{\mathbf{x}}(t_1^-) = \begin{bmatrix} -18,101 \\ 501.2 \end{bmatrix} - \begin{bmatrix} 0 \\ 0 \end{bmatrix} = \begin{bmatrix} -18,101 \\ 501.2 \end{bmatrix}$$

Multiplying by the gain matrix and adding in the previous error state vector yields

$$\hat{\mathbf{x}}(t_1^+) = \hat{\mathbf{x}}(t_1^-) + \mathbf{K}(t_1)\left[\mathbf{y}(t_1) - \mathbf{H}(t_1)\hat{\mathbf{x}}(t_1^-)\right]$$

$$= \begin{bmatrix} 0 \\ 0 \\ 0 \\ 0 \end{bmatrix} + \begin{bmatrix} -1.990\text{E}-8 & -5.251\text{E}-3 \\ -4.900\text{E}-13 & -5.252\text{E}-3 \\ 9.999\text{E}-1 & -2.878\text{E}-3 \\ 1.174\text{E}-12 & 9.971\text{E}-1 \end{bmatrix} \begin{bmatrix} -18,101 \\ 501.2 \end{bmatrix}$$

$$= \begin{bmatrix} -2.632 \\ -2.632 \\ -18,102.6 \\ 499.7 \end{bmatrix}$$

Adjust the Covariance of the Current Estimate $(\sigma_{\hat{x}}^2)$
The covariance of the new estimate is computed using the equation

$$\mathbf{P}(t_1^+) = \left[\mathbf{I} - \mathbf{K}(t_1)\mathbf{H}(t_1)\right]\mathbf{P}(t_1^-)$$

$$\mathbf{P}(t_1^+) = \left[\mathbf{I} - \mathbf{K}(t_1)\mathbf{H}(t_1)\right]\mathbf{P}(t_1^-) = \begin{bmatrix} 500.70 & 99.71 & 274.40 & 54.64 \\ 99.71 & 99.72 & 54.65 & 54.65 \\ 274.40 & 54.64 & 151.40 & 29.95 \\ 54.64 & 54.64 & 29.96 & 29.96 \end{bmatrix}$$

Apply the Corrections and Reset the Error State Vector

$$\delta x = 1,527,397 + (-2.63) = 1,527,394\text{m}$$
$$\delta \dot{x} = 0 + (-2.63) = -2.6 \text{ m/s}$$
$$ct_u = 0 + (-18,103) = -18,103\text{m}$$
$$c\dot{t}_u = 0 + 499.7 = 499.7 \text{ m/s}$$

$$\hat{\mathbf{x}}(t_1^+) = \begin{bmatrix} 0 \\ 0 \\ 0 \\ 0 \end{bmatrix}$$

After the first iteration, we can see that almost all of the correction from the GPS receiver has been placed into the clock bias and clock drift. As we proceed with further iterations, the error will be placed in the clock, position, and velocity error. After a few hundred iterations, the filter should stabilize (if the noise parameters have been properly set and truncation/roundoff errors have been minimized). The errors in the position and velocity will not greatly exceed the errors in the pseudorange and pseudorange rate measurements.

9.2.4.6 Carrier Loop Aiding

As previously mentioned, aiding a phase lock loop with inertial velocity is quite difficult, due to the small GPS wavelength (20 cm). A simplified, linear continuous time model for an aided carrier loop can be constructed in a manner very similar to that used for the aided code loop. In Figure 9.11, the range delay ρ and related quantities (i.e., ρ_{est} and $\delta\rho$) are replaced by their counterparts θ, θ_{est} and $\delta\theta$, respectively. The code loop filter K_c is replaced by the carrier loop filter (also a gain K_θ in this simple model), and the rate of change of the range delay $d\rho/dt^{INS}$ is replaced by $d\theta/dt^{INS}$. The resultant model for an aided carrier loop can be used to derive (9.6), expressed in terms of Laplace (continuous time) transforms:

$$\delta\Theta(s) = \left[s/(s + K_\theta) \right]\Theta(s) - \left[s/(s + K_\theta) \right]\Theta^{INS}(s) \tag{9.6}$$

where Θ^{INS} represents a carrier phase estimate constructed from the INS velocity following initialization. Note that $\Theta^{INS}(s)$ is simply a mathematical construct introduced in the equation derivation: it is not calculated in the carrier phase aiding process. The INS constructed carrier phase estimate can be expanded as:

$$\Theta^{INS}(s) = \Theta(s) + \delta\Theta^{INS}(s) \tag{9.7}$$

Substituting into (9.6), we see the aided tracking loop error is independent of $\Theta(s)$, the actual carrier phase history, and dependent only upon the INS error. (We have neglected the effects of noise and clock error in starting with (9.6) to reach a conclusion about the required INS velocity accuracy.)

$$\delta\Theta(s) = -\left[s/(s + K_\theta) \right]\delta\Theta^{INS}(s) \tag{9.8}$$

But $\delta\Theta^{INS}(s)$ can be related to the satellite LOS component of INS velocity error using:

$$\delta\Theta^{INS}(s) = \mathbf{u}^T \delta\mathbf{v}^{INS}(s)/s \tag{9.9}$$

Finally, we can express the carrier phase error of an aided loop in terms of the INS velocity error:

$$\delta\Theta(s) = -\left[1/(s + K_\theta) \right]\mathbf{u}^T \delta\mathbf{v}^{INS}(s) \tag{9.10}$$

The carrier phase error in steady state, determined by setting s to 0 in (9.10), is the LOS INS velocity error component divided by K_θ. Equivalently, the aided carrier phase error is the LOS INS velocity error times the time constant of this simple loop model (the time constant is just the inverse of the gain K_θ in this first order loop model). Thus, limiting carrier phase error to 90° (assuming a time constant of 10 seconds is used) requires a LOS velocity error in steady state of no greater than 5.0 mm/sec, a very tight requirement indeed. As the aided loop time constant is increased (and the corresponding loop bandwidth is reduced to further attenuate the effects of jamming), the INS velocity requirement becomes more difficult to meet. Of course, corresponding requirements for peak transient velocity errors are less stringent (e.g., a velocity error component as large as 5 cm/s, if it persists for less than 1 second, may not induce loss of track, depending on the tracking state when the velocity transient occurred).

This very tight requirement for INS velocity error implies that certain error sources are carefully controlled, including the nonstatic component of accelerometer bias (the static component is generally cancelled by the platform misalignments generated during initial alignment), accelerometer scale factor and misalignments, and even the quantization level associated with the delta velocity derived from each accelerometer. For example, consider a residual accelerometer scale factor of 100 parts per million (ppm). Assume the host vehicle is a high-performance fighter aircraft doing a highly dynamic maneuver, producing a 5g acceleration along its lateral axis for 5 seconds. This single error source integrates to a velocity error of 2.5 cm/s, which could jeopardize carrier phase aiding with a bandwidth as narrow as that considered in our simplified analysis. Recall in the introduction that it was mentioned that oscillator instability also limited the potential bandwidth reduction that can be generally be achieved when receiver aiding. For the dynamic example here, it is possible that the g sensitivity of the local oscillator (see Section 5.6.1.5) will limit the utility of carrier phase aiding to as great an extent as the identified INS error sources. This point will be addressed in more detail in Section 9.2.4.8.

Common output rates of delta angle and delta velocity information from an IMU range from 10 to 100 Hz. These output rates may be unacceptable for carrier phase aiding and can lead to large transient errors in the aiding source under worst-case dynamics. This transient error can be reduced using an extrapolation algorithm. For example, a *constant jerk* model could be hypothesized for the delta velocity history, and the coefficient of the jerk term can be periodically determined from sets of delta-velocities output from the IMU; the model would then be used to generate modeled delta velocities to supply to the carrier loop at a higher rate. Notwithstanding these technical challenges, carrier phase aiding is possible and can extend track by as much as 9 dB [10].

Given the difficulties associated with aiding the phase lock loop, it is attractive to consider aid of the frequency tracking loop as a "fall back" position. Frequency track, as discussed in Section 5.3.3, is more tolerant of dynamic and interference induced errors than is phase track. A typical error detector (see Table 5.4) used for frequency track can tolerate up to 50 Hz of frequency error. It is in fact the use of frequency track that enables many commercial GPS receivers to maintain track under foliage. Obviously, maintaining an INS velocity aiding error less than 10 m/s (corresponding to the 50-Hz limit at L1) is relatively easy to do and will guarantee frequency lock as long as excessive frequency error is not induced by the receiver's oscillator. Enhancements of at least 10 dB in antijam performance are expected.

9.2.4.7 Code Loop Aiding

As mentioned in Section 9.2.1, code loop aiding is the most commonly exercised option. To gain additional insight into the operation of an aided code loop, let us return to Figure 9.11 and consider the decomposition of the aided range delay estimate, ρ_{est}, in terms of an INS component and a GPS component:

$$P_{est}(s) = \left[K_c / (s + K_c) \right] P_{rcvr}(s) + \left[s / (s + K_c) \right] P_{INS}(s) \qquad (9.11)$$

Equation (9.11) is an expression for a classic complementary filter in the frequency (i.e., Laplace) domain, in that it represents the combination of a lowpass filter operation on receiver information with a highpass filter operation on INS information. Thus, as the bandwidth of the receiver is reduced (i.e., K_c is reduced, or the loop's time constant is increased), the aided loop is constructing an estimate of the range delay based largely on simply integrating the INS velocity from the estimated range delay when the loop was unaided. Thus, in the limit, as K_c approaches zero, the loop's estimated range delay is completely determined from the INS behavior since the onset of aiding. This observation should assist in understanding some of the problems that are encountered when attempting to process the estimated range delay in a conventional Kalman filter design. These problems are discussed in [11].

Consider the aided code loop, including the Kalman filter operation, depicted in Figure 9.12, referred to in the discussion that follows as a *partitioned design*. The estimated range delay, ρ_{est}, is used to close the code loop, with its filter represented as the gain K_c as before; it is also used as a code phase measurement input to the Kalman filter. The Kalman filter generates an estimate of the INS velocity error δv_{est}, which is used to correct the INS velocity. The "known" satellite velocity v_s is then subtracted from the corrected INS velocity and projected along the LOS (represented by the unit vector **u**) to the satellite tracked by this loop. Based on the complementary filter model derived for the aided code loop model, the utility of the Kalman filter correction when aided can be questioned. In fact, the aided configuration can become unstable as the bandwidth is lowered below the effective bandwidth of the Kalman filter [11, 12]: This is also driven by the fact that there are two loop filters.

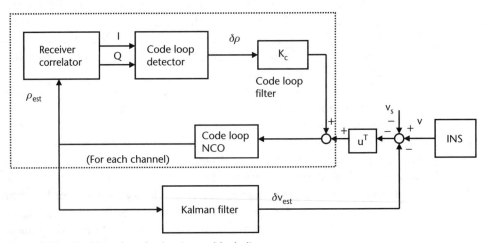

Figure 9.12   Partitioned tracker/navigator block diagram.

The first, the code loop itself, is using a very low gain (K_c) closure; the second loop closure is through the Kalman filter. The Kalman filter, expecting to receive measurements corrupted by uncorrelated measurement error, is processing measurements whose error is strongly correlated in time. This is a classical filter-modeling problem and contributes to the potential for instability.

A number of approaches can be used to stabilize the aided code loop [12]. Two of the more straightforward include simply turning off the Kalman filter corrections to the INS while the loop is aided and reducing the effective bandwidth of the Kalman filter (i.e., reducing its gains) to be less than the lowest bandwidth that the code loop itself (determined by the lowest value used for K_c) can achieve. The referenced analysis [12], which represents the Kalman filter as a fixed gain Butterworth filter (to enable conventional stability analysis), motivates the frequency domain interpretation in Figure 9.13. Stability problems generally arise when the Kalman filter effective bandwidth exceeds the code loop bandwidth, as illustrated in Figure 9.13(b).

The aided code loop depicted in Figure 9.12 is referred to as a *partitioned* design because the tracking loop and navigation filter are considered separate functions—the bandwidth of the tracking loop can be varied as a function of sensed SNR, but it is independent of the Kalman filter operation. In the next section, the navigation and tracking functions will be considered a single, integrated function, which will lead to a receiver aiding formulation that has been referred to as *ultratight integration*.

9.2.4.8 Integrated Tracking/Navigation Functions

Figure 9.14 provides a block diagram of the so-called integrated tracker/navigator, also referred to in the literature as *ultratight* or *deeply integrated*. The very first recognition of the benefits of this level of integration occurred in [13]. In that paper, the essential observation is made that the optimal estimators for navigation and signal tracking differ only in their coordinates (i.e., that a best estimator for position, velocity, and clock phase and frequency error should be equivalent to a best estima-

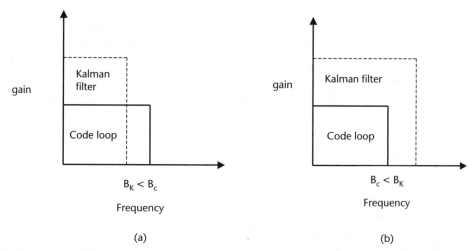

(a)   (b)

Figure 9.13 Aided code loop frequency domain perspective: (a) "safe" and (b) "dangerous" conditions.

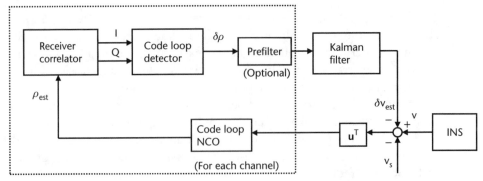

Figure 9.14 Integrated tracker/navigator block diagram.

tor for the set of satellite code phases and Dopplers). This essential observation does not depend upon the inertial augmentation of GPS. Applications of this high-level concept have therefore arisen in commercial applications of GPS [14, 15], where the INS is absent. Such implementations are sometimes referred to as *vector tracking*, since the individual tracking loops within the GPS receiver are no longer independent—they are coupled through their response to the position and velocity of the host vehicle, as well as the common clock errors.

Returning to Figure 9.14, it can be seen that this architecture removes the conventional code tracking loop, replacing it with a single loop that is closed through the Kalman filter. A byproduct of this new architecture is a solution for the stability problem: without the separate loop that produces an unmodeled measurement error correlation for the Kalman filter, a well-designed filter will not cause stability problems in this aided configuration. Note the optional prefilter. The receiver correlator outputs in-phase (I) and quadrature (Q) correlations at a rate typically ranging from a few milliseconds to up to 20 ms. This is obviously an extremely high rate for Kalman filter execution: one solution to this problem is to average the outputs of the detector up to a more typical processing rate for a Kalman filter (e.g., once per second). Recent applications of ultratight coupling have made use of reduced-order Kalman prefilters to feed the Kalman tracking and navigation filter (the centralized filter) in a federated filter architecture [16, 17]. Alternatively, a multirate mechanization for the Kalman filter can be used, where the state propagation and update occur at the highest rate at which the code loop detector output is generated, but gain calculation, covariance propagation, and update (where the bulk of the Kalman computations occur) are performed at a more typical lower rate (e.g., 1 Hz).

Simulations are used to compare the performance of the integrated, or tightly coupled and partitioned, designs in [13]. Although the improvements in its response to increasing noise levels are not significant (the first simulation case considered in [13]), substantial improvements are realized when significant dynamics are combined with near threshold noise levels (the second simulation case considered). The results are somewhat intuitive: in the first case, since both designs are able to adapt to an increasing noise level by lowering the effective aided receiver bandwidth, their performance is quite similar. In the second simulation case, it is in fact the recognition of the receiver oscillator's g sensitivity by the integrated design that leads to the substantial performance improvement. Recall from Section 9.2.1 that tracking the dynamics of the local oscillator is a requirement that sets the floor on the aided bandwidth. As the host vehicle performs highly dynamic maneuvers near threshold tracking conditions, the ultratightly coupled design increases the aided bandwidth just enough to maintain lock. Even though the Kalman filter of the partitioned design similarly correctly models the clock g sensitivity (its model is identical to that of the integrated design), its tracking loop does not adapt in recognition of this error source. The ultratightly coupled design thus affords another dimension of band-width adaptivity. More generally, the improvements of the integrated design can be understood by observing that its bandwidth adapts to everything that is modeled by the Kalman filter, including INS quality and clock dynamics. The maturity of the simulations used in [13] for the comparative evaluations was questionable in that the receiver motion and satellite geometry were limited to a plane; however, more thorough and detailed evaluations have been reported fairly recently [18] and confirm the fundamental conclusions of this very early paper.

Given the potential performance improvements reported in [13], it is natural to ask why it has taken so long (i.e., more than 20 years) for the ultratightly coupled design to gain wide acceptance (it was at least considered in a succeeding generation design to [1] by Rockwell-Collins). The reason for its delay in recognition as a worthy design approach may in part be cultural: not many individuals are skilled in both the art of Kalman filtering and receiver design. A more technical reason for the lack of acceptance is some of the significant modeling issues for the ultratightly coupled design, two of which can be addressed here. The first technical issue is the modeling of the code loop nonlinearity by the Kalman filter; the second is loss of lock detection. The code loop model embedded in the Kalman filter is quite important, especially as the loop thresholds are approached. Ignoring the nonlinear nature of the detector generally leads to performance degradations. A *quasi-linear* or describing function-based [19] approach is preferred, where the representation of the detector gain or the associated assigned error variance to the code phase measurement depend on the input SNR. As the SNR is lowered, the quasi-linear gain approach calculates a probability that the detector may be operating outside of its linear range—denoted p_l in the following equation—and weights the gain in this region (often zero) by the probability in computing a quasi-linear gain:

$$K_q = (1 - p_l)K_l + p_l K_n$$

where K_l is the detector gain in the linear range, and K_n is the detector gain in the nonlinear range of the detector. The probabilities are evaluated using the uncertainty, embedded in the filter's covariance matrix, projected along the LOS to the satellite that is tracked. Thus, as loss-of-lock conditions are approached, the integrated design recognizes the limited utility of each code phase measurement: in the limit as the effective detector gain become zero, it is using only INS information to close the code loop.

Finally, loss-of-lock becomes difficult for either the partitioned or integrated designs as threshold conditions are approached. This is fundamentally because all parameters that can be used to assess lock (see Section 5.11.2) are unreliable. Sophisticated approaches based on hypothesis testing and parallel filter operations can be considered. Such approaches, for the one or more receiver channels close to threshold, consider the lock state unknown and process the receiver ouputs with parallel filters—one assuming the channel (or channels) is (are) in lock, the other assuming that lock has been lost. This can obviously become computationally intractable very quickly, especially as most of the channels are near thresholds and passing in and out of a lock state. Use of the quasi-linear model for the code (or other tracking loop) detector as described here can make the design highly resistant to missed loss-of-lock detection, as the loop gain becomes zero as that condition is approached. Thus appropriate modeling of the code (or carrier) loop nonlinearity can remove loss-of-lock detection as a critical design issue.

9.2.5 Reliability and Integrity

It is difficult for a GPS receiver to determine the precise point at which it loses lock. A capability that prevents erroneous measurements from entering the filter is thus required. With filter processing, a check can be made using the observed error in the GPS signal compared to the predicted covariance to see if the measurement being processed is within reasonable limits. The extrapolated covariance at the time of the measurement is calculated in a similar manner to the formulation used in our filter, $\mathbf{P}(t_1^-) = \mathbf{\Phi}\mathbf{P}_0\mathbf{\Phi}^T + \mathbf{Q}(t_0)$. Since we are dealing with a single measurement, the equation of the range and range rate can be separated from the matrix calculation and reduced as follows:

$$\mathbf{\Phi}\mathbf{P}_0\mathbf{\Phi}^T + q_{33} = \begin{bmatrix} 0 & 0 & 1 & \phi_{23} \end{bmatrix} \begin{bmatrix} p_{00} & p_{01} & p_{02} & p_{03} \\ p_{10} & p_{11} & p_{12} & p_{13} \\ p_{20} & p_{21} & p_{22} & p_{23} \\ p_{30} & p_{31} & p_{32} & p_{33} \end{bmatrix} \begin{bmatrix} 0 \\ 0 \\ 1 \\ \phi_{23} \end{bmatrix} + q_{33}$$

$$= \begin{bmatrix} (p_{20} + \phi_{23}p_{30})(p_{21} + \phi_{23}p_{31}) \\ (p_{22} + \phi_{23}p_{32})(p_{23} + \phi_{23}p_{33}) \end{bmatrix} \begin{bmatrix} 0 \\ 0 \\ 1 \\ \phi_{23} \end{bmatrix} + q_{33}$$

$$= p_{22} + \phi_{23}p_{32} + \phi_{23}(p_{23} + \phi_{23}p_{33}) + q_{33}$$

Since $p_{ij} = p_{ji}$, let

$$\alpha_\rho = p_{22} + 2\phi_{23}p_{23} + (\phi_{23})^2 p_{33} + q_{33}$$

One can do the same thing for the GPS velocity measurement and get

$$\alpha_{\dot\rho} = p_{33}q_{33} + p_{44}$$

The error in the observation that we earlier called the innovations process we will denote as gamma ($\mathbf{\Gamma}$), which can be calculated by subtracting the predicted observation $\mathbf{H}(t_1)\hat{\mathbf{x}}(t_1^-)$ from the observation. The value $\mathbf{\Gamma}^2$ is compared to $m^2\alpha$, where m is the $m\sigma$ limit (typically $3 \le m \le 6$). If $\mathbf{\Gamma}^2$ exceeds the $m^2\alpha$ limit, the measurement is declared bad and not processed by the filter.

Another technique that is used is a function of the GPS receiver. Most bad measurements are caused by disruptions in the GPS signal. These disruptions result in changes in the power levels of the GPS signal being received. By calculating the received power level during each GPS sub dwell (1 ms) and comparing these levels to set thresholds, the receiver can recognize significant fluctuations. When thresholds are exceeded, the measurement is declared bad and not utilized by the filter.

9.2.6   Integration with CRPA

This section discusses the integration of a CRPA antenna, originally discussed in Chapter 6, with a GPS/inertial system. The gain pattern of the CRPA antenna as compared to a standard FRPA when a source of interference is present is illustrated in Figure 9.15.

The CRPA antenna minimizes gain toward the interference source adaptively by utilizing an array of N antenna elements, as shown in Figure 9.16. The signal from each element is weighted and combined in such a fashion that signals coming from the direction of jamming source are greatly attenuated (or *nulled*, using the terminology prevalent in adaptive antenna literature) to minimize the effects of the interference on the GPS receiver. Another aspect of this antenna is that the gain toward the GPS satellites can be increased, improving the GPS signal strength. This technique is generally referred to as *beam steering*. Null steering and beam steering antennas have been successfully used to mitigate the effects of interference and multipath for GPS applications for a number of years. Null steering antennas are currently used on a number of military platforms. Drawbacks of the use of CRPAs include high cost (relative to FRPAs), and weight/size issues. A number of programs have been trying to address these concerns by reducing the size of the antenna from 14 inches to 5.5 inches [20–22]. The majority of current CRPA applications implement null steering without beam steering. The reason is that beam steering requires knowledge of the platform attitude, which is not always available or easily accessed.

A diagram of the *antenna electronics* (AE), which in airborne installations is usually housed within the aircraft rather than in the antenna, is shown in Figure 9.17. The electronics consists of circuitry to control the weighing of the signal from

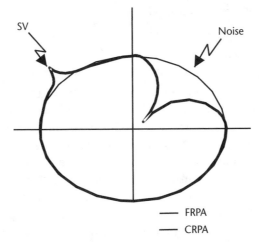

Figure 9.15   Antenna pattern of a FRPA and CRPA antenna.

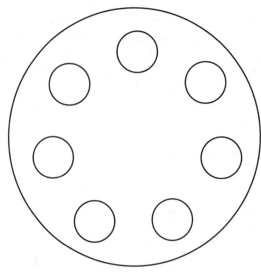

Figure 9.16 Layout of seven-element CRPA antenna.

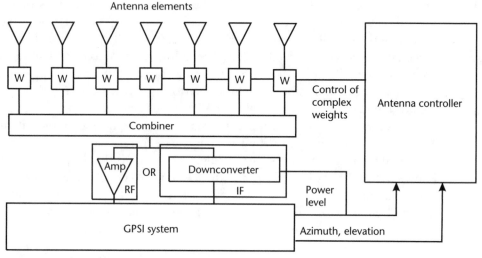

Figure 9.17 CRPA antenna block diagram.

each element, a combiner used to combine the weighed signal from each antenna element, a microprocessor (occasionally referred to as an antenna controller), a combiner to reconstruct the GPS signal, and optionally a downconverter and a power detector to measure the amount of jamming coming into the receiver if not available from the GPS receiver. The microprocessor used within the antenna controller executes an iterative algorithm that computes the weight applied to each element, which will minimizes the jamming coming in from the antennas. Since the received power coming in from a jamming source is above the ground floor, the AE tries to minimize any incoming power. AE used to implement beam forming additionally must incorporate platform attitude and satellite location information into the adaptive algorithm, in combination with the measured voltages from each antenna element, to optimize the weighting applied to each element. Electronics used for currently available CRPA antennas also include the first down conversion and AGC electronics of the GPS receiver (see Figure 6.1). This allows the power detector of the AGC circuitry to be included in the AE.

In some implementations, a time delay line with M taps are added to each of the N antenna elements. The combiner then weights the $M \times N$ delay line taps. This technique, referred to as *space-time adaptive processing* (STAP), can significantly improve nulling and beamforming performance. STAP improves performance by allowing a null to be created in a certain direction only for a certain band of frequencies, which is sufficient to suppress the interference while possibly allowing enough desired signal power to remain so that the receiver can track a satellite visible in the same direction.

As mentioned earlier, to implement beam steering, the AE must know the LOS direction to the satellites being utilized by the GPS receiver. This is accomplished by means of a serial interface between the navigation processor and AE. Satellite azimuth and elevation relative to the antenna and usually the vehicle are periodically sent to the AE to use in optimizing the gain toward the satellites.

9.3   Sensor Integration in Land Vehicle Systems

This section examines integrated positioning systems found in vehicle systems, automotive electronics, and mobile consumer electronics. Low-cost sensors and methods used to augment GPS solutions are presented, and example systems are discussed.

9.3.1   Introduction

Ever since GPS was first conceived, it was envisaged that receivers would be used for positioning in motor vehicles. By the early 1990s, GPS receiver technology had advanced to the point where GPS products functioned reliably in automotive environments and costs had dropped to a point where widespread use was possible. GPS is now used in automotive systems for locating vehicles, tracking vehicles, and providing navigation assistance to drivers.

Vehicle navigation systems are available on dozens of vehicle models in the market today. The purpose of these systems is quite simply to help a driver get to a destination. A generic vehicle navigation system architecture is depicted in Figure 9.18. Major components include a user interface to enter a destination, a GPS receiver to determine the absolute position of the vehicle, possible auxiliary sensors for augmenting the positioning solution, access to a digital map database for planning routes and determining maneuvers, and means to present the directions to the driver by voice, graphics, or both via the user interface. Access to digital map data is essential for route planning and guidance, and when available in the vehicle may also be used to improve the positioning, as will be discussed in this chapter. GPS is used for positioning in virtually every vehicle navigation system on the market. Differential GPS corrections may be provided and applied to improve the positioning accuracy of the solution.

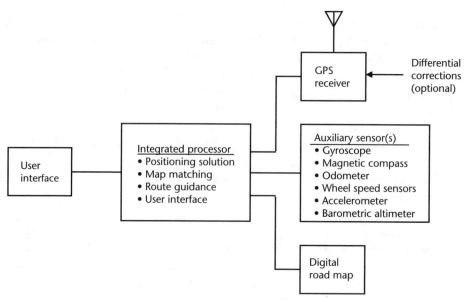

Figure 9.18   Generic vehicle navigation system architecture.

Many diverse applications involve vehicle tracking, most of which use GPS for positioning. In vehicle tracking applications, the position of the vehicle is determined and then sent via wireless data connection to a centralized monitoring facility or fleet dispatcher. A typical vehicle tracking system architecture is shown in Figure 9.19. Like the navigation system, the tracking system has a GPS receiver, auxiliary sensors, and a computer processor to control the components and calculate the optimized position solution. In addition, there is a wireless data radio for communicating the vehicle position data and possible status to the central monitor. At the central monitor, the vehicle position and other attributes may be displayed or overlaid on a

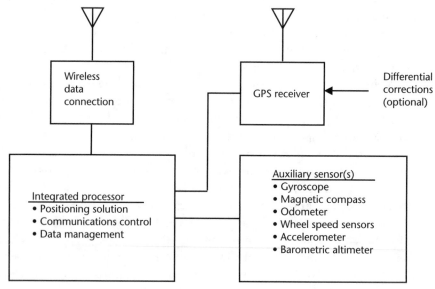

Figure 9.19   Generic vehicle tracking system architecture.

digital map. The digital map can also be used to look up the nearest street address, a process known as *reverse geocoding.*

There are many wireless technologies that may be used as the data radio, including cellular modems, cellular packet data, two-way paging, satellite links, and private data networks. Some systems track the vehicles on a continuous basis with position reports broadcast at certain intervals, while other systems are designed to record data to be uploaded periodically or on demand. Enterprises that own or operate fleets of vehicles (e.g., taxis, delivery trucks, or service vehicles) use vehicle tracking systems to monitor the usage of the vehicles and improve efficiency in logistics through optimum dispatching. Public safety departments (e.g., police, fire, or ambulance) use vehicle tracking to reduce call response time and to locate workers in the case of distress calls.

Individual vehicles can be located in emergency situations using GPS and wireless communications. These emergency messaging systems, also known as telematics systems, are offered by many automobile manufacturers today. A generic emergency messaging system architecture is shown in Figure 9.20. Typically, these systems use a cellular phone for wireless data communications because of the dual-purpose voice and data capabilities, extensive coverage throughout most developed countries, and relative low cost. These devices are connected to vehicle systems or to the vehicle bus and can notify a service provider automatically when an air bag is deployed or some other crash sensor is triggered. The user interface includes one or more buttons to activate the system, a hands-free voice call capability, and possibly a display to indicate status. The GPS position of the vehicle is sent via the cellular phone so that emergency services or other assistance can be sent to the exact location of the vehicle. These devices are also used for crash notification, roadside assistance, theft tracking, and direction assistance.

In navigation, tracking, and emergency location, the availability of an accurate GPS position fix is essential. In all of these applications, a GPS C/A code receiver

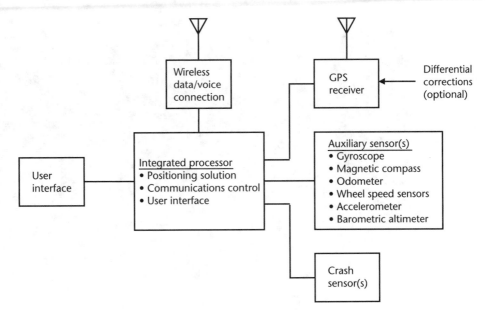

Figure 9.20   Generic emergency messaging system architecture.

with 8 to 12 channels should be used. The receiver should have rapid signal reacquisition to minimize the effects of urban canyon signal blockage from buildings and structures. The removal of SA has had a large impact on the accuracy of low-cost GPS sensors, but differential GPS is sometimes still used to improve the accuracy. A separate radio can be used to receive differential corrections, such as the RTCM corrections (see Section 8.5) broadcast by the NDGPS service in the United States (see Section 8.6.1.1). Some newer GPS receivers have the ability to directly acquire corrections from WAAS in North America. As discussed in Section 8.6.1.2, WAAS is a free service and adds little cost to the GPS receiver. The improvement in accuracy due to WAAS is not dramatic now that SA has been turned off; however, the WAAS integrity information may warrant its use.

GPS signal blockage in urban canyons and in parking garages can still severely impact the availability of GPS positions. Figure 9.21 shows the results of a GPS drive test in downtown Phoenix, a moderate urban canyon environment. Figure 9.22 shows the results of a GPS drive test in downtown Chicago, a severe urban canyon environment due to the taller and more numerous buildings. The GPS receiver used is a commercially available conventional 12-channel C/A code receiver and the positioning is determined by least squares with no filtering applied in the position domain. Of course, some level of filtering and the use of a high-sensitivity receiver design (whose enhanced acquisition capabilities are discussed in Chapter 5) can be expected to improve the performance. As can be seen, there are several position jumps and gaps, which are caused by signal blockage and reflection due to the tall buildings. In the moderate urban canyon, the jumps are as large as half a block, or 50–70m, and there are at least a few position fixes in each block. In the severe urban canyon, the jumps reach 500m and sometimes the receiver goes a block or more without a position fix. Clearly, it is highly desirable to augment the performance of GPS with additional sensors and filtering methods. Integration of one or more of the

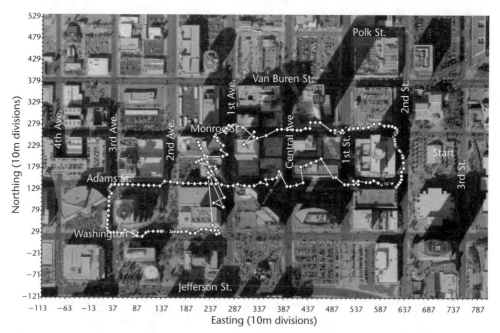

Figure 9.21 GPS performance in moderate urban canyon (Phoenix).

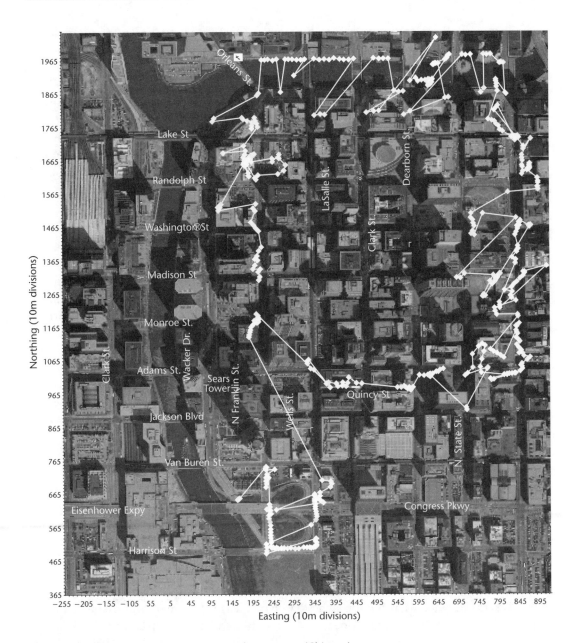

Figure 9.22 GPS performance in severe urban canyon (Chicago).

auxiliary sensors listed in Figure 9.18 should ensure complete position coverage, as well as improve navigation accuracy and reduce susceptibility to gross positioning errors—these issues are discussed further in the following sections.

Only one factor is as important in system design as performance: cost. The overall cost of the system impacts market adoption, and then once the systems are made in high volume, every dollar saved in system cost represents a large improvement in profitability. The total annual volume of navigation and telematics systems is in the millions of devices, and the cost of the GPS components is dropping below $10 per unit. There is a natural reluctance among equipment manufacturers to include expensive augmentation sensors. Systems integrators are finding ways to use lower grade (and lower cost) sensors and still achieve complete coverage and improved accuracy over the performance provided by GPS alone.

In recent years, small, low-cost GPS receivers have been integrated into cellular phones for emergency location in 911 calls (E-911). These cellular phones are in high demand for personal navigation, tracking workers, friends and family members, and finding nearby services (gas stations, restaurants, shops, and such). As the cost and size of auxiliary sensors decreases, it is likely that these too will be integrated into cellular phones, further increasing the performance and utility of these systems.

9.3.2 Review of Available Sensor Technology

9.3.2.1 Inertial Systems and Sensors

The use of inertial and various automotive sensors to augment GPS performance in automotive applications is often termed *dead reckoning*. Since this term may appear strange to the reader, and since there is some controversy associated with its origin, some explanation is in order. The term is much broader than automotive in its application and in fact originated long before automobiles were invented. A popularly held belief is that it derives from "deduced reckoning," and it is often abbreviated as "ded. reckoning," consistent with this interpretation. Certainly, this view is consistent with its meaning (i.e., to deduce one's current position by applying course and distance traveled to a previously determined position). However, according to the *Oxford English Dictionary*, the phrase *dead reckoning* dates from Elizabethan times, in 1605–1615. At that time, it applied to navigation in ships in the absence of stellar observations. With stellar observations, navigation was viewed as navigating "live," working with the stars and the motion of the Earth; in comparison, navigating without sky visibility, by using logs (the process of determining speed by timing the transit of a log dropped in the water from bow to stern), compasses, and clocks, was viewed as navigating "dead," and hence dead reckoning. So either expression is valid; both are consistent with the modern day application, and both are consistent with the abbreviation DR.

The use of inertial sensors to augment GPS in automotive applications offers several advantages over approaches based on measuring tire rotation. The quality of inertial sensor information does not vary with tire wear or road conditions, whereas measures of distance traveled certainly do, as their performance will vary with tire wear and tire slipping or skidding due to nonideal road conditions. However, inertial sensors useful for navigation aiding generally are not preinstalled in the car. In addition, very-low-cost inertial sensors require nearly continuous calibration: large bias and scale factor errors are typical, as are high sensitivities to temperature variations.

In terms of their usage in automotive and other land vehicle applications, the following inertial system options have emerged as attractive alternatives, with varying limits of practicality:

- Three orthogonal gyros and three orthogonal accelerometers;
- Three orthogonal gyros and two level axis orthogonal accelerometers;

- All (six or more) accelerometer systems;
- Two level axis orthogonal accelerometers;
- Single longitudinal axis accelerometer and a vertical gyro;
- Single lateral axis accelerometer with an interface to the vehicle's odometer;
- A single vertical gyro with an interface to the vehicle's odometer.

Obviously, the last two options do not take full advantage of inertial instrumentation, since they make use of an interface to the vehicle's odometer and so are sensitive to both tire wear and road conditions. To better understand the relative strengths and weaknesses of the various options, it is helpful to first review the basics of inertial sensing. An in-depth treatment of inertial sensors and systems is beyond the scope of this text and can be found in [4].

A common misconception is that an accelerometer directly measures a component of acceleration: in fact, the accelerometer senses what is often referred to as *specific force* [4], the difference between the component of acceleration along its input (sensitive) axis and the component of gravity along the same axis. Figure 9.23 illustrates the specific force measurement for an accelerometer mounted along the lateral axis of an automotive vehicle. Note that it is implicitly assumed that the input axis of the accelerometer is perfectly aligned with the vehicle's lateral dimension in the figure, which is not realistic. More generally, the misalignment between the accelerometer's sensitive axis and the vehicle's lateral axis is a source of error that must be considered in the design of the navigation system. Neglecting this misalignment in Figure 9.23, the angle φ (in radians) represents the *roll* of the automobile, or the rotation of the vehicle's vertical axis about its longitudinal axis with respect to the local vertical, b_L, the inherent bias of the accelerometer (in m/s^2), and a_L, the lateral acceleration component (also in m/s^2). Accounting also for a dimensionless scale factor error s_L, the output of the accelerometer can be modeled (in m/s^2) as:

$$a_L^m = (1 + s_L)a_L + b_L - g\sin\varphi \approx (1 + s_L)a_L + b_L - g\varphi \tag{9.12}$$

where the indicated approximation is valid for small roll angles, and the *m* superscript denotes measured value. A similar equation exists for an accelerometer mounted along the longitudinal axis of the vehicle, with independent bias and scale factor errors and with the roll angle replaced by the pitch angle of the vehicle. Equation (9.12) and Figure 9.23 illustrate the difficulty in directly measuring acceleration.

A similar misconception exists relative to the gyro (i.e., that it simply measures the rate of rotation of the vehicle in which it is mounted along its sensitive axis).

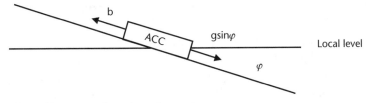

Figure 9.23   Error effects upon lateral accelerometer.

While this is true to excellent approximation even for low-cost gyros, the gyro, in theory, senses inertial angular velocity along its sensitive axis, which will include a component of the Earth's rotation rate. It is, in fact, this property that has been exploited in initializing the heading of inertial systems, using a process generally referred to as *gyrocompassing* [4]. Because the sources of error associated with low-cost gyros are orders of magnitude greater than Earth rate (e.g., drift rates approaching 1°/second, as contrasted with 15°/hour), an alternate means of initializing heading is necessary until low-cost gyro technology dramatically improves.

Let's return now to the issue of gyro and accelerometer initial alignment. Any misalignment of either sensor, due either to imperfect mounting of the sensitive element(s) within the sensor's housing or imperfect alignment of the sensor housing within the vehicle upon installation, will lead to a cross-axis sensitivity, which can be significant. From (9.12), a misalignment about the vertical axis of the host will cause the accelerometer to sense a component of longitudinal acceleration, and a misalignment about the roll axis will cause the accelerometer to sense gravitational acceleration, even when the vehicle is level (i.e., at zero roll angle). In each case, the magnitude of the error, for small misalignment angles, is the product of the angle (in radians) and the off-axis acceleration. For example, a 5° misalignment about the vehicle's roll axis will produce an error in the lateral accelerometer of roughly 0.1g, or about 1 m/s^2. A gyro mounted with its sensitive axis in the vertical direction, intended to sense the turns of the vehicle, will produce an output that may be modeled (in units of radians/second) as:

$$\omega_H^m = (1 + s_H)\omega_H + b_H + m_\varphi \omega_\theta + m_\theta \omega_\varphi \qquad (9.13)$$

where s_H is the gyro's scale factor error, b_H is the gyro bias, m_φ and m_θ are the small angle misalignments (in radians) of the gyro sensitive axis about the roll and pitch axes, respectively, and ω_θ and ω_φ are pitch and roll rate (in radians/second), respectively. In addition, any misalignment of the gyro with respect to the local vertical will appear as a component of gyro scale factor error, since it will contribute an error that is proportional to the angular rate about its sensitive axis. The scale factor error term is expressed in (9.14), where α (in radians), is the misalignment value:

$$\delta s_H = \cos\alpha - 1 = -\alpha^2/2 \qquad (9.14)$$

So, for a gyro that is misaligned by 5° relative to the vertical axis of the car, the effective scale factor error is changed by 0.5%, which is generally not significant for low-cost gyros (the nominal scale factor error can be 10 times this level).

Now, given this very basic review of inertial sensing technology, we can return to the issues associated with the options for inertial sensor augmentation of GPS in automotive vehicles. The first two options differ only in that the second abandons the vertical accelerometer, as the vertical motion of an automobile is not expected to be significant, and GPS aided by an altitude constraint may suffice. Referring to (9.12) and Figure 9.23, initialization of the pitch and roll angles for both systems begins (upon turn-on of the system) by assuming that the car is stationary and level, which implies that the accelerometers (after gravity compensation for the vertical axis for the first option) should read zero. Of course, under zero acceleration, the accelerometers will read the bias error level associated with their current operation. The assumptions of initial level operation, while probably good for an aircraft on a runway or in a hangar, are generally not good for an automobile. Even if the road on which the car is parked is level, the road crown will induce a nonzero roll angle. In general, both the car's pitch and roll angles will be nonzero at IMU turn on. From (9.12), this implies that each level accelerometer will sense a component of gravity. The sum of the sensed gravity component will be nulled by assumed roll and pitch angles as part of the process that initializes the vehicle's attitude: this so determined pitch and roll will not, of course, in general, match the actual pitch or roll of the vehicle. These initial attitude errors, through the actions of the inertial system, will induce a *Schuler oscillation* [4] in both attitude and position and velocity error in the level axes. The Schuler oscillation period is 84 minutes. This error oscillation, if not disturbed by other error-inducing effects (e.g., maneuvers), will persist until the Kalman or integration filter has had time to estimate the sensor errors. Typical Kalman filter designs will be addressed in Section 9.3.3.

Unlike the initialization of pitch and roll, however, because low-cost gyros have bias errors that are very large relative to Earth rate, the heading of the vehicle must be initialized by an auxiliary sensor (e.g., a magnetic compass), use of a GPS determined heading, or use of the vehicle heading as last computed by the navigation system. In the case of a GPS heading, care should be taken that a minimum speed has been attained and that at least four GPS satellites are tracked to ensure adequate accuracy.

Returning to the two-accelerometer INS, use of a vertical accelerometer in an INS brings a potential stability problem. As is well known [4], an INS vertical channel is inherently unstable due to the dependence of gravitational acceleration upon altitude (in general, a gravity model is needed to remove gravitational acceleration from the accelerometer outputs to enable sensing of inertial acceleration). The fact that modeled gravitational acceleration may decrease with altitude increase leads to an effective *positive feedback loop* in the error equations for the vertical channel [4], which produces an exponential error growth. This error growth will produce more than a doubling of altitude error roughly every 10 minutes if not corrected. Thus, an independent source of altitude information is needed, which could be provided by an additional sensor (e.g., a barometric altimeter) or an altitude constraint (e.g., the assumption that the vehicle is at mean sea level or at the known altitude for a certain road).

Because gyro design and development is generally more complex and less reliable than accelerometer design and development [23], it is attractive to consider an accelerometer-only INS, which develops angular acceleration estimates by placing dual accelerometers at known displacements (referred to as *lever arms*) from the vehicle's center of gravity. For example, as illustrated in Figure 9.24, the two accelerometers illustrated could be used to sense both linear and angular acceleration. Before discussing a recent reference [24] where such a prototype system is constructed, some high-level comments are worth making. First, since we have replaced the gyro, an angular rate sensor, with an angular acceleration sensor, accelerometer errors will have a different effect on the INS position and velocity error. Any biases in the accelerometers will produce a time-varying rate error in angular velocity: the accelerometer biases add, while error effects due to sensing of gravitational acceleration from pitch or roll error is largely cancelled. The quality of the angular acceleration sensing improves as the separation between the accelerometers increases. To understand this, consider the treatment in (9.15), valid for two accelerometers placed along the longitudinal axis of the vehicle:

$$a^m = (f_1 - f_2)/2 \tag{9.15a}$$

$$d\omega/dt^m = (f_1 + f_2)/2L \tag{9.15b}$$

$$f_1 = (1 + s_1)a + Ld\omega/dt + b_1 - g\sin\varphi \tag{9.15c}$$

$$f_2 = -(1 + s_2)a + Ld\omega/dt + b_2 + g\sin\varphi \tag{9.15d}$$

$$\delta(d\omega/dt) = \left[(s_1 - s_2)a + b_1 + b_2\right]/2L \tag{9.15e}$$

In (9.15), (9.15a) and (9.15b) represent the equations that would be used to measure linear and angular acceleration, labeled a^m and $d\omega/dt^m$, respectively; (9.15c) and (9.15d) represent the error equations associated with the measured quantities in (9.15a) and (9.15b). Thus, a represents the true acceleration of the vehicle along the sensitive (lateral) axis, b_1 and b_2 are the accelerometer biases, all preferably represented in units of m/s^2. As used previously, φ is the roll angle of the vehicle in radians, and g represents gravitational acceleration in m/s^2. The accelerometer scale factor errors (unitless quantities) are denoted s_1 and s_2, respectively. The lever arm is represented by the variable L, expressed in meters to maintain consistent units. Finally, note that (9.15c) is an equation for the rate of change of the error in sensing angular rate (i.e., yaw rate, which is roughly heading rate), which would typically be modeled in a Kalman filter that attempted to reduce this error by processing GPS measurement data.

Thus, the error contributors to angular acceleration—the individual accelerometer bias and scale factor errors, b_1 and b_2 and s_1 and s_2—are reduced by increasing the lever arm, L, between each sensor and the center of gravity of the vehicle. In the specific case illustrated in Figure 9.24, best performance would be achieved by placing one accelerometer near the front of the car and the second near the rear of the car. Of course, the lever arm does not affect the quality of the determined linear acceleration. Because the accelerometer bias contributes to an angular rate bias in this formulation, it produces different position and velocity error behavior than its gyro bias counterpart. As is well known [4], level axis gyro bias errors produce biased velocity errors superimposed on a Schuler oscillation in the level axes. The bias component of the velocity error can dominate the INS drift for periods that are less than the Schuler period, leading to the familiar "nmi/h" rating often associated with inertial systems [2]. A bias angular acceleration error can therefore be expected to produce a ramping velocity error over a similar time period.

The concept of using accelerometers to sense angular acceleration is not new [25]. Only fairly recently, however, has this concept received new attention, driven largely by the presence of very-low-cost microelectromechanical sensors (MEMS) accelerometer technology for cars and the ability to fabricate accelerometers for a fraction of the cost of gyros [26, 27]. Recent work has also focused on the placement of accelerometers within the vehicle for best performance [28]. The most recent

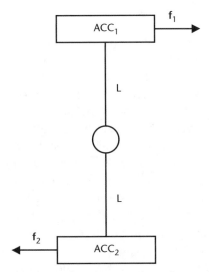

Figure 9.24   Dual-accelerometer approach to linear and angular acceleration sensing.

treatment [24] attempts to make use of existing accelerometers (e.g., as could be associated with air bag deployment or the vehicle's ABS) distributed throughout the car to support an inertial navigation capability. Tests of a prototype system have demonstrated that the accuracy of measured angular accelerations using accelerometers is nearly equivalent to that provided by low-cost gyro sensors.

Use of single accelerometers aligned with the lateral or longitudinal axis of the vehicle is an option worthy of consideration. The longitudinal accelerometer measures vehicle accelerations and decelerations, which, once integrated, could potentially replace use of the vehicle's odometer. The lateral accelerometer could potentially replace a heading or heading rate sensor, since a lateral acceleration is generally indicative of a turn: the product of the vehicle's speed and the turn rate is the lateral acceleration of the vehicle. However, use of single accelerometers has its drawbacks. As previously discussed, both accelerometers will generally sense a component of gravity, due either to initial misalignment of the sensor as installed in the vehicle or the pitch (affecting the longitudinal accelerometer) and roll (affecting the lateral accelerometer) of the vehicle. Although the pitch and roll of a vehicle during normal operation are expected to be small, the error effect, if uncompensated, can be significant. Relatively high frequency pitch and roll variation, as could be induced by road or speed bumps, is not as troublesome as a steady offset. A 5° steady roll angle induced by the crown of the road induces an effective acceleration error of 0.1g, or roughly 1 m/s^2. Without compensation, this will integrate to a velocity and position error, even when the vehicle is stationary (e.g., in 10 seconds, roughly 50m of cross track error will develop). In addition, since the lateral accelerometer measures the product of heading rate with the vehicle's speed, heading changes may be very difficult to detect at low speed. Similarly, a steady climb or descent on a road will be incorrectly interpreted as an acceleration or deceleration of the vehicle by the longitudinal axis accelerometer, which, without compensation, will be integrated into significant along track velocity and position error.

Finally, the use of a low-cost gyro to track the heading changes of the vehicle is an attractive option used in several of the current navigation systems. The vehicle's pitch and roll has a second-order effect upon the gyro scale factor, as indicated in (9.14), but this should be small relative to its nominal scale factor error.

Given the preceding discussion on inertial system options, the error characteristics of gyros and accelerometers can now be addressed. For the low-cost sensors considered for automotive applications, the bias and scale factor errors can be very large relative to those of gyros and accelerometers associated with navigation grade systems (e.g., for the gyro, a bias of several degrees per second is expected, and a scale factor error as large as 5% is possible). A summary of gyro and accelerometer bias and scale factor errors for different applications may be found in [25]. Of course, these errors can be calibrated using GPS and other means. For instance, an estimate of the gyro bias can be obtained each time the vehicle is stationary in a calibration procedure referred to as a *zero velocity update* (ZUPT). However, the errors can also be quite unstable and have high temperature sensitivities.

Figure 9.25 illustrates the laboratory-measured gyro bias temperature sensitivities for two samples of a low-cost, vibrational gyro. The term *vibrational* indicates that the gyro has a vibrating element that senses angular rate through a Coriolis force exerted on the vibrating element. This force is directly proportional to the angular rate and is measured through the actions of the gyro electronics. Figure 9.26, abstracted from [29], illustrates the driving and detection and control mechanisms for the Murata Gyrostar gyro as an example of vibrational gyro technology.

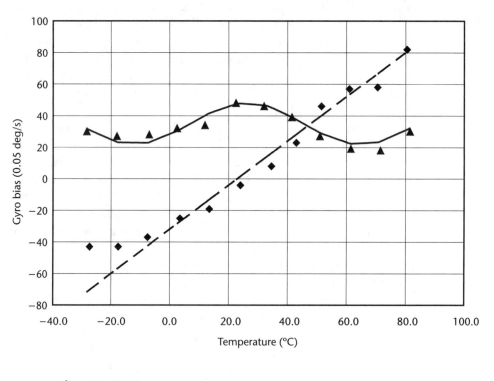

Figure 9.25   Bias versus temperature for two low-cost vibrational gyro samples.

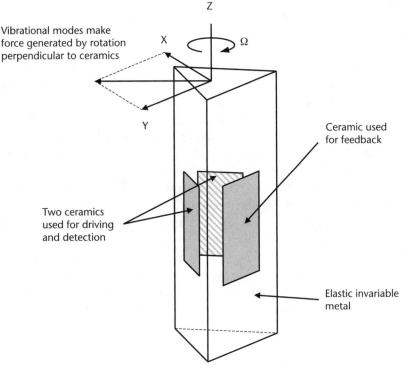

Figure 9.26   Gyrostar free-free bar and ceramics. (*From:* [29]. © 2000 University of Calgary. Reprinted with permission.)

The illustrated bar has a triangular cross section, with the bar faces forming an equilateral triangle. Two sides are used for driving the beam at a resonant frequency and detecting the Coriolis force; the third face is used to close the vibration control loop.

Returning to Figure 9.25, several conclusions relative to temperature sensitivities can be drawn from just these two gyro samples. First, the temperature sensitivity can be very large. For the sample denoted EM 0, the sensitivity is roughly linear over the temperature range, and its magnitude is 0.07°/sec/°C. If the sensitivity is ignored, and the gyro is in an agile temperature environment (e.g., a car left outside overnight in the winter in Boston heating up), the gyro will require frequent calibration. At constant speed, an uncompensated gyro bias error will produce a quadratic growth in cross-track position error proportional to the product of the bias and the speed of the vehicle. Second, the temperature sensitivity is individualized to each gyro (i.e., if compensation is desired, every gyro must be tested prior to installation in the vehicle, unless this requirement is levied upon the manufacturer). Such requests inevitably increase the cost of the gyro. The sample denoted EM 4 has a nearly sinusoidal variation, which is relatively minor over the temperature range tested. Given a temperature curve for a gyro or accelerometer bias or scale factor, it is tempting to use a curve fit or other means to compensate its output in real time. There are several issues here, in addition to the expense associated with the curve fit generation for each gyro sample. First, a temperature sensor will be needed to perform the compensation, and the sensor must certainly be installed near the gyro or accelerometer sensitive element. Although some sensor assemblies may provide temperature information, not all do. The second issue that must be considered is the stability of the underlying sensitivity itself. Can the temperature compensation curve, without adjustment, be used for several months or even several years? The answer to such a question may not be known by the manufacturer, so it is therefore advisable to at least monitor the curves for stability. This subject is addressed further in Section 9.3.3.

The use of gyros and accelerometers based upon MEMS technology is currently receiving much attention for military systems [30] as a result of expected cost, weight, size, and power savings. Due largely to their use as sensors for air bag deployment in cars, accelerometer development is more mature than that for gyros. Until fairly recently, however, performance has been a limiting factor. In [31–35], accelerometer developments are described that achieve navigation grade accuracies (i.e., with bias errors as low as 20 μg, and scale factor errors approaching 50 ppm). Gyro technology is not there yet, however; [36–38] summarize key developments. Although 1°/hour gyro bias performance is predicted, reported performance levels are limited to 10°/hour, with scale factor errors approaching 500 ppm. MEMS applications in the commercial world appear very promising [39]. Automotive navigation systems could certainly make use of MEMS technology, given the performance improvements expected, as the gyros and accelerometers are cost competitive with existing inertial sensors. Characterization of MEMS-based sensors for land vehicle applications is treated in [40]. Like the existing sensors (e.g., the vibrational gyros), MEMS gyros, as well as accelerometers, are expected to have significant temperature sensitivities that must be compensated to realize their full performance potential.

9.3.2.2   Map Databases

As mentioned in Section 9.3.1, the emergence of high-quality, affordable, digital maps has been a significant factor in the wider acceptance of automotive navigation. Digital road maps are not only an essential component for pathfinding and route guidance in navigation systems, but also a high-value addition to the positioning subsystem.

At the time of this writing, two primary companies were developing digital road map databases for vehicle navigation: Navteq and TeleAtlas. TeleAtlas acquired Etak in 2000 and acquired Geographic Data Technology in 2004. Both Navteq and TeleAtlas have extensive databases covering most of the United States, Canada, Europe, some countries in Asia and the Middle East, and other emerging markets worldwide. The accuracy of these databases, as determined by comparing road centerline vectors to ground truth, ranges from under 12m in urban areas to 50m or more in rural areas. New initiatives are underway to map road centerlines to better than 5-m accuracies and to include vertical information for use in advanced driving systems. Over time, both the positional and topological accuracies are being improved through GPS surveying, photogrammetry, and other data acquisition methods [41].

Even before GPS became a viable positioning system for use in commercial products, digital road maps were used as a component in the positioning subsystem of navigation systems. The Etak Navigator, introduced in 1984, consisted of a cassette tape player, an 8086-based computer, dual odometers, a compass, and a small cathode ray tube display. A digital road map was stored on the cassette tape. The system used the compass, differential odometry, and map matching to position the vehicle [42–44]. Map matching is the process of correlating the vehicle path with a drivable path in the digital road map [45]. The map and the vehicle position were displayed, and as the vehicle moved, the map would move, keeping the vehicle symbol in the center of the screen. With map matching, a basic assumption made is that the vehicle is on the road network so that the DR position is constrained to one of the road segments in the map. As the vehicle travels, the DR sensors provide a path of the vehicle, which is matched up with road segments in the map database that have the same approximate shape in order to determine the position of the vehicle.

One major challenge with map matching before GPS was available was the initialization of the system when the starting position was not known. In early navigation systems, the user sometimes had to be prompted to enter the current position. Of course this was difficult if the user did not know where they were! With GPS, the absolute position is readily determined, and, in time, GPS receivers were added to navigation systems. Initially, GPS was only used to get the DR/map matching system started or to detect large errors. Then systems emerged where the GPS/DR trace was compared with the digital road map in order to find the most probable location of the vehicle [46]. Today, most navigation systems rely primarily on GPS and use DR and map matching to correct GPS errors and bridge the coverage gaps.

A robust map matching implementation uses confidence measures to determine all possible road segments in the map on which the vehicle could be traveling, as illustrated in Figure 9.27 [47]. As the vehicle travels, distance traveled and changes in direction are used to continuously determine the shape of the route traveled; this shape is used to match the road network in the map through shape correlation. When an accurate heading is known, the list of roads is reduced to those that have a

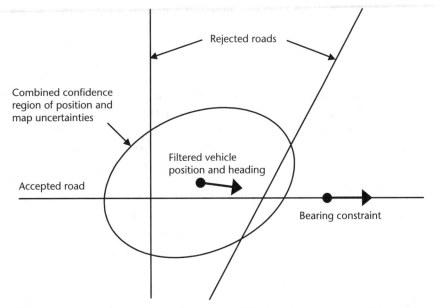

Figure 9.27 Road selection and map aiding. (*From:* [47]. © 1995 University of Calgary. Reprinted with permission.)

bearing within a tolerance of the vehicle heading. When the vehicle makes a turn, the list of candidate segments is further reduced based on examining the topology of the road network to find candidate segments that have a turn in the direction the vehicle turned. Through this process, the list of possible vehicle positions is eventually reduced to a unique segment, and the confidence in the positioning solution increases accordingly. When there is only one possible vehicle position, the map-matched position solution will have a small confidence region and therefore can be considered highly reliable. If a position jump or a turn occurs that introduces additional potential positions in the road network, then the confidence region should grow, reflecting a lower confidence in the map-matched solution.

In order to support map matching, the map data should have high position accuracy, ideally better than 15m, to minimize incorrect road selections. The map data should also be topologically correct, reflecting the real-world road network, so that the algorithm does not get confused if the user drives on a road that is not in the database. The expected accuracy of the road centerline data should be used in the map-matching process to determine the overall confidence region of the map-matched position solution.

Once a match is determined, the vehicle position is then displayed on the matched road segment and used for the route guidance instructions. The map can also be used as a sensor itself to provide useful information to the positioning sub-system or to calibrate inertial and other DR sensors. These capabilities are broadly referred to as *map aiding* [47] and *map calibration.*

Map aiding is most useful when map matching has determined that the vehicle has just turned a corner, in which case its position is in close proximity to the inter-section of two streets of a known location in the map database. This reference position may be treated as a single position fix by the integration filter (see Section 9.3.3 for further discussion), which serves to correct or improve the accuracy of the absolute position determined by GPS. Further, if map matching has determined, with high probability, that the vehicle is traveling on a specific road in the database and that road is straight, then a heading fix may be generated for the integration filter (see Section 9.3.3) based on the bearing of that road segment according to the map database, as shown in Figure 9.27. Another way to utilize the heading information after a turn is to impose a constraint on the model to force the heading of the vehicle to match the bearing of the road. Map feedback can be used instead of DR sensors to improve the performance of GPS in low-cost navigation systems [47].

In addition to the horizontal position components of road vectors, ground eleva-tion data may be used to augment the performance of GPS. A digital terrain model (DTM) is a representation of the Earth's surface that can be used to extract elevation data. A digital elevation model (DEM) is a type of DTM with a regularly spaced grid of elevations corresponding to the elevation of the Earth's terrain at that point. Modern DTMs are derived from airborne or satellite-based remote sensors, are georeferenced using GPS coordinates, and have vertical accuracies better than 10m.

Terrain elevation can be used to improve the accuracy associated with GPS fixes for land applications. As is well known, and addressed previously in the text, the vertical axis is the weakest part of the GPS solution. Terrain elevation data, if suffi-ciently accurate, can be added as a constraint to a least squares or WLS GPS fix or added as a measurement to a real-time Kalman filter. To apply a height constraint, an approximate or previous position can be used to extract the corresponding eleva-tion from a DTM, DEM, or other source of elevation data. If the terrain elevation varies greatly in the vicinity of the position, iteration may be necessary. Using a DEM for this purpose may be easier from a computational perspective, since it would involve a simple value lookup and interpolation based on the coordinates; however, a large amount of storage would be required for the DEM. A DTM that has the elevation data organized into vectors would use less storage but would require more complicated computations to determine the elevation at a specific point. Elevation data can also be integrated into digital road maps as attribute data, which would simplify elevation lookup and keep the storage requirements lower. Terrain elevation data has not yet been used widely to augment GPS; this will likely change in navigation and driver safety systems once elevation information is integrated into digital road maps.

Map calibration is very similar to the process of using GPS data to calibrate iner-tial and other DR sensors. For example, with the same set of conditions that support the heading fix generation, the constant road heading may be used to calibrate a low-cost gyro or magnetic compass. Since the road heading is constant, the gyro read-ing is then a direct measure of its bias. Another example is when the vehicle makes a turn at an intersection, the change in heading between the inbound segment and the outbound segment can be used to calibrate a heading sensor. With the current perfor-mance of GPS, map calibration of sensors is less common than it once was.

9.3.2.3   GPS

As mentioned in Section 9.3.1, the discontinuance of SA enabled commercial use of GPS at close to full accuracy, except for the inability to remove the majority of the ionospheric delay (awaiting availability of the second civilian frequency). Previous sections in the text have identified and discussed the major sources of GPS errors, both in the measured pseudoranges and delta ranges or Doppler measurements, and the determined positions and velocities. Of interest here are the sources of error in the GPS-determined speed and heading and sources of error that may be unique to the automotive environment. GPS-determined speed and heading are most useful in calibrating automotive sensors that are typically sources of speed and heading infor-mation: this direct comparison enables rapid calibration of sensor errors when GPS is accurate. For errors that are small relative to the vehicle speed, the error in the GPS-determined speed and heading can be expressed as:

$$\delta v = \left(v_n \delta v_n + v_e \delta v_e \right) / v \tag{9.16}$$

$$\delta H = v_n \left(v_n \delta v_e - v_e \delta v_n \right) / v^2 \tag{9.17}$$

where:

  δv_n and δv_e are the north and east velocity error components
  v_n and v_e are the north and east velocity components
  δH and δv are the heading and speed errors, respectively
  v is the vehicle speed in a horizontal plane

All velocity components (both whole value and error quantities) in (9.16) and (9.17) should be expressed in consistent units (e.g., meters per second for velocity, and radians for the heading error). Equations (9.16) and (9.17) can be derived by simply perturbing the equations for speed and heading expressed in terms of the velocity components.

An additional source of error in the GPS-determined heading is worthy of mention and can be a significant error, depending upon the antenna placement in the vehicle. The GPS antenna will generally not be installed close to the center of rotation of the car. As illustrated in Figure 9.28, where the antenna is installed a distance L from the center of rotation of the vehicle, the GPS receiver will detect the heading rate multiplied by the distance L as a velocity component orthogonal to the true velocity of the vehicle. Since GPS (in a nonmultiantenna configuration) can only derive heading from the determined velocity components, a heading error given by (9.18) results:

$$\delta H = \omega L / v \qquad\qquad (9.18)$$

where:

ω is the heading rate of the vehicle, typically represented in radians/second

L is the distance from the center of rotation in meters

v is the vehicle's speed in meters per second

δH is the resultant heading error in radians

To assess the magnitude of this error source, assume that the GPS antenna is 1m from the center of rotation, the heading rate is 30°/second, and the vehicle speed is 5 mph. A heading error of more than 10° results, which is generally unacceptable for

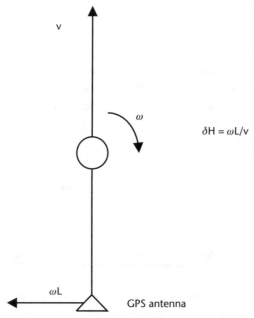

Figure 9.28   Effect of antenna placement on GPS heading.

navigation purposes, producing cross-track error that is more than 15% of distance traveled. Of course, the error persists only as long the vehicle is turning. If the lever arm L can be measured, the error effect can be compensated. As a minimum, however, the real-time navigation filter should recognize this error effect in its weighting of GPS headings in turns.

As efforts continue to lower acquisition and tracking thresholds for GPS receivers, additional sources of error must be considered, including false signal acquisitions and tracking of reflected signals (commonly referred to as multipath). As discussed in Section 5.13, acquisition of signals below normal thresholds requires longer coherent and noncoherent integration times. As SNR thresholds for acquisition and tracking are lowered by more than 20 dB, the potential for cross-correlation (i.e., declaring detection of a higher power signal with an incorrect PRN code) increases. In addition, the conservatism associated with normal detection thresholds (i.e., the threshold placed upon the peak-to–noise floor ratio) may be relaxed in order to increase coverage. Alternate tests may also be employed (e.g., use of a *neighbor test*, where a detection may be declared if the peak magnitude and the next largest peak magnitude are in neighboring code phase positions—separated by one-half chip). Such relaxations of conservatism in detection inevitably bring a higher probability of false signal acquisition (i.e., interpreting integrated noise as a signal). Both false signal acquisition and cross-correlation will produce pseudoranges that are grossly in error; generally, these errors do not persist as the transition is made to tracking the signal. If this should happen for a short period of time, however, statistical rejection tests employed by the navigation filter should remove them.

Reflected signal tracking is a serious problem that can arise in urban canyons. It can occur when the direct signal path is obscured by a high-rise building, yet a reflected signal path is visible to the GPS receiver. Note that this condition cannot be labeled as multipath, as the direct path cannot be seen, and only the reflected version is tracked. Of course, the reflected signal will be attenuated relative to the direct path, and the geometry of the reflection cannot persist indefinitely. Pseudoranges presented to the navigation filter will have additional, unexpected error due to the additional range delay associated with the reflected path, and Doppler measurements derived from the reflected signal can be significantly in error. In fact, the measured Doppler component due to receiver motion may be opposite in sign to the actual Doppler component induced by the receiver motion. It is generally a function of the velocity of the vehicle relative to the surface that is supporting the reflection, as illustrated in Figure 9.29. In Figure 9.29, as was the case with the false acquisitions, we must rely upon the integration filter's statistical rejections to preserve acceptable navigation performance.

9.3.2.4 Transmission and Wheel Sensors

The use of elapsed distance traveled information available in the vehicle is generally a low-cost, high-value augmentation of GPS. Vehicle transmission and wheel sensors can be used to determine the speed and heading changes of the vehicle. Depending on the type of sensor utilized, the distance determination can become unreliable at low speed; if variable reluctance sensing [48] is used, the sensor output becomes

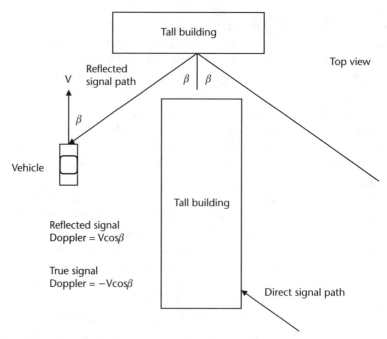

Figure 9.29 Illustration of reflected signal tracking geometry.

zero as the magnetic flux change becomes small, as illustrated in Figure 9.30. When the motion of the protruding tab through the magnetic field becomes too slow, the signal processor will not be able to detect a pulse, corresponding to a certain distance moved by the wheel. Depending on the specific sensor utilized and the signal processing circuitry, speeds of 0.5 to several meters per second may be undetectable. On the other hand, Hall-effect sensors [48], whose output is position rather than rate sensitive, can detect vehicle speed reliably down to stationary conditions. For this reason, Hall-effect sensors are preferred, but they are generally more expensive to install.

Independent of the type of sensor utilized, transmission odometer-based speed determination can be unreliable under three distinct conditions:

• Wheel slipping;
• Wheel skidding;
• Vehicle motion when the tires are stationary.

The first problem can be reduced by installing sensors so they detect the motion of the nondriven wheels (e.g., the nondriven wheels of a front-wheel drive vehicle are the rear wheels, and vice versa). Otherwise, tire slippage can lead to gross positioning errors in the DR system, since the sensed speed will generally greatly exceed the actual speed of the vehicle. Some slippage will occur, even with nondriven wheel installation, but generally only during braking and cornering. The second problem, wheel skidding, is much more difficult to solve; however, the potential for it can be reduced but not eliminated by use of an ABS. Detection of and recovery from skidding conditions should be an important consideration in the design of the sensor

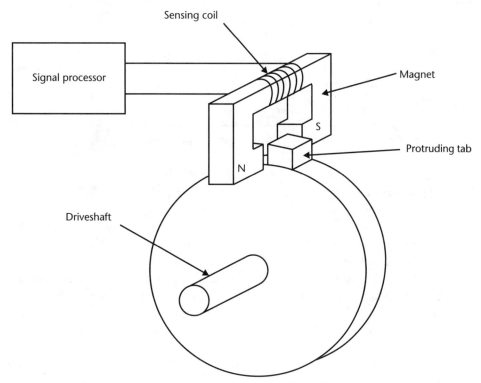

Figure 9.30 Variable reluctance rotation sensor. (*From:* [29]. © 2000 University of Calgary. Reprinted with permission.)

integration algorithm (this concern is discussed further in the next section). Finally, motion of the vehicle when the tires are stationary (e.g., as could occur when the vehicle is transported with a tow truck or onboard a ferry) can also lead to excessive positioning error; this is a second recovery mode for the sensor integration algorithm.

Excepting these anomalies, speed determination is affected by the ability to measure distance traveled using the circumference of the wheel. Typically, 24 to 48 pulses are generated for each wheel revolution. The scale factor that converts pulse counts to distance traveled can be accurately calibrated at installation by driving a known distance. However, slow variations in tire pressure can degrade the initial calibration and, over time, affect the accuracy of the scale factor. Wheel sensors suffer from the same problems described for the transmission sensors—however, with potentially more serious error conditions. Individual wheel sensors can be used to determine heading changes of the vehicle as well as speed. This is done by measuring the difference in the distance traveled by each nondriven wheel, a technique known as differential odometry. If the vehicle is making a right turn, the left wheel has to travel farther than the right wheel to complete the turn and vice versa. Assuming that the sensors are installed on nondriven rear wheels, the following equation can be used to compute heading change, ΔH, and is illustrated in Figure 9.31:

$$\Delta H = \left(d_R - d_L \right)/T \qquad (9.19)$$

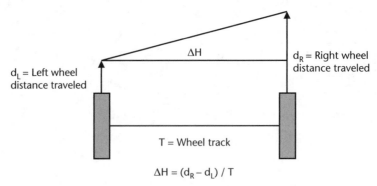

Figure 9.31 Heading change determination using rear wheels.

where d_R and d_L are the distances traveled by the right and left wheels, respectively, and T is the wheel track (the distance between the tires).

In (9.19), the right and left wheel distances are generally represented in meters, as is the wheel track, resulting in the computed heading change ΔH in radians. Note that (9.19) is valid only when the sensors are installed on the rear wheels. When the front wheels are used, the geometry changes, since the front wheels develop *wheel angles,* denoted γ in Figure 9.32.

Because of the wheel angles, the original wheel track, T, is no longer perpendicular to the tires, and the effective wheel track, denoted T' in Figure 9.32, is reduced by $\cos \gamma$. This shortening of the wheel track becomes more significant as the wheel angle increases (i.e., the heading rate is more rapid). Ignoring this effect for front wheel installations can induce significant heading errors in turns. Since the wheel angles are generally not known to the DR system, an approximate method for computing the effective track width is required. Several such methods are described in [49]. The track width variation with vehicle speed is also referenced in [49].

Heading determination via differential odometry is susceptible to gross errors when the pulse count difference is induced by either tire slipping or skidding, as discussed for the transmission odometer, but also when there is significant differential tire pressure. A relatively small difference in tire pressure, if not calibrated, can lead to significant error growth: a difference in tire size of 1% produces a heading rate

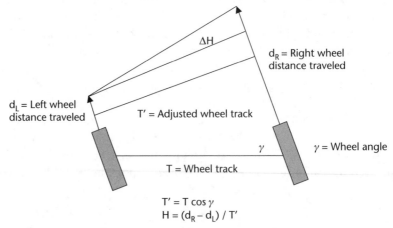

Figure 9.32 Heading change determination using front wheels.

error of roughly 3°/second at 20 mph, assuming a 2-m wheel track. Calibration of this error source by the integration filter is therefore essential and will be discussed in Section 9.3.3. The effects of wheel sensor pulse count quantization are not a significant error contributor to accumulated heading error, as recently demonstrated [50]. The reason for this is that a quantization error, which can induce a heading error of one distance quantum divided by the wheel track in one sampling interval, will tend to correct itself in the following sampling interval. For example, if the left tire had just missed registering a pulse in the current sum of pulse counts, it will certainly register that pulse in the next pulse count, and so "catch up" in its measure of accumulated heading change. In statistical parlance, successive quantization-induced heading errors are strongly negatively correlated; hence, their summation approaches zero. However, ABSs will sometimes exhibit a random heading error, whose 1-sigma level is roughly the size of the pulse quantization and so behaves like an uncorrelated, quantization error. The error can be attributed to noise in the sensor, which generates the pulses; this seems to be accurate, by design, to the pulse quantum level. Thus, (9.20), though not representative of the effects of true pulse quantization, may still be representative of the actual heading error growth; thus, it is generally recommended for consideration in the design of any real-time Kalman filter algorithm for conservatism.

$$\sigma_H = \sigma_q \sqrt{t} \qquad\qquad (9.20)$$

where:

σ_H = one-sigma heading error (rad)

σ_q = quantization level (rad)

Table 9.3, abstracted from [29], assesses the magnitudes of various factors affecting differential tire size.

9.3.2.5 Barometric Altimeter

As mentioned in Section 9.3.2.3, a barometric altimeter can be used to stabilize an inertial indication of altitude derived by a vertical accelerometer and a gravity model. In addition, it can be used to augment a GPS-based altitude, as with a gyro/odometer, or ABS-based augmentation of GPS. Because of the relative geome-

Table 9.3 Factors Affecting Wheel Scale Factor

Error Factor	Possible Error in Radius
Pressure	1 mm/lbf/in^2
Temperature	1 mm/5°C
Wear	5 mm
Speed	1 mm
Weight	1 mm/100 kg

Source: [29].

try of the satellites (i.e., none are likely to be visible below the local horizon), GPS-based altitude estimates are less accurate than lateral position estimates, so an augmentation for improved altitude estimation is attractive. Relatively low-cost barometric altimeters are available [51], which can sense changes as low as 1m in altitude and, with proper calibration, can provide absolute altitude measurements as good as 10m. Both the absolute and relative altitude information are valuable in aiding GPS, whether or not inertially augmented.

Since any barometric altimeter determines altitude through sensing air pressure, calibration (which associates pressure readings and altitudes) is necessary, and the calibration information will degrade relatively slowly with time, as local weather conditions change. The calibration accuracy will also degrade as the physical separation between the vehicle and the reference location for the calibration increases. Thus, operation of a vehicle navigation system that makes use of a barometric altimeter as a source of absolute altitude information will require either that calibration data from a reference station be supplied to it or that similar calibration information be supplied by GPS. If the navigation system is integrated with a cellular phone or other communication means within the car, then the communications network can provide the calibration information, if located relatively close to the car (most cellular phone service areas are limited to mobile separations less than 10 km). Air pressure sensors can be implemented on a small silicon chip at low cost [51]. Unfortunately, at the time of this writing, cellular phone base stations (BSs) did not support such a capability, although proposals have been made fairly recently [52]; thus, calibration using GPS will be required. This is preferably done by inclusion of a barometric altimeter bias state in the Kalman filter, which compares GPS altitudes (when relatively accurate altitudes are available with the barometric altimeter reading) with barometric altimeter readings: an appropriate level of process noise associated with the barometric altimeter bias will ensure that the calibration is not static. In addition, if the barometric altimeter-derived pressure changes are used as a source of vertical velocity information by the integration filter, a scale factor error state that calibrates altitude change derived by pressure change using GPS-determined vertical velocity may be necessary.

9.3.2.6 Magnetic Compass

Magnetic compasses provide an inexpensive means of determining vehicle heading and have been used to augment early DR systems [53]. The major problem associated with the use of a magnetic compass as a primary or sole heading reference is its sensitivity to magnetic anomalies. Although compass designs can be self-calibrating, this calibration serves only to remove the *static* disturbance of the Earth's magnetic field (e.g., as could be induced by the vehicle itself). The error induced by the tilt of the sensor can also be compensated [29]. Dynamic sources of disturbance, which could be generated by other passing cars or the steel trusses of a bridge, can induce very significant errors in the compass' heading indication. Thus, the compass is usually relegated to a backup role or as a complement to another system. If integrated with a source of heading rate information (e.g., as could be supplied by a low-cost gyro or an ABS), the integration filter's residual test, which compares the current magnetic compass reading with the current best estimate of heading (propagated forward in time using the heading rate information), can usually be used to screen gross errors induced by magnetic disturbances.

9.3.3   Sensor Integration Principles

9.3.3.1   Position Versus Measurement Domain Integration

Integration of GPS with any of the systems and sensors discussed in the previous section can generally be done by either position or measurement domain integration. Position domain integration means that GPS positions and velocities are processed by the navigation filter, along with data from additional sensors. Measurement domain integration means that individual GPS satellite pseudorange and Doppler measurements are processed by the navigation filter, along with data from additional sensors. Generally speaking, measurement domain processing is preferred, but it is not necessarily required for acceptable performance (see [54] for a description of a gyro-based DR system that uses position domain integration). The measurement domain approach enables "partial" updates of the DR system using less than the number of satellites required for a position fix (i.e., three for a two-dimensional fix or four for a three-dimensional fix); thus, performance should be improved. However, this improvement comes at a cost. The cost is the requirement for the integration filter to either compute the satellite positions and velocities from the ephemeris data decoded by the GPS receiver or request this from the GPS receiver. If the integration filter shares a processor with the GPS receiver, the cost is zero.

A commonly held myth by newcomers to GPS integration with inertial or automotive sensors is that a measurement domain integration is needed for sensor calibration. In fact, both integration approaches enable calibration of the DR sensors. For example, GPS heading and speed information (derived from the GPS-determined velocity), as well as individual Doppler measurements, can be used to calibrate the gyros, accelerometers, and wheel sensors of the DR system.

9.3.3.2   The Ubiquitous Kalman Filter

The Kalman filter remains the most widely used tool in integrated navigation systems. In this section, the key aspects of Kalman filter designs for three of the integrated systems identified in the previous section will be provided. It is assumed that the reader is familiar with Kalman filters or can consult one of the many excellent textbooks on the subject [5, 55] as well as the overview in Section 9.2.3. The three systems that will be examined in detail include an INS with GPS, three gyros, and two accelerometers; a system with GPS, a single gyro, and an odometer; and a system with GPS and differential odometers using an ABS.

Two-Accelerometer INS Kalman Filter Model

The error equations for an INS are well known and will not be repeated here [56]. Suitable error models for automotive quality sensors should, of course, include the basic nine error states associated with the unforced error dynamics of any INS, excepting the two states specific to the vertical axis (i.e., two INS position errors, two INS velocity errors, non-INS altitude and vertical velocity errors, and three attitude errors). The fundamental (**F**) matrix associated with the INS error dynamics has two distinct frequencies of oscillation when the INS is at rest: the Schuler frequency, with an 84-minute period, and Earth rate, with a 24-hour period. Because the longest GPS outages in the automotive environment are expected to be no more than several minutes long, the Earth rate dynamics can be ignored, and the Schuler dynamics well approximated by much simpler equations. Now returning to the state vector selection, the basic nine error states (i.e., three position errors, three velocity errors, and three attitude errors) will be augmented by three gyro bias states, two accelerometer biases, three gyro scale factor errors, and two accelerometer scale factors, resulting in a total of 19 states. The resulting state vector is summarized here:

$$\mathbf{x}^T = \begin{bmatrix} \delta\mathbf{p}^T \delta\mathbf{v}^T \delta\boldsymbol{\theta}^T \mathbf{b}_\theta^T \mathbf{s}_\theta^T \mathbf{b}_a^T \mathbf{s}_a^T \end{bmatrix} \tag{9.21}$$

Of course, the 19 states must be augmented by GPS clock phase and frequency errors if a measurement domain integration approach is chosen, resulting in a total of 21 states. Preferably, the modeled position errors ($\delta\mathbf{p}$) in (9.21) are represented in meters, velocity errors ($\delta\mathbf{v}$) in meters per second, attitude errors ($\delta\boldsymbol{\theta}$) in radians, gyro biases ($\mathbf{b}_\theta$) in radians per second, and accelerometer biases ($\mathbf{b}_a$) in m/s². Note that scale factor errors for both the gyro ($\mathbf{s}_\theta$) and accelerometer ($\mathbf{s}_a$) are unitless.

Given that most GPS outages due to signal blockage are less than a few minutes in duration, the sine or cosine of the Schuler angle, which appear in various terms in the INS error dynamics equations, can be well approximated by (9.22) and (9.23):

$$\sin(\omega_s t) = \omega_s t \tag{9.22}$$

$$\cos(w_s t) = 1 - \omega_s^2 t^2 / 2 \tag{9.23}$$

Given these substitutions, the INS error dynamics simplify significantly and become more intuitive:

$$d\delta\mathbf{p}/dt = \delta\,\mathbf{v} \tag{9.24}$$

$$d\delta\mathbf{v}/dt = \mathbf{b}_a + g\delta\boldsymbol{\theta} + \mathbf{S}_a\mathbf{a} \tag{9.25}$$

$$d\delta\boldsymbol{\theta}/dt = \mathbf{b}_\theta + \mathbf{S}_\omega\boldsymbol{\omega} \tag{9.26}$$

where $\mathbf{S}_a$ and $\mathbf{S}_\omega$ are matrices with the scale factor elements on the diagonal, and instrument input axis misalignments as off-diagonal terms, with g representing gravitational acceleration in m/s². Our Kalman filter state vector per (9.21) only estimates the accelerometer and gyro scale factor errors (i.e., the misalignments are set to zero in these equations). A real-time Kalman filter would generally have a very difficult time observing these misalignments, as controlled maneuvers are generally required for observability, so they are generally assumed to be calibrated to negligible levels prior to the filter's operation. The altitude and vertical velocity error behavior is noninertial, yet must be modeled by the filter, since errors in these states drive the inertial errors. A simplified model providing acceptable performance for many applications is

$$d\delta p_3/dt = \delta v_3 \qquad (9.27)$$

$$d\delta v_3/dt = -\beta \delta v_3 + w \qquad (9.28)$$

In (9.27) and (9.28), units are consistent with those already referenced, with position errors in meters, and velocity errors in meters per second.

In (9.28), the velocity error is modeled as a Markov process [56], which, through appropriate choice of the variance associated with the white noise, w, reaches a steady-state error variance in the absence of updates. This error variance represents the expected variation in the vertical velocity of the car. Altitude and vertical velocity can be maintained through GPS measurement processing and can also be augmented with barometric altimeter measurements. In this case, as discussed in Section 9.3.2.5, a barometric altimeter bias state should be added to the state vector, resulting in a total of 22 states.

Implementing a Kalman filter with 21 or 22 states may pose some problems from a computational burden standpoint, depending on the processing bandwidth available to the filter. Some of the states can perhaps be removed. Leading candidates for removal are the scale factor errors associated with the pitch and roll gyros, since pitch and roll rates are not expected to be large for car maneuvers (except for relatively high frequency effects, as could be induced by speed bumps, but which do not integrate to significant attitude error). It may also be worthwhile to consider removing the accelerometer bias states, since the initial determination of vehicle pitch and roll will remove their effect. Their inclusion is therefore largely a function of the bias instability and the expected pitch and roll agility of the vehicle.

Because of the potentially significant temperature sensitivities associated with the gyro and accelerometer bias and scale factor errors, it is highly desirable that temperature information be supplied with their high-rate outputs (i.e., the gyro measured delta-angles and the accelerometer measured delta-velocities). The temperature sensitivities can be measured in a laboratory environment (as previously discussed, this must be done for each gyro and accelerometer), and the resulting bias and scale factor error estimates will be comprised of a precomputed temperature-dependent component, preferably represented as a curve fit, and a correction to that generated by the Kalman filter from processing GPS. A consistent and statistically significant trend in the correction component away from the sensitivity curve may result in a modification of the temperature sensitivity curve, as could be determined using the following statistic for the gyro bias:

$$S_t = \sum \left(\delta b_\theta / \sigma_{bg} \right) / n \qquad (9.29)$$

In (9.29), δb_θ represents the corrections to a component of the gyro bias vector $\mathbf{b_\theta}$, preferably represented in radians per second, over the most recent set of n Kalman filter updates. The value in the denominator of the summation, σ_{bg} in (9.29) represents the a priori uncertainty associated with each gyro bias component correction, representing the designer's best knowledge about its temporal stability. If the process noise associated with the gyro bias state considered in (9.29) assumes that the factory-generated temperature compensation curve is effective in removing the gyro bias sensitivity, then the value of the normalized statistic in (9.29) can be used to detect a departure from those conditions. Such a detection must be *gated* by two conditions: a significant temperature change occurring over the set of *n* updates used in (9.29) and the establishment of an upper limit, or threshold, for the statistic. Such a threshold selection will typically be chosen to represent a 3-*sigma* condition, dictating use of a value of nine for testing S_t. Simulation study and test experience will generally be required, however, to achieve the desired response characteristics from the test. When the threshold is exceeded, the precomputed temperature curve for this error source can be revised. Such revisions are generally done cautiously: incorrectly revising the temperature sensitivity curve can adversely affect performance for a long time until the erroneous adjustment is detected and removed. Similar statistics and tests can be generated for each error source for which a predetermined temperature compensation exists.

Low-cost sensors may also exhibit significant scale-factor asymmetry (i.e., it may be advisable to separately model gyro and accelerometer scale factors for positive and negative rotations and accelerations, respectively). Usually, however, the component of the scale factor that is common for both directions is dominant, and the asymmetry can barely be observed in the normal operation of the vehicle.

Given the state vector definition in (9.21), the process noise selection should consider all sources of error that have been excluded (i.e., scale factor asymmetry, sensor misalignments, and gyro g-sensitivity, if significant). Of course, the expected noise floor of each sensor is also included. Since most of the unmodeled effects behave more like biases than noise, caution must be exercised to select appropriate levels. As is well known, bias errors do not behave like white noise (e.g., a bias acceleration error produces a velocity error that grows linearly or an error variance that grows quadratically). By contrast, representing a bias acceleration error as white noise (implied through a process noise representation) produces a velocity error with a variance that grows linearly.

Consider the misalignment of the roll gyro about the lateral axis of the vehicle as an illustrative example. This error source is generally expected to be constant, assuming that the gyro case is rigidly attached to the vehicle and does not experience significant shock (which could change the sensitive element's alignment within the case). During a heading maneuver, for example, this error source produces an angular velocity error in the roll gyro's output:

$$\delta\varphi = \Delta H m_\theta \qquad (9.30)$$

where m_θ is the misalignment of the roll gyro about the pitch (or lateral) axis of the vehicle, measured here in degrees; ΔH represents the magnitude of the heading maneuver in radians; and $\delta\varphi$ is the resultant roll error in degrees. If the vehicle makes a u-turn at a stoplight, the heading change will be π radians, and let us assume that the maneuver is completed in 5 seconds. The actual roll error that is induced, assuming a 1° misalignment, will be slightly more than $3\pi°$. If we select a process noise variance as in (9.31):

$$q_\varphi = \Delta H^2 \sigma_m^2 \qquad (9.31)$$

where σ_m^2 is the error variance assigned to the misalignment, and ΔH is the sensed heading change of the gyro in each assumed 1-second propagation step. Use of the (9.31) representation will increase the roll error variance by less than 2.0 degrees squared at the end of the turn, or roughly 1.4°, 1 sigma, compared to the actual error, which is more than double this predicted 1-sigma value. The reason for this optimistic prediction is that the filter assumes a white noise model, such that the error accumulation root-sum-squares from second to second. However, the actual error is a bias, which adds each second. A way to force the filter to be more conservative, and thus more realistic, is to assume a maneuver duration associated with the heading change and scale the process noise variance by this amount. If a 3-second average maneuver change is assumed, the resulting prediction will be 2.4°, 1 sigma, closer to the actual induced roll error.

Gyro/Odometer

Integration of a vertical gyro (to sense heading changes) with an interface to the vehicle's odometer is one of the first GPS augmentations considered [54] and still one of the most popular options. A commonly selected state vector for the Kalman filter is given as (9.32) in row vector form:

$$\mathbf{x}^T = \begin{bmatrix} \delta\mathbf{p}^T \delta v_o & \delta v_z & \delta H & b_H & s_H \end{bmatrix} \tag{9.32}$$

where $\delta\mathbf{p}$ is the three-dimensional position error vector, δv_o is a scale factor error associated with the odometer, δv_z is vertical velocity error, δH is heading error, and b_H and s_H are the gyro bias and scale factor errors, respectively. In (9.32), position errors are represented in meters, velocity errors in meters per second, heading error in radians, and gyro bias error in radians per second. In general, temperature error curves can be derived and applied for both the gyro bias and scale factor errors, if temperature information in the vicinity of the gyro is available. The state vector definition in (9.32) implies a centralized filter approach—where a single filter (eight state) is used—however, adequate performance can be obtained using a decentralized approach [54]. In this system, individual, mostly single-state filters are used.

Appropriate levels of process noise are required to force the filter to track variations in average tire pressure due to changes in temperature and driving conditions, which affect the scale factor error associated with the odometer. In addition, if the odometer cannot accurately track very low velocities due to sensor limitations (see Section 9.3.2.4), additional process noise can be injected into the horizontal position error states directly (the velocity error is therefore represented as the sum of the odometer scale factor induced error plus other, unmodeled effects that are represented as white noise). Any filter designed to operate with sensors that derive velocity information from the vehicle's wheels must deal with the anomalous sensor performance induced by wheel skidding and slipping. As mentioned in Section 9.3.2.4, the preferred solution to tire slipping is to derive information from the nondriven wheels; however, this may not always be possible. For tire skidding, there may be an indication of ABS activity (if the car has an ABS), which can be made available to the filter. This serves as an alert, and conservatism would dictate that additional process noise should be injected to keep the filter aware of potential error in its propagation. The amount should be derived from test experience.

For either skidding or slipping, then, the Kalman filter may have to adjust to a potentially significant and unmodeled source of error. Since its a priori levels of process noise do not reflect the presence of either condition, they must be treated as failure conditions by the filter. Generally, gross discrepancies between the GPS measurements (in this case, a Doppler or velocity component) and the reference speed and heading may indicate such a failure; however, distinguishing between slipping or skidding and a large Doppler error (as could be induced by tracking a reflected signal or tracking beyond the limits of the lock detector) is not straightforward. Failures are generally detected by a Kalman filter through a statistical test applied to the measurement residual, as explained in Section 9.2.

$$\text{if } (D^2_{res} > r_{scale}\, r_{var}) \text{ bypass this Doppler measurement} \qquad (9.33)$$

where D_{res} is the Doppler residual for the current satellite represented in meters per second, and r_{var} is the Kalman filter computed residual variance [in $(m/s)^2$]. The parameter r_{scale} is typically set to 9, implying that the probability of a residual failing the test (under the assumed unfailed error conditions of a Gaussian process) is roughly 0.01. If the failure condition is the reference trajectory (as would be the case if significant tire slipping or skidding was occurring), then several, or perhaps all, Doppler measurement residuals should fail. This is therefore a way to distinguish skidding and slipping from Doppler failure, since it is unlikely that several or all Doppler measurements would fail at the same time. In this case, two approaches can limit the errors induced in the integrated trajectory: reinitialization to a GPS position and velocity (if that is possible, given the GPS coverage at the time of the failure), or addition of sufficient process noise such that measurement rejections no longer occur. The appropriate level can be determined through experiments conducted with test data, or it may be possible (depending on the number of Doppler measurements available during the failure condition, to solve for the needed amount of process noise:

$$\mathbf{h}^T \mathbf{\Delta Q} \mathbf{h} = r_{var} - D^2_{res} \qquad (9.34)$$

The vector $\mathbf{h}$ in (9.34) represents the measurement gradient for each measurement that produces a detected failure using the test of (9.33). Since (9.34) is a single equation, each residual that produces a failure detection through (9.33) should be included to enable a possible solution for the process noise increment $\mathbf{\Delta Q}$, which will generally have more than a single nonzero component. An overdetermined set of equations for $\mathbf{\Delta Q}$ may be ensured if we limit the increment to the horizontal velocity components, or further limit the increment to a speed adjustment or a scale factor adjustment to the a priori process noise levels. Once determined, the covariance propagation can be repeated and the Doppler measurements reprocessed, if sufficient processor throughput exists.

ABS

Integration of the sensed wheel speeds, or distances traveled from an ABS in a vehicle, is perhaps the most cost-effective augmentation of GPS, since no additional sensors are required. A commonly selected state vector for the Kalman filter is given as (9.35) in row vector form:

$$\mathbf{x}^T = \begin{bmatrix} \mathbf{\delta p}^T & \delta v_L & \delta v_R & \delta v_z \end{bmatrix} \qquad (9.35)$$

where **δp** is the three-dimensional position error vector, represented in meters; δv_L is a scale factor error associated with the left wheel; δv_R is a scale factor error associated with the right wheel; and δv_z is vertical velocity error in meters per second. Of course, it is possible to include information from more than two wheels: Inclusion of separate scale factors for each wheel can then lead to observability problems for the integration filter. Essentially, the average of the left and right scale factors is estimated by comparison with GPS-derived speed, while the difference is determined using GPS-derived heading.

Of course, ABS-determined speed and heading is also subject to failures induced by slipping and skidding—but in a potentially more damaging way than for the gyro/odometer system. Because heading is also determined from the wheels, the potential exists for very large heading errors to develop (e.g., one wheel slipping over ice while the other is stationary produces a heading error rate equal to the wheel speed divided by the track). A slipping rate of 20 mph corresponds to a heading error rate of almost 300°/hour! In general, heading errors are more of a concern in the use of DR systems than speed errors, due to the potential for excessive error growth as heading errors become large.

Another issue worthy of mention is the possible adjustment of the covariance equations as heading errors become large. Because of the additional failure mechanisms just discussed, heading errors exceeding the expected *linear range* (e.g., 10°) can and will occur. In these cases, filter conservatism can be lost with a linear model. In developing a linear model involving the sine and cosine of heading, the usual (linear) approximations are:

$$\sin(\delta H) = \delta H \tag{9.36a}$$

$$\cos(\delta H) = 1 \tag{9.36b}$$

In (9.36), the heading error is represented in radians. As heading error becomes large, the cosine function can be better approximated as $1 - \delta H^2/2$. The error variance propagation equations have become nonlinear, since expressions involving error variances associated with the sine and cosine of heading error can no longer can be linearized. These expressions can be approximated by including additional terms that involve the variance of $\delta H^2/2$. Its variance can be approximated using a Gaussian assumption and noting that:

$$var(\delta H^2) = 3\sigma_{\delta H}{}^4 \tag{9.37}$$

Thus, the traditionally linear variance propagation equations can be replaced with equations that approximate the nonlinear distortion of the statistics.

Gyro/ABS Performance Comparisons

A comparison of urban canyon performance for experimental gyro- and ABS-based DR systems is performed in [29]. Both are integrated with two types of GPS receivers: wide and narrow correlator spacing. As discussed in Section 6.3, the receiver with narrow correlator spacing is expected to reduce the effects of multipath on each pseudorange measurement. Many sets of comparison data are generated and discussed in [29]; however, only a small subset of the performance data is summarized here. The reported tests of primary interest are those tests performed in downtown areas, as these are expected to be most limiting for GPS coverage. Figure 9.33 is a sample result from the gyro/odometry integration, where the map truth and unaided GPS trajectories are also shown. Corresponding results for the ABS integration are shown in Figure 9.34. Both tests were performed with narrow correlator receivers.

Since it is difficult to make quantitative comparisons from the plots, Table 9.4 is also abstracted from [29] and provides a rough characterization of the relative performance of the integrated systems. The results represent a summary of roughly a dozen tests and indicate that the gyro-based system has performance advantages, particularly in reducing the maximum excursions from the road.

Both DR systems can provide complete solution availability under nominal sensor performance conditions. However, both systems are subject to conditions that can lead to excessive error growth, which inevitably forces a reset to a GPS solution in order to recover. For the ABS, road conditions can induce such error behavior, while, for the gyro-based system, a gyro failure or abrupt and unknown temperature change can induce this behavior. Generally speaking, this is expected to occur more frequently for the ABS. The choice, then, for the systems designer, may simply be whether or not the cost of the gyro is worth the expected reduction in excessive drift conditions.

9.4 Network Assistance

Network-assisted GPS methods grew out of a need to simultaneously reduce the time to produce a position solution and increase the sensitivity of the GPS receiver.

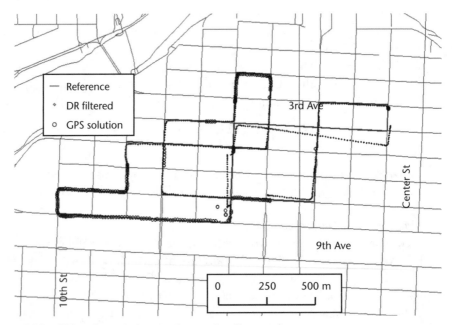

Figure 9.33   GPS and gyro/odometry integration filter results.

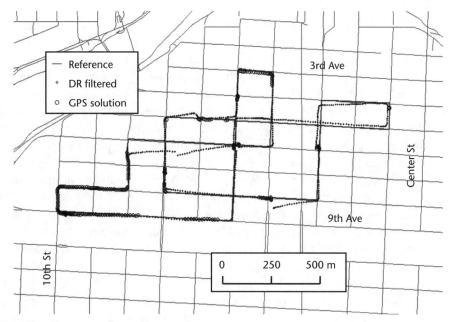

Figure 9.34 GPS and ABS integration filter results.

Table 9.4 Summary Comparison, Gyro Odometry, and ABS Integrations

DR	Maximum Error	RMS Error
ABS	115m	17m
Gyro/odometry	69m	13m

Source: [29].

One drawback of "standard" GPS is the long time to demodulate the satellite orbit parameters (ephemeris) and satellite clock correction parameters directly from the satellites. If a GPS receiver could acquire the satellites instantly, an additional 18–30 seconds of continuous tracking would be required to demodulate the 50-bps navigation data message for each satellite to extract the required orbital elements and satellite clock correction terms. In applications in which the GPS receiver is part of an emergency response system, waiting 30 seconds for data demodulation can seem like an eternity. As such, methods to eliminate the need to demodulate the satellite navigation data message directly and to decrease the acquisition time of the signals in weak signal environments has been the basis for all assisted GPS work.

There are two basic methods of assisted GPS employed in cellular handsets, *mobile station (MS)-assisted* and *MS-based*. In cellular telephone terminology, MS refers to a cellular phone. The two methods are quite different, but both require a complete or nearly complete GPS receiver to be integrated into the cellular handset.

In the MS-assisted method, the position solution is computed in the network. The MS-assisted handset shifts some of the functions of the traditional GPS receiver to a network-based processor or server. This method requires most of the hardware elements of a stand-alone GPS receiver (an antenna, RF section, and digital processor for making pseudorange measurements), but generally can get by with less embedded RAM and read-only memory (ROM) as the firmware required to compute the position solution exists elsewhere in the network. The network transmits a very short assistance message to the MS, consisting of time, visible satellite list, predicted satellite Doppler, and code phases, among other things. This visible satellite list helps the embedded GPS sensor reduce its acquisition time considerably, since the receiver does not need to use what is, in essence, a trial and error approach to determining the visible satellites. In addition, the other parameters will enable significant reduction of the search regions used for the visible satellites. This point will be explained in detail in Section 9.4.3. The MS-assisted handset simply acquires the signals and returns the measured pseudorange data for all detected satellites to the network. There, a position determining entity (PDE) such as a server does the work of computing the position solution. MS-assisted solutions are inherently differential in nature, since the PDE can have access to DGPS corrections, either from a local receiver or via the Internet.

In the MS-based method, the position solution is computed in the handset. The MS-based handset solution maintains a fully functional GPS receiver in the handset. This requires the same functionality as described in MS-assisted handset with the additional means for computing the position of the mobile station. Computing position locally to the handset generally adds to the handset's total memory (RAM, ROM) requirements in addition to increasing the loading on the host processor [e.g., as might be measured in millions of instructions per second (MIPS)]. The MS-based handset may work in an autonomous mode as well, providing position solutions to the user or embedded applications without the cellular network provided aiding data. MS-based methods are better for applications requiring the position solution in the handset, an example of which is personal navigation that can provide the user with turn-by-turn real-time directions. Turn-by-turn navigation is difficult in MS-assisted technology due to required network interaction between each position update. In the MS-based case, significantly more data needs to be delivered to the handset in the form of the precise satellite orbital elements (ephemeris, or its compressed equivalent), but once it is transferred to the handset, little or no additional data is needed to perform periodic fixes as long as the ephemeris remains vaild (several hours). MS-based solutions can be differentially corrected if DGPS corrections are sent to the handset, but DGPS is not implemented in most current MS-based networks.

These two methods, and the supporting handset input and output data messages corresponding to each, are depicted in Figure 9.35.

In both cases, some portion of the solution is accomplished by the in-network element. The network server needs, at a minimum, access to GPS satellite information in the form of the real-time ephemeris data so that it can deliver it to the MS-based handset when needed; or it needs to be able to compute predicted Doppler and code phase estimates for the MS-assisted handset. The simplest implementation installs a fixed-site GPS receiver with clear-view of the sky that can operate continuously somewhere in the network. This reference network is also connected with the cellular infrastructure and continuously monitors the real-time constellation status and provides precise data such as satellite visibility, Doppler, and even the pseudorandom noise code phase for each satellite at a particular epoch time. At the request of the mobile phone or location-based application, the assist data derived

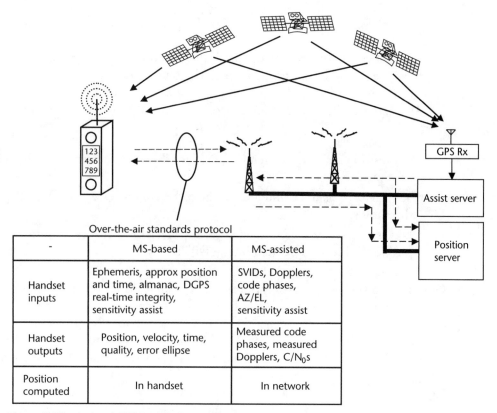

Figure 9.35 Assisted GPS positioning methods.

Over-the-air standards protocol

-	MS-based	MS-assisted
Handset inputs	Ephemeris, approx position and time, almanac, DGPS real-time integrity, sensitivity assist	SVIDs, Dopplers, code phases, AZ/EL, sensitivity assist
Handset outputs	Position, velocity, time, quality, error ellipse	Measured code phases, measured Dopplers, C/N_0s
Position computed	In handset	In network

from the GPS reference network are transmitted to the mobile phone GPS sensor to aid fast start-up and to increase the sensor sensitivity. Acquisition time is reduced because the Doppler and code phase uncertainty space is much smaller than in conventional GPS because the search space has been predicted by the network. This allows for rapid search speed and for a much narrower signal search bandwidth, which enables enhanced sensitivity by allowing the receiver to dwell longer in each of the reduced Doppler/code phase uncertainty cells. Once the embedded GPS sensor acquires the available satellite signals, the pseudorange measurements can be delivered to a network-based PDE or used internally to compute position in the handset.

Additional assistance data, such as DGPS corrections, approximate handset location or cell BS location, and other information such as the satellite ephemeris data and clock correction can be transmitted to improve the location accuracy, decrease acquisition time, and allow for handset-based position computation. Several schemes have been proposed in the standards that reduce the number of bits necessary to be exchanged between the handset and the network by using compression techniques such as transmitting only the changes to parameters instead of the raw parameters themselves. Other satellite systems could be used, such as the Russian GLONASS system (see Section 11.1), but current standards only provide for GPS and WAAS (see Section 8.6.1.2) signals. Besides adding a GPS reference network and additional location determination units in the network, the mobile phone must embed, at a minimum, a GPS antenna and RF downconverter circuits, as well as make provision for some form of digital signal processing software or dedicated hardware.

The reduction in search space allows the receiver to spend its search time focusing on where the signal is expected to be, which in turn allows it to search at a much narrower bandwidth, hence increasing signal detection sensitivity.

As referenced in this section, network assistance can refer to any one of three forms:

- Acquisition assistance, intended to reduce the GPS receiver's time to generate a fix—time to first fix (TTFF);
- Sensitivity assistance, intended to help the GPS receiver lower its acquisition thresholds;
- Navigation assistance, intended to improve the accuracy or integrity of the position solution generated by the GPS receiver.

Of course, certain types of information can qualify as more than a single type of assistance: for example, supplying the GPS receiver with an initial, coarse position estimate that represents the general location of the network infrastructure providing the assistance data can assist both acquisition and navigation.

In this section, following a brief, historical view of GPS network assistance through a discussion of example systems, the fairly recent FCC mandate [57] for cellular telephone emergency call location is reviewed. The FCC mandate is driving the needs and development of network assistance to unprecedented levels: each type of cellular network assistance is generally provided to optimize the TTFF and achievable accuracy of the determined location. Following this review, the fundamental issues of GPS receiver integration in cell phones as they relate to the use of network assistance are reviewed and discussed. In the last section, example cellular network architectures are reviewed, including discussions of their forms of network assistance, the applicable standard for over-the-air protocol, and their current status and expected performance.

9.4.1 Historical Perspective of Assisted GPS

Examples of the earliest uses of network assistance predate the introduction of cellular telephones. Perhaps the earliest formal reference to the use of assistance information is disclosed in [58]. In this patent, NASA inventors realized the potential benefit of transmitting an initial almanac or ephemeris to a mobile GPS receiver to enable prediction of satellite visibility and Doppler and eliminate the long data demodulation time inherent in collecting the required data bits from the signals directly. An Earth-based station in the vicinity of the mobile GPS receiver was used to send this information through a geostationary satellite link. Of course, an initial, coarse estimate of the mobile's location was required to generate the predictions. The very first standard for sending ephemeris data over a wireless link was included as part of the RTCM DGPS Standard [59]: message type 17 includes the ephemeris data for all satellites visible to the DGPS reference station receiver. One of the earliest references to sending measured pseudorange data over a wireless link to support location determination external to the GPS receiver is described in [60]. It describes a vehicle tracking system in which pseudoranges can be sent over a wireless link to a workstation that calculates the position of the host vehicle. In determining the vehicle's position, altitude information derived from a terrain map of the local area can be used to improve the accuracy and reliability of the solution.

An early example of ephemeris-aiding was the Motorola EAGLE line of GPS receivers. Introduced in 1985, it was one of the first commercially available GPS receivers to offer a form of ephemeris aiding [61] in one of its operational modes. Inherent in its design, and when two receivers were used in a differential master/slave configuration, the master station sent DGPS range and range rate data for all satellites tracked by the master station. In addition to this information, the master station transmitted the ephemeris data for all satellites tracked by the master station using a commutated message structure. A few parameters of each ephemeris were sent with each DGPS correction message, allowing eventual broadcast of all ephemeris data for all visible satellites to the slave receiver. The master-station ephemeris information was used by the DGPS slave receiver to:

- Enable the best DGPS position performance by ensuring both master and slave units were using the same ephemeris set for each satellite (this was prior to the development of the RTCM-104 DGPS messaging standard discussed in Chapter 8).
- Ensure that the slave unit acquired the ephemeris data for all satellites visible by the master, maximizing the availability of DGPS solutions.

The latter was especially useful when the slave unit was partially blocked from acquiring the data directly from the satellite because of blocked or reduced signal power to one or more satellites, which occurs near tall mountains, in canyons, under trees, or near buildings. Many times in these environments, the signal is strong enough to detect code phases and track but not strong enough to reliably demodulate the ephemeris data. Transmitting the ephemeris data from the master to the slave unit alleviated this problem.

In 1990, a system was patented [62] that transmitted almanac data via an over-the-air message from a master station to many slave units called *pseudorangers*. The pseudorangers would accept the almanac data, use it to acquire and track GPS satellites, then transmit back to the master station the measured pseudoranges and a time stamp. The master station, remote from the movers, would then compute position of each mover from the pseudoranger unit–measured pseudoranges. This idea is a precursor of the current MS-assisted method of assisted GPS (A-GPS) for cellular telephones (the preferred method in the United States in CDMA phones) in which the handset outputs pseudoranges instead of position, and the network then uses the measured pseudoranges to compute the location of the cell phone.

Approximate position, ephemeris, almanac, and approximate time-assist information was present in a White Sands Missile Range system [63]. The White Sands system used GPS to measure the performance of missiles. When a missile is fired, it has little time to acquire and track GPS satellites and cannot tolerate the 30-second ephemeris acquisition period. Thus, a wireless message was sent from a master station to the just-launched missile consisting of approximate position, approximate time, almanac data, and ephemeris data, all of which was used by the missile to acquire GPS signals rapidly and produce a string of position reports while in flight.

9.4.2 Requirements of the FCC Mandate

The original FCC mandate allowed for two types of solutions: network-based solutions to work with all legacy phones (non-GPS), and handset-based solutions (such as assisted GPS and E-OTD) in which the user was required to have a new handset that is augmented with the location technology. Of course, the location determination for legacy phones must be performed within the cellular infrastructure based on TOA measurements derived using the cellular signals. Here, the FCC set accuracy requirements to be less stringent than for future, handset-based solutions: 67% of emergency calls needed to be located to within 100-m accuracy, while 95% of all emergency calls required a 300-m accuracy. For handset-based solutions, the corresponding accuracies were 50m and 150m, respectively. Although these numbers appear relatively easy for a GPS receiver to meet, especially with SA deactivated, the location determination must ideally be performed wherever a cellular phone emergency call can be made, which includes indoor locations, where the GPS system was not designed to operate.

Note that there is a degree of ambiguity in the accuracy requirement (e.g., if 95% of cellular emergency calls were made outside, and an accurate GPS solution is provided there that satisfies the accuracy constraints, but indoor location attempts are never successful, is the requirement met?). The FCC published guidelines [64] for validation of accuracy and availability, but it still leaves to interpretation how to weight or proportion outside and in-building cases for test. A possible interpretation of the accuracy requirement across the multiple environments for which the cell phone can make E-911 calls is the following: each environment is weighted by the relative frequency of E-911 calls made from that environment in deriving a composite accuracy number. Hence, it is important to understand GPS signal characteristics in the environments in which cellular phones can be expected to operate.

9.4.2.1 Characterization of Environments

A characterization of L-band signal environments was previously reported in [65–70], which summarize data collection campaigns at 1,600 MHz in support of satellite telephone communications link margin studies. The proximity of the test frequency to the GPS frequency makes this research applicable. More recent GPS in-building cumulative distribution function (CDF) fade data has been presented in [71, 72]. In all cases, extensive radio propagation data was collected at L-band and analyzed to characterize the shadowing, scattering, and blocking effects of trees, cars, and buildings. Hundreds of hours of test data were collected and analyzed. Table 9.5 lists the environments characterized in the previously mentioned references and summarizes the 50% median fade of the signal due to the environment. The data in the table were extracted from charts showing fade depth versus probability charts presented in the multiple references listed.

"Heavy Urban" with the portable unit and the three in-building environments was chosen for the basis of further calculations as the median attenuation values were large and expected to produce reduced GPS satellite signal availability. Mobile and in-vehicle data in an open environment were also chosen to show the trivial case where the received signal strength is so high that fix percentage will surely be 100% and the important case of a unit employed inside of a car.

Table 9.5   Environments Characterized for L-Band Signal Transmission

Environment	Description	Median Signal Attenuations in Decibels for Mobile/ Portable/In-Vehicle[1]
Open	Almost no trees or buildings	2.5/0.0/12.0
Rural light	Moderate to large number of trees, very few buildings	3.0/3.5/12.0
Rural moderate	Moderate to large number of trees, very few buildings	8.0/7.0/16.0
Rural heavy	Light to moderate forested area	16.0/10.0/18.0
Suburban light	Scattered trees and building structures (e.g., homes far from mobile receiver or new residential areas with little vegetation)	2.0/1.5/14.0
Suburban moderate	Suburban area with one- and two-story homes with moderate amount of trees	3.5/6.5/13.5
Suburban heavy	Older suburban areas with large numbers of trees and homes close to roads (e.g., older subdivisions in a city like Chicago)	7.0/2.5/11.0
Urban light	Small, sparse urban areas (e.g., urban areas of smaller cities)	2.0/2.0/16.0
Urban moderate	Urban areas from moderate-sized cities (e.g., Phoenix)	4.0/4.0/15.5
Urban heavy	Steel canyons (e.g., downtown Chicago)	5.0/15.0/16.0
In-building residential	Buildings made of wood or stucco (e.g., Phoenix and California residences)	12.5[2]
In-building commercial	One- to three-story motels, airports, and commercial buildings	24.0[2]
In-building high-rise	High-rise buildings	30.0[2]

1. The numbers in the column correspond to decibels of attenuation for the indicated conditions. The mobile case corresponds to the reception conditions in an automobile with an antenna installed on its roof, while, for the in-vehicle case, the antenna is used inside the car. The portable case corresponds to an antenna from a transportable satellite receiver with a large quad helix antenna, not typical of GPS antennas embedded into cell phones.
2. These numbers correspond to the "Portable" case.

It should be noted that due to the requirement for reasonable transmitter efficiency "Portable" antennas used for the data collection experiments are fairly large and mounted to minimize head blockage. The result is some attenuation numbers that are similar to "Mobile" attenuations. Due to the size of these antennas, they are not considered acceptable for the GPS needs of a cellular handset. Appropriately sized GPS antennas for handsets have significantly less gain than any antennas used in the collection of the data discussed from [71, 72] or, for that matter, than conventional GPS antennas for mobile or automotive applications.

As cellular telephones continue to shrink, the problem of integrating adequate-performing GPS antennas becomes even more difficult. To perform well, the antenna needs to present uniform gain in the up direction covering the full hemisphere where GPS signals emanate. Simple patch antennas are used in automotive applications and can be hidden under the dash or under the rear deck with little effort and provide the ideal RHCP to match the satellite transmitted signal. However, placement of a dedicated GPS antenna in a cell phone forces compromises in performance with regard to antenna efficiency and gain pattern, especially when the user can hold it in many different orientations (handheld next to head, in the dialing position, and using different hand grips). Antenna efficiencies in the 30% to 40% range are typical, with attenuation profiles in the 5- to 15-dB range, depending on orientation and use pattern. Figure 9.36 shows a photograph (courtesy of Motorola) of an embedded inverted-L GPS antenna in a cellular handset—in this case, a Motorola A835, in which the antenna is mounted on the upper end of the unit. The element is made to snake around the phone's digital camera aperture. Note the SMA connector on the side of the unit is strictly for test purposes on this engineering unit and is not present in the final product. The top-end antenna placement is ideal for the dialing position or while using embedded navigation features as the user must look at the screen, forcing a sky view to the antenna. Antennas have been placed on the back side and in the upper and lower portions of flip-style phones, each presenting unique and challenging integration issues.

Depending on how the user holds the product in operation, it's possible for the user's hand to completely cover the antenna, which tends to attenuate the signal further and detune the antenna to even worse efficiency. The product styling team is usually forced to make compromises as well simply to make room for the antenna, and in a world where product styling is very important, these types of compromises are difficult. As such, some cell phone types reuse the cellular communications whip or stub antenna as a GPS antenna, coupling into the device with tuning elements but compromising the pattern even more, as the circular polarization can be lost.

9.4.2.2 Characterizing Signal Attenuations

This section presents the results of a measurement campaign that was conducted to statistically characterize L-band and GPS signal attenuation in various environments. Preprocessing of the raw, measured signal amplitude data was corrected to remove the effect of the transmit antenna pattern as its angle to the receiver changed.

Figure 9.36   GPS antenna embedded into cell phone. (Courtesy of Motorola.)

Measurements in high-rise buildings included a reference receiver on the roof. The resulting fade data was a differential measurement from the two receivers. The preprocessed data output that is of interest here is fade magnitude versus time. Traces were typically 4 to 8 minutes long and can be interpreted as signal attenuation versus time relative to an unattenuated outdoor received signal. Plots of two such traces are shown in Figure 9.37. Note the relatively high frequency variation in the traces, corresponding to vehicle motion through its signal environment.

Two CDFs corresponding to the traces in Figure 9.37 are shown in Figure 9.38. The mobile curve on the left has an extremely steep slope with very few fades exceeding 8 dB. The in-vehicle curve on the right has a gentle slope characteristic of a greater standard deviation of fade value.

An alternate way to look at the signal attenuation profile is to directly use GPS signals detected by a high-sensitivity receiver. In most cases, 8–12 satellite signals are available for measurement at any one time. In order to profile the signal attenuation characteristics in a particular environment, 12 to 24 hours of data needs to be mapped out to capture the effects of the GPS satellite constellation repeat time. The GPS receiver-reported SNR for each satellite (typically in units of dB-Hz) is collected and then translated to an equivalent signal power on the antenna in units of dBm by making an estimate of the receiver noise figure and equivalent bandwidth. If desired, one can map the attenuation profile of the environment as a function of satellite azimuth and elevation angle to provide even more detail on the environment and identify directions of low and high attenuation. Signal power CDF curves are produced and used to predict the availability of location fix within the environment by determining the probability of at least four satellites offering signal power above the receiver's raw detection threshold.

Figure 9.39 shows the signal power CDF curves for the eight strongest satellites detected from a rooftop antenna over a 12-hour period. As can be seen, the 95%

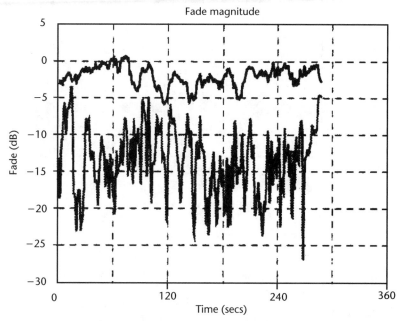

Figure 9.37   Typical fade magnitude versus time for mobile (top line) and in-vehicle (bottom line).

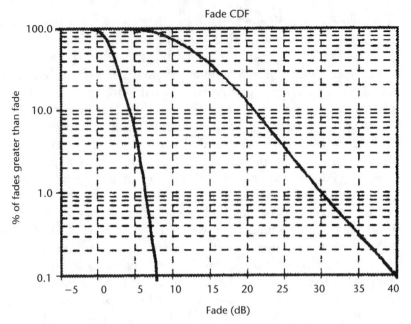

Figure 9.38   Fade CDFs for mobile (left line) and in-vehicle (right line).

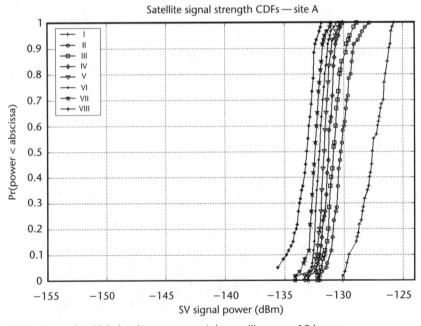

Figure 9.39   Open-sky CDFs for the strongest eight satellites over 12 hours.

probability for the fourth satellite is stronger than about –132 dBm in this open-sky condition. As expected, the signal power spread from the strongest to weakest is only a few decibels.

By contrast, Figure 9.40 shows the same corresponding CDF curves for the strongest eight satellites observed in-building. The environment is the second floor

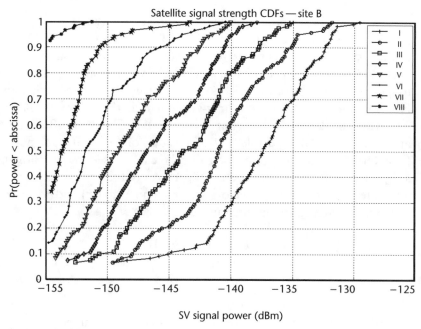

Figure 9.40 In-building (moderate indoor) CDFs for the strongest eight satellites over 12 hours.

of a three-story apartment building, in the center of the main living room away from windows, with wood and brick construction. In this environment, the 95% probability for the fourth strongest satellite is at >= −152 dBm. Other notable items include that the strongest signal is approximately 10 dB below that from the roof antenna (50% point), and the spread from the strongest to the weakest is much larger, on the order of 20 dB or more in this particular environment. The large spread implies that the algorithm to detect indoor signals should be adaptive as the integration dwell time to detect the stronger signals can be shorter than the dwell time to detect the weaker signals. As will be shown later, common-mode error parameters associated with each satellite signal (code phase error due to time error and Doppler error due to oscillator error) can be exploited to reduce the total search space after one or more satellites are detected; thus, the already detected stronger signals can be used to further reduce the search space in order to detect the weaker signals.

For every environment tested in this way, a unique set of CDF curves will be produced. Thus, it is very difficult to project success or failure in a particular environment based on Table 9.5 or Figures 9.37 through 9.40 without first collecting data and generating CDF curves within the environment in question. The data in the table and figures should only be used as an example of the specific location tested and should not be used to project other environments, although the trends shown are useful. Of course, it's impossible to collect data from every location that might host an emergency cellular telephone call, and there is insufficient space to include the complete set of measured CDF curves here. Thus, some form of statistical averaging or site weighting is generally used to extend or predict the coverage from one environment to another, the weight generally determined by estimates of emergency calling patterns.

Table 9.6 presents a very coarse estimate for typical relative frequencies of E-911 calls based in part on speculation. Unfortunately, a more detailed mapping of call probabilities to reception environment is not available, as such data is not normally logged for emergency calls. As evident from the table, and fortunately for GPS usage, calls generally occur less frequently as signal reception becomes more difficult. For example, in the heavy indoor environment, in the basement of a high-rise building, where signal attenuations at L-band can easily reach 40 dB (note its median attenuation of 30 dB in Table 9.5), acquisition of the requisite signals required for a fix is very difficult. The results of Table 9.6 can be used in the following way to test adherence to the E-911 requirement: perform N fix attempts in each environment, and note the number whose errors are less than 50m (m) and 150m (n). Composite probabilities are then computed using:

$$P_c^{(1)} = \left(\sum p_i m_i\right)/N \tag{9.38}$$

$$P_c^{(2)} = \left(\sum p_i n_i\right)/N \tag{9.39}$$

where the summations are indexed over the test environments, with p_i representing the frequency of occurrence in the environment, and m_i and n_i the number of successes in each environment. The test results would be considered a success for the candidate GPS receiver if the composite probabilities were greater than the specified values (i.e., 0.67 for $P_c^{(1)}$, and 0.95 for $P_c^{(2)}$).

However, the approach described earlier, resulting in the use of (9.38) and (9.39), is only one way of interpreting the FCC mandate and demonstrating success or failure. Alternate approaches for testing adherence have been proposed (e.g., the so-called dart board test, where an area of cell phone coverage is given and test sites are selected randomly within that area by assuming a uniform distribution of emergency calls within that area).

TTFFs in excess of reasonable response times for an emergency call (e.g., TTFFs of several minutes time) are obviously unacceptable. The FCC guidelines [64] discuss a 30-second TTFF that is location method neutral, but leaves just enough room for autonomous GPS given its 30-second ephemeris data demodulation time. A consortium of CDMA cell phone vendors and suppliers, together with representatives from cell phone carriers, have defined a set of minimum performance tests that must be met [73]. These tests define specific signal simulation scenarios and requirements for both position accuracy and TTFF. For example, the sensitivity test of the IS-916 specification requires that the GPS function embedded in a CDMA telephone acquire

Table 9.6 E-911 Call Distribution by Environment

Environment	Call Probability
Outdoors or in-vehicle	0.70
Light indoor or in-vehicle	0.15
Moderate indoor	0.10
Heavy indoor	0.05

four GPS satellite signals at −147 dBm within 16 seconds with success rate of 95% or better. Corresponding minimum performance specifications for other cellular technologies (CDMA, TDMA, GSM, AMPS, or WCDMA) have not yet been established but are being pursued. The collection of various types of cell phone technologies are sometimes referred to as "MA" because of the last two letters of CDMA and TDMA; thus, each handset type can be referred to as being of an *MA type*. The standards body for each cellular MA technology is addressing the custom requirements and unique capabilities of each type to create its own minimum performance test. For CDMA handsets, its precise time knowledge (to approximately 100 ns) provides an advantage to minimizing the total number of code phase/Doppler search cells because the projection of the 100-ns time error into the search space is less than one-half of one GPS chip. Adherence to an MA's minimum performance test does not, in any way, guarantee that the particular handset meets the FCC mandate.

The FCC mandate is not the only driver for high-sensitivity GPS: Use of a cell phone within a car as a navigation aid to drivers is an emerging application for GPS embedded in cellular phones, as referenced in Section 9.3. A nonoptimal GPS antenna design is expected, with losses ranging from 5 to 15 dB relative to conventional, stand-alone GPS antennas; in addition, operation within the car is expected to contribute an additional 3- to 5-dB attenuation. Thus, embedded handset applications alone requires that acquisition and tracking thresholds be extended roughly 10 dB relative to those for GPS operating in more conventional open-sky environments.

In Section 5.13, the benefits of extended coherent and noncoherent integration in reducing signal acquisition thresholds have been addressed. In order to maximize GPS coverage in an effort to satisfy the FCC mandate, maximizing the use of extended integration is highly desirable. Ideally, use of the assistance information will enable coverage of the search space with the number of correlators in the receiver to permit parallel searching across satellites and stationarity with respect to the correlator bin location during the extended integration interval. If sufficient correlators are not available to cover the total uncertainty space in parallel, some form of sequential processing is required.

9.4.3   Total Uncertainty Search Space

For a given scenario, one can compute the total Doppler-code phase uncertainty space required to be searched and, consequently, the number of correlators required to cover the entire search space in parallel. The initial parameters of position, time, and frequency uncertainty, along with the particular orientation of the satellite constellation at the time, can be used to compute the total uncertainty search space. Figure 9.41 depicts the two-dimensional search space for each satellite, the x-axis representing the total Doppler uncertainty, and the y-axis showing the total code phase uncertainty. For each satellite, the number of Doppler search bins (N_{dopp}) and code phase search bins (N_{cp}) is computed.

The number of required correlators N_c to cover the search space in parallel is given by:

$$N_c = \sum_{i=1}^{M} N_{dopp_i} \times N_{cp_i} \qquad (9.40)$$

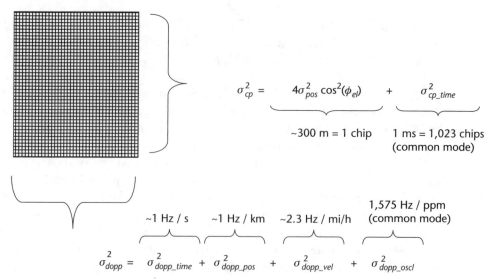

Figure 9.41 Two-dimensional Doppler/code phase search space.

For each satellite, the number of Doppler search bins N_{dopp} is dependent on the total Doppler uncertainty (in hertz) for each satellite, and the coherent integration (PDI) period in seconds, which is the same as the PDI period T discussed in Section 5.2.1.

$$N_{dopp_i} = \frac{\sigma_{dopp_i}}{\left(\dfrac{k}{PDI}\right)} \tag{9.41}$$

The parameter k is based on the desired overlap of the Doppler search bins and can generally range between 0.5 and 1. The computation of total Doppler uncertainty $\sigma^2_{dopp_i}$ for each satellite is then dependent on the contributions of Doppler uncertainty due to position uncertainty, time uncertainty, reference oscillator uncertainty, and user motion (velocity) uncertainty. Thus, one can write a simple equation for the total Doppler uncertainty per satellite as:

$$\sigma^2_{dopp_i} = \sigma^2_{dopp_i\_time_i} + \sigma^2_{dopp\_pos_i} + \sigma^2_{dopp\_vel_i} + \sigma^2_{dopp\_oscl} \tag{9.42}$$

The first term, the sensitivity of Doppler uncertainty to time uncertainty, can be computed for each satellite [74], but as a general rule, it is no larger than 1 Hz per second of time uncertainty. Likewise, the second term, the sensitivity of Doppler to initial position error, is about 1 Hz/km worst case. In [74], equations are presented for the precise computation of $\sigma^2_{dopp\_pos_i}$ for each individual satellite, which is generally much less than 1 Hz/km. The effects of user platform motion are accounted for by the third term, which represents the Doppler error induced on the GPS signal due to user motion. The term $\sigma^2_{dopp\_vel_i}$ is a maximum for low elevation angle satellites if the user is heading directly at or away from the satellite, and it is very small for high elevation angle satellites. Worst case, $\sigma^2_{dopp\_vel_i}$ contributes no more than 2.3 Hz/mph of user motion and can be generally multiplied by the cosine of the elevation angle to limit its effect.

$$\sigma^2_{dopp\_vel_i} \sim 2.3 \times \cos(el) \, \text{Hz/mph} \tag{9.43}$$

The first three terms of (9.42) are dependent on the satellite constellation, the user position, and the user motion. The last term, $\sigma^2_{dopp\_oscl}$, is dependent on the reference oscillator and thus is common mode with respect to all satellites. $\sigma^2_{dopp\_oscl}$ is typically 1,575 Hz/ppm of reference oscillator frequency uncertainty and is by far the most dominant element of (9.42).

To compute the total code phase dimension uncertainty (see Figure 9.41), the two dominant terms are proportional to the position uncertainty and time uncertainty. Thus,

$$\sigma^2_{cp} = 4\sigma^2_{pos} \cos^2(\phi_{el}) + \sigma^2_{cp\_time} \tag{9.44}$$

where the term σ_{cp_time} is in units of half-chips by multiplying the time uncertainty by the conversion 2,046 half-chips per millisecond, and the first term of (9.44) is computed as shown in Figure 9.42. Figure 9.42 shows the simple relationship of the effect of position uncertainty and satellite elevation angle to transform to the dimension of code phase uncertainty in units of half-chips in the direction of the satellite LOS vector (conversion factor: 1 half-chip $\cong$ 150m).

The other element of code phase uncertainty is common mode across all satellites and directly proportional to time uncertainty. A 1-ms error in time transforms into a 2,046 half-chip error in code phase. For the typical assisted case in which the position uncertainty is relatively small (e.g., 6 km), the largest term of (9.42) is that contributed by the time error.

For the time dimension, we first recognize that the GPS signals are all synchronized in time, which means that, except for the relative drift between the satellite clocks, the first PRN bit and the first navigation data message bit (subframe 1) are transmitted from each satellite at precisely midnight Saturday in the GPS time coordinate system. Each PRN bit and each navigation data message bit is then predictable in time in the following manner:

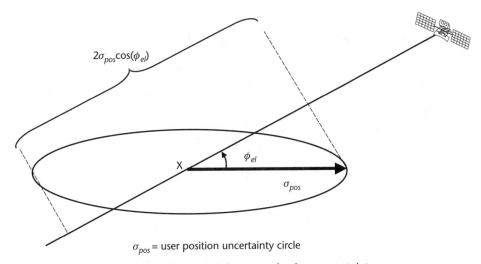

Figure 9.42 Relationship of position uncertainty to code phase uncertainty.

$$Subframe\_Number = 1 + MOD(GPS\_Time/6, 5)$$
$$Word\_Number = 1 + MOD(GPS\_Time/(30 \times 0.020), 10)$$
$$Bit\_Number = 1 + MOD(GPS\_Time, 0.020) \qquad (9.45)$$
$$Integer\_PN\_Rolls = MOD(GPS\_Time/0.001)$$
$$Code\_Phase = MOD(2,046 \times GPS\_Time \times 1,000, 2,046)$$

The equations shown in (9.45) enable the user to precisely compute the *Code_Phase*, *Bit_Phase*, *Bit_Number*, *Word_Number*, and *Subframe_Number* of the signal leaving the satellite at precisely any time into the week based on a *GPS_Time*. Of course, the user will observe this code phase on the ground later in time after it propagates from the satellite to the user by the propagation time, *Dtprop*. *Dtprop* is easily computed, as shown in (9.47), based on the geometric range between satellite and user divided by the speed of light. In addition, the signal will be slipped forward or backward in time an amount proportional to the satellite clock correction *Tcorr* to the tune of a few milliseconds. Thus, the user will always be able to predict the code phase to all satellites observed on the ground at any instantaneous *GPS_Time* by the pseudocode:

$$Code\_Phase\_observed = MOD(2,046 \times (GPS\_Time + Tcorr - Dtprop) \times 1,000, 2,046)$$

where:

$$Tcorr = a_{f0} + a_{f1} \times (GPS\_Time - t_{oc}) + a_{f2} \times (GPS\_Time - t_{oc})^2 \qquad (9.46)$$

$$Dtprop = |SV\_POS - USER\_POS|/SOL \qquad (9.47)$$

a_{f0}, a_{f1}, a_{f2} are the zeroth through second-order satellite clock correction terms from navigation data message subframe 1, and t_{oc} is the reference GPS time for the satellite clock correction terms.

Likewise, all equations of (9.45) can be modified to include the user-observed parameters as follows:

$$Subframe\_Number\_observed = 1 + MOD\left(\left(\begin{matrix}GPS\_Time + \\ Tcorr - Dtprop\end{matrix}\right)/6, 5\right)$$

$$Word\_Number\_observed = 1 + MOD\left(\left(\begin{matrix}GPS\_Time + \\ Tcorr - Dtprop\end{matrix}\right)/(30 \times 0.020), 10\right)$$

$$Bit\_Number\_observed = 1 + MOD\left(\left(\begin{matrix}GPS\_Time + \\ Tcorr - Dtprop\end{matrix}\right), 0.020\right) \qquad (9.48)$$

$$Integer\_PN\_Rolls\_observed = MOD\left(\left(\begin{matrix}GPS\_Time + \\ Tcorr - Dtprop\end{matrix}\right)/0.001\right)$$

$$Code\_Phase\_observed = MOD\left(2046 \times \left(\begin{matrix}GPS\_Time + \\ Tcorr - Dtprop\end{matrix}\right) \times 1,000, 2,046\right)$$

in which the "_observed" described by (9.48) represents what a ground-based user located at USER_POSITION on the Earth would observe at the instant of time "GPS_Time." Equations (9.48) ignore the small effects of Earth rotation rate as well as tropospheric and ionospheric delay on the signal. But from a macro level, (9.48) are useful in determining the most likely initial receiver state for the signal detection function to initialize the starting code phase and bit phase. The computed code phase uncertainty from (9.44) then defines the range of code phase to search over, specifically

$$Code\_Phase\_Search\_range = Code\_Phase\_Observed +/- \sigma_{pos} \cos(\phi_{el})$$

Equation (9.40) can be used to determine the search time for a particular scenario based on signal power, number of satellites, and the required PDI and noncoherent integration dwell time required to positively detect the signal. Section 5.13 previously showed that as signals get weak, the integration dwell time required to positively detect the signal increases substantially. For example, if the signal is −130 dBm (typical clear view of the sky conditions), the signal can be positively detected with a 1-ms PDI and a 2-ms noncoherent integration dwell time. As the signal gets weaker, the required PDI and noncoherent integration time increases substantially (e.g., if the signal is −150 dBm, then a PDI of 10–12 ms and a noncoherent integration time of 1 or more seconds is required). Tables 9.7 through 9.9 illustrate this effect.

Equation (9.33) describes N_c as the number of total Doppler/code phase search bins for all satellites for a particular scenario. Given that the dwell time per bin is indicated by T_{dwell}, and the number of available correlators for the search is given by N_{corr}, then the maximum total search time is approximately indicated by

Table 9.7   Maximum Search Times

Signal dBm	PDI (seconds)	T_{dwell} per Bin (seconds)	N_{cp} per SV (half-chips)	N_{dopp} per SV	N_c for 8 SVs	T_{search} 12 (seconds)	T_{search} 32K (seconds)
−130	0.001	0.002	2,046	2	32,736	5.4	0.002
−145	0.006	0.050	2,046	12	196,416	818	0.3
−150	0.012	1.0	2,046	25	409,200	9.4 hours	13
−155	0.020	5.0	2,046	42	687,456	80 hours	107

Time uncertainty = 1 ms; frequency uncertainty = 0.5 ppm; 8 satellites; position uncertainty = 30 km; ignoring code-phase and Doppler search range reductions after finding a first satellite.

Table 9.8   Maximum Search Times

Signal dBm	PDI (seconds)	T_{dwell} per Bin (seconds)	N_{cp} First SV (half-chips)	N_{dopp} First SV	N_c for 8 SVs	T_{search} 12 (seconds)	T_{search} 32K (seconds)
−130	0.001	0.002	2,046	2	6,240	1	0.002
−145	0.006	0.050	2,046	12	26,700	111	0.05
−150	0.012	1.0	2,046	25	53,300	1.23 hours	1.7
−155	0.020	5.0	2,046	42	90,230	10.4 hours	14

Time uncertainty = 1 ms; frequency uncertainty = 0.5 ppm; 8 satellites; position uncertainty = 30 km; taking advantage of reduced code-phase and Doppler search range after finding a first satellite; number of code phase delays and Doppler bins is reduced after finding first satellite by and reflected in total N_c.

Table 9.9   Maximum Search Times

Signal dBm	PDI (seconds)	T_{dwell} per bin (seconds)	N_{cp} per SV (half-chips)	N_{dopp} per SV	N_c for 8 SVs	T_{search} 12 (seconds)	T_{search} 32K (seconds)
−130	0.001	0.002	~300	1	1,636	0.27	0.002
−145	0.006	0.050	~300	1	1,636	6.8	0.05
−150	0.012	1.0	~300	2	1,841	153	1
−155	0.020	5.0	~300	4	3,682	1,535	5

Time uncertainty = 100 μs; frequency uncertainty = 0.05 ppm; 8 satellites; position uncertainty = 30 km; taking advantage of reduced code-phase and Doppler search range after finding a first satellite; number of code phase delays and Doppler bins is reduced after finding first satellite and reflected in total N_c.

$$T_{search} = T_{dwell} \times (N_c / N_{corr}) \qquad (9.49)$$

For a particular scenario in which the time uncertainty is 1 ms or more, full code phase search of 2,046 half-chips is required to find the first satellite. Given a condition of a 0.5-ppm oscillator, the number of Doppler bins is dominated by the oscillator uncertainty; thus, column N_{dopp} in Table 9.7 indicates the number of Doppler bins per satellite and N_{cp} the number of code phase search bins. The initial conditions of time, position, and frequency uncertainty are shown. Column N_c indicates the number of Doppler-codephase search bins for an eight-satellite case in which the receiver does not take advantage of the code phase learned from a first detected satellite to reduce the code phase search range on the remaining. Finally, two conditions are highlighted—the total search time T_{search} using (9.49) for two cases: that of a typical automotive-grade receiver containing 12 searchers, and a modern high-performance flash correlator receiver that can search up to 32,000 bins simultaneously.

As described earlier, when a first satellite is detected, it's possible to substantially reduce the code phase and Doppler search range for the remaining $N_{sv} - 1$ satellites. Table 9.8 illustrates the gain achieved as reflected in reduced N_c and T_{search} cases by using the full code phase and Doppler search space to find the first satellite and reducing the remaining seven satellite uncertainties to approximately 300 half-chips in code phase and 100 Hz in Doppler.

Finally, Table 9.9 illustrates further reductions in the search space and search time by changing the reference oscillator to 0.05 ppm (for example, taking advantage of handset AFC tuning) and reducing the time uncertainty to 100 μs (such as taking advantage of precise time transfer).

9.4.4 GPS Receiver Integration in Cellular Phones—Assistance Data from Handsets

As shown in (9.42), much of the total code-Doppler uncertainty space for N satellites is represented by common-mode error terms of time error and oscillator frequency error. Typical low-cost reference oscillators are in the 0.5- to 1-ppm stability range, and at this level, the oscillator frequency uncertainty is by far the largest element of the total Doppler uncertainty search space. Likewise, a 1-ms or more time uncertainty is common mode across all satellites and forces full code phase (2,046 half-chips) scan for each satellite, as time error is the largest of the possible contributors to code-phase uncertainty. There are methods to remedy this common-mode frequency and time problem that are unique in a cellular handset.

Time.   Some types of handsets, such as CDMA, have precise knowledge of GPS time internally as long as the handset is monitoring at least one paging channel. CDMA cell towers are synchronized in time using GPS receivers in each cell tower. The handset uses the precise time information when handing over from one cell tower to another so that it can align the cell signal spreading code phase and maintain seamless communication as the user moves from one cell to the next. By transferring the precise time information into the GPS function, it becomes possible to substantially reduce the contribution of time error as it reflects into the code phase uncertainty dimension, leaving (mostly) the contributions to position uncertainty as shown in Figure 9.41.

Certain types of handsets, such as GSM, do not have precise time information available internally. As such, methods have been devised by which precise time can be delivered to a GSM handset via the network to handset messaging protocol so that it too can be time synchronized as in CDMA.

The GSM over-the-air protocol is time-division multiplex—each handset is assigned a timeslot in which it receives and transmits packets of data between itself and the network. To accomplish precise time transfer in the asynchronous GSM network, an additional hardware element is installed in the network called a *location measurement unit* (LMU). The LMU contains a GPS receiver for time synchronization. It also contains a GSM phone receiver that it uses to measure the absolute timing of certain data packets that it receives from each cell tower it can "hear"—in effect, time tagging the bits received with GPS time. The LMU measures the time shift or time offset of each cell tower signal that it can hear and makes this time-shift information available to the cell network for delivery to those handsets desiring precise time correction. The handset accepts parameters via a network-to-handset message that allows it to instantiate a particular portion of the network-to-handset message with a precise time tag. As such, when the handset receives the particular portion of the network-to-handset message, it can associate the event of receiving the bits with the precise time tag (derived from the LMU), thus providing a method of time transfer that is much better than 1 ms, or 1 GPS PRN-code time period.

Installing LMUs into a GSM network is a rather expensive proposition, so not all GSM networks will have LMUs. Network operators prefer a lower cost alternative—to deliver an approximate time estimate to the handset via a standard network-to-handset message. Network latencies in delivering the message to the handset establish the best possible accuracy of no more than ±2 seconds; thus, approximate time is useful in computing satellite Doppler when satellite ephemeris and approximate position is available, but it is generally useless in computing precise code phase estimates for each satellite so as to avoid searching the entire code phase space.

All is not lost, however, because as described earlier, most receivers take advantage of the common-mode nature of time uncertainty once one satellite is detected. After detecting a first satellite generally using a full-code phase scan, the code phase uncertainty region for the remaining satellites is reduced substantially because the measured code phase from the detected satellite can be differenced with the predicted code phase (computed using the 2-second error approximate time) to provide a first estimate of the common-mode time error. This correction represents most of the common-error time contribution to code phase in Figure 9.41; thus, the remaining satellites can be searched for using constrained or limited code phase search space, substantially reducing the size of the total Doppler/code phase uncertainty search space.

Frequency.   Figure 9.41 shows that the frequency uncertainty dimension of the satellite search process is dominated by the reference oscillator uncertainty. The other contributions are small, with position uncertainties of tens of kilometers assumed. If one assumes a 0.5- to 1.0-ppm reference oscillator is used for GPS, it is by far the largest contributor to Doppler uncertainty and is common mode across all satellites.

A cellular handset also contains a reference oscillator for its communication function, and sharing or reusing the oscillator for GPS offers a compelling cost advantage. Sharing the oscillator also enables substantial reduction in the reference oscillator frequency uncertainty because all modern cellular telephones employ a method of an AFC control loop to correct the oscillator frequency. This is based on a frequency error relative to the cellular BS-to-handset signal, as shown in Figure 9.43. The frequency of the cellular BS-to-handset signal is precisely controlled by the network to better than 0.05 ppm within each network tower. As such, the handset AFC control loop adjusts the frequency of the reference oscillator (via VCO in Figure 9.43) until the frequency difference is zero. Thus, the AFC function calibrates the reference VCO oscillator to the same accuracy as the network-to-handset signal, or 0.05 ppm. Reusing this high-accuracy clock for GPS purposes enables significant reduction in the number of Doppler uncertainty search bins, contributing to lower overall TTFF and minimizing the number of required correlators needed to meet a minimum performance criteria.

Some handsets physically adjust the frequency of the reference oscillator as shown in Figure 9.43. Other handsets do not do so; instead, they let the oscillator free-run and then adjust the control registers on a fractional-N synthesizer to pro-

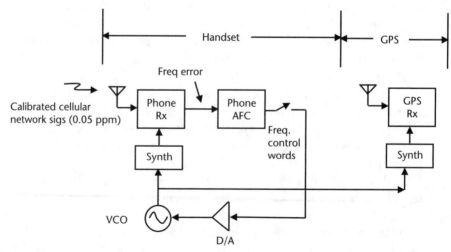

Figure 9.43   Typical handset AFC tuning of reference oscillator.

duce an adjusted frequency inside the phone receiver. The control registers of the fractional-N synthesizer are translatable into a known frequency of operation of the handset reference oscillator. This frequency is known to better than 0.05 ppm, achieving the same goal as long as the synthesizer tuning parameters are made available to the GPS function. The latter method offers significant advantages over the former, as the discrete jumps in frequency attributed to manually adjusting the reference oscillator frequency can cause data demodulation and tracking problems to the GPS function. The frequency jumps cause instantaneous phase rotation of the received GPS biphase modulated signal. If large enough, the instantaneous phase rotation due to the frequency jump cannot be discriminated from the $\pm 180°$ phase rotations due to signal PRN modulation or navigation data bit modulation, thus confusing the data demodulation process and causing possible loss of lock.

As with time, using handset-based frequency aiding information is not absolutely necessary in order to meet the acquisition time goals of cellular A-GPS. In all cases, the battle can be won by having sufficient correlators available to search out the uncertainty space in sufficient time. However, there is a cost and power consumption penalty associated with a maximum correlator solution that is painful to overcome, at least in the near term until IC technology evolves further. As with time, one can take advantage of the common-mode nature of the reference frequency uncertainty for applications by choosing to install a separate GPS reference oscillator. In this case, most of the Doppler uncertainty is due to reference oscillator uncertainty and can be solved for as soon as one satellite is detected. Thus, the total uncertainty search space collapses significantly once a first satellite is detected and a precise Doppler measurement to it is made.

9.4.5   Types of Network Assistance

The specifics of assistance information that are available from a cellular network are governed by applicable standards that can vary with cellular telephone technology type (e.g., AMPS, CDMA, TDMA, GSM, or WCDMA). Generally, the individual standards messaging protocols are similar across the MAs, with the possible exception of the CDMA standard in which additional assist data types and location methods are included. In order to simplify the discussion, we will focus on the GSM cellular standard, since it is the most widely deployed standard.

The possible forms for acquisition assistance include the following:

- A list of visible satellites;
- Predicted GPS satellite Dopplers and Doppler rates;
- Azimuth and elevation angles for the visible satellites;
- Local oscillator offset information (through the handset AFC function);
- Approximate mobile location;
- GPS satellite ephemeris information;
- GPS almanac;
- Satellite clock correction terms;
- Approximate GPS time;
- Precise GPS time;

- Predicted codephases;
- Predicted codephase search window;
- Navigation data bit timing information (bit number, fractional bit);
- Navigation data bits (sensitivity assistance).

This list is redundant, as a mobile receiver will only use a subset of this information in attempting to acquire the requisite number of satellites for a fix (e.g., predicted Doppler and Doppler rate information is not needed if an ephemeris, coarse location, and coarse GPS time are provided). For example, the MS-assisted handset could use visible satellite list, predicted Doppler (and sometimes rate), and predicted code phase. The MS-based handset could use approximate position, ephemeris, and approximate time. Both can transform these parameters into corresponding Doppler and Doppler uncertainty and code phase and code phase uncertainty, as discussed earlier. The GPS receiver then conducts its satellite search algorithm over the search region of interest in a parallel manner if sufficient correlators are available (or sequentially if not).

The visible satellite list is generated within the cellular network by simply reporting the visible satellites at a GPS reference receiver within or in the vicinity of the cellular network. The reference receiver should be positioned to ensure an unobstructed view of the sky. Because of the relative proximity of the network and the mobile with which it is communicating (i.e., a maximum separation of 20–30 km is expected), the visible satellite list is virtually the same for the reference and mobile receiver, except possibly for a satellite very close to the horizon (i.e., less than the separation distance divided by the radius of the Earth, or roughly a 0.2° elevation for a 20-km separation) and with an azimuth opposite to the LOS between the reference receiver and the mobile. Knowledge of the satellites that are potentially visible permits the mobile receiver to focus its search and avoid wasting time searching for satellites that are not visible, thus reducing its time to acquire sufficient satellites for a fix.

Because the GPS satellite Doppler has such a large dynamic range relative to the Doppler attributable to Earth-borne vehicle motion, providing this information to a mobile receiver drastically reduces the required number of Doppler bins (and so correlators) required to cover the search space. The magnitude of the satellite Doppler can approach 4.2 kHz in the worst case. Assuming that a coherent integration time of 20 ms (the largest value generally possible without knowledge of the navigation data bits) is required to acquire a weak GPS signal, the Doppler bin size must be restricted to 50 Hz due to the well-known Doppler error modulation through the sinc function. This Doppler bin size thus implies a requirement for 100 Doppler bins per code phase bin for acquiring this satellite. In contrast, given knowledge of the satellite Doppler and Doppler rate, the Doppler range can be restricted to a level that is consistent with maximum expected host velocity (i.e., 250 Hz, or only about 5 Doppler bins). Because satellite Doppler rate is relatively small compared to the Doppler itself [74], it is generally not needed as part of the assistance data. Only for very long noncoherent accumulations is the satellite Doppler rate potentially significant (e.g., a total integration time of 20 seconds can produce a maximum Doppler error of 20 Hz in the worst case).

Satellite azimuth and elevation angles can be used by a mobile receiver in its assignment of search ranges. For example, in the previous paragraph, the number of

Doppler bins assigned was computed solely as a function of the maximum expected host velocity. This calculation ignores the fact that Earth-borne host velocities are largest in the horizontal plane; a more realistic assignment of search range could therefore have been made using the elevation angle of the to-be-acquired satellite, E, as indicated in the following equation:

$$\Delta D = v_{H\max} \cos E + v_{z\max} \sin E \qquad (9.50)$$

Since maximum vertical velocities (i.e., $v_{z\max}$ above) are expected to be small relative to maximum horizontal velocities (i.e., $v_{H\max}$ above), smaller search ranges would generally be assigned to higher elevation satellites using (9.50).

Providing the mobile receiver with an approximate location is most useful for acquisition assistance when combined with either ephemeris or almanac data for the satellites expected to be visible. The position provided by the network is generally either the location of the serving BS or the center of the service area; it is therefore expected to be within 20 km of the mobile's actual location. Given this position, and either an ephemeris or almanac representation for each satellite, Doppler and Doppler rate information can be computed by the mobile with satisfactory accuracy (the sensitivity of Doppler prediction error to position error is generally less than 1 Hz/km [74]), the value of which for acquisition assistance has already been discussed.

As referenced in the preceding paragraph, satellite ephemeris or almanac information enables accurate Doppler prediction, given relatively coarse position information. In addition, if GPS time is known such that the satellite positions can be accurately computed (a 1-second error in knowledge of GPS time translates to 1 km of ranging error in the worst case), an accurate range to the GPS satellite can be determined. If, additionally, the handset has been time-synchronized to GPS time and the error of each satellite's time relative to GPS time can be accurately predicted (i.e., via the satellite clock correction polynomial coefficients that enable this, which are also provided in the navigation model assistance data), prediction of the satellite code phase can be made as described in (9.49) to substantially reduce the range of code phases to search. For example, if the local oscillator has been synchronized to GPS time, and GPS time-of-week is known to 1 second, the relative code phases can be resolved to roughly 140 half-chips (i.e., 21 km of ranging error) after finding a first satellite, representing a significant savings relative to a full code phase search of 2,046 half-chips.

The information, provided to assist acquisition, can also increase sensitivity (i.e., enable acquisition of weaker signals). This is because the assistance information is likely to reduce the search ranges in Doppler and code phase such that the receiver has sufficient correlators to cover all cells in a parallel search and thus can spend more time searching the remaining space.

Independent of the acquisition assistance types already discussed, the primary form for actual sensitivity-increasing assistance data is the provision of navigation data bits over the cellular network. Given that the navigation data bits can be synchronized with the knowledge of the data bit edges for each satellite for which acquisition is attempted, the PDI can be extended beyond one navigation data bit: each doubling of the coherent integration time lowers the acquisition threshold by 3 dB. However, each doubling of the coherent integration period requires a correspondingly narrower Doppler size due to the sinc function, and so more Doppler bins (and more correlators) will be required to cover the same uncertainty range.

The over-the-air protocols for A-GPS have provisioned methods of sending the entire navigation data message to the handset so it has a priori knowledge of each bit and can subsequently wipeoff the data if needed for additional signal processing gain. The handset has to assemble the total bit sequence through a number of different messages. For example, in the GSM protocol, most of the bits for each satellite from subframes 1–3 (words 3 through 10) are delivered via the "Navigation Model" assist data message. Most of the bits for subframes 4 and 5 (words 3 through 10) are delivered via the "Almanac" assist data message. The bits contained in each word's 6-bit parity field are not sent, as these are computable after the handset has the data elements. Each subframe has a constant preamble that does not need to be sent, and the 17-bit HOW word contained in each subframe (word 2) is predictable with time. Thus, the remaining missing bits in the navigation message, primarily the TLM Message (14 bits), the antispoof flag (1 bit), the alert flag (1 bit) and the TLM-reserved bits (2 bits) have been accumulated into one additional *garbage collection* message and appended at the end of the "Reference Time" network-to-handset message.

At least two alternatives exist to sending and receiving navigation data bits over the network that achieve most of the benefit: predicting the navigation data bits, as discussed earlier, and guessing the navigation data bits. Estimated bits [75] can substantially increase the required number of correlators for longer coherent integrations. In guessing the navigation data bits, a hypothesis corresponding to each possible bit transition is formulated, and parallel integrations are performed, with the integration resulting in the largest signal correlation peak determined to be the correct bit sequence. For a sequence of n data bits, 2^n parallel integrations are required, corresponding to each hypothesized bit sequence. This increases the number of correlators dedicated to each satellite for which bits are guessed by 2^n. In [75], a practical limit of 5 estimated bits is imposed, corresponding to 32 parallel integrations.

Modernized future signals such as the L2C signal will offer a dataless component to the signal, which allows for long coherent integration periods without regard to data bit modulation interference, eliminating the need to transmit the bits to the mobile user through a cellular network.

The possible forms for navigation assistance include the following:

• DGPS correction data;
• Approximate altitude of the mobile;
• Approximate mobile location;
• Real-time satellite integrity information;
• Fine GPS timing information;
• Satellite clock correction coefficients;
• GPS satellite ephemeris information.

Although the improvements derived through the application of DGPS corrections to each measured pseudorange have diminished since the presidential directive to deactivate SA, the benefit may still be worthy of consideration in the E-911 environment. Here, the solution geometry can be significantly degraded relative to open-sky conditions. Hence, each meter of ranging error can be scaled by a large multiplier related to the geometry (e.g., HDOP for the HPE), resulting in a significant navigation error, which DGPS can reduce.

The approximate altitude of the mobile can be provided as either the altitude (above the WGS-84 reference ellipsoid) of the serving cell or an average altitude over the cellular network service area (e.g., the average of the altitudes of each BS in the network). It is reasonably important that an accuracy measure be provided for the altitude, generally represented as a 1-sigma error: the applicable standards allow for this, as discussed in [76]. This error measure is then most readily incorporated into a WLS solution for the mobile position (see Section 7.3.3 and Appendix A). Thus, the altitude is added as an additional measurement to the m pseudorange measurements, z_{m+1}, with an error variance set to the square of the 1-sigma value from the network:

$$x = \left(H^T R^{-1} H\right)^{-1} H^T R^{-1} z \qquad (9.51)$$

Note that bold letters denote vectors in (9.51)—the $m + 1$ dimensional measurement vector, z, and the four-dimensional vector of state corrections, x. The measurement gradient matrix H is of dimension $m + 1$ by 4, with its first m rows corresponding to the m pseudorange measurements, and the last row corresponding to the altitude, and R is the $m + 1$ dimensional diagonal measurement error variance matrix, with each element representing an error variance assigned to the corresponding measurement. The importance of assigning the error variance to the altitude measurement can be illustrated by an example. Suppose the emergency call is made from the tenth floor of a high-rise building, and the mean altitude of the cellular network coverage area is only slightly above mean sea level—in this case, the altitude aiding information is grossly in error, and the only mechanism for informing the mobile is through the assignment of a large error variance to the altitude aiding. Thus, the communicated network 1-sigma altitude error must reflect the presence of high-rise buildings in the service area.

The approximate location that is communicated to the mobile can serve two functions for the navigation solution. The first is simply to *initialize* the WLS solution, or provide a starting point for its iterations—the x value in (9.51)—which is defined as a set of corrections relative to this initial supplied location. In order for (9.51) to be valid, the approximate location must be sufficiently accurate such that the pseudorange measurements are effectively *linearized*. A second function is to add horizontal position domain constraints to the WLS solution, in the same way in which the altitude constraint is added. The dimension of the measurement vector, z, is then increased to $m + 3$, where m is the number of pseudorange measurements, and the R matrix elements corresponding to the position constraints are assigned error variances that reflect the accuracy of the approximate location. As referenced in (9.41), error variances, perhaps in the form of an error ellipse, are communicated with the approximate position. The error ellipse can be communicated (as an orientation angle and 1-sigma errors in principal axes), as illustrated in Figure 9.44, when the approximate position is determined from a coarse fix (e.g., based upon

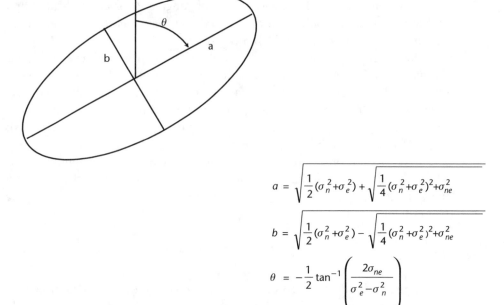

$$a = \sqrt{\frac{1}{2}(\sigma_n^2 + \sigma_e^2) + \sqrt{\frac{1}{4}(\sigma_n^2 + \sigma_e^2)^2 + \sigma_{ne}^2}}$$

$$b = \sqrt{\frac{1}{2}(\sigma_n^2 + \sigma_e^2) - \sqrt{\frac{1}{4}(\sigma_n^2 + \sigma_e^2)^2 + \sigma_{ne}^2}}$$

$$\theta = -\frac{1}{2} \tan^{-1}\left(\frac{2\sigma_{ne}}{\sigma_e^2 - \sigma_n^2}\right)$$

Figure 9.44 Error ellipse relationship to covariance matrix.

ranging off the cellular signals). In the figure, σ_e^2, σ_n^2, and σ_{ne} denote the elements of the covariance matrix corresponding to east and north position error. In the case of an error ellipse, the east and north position error components will generally be correlated (i.e., a nondiagonal measurement error variance will be needed if the constraints are expressed directly in terms of east and north position error components). Preferably, the measurement error variance matrix can remain diagonal if the measurements are expressed in the principal axes. Adding the approximate location information as measurements cannot be expected to improve the accuracy of the resultant fix, but it can assist in the identification of failed pseudorange measurements corresponding to false signal detections.

In a manner completely analogous to the addition of position constraints as additional measurements in the WLS solution for location, a timing constraint can be added to the clock offset solution, if fine timing information is available and sufficiently accurate (i.e., submillisecond).

Finally, the mobile's navigation solution can be aided by the transmission of satellite clock correction and ephemeris data, which may already be part of the acquisition assistance. However, for a handset-based solution in response to an emergency call, both are generally required for an accurate solution, since time does not permit decoding of the equivalent information from the navigation data bits.

9.4.5.1 Over-the-Air Location Protocol Standards

It is important to develop common over-the-air messaging standards to support assisted GPS technology in a handset in order to guarantee interoperability among various handset and location technology developers. As such, telecommunication standards organizations, location technology developers, handset manufacturers, and carriers have been busy incorporating location technologies into their standards, whether it is GSM, TDMA, CDMA, CDMA2000, WCDMA/UMTS, or even AMPS. The process to create a new over-the-air protocol to support a new technology can take years (e.g., the process to develop the CDMA protocol IS-801 began in late 1998 and completed with the first revision of the document in early 2000). Work to upgrade the document to IS-801a status to include new features and capabilities continued through 2003. The process of creating a new standard is contribution driven: interested parties contribute written descriptions of candidate features to regular meetings. The contribution is discussed, merits of each idea are judged, and the idea is voted upon for inclusion or exclusion. Needless to say, it's a long process to obtain agreement among all parties and to publish the final specification; ideas that are initially accepted can be removed when better ideas are created before final publication is achieved.

Many requirements are generally covered by a standard. First, the methods and procedures must be technically sound and have no holes. Second, messaging efficiency is important—transporting the maximum of useful information in the least number of bits is highly valued by the cellular carriers to minimize the incremental feature burden on the cellular infrastructure and support the most number of users without consuming all of the available bandwidth. Sometimes, a carrier's vote carries more weight, as ultimately they are the final customer of the specification and have to live with its ramifications as it impacts their cellular customer base.

Standards organizations involved are the Third Generation Partnership Project (3GPP), 3GPP2, the European Telecommunications Standards Institute (ETSI), Telecommunications Industry Association (TIA), and the T1P1 Committee. Listed in Table 9.10 are technologies being standardized by these organizations.

As discussed earlier, there are two main types of A-GPS technology, MS-assisted and MS-based. The GSM over-the-air protocol information elements to support each will be discussed next.

MS-Assist Exchange

Referring to Figure 9.35, recall that the MS-assist method moves the position computation element to the network-based position computation server, called a PDE in a CDMA network or an serving mobile location center (SMLC) in a GSM network. Information flows from the network to the handset to enable the handset-based GPS receiver to acquire, detect, and measure pseudoranges to multiple satellites.

Table 9.10 Standardized Location Technologies

Handset Technology (MA)	Organization	Standards Documents	Location Technology	Reference
AMPS	TIA TR45.1	TIA/EIA/IS-817	A-GPS	[77]
CDMA (IS-95)	TIA TR45.5	IS-801/IS-801A	A-GPS/AFLT	[78]
CDMA-2000	3GPP2	IS-801/IS801A	A-GPS/AFLT	[78]
TDMA	TIA TR45.3	TIA/EIA-136-740-C	A-GPS	[79]
GSM	ETSI & T1P1.5	04.31	A-GPS/EOTD	[76]
WCDMA/UMTS	3GPP GERAN/ 3GPP RAN2	25.331	A-GPS	[80]

The handset then returns measured code phases, Doppler, and signal power estimates for each detected satellite.

In MS-assist mode, the GSM exchange begins when the handset requests an "Acquisition Assistance" message from the GSM network. Tables 9.11 and 9.12 showcase the information content of the "Acquisition Assistance" message that is promptly delivered from the network to the handset via a short digital message. The data in Table 9.11 is sent once, while the data in Table 9.12 is sent for each visible satellite data in the assist message set.

The parameters "Doppler uncertainty" and "code phase search window" correspond to the network's estimate of Doppler uncertainty and code phase uncertainty depicted in Figures 9.3 through 9.7. The parameters "code phase," "integer code phase," and "GPS bit number" correspond to "Code_Phase_observed," "Integer_PN_Rolls_observed," and "Bit_Number_observed" in (9.48); however, "GPS_Bit_number" is truncated further to just two bits by a modulo function, such that GPS_Bit_number = MOD(Bit_Number_observed, 4). In Table 9.11, the parameter "GPS TOW" represents the time-tag corresponding to the data contained in Table 9.12 and is analogous to "GPS_Time" in (9.48). In Table 9.11, the parameters "BCCH carrier," "BSIC," "frame number," "timeslot number," and "bit number"

Table 9.11   GPS Acquisition Assist—Parameters Appearing Once Per Message

Parameter	Range	Bits	Resolution	Incl.
Number of Satellites	0–15	4	—	M
Reference Time				
GPS TOW	0–604,799.92 seconds	23	0.08 second	M
BCCH Carrier	0–1,023	10	—	O
BSIC	0–63	6	—	O
Frame Number	0–2,097,151	21	—	O
Timeslots Number	0–7	3	—	O
Bit Number	0–156	8	—	O

Source: [76].

Table 9.12   GPS Acquisition Assist—Parameters Appearing (Number of Satellites) Times Per Message

Parameter	Range	Bits	Resolution	Incl.
SVID/PRNID	1–64 (0–63)	6		M
Doppler (zero-order term)	−5,120 to 5,117.5 Hz	12	2.5 Hz	M
Doppler (first-order term)	−1–0.5	6		O
Doppler uncertainty	12.5 Hz – 200 Hz $[2^{-n}(200)$ Hz, $n = 0 - 4]$	3		O
Code phase	0–1,022 chips	10	1 chip	M
Integer code phase	0-19	5	1 C/A period	M
GPS bit number	0–3	2		M
Code phase search window	1–192 chips	4		M
Azimuth	0–348.75°	5	11.25°	O
Elevation	0–78.75°	3	11.25°	O

Source: [76].

represent the LMU-generated parameters that link the asynchronous GSM cellular messaging protocol state at an instant in time to the corresponding GPS-TOW time tag (i.e., the cellular messaging protocol state defined by these parameters existed at the precise GPS-TOW time tag that enables precise time transfer). The use of the time transfer parameters are optional, (marked "O" in the table), which means the handset does not necessarily need to use the data, and, in fact, the parameters may be missing from certain cellular networks if the network operator does not want to deploy LMUs. Those elements marked "M" are mandatory.

The parameters "azimuth" and "elevation" provide the MS-assisted handset with the ability to compute approximate HDOP (see Chapter 7) as it acquires satellites. Without some form of geometry quality indicator, the MS-assisted handset does not know when it has detected sufficient satellites for a good fix. Thus, being able to compute HDOP after each subsequent new satellite detection enables the MS-assisted handset to know when it has detected sufficient satellites for a quality fix and to deliver the pseudorange measurement response message to the network.

When the MS-assisted handset acquires sufficient satellites for a good fix, it returns the measured pseudorange data to the network via a *measurement information element* response message, depicted in Tables 9.13 and 9.14. As before, Table 9.13 data is sent one time and Table 9.14 data is sent N-SAT times. Table 9.14 represents the actual receiver measured range data that the network-based SLMC will use to compute the position of the handset.

MS-Based Exchange

Referring to Figure 9.35, recall that the MS-based method provides the position computation element in the handset, enabling local applications such as personal

Table 9.13   GPS TOW Field Contents

Parameter	Number of Bits	Resolution	Range	Units
Reference frame	16	—	0–65,535	Frames
GPS TOW	24	1 ms	0–14,399,999	ms
N_SAT	4	—	1–16	—

Source: [76].

Table 9.14   Measurement Parameters Field Contents

Parameter	Number of Bits	Resolution	Range	Units
Satellite ID	6	—	0–63	—
C/N_0	6	1	0–63	dB-Hz
Doppler	16	0.2	±6,553.6	Hz
Whole chips	10	1	0–1022	chips
Fractional chips	10	2^{-10}	$0–(1–2^{-10})$	chips
Multipath indicator	2	4 levels		—
Pseudorange RMS error	6	3-bit mantissa 3-bit exp	0.5–112	m

Source: [76].

navigation or mapping to operate within the handset. To do so, the handset will need a fresh copy of satellite ephemeris data, as it needs to know precise satellite positions in order to compute range residuals and update its local estimate of user position. Thus, one of the data elements the MS-based handset will need from the cellular network is the real-time (current) ephemeris data. The ephemeris is also useful in computing local acquisition assist data, given that the handset also knows approximate position and time. Two other data elements that are obtainable by the handset include this additional data.

The MS-based handset has a number of things it can request from the cellular network. Table 9.15 describes the suite of assistance data elements that can be requested by the handset. The handset can individually select each or all data elements listed in the table in one uploaded request to the network, thus, the handset that is *cold* (i.e., no time, position, ionosphere correction, or ephemeris data) can request the entire load in one uploaded message and then accept each *assist* data element as it is delivered from the network message.

Each data element is formatted into a unique data message before being sent to the handset. For a detailed description of each data element message, refer to [76]. The handset uses the assist data, transforms it into Doppler, code phase estimates, and uncertainties, as described in Figure 9.41 and (9.48). The signals are acquired and position determined using the locally stored ephemeris and ionospheric correction constants. The handset then can return the position to the network via one of five different digital messages [81]. The messages contain the user position data along with optional uncertainty and altitude. The optional messages include:

- Ellipsoid point;
- Ellipsoid point with uncertainty circle;
- Ellipsoid point with uncertainty ellipse;
- Ellipsoid point with altitude;
- Ellipsoid point with altitude and uncertainty ellipse.

The most general option, ellipsoid point with altitude and uncertainty ellipse from [80], is detailed in Table 9.16.

Table 9.15 Fields in the GPS Assistance Data Element

Parameter	Presence
Reference time	O
Reference location	O
DGPS corrections	O
Navigation model	O
Ionospheric model	O
UTC model	O
Almanac	O
Acquisition assistance	O
Real-time integrity	O

Source: [76].

Table 9.16 Position Response Data Element

Information Element/ Group Name	Type and Reference	Semantics Description
Latitude sign	Enumerated (north, south)	
Degrees of latitude	Integer $(0...2^{23}-1)$	The IE value (N) is derived by this formula: $N \leq 2^{23} X /90 < N + 1$ X is the latitude in degrees $(0°...90°)$
Degrees of longitude	Integer $(-2^{23}...2^{23}-1)$	The IE value (N) is derived by this formula: $N \leq 2^{24} X /360 < N + 1$ X is the longitude in degrees $(-180°...+180°)$
Altitude direction	Enumerated (height, depth)	
Altitude	Integer $(0...2^{15}-1)$	The IE value (N) is derived by this formula: $N \leq a < N + 1$ a is the altitude in meters
Uncertainty semimajor	Integer $(0...127)$	The uncertainty r is derived from the uncertainty code k by $r = 10 \times (1.1^k-1)$
Uncertainty semiminor	Integer $(0...127)$	The uncertainty r is derived from the uncertainty code k by $r = 10 \times (1.1^k-1)$
Orientation of major axis	Integer $(0...89)$	The IE value (N) is derived by this formula: $2N \leq a < 2(N + 1)$ a being the orientation in degree $(0°...179°)$
Uncertainty altitude	Integer $(0...127)$	The uncertainty in altitude, h, expressed in meters, is mapped from the IE value (K), with the following formula: $h = C((1 + x)^K -1)$ with $C = 45$ and $x = 0.025$.
Confidence	Integer $(0...100)$	In percentage

Source: [80].

One example of how the cellular over-the-air protocol can be used to solve a particular handset application problem is demonstrated by the "Real-Time-Integrity" acquisition assist data element. In Section 7.5, the importance of ensuring integrity for GPS is discussed, since GPS satellite clocks can fail, resulting in significant error in unprotected receiver solutions. A GPS receiver embedded in a cellular handset cannot generally be expected to perform its own RAIM (e.g., see Section 7.5.3) function, since signal reception conditions may be poor and the luxury of redundant measurements may not exist. For this reason, the cellular standards have allowed for integrity information to be communicated to the handset, since a network-based GPS receiver will certainly be able to perform the RAIM function and identify which satellites are failed or failing. It should be noted that the historical failure rate of GPS satellites or ephemeris uploads to those satellites has been very low—approximately one event every 18 to 24 months. However, when GPS is used for high-frequency E-911 emergency location function, it is certain that someone will need the system at precisely the time a satellite fails. Consequently, a real-time integrity function was added to the Radio Resources Location Services Protocol (RRLP) to prevent such failures.

An MS-based handset can be particularly vulnerable to GPS satellite failures. The handset can request real-time ephemeris data from the cellular network and then subsequently use the data for several hours. One mode that may be used by the handset is a periodic fix mode, in which the handset accepts the ephemeris assist data and then computes position at some periodic rate (e.g., once per minute). The handset only needs to get current ephemeris for each satellite at the start, as its useful life is ±2 hours around the TOE time. In an assisted mode, the handset may never observe the satellite-broadcast real-time integrity data that is available in the 50-bps satellite navigation data message. Thus, if a particular satellite fails between the time the handset accepts ephemeris and the time it wants to use it for a position solution, the handset will not have knowledge of the failed state and could produce erroneous position data.

To combat this potential problem, a short real-time integrity message was added to the RRLP protocol to inform the handset when a particular satellite has failed. The real-time-integrity message is requested at the start of each location attempt and consumes only a few bits of the available bandwidth. The network-generated real-time-integrity message is then sent to the handset. For the case of no failed satellites, this message returns one zero bit. For the case of a failed satellite or group of failed satellites, the satellite IDs of the failed satellite(s) are returned to the handset; the handset excludes those failed satellites from any subsequent position solution. As such, the MS-based handset needs to request real-time integrity information at the start of each location attempt to ensure solution integrity.

References

[1]   Hemesath, N. B., et al., "Anti-Jamming Characteristics of GPS/GDM," *Proc. of the National Telecommunications Conference*, Dallas, TX, November 1976.

[2]   Greenspan, R. L., "Inertial Navigation Technology from 1970–1995," *NAVIGATION: Journal of The Institute of Navigation*, Vol. 42, Spring 1995.

[3]   Evans, F. A., et al., "Experimental Strapdown Redundant Sensor Inertial Navigation System," *Proc. of AIAA Guidance, Control, and Flight Mechanics Conference*, Princeton, NJ, August 18–20, 1969.

[4]   Lawrence, A., *Modern Inertial Technology: Navigation, Guidance, and Control*, New York: Springer-Verlag, 1998.

[5]   Gelb, A., et al., *Applied Optimal Estimation*, Cambridge, MA: MIT Press, 1992.

[6]   Kalman, R. E., "A New Approach to Linear Filtering and Prediction Problems," *Journal of Basic Engineering (ASME)*, Vol. 82D, March 1960, pp. 35–37.

[7]   Frazer, D. E., et al., "T-33 Aircraft Demonstration of GPS Aided Inertial Navigation," *Proc. of The Institute of Navigation Satellite Division Technical Meeting*, Colorado Springs, CO, September 1987.

[8]   Thornton, C. L., and G. J. Bierman, UDU^T *Covariance Factorization for Kalman Filtering*, New York: Academic Press, 1980.

[9]   Nielson, J. T., "GPS Aided Inertial Navigation," *Proc. of IEEE NAECON*, Dayton, OH, 1986, p. 20.

[10] Cox, D. B., "Integration of GPS with Inertial Navigation Systems," *Global Positioning System: Papers Published in Navigation, Volume I*, Fairfax, VA: Institute of Navigation, 1980.

[11] Carroll, R. W., et al., "Velocity Aiding of Non-Coherent GPS Receiver," *Proc. of 1977 National Aerospace Conference*, Dayton, OH, May 1977.

[12] Widnall, W. S., "Alternate Approaches for Stable Rate Aiding of Jamming Resistant GPS Receivers," *NAECON Proc.*, Dayton, OH, May 1979.

[13] Copps, E. M., et al., "Optimal Processing of GPS Signals," *NAVIGATION: Journal of The Institute of Navigation*, Fall 1980.

[14] Sennott, J. W., et al., "Navigation Receiver with Coupled Signal Tracking Channels," U.S. Patent 5,343,209, May 1992.

[15] Leimer, D., "Receiver Phase Noise Mitigation," U.S. Patent 6,081,228, SiRF Technology, September 1998.

[16] Beser, J., et al., "TRUNAV: A Low Cost Guidance/Navigation Unit Integrating a SAASM Based GPS and MEMS in a Deeply Coupled Mechanization," *Proc. of The Institute of Navigation ION-GPS 2002*, Vol. 24–27, Portland, OR, September 2002.

[17] Abbott, T., et al., *Ultra-Tight GPS/IMU Coupling Method*, The Aerospace Corporation, TOR-2001(1590)-0846e, El Segundo, CA, April 10, 2001.

[18] Gautier, J. D., et al., "Using the GPS/INS Generalized Evaluation Tool (GIGET) for the Comparison of Loosely Coupled, Tightly Coupled, and Ultra-Tightly Coupled Integrated Navigation Systems," *Proc. of The Institute of Navigation 59th Annual Meeting*, Albuquerque, NM, June 2003.

[19] Gelb, A., et al., *Multiple Input Describing Functions and Nonlinear System Design*, New York: McGraw-Hill, 1968.

[20] Manry, C. W., et al., "Advanced Mini Array Antenna Design Using High Fidelity Computer Modeling and Simulations," *Proc. of The Institute of Navigation ION GPS-2000*, Salt Lake City, UT, September 2000, pp. 2485–2490.

[21] Tseng, H.-W., et al., "Test Results of a Dual Frequency (L1/L2) Small Controlled Reception Pattern Antenna," *Proc. of The Institute of Navigation ION GPS-2002*, San Diego, CA, January 2002.

[22] Kunysz, W., "Advanced Pinwheel—Compact Controlled Reception Pattern Antenna (AP-CRPA) Designed for Interference and Multipath Mitigation," *Proc. of The Institute of Navigation ION GPS-2002*, Portland, OR, September 2002.

[23] Yazdi, N., et al., "Micromachined Inertial Sensors," *Proc. of IEEE*, Vol. 86, No. 8, August 1998, pp. 1640–1659.

[24] Peng, K. "A Vector-Based Gyro-Free Inertial Navigation System by Integrating Existing Accelerometer Network in a Passenger Vehicle," *Proc. of IEEE Position Location and Navigation Symposium (PLANS)*, Monterrey, CA, April 26–29, 2004, pp. 234–242.

[25] Schuler, A. R., "Measuring Rotational Motion with Linear Accelerometers," *IEEE Trans. on Aerospace and Electronic Systems*, Vol. AES-3, 1967, pp. 465–471.

[26] Weinburg, H., "MEMS Sensors Are Driving the Automotive Industry," *Sensors*, Vol. 19, No. 2, February 2002, pp. 36–41.

[27] Mostov, K. S., A. A. Soloviev, and T. J. Koo, "Accelerometer Based Gyro-Free Multi-Sensor Generic Inertial Device for Automotive Applications," *Proc. of IEEE Conference on Intelligent Transportation Systems*, Boston, MA, November 1997, pp. 1047–1052.

[28] Chen, T. H., "Gyroscope Free Strapdown Inertial Measurement Unit by Six Linear Accelerometers," *Journal of Guidance, Control, and Dynamics*, Vol. 17, No. 2, 1994, pp. 286–290.

[29] Stephen, J., "Development of a Multi-Sensor GNSS Based Vehicle Navigation System," M.Sc. thesis, UCGE Report No. 20140, Department of Geomatics Engineering, University of Calgary, Canada, August 2000.

[30] U.S. Department of Defense, "Micromachined System Opportunities," a Department of Defense Dual-Use Technology Industrial Assessment, 1995.

[31] Helsel, M., et al., "A Navigation Grade Micro-Machined Silicon Accelerometer," *Proc. of IEEE Position Location and Navigation Symposium (PLANS)*, Las Vegas, NV, April 11–15, 1994, pp. 51–58.

[32] Lemkin, M. A., et al., "A Three Axis Surface Micromachined Sigma-Delta Accelerometer," *ISSCC Digest of Technical Papers*, February 1997.

[33] Gustafson, D., et al., "A Micromechanical INS/GPS System for Guided Projectiles," *Proc. ION 51st Annual Meeting*, Colorado Springs, CO, June 5–7, 1995, pp. 439–444.

[34] Warren, K., "High Performance Silicon Accelerometers with Charge Controlled Rebalance Electronics," *Proc. of IEEE Position Location and Navigation Symposium (PLANS)*, Atlanta, GA, April 22–26, 1996, pp. 27–30.

[35] Le Traon, O., et al., "The VIA Vibrating Beam Accelerometer: Concept and Performances," *Proc. IEEE Position Location and Navigation Symposium (PLANS)*, Palm Springs, CA, April 20–23, 1998, pp. 25–29.

[36] Hulsing, R., "MEMS Inertial Rate and Acceleration Sensor," *Proc. of The Institute of Navigation National Technical Meeting*, Long Beach, CA, January 1998, pp. 353–360.

[37] Clark, W., R. Howe, and R. Horowitz, "Surface Micromachined Z-Axis Vibratory Rate Gyroscope," *Proc. Solid-State Sensors and Actuators Workshop*, Hilton Head, SC, June 13–16, 1996, pp. 283–287.

[38] Kourepenis, A., et al., "Performance of MEMS Inertial Sensors," *Proc. IEEE Position Location and Navigation Symposium (PLANS)*, Palm Springs, CA, April 20–23, 1998, pp. 1–8.

[39] Barbour, N., "Operational Status of Inertial," *Proc. of The Institute of Navigation National Technical Meeting*, Santa Monica, CA, January 22–24, 1996, pp. 7–15.

[40] Park, M., "Error Analysis and Stochastic Modeling of MEMS Based Inertial Sensors for Land Vehicle Applications," M.Sc. Thesis, UCGE Report No. 20194, Department of Geomatics Engineering, University of Calgary, Canada, April 2004.

[41] Bullock, J. B., and E. J. Krakiwsky, "Analysis of the Use of Digital Road Maps in Vehicle Navigation," *Proc. of IEEE Position Location and Navigation Symposium (PLANS)*, Las Vegas, NV, April 11–15, 1994, pp. 494–501.

[42] Zavoli, W. B., and S. K. Honey, "Map Matching Augmented Dead Reckoning," *Proc. IEEE Position Location and Navigation Symposium (PLANS)*, Las Vegas, NV, 1986, pp. 359–362.

[43] Honey, S. K., et al., "Vehicle Navigation System and Method," U.S. Patent 4,796,191, Etak Incorporated, January 3, 1989.

[44] Mathis, D. L., et al, "Combined Relative and Absolute Positioning Method and Apparatus," U.S. Patent 5,311,195, Etak Incorporated, May 10, 1994.

[45] French, R. L., "Map Matching Origins, Approaches and Applications," *Proc. Land Vehicle Navigation*, Verlag TUV Rheinland GmbH., Koln, Germany, July 4–7, 1989, pp. 91–116.

[46] Harris, C. B., "Prototype for a Land Based Automatic Vehicle Location and Navigation System," M.Sc. Thesis, Department of Geomatics Engineering, University of Calgary, Canada, 1989.

[47] Bullock, J. B., "A Prototype Portable Vehicle Navigation System Utilizing Map Aided GPS," M.Sc. Thesis, Department of Geomatics Engineering, University of Calgary, Canada, 1995.

[48] Ribbens, W. B., "Understanding Automotive Electronics," *SAMS*, 1992, pp. 138–143.

[49] Zavoli, W. B., et al., "Method and Apparatus for Measuring Relative Heading Changes in a Vehicular Onboard Navigation System," U.S. Patent 4,788,645, Etak Incorporated, November 29, 1988.

[50] Carlson, C. R., J. C. Gerdes and J. D. Powell, "Error Sources When Land Vehicle Dead Reckoning with Differential Wheelspeeds," *NAVIGATION: Journal of The Institute of Navigation*, Vol. 51, No. 1, Spring 2004, pp. 13–27.

[51] Honeywell silicon pressure sensors, http://content.honeywell.com/sensing/prodinfo/pressure.

[52] Vannucci, G., "Inclusion of Atmospheric and Barometric Pressure Information for Improved Altitude Determination," *TIA TR45 Cellular Network Standards Proposal TIA 45:1.1.1 LocTaskG*, March 2000.

[53] Wald, M., "An Automobile Option for Self-Navigating Car," *New York Times*, January 5, 1995, p. D2.

[54] Geier, G. J., et al., "Integration of GPS with Dead Reckoning for Vehicle Tracking Applications," *Proc. of 49th Annual Meeting of the Institute of Navigation*, Cambridge, MA, June 21–23, 1993, pp. 75–82.

[55]   Brown, R. G., and P. Hwang, *Introduction to Signal Processing and Applied Kalman Filtering*, New York: John Wiley & Sons, 1992.

[56]   Britting, K. R., *Inertial Navigation System Analysis*, New York: Wiley-Interscience, 1971.

[57]   Monteith, K. A., "Wireless E911: Regulatory Framework, Current Status and Beyond," *IBC Mobile Location Services Conference,* McLean, VA, April 2001.

[58]   Taylor, R. E., et al., "Navigation System and Method," U.S. Patent 4,445,118, May 1981.

[59]   RTCM Recommended Standards for Differential GPS Service, Version 2.0, January 1990.

[60]   Brown, A. K., et al., "Vehicle Tracking System Employing GPS Satellites," U.S. Patent 5,225,842, NAVSYS Corporation, May 1991.

[61]   *Motorola EAGLE GPS Receiver Users' Manual*, January 1986.

[62]   Bryant, R. C., "Position Reporting System," Auspace Limited, Australian patent number AU-B-634587, November 1989.

[63]   "White Sands Missile Range (WSMR) Interface Control Document (ICD)," ICD 3680090, April 28, 1994.

[64]   "OET Bulletin 71—Guidelines for Testing and Verifying the Accuracy of Wireless E-911 Systems," Federal Communications Commission, Washington, D.C., March 2000.

[65]   Vogel, W. J., G. W. Torrance, and N. Kleiner, "Measurement of Propagation Loss into Cars on Satellite Paths at L-Band," *Proc. of EMPS '96*, Rome, Italy, October 1996.

[66]   Vogel, W. J., and N. Kleiner, "Propagation Measurements for Satellite Services into Buildings," *European Mobile/Personal Satcoms Conference*, Rome, Italy, October 1996.

[67]   Vogel, W. J., "Satellite Diversity for Personal Satellite Communications—Modeling and Measurements," *10th International Conference on Antennas and Propagation*, Edinburgh, U.K., April 14–17, 1997.

[68]   Vogel, W. J., and R. Akturan, "Elevation Angle Dependence of Fading for Satellite PCS in Urban Areas," *Electronic Letters*, Vol. 31, No. 25, December 7, 1995.

[69]   Vogel, W. J., and J. Goldhirsh, "Mobile Satellite System Fade Statistics for Shadowing and Multipath from Roadside Trees at UHF and L-Band," *IEEE Trans. on Antennas and Propagation*, Vol. 37, No. 4, April 1989.

[70]   Vogel, W. J., and G.W. Torrence, "Propagation Measurements for Satellite Radio Reception Inside Buildings," *IEEE Trans. on Antennas and Propagation*, Vol. 43, No. 7, July 1993.

[71]   "Update of Indoor Measurement Results," Phillips Contribution number R4-040285 3GPP TSG RAN WG4 (Radio) Meeting #31, Beijing, China, May 2004.

[72]   "GPS Satellite Signal Strength Measurements in Indoor Environments," Motorola Contribution number R4-040310, TSG-RAN WG4 meeting #31, Beijing, China, May, 2004.

[73]   TIA Standard TIA-IS-916, "Recommended Minimum Performance Specification for TIA/EIA/IS801-1 Spread Spectrum Mobile Stations," Telecommunications Industry Association, Arlington, VA, April 2002.

[74]   Smith, C. A., et al., "Sensitivity of GPS Acquisition to Initial Data Uncertainties," *ION GPS Papers*, Volume III, 1986.

[75]   Ziedan, N., et al., "Unaided Acquisition of Weak GPS Signals Using Circular Correlation or Double Block Zero Padding," *IEEE Plans 2004*, Monterey, CA, April 26–29, 2004.

[76]   3GPP Technical Specification TS 04.31 3rd Generation Partnership Project, "Technical Specification Group GSM/EDGE Radio Access Network, Location Services (LCS), Mobile Station (MS), Serving Mobile Location Centre (SMLC), Radio Resource LCS Prococol (RRLP)," Release 1999.

[77]   TIA45.1, Technical Specification TIA/EIA/IS-817, "A Position Determination Standard for Analog Systems (2001)," February 1, 2002.

[78]   TIA45.5, Technical Specification IS-801/IS-801A, "Position Determination Service Standard for Dual-Mode Spread Spectrum Systems," Telecommunications Industry Association, February 2002.

[79] TIA45.3, Technical Specification TIA/EIA-136-740, "TDMA Third Generation Wireless—System Assisted Mobile Positioning Through Satellite (SAMPS) Teleservices" (ANSI/TIA/EIA-136-740-2001), April 1, 2001.

[80] 3GPP Technical Specification TS 25.331, 3rd Generation Partnership Project, "Technical Specification Group Radio Access Network, Radio Resource Control (RRC) Protocol Specification," Release 1999.

[81] 3GPP Technical Specification TS 23.032, 3rd Generation Partnership Project, "Technical Specification Group Core Network; Universal Geographic Area Description (GAD), Release 4," 2001.

CHAPTER 10

GALILEO

Marco Falcone and Philippe Erhard
European Space Agency, ESA/ESTEC
Noordwijk, the Netherlands

Guenter W. Hein
Institute of Geodesy and Navigation
University FAF Munich, Germany

10.1 GALILEO Program Objectives

Satellite navigation, positioning, and timing have already found widespread applications in a large variety of fields. Recognizing the strategic importance of its applications, a European approach was developed in the early 1990s. It started with the European contribution to the first generation of Global Navigation Satellite Systems (GNSS-1), the EGNOS program, and continues with the future generation of Global Navigation Satellite Systems (GNSS-2), the GALILEO program.

GNSS-1 provides Europe with early benefits but does not offer a sufficient level of control over GNSS; nor does it offer signals with guaranteed availability and performance, as it depends upon the GPS or GLONASS. This has led to the definition of GALILEO, a satellite constellation providing worldwide coverage, which is proposed as the European contribution to GNSS-2.

The combined use of GALILEO, EGNOS, and GPS/GLONASS will increase the overall performance, robustness, and the inherent safety of the services achieved from GNSS, and it will allow for worldwide acceptability of the exploitation and use of satellite navigation for the benefit of all potential users.

10.2 GALILEO Services and Performance

The GALILEO system is being designed to meet a variety of user needs, out of which a number of representative services has been identified to form the basis of the design and to allow the definition of the main features of GALILEO. However, the capabilities of the system will allow the realization of a larger number of services, well beyond the scope of the ones defined here. In addition, the system architecture is flexible and scalable so that evolution of user needs can be accommodated.

This section focuses on GALILEO services: these services will be provided worldwide and independently from other satellite navigation systems by using only the signals broadcast by the GALILEO satellite constellation. Five reference services are defined: open service (OS), safety of life (SOL), commercial service, public regulated service (PRS), and the support for a search and rescue (SAR) service. Table 10.1 highlights the anticipated performances for these services derived from the GALILEO Mission High Level Definition [1].

10.2.1 Open Service (OS)

The OS will provide positioning, velocity, and timing information that can be accessed free of direct charge. This service is suitable for mass-market applications, such as in-car navigation. This service is also particularly suitable with integration in

Table 10.1 Performance for the GALILEO Services

GALILEO Global Services	OS	Commercial Service	SOL Service	PRS
Coverage	Global	Global	Global	Global
Positioning accuracy (Horizontal, 2 dRMS, 95%) (Vertical, 95%)	15m or 24m H–35m V (single frequency) 4m H–8m V (dual frequency)		4m H–8m V (dual frequency)	15m or 24m H–35m V (single frequency) 6.5m H–12m V (dual frequency)
Timing accuracy (95%)	30 ns	30 ns	30 ns	30 ns
Integrity[1] Alert limit Time to alert Integrity risk	None	None	12m H–20m V 6 seconds 3.5×10^{-7}/150 seconds	20m H–35m V 10 seconds 3.5×10^{-7}/150 seconds
Continuity risk[2]			1×10^{-5}/15 seconds	1×10^{-5}/15 seconds
Service availability[3]	99.5%	99.5%	99.5%	99.5%
Access control	Free open access	Controlled access of ranging codes and navigation data message	Authentication of integrity information in the navigation data message	Controlled access of ranging codes and navigation data message
Certification and service guarantees	None	Guarantee of service possible	Build for certification and guarantee of service	Build for certification and guarantee of service

Single frequency accuracy depends on the frequency used: 15-m horizontal accuracy when using the L1 signal or 24m when using the other frequencies (E5a, E5b, E6).

1. Integrity is defined by the following parameters:
   - *Alert limit:* the maximum allowable error in the user position solution before an alarm is to be raised within the specific time to alert;
   - *Time to alert:* the time from when an alarm condition occurs until when the alarm is received at the user level (including the time to detect the alarm condition);
   - *Integrity risk:* the probability, during any continuous period of operation, that the computed vertical or horizontal positioning error exceeds the corresponding alert limit and the user is not informed within the specified time to alert (note that the value reported in the table includes the user contribution of 1.5×10^{-7}/150 seconds).

2. Continuity risk is the probability that the specified performances (accuracy and integrity) are supported by the system over the time interval applicable and within the coverage area, given that they are supported at the beginning of the operation and that they are predicted to be supported all along the operation duration (note that the value reported in the table includes the user contribution of 0.2×10^{-5}/15 seconds).

3. Service availability represents the percentage of time averaged over the design lifetime (20 years) when the service is within the specified performance (accuracy, integrity, and continuity) for any point within the service volume. It is derived from the availability of each operational configuration (nominal, without failures, or nonnominal, with one or more failures), weighted by its probability of occurrence, averaged over the design lifetime.

mobile telephones. In Table 10.1, service performance is defined for single- as well as dual-frequency users. Three signals (E5a, E5b, and L1) will be broadcast for the OS. These signals are shown in Figures 10.1 and 10.2. By using these three signals with differential techniques based on carrier phase processing, a very high accuracy can be achieved. This performance will be realizable by users at any point in the world and at any time, provided the users are equipped with receivers that process

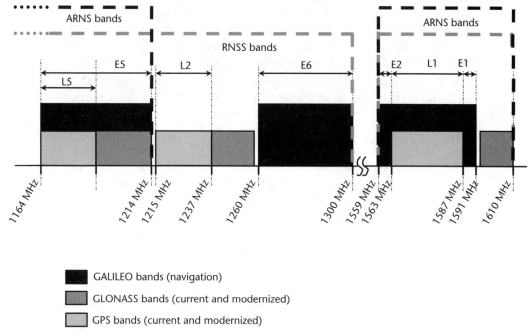

Figure 10.1 GALILEO frequency plan.

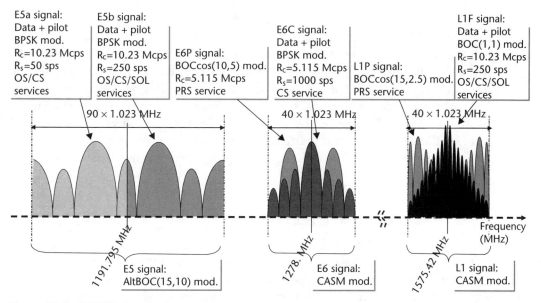

Figure 10.2 GALILEO frequency spectrum.

all GALILEO satellite signals visible 10° above the horizon (i.e., 10° mask angle). In contrast, single-frequency user performance represents the worst case.

10.2.2 Commercial Service (CS)

The commercial service will allow the development of professional applications by supporting the dissemination of value-added data on a dedicated commercial service signal that can be used for supporting high-accuracy positioning applications. The GALILEO Operating Company, in charge of deploying, financing, and operating the system, will determine the level of performance and guarantee of service it can offer for each commercial service on the basis of the market potential of the applications. Contractual arrangements might exist, for instance, between the GALILEO Operating Company and third party service providers for value-added services such as weather alerts, accident warnings, traffic information, and map updates.

10.2.3 Safety of Life (SOL) Service

The SOL service is intended for safety-critical users (e.g., those involved in maritime, aviation, and railway modes of transportation whose applications or operations require stringent performance and safety levels). This service will be offered unencrypted, and the system will have the capability to authenticate the included signals to assure that the received signals are truly those broadcast by GALILEO. This will allow the user to periodically verify in a cryptographic way that the information broadcast by the spacecraft is genuine. In addition to signal authentication, the SOL service will include integrity monitoring and notification (i.e., a timely warning will be issued to the users when the safe use of the SOL signals cannot be guaranteed according to specifications). All of these features, together with adequate service guarantees, will facilitate the development and certification of SOL applications. E5b and L1 are the frequencies used for SOL services. As with the OS, the SOL specifications are given for a worst-case user anywhere in the world at any time of the day. This critical service level performance has been one of the drivers for the design of the system. This level can support critical operations, such as aviation precision approach, with vertical guidance where stringent levels of safety are demanded. In addition, it will also be possible for regional service providers to monitor integrity of the GALILEO signals over their region. Regional integrity data can be broadcast directly by regional service providers using up to five authorized integrity uplink channels provided by the GALILEO satellites. Alternatively, regional integrity data can also be transmitted by regional service providers to the GALILEO Control Centers (GCC) for indirect uplink, together with the integrity data computed centrally.

10.2.4 Public Regulated Service (PRS)

The PRS will be offered only to government-authorized users requiring a higher level of protection (e.g., increased robustness against interference or jamming). The PRS signals will be encrypted, and access to the service will be controlled through a government-approved secure key distribution mechanism.

10.2.5 Support to Search and Rescue (SAR) Service

The GALILEO constellation of satellites will be equipped with transponders that will allow the relay of alarms from distress beacons to SAR organizations. An interface with those centers will also be implemented so that the system will be capable of relaying back to the users an acknowledgment that the rescue operation is engaged. This acknowledgment will be provided through the GALILEO navigation signals themselves. This GALILEO SAR service will be integrated into the international COSPAS/SARSAT cooperative effort on SAR activities.

10.3 GALILEO Frequency Plan and Signal Design

This section presents a summary description of the GALILEO frequency plan and signal structure. The main considerations in the selection of the GALILEO signal characteristics were [2–5]:

- Transmission of wide bandwidth signals in the L-band spectrum, enabling precise and robust tracking performance and multipath mitigation capability;
- Minimization of interference from and to existing satellite navigation systems (e.g., GPS, GLONASS) for the purpose of radio frequency compatibility;
- Selection of frequencies with good performance and small tracking errors in the upper L-band frequencies for the purpose of ionospheric compensation in dual-frequency receivers;
- Interoperability with GPS;
- Security aspects with respect to the military GPS M code and the GALILEO PRS (i.e., the separation of military and specially protected services from civil services).

The EU and the United States concluded an agreement on GALILEO and GPS at the EU-U.S. Summit held in Ireland on June 26, 2004. The agreement on the promotion, provision, and use of the two satellite-based navigation systems and related applications was signed by EC Vice President Loyola de Palacio and U.S. Secretary of State Colin Powell. The provisions of this agreement will allow each system to work alongside the other without interfering with its counterpart's signals, thus providing interoperability between GPS and GALILEO.

10.3.1 Frequencies and Signals

GALILEO will provide six navigation signals with RHCP in the frequency ranges 1,164–1,215 MHz (E5 band), 1,260–1,300 MHz (E6 band), and 1,559–1,592 MHz (E2-L1-E1 band), which are each internationally allocated for radionavigation satellite services (RNSS). The GALILEO frequency plan is shown in Figure 10.1 (the frequency band E2-L1-E1 is sometimes denoted as L1 for convenience). All satellites will make use of the same carrier frequencies with different ranging codes through CDMA transmission.

The E5 and L1 bands have international coprimary allocations for ARNS, so that transmitted GALILEO signals in those bands can be used for dedicated aviation-related safety-critical applications. Moreover, Figure 10.1 highlights common frequencies with GPS (L1 and E5a), which are beneficial for interoperability at the user equipment level.

Figure 10.2 illustrates the baseline GALILEO signal's spectral characteristics as well as modulation, chip rate, and data rate at the time of this writing. Some of those parameters are still subject of further tradeoff analysis (L1F modulation, for instance).

Each GALILEO satellite will transmit six navigation signals denoted as L1F, L1P, E6C, E6P, E5a, and E5b signals.

- *L1F signal:* L1F is an open-access signal transmitted in the L1 band comprising a data channel and a pilot (or dataless) channel. It has unencrypted ranging codes and navigation data, which are accessible to all users. The L1F data stream also contains integrity messages and encrypted commercial data. The L1F data rate is 125 bps. The L1F signal will support the OS, commercial service, and the SOL.

- *L1P signal:* L1P signal is a restricted-access signal transmitted in the L1 band. Its ranging codes and data are encrypted using a governmental encryption algorithm. The L1P signal will support the PRS.

- *E6C signal:* E6C is a commercial-access signal transmitted in the E6 band that includes a data channel and a pilot (or dataless) channel. Its ranging codes and data are encrypted using a commercial algorithm. A data rate of 500 bps will allow the transmission of added-value commercial data. The E6C signal is a dedicated signal for supporting the commercial service.

- *E6P signal:* E6P is a restricted-access signal transmitted in the E6 band. Its ranging codes and data are encrypted using a governmental encryption algorithm. The E6P signal will support the PRS.

- *E5a signal:* E5a signal is an open-access signal transmitted in the E5 band that includes a data channel and a pilot (or dataless) channel. The E5a signal has unencrypted ranging codes and navigation data, which are accessible by all users. It transmits the basic data to support navigation and timing functions, using a relatively low 25-bps data rate that enables more robust data demodulation. The E5a signal will support the OS.

- *E5b signal:* E5b is an open-access signal transmitted in the E5 band that includes a data channel and a pilot (or dataless) channel. It has unencrypted ranging codes and navigation data accessible to all users. The E5b data stream also contains integrity messages and encrypted commercial data. The data rate is 125 bps. The E5b signal will support the OS, commercial service, and SOL services.

The E5a and E5b signals are modulated onto a single E5 carrier using a technique known as AltBOC [4] (see description of alternative BOC modulation in Section 10.3.2.3). The composite of the E5a and E5b signals is denoted as the E5 signal and can be processed as a single large-bandwidth signal with an appropriate user receiver implementation. A rate half convolutional coding scheme is used for all signals before transmission of the message data onto their carriers so that the data symbol rate on each signal in symbols per second (sps) is twice the data rate in bits per second (bps). The data contained in the navigation message are summarized next.

- Navigation and timing data are generated by the GALILEO Ground Mission Segment (GMS) and uploaded to all satellites for dissemination through all signals data channels.
- Integrity data are also generated by the GALILEO GMS and uploaded to all satellites for dissemination through the E5b and L1F signals data channels.
- Commercial data will be provided by external service providers that will interface with the GALILEO Control Center (GCC) before dissemination through all GALILEO satellites. The service providers will give access to the data directly to the CS users through the E5b, E6C, and L1F signals data channels.
- PRS data will be transmitted on the E6P and L1P signals.

Table 10.2 is a summary of the primary GALILEO navigation signal parameters (see Section 4.2.3 for an overview of BPSK-R and BOC modulations).

10.3.2   Modulation Schemes

10.3.2.1   L1 Signal

The transmitted GALILEO L1 signal $s_{L1}^{tx}(t)$ consists of the multiplexing of three components as follows:

- *The L1F data channel (L1F-d):* The modulation on this channel results from the modulo-two addition of three components—the L1F navigation data stream $d_{L1F}(t)$, the L1F-d channel PRN code sequence $c_{L1F\text{-}d}(t)$, and the L1F-d subcarrier $sc_{L1F\text{-}d}(t)$. The BOC subcarrier has sine phasing. The signal corresponds to $\text{BOC}_s(1,1)$ modulation by the d-channel code sequence and the d-channel data signal.

Table 10.2   Primary GALILEO Navigation Signal Parameters

Frequency Bands	Channel	Modulation Type	Chip Rate (Mchip/s)	Symbol Rate (sps)	User Minimum Received Power Above 10° Elevation (dBW)
E5	E5a data			50	
	E5a pilot	AltBOC(15,10)	10.23	N/A	−155
	E5b data			250	
	E5b pilot			N/A	−155
E6	E6P	$\text{BOC}_c(10,5)$	5.115	To be decided	−155
	E6C data	BPSK-R(5)	5.115	1,000	
	E6C pilot			N/A	−155
E2-L1-E1	L1P	$\text{BOC}_c(15,2.5)$	2.5575	To be decided	−157
	L1F data	$\text{BOC}_s(1,1)$	1.023	250	
	L1F pilot			N/A	−157

- *The L1F pilot channel (L1F-p):* The modulation on this channel results from the modulo-two addition of the L1F-p channel PRN code sequence $c_{L1F\text{-}p}(t)$ with the L1F-p subcarrier $sc_{L1F\text{-}p}(t)$. The BOC subcarrier has sine phasing. The signal corresponds to $\mathrm{BOC}_s(1,1)$ modulation by the p-channel code sequence.
- *The L1P channel:* The modulation on this channel results from the modulo-2 addition of three components—the L1P navigation data stream $d_{L1P}(t)$, the L1P channel PRN code sequence $c_{L1P}(t)$, and the L1P subcarrier $sc_{L1P}(t)$. The BOC subcarrier has cosine phasing. The signal corresponds to $\mathrm{BOC}_c(15,2.5)$ cosine modulation by the code sequence and data signal.

The L1 signal components are multiplexed into the L1 carrier using the modified hexaphase modulation [6]. The L1F signal is modulated onto the carrier in-phase component while the L1P signal is modulated onto the quadrature component. The composite signal may be expressed as:

$$S_{L1}^{tx}(t) = \frac{\sqrt{2 \cdot P_{L1}^{tx}}\left[\alpha_{L1} \cdot s_{L1F\text{-}d}^{tx}(t) - \alpha_{L1} \cdot s_{L1F\text{-}p}^{tx}(t)\right] \times \cos(2\pi f_{L1}t) -}{\sqrt{2 \cdot P_{L1}^{tx}}\left[\beta_{L1} \cdot s_{L1P}^{tx}(t) + \gamma_{L1} \cdot s_{L1,\mathrm{int}}^{tx}(t)\right] \times \cos(2\pi f_{L1}t)}$$

where:

$\text{L1F-}d\text{: } s_{L1F\text{-}d}^{tx}(t) = d_{L1F}(t) \cdot c_{L1F\text{-}d}(t) \cdot sc_{L1F\text{-}d}(t)$

$\text{L1F-}p\text{: } s_{L1F\text{-}p}^{tx}(t) = c_{L1F\text{-}p}(t) \cdot sc_{L1F\text{-}p}(t)$

$\text{L1P: } s_{L1P}^{tx}(t) = d_{L1P}(t) \cdot c_{L1P}(t) \cdot sc_{L1P}(t)$

$s_{L1,\mathrm{int}}(t) = s_{L1F\text{-}d}^{tx}(t) \cdot s_{L1F\text{-}p}^{tx}(t) \cdot s_{L1P}^{tx}(t) = $ the intermodulation product in the

modified hexaphase modulation, which ensures the constant envelope property of the transmitted carrier signal

The coefficients, α_{L1}, β_{L1}, and γ_{L1}, adjust the relative power of the four components. The values determine the distribution of the total useful power among signal channels. The power distribution, shown in Table 10.3, aims at an equal sharing between L1P and L1F transmit power.

At reception, the L1 modulation scheme allows independent processing of the L1F and L1P signals in a GALILEO receiver.

The L1F received signal can be written as:

$$S_{L1F}^{rx}(t) = \alpha_{L1}\sqrt{2P_{L1}^{rx}}\left[s_{L1F\text{-}d}^{tx}(t - \tau_{L1}) - s_{L1F\text{-}p}^{tx}(t - \tau_{L1})\right]$$
$$\times \cos\left(2\pi(f_{L1} - \Delta f_{L1})(t - \tau_{L1}) + \theta_{L1}\right)$$

where P_{L1}^{rx} is the L1 total received power, τ_{L1} is the transmission delay at L1, Δf_{L1} is the carrier frequency offset (including Doppler offset), and θ_{L1} is the received phase.

Equivalently, the L1P received signal can be written as:

$$s_{L1P}^{rx} = \beta_{L1}\sqrt{2P_{L1}^{rx}} \cdot s_{L1P}^{tx}(t - \tau_{L1}) \cdot \sin\left(2\pi(f_{L1} - \Delta f_{L1})(t - \tau_{L1}) + \theta_{L1}\right)$$

Table 10.3 Distribution of L1 Useful Power Among Channels

Channel	Relative Signal Power
L1P	50%
L1F-d	25%
L1F-p	25%

10.3.2.2 E6 Signal

The transmitted GALILEO E6 signal $S_{E6}^{t_x}(t)$ consists of three components:

- *The E6C data channel (E6C-d):* The modulating signal is the modulo-two addition of the E6C navigation data stream $d_{E6C}(t)$ with the E6C-d channel PRN code sequence $c_{E6C\text{-}d}(t)$. The resulting signal is binary phase shift keyed onto the E6 carrier at 5.115×10^6 chip/s – BPSK-R(5).
- *The E6C pilot channel (E6C-p):* The modulating signal is the E6C-p channel PRN code sequence $c_{E6C\text{-}p}(t)$. This is binary phase shift keyed onto the E6 carrier at 5.115×10^6 chip/s – BPSK-R(5).
- *The E6P channel:* The modulating signal is the modulo-two addition of the E6P navigation data stream $d_{E6P}(t)$, the E6P channel PRN code sequence $c_{E6P}(t)$, and the binary E6P subcarrier $sc_{E6P}(t)$. This is binary phase shift keyed onto the E6 carrier with a code chipping rate of 5.115×10^6 chips/s and a subcarrier of 10.23 MHz – $BOC_c(10,5)$.

E6 signal components are multiplexed onto the E6 carrier signal by means of a modified hexaphase modulation [6]. E6C signal channels are modulated onto the in-phase component and the E6P channels are modulated on to the quadrature component of the E6 carrier signal.

$$S_{E6}^{t_x}(t) = \frac{\sqrt{2P_{E6}^{t_x}}\left[\alpha_{E6} \cdot s_{E6C\text{-}d}^{t_x}(t) - \alpha_{E6} \cdot s_{E6C\text{-}p}^{t_x}(t)\right] \times \cos(2\pi f_{E6}t) -}{\sqrt{2P_{E6}^{t_x}}\left[\beta_{E6} \cdot s_{E6P}^{t_x}(t) + \gamma_{E6} \cdot s_{E6,\text{int}}^{t_x}(t)\right] \times \sin(2\pi f_{E6}t)}$$

where:

$s_{E6C\text{-}d}^{t_x}(t) = d_{E6C}(t) \cdot c_{E6C\text{-}d}(t)$ = the E6C-d signal component

$s_{E6C\text{-}p}^{t_x}(t) = c_{E6C\text{-}p}(t)$ = the E6C-p signal component

$s_{E6P}^{t_x}(t) = d_{E6P}(t) \cdot c_{E6P}(t) \cdot sc_{E6P}(t)$ = the E6P signal component

$s_{E6,\text{int}}(t) = s_{E6C\text{-}d}^{t_x}(t) \cdot s_{E6C\text{-}p}^{t_x}(t) \cdot s_{E6P}^{t_x}(t)$ = the intermodulation product that ensures the constant envelope property of the transmitted signal

The coefficients, α_{E6}, β_{E6}, and γ_{E6}, adjust the relative power of the four components. The values determine the distribution of the total useful power among the sig-

Table 10.4 Distribution of
E6 Useful Power Among
Channels

Channel	Relative Signal Power
E6P	50%
E6C-d	25%
E6C-p	25%

nal channels. The distribution of the useful power, as shown in Table 10.4, aims at an equal sharing between E6C and E6P.

At reception, the E6 signal multiplexing scheme allows the independent processing of E6C and E6P signals.

The E6C received signal can be expressed as:

$$s_{E6C}^{r_x}(t) = \alpha_{E6}\sqrt{2P_{E6}^{r_x}}\left[s_{E6C\text{-}d}^{t_x}(t - \tau_{E6}) - s_{E6C\text{-}p}^{t_x}(t - \tau_{E6})\right]$$
$$\times \cos\left(2\pi(f_{E6} - \Delta f_{E6})(t - \tau_{E6}) + \theta_{E6}\right)$$

where $P_{E6}^{r_x}$ is E6 total received power, τ_{E6} is the delay between transmission and reception for E6, Δf_{E6} is the carrier frequency offset, and θ_{E6} is the received phase.

Also, the E6P received signal can be written as:

$$s_{E6P}^{r_x}(t) = \beta_{E6}\sqrt{2P_{E6}^{r_x}} \cdot s_{E6P}^{t_x}(t - \tau_{E6}) \times \sin(2\pi\Delta f_{E6}t + \theta_{E6})$$

10.3.2.3 E5 Signal

The transmitted GALILEO E5 signal $S_{E5}^{t_x}(t)$ consists of the multiplexing of four components:

- *The E5a data channel:* This is the modulo-two addition of the E5a navigation data stream $d_{E5a}(t)$ with the E5a data channel PRN code sequence $c_{E5a\text{-}d}(t)$, which has a chipping rate of 10.23 MHz.
- *The E5a pilot channel:* This is the E5a pilot channel PRN code sequence $c_{E5a\text{-}p}(t)$, which has a chipping rate of 10.23 MHz.
- *The E5b data channel:* This is the modulo-two addition of the E5b navigation data stream $d_{E5b}(t)$ with the E5b data channel PRN code sequence $c_{E5b\text{-}d}(t)$, which has a chipping rate of 10.23 MHz.
- *The E5b pilot channel:* This is the E5b pilot channel PRN code sequence $c_{E5b\text{-}p}(t)$, which has a chipping rate of 10.23 MHz.

The multiplexing of the four channels is achieved by means of the AltBOC(15,10) modulation according to the baseband expression [6, 7]:

$$S_{E5}^{t_x}(t) = \text{Re}\left[s_{E5}^{t_x}(t)\right]\cos(2\pi f_{E5}t) - \text{Im}\left[s_{E5}^{t_x}(t)\right]\sin(2\pi f_{E5}t)$$

with

$$s_{E5}^{tx}(t) = \frac{1}{2 \cdot \sqrt{2}} \cdot \left(s_{E5a\text{-}d}^{tx}(t) + j \cdot s_{E5a\text{-}p}^{tx}(t) \right) \cdot \left[sc_{E5\text{-}d}(t) - j \cdot sc_{E5\text{-}d}\left(t - T_{sc_{ES}}/4 \right) \right]$$

$$+ \frac{1}{2 \cdot \sqrt{2}} \cdot \left(s_{E5b\text{-}d}^{tx}(t) + j \cdot s_{E5b\text{-}p}^{tx}(t) \right) \cdot \left[sc_{E5\text{-}d}(t) - j \cdot sc_{E5\text{-}d}\left(t - T_{sc_{ES}}/4 \right) \right]$$

$$+ \frac{1}{2 \cdot \sqrt{2}} \cdot \left(\overline{s}_{E5a\text{-}d}^{tx}(t) + j \cdot \overline{s}_{E5a\text{-}p}^{tx}(t) \right) \cdot \left[sc_{E5\text{-}p}(t) - j \cdot sc_{E5\text{-}p}\left(t - T_{sc_{ES}}/4 \right) \right]$$

$$+ \frac{1}{2 \cdot \sqrt{2}} \cdot \left(\overline{s}_{E5b\text{-}d}^{tx}(t) + j \cdot \overline{s}_{E5b\text{-}p}^{tx}(t) \right) \cdot \left[sc_{E5\text{-}p}(t) - j \cdot sc_{E5\text{-}p}\left(t - T_{sc_{ES}}/4 \right) \right]$$

where the useful signal components are:

$$s_{E5a\text{-}d}^{tx}(t) = d_{E5a}(t) \cdot c_{E5a\text{-}d}(t) = \text{the E5a-d signal component}$$

$$s_{E5a\text{-}p}^{tx}(t) = c_{E5a\text{-}p}(t) = \text{the E5a-p signal component}$$

$$s_{E5b\text{-}d}^{tx}(t) = d_{E5b}(t) \cdot c_{E5b\text{-}d}(t) = \text{the E5b-d signal component}$$

$$s_{E5b\text{-}p}^{tx}(t) = c_{E5b\text{-}p}(t) = \text{the E5b-p signal component}$$

The respective dashed signal components $\overline{s}_{E5a\text{-}d}^{tx}(t)$, $\overline{s}_{E5a\text{-}p}^{tx}(t)$, $\overline{s}_{E5b\text{-}d}^{tx}(t)$, and $\overline{s}_{E5b\text{-}p}^{tx}(t)$, are product signals according to the following equations:

$$\overline{s}_{E5a\text{-}d}^{tx}(t) = s_{E5a\text{-}p}^{tx}(t) \cdot s_{E5b\text{-}d}^{tx}(t) \cdot s_{E5b\text{-}p}^{tx}(t)$$

$$\overline{s}_{E5a\text{-}p}^{tx}(t) = s_{E5a\text{-}d}^{tx}(t) \cdot s_{E5b\text{-}p}^{tx}(t) \cdot s_{E5b\text{-}d}^{tx}(t)$$

$$\overline{s}_{E5b\text{-}d}^{tx}(t) = s_{E5b\text{-}p}^{tx}(t) \cdot s_{E5a\text{-}d}^{tx}(t) \cdot s_{E5a\text{-}p}^{tx}(t)$$

$$\overline{s}_{E5b\text{-}p}^{tx}(t) = s_{E5b\text{-}d}^{tx}(t) \cdot s_{E5a\text{-}d}^{tx}(t) \cdot s_{E5a\text{-}p}^{tx}(t)$$

The parameters $sc_{E5\text{-}d}(t)$ and $sc_{E5\text{-}p}(t)$ are the four-level subcarrier functions used for the AltBOC modulation and represented in Figure 10.3:

$$sc_{E5\text{-}d}(t) = \sum_{k=1}^{8} a_k \cdot rect_{T_{sc_{ES}}}\left(t - k \cdot T_{sc_{ES}}/8 \right)$$

$$sc_{E5\text{-}p}(t) = \sum_{k=1}^{8} b_k \cdot rect_{T_{sc_{ES}}}\left(t - k \cdot T_{sc_{ES}}/8 \right)$$

with $T_{sc_{ES}}$ being the E5 subcarrier period and coefficients a_k and b_k according to Table 10.5.

The relative sharing of the total useful power in E5 among the four signal channels is as shown in Table 10.6.

At reception, the multiplexing adopted for the transmission of the E5a and E5b signals allows three alternative receiver implementations and processing:

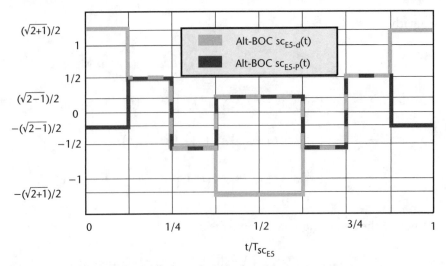

Figure 10.3 Periodic AltBOC modulation subcarrier functions.

Table 10.5   AltBOC Modulation Subcarrier Coefficients

k	1	2	3	4	5	6	7	8
$2 \cdot a_k$	$\sqrt{2}+1$	1	-1	$-\sqrt{2}-1$	$-\sqrt{2}-1$	-1	1	$\sqrt{2}+1$
$2 \cdot b_k$	$-\sqrt{2}+1$	1	-1	$\sqrt{2}-1$	$\sqrt{2}-1$	-1	1	$-\sqrt{2}+1$

Table 10.6   Distribution of E5 Useful Power Among Channels

Channel	Relative Signal Power
E5a-d	25%
E5a-p	25%
E5b-d	25%
E5b-p	25%

1. E5a single sideband reception;
2. E5b single sideband reception;
3. E5 (or E5a + E5b) wideband reception.

As a matter of fact, the E5a signal can be received and processed in isolation from the E5b signal, as if it was transmitted alone as a signal with in-phase and quadrature components according to the following:

$$s_{E5a}^{r_x}(t) = \sqrt{2 P_{E5a}^{r_x}} \cdot \left[\begin{array}{l} s_{E5a-d}^{t_x}\left(t - \tau_{E5a}\right) \times \cos\left(2\pi\left(f_{E5a} - \Delta f_{E5a}\right)\left(t - \tau_{E5a}\right) + \theta_{E5a}\right) - \\ s_{E5a-p}^{t_x}\left(t - \tau_{E5a}\right) \times \sin\left(2\pi\left(f_{E5a} - \Delta f_{E5a}\right)\left(t - \tau_{E5a}\right) + \theta_{E5a}\right) \end{array} \right]$$

where $P_{E5a}^{r_x}$ is the E5a total received power, τ_{E5a} is the delay between transmission and reception for L1, Δf_{E5a} is the carrier frequency offset, and θ_{E5a} is the received phase.

In the same way, the E5b signal can be received and processed in isolation from the E5b signal, as if it was transmitted alone as a signal with in-phase and quadrature components according to the following:

$$s_{E5b}^{r_x}(t) = \sqrt{2P_{E5b}^{r_x}} \cdot \left[\begin{array}{l} s_{E5b-d}^{t_x}(t - \tau_{E5b}) \times \cos(2\pi(f_{E5b} - \Delta f_{E5b})(t - \tau_{E5b}) + \theta_{E5b}) - \\ s_{E5b-p}^{t_x}(t - \tau_{E5b}) \times \sin(2\pi(f_{E5b} - \Delta f_{E5b})(t - \tau_{E5b}) + \theta_{E5b}) \end{array} \right]$$

where $P_{E5b}^{r_x}$ is the E5b total received power, τ_{E5a} is the delay between transmission and reception for L1, Δf_{E5a} is the carrier frequency offset, and θ_{E5a} is the received phase.

Finally, and as said previously, the E5 signal can be processed as a single large bandwidth signal into a receiver with an adequate processing that would generate a local replica with an AltBOC modulation. The receiver then would perform a complex correlation between the received signal and the local replica, using all four codes of the E5a and E5b signals.

A simplified implementation technique for the generation of the local replica is possible in the receiver, considering that the E5 AltBOC baseband signal $S_{E5}^{t_x}(t)$ can be also described as an 8-PSK signal with values [4]:

$$S_{E5}^{t_x}(t) = \exp\left(j \cdot \frac{\pi}{4} \cdot k \right) \text{ with } k \in \{1, 2, 3, 4, 5, 6, 7, 8\}$$

The relation of the 8-phase states to the 16 different possible states for the quadruples $s_{E5a-d}^{t_x}(t)$, $s_{E5a-p}^{t_x}(t)$, $s_{E5b-d}^{t_x}(t)$, $s_{E5b-p}^{t_x}(t)$ depends also on time. Therefore, time is partitioned first in subcarrier intervals $T_{sc_{E5}}$ and further subdivided in eight equal subperiods. The index i_{T_s} of the actual subperiod is given by:

$$i_{T_s} = \text{integer} - \text{part}\left[\frac{8}{T_{sc_{E5}}} \cdot (t \text{ modulo } T_{sc_{E5}}) \right] \text{ with } i_{T_s} \in \{1, 2, 3, 4, 5, 6, 7\}$$

and determines which relation between input quadruple and phase states has to be used.

The dependency of phase-states from input-quadruples and time is given in Table 10.7.

This representation allows the implemention and generation of the E5 signal using a look-up table according to the diagram shown in Figure 10.4.

GALILEO Spreading Codes

The PRN code sequences used for the GALILEO navigation signals determine important properties of the system. Therefore, a careful selection of GALILEO code design parameters was necessary. These parameters include the code length and its relation to the data rate, as well as the auto- and cross-correlation properties of the code sequences. The performance of the GALILEO codes is also given by the target acquisition time.

Table 10.7 Look-Up Table for AltBOC Phase States in Dependency of Input Quadruples and Time

	Input Quadruple															
$s_{E5a\text{-}d}^{tx}(t)$	−1	−1	−1	−1	−1	−1	−1	−1	1	1	1	1	1	1	1	1
$s_{E5b\text{-}d}^{tx}(t)$	−1	−1	−1	−1	1	1	1	1	−1	−1	−1	−1	1	1	1	1
$s_{E5a\text{-}p}^{tx}(t)$	−1	−1	1	1	−1	−1	1	1	−1	−1	1	1	−1	−1	1	1
$s_{E5b\text{-}p}^{tx}(t)$	−1	1	−1	1	−1	−1	−1	1	−1	1	−1	1	−1	1	−1	1

i_{T_s}	$t' = t$ modulo $T_{sc_{E5}}$ t'	k according to $S_{E5}^{tx}(t) = \exp(jk\pi/4)$														
0	$[\,0, T_{sc_{E5}}/8]$	5	4	4	3	6	3	1	2	6	5	7	2	7	8	8	1
1	$[T_{s,E5}/8, 2 \times T_{sc_{E5}}/8]$	5	4	8	3	2	3	1	2	6	5	7	6	7	4	8	1
2	$[2 \cdot T_{s,E5}/8, 3 \times T_{sc_{E5}}/8]$	1	4	8	7	2	3	1	2	6	5	7	6	3	4	8	5
3	$[3 \cdot T_{s,E5}/8, 4 \times T_{sc_{E5}}/8]$	1	8	8	7	2	3	1	6	2	5	7	6	3	4	4	5
4	$[4 \cdot T_{s,E5}/8, 5 \times T_{sc_{E5}}/8]$	1	8	8	7	2	7	5	6	2	1	3	6	3	4	4	5
5	$[5 \cdot T_{s,E5}/8, 6 \times T_{sc_{E5}}/8]$	1	8	4	7	6	7	5	6	2	1	3	2	3	8	4	5
6	$[6 \cdot T_{s,E5}/8, 7 \times T_{sc_{E5}}/8]$	5	8	4	3	6	7	5	6	2	1	3	2	7	8	4	1
7	$[7 \cdot T_{s,E5}/8, T_{sc_{E5}}]$	5	4	4	3	6	7	5	2	6	1	3	2	7	8	8	1

A first set of reference codes has been developed for GALILEO (referred to as the reference spreading codes) that offer a good compromise between acquisition time and protection against interference. These codes may be generated using linear feedback shift registers on-board the satellites and within GALILEO user equipment.

The reference ranging codes are constructed tiered codes, consisting of a short-duration primary code modulated by a long-duration secondary code (see Figure 10.5). As illustrated in Table 10.8, the resulting code then has an equivalent duration equal to one of the long-duration secondary codes. The primary codes are based on classical Gold codes, with register lengths up to 25. The secondary codes are predefined with sequences of lengths up to 100 bits.

At the time of this writing, alternative codes were being investigated. A strong consideration for the selection is flexibility of both spacecraft navigation payload and user receiver implementation with, for instance, the capability for on-board reconfiguration from ground.

The PRN code length for GALILEO channels carrying a navigation data message shall fit within one symbol for avoiding code ambiguity. The resulting code lengths are shown in Table 10.8.

For the dataless channels, the baseline approach is to consider long codes of 100-ms length. For the data channels, the overall code length is equivalent to one data symbol duration.

The transmitted L1F, E6C, E5a, and E5b signals for a particular GALILEO satellite are coherently derived from the same on-board frequency standard. All digital signals are clocked in synchronism with the PRN code chips and subcarrier transitions. Symbol bit edges for data channels are aligned with primary and secondary codes sequences, as illustrated in Figure 10.6.

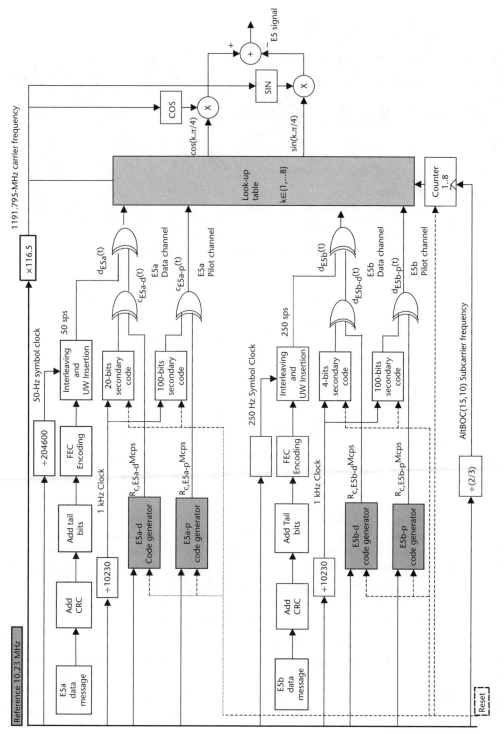

Figure 10.4 Possible AltBOC modulation implementation scheme.

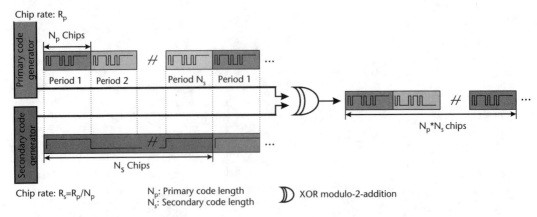

Figure 10.5 Structure of tiered codes.

Table 10.8 Main Characteristics of Spreading Codes

Channel	Code Sequence Duration (ms)	Primary Code Length (chips)	Secondary Code Length (bits)
E5a data	20	10,230	20
E5a pilot	100	10,230	100
E5b data	4	10,230	4
E5b pilot	100	10,230	100
E6P	Not public	Not public	Not public
E6C data	1	5,115	N/A
E6C pilot	100	5,115	100
L1P	Not public	Not public	Not public
L1F data	4	4,092	N/A
L1F pilot	100	4,092	25

GALILEO Message Frame Structure

The complete navigation messages will be transmitted on each data channel as a sequence of superframes. A superframe is composed of several frames, and a frame is composed of several subframes. The subframe is the basic structure for building the navigation message and contains the following fields:

- A synchronization word called *unique word* (UW);
- Cyclic redundancy check (CRC) bits for error detection;
- Tail bits for the FEC encoder, in a defined fixed state, containing all zeros.

All subframes are protected by rate half convolutional FEC encoding and block interleaving. The resultant symbol sequence is then summed with the corresponding PRN code and used to modulate the navigation signal component.

The GALILEO message frame structure is illustrated in Figure 10.7. The current baseline is to use a fixed frame format that allows flexibility in allocation of the subframes to a given message data content (integrity, almanac, ephemeris, clock correction data or ionospheric correction data). Parallel investigations are ongoing for

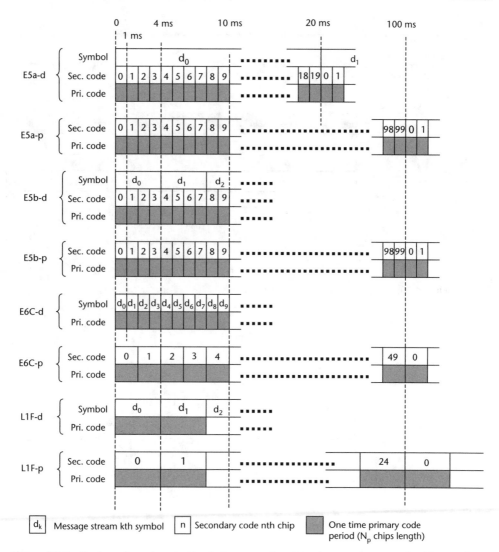

Figure 10.6 On-board synchronization between code subcarrier waveforms, code chips, and data symbols.

the GALILEO frame structure, aiming at increasing the transmission rate efficiency for the E5b and L1F signals in particular.

The subframe synchronization field is a fixed pattern (UW) that allows the receiver to achieve synchronization to the data field boundaries. The synchronization pattern is applied as uncoded data symbols at the transmitter.

The navigation message bit train, excluding the synchronization word, is rate 1/2 convolutional encoded with a FEC code. Therefore, the symbol rate is twice the original data rate. The convolutional coding has constraint length 7 and is characterized by polynomials $G_1 = 171$ (octal) and $G_2 = 133$ (octal), with a convolutional logic arrangement as illustrated in Figure 10.8.

As shown in Figure 10.7, each subframe contains a CRC parity block consisting of 24 bits covering the frame data field (excluding the synchronization pattern and the tail bits). To compute the CRC, the subframe is written as a polynomial in x,

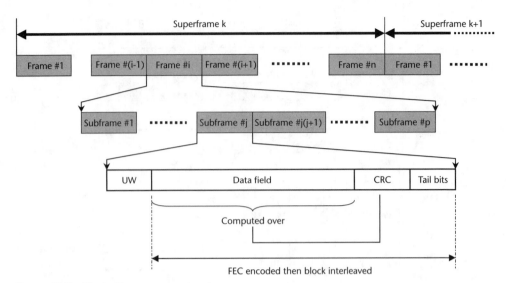

Figure 10.7   Navigation message structure.

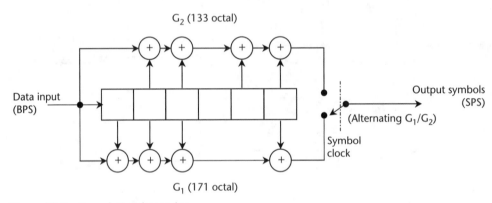

Figure 10.8   Convolutional encoder.

where the coefficient on X^N is the first transmitted bit of the subframe header and the coefficient of x^{12} is the last transmitted bit of the navigation data (N is the number of bits in the frame, including the CRC). This polynomial is divided by the generator polynomial $G(x)$ using modulo-2 arithmetic. The remainder is a polynomial of degree 11 in X. The first bit of the CRC is the coefficient of X^{11} in this polynomial, and the last bit of the CRC is the coefficient of X^0.

Finally, block interleaving is applied after convolutional encoding to all subframes, excluding the synchronization pattern. The block interleaver uses block sizes of $n \times k$ bits, where a $n \times k$ block interleaver takes $n \times k$ symbols and fills a matrix having k rows and n columns column by column; symbols are then transmitted row by row.

10.3.3   SAR Signal Plan

The SAR distress messages (from distress-emitting beacons to SAR operators) will be detected by the GALILEO satellites in the 406–406.1-MHz band and then broadcast to the dedicated receiving ground stations in the 1,544–1,545-MHz band, called L6 (below the E2 navigation band and reserved for the emergency services). The SAR data, from SAR operators to distress-emitting beacons, will be used for alert acknowledgment and coordination of rescue teams, and it will be embedded in the OS data of the signal transmitted in the E2-L1-E1 carrier frequency.

10.4   Interoperability Between GPS and GALILEO

Interoperability simply means combining information (e.g., pseudorange measurements, navigation data) from both the GPS and GALILEO systems at the user receiver to achieve better performance than employing either system separately.

The level of interoperability is a result of an optimization process. Factors considered in this process were radio frequency compatibility (RFC), complexity of the user equipment (receiver design), market prospects, vulnerability (common mode of failures), independence of the systems, and national security compatibility issues.

Looking closer to the interoperability of GPS and GALILEO, three topics are of primary importance:

- Signal in space;
- Geodetic coordinate reference frame;
- Time reference frame.

10.4.1   Signal in Space

The software implementation of the navigation message data processing in a user receiver allows de facto interoperability between GALILEO and GPS for the message data layer, at reduced receiver implementation cost and complexity. However, more consideration was needed for the physical layer for the choice of GALILEO signals carrier frequencies with respect to the GPS signals carrier frequencies. Processing two signals with different carrier frequencies requires increased receiver front-end complexity, as two separate down-conversion channels would be required. Furthermore, processing two signals with different carrier frequencies may cause frequency biases in the navigation solution. In particular, the high-precision position solutions that use carrier phase data may be degraded in terms of accuracy. GALILEO/GPS interoperability will be realized by a partial frequency overlap with sometimes different signal structures or different code sequences. At E5a and E2-L1-E1, GALILEO and GPS signals will be broadcast using identical carrier frequencies to L5 and L1, respectively. This will drastically simplify user receiver RF front-end design.

This simplification in RF front-end design comes, however, at the cost of intersystem interference between both systems due to the overlapping of signal spectrum accounting for their respective modulations. In the L1 band, the level of intersystem interference between secured or restricted-access signals and nonsecured or open-access signals has been limited by ensuring a sufficient spectral separation between them. This will allow, for instance, the jamming of civil signals without affecting GPS M code or the GALILEO PRS signal. By contrast, the choice for increased interoperability between GALILEO L1F and GPS modernized L1C (GPS III) open-access signal in the L1 band has been made, for the time being, since a common BOC(1,1) modulation was adopted out of the EU-U.S. negotiations on GALILEO and GPS. Starting from this baseline assumption, a process that is allowed by the EU-U.S. agreement is being put in place for further cooperation between both parties for a joint or isolated optimization of their respective signals modulation.

Another area of interest for interoperability at signal level is the selection of the PRN code families. Currently, GALILEO E5a and L1F signals have the same modulation and carrier frequency as the GPS L5 and modernized L1C signals (on GPS III), respectively. Having common code families could bring some more benefit to the user community.

10.4.2 Geodetic Coordinate Reference Frame

International civilian standards will be adopted for the GALILEO coordinate reference system. The realization of the GALILEO coordinate and time reference frame will be based on stations and clocks different from those of GPS.

The GALILEO Terrestrial Reference Frame (GTRF) shall be an independent realization of the International Terrestrial Reference System (ITRS). The ITRS is defined and monitored by the Central Bureau of the IERS.

The ITRF is based on a set of station coordinates and velocities derived from observations of very long baseline interferometry, satellite laser ranging, lunar laser ranging, GPS, and DORIS (the French Doppler system). A reduction of the individual station coordinates to a common reference epoch considering their station velocity models is performed using fixed plate motion models or estimated velocity fields. WGS-84 is the coordinate reference frame for GPS. WGS-84 is also a realization of the ITRS. Coordinates of both the GPS CS and NGA monitoring stations serve as a reference for WGS-84. The differences between WGS-84 and the GTRF are expected to be on the order of a few centimeters [8]. This implies that the WGS-84 and GTRF will be identical within the accuracy of both realizations (i.e., the coordinate reference frames are compatible). This accuracy is sufficient for navigation and most other user requirements. The remaining discrepancies are in the 2-cm level and are only of interest for very special research in the geosciences.

Coordinate reference frames often include Earth gravity models. For example, the WGS-84 uses a spherical harmonic expansion of the gravity potential up to the order and degree 360 [9]. For GALILEO, a similar model must be considered. In that context, the European satellite gravity missions Gravity Field and Steady-State Ocean Circulation Explorer and Challenging Mini-Satellite Payload for Geo-Scientific Research and Applications Program are of importance. The American Gravity Recovery and Climate Experiment will also provide data. The findings from these missions will serve as a basis for the GTRF Earth gravity model.

10.4.3 Time Reference Frame

GALILEO System Time (GST), modulo 1 second, is planned to be steered to a prediction taken from a number of UTC laboratories obtained through an external

GALILEO time service provider. GST is specified to be kept to within 50 ns (95%) of TAI over any 1-year time interval. The offset between TAI and GST will be known with a maximum uncertainty of 28 ns (2 sigma), assuming the estimation of TAI six weeks in advance. Users equipped with a GALILEO timing receiver will be able to predict UTC to 30 ns for 95% of any 24 hours of operation.

GPS System Time is the internal GPS navigation time scale, which is not adjusted for leap seconds and which is steered to UTC (USNO) modulo 1 second. GPS System Time is specified to be maintained to within one microsecond modulo integral seconds, and for the past eight years it has been maintained to within (+/–25 ns) of this goal. Once GALILEO is operational, it is anticipated by many that most users will use a combined GPS and GALILEO positioning, navigation, and timing service. There are two options for obtaining the GALILEO/GPS time offset:

- The user is able to determine the GALILEO/GPS time offset in the position and navigation processing at the cost of one additional satellite tracked (fifth satellite when determining a three-dimensional position).
- The offset could be measured by traditional time transfer techniques (e.g., two way, common view) or precisely estimated in near real time at the monitor station of both systems using a combined GPS/GALILEO receiver.

The latter option was adopted as part of the EU-U.S. agreement on the GALILEO/GPS interoperability. An interface control document (ICD) was jointly developed that will allow precise estimation of the GALILEO/GPS time offset and inclusion of it in each system's navigation message. The accuracy of this time offset modulo 1 second is specified to be less than 5 ns with 2-sigma confidence interval over any 24-hour period [10].

10.5   System Architecture

The GALILEO system will comprise a number of segments as illustrated in Figure 10.9.

- The space segment will consist of 30 satellites distributed over three planes. The design calls for nine satellites plus one (nonactive) spare satellite per plane.
- The ground segment will comprise a network of sensor stations, the control centers, and uplink stations. A global communication network will interconnect the centers and the stations.
- The user segment will consist of the satellite navigation receivers, a variety of which can be envisaged for exploiting the different types of GALILEO services.

Each segment is described in detail in the following sections.

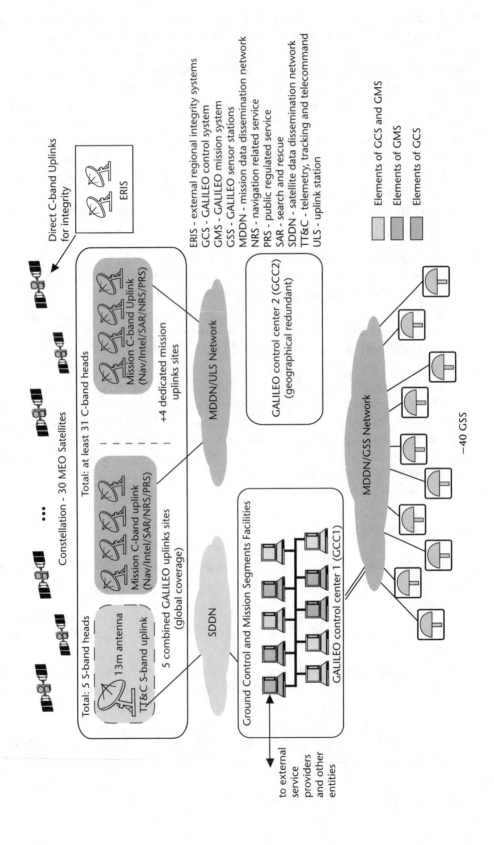

Figure 10.9 GALILEO system architecture.

10.5.1 Space Segment

The GALILEO space segment will comprise 27 operational satellites in a Walker constellation (see Section 2.3.2.3) with three orbital planes, equally spaced and with 56° nominal inclination. Each plane will contain nine satellites, nominally 40° apart. It is planned to keep a spare, nonoperational satellite in each orbit plane, so that a failure in the constellation may be repaired quickly by moving the spare to replace the failed satellite, which can be done in a matter of days, rather than waiting for a new launch to be arranged, which could take many months.

The orbit altitude above Earth of 23,222 km has been chosen so that the constellation has a repeat cycle of 10 orbits in 17 days. This is short enough to allow repeatability of measured characteristics while being long enough to avoid gravitational resonances; thus, after initial orbit optimization, station-keeping maneuvers will not be needed during the lifetime of a satellite. The position constraints for individual satellites are set by the need to maintain a uniform constellation, for which it is specified that each satellite should be within +/–2° of its nominal position relative to the adjacent satellites in the same orbit plane and should be within 2° of the orbit plane. The in-plane accuracy is equivalent to a relative tolerance of over 1,000 km but requires very careful adjustment of the satellite velocity to ensure that the orbit period of all of the satellites is kept precisely the same. The across-track tolerance allows the inclination and RAAN of each satellite to be biased at launch so that natural drifts remain within the tolerance without the need for orbit plane changes requiring major expense of fuel [11]. Table 10.9 lists the primary constellation parameters.

10.5.1.1 Satellite Description

The GALILEO satellite is a 680-kg/1,500-W class satellite. The satellite dimensions in launch configuration are shown in Figure 10.10.

The main drivers for the satellite design have been:

- Direct injection in MEO orbit;
- Optimization of the satellite size and mass for multiple launch;
- Modularity for assembly, integration, and verification (AIV) and series production;

Table 10.9 Primary Constellation Parameters

Constellation Parameters*		
Constellation	Walker 27/3/1 + 3 spare satellites	
Orbit	10 day/17 orbits repeat cycle	
Orbit parameter	Semimajor axis a	29,600.318 km
	Eccentricity e	0.002
	Inclination i	56°

*For altitudes above 23,000 km, the minimum number of satellites to achieve the required vertical accuracy is 24, with no major benefit beyond 30 satellites. For this range of altitude and number of satellites, three-plane constellations show the best performance. Furthermore, limiting the number of planes allows lower deployment costs and easier maintenance and replenishment strategies. The chosen inclination of 56° ensures a good coverage at Northern Europe latitudes.

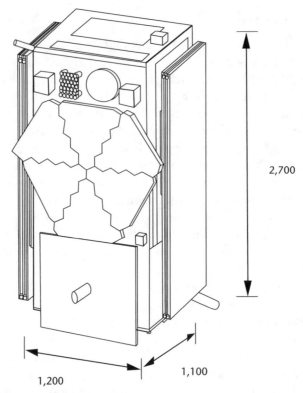

2,700

1,200   1,100

Figure 10.10 GALILEO satellite dimensions.

- Thermal stability for atomic clocks.

The satellite is based on modular elements in order to separate payload and platform and to allow parallel assembly, integration, and test (AIT) activities. An artistic picture of the satellite is shown in Figure 10.11.

The data handling and control is based on an integrated control and data unit that performs the control of the platform and payload. The attitude and orbital control system (AOCS) strategy is based on the steering of the MEO spacecraft to maintain the solar panels oriented towards the Sun (yaw steering). The AOCS will provide three-axis attitude control during all phases and maneuvers. Several operational modes are derived from the mission sequence of events.

- The normal mode is the nominal operational mode with full nadir pointing performance. A yaw steering capability is included to optimize the use of the solar panels and to support the thermal control of the satellite.
- An orbit change mode is provided for orbit acquisition, station-keeping maneuvers, and end-of-life (EOL) decommissioning. In the current GALILEO constellation design, very limited need for station-keeping maneuvers is anticipated.
- Finally, there are also dedicated Earth and Sun acquisition modes to be used during launch and early orbit phase (LEOP) as well as in contingency situations and safe modes for Earth reacquisition and survival mode.

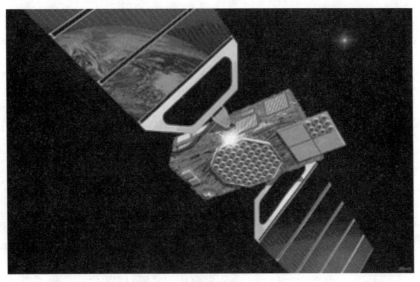

Figure 10.11 GALILEO satellite. (Courtesy of ESA.)

In normal mode, the AOCS sensor/actuator configuration is based on Earth and Sun sensors for attitude sensing together with reaction wheels for control. The angular momentum accumulated by the reaction wheels will be unloaded with magneto-torquers. In all other modes, a single-axis gyro is used for additional rate sensing, together with monopropellant thrusters for impulse and attitude control. Several of the modes can also operate in redundant configurations.

The propulsion subsystem is based on monopropellant thrusters. The baseline of direct injection means that no boost from a lower transfer orbit is needed. The propulsion subsystem is equipped with a set of eight thrusters; each thruster provides, under beginning of life (BOL) conditions, a nominal thrust of 1N. The propellant and pressurant masses are stored in a common tank. The tank is sized for up to 78 kg of usable monopropellant-grade hydrazine.

The power subsystem is responsible for the generation, storage, conditioning, and distribution of relevant power to the satellite. A power subsystem classical regulated 50-V bus architecture has been selected and it is composed of:

- A power conditioning and distribution unit;
- A single Li-Ion battery;
- Two solar array wings, each one composed of three panels (2,300 mm × 1,000 mm) equipped with silicon high-efficiency cells, providing 1,525W at 53V in EOL conditions, including one string failure as required by the power budget. Total solar array area is around 14 m^2.

The TT&C subsystem will provide redundant command reception, telemetry transmission, and turnaround ranging at S-band. The TT&C subsystem operates in two modes:

- ESA standard TT&C mode to be used during LEOP;
- Spread-spectrum mode to be used for nominal operations.

Furthermore, accurate range-rate (Doppler) measurements are possible when the S-band transponder is operated in coherent mode. S-band TT&C operations will be provided via two separate hemispherical-coverage helix antennas situated on opposite sides of the satellite. Designed for orthogonal circular polarization, together they will provide omnidirectional coverage for reception and transmission. The S-band antennas are provided with RHCP and LHCP, respectively. Ranging operation will be performed simultaneously with telemetry transmission.

Satellite Payload Description

The GALILEO satellite carries two payloads: a navigation payload and a SAR payload.

The navigation payload will broadcast navigation data on four carrier frequencies in the L-band, with each carrier modulated with the navigation data for a number of services. Refer to the navigation signal description in Section 10.3 for more detailed information.

The navigation data are uploaded to the GALILEO satellite by means of a dedicated CDMA C-band uplink. This enables uplinking several simultaneous signals.

The navigation payload features two different types of on-board clock technologies, a RAFS and a Passive Hydrogen Maser (PHM). Each type of technology has a redundant unit. These are shown in Figures 10.12 and 10.13, respectively, along with their measured stability in laboratory tests [12]. These tests indicated that both clocks largely exceed their respective design specifications.

The SAR transponder on GALILEO satellites will detect the distress alert from any COSPAS-SARSAT beacon emitting an alert in the 406–406.1-MHz band. The SAR transponder will rebroadcast this information to dedicated ground stations in the L-band (1,544 MHz). Particular emphasis is given to the SAR payload design to avoid negative mutual effects with respect to the navigation payload.

Once the beacon information has been received by the dedicated ground segment, COSPAS-SARSAT mission control centers (MCCs) carry out the position determination of the distress alert-emitting beacons. This is further discussed later in this chapter.

10.5.1.2   Launch Vehicle Description

In order to enable a cost-optimized placing of the spacecraft into orbit, a *launcher family* has been selected. This family is comprised of large launchers having the

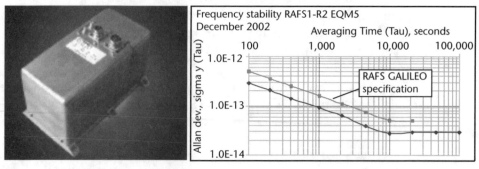

Figure 10.12   GALILEO RAFS and stability results.

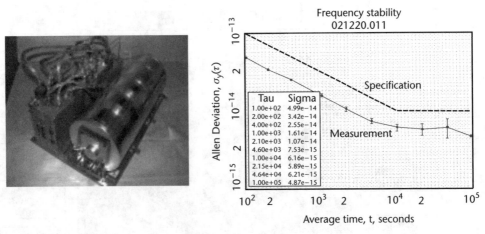

Figure 10.13   GALILEO PHM and stability results.

capability to carry up to six SVs per launch, and small launch vehicles to carry one or two SVs.

The currently identified launch vehicle configurations are as follow:

- Ariane 5: six satellites;
- Proton: six satellites;
- Soyuz 2 ST: one or two satellites;
- Zenit: one or two satellites with the possibility to extend up to three or four.

10.5.2   Ground Segment

The GALILEO Ground Segment comprises two major ground systems, the Ground Control Segment (GCS) and the Ground Mission Segment (GMS). It is implemented through:

- A global network of GALILEO Sensor Stations (GSSs) used for one-way ranging measurements and monitoring of the signal in space of the GALILEO satellites for orbit determination, time synchronization, integrity determination and supervision of provided services;
- A global network of TT&C stations for control of the GALILEO satellites and constellation;
- A global real-time oriented network of uplink stations (ULSs) for mission data (navigation, integrity, SAR, and other navigation-related services);
- An interconnecting high-performance communication network;
- Two geographically redundant GCCs for all the centralized processing, monitoring, and control.

LEOP and in-orbit testing (IOT) activities will be supported through renting or refurbishing of an existing infrastructure from LEOP and IOT service providers. Figure 10.14 provides an illustration of the physical architecture concept.

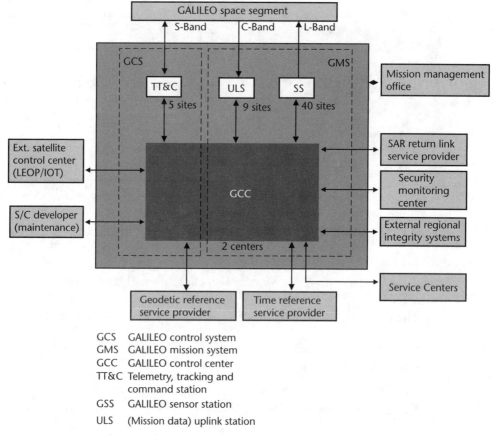

GCS   GALILEO control system
GMS   GALILEO mission system
GCC   GALILEO control center
TT&C   Telemetry, tracking and
       command station
GSS   GALILEO sensor station
ULS   (Mission data) uplink station

Figure 10.14 Ground Segment external interfaces.

The GALILEO Ground Segment will be implementing a number of GALILEO interfaces to external entities and to the other GALILEO segments as follows:

1. Interfaces to reference service providers:
   - Geodetic reference service providers to support the maintenance of the GTRF within the maximum offset to the ITRF and the independent verification/calibration of the orbital products of GALILEO using satellite laser ranging;
   - Time service providers to support the maintenance of GST to provide steering parameters for steering GST toward TAI and to validate GST.

2. Interfaces for service implementations of GALILEO:
   - Interface to service centers implementing commercial navigation service(s) of GALILEO;
   - Interface to GALILEO security monitoring centers monitoring the overall security functions and status of the GALILEO system to ensure its compliance with EU security policy;
   - Interface to external regional integrity service providers for using GALILEO for centralized dissemination of independently determined

integrity information of GALILEO through the GALILEO navigation signals;

- Interface to COSPAS/SARSAT for dissemination of SAR return-link messages through the GALILEO navigation signals.

3. Interfaces for satellite command and control:
   - Interface to the satellite/payload manufacturers of GALILEO for onboard software maintenance or support in contingency operations;
   - Interface to external satellite control centers for support to LEOP/IOT or contingency special operations.

10.5.2.1   GALILEO GCS

The GCS will perform all functions related to command and control of the satellite constellation:

1. Constellation management, dealing with all aspects of populating, maintaining, and replenishing the GALILEO satellite constellation, which include:
   - Long- and medium-term mission planning to ensure global coverage and continuity of the GALILEO signal in space;
   - Maintenance of the overall GALILEO satellite constellation;
   - Implementation of an adequate satellite replenishment strategy;
   - Recovery from contingencies and satellite failures minimizing the effects on the service provision.

2. Satellite control, dealing with all aspects of monitoring and controlling individual satellites for routine platform and payload operations or any unplanned critical operations in a contingency case, which include:
   - Satellite TT&C;
   - Scheduling of TT&C, ranging, or contingency access to individual satellites using the global network of TT&C stations;
   - Planning and execution of individual orbit maneuvers, platform maintenance, and payload commands;
   - Support for onboard software maintenance.

A TT&C station network will service the GALILEO satellite constellation. The TT&C network is composed of five ground stations with 13-m antennas working in the S-band and providing global coverage of the GALILEO constellation.

The design of the GCS is determined by the requirements for routine contacts with all satellites of the GALILEO constellation, the amount of telemetry data to be downloaded, the required number and volume of telecommands, and the capacity of the TT&C network to support nonroutine and contingency operations. Table 10.10 summarizes those drivers.

Table 10.10   Design Drivers for the GCS

Design Driver	Value
Routine operations	
• Telemetry data volume	1.5 MB/SV/orbit
• Telemetry downlink data rate	20 Kbps (information rate)
• Ground contact required	20–45 minutes/orbit (nominal); 60 minutes/orbit (worst case)
• Telecommand uplink data rate	1 Kbps (information rate)
Special Operations	
• Number of simultaneous contact	4
• Maximum contact duration	4 hours/orbit
• Maximum visibility gap duration	2 hours
TTC masking angle	5°

10.5.2.2   GALILEO GMS

The GMS implements the functions for providing the main services of GALILEO.

A real-time worldwide-distributed network of sensors (GSSs) will permanently monitor the GALILEO signal in space. The monitoring data obtained with these sensor stations will be used for orbit determination, time synchronization, and integrity monitoring.

The performance and sizing of such a network is driven by the SOL service integrity requirements. At present, the proposed GALILEO sensor network will be composed of approximately 40 worldwide-distributed stations.

The GSS network will collect one-way pseudorange raw measurements referenced to a local atomic reference clock with navigation messages received from the satellites. The GSS network provides this data with local meteorological and other data (such as monitor and control information and navigation data message) to the GCC.

Clock and Ephemeris Prediction

The GCC will host a centralized orbitography and synchronization processing facility (OSPF) that periodically computes the ephemeris data for each satellite and the clock data for each onboard clock.

The allocated contribution of ephemeris and clock determination and models to the UERE is predicted to be less than 65 cm (1σ). This results in the following main drivers:

- The prediction of orbits resulting in ephemeris data for broadcast to users will be valid for 12 hours and are, therefore, required to be uplinked to the satellites once per orbit (approximately 12 hours).
- The prediction of the onboard clock behavior resulting in the onboard clock correction data (OCCD) for broadcast to users depends on the stability of the frequency standard used onboard. Both PHMs and RAFS will be installed onboard the satellites. The use of the PHM is the current baseline. However, RAFS are short-term stable and therefore drive the Ground Segment capability

to uplink the OCCD. That is, RAFS corrections are valid for 100 minutes and, therefore, need to be uploaded to the satellites for dissemination to the users in 100-minute intervals.

Table 10.11 summarizes the navigation control drivers.

The GCC also hosts the precision timing facility (PTF), which represents an ensemble of high-performance atomic clocks of different types (currently two active hydrogen maser and four cesium) operated in a carefully controlled environment to ensure maximum clock stability. GST is computed by the OSPF, based on averaging of the different clock contributions (onboard and on the ground) with different weights. The clocks of the PTF participate in the establishment of the GST with the highest weight due to their high stability.

GALILEO time receivers are also installed with UTC(k) laboratories participating with the time service provider to determine the offset of GST with regard to their representation of UTC for steering of GST to TAI.

GALILEO Integrity Determination

In addition to SIS authentication, integrity determination for GALILEO will be achieved through the GSS network. The GSS network will monitor the navigation signal transmissions from all GALILEO satellites. With the known positions of the GSSs, the actual position of the SV can be determined. This SV position will enable the maximum error on the range measurement—the signal-in-space error (SISE)—to be estimated.

It is assumed that the prediction of the SISE distribution (which may not necessarily be Gaussian) can be overbounded by a nonbiased Gaussian distribution with the minimum standard deviation, called signal-in-space accuracy (SISA). With this distribution, the difference between the actual four-dimensional position (orbit and clock) of the SV and the predicted four-dimensional position on the navigation message is described in Figure 10.15.

The estimation of the SISE is also a statistical process. The assumption made in this case is that the distribution of the actual SISE around the value of the estimated SISE can be described with a Gaussian distribution with the standard deviation called signal-in-space monitoring accuracy (SISMA). The determination of the

Table 10.11 Design Drivers for Navigation Control

Design Driver	Value
Measurement data acquisition	
• Sampling frequency	30 seconds
• Minimum elevation angle	12.5°
• Number of receivers	1 nominal and 1 backup
• Number of carriers acquired	All (E5a, E5b, E6, L1)
• Maximum number of receiver channels	15
Navigation message generation	
• Clock and ephemeris contribution to UERE	65 cm
• Ephemeris prediction validity time	12 hours
• Clock prediction validity time	100 minutes (RAFS); 8.3 hours (PHM)

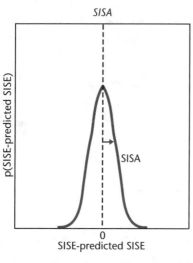
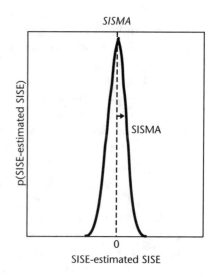

Figure 10.15   Illustration of SISA and SISMA.

SISMA values is dependent of the geometry between the available GSSs and the SVs. Thus, the difference between the true SISE and the estimated SISE can be described with this Gaussian distribution with the standard deviation SISMA (see Figure 10.15) [13].

The dimensioning of the GSS network is related to the SISMA value—the design goal is 70 cm with all GSS available and 1.3m in case of one GSS failing. At the GCC, an integrity processing facility estimates the SISE using the measurements of the GSSs to detect faulty satellites. If the estimated SISE for a satellite is larger than a certain threshold, the satellite will be flagged "don't use."

The system navigation function provides the quality of the SIS broadcast by SVs (i.e., SISA).

The system integrity function provides integrity information to the users containing:

- Accuracy of the GSS monitoring of the SIS broadcast by the SVs (i.e., SISMA);
- SIS broadcast by SVs that should not be used (i.e., integrity flag).

From this information, the user can derive his or her individual integrity risk. This integrity risk is always calculated for a given alert limit. The alert limit is the maximum allowed position deviation for which no alert has to be raised. Whenever the derived integrity risk at the alert limit is larger than the allowed integrity risk, the user equipment will raise an alert.

The dissemination of integrity information to users is driven by the following requirements:

- Three satellites in view of a user with a minimum elevation angle of 10° are located at a so-called worst-user location, ensuring that with a failure of one dissemination path, two independent paths are always maintained.
- Time to alarm (TTA) is less than 5.2 seconds from occurrence of the event until detection and dissemination by the GALILEO system to any user.

Table 10.12 summarizes control drivers for integrity determination and dissemination.

The navigation and integrity data sets, which are included in the navigation data message, are multiplexed and uplinked via the ULS network for dissemination to users through selected satellites. The uplink of integrity data requires real-time connectivity with the selected satellites for integrity dissemination.

The function of the ULS network is:

- To upload updated navigation data every 100 minutes (corresponding to the worst-case clock prediction validity time);
- To uplink to a subconstellation of satellites for the dissemination of integrity data in real time.

For this purpose, some nine stations fitted with five to six antennas[1] will be deployed worldwide in order to fulfill the global dissemination of integrity signals. The mission ULS are 3m antennas transmitting spread-spectrum signals in the C-band, without downlink implementation.

10.6 GALILEO SAR Architecture

GALILEO will contribute to the international SAR architecture and its associated provided services. It is planned to provide a SAR payload on each GALILEO satellite, which will be backward compatible with the present COSPAS/SARSAT system and provide a rich set of additional capabilities. The GALILEO Ground Segment will interface with Rescue Coordination Centers (RCCs) to allow for the dissemination of feedback messages to distress-emitting beacons. This architecture will fulfill

Table 10.12 Design Drivers for the Integrity System

Design Driver	Value
TTA	5.2 seconds
Integrity determination	
• Sampling frequency	1 second
• SISA	85 cm
• SISMA	0.7m (nominal GSS network); 1.3m (one GSS failure)
Integrity dissemination	
• Integrity flag update rate	1 Hz
• Integrity user masking angle	10°
• Minimum number of SVs in view broadcasting integrity data (diversity)	2 (user requirement)
• Uplink station masking angle	5°

1. The total number of ULS antennas is a function of the subconstellation broadcasting integrity data: in the case of a 15-satellite subconstellation, three to four antennas per ULS site are considered sufficient. The quoted number of five to six is related to all satellites broadcasting integrity data.

the requirements and regulations of the International Maritime Organization (IMO) and the ICAO for the detection of emergency beacons. It will be backward compatible with the COSPAS-SARSAT system to efficiently contribute to this international SAR effort.

GALILEO SAR services will provide enhanced service offerings with significant improvements:

* Reduced detection, localization, and confirmation delay;
* Extended distress message with additional information to improve SAR operations;
* Multiple satellite coverage to avoid terrain blockage in severe conditions;
* Increased availability of the SAR space segment;
* New return-link service from RCC to the distress-emitting beacon;
* Forward link via stand-alone payload (with SAR-dedicated up/downlink antenna);
* Return link integrated into navigation messages on L1 (up to six messages per minute), uplinked by the GALILEO Ground Segment.

Figure 10.16 depicts the defined architecture and the sequence of steps from distress message emission by the emergency beacon up to transmission of acknowledgment from the RCC.

10.7 GALILEO Development Plan

The GALILEO development has been structured according to the following phases:

* Overall development and validation phase (phases C/D/E1);

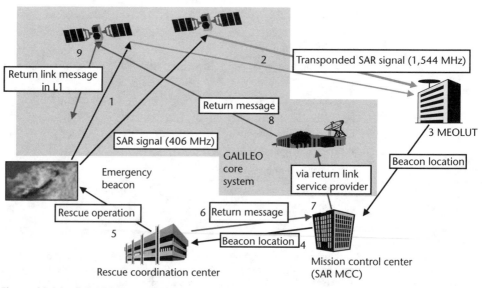

Figure 10.16 GALILEO SAR architecture.

   • Full deployment and operations phase (phase E2).

   The development and validation phase consists of the design, development, and in-orbit validation (IOV) of the so-called IOV system configuration. This configuration consists of a limited number of GALILEO satellites with the associated Ground Segment and initial operations. Following successful completion of this phase, additional satellites and Ground Segment elements will be deployed to achieve the so-called FOC system configuration leading to FOC.
   The activities contained under phases C/D/E1 address the following:

   • Overall system engineering, verification, and operations;
   • Development and IOV of the Space Segment, including the launch of a proto-type flight model satellite followed by three flight model satellites, IOT, and initial operations;
   • Development and validation of the GCS, including in particular S-band TT&C stations, associated communications network, and satellite control facilities within the GCC, including deployment and initial operations;
   • Development and validation of the GMS, including in particular L-band GSS, C-band ULS, associated communications network, processing, and mission control facilities within the GCC such as deployment and initial operations;
   • Development of test user equipment in support of system experimentation and validation.

   The configuration of the GALILEO system during IOV is scaled down from the full-operational configuration. Figure 10.17 shows the configuration for the IOV GALILEO system.

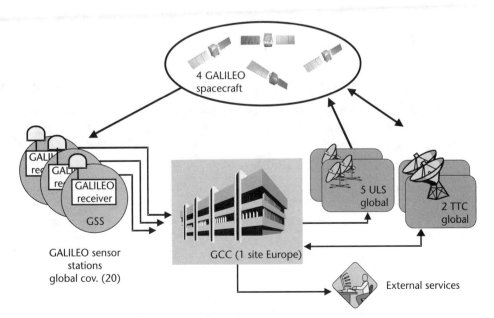

Figure 10.17   IOV GALILEO system configuration.

The activities contained under phase E2 address full system deployment (lasting around 24 months), long-term operations, and replenishment. It will consist of the launch of all remaining satellites (up to 30) and deployment of the full operational Ground Segment, including all required redundancies in order to comply with the full mission requirements in terms of performance and service area. The operations phase is planned to start during deployment of the full system, and it will consist of routine operations as well as Ground Segment maintenance and replenishment of the satellite constellation upon failure of one or more spacecraft. This phase is planned to last over the design lifetime of the system, about 20 years.

References

[1] GALILEO Mission High Level Definition, September 2003.

[2] Ries, L., et al., "A Software Simulation Tool for GNSS2 BOC Signals Analysis," *Proc. of ION GPS 2002,* Portland, OR, September 24–27, 2002, pp. 2225–2239.

[3] Pratt, A. R., and J. I. R. Owen, "Performance of GPS/Galileo Receivers Using m-PSK BOC Signals," *Proc. of ION NTM 2004,* 2004.

[4] Issler, J.-L., et al., "Spectral Measurements of GNSS Satellite Signals Need for Wide Transmitted Bands," *Proc. of ION GPS 2003,* 2003.

[5] Hein, G. W., et al., "Status of GALILEO Signal Design and Frequency Plan," *Proc. of ION GPS 2002,* Portland, OR, September 24–27, 2002.

[6] Soellner, M., "Comparision of AWGN Code Tracking Accuracy for Alternative BOC: Complex LOC and Complex-BOC Modulation Options in Galileo E5-Band," *Proc. of GNSS 2003,* 2003.

[7] Erhard, P., and E. Armengou-Miret, "Status and Description of Galileo Signals Structure and Frequency Plan," European Space Agency Technical Note, April 2004.

[8] Merrigan, M. J., et al. "A Refinement of the World Geodetic System 1984 Reference Frame," *Proc. of ION GPS 2002,* Portland, OR, September 24–27, 2002, pp. 1519–1529.

[9] Lemoine, F. G., et al., "The Development of the Joint NASA GSFC and NIMA Geopotential Model EGM96," NASA/TP-1998-206861, NASA Goddard Space Flight Center, Greenbelt, MA, July 1998.

[10] Hahn, J., and E. Powers, "GPS and Galileo Timing Interoperability," *Proc. of GNSS 2004,* Rotterdam, the Netherlands, May 2004.

[11] Zandbergen, R., et al., "Galileo Orbit Selection," *Proc. of ION GNSS 2004,* Long Beach, CA, September 2004.

[12] Emma, F., "Onboard Clocks for Galileo Development Status," *Proc. of International Workshop on Galileo Time,* Turin, Italy, September 27–28, 2004.

[13] Oehler, V., et al., "The Galileo Integrity Concept," *Proc. of ION GNSS 2004,* Long Beach, CA, September 2004.

CHAPTER 11

Other Satellite Navigation Systems

Scott Feairheller and Richard Clark
U.S. Air Force

11.1 The Russian GLONASS System

11.1.1 Introduction

GLONASS is the Russian counterpart to the U.S. GPS. Like GPS, the Russians designed GLONASS to provide PVT information to suitably equipped civil and military users. Unlike GPS, the Russians have been unable to sustain the satellite constellation at full strength, and, therefore, users can only navigate with GLONASS part of the time. The Russians are currently developing several new generations of modernized GLONASS spacecraft to replenish the constellation. The Russians do not expect to fully replenish the GLONASS constellation up to 24 satellites until 2011–2012.

As designed, the GLONASS space segment consists of 21 satellites plus 3 active spares. The ground support segment consists of a number of sites scattered throughout Russia that control, track, and upload ephemeris, timing information, and other data to the satellites. Each satellite currently transmits two L-band navigation signals. At the time of this writing, the Russians were planning to add a third L-band signal near the radio frequency of the new L5 signal planned for GPS, beginning in 2008. The Russians are developing a variety of user equipment for both civil and military applications. Other parties outside of Russia are also developing GLONASS civil user equipment.

11.1.2 Program Overview

The history of the GLONASS program is similar to GPS. Like GPS, the Soviet military initiated the GLONASS program in the mid-1970s to support military requirements. Originally, GLONASS was funded to support naval demands for navigation and time dissemination. Early system testing convincingly demonstrated that GLONASS could also support civilian use while concurrently meeting Soviet defense needs. Thus, the mission was broadened to include civilian users [1].

The Soviets launched the first GLONASS satellite on October 12, 1982. An initial test constellation of four satellites was deployed by January 1984. Normally, three satellites are launched simultaneously on an SL-12 Proton launch vehicle from

Kazakhstan. However, early in the program, the Soviets launched ballast payloads, instead of real satellites, to save production costs while the system was under development.

At a meeting of the Special Committee on Future Air Navigation Systems (FANS) of the ICAO in 1988, the USSR offered the world community free use of GLONASS navigation signals. A similar offer was made at the 35th Session of the IMO Subcommittee of Navigation Safety in the same year [1].

After the demise of the Soviet Union (SU), in 1990–1991, the Russians established a test constellation of 10 to 12 satellites. Extensive testing of the system followed this. As a result, in September 1993, Russian President Boris Yeltsin officially proclaimed GLONASS to be an operational system, part of the Russian Armory and the basis for the Russian Radionavigation Plan [2].

During the development, it became clear that GLONASS signals interfered with radio astronomy observations in the 1,610.6–1,613.8-MHz band. The international scientific community protested, and the Russians agreed to modify the future GLONASS frequency plan in November 1993. Under the plan, the Russians quickly ceased transmitting directly in the band, doubling up on navigation signal frequency-channel assignments, and they promised to gradually move the GLONASS signals out of the radio astronomy band as they depleted the stock of older satellites and replenished the constellation with new satellites. At the time of this writing, the Russians were continuing to follow through on their commitments to this plan [1, 3].

In April 1994, the Russians initiated the first of seven launches to complete the constellation. In December 1995, the Russians successfully launched the last set of three satellites to complete the 24-satellite constellation. In February 1996, these satellites were declared operational, and the constellation was fully populated for the first and only time. However, a number of older satellites soon thereafter failed, and the constellation quickly degraded. From 1996 through 2001, the Russians only launched two sets of three satellites. This was insufficient to maintain the constellation. The constellation degraded to six to eight satellites in 2001. To date, the constellation has not been restored to full operational strength.

During the buildup, the government of Russia issued Decree 237 on March 7, 1995, which opened the GLONASS C/A code signals up to the civil use and guaranteed it would be available free of charge, affirming the Soviet 1988 statement. (Section 11.1.9 contains signal characteristic descriptions.) The Russians also published and made publicly available an Interface Control Document, which detailed the structure of the GLONASS signals [4, 5].

Later, on February 18, 1999, the Russian president issued a decree 38-RP, which declared GLONASS a dual-use system. This was followed by a decree on March 29, 1999, opening GLONASS up for international cooperation. This allowed the Russians to negotiate with the EU for possible inclusion of GLONASS in the GALILEO program [6, 7].

The Russian Space Agency attempted to broker a deal with the Europeans on incorporating GALILEO into the GLONASS program. Separately the Russians conducted talks with China to fund GLONASS; however, neither effort appears to have succeeded.

On August 20, 2001, the Russian government passed Decree Number 587 entitled "Federal Dedicated Program (FTsP) Global Navigation System—2002–2011." This decree established a 10-year program to rebuild the GLONASS program. The program has a dedicated funding line in the Russian budget and is subject to Russian Parliamentary oversight. GLONASS is one of approximately 50 Russian programs, and the only Russian space program that receives this level of attention within the budgetary process. The GLONASS FTsP is a comprehensive program designed to fund the space segment, ground segment, user segment, user equipment manufacturing industry, transportation applications industry, and geodetic applications industry. Specifically, under the program, the GLONASS constellation will be replenished with 10–12 modernized GLONASS-M spacecraft and 18–27 new lightweight GLONASS-K spacecraft. The first visible fruits of this program came with the successful launch of a GLONASS-M satellite in late 2003. However, the long-term viability of GLONASS depends on successful transition to GLONASS-K in the 2008 time frame [8–12].

As of mid-2005, there had been 31 successful launches (2 launch vehicle failures) in the program, placing in orbit a total of 81 GLONASS satellites, 2 GLONASS-M satellites, 2 Etalon passive geodetic satellites, and 8 ballast payloads. (Ballast payloads are used to balance the payload if fewer than 3 satellites are launched.)

11.1.3   Organizational Structure

At the time of this writing, the Russian Ministry of Defense and the Russian Space Agency had jointly managed the GLONASS program since approximately 2002. The Russians have established an organization called the Interagency GLONASS Coordination Board (IGCB) to develop Russian national policy and facilitate international cooperation. The IGCB is similar in mission and structure to the U.S. Interagency GPS Executive Board (IGEB) established from 1996 through 2005. As of 2005, the Russians have not responded with similar changes in GLONASS management that correspond to U.S. government's expansion of GPS management from the IGEB to the GPS Executive Committee.

Prior to establishment of the IGCB, the Russian Ministry of Defense was both the principal user and owner of GLONASS. Within the Ministry of Defense, responsibility for GLONASS policy and operation fell under the Military Space Forces (VKS). GLONASS responsibility was further delegated within the VKS to the State Department of Space Means (GUKOS). GUKOS approved all GLONASS-related policies prior to 1999. GUKOS had management responsibility in the following areas: (1) system control center, (2) master system time clock, (3) command and tracking stations, (4) laser tracking stations, and (5) GLONASS Coordinating Scientific Information Center (CSIC) [1].

11.1.4   Constellation and Orbit

The GLONASS constellation will consist of 21 active satellites plus 3 active on-orbit spares. A depiction of the constellation is provided in Figure 11.1. The 24 satellites will be uniformly located in three orbital planes 120° apart in right ascen-

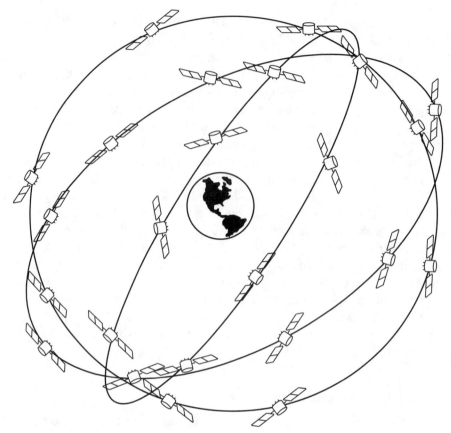

Figure 11.1 GLONASS satellite constellation.

sion. A 21-satellite constellation provides continuous 4-satellite visibility over 97% of the Earth's surface, whereas a 24-satellite constellation provides continuous observation of no fewer than 5 satellites simultaneously from more than 99% of the Earth's surface. Under the 21-satellite concept, the performance of all 24 satellites will be determined by GLONASS controllers and the "best" 21 will be activated. The remaining three will be held for backup or in reserve. Periodically, the mix will be evaluated and, if necessary, a new best set of 21 will be defined [1, 2, 13, 14].

Once the permanent system of 21 operational and 3 spare satellites is established, a single satellite failure would not lower the system design probability of successful fix determination below 94.7%. (Available reference material did not specify whether the term "successful fix determination" is referring to a two-dimensional and/or a three-dimensional fix.) When necessary to maintain system accuracy, new satellites will be launched and used either to replace malfunctioning satellites or held in reserve for future use [1].

Each GLONASS satellite is in a 19,100-km circular orbit referenced to the Earth's surface with an inclination of 64.8°. The orbital period is 11 hours and 15 minutes. The current orbital configuration and overall system design (including satellite nominal L-band antenna beamwidths of 35° to 40°) provide navigation service to users up to 2,000 km above the Earth's surface [1].

11.1.5   Spacecraft Description

The Russians are currently populating the GLONASS constellation with two types of spacecraft, the original GLONASS satellite-series design and the new GLONASS-M satellite-series design. Within each series, there are different blocks that denote subtle changes in the spacecraft payloads and electronics. These changes were introduced to increase satellite lifetime [9–12].

11.1.5.1   GLONASS

From 1982 through 2005, the Russians planned to launch GLONASS series satellites. This satellite is a traditional Russian design consisting of a pressurized, hermetically sealed cylinder that is three-axis stabilized (i.e., oriented in all three axes of motion, usually measured as in-track, cross-track, and radial from the satellite's point of view). Circulation of gas inside the pressurized vessel allows for cooling of the satellite electronics. Attached to the bottom of the spacecraft is the payload assembly. This assembly consists of the horizon sensor, laser retroreflectors, a 12-element navigation signal antenna, and various command and control antennas. Attached to the sides of the pressurized cylinder are the solar panels, orbital correction engines, a portion of the attitude control system, and the thermal control louvers [1]. A GLONASS satellite is shown in Figure 11.2.

Within the original GLONASS series, there have been two major block changes (referred to as types I and II by the Russians) and three variants (referred to as a, b, and c) within the second block. The main difference between the spacecraft blocks is the design lifetime. Early satellites had design lifetimes of 1 to 2 years. At the time of this writing, the Russians were launching GLONASS type IIc spacecraft with a 3-year design lifetime. A tabulation of the GLONASS satellites, their respective orbital locations, and frequency assignments is contained in Table 11.1. Unlike GPS, which transmits CDMA format, GLONASS employs frequency division multiple access (FDMA) [1]. (Details on this scheme are provided in Section 11.1.9.)

Figure 11.2   GLONASS satellite.

Table 11.1 GLONASS Constellation Status as of February 25, 2005

Spacecraft Number	Cosmos Number	Orbital Plane/Slot	Frequency Channel	Launch Date	Introduction Date	Status
796	2413	1/01	02	Dec. 26, 2004	Feb. 6, 2005	Under test
794	2402	1/02	04	Dec. 10, 2003	Feb. 2, 2004	Operating
789	2381	1/03	12	Dec. 1, 2001	Jan. 4, 2002	Unusable
795	2403	1/04	06	Dec. 10, 2003	Jan. 30, 2004	Operating
711	2382	1/05	02	Dec. 1, 2001	Apr. 15, 2003	Operating
701	2404	1/06	10	Dec. 10, 2003	Dec. 10, 2004	Operating
712	—	1/07	—	Dec. 26, 2004	—	Under test
797	—	1/08	06	Dec. 26, 2004	Feb. 6, 2005	Operating
787	2375	3/17	05	Oct. 13, 2000	Nov. 4, 2000	Operating
783	2374	3/18	10	Oct. 13, 2000	Jan. 5, 2001	Operating
792	2395	3/21	05	Dec. 25, 2002	Jan. 31, 2003	Operating
791	2394	3/22	10	Dec. 25, 2002	Feb. 10, 2003	Operating
793	2396	3/23	11	Dec. 25, 2002	Jan. 31, 2003	Operating
788	2376	3/24	03	Oct. 13, 2000	Nov. 21, 2000	Operating

The onboard navigation complex (OBNC) is the nucleus of the satellite. The OBNC is composed of an information logical complex (ILC) unit, a set of three spacecraft atomic clocks, a memory unit, a TT&C link receiver, and navigation signal transmitters. The complex operates in one of two modes: recording mode or transmission mode. In recording mode, navigational information is uplinked to the satellite and then stored in onboard memory. Under normal conditions, new navigational data is uplinked to the satellite every orbit. In transmission mode, the OBNC generates navigational signals on two carrier frequencies, one frequency from each band: 1,246–1,257 MHz and 1,602–1,616 MHz. As in GPS, these navigational signals supply the users with information such as satellite ephemeris data, atomic clock corrections, and almanac data, and provide a satellite-to-user ranging capability [1].

The ILC performs three primary functions [1]:

1. Recording of satellite ephemeris and system almanac data uplinked from the ground stations;
2. Controlling of navigation signal formulation, including the navigation frames, which are analogous to the GPS navigation message;
3. Performing of regular diagnosis of OBNC performance.

The onboard clock is the most critical element of the GLONASS satellite. It is the long-term stability and predictability of modern atomic clocks that makes the concept of navigation satellite systems possible. The current block IIc spacecraft carry three "Gem" cesium-beam frequency standards, which are produced by the Russian Institute of Navigation and Time. The standards have dimensions of 370 by 450 by 500 mm, weigh 39.6 kg, and have an operational lifetime of 17,500 hours. Each standard has the following frequency stability (i.e., Allan variance) characteristics for the following averaging times: 5×10^{-11} at 1 second, 1×10^{-11} at 100 seconds, 2.5×10^{-12} at 1 hour, and 5×10^{-13} at 1 day [1, 15]. Appendix B contains a detailed description of the Allan variance and its applicability to satellite navigation.

11.1.5.2   GLONASS-M

In 2003, the Russians began launching the new GLONASS-M spacecraft, where "M" stands for *Modified*. The GLONASS-M is a modernized version of the GLONASS spacecraft using more modern electronics and supporting a number of new features. Although the first launch occurred in 2003, GLONASS-M is an older spacecraft design, first conceived in the early 1990s but not sufficiently funded until 2001. GLONASS-M continues the design practice of housing the satellite electronics in a heavy pressurized gas-filled vessel, similar to the original GLONASS spacecraft design. The older design requires the continued use of the expensive Proton launch vehicle to launch a set of three satellites into orbit. As a result, the Russians plan only to build and launch a total of 10 to 12 GLONASS-M satellites over the next several years to act as a gap-filler until they complete the design and production of the next generation of satellites, GLONASS-K. The GLONASS-K spacecraft is projected to be much smaller and half the weight, thus reducing program costs significantly [9–12, 16–18]. The GLONASS-M has a number of new features. These include:

1. *Improved navigation performance.* GLONASS-M carries a more accurate satellite clock (Allan variance of 1×10^{-13} at 1 day), a better attitude control system, and intersatellite navigation links (incorporated after the second GLONASS-M satellite). These features will improve user PVT accuracy by reducing errors in measurements of time and ephemeris calculation [9–12, 16–18].

2. *Longer lifetime.* GLONASS-M carries an increased propellant loading, improved onboard batteries, and modernized spacecraft electronics. These features support a longer design-lifetime of 7 years [9–12, 16–18].

3. *Improved navigation signals.* This feature will add a second civil modulation on L2 signal and capability to shift the signals from channels –7 to +12. The addition of a second civil frequency will allow civil users to make ionospheric corrections, thus improving accuracy. The additional channels will allow the Russians to fulfill international commitments to move the navigation signals out of the radio astronomy frequency band. In addition, the satellite will carry filters, which will remove out-of-band emissions in the 1,610.6–1,613.8-MHz and 1,660.0–1,670.0-MHz radio astronomy bands [9–12, 16–18].

4. *Improved navigation message.* This feature will transmit corrections between GPS and GLONASS time to facilitate joint use; navigation data authentication information every 4 seconds; navigation age-of-data information; and warnings about the future adjustment of the GLONASS time scale with leap-second correction [9–12, 16–18].

Like the original GLONASS spacecraft, the GLONASS-M spacecraft consists of a pressurized, hermetically sealed cylinder that is three-axis stabilized. Figure 11.3 is a depiction of the GLONASS-M spacecraft. By contrast, the solar panels are attached to the top of the cylinder, and the payload assembly (attached on the bottom of the spacecraft) is much larger in one dimension. The spacecraft mass will be increased from the current satellite mass of approximately 1,300 kg to approximately 1,480 kg. This assembly consists of the horizon sensor, laser retroreflectors, a 12-element navigation signal antenna, a cross-link antenna, and various command and control antennas. The longer assembly allows the navigation payload and laser retroreflector arrays to be mounted separately instead of interleaved. Attached to the sides of the pressurized cylinder are the orbital correction engines, a portion of the attitude control system, and the thermal control louvers [1, 9–12, 16–18].

11.1.6 Ground Support

The ground-based control complex (GBCC) is responsible for the following functions [1]:

1. Measurement and prediction of individual satellite ephemeris;
2. Uploading of predicted ephemeris, clock corrections, and almanac information into each GLONASS satellite for later incorporation into the navigation message;
3. Synchronization of the satellite clocks with GLONASS system time;
4. Calculation of the offset between GLONASS system time and UTC (Soviet Union);
5. Spacecraft command, control, housekeeping, and tracking.

The functions of the ground control segment had been performed by a number of sites located within the former Soviet Union. With the demise of the USSR, the

Figure 11.3 GLONASS-M spacecraft.

ground support segment has been reduced to sites within Russia, with the exception of one laser tracking site as indicated in Table 11.2. Further changes may also occur in the future, including the addition of other control sites within the VKS control network [1–4].

11.1.6.1   SCC

The SCC is a military complex run by the Russian Space Forces and is located in Golitsyno-2, about 70 km southwest of Moscow. The SCC schedules and coordinates all system functions for GLONASS [1].

11.1.6.2   Central Synchronizer

The central synchronizer forms GLONASS system time. Signals from the central synchronizer are relayed to the phase control system (PCS), which monitors satellite clock time/phase as transmitted by the navigation signals. The PCS performs two types of measurements to determine the satellite time/phase offsets. The PCS directly measures the range to the satellites by use of radar techniques. The PCS also simultaneously compares the satellite transmitted navigation signals to a reference time/phase generated by a highly stable frequency standard (relative error approximately 10^{-13}) at the ground site. These two measurements are then differenced to determine the satellite clock time/phase offsets. The range of the satellite can only be measured with an accuracy of 3m to 4m, which limits the accuracy of the time/phase measurements. Measurements from the PCS are used to predict the satellite clock time/phase corrections, which are uploaded by the ground station into the satellite. This comparison of each satellite's time/phases errors is carried out on at least a daily basis [1, 19].

11.1.6.3   Command and Tracking Stations

The command and tracking stations (CTSs) measure individual satellite trajectories and uplink required control and payload information to the satellite's onboard processor. Trajectory tracking is carried out every 10 to 14 orbits. Tracking involves between three and five measurement sessions, each lasting 10 to 15 minutes. Range

Table 11.2   GLONASS Ground Control Support Network

Site Function	Former USSR Network	Current Russian Network
System control center (SCC)	Golitsyno-2	Golitsyno-2
Central synchronizer	Moscow	Moscow
Phase control system	Moscow	Moscow
Command and tracking stations	St. Petersburg, Yeniseisk, Komsomolsk, Balkhash, and Ternopol	St. Petersburg, Yeniseisk, and Komsomolsk
Laser tracking stations	Komsomolsk, Balkhash, Kitab, Evpatoria, and Ternopol	Komsomolsk and Kitab
Navigational field control equipment	Moscow, Komsomolsk, and Ternopol	Moscow and Komsomolsk

of the satellite is measured by radar techniques with a maximum error of between 2m and 3m. These radio-frequency ranges are periodically calibrated using a laser ranging device at the laser tracking stations. Each satellite carries laser retroreflectors specifically for this purpose. Ephemeris is predicted 24 hours in advance and uploaded once per day. The spacecraft clock correction parameters are renewed twice a day. Therefore, timing errors of the satellites' ranging signals can lead to a pseudorange measurement error of at most 5m to 6m. Any interruption in the normal operation of the ground segment interrupts the accuracy of GLONASS signals. Tests have shown that the spacecraft clock can maintain acceptable accuracy (one part in 5×10^{13}) for no more than two to three days of autonomous operations. Although the satellite's central processor is capable of 30 days of autonomous operations, this variability in the time standard is the limiting component for autonomous GLONASS operations [1].

11.1.6.4   Laser Tracking Stations

GLONASS is supported by the Etalon (Komsomolsk) and Maidanak (Kitab) laser stations. These stations calibrate radio-frequency tracking measurements. These systems may be third generation laser systems.

Etalon stations are able to measure the position of satellites visible in reflected solar light down to stellar magnitudes of less than 13. Range errors based on a 15-second averaging interval are about 1.5–2 cm and between 2 and 3 arcsec in angular position. Detailed specifications of these third generation military systems remain classified [1].

GLONASS is supported by an experimental multifunctional optical and laser complex located near Kitab in southern Uzbekistan on Mt. Maidanak. Cameras located on Mt. Maidanak are capable of measuring ranges to an object up to an altitude of 40,000 km and down to a visible stellar magnitude of 16. Maximum error of satellite angular coordinate determination does not exceed 1–2 arcsec under normal operating conditions and 0.5 arcsec under special experimental conditions. Maximum ranging error is not more than 1.5–1.8 cm, and the error of the fix to the UTC(SU) scale is not more than +/–1 μs. GLONASS measurements are relayed via secure radio link to the system control center once per hour. Mt. Maidanak provides unique climatic characteristics with more than 220 clear days annually, thus making it a reliable source of correction data to the system control center [1, 2].

11.1.6.5   Navigation Field Control Equipment

The navigation field control equipment stations monitor the GLONASS navigation signals. If anomalies are observed, they are reported back to the SCC [1].

11.1.7   User Equipment

The Russian GLONASS user segment is small and concentrated primarily in Russia. Russian industry has designed many different types of GLONASS and GPS-GLONASS user equipment and listed these for sale on the Russian Internet. However, since the mid-1990s, the Russian press has carried numerous complaints about the lack of development of the GLONASS user segment, indicated by a lack of users. Outside of Russia, only a few types of GPS-GLONASS user equipment are manufactured, primarily for high-end geodetic applications. As a result, the Russians plan to invest in development of the GLONASS user equipment and in the GLONASS applications industry under the FTsP Global Navigation System—2002–2011. Under current plans, the Russians project that the number of future GLONASS civil users will grow but will remain significantly less than for GPS outside Russia.

11.1.8   Reference Systems

GLONASS provides position and time in Russian reference systems.

11.1.8.1   Geodetic References

Since August 1993, GLONASS has transmitted ephemeris data in the Earth Parameter System 1990 (PZ-90). Prior to that time, GLONASS provided data in the Soviet Geodetic System 1985 (SGS-85). PZ-90 is similar in quality to the Earth model employed in WGS-84 used by GPS [3].

The basic characteristics of PZ-90 are provided in Table 11.3 [3, 20, 21].

Details on the SGS-90 are provided in the Russian document "Parameters of the General Earth Ellipsoid and Earth Gravity Field SGS-90" by the Military Topographic Department of the General Staff, Editorial Department, Moscow 1991. To date, the Russians have not made this document publicly available. Although GLONASS transmits ephemeris and almanac data using PZ-90, the output of most

Table 11.3   PZ-90 Characteristics

Name and Designation of the Constant	Unit of Measurement	Value
Fundamental Geodetic Constants		
Angular rate of rotation of Earth (ω)	rad/s	$7.292\ 115 \times 10^{-5}$
Geocentric gravitational constant, including atmosphere (GM)	m^3/s^2	$398{,}600.44 \times 10^9$
Geocentric gravitational constant of atmosphere (GM_A)	m^3/s^2	0.35×10^9
Speed of light (c)	m/s	$299{,}792{,}458$
Parameters of the Common Terrestrial Ellipsoid		
Semimajor axis (a_e)	m	$6{,}378{,}136$
Denominator of compression ($1/\alpha$)	Unit of denominator	298.25784
Acceleration of gravity at the equator ($\gamma\varepsilon$)	mgal	$978{,}032.8$
Correction in the acceleration of gravity, γ, due to the attraction of atmosphere at sea level ($\delta\gamma_a$)	mgal	-0.9
Other Constants		
Second harmonic coefficient (J^0_2)	—	$1{,}082{,}625.7 \times 10^{-9}$
Fourth harmonic coefficient (J^0_4)	—	$-2{,}370.9 \times 10^{-9}$
Normal potential on the surface of the common terrestrial ellipsoid (U_0)	m^2/s^2	$62{,}636{,}861$

Russian-built receivers is in the Soviet Krasovskiy-1942 (SK-42) reference coordinate system. SK-42 is used as the reference for Russian and former Soviet Bloc maps in Eastern Europe and Asia [21].

The Russians have performed a limited number of measurements within western Russia and determined a preliminary rotation matrix between PZ-90 and WGS-84. Details of this rotation matrix are contained in [21].

The Russians believe that this matrix is good to within 5m to 10m, but caution that measurements should be made in a number of locations throughout the world in order to verify the rotation matrix and the magnitude of its error [21].

11.1.8.2   Time References

GLONASS provides time in both GLONASS system time, which is kept in Moscow, and in UTC(SU), which is kept at the All Union Institute for Physical, Technical, and Radio-Technical Measurements in Mendeleevo near Moscow [1, 7].

11.1.9   GLONASS Signal Characteristics

Unlike GPS, where each satellite transmits a unique PRN code pair—C/A and P(Y)—on the same frequency in a CDMA format, each GLONASS satellite transmits the same PRN code pair on a different frequency. This process, FDMA, is the same method used by commercial radio and television stations. Each station is analogous to a GLONASS satellite, and the radio receivers are analogous to GLONASS receivers. A GLONASS receiver "tunes in" a particular GLONASS satellite in the same manner one would tune in their favorite radio station—by tuning in the frequency allocated to the desired satellite.

The choice of FDMA over CDMA is one of the design tradeoffs. FDMA typically results in larger, more expensive receivers because of the extra front-end components required to process multiple frequencies. By contrast, CDMA signals can be processed with the same set of front-end components. FDMA does have some redeeming qualities in terms of interference rejection. A narrowband interference source that disrupts only one FDMA signal would disrupt all CDMA signals simultaneously. Furthermore, FDMA eliminates the need to consider the interference effect between multiple signal codes (cross-correlation). Thus, GLONASS offers more frequency-based interference rejection options than GPS and has a more simplified code-selection criterion. Each GLONASS satellite transmits signals centered on two discrete L-band carrier frequencies. Each carrier frequency is modulated by the modulo-2 summation of either a 511-kHz or 5.11-MHz PRN ranging code sequence and a 50-bps data signal. This 50-bps data signal contains the navigation frames and is denoted as the navigation message. Figure 11.4 shows a simplified block diagram of the signal generator. Details of the frequencies, modulation, PRN code properties, and navigation message are covered next [1, 22, 23].

11.1.9.1   GLONASS Frequencies

Each GLONASS satellite is allocated a pair of carrier frequencies, referred to as L1 and L2, according to the following equation:

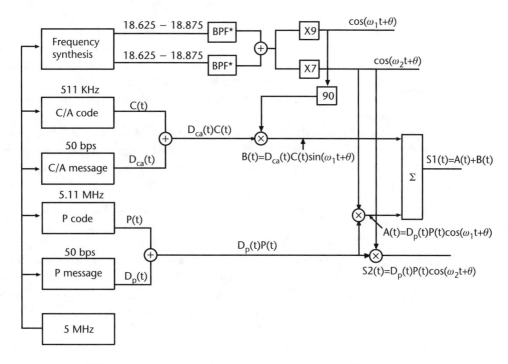

*BPF = Passband determined by satellite frequency assignment number.
Frequency synthesis is for k = 0 to 24; this will change for new satellites.

Figure 11.4   GLONASS signal generator.

$$f = \left(178.0 + \frac{K}{16}\right) \cdot Z \quad (\text{MHz})$$

where:

K = an integer value between −7 and +12

Z = 9 for L1, 7 for L2.

The spacing between adjacent frequencies on L1 is 0.5625 MHz and L2 is 0.4375 MHz. Originally, K was a unique integer for each satellite and varied from 0 to 24. But, due primarily to interference with radio astronomy measurements, the Russians have proposed the following modifications to their frequency assignments [24]:

• Through 1998: K = 0 to 12;
• From 1998–2005: K = −7 to 12;
• After 2005: K = −7 to 4.

The end result is to move the frequencies away from the radio astronomy band. Additionally, the final configuration will only use 12 values of K (K = −7 to 4) for the 24 satellites. The plan is to have satellites on opposite sides of the Earth (antipodal) share the same K number (i.e., broadcast on the same frequency). This center frequency modification will have little effect on terrestrial users who cannot see antipodal satellites simultaneously. Space-based receivers may require special discriminating functions, such as Doppler checks, in order to track the proper satellite. This ability to discriminate antipodal satellites is important, since the antenna beamwidths on the GLONASS-M satellites are specifically designed to accommodate space-based users [1, 25].

The values of K listed earlier are the proposed values for satellites operating under normal conditions. Other values of K may be assigned for certain command and control processing tasks or under "exceptional circumstances," according to the Russians [1].

11.1.9.2 Modulation

In a similar manner as GPS, each satellite modulates its L1 carrier frequency with two PRN ranging sequences. (As shown in Figure 11.4, both sequences are modulo-2 added with navigation data before modulating the carrier.) One sequence, called the P code, is reserved for military purposes. The other sequence, called the C/A code, is for civil use and aids acquisition of the P code. Each satellite modulates its L2 carrier frequency solely with the modulo-2 summation of P code and navigation data. The P code and C/A code sequences are the same for all satellites [1, 22, 23].

11.1.9.3 Code Properties

Both GLONASS and GPS use pseudorandom codes that facilitate satellite-to-user ranging and have inherent interference rejection. GLONASS C/A code and P code sequences are described next [1, 22, 23].

GLONASS C/A Code
The GLONASS C/A code has the following characteristics:

- Code type: Maximal length 9-bit shift register;
- Code rate: 0.511 Mchips/s;
- Code length: 511 chips;
- Repeat rate: 1 ms.

A maximal-length code sequence exhibits predictable and desirable auto-correlation properties (see Section 4.3). The 511-bit C/A code is clocked at 0.511 Mchips/s; thus, the code repeats every millisecond. This use of a relatively short code clocked at a high rate produces undesirable frequency components at 1-kHz intervals that can result in cross-correlation between interference sources, reducing the interference rejection benefit of the spread frequency spectrum. On the plus side, the FDMA nature of the GLONASS signal significantly reduces any cross-correlation between satellite signals due to the frequency separation. The reason for the short code is to allow quick acquisition, requiring a receiver to search a maximum of 511 code phase shifts. The fast code rate is necessary for range discrimination, with each code phase representing approximately 587m.

GLONASS P Code

The Russians have emphatically stated numerous times that the P code is strictly a military signal. As such, there is very little Russian information available on the GLONASS P code. Most P code information is derived from analysis of the code performed by various independent individuals or organizations such as that provided in [23]. Based on [23], the P code characteristics are:

- Code type: Maximal length 25-bit shift register;
- Code rate: 5.11 Mchips/s;
- Code length: 33,554,432 chips;
- Repeat rate: 1 second (repeat rate is actually at 6.57-second intervals, but chipped sequence is truncated such that it repeats every 1 second).

As with the C/A code, the maximal length code has exceptional, predictable auto-correlation properties. The significant difference between the P code and the C/A code is that the P code is much longer compared to its clock rate, thus repeating only once every second. Although this produces undesirable frequency components at 1-Hz intervals, the cross-correlation problem is not as severe as with the C/A code. As with the C/A code, FDMA virtually eliminates any problems involving cross-correlation between GLONASS satellite signals. While the P code gains in terms of correlation properties, it sacrifices in terms of acquisition. The P code contains 511 million code phase shift possibilities. Thus, a receiver typically acquires C/A code first and then uses the C/A code to help narrow the number of P code phase shifts to search. Each P code phase, clocked at 10 times the C/A code, represents 58.7m in range. A HOW like the one used in GPS to facilitate handover to P(Y) code is not necessary. The GLONASS P code repeats once every second, making it possible to use the timing of the C/A code sequence to assist in the handover process. This is an example of one more design tradeoff between the desired security and correlation properties of a long sequence and the desire for a faster acquisition scheme. GPS employs the former implementation, while GLONASS employs the latter [23].

Comparison of GLONASS Codes to GPS Codes

Because of the CDMA nature of GPS, the GPS design could not ignore the effect of cross-correlation between satellite signals. The Gold codes used by GPS were specifically chosen because of the ability to mathematically bound the auto-correlation and cross-correlation properties of the C/A codes. Nonetheless, in most respects, the GLONASS and GPS C/A codes are comparable in terms of correlation properties. By contrast, the longer GPS P code means GPS has better correlation properties than GLONASS P code. However, under certain configurations, the shorter GLONASS P code may make it easier to directly acquire than the GPS P(Y) code.

11.1.9.4 Navigation Message

Unlike GPS, GLONASS has two types of navigation messages. The C/A code navigation message is modulo-2 added to the C/A code at the satellite, whereas a P code unique navigation message is modulo-2 added to the P code. Both navigation messages are 50-bps data streams. The primary purpose of these messages is to provide information on satellite ephemeris and channel allocations. The ephemeris information allows the GLONASS receiver to accurately compute where each GLONASS satellite is located at any point in time. Although ephemeris is the predominant navigation information, there is an assortment of other items provided, such as:

- Epoch timing;
- Synchronization bits;
- Error correction bits;
- Satellite health;
- Age of data;
- Spare bits.

In addition, the Russians plan on providing data that will facilitate the combined use of GPS and GLONASS, particularly differences between GLONASS system time and GPS system time as well as differences between WGS-84 and PZ-90. An overview of the C/A code and P code navigation messages is provided next [22, 23].

C/A Navigation Message

Each GLONASS satellite broadcasts a C/A code navigation message that contains a superframe consisting of five frames. Each frame contains 15 lines, with each line containing 100 bits of information. Each frame takes 30 seconds to broadcast, so the entire superframe is broadcast once every 2.5 minutes [22].

The first three lines of each frame contain the detailed ephemeris for the satellite being tracked. Since each frame repeats every 30 seconds, a receiver will receive a satellite's ephemeris within 30 seconds once data reception begins [22].

The other lines of each frame consist primarily of approximate ephemeris (i.e., almanac) information for all of the other satellites in the constellation. Each frame can hold the ephemeris for five satellites. Since the constellation will have 24 satellites, all five frames must be read in order to get the approximate ephemeris for all the satellites. This takes approximately 2.5 minutes [1, 22].

The approximate ephemeris information is not as accurate as the detailed ephemeris and is not used for the actual ranging measurement. Nonetheless, the approximate ephemeris is sufficient to allow the receiver to quickly align its code phase and acquire the desired satellite. Once acquired, the satellite's detailed ephemeris is used for the ranging measurement. As with GPS, the ephemeris information is often valid for hours. Therefore, a receiver does not need to continually read the data message in order to compute accurate position.

P Code Navigation Message

The Russians have not publicly published any specifics on their P code. Nonetheless, a number of independent organizations and individuals have investigated the P code waveform and published their results [22]. The following information is extracted from the published information. The important thing to remember is the Russians publicly provided the detailed information on their C/A code data message and have given certain guarantees regarding its continuity. No such information or guarantees exist regarding the P code data. Thus, the P code data structure described here may change at any time without notice.

Each GLONASS satellite broadcasts a P code navigation message that contains a superframe consisting of 72 frames. Each frame has five lines, with each line containing 100 bits of information. Each frame takes 10 seconds to broadcast, so the entire superframe is broadcast once every 12 minutes [22].

The first three lines of each frame contain the detailed ephemeris for the satellite being tracked. Since each frame repeats every 10 seconds, a receiver will receive a satellite's ephemeris within 10 seconds once data reception occurs. The other lines of each frame consist primarily of approximate ephemeris information for the other satellites in the constellation. All 72 frames must be read to get all the ephemeris, which takes 12 minutes [22].

The two most distinguishing differences between the data messages deal with the length of time required to obtain ephemeris information. The time to obtain detailed ephemeris is:

- P code: 10 seconds;
- C/A code: 30 seconds.

The time to obtain almanac (approximate ephemeris) for all satellites is:

- P code: 12 minutes;
- C/A code: 2.5 minutes.

11.1.10   System Accuracy

GLONASS provides two levels of accuracy similar to GPS. The high-accuracy service is exclusively for Russian military use, while the lower accuracy service is for civil use. The high-accuracy service has an antispoofing capability that is under the control of the Russian Ministry of Defense. Based on Western observations, this feature is typically not activated, and the service is available for navigation. Observations by the University of Leeds in the United Kingdom and 3S Corporation during the mid-1990s, when the constellation was almost fully populated, indicate that the accuracy provided by the military service is similar to the specification for the GPS PPS—approximately 20m (2 drms, 95% probability) in the horizontal plane and 34m (2 sigma), in the vertical dimension. However, according to the Russians, the military accuracies for GLONASS remain classified [1, 22].

The specification for GLONASS civil accuracy is 100m (2 drms, 95% probability) in the horizontal, 150m (2 sigma) in the vertical, and 15 cm/sec (2 sigma) in velocity. A full GLONASS constellation (21 satellites plus 3 active spares) is designed to have a 94.7% probability of providing civilian navigational information to the previously mentioned design accuracy. The specification for derived time is within 1m of GLONASS system time and within 5 ms of UTC (SU) [1].

In practice during the mid-1990s when the constellation was almost fully populated, GLONASS accuracy was much better than the specified values cited here. Tests of the operational system have demonstrated civil accuracies of 26m (2 drms,

95% probability) in the horizontal plane and 45m (95% probability) in the vertical plane [26]. Velocity measurement accuracy is between 3 and 5 cm/sec [1, 27].

11.1.11   Future GLONASS Development

The Russians plan a number of changes to the GLONASS program in the future. These changes include improvements to the ground support segment, the space segment, and augmentation to provide differential services and to support SAR [1].

11.1.11.1   Space Segment Enhancements

The Russians plan to introduce two new generations of spacecraft to the constellation designated GLONASS-K and GLONASS-KM (sometimes referred to as the GLONASS-NG). The GLONASS-K is in the late stages of design and development with the first launched planned in 2007–2008. The GLONASS-KM is in a conceptual phase with the first launch planned in 2015. No other information is available on the GLONASS-KM. The GLONASS-K is described in detail next [9–12, 16–18]:

GLONASS-K
In 2007 to 2008, the Russians plan to start launching the new GLONASS-K spacecraft series. Currently, the Russians plan to produce 18–27 satellites in this series. The GLONASS-K represents a radical change in GLONASS spacecraft design, adopting a Western-style nonpressured and modular spacecraft bus design. Figure 11.5 is a depiction of the GLONASS-K spacecraft. As a result, the GLONASS-K

Figure 11.5   GLONASS-K spacecraft.

spacecraft, at the time of this writing, was projected to weigh 825 kg, half the weight of the GLONASS-M spacecraft. The smaller mass will allow Russians to launch GLONASS-K satellites six at a time on a single Proton launch vehicle, or two at a time on a Soyuz launch vehicle. The satellites are also projected to have a design lifetime of 10–12 years. The reduced mass and increased lifetime will reduce the overall program launch and operating costs significantly [9–12, 16–19].

The navigation payload will be improved in several ways. The satellite atomic clock is projected to provide improved stability on the order of 1×10^{-14}. The satellite will carry a third civil and military signal in the 1,190–1,212 MHz range, near GPS L5. In addition to transmitting navigation-message data, the two new signals will also transmit GLONASS integrity and GLONASS wide-area differential correction information to enhance the accuracy and reliability of the navigation services. GLONASS-K is also projected to carry an intersatellite link similar to the intersatellite link planned for GLONASS-M (after the third satellite) [9–12, 16–18, 28].

The Russians also plan to add a new SAR payload to the GLONASS-K series. The payload will relay the 406-MHz SAR beacon transmissions that are designed to work with the currently deployed COSPAS-SARSAT system. This payload is similar in design and concept to the payload planned for the European GALILEO satellite navigation system [9–12, 16–18].

11.1.11.2   Differential GLONASS Improvements

The Russians have developed several types of GLONASS differential services. They have deployed a coastal differential service for GLONASS and GPS using maritime radio beacons, similar to other services set throughout most of the world. The Russians actively participated in RTCM Special Committee SC-104, which developed the series of standards that permit the seamless use of DGPS, differential GLONASS, and differential GPS/GLONASS services [1].

A second scheme proposes to use the network of the existing Russian Military Space Force's Command and Control sites to double as differential reference sites. At the time of this writing, the Russians had not provided any details on the status or plans of the program. One advantage of this plan from the Russian perspective is that it would use preexisting accurately surveyed sites as reference points. The plan would also use the CSIC as a hub for computing differential corrections and extending the coverage over Asia, Europe, and Northern Africa. The differential radio communications links to transmit the differential corrections currently have not been selected or installed [5, 29].

A third scheme is comparable to the U.S. FAA plans for local-area differential GPS for category II and III landing approaches. The Russians plan to use differential GLONASS and differential GPS/GLONASS for categories I, II, and III, all categories of landing approach. At the time of this writing, the Russians indicated that they were pursuing this concept but had not deployed ground equipment [3].

A fourth scheme proposes the use of the existing ground-based radionavigation aid, Chaika, to transmit differential GLONASS corrections in addition to its navigation service. Chaika is the Russian counterpart to Loran-C. This concept is similar to the Eurofix concept. The status of the Russian program is unclear, but is discussed extensively in the 1994 CIS Federal Radionavigation Plan. The Russians will likely follow the European lead and deploy their system only if the Europeans deploy Eurofix. Eurofix is a proposal by Delft University of Technology, in the Netherlands, for upgrading Loran-C with integrated differential and communication services. Under the concept published on the Eurofix Web site, Loran-C or Chaika could be upgraded to broadcast low-data-rate differential corrections. Delft assigned eight possible channels: DGPS, DGLONASS, Differential Loran-C/Differential Chaika, navigation integrity messages, short-text message services, and three channels reserved for future applications [10].

11.1.12 Other GLONASS Information Sources

In addition to the materials provided in this chapter, other resources are available on the GLONASS program and signal structure. These include books [30, 31] published by the Russians on GLONASS, the availability of the GLONASS Interface Control Document (ICD), which is a living specification of the navigation signal, and various information centers that provide information on GLONASS over the Internet. The ICD and a number of information centers are presented in the following sections.

11.1.12.1 GLONASS ICD

The specifications for the GLONASS signals are documented in the GLONASS ICD. The ICD provides the specifications to build a properly functioning GLONASS user set. To date, the Russians have published five versions of the GLONASS ICD; the latest was published on September 30, 2002. The fifth version covers the GLONASS civil signals on L1 and L2 corresponding to GLONASS and GLONASS-M satellites. A new version is not expected until shortly before the first GLONASS-K launch in the 2008 time frame. The current GLONASS ICD is available in English at [32].

11.1.12.2 GLONASS Information Centers

The Russians operate various information centers that provide information on GLONASS on the Internet. Most of the Web sites provide information in English and Russian. The maintenance of the Web sites, especially the English portions of the Web sites, is intermittent. The four major information centers and associated Web addresses are listed next.

CSIC of Russian Space Forces
The CSIC is the official public interface for GLONASS. The CSIC is operated by the Russian Space Forces and was set up to be the Russian counterpart to the U.S. Coast Guard's GPS Information Center. The CSIC acts as the main interface between the military operators of GLONASS and the Russian Department of Air Traffic and the Ministry of Transport. The CSIC can provide assistance in the following areas [5, 33]:

- Provide consultations, information, and expertise to increase the effective use of the GLONASS system;

- Provide official representation of the GLONASS system and its users at conferences, symposiums, and negotiations;
- Facilitate dialogue with domestic and foreign users of the GLONASS;
- Issue licenses for the use of the navigational services provide by the GLONASS;
- Certify GLONASS and GPS/GLONASS user equipment;
- Provide official research on the utility of the GLONASS system;
- Promote combined use of the GLONASS and GPS systems.

Information Analytical Center of Coordinate-Time Support
The Information Analytical Center of Coordinate-Time Support is part of the Russian MCC located in Moscow and provides real-time and a posteriori analysis of the accuracy and integrity of the GLONASS navigation signals independent of the GLONASS ground control system [34].

Multifunctional Navigation-Information Center (MNIC) of Rosaviacosmos
The MNIC is part of the Russian Institute of Space Device Engineering (RISDE). RISDE is the agency responsible for the design of the GLONASS satellite navigation payload and ground command and control equipment. The MNIC appears to be primarily tasked with developing the infrastructure for generating differential corrections and integrity information for GNSS, including GLONASS. However, at the time of this writing, the MNIC Web site was still under construction [35].

Intergovernmental Navigation Information Center (INIC)
The INIC is operated by the Intergovernmental Navigation Research Center and was established to exchange navigation data between the departmental navigation centers in Russia and foreign countries. The INIC is responsible for drafting the Russian and CIS Federal Radio Navigation Plans and hosting international navigation symposiums. At the time of this writing, the INIC Web site was only hosted in Russian and was not currently maintained [36].

11.2   The Chinese BeiDou Satellite Navigation System

11.2.1   Introduction

BeiDou is the Chinese name for the multistage satellite navigation program designed to provide positioning, fleet-management, and precision-time dissemination to Chinese military and civil users. Currently, BeiDou is in a semioperational phase, with three satellites deployed in geostationary orbit over China. The official Chinese press has designated the constellation as the BeiDou Navigation Test System (BNTS). The BNTS supports two types of satellite navigation capabilities: RDSS and SBAS. The RDSS capability is operational, and the status of SBAS is unknown. The BNTS provides limited coverage and only supports users in and around China. The BNTS should be operational by the end of the decade. In the long term, the Chinese plan to deploy a regional or worldwide navigation constellation of 14–30 satellites under the BeiDou-2 Program. The Chinese did not plan to finalize the design for BeiDou-2 until 2005.

11.2.3 Program History

The BeiDou program was first proposed by Chinese academic Chen Fangyun in 1983 to provide navigation support to Chinese marine vessels. The program was originally named Double Star Positioning and Communications System. The Chinese government, including the military, initially rejected the concept. The proposal resurfaced in 1985 at a meeting where Chen was an invited speaker. The second proposal attracted the interest of the Central Committee of the Peoples Liberation Army Mapping Bureau. In March 1986, Chen and three other prominent Chinese scientists authored a letter to the Central Committee of the Communist Party of China, suggesting ways to acquire Western technology to accelerate China's science and technology development, giving China time to develop its own technical industry. Chinese leader Deng Xiaoping accepted the suggestion, which became the famous Chinese "863 Program." Chen's involvement in suggesting the 863 Program very likely secured and accelerated the development of BeiDou, due to his newly gained prestige. The program entered the advance research phase in 1986. The first major scientific paper on the proposal was published in the June 1987 issue of *China Space Science and Technology* magazine. In September 1989, the Double Star concept was demonstrated by using two DHF-2 geostationary communication satellites. The success of the experiment was reported in the Chinese press. In 1993, the Double Star Positioning System program officially entered the development phase in the Chinese budgetary process in 1994 [37, 38].

At the same time as Chen developed the Double Star Positioning System, the RDSS concept was patented by Professor Gerard O'Neill in November 1982. O'Neill founded Geostar Corporation in 1983 to implement the RDSS concept. Geostar envisioned seamless worldwide coverage and attempted to set up various cooperative arrangements with other possible service providers, including China. By 1985, Geostar applied for patents on the specific RDSS implementation planned for the Geostar in both the United States and China simultaneously. In May 1987, at the first Global RDSS conference, the Chinese presentation touted the close working relationship China had with Geostar and predicted an optimistic future for their cooperation. In a July 25, 1988, interview, Martin Rothblatt, then Geostar's chief executive officer, told *Aviation Week* that Geostar Corporation planned to seek permission from the U.S. government to enter into a formal agreement with the Chinese Academy of Space Technology (CAST) after the terms of the agreement became mature. Under the draft agreement, Geostar planned to supply U.S.-built RDSS payloads for CAST to host on unspecified Chinese geostationary satellites. In 1991, Geostar was declared bankrupt. In a 1993 conference paper, the Chinese mentioned their plans to continue pursuing an RDSS constellation despite the bankruptcy of Geostar Corporation. Further evidence on this can be found in Chinese papers, theses, and journal articles from 1984 to 2000, which make numerous references to Geostar [39–41].

The BeiDou program was established in 1994 under sponsorship of the General Staff of the CCPLA Mapping Bureau after completion of the developmental phase of the Double Star Positioning System. The Chinese indicated the system would support mapping, aeronautics, aviation, navigation, mining, shipping, emergency disaster relief applications, and national defense [37].

The first BeiDou satellite was launched in October 2000, and the second in December 2000. The third BeiDou satellite was launched in May 2003. There are some Chinese press references to a fourth spare satellite, but these are unconfirmed [42].

After the launch in late 2000, the system went through an on-orbit validation. In 2001, the Chinese government issued a series of contracts for development and operation of the military fleet management service, the civil fleet management service, the SBAS ground-monitoring network, and for various types of user equipment. The RDSS system also went through a series of system validations from 2001 to 2002. In December 2001, the Chinese began advertising user equipment for the BNTS. However, to date, there were only a few claims of sales of the user sets to the Chinese military. The Chinese contractor completed the military service in late 2003. The civil service was declared operational in conjunction with the launch of the third satellite in June 2003. As stated earlier, the status of Chinese SBAS is unknown [43–45].

11.2.4   Organization Structure

The BeiDou system is owned and operated by the Chinese government as a dual-use system. However, the Chinese have not provided specific details or an official point of contact within the Chinese government for BeiDou. The Chinese identify two private companies under contract from the government providing the BeiDou RDSS positioning and fleet-management services. ChinaTopComm operates the civil fleet-management services. BDStar operates the military fleet-management services. BDStar has also expressed interest in developing commercial services in the future. The operators of the BeiDou SBAS services have not been made known to the international community [43, 44].

11.2.5   Constellation and Orbit

BNTS is composed of three satellites. The first two satellites, launched in October and December 2000, were placed at 80°E and 140°E longitude on the geostationary belt and carry a RDSS transponder payload. The RDSS transponders operate using an L-band (1,610–1,626.5-MHz) uplink and S-band (2,483.5–2,500-MHz) downlink. The third BeiDou-1 satellite was launched in May 2003 and placed at 110°E longitude. It carries both an RDSS and SBAS transponder payload. The SBAS payload operates in the GPS L1 and L2 radio frequency bands and is likely used to augment both GPS and GLONASS [46, 47].

11.2.6   Spacecraft

The BNTS satellites use the Chinese standard DJS-1 spacecraft bus, which is also used by Chinese DFH-3, CHINASAT, Zhongxing-20, and Zhongxing-22 communications satellites. The spacecraft uses a box-shaped bus with the dimensions of

2.2m × 1.72m × 2.0m, and twin solararrays with a span of 18.1m. The twin solar arrays are composed of three panels each and are designed to generate 2,049W of power at the start of the mission and 1,688W EOL power. During periods of eclipse, two 45-Ah nickel hydrogen (NiH$_2$) batteries provide power. DJS-1 carries an apogee kick motor for postlaunch orbit-transfer maneuvers. The spacecraft has an on-station BOL mass of 1,145 kg and a dry mass of 745 kg. Thus, the mass of the fuel is 400 kg. The DJS-1 has a minimum design life of 8 years, but too few spacecraft have been launched to independently determine the expected on-orbit lifetime [48–50].

The DJS-1 spacecraft bus carries an apogee kick motor for orbital transition and station keeping for north/south station-keeping maneuvers. The motor is used initially during launch to finalize the spacecraft orbit. The thrust output is 490 N. The propellant is monomethyl hydrazine and has a mass of 200 kg [49].

The DJS-1 spacecraft bus carries a three-axis attitude control system (ACS) comprised of Earth sensors, momentum wheels, and 14 ACS thrusters. During the on-station operation, the ACS maintains the satellite pointing toward China with both a northward and inward angle. The satellites are maintained to within 0.10° beam pointing error [50].

During the preoperational mode, from launch vehicle separation through Earth acquisition, the satellite is spin-stabilized. Data from the horizon and Sun sensors is telemetered to the ground for determination of the satellite attitude. The satellite transitions from spin-stabilized to three-axis stabilized with a dual-spin turn maneuver [48].

In the normal mission mode, the satellite is in an off-nadir Earth-oriented attitude with the momentum wheels. The satellite is three-axis stabilized, with an Earth sensor providing the attitude reference, a momentum wheel providing the required gyroscopic stiffness as well as momentum exchange for pitch control, and autonomous magnetic torquing providing roll and yaw control. Thrusters provide the backup three-axis control during station-keeping maneuvers and momentum unloading [49].

11.2.7 RDSS Service Infrastructure

The BNTS is designed to provide regional two-dimensional communications, positioning, and fleet management services over China and Taiwan using a RDSS technique. Under the RDSS concept, the Payload Operations Center (POC) sends out a navigation or polling signal through one of the BeiDou satellites. Subsets of users respond to this signal via both satellites. The travel time is measured as the navigation signals loop from POC to the satellite, to the receiver on the user platform, and back around. With this time-lapse information, the known locations of the two satellites and an estimate of the user altitude, the user's location can be determined by the POC. Once calculated, the POC transmits the positioning information to the user. Since the POC must calculate the positions for all subscribers to the system, BeiDou can also be used for fleet management and communications [43, 44].

To support the RDSS positioning, the Chinese BNTS is composed of:

• A two or three geostationary satellite constellation;

- The POC;
- Handheld, mobile, and integrated user transmission and reception sets;
- Fixed ground sites used to calibrate the navigation signals, called benchmarks;
- Fleet management centers connected by a wide-area communications network or via BeiDou itself;
- Ground support and tracking system for spacecraft support [43, 44].

11.2.7.1   BNTS Constellation

As stated earlier, the BNTS is composed of two BeiDou satellites placed at 80°E and 140°E longitude. A spare third satellite is currently at 110°E longitude. While in this position, the spare satellite enhances the basic RDSS coverage in areas where one or the other primary satellite is blocked by terrain or buildings (urban canyons). The third satellite can allow testing of an experimental three-dimensional RDSS capability and act as an on-orbit spare to replace either of the primary RDSS satellites if either fail [43, 44].

11.2.7.2   POC

The tasks performed by the BNTS POC have been described in the introduction to Section 11.2.7. Its location has not been identified by the Chinese.

11.2.7.3   BNTS User Equipment

The Chinese are developing and marketing handheld, mobile, and integrated user sets for both Chinese military and civil applications. Originally, the Chinese issued a set of industry standards for 11 types of user sets grouped into five classes. The five classes are listed here and detailed in Table 11.4 [43, 44]:

- *General mobile class* for positioning, communications, and fleet management;
- *Communication class* for text messaging;
- *Time synchronization class* for one- and two-way time transfer;
- *Fleet management class* for low-volume fleet management that do not require wide area network (WAN) connections;
- *Multimode class*, which is a combined use of BeiDou with GPS and GLONASS [43, 44].

Currently, a number of companies are marketing various types of user equipment.

11.2.7.4   BNTS Benchmarks

Benchmarks are a network of fixed ground sites used to calibrate the errors in the RDSS signals. In a similar manner as DGPS, the POC uses data from the benchmark sites to improve the user accuracy. The POC applies corrections to the calculated position fixes and then transmits these to the mobile users near the benchmark.

Table 11.4   BeiDou User Equipment Classes and Types

Class 1: General User Terminals	*Land vehicle terminal:* The user equipment is designed to support all types of land vehicles. The user equipment consists of an antenna and user terminal with liquid crystal display (LCD) and built-in keypad. The terminal uses the vehicle's power and has a data port to interface with an onboard computer. The user equipment provides all-weather rapid-positioning, real-time navigation, and bidirectional short-text-message communication capability.
	Ship terminal: The user equipment is designed to support ships within the BeiDou coverage area. The user equipment consists of an antenna and user terminal with LCD and built-in keypad. The terminal uses the ship's power and has a data port to interface with an onboard computer. The user equipment provides all-weather rapid-positioning, real-time navigation, and bidirectional short-text-message communication capability.
	Handheld terminal: The user equipment is designed to support handheld applications. The user equipment consists of the dual-mode antenna, the user terminal (with LCD), PDA (or other handwriting device), and battery. The terminal has a data port to interface with a remote computer. The terminal provides all-weather rapid-positioning, real-time navigation, and bidirectional short-text-message communication capability.
	Emergency reporting terminal: The user equipment is designed to make emergency reports to police. The user equipment consists of the dual-mode antenna, the user terminal (with LCD), PDA (or other handwriting device), and battery. The terminal provides all-weather positioning, real-time navigation and bidirectional short-text message (up to 120 Chinese characters) communications capability.
Class 2: General Communications User Terminals	*One-way communication user terminal:* The user equipment is designed to receive messages over the BeiDou system. The user equipment consists of the receive-only antenna, the user terminal (with LCD), PDA (or other handwriting device), and battery. The terminal also has a data port to interface with an onboard computer. The terminal can receive up to 120 Chinese characters and has a storage capacity of 4,800 Chinese-character short-text messages.
	Two-way correspondence user terminal: The user equipment is designed to send and receive messages over the BeiDou system. The user equipment consists of the send/receive antenna, the user terminal (with LCD), PDA (or other handwriting device), and battery. The terminal also has a data port to interface with an onboard computer. The terminal can send or receive short-text messages (up to 120 Chinese characters). The user equipment can also provide all-weather positioning and real-time navigation.
Class 3: Time Dissemination Terminals	*One-way time service user terminal:* The user equipment is designed for time synchronization using the BeiDou system in a passive mode. The user equipment consists of the receive-only antenna, the user terminal, and battery. The terminal provides time and frequency synchronization with 100-ns time accuracy.
	Two-way time service user terminal: The user equipment is designed for time synchronization using the BeiDou system in an active mode. The user equipment consists of the send/receive antenna, the user terminal, and battery. The terminal provides time and the frequency synchronization with 20-ns time accuracy.
Class 4: Central Dispatcher User Terminals	*Dispatcher terminal:* The dispatcher terminal is designed to communicate with and monitor the locations of users of the BeiDou system. The equipment consists of an antenna and user terminal with a port for special data network connections. The terminal supports fleet management, real-time navigation, and bidirectional short-text-message communications, and can monitor BeiDou user equipment in the field in real time.
Class 5: Multimode User Terminals	*Multimode terminal:* The multimode terminal is designed to use the BeiDou, GLONASS, and GPS systems. The user equipment consists of the antenna and the user terminal capable of working with BeiDou, GLONASS, and GPS. The terminal supports both BeiDou-based and GLONASS/GPS-based fleet management, real-time navigation, and bidirectional short-text-message communications.
	Enhancement user terminal: The enhanced user terminal is designed to improve GLONASS and GPS with differential corrections transmitted over the BeiDou system. The user equipment consists of the antenna and the user terminal capable of working with GPS, GLONASS, and BeiDou. The terminal supports all-weather rapid-positioning, real-time navigation, and bidirectional short-text-message communications.

Essentially, the benchmarks are a special class of user sets deployed in a network at fixed sites with known presurveyed geodetic locations across China [43, 44].

11.2.7.5   BNTS Fleet Management Centers

The BNTS is designed to allow civil fleet managers to monitor, determine locations of, and communicate with mobile users of the system. Currently, there are two networks, one for military users and a second for civil users. BDstar is developing the military fleet management service under a contract signed in April 2002. ChinaTopComm is developing a civil service as part of a joint venture initiated in December 2001. Company literature indicates that BDstar may also enter the civil fleet management market at a later date. Each company plans to provide two levels of service for military and civil users: one targeted for high-volume fleet managers and a second targeted for low-volume fleet managers. The main difference between the two levels of service is the complexity of the fleet management center and the communication links used to connect the fleet manager with the POC [43, 44].

- *Low-volume service architecture.* Both BDstar and ChinaTopComm are also developing similar low-capacity fleet management services using the BeiDou system to communicate between the POC and the individual fleet management centers [43, 44].
- *High-volume service architecture.* Both BDstar and ChinaTopComm are developing similar high-capacity fleet-management services. The high-volume service uses traditional communications links (like very small aperture terminals, terrestrial, microwave, fiber-optic, and landline) to establish wide-area computer network connectivity between the POC and the individual fleet management centers. The Chinese have provided limited details on the design and capability of a fleet management center. The high-volume center consists of several map displays and communications consoles [43, 44].

11.2.8   RDSS Navigation Services

The Chinese plan five basic positioning and communication services using the BeiDou RDSS capability. The Chinese service providers indicate that these services are currently operational. These are [43, 44]:

- *RDSS positioning of mobile users for navigation and fleet management.* The BNTS provides about 20–100-m two-dimensional accuracy in areas where the system is calibrated with benchmarks in a transmit and receive mode. Because the positions are calculated at the POC, the system can also be used for fleet management [43, 44].
- *Broadcast of accuracy corrections and integrity information for use with the GPS and GLONASS systems.* The BNTS RDSS also provides accuracy corrections for and information on the integrity of U.S. GPS and Russian GLONASS so that the Chinese military and civil users can use these systems more reliably. In this mode of operation, the users need only to passively receive the BNTS (S-band) and GPS (L-band), or GLONASS (L-band) signals [43, 44].

• *Two-way text messaging.* The BNTS RDSS also provides an on-demand text-messaging capability for civil users in and around China. The BNTS should be able to provide a text-messaging service similar to the text-messaging service offered by Blackberry. The BNTS is designed to send or receive short messages (up to 120 Chinese characters) in the text mode, or up to 480 numeric characters in the data mode. The Chinese indicate that the BNTS can encrypt the data for secure communications [43, 44].

• *Dissemination of Chinese atomic time for synchronization.* The BNTS RDSS provides both passive-mode (users receive only) and active-mode (users transmit and receive) time dissemination and synchronization for military and civil users in China. The Chinese indicate that the BNTS provides 100-ns time accuracy in the passive mode and 20-ns time accuracy in the active mode. BNTS allows remote users to synchronize to Chinese atomic time for use by communications networks, computer networks, and power grids. Typically, the Chinese equipment also uses GPS and GLONASS as part of the time synchronization ensemble [43, 44].

• *Communication of GPS-derived mobile users' positions for civil fleet management.* The Chinese indicate that BNTS RDSS is used to relay GPS- or GLONASS-derived positions from the users to the fleet management center. Typically, GPS and GLONASS provide positions to within 5–10m. The current marketing strategy in China is to use cellular phone networks for local fleet management communications and BeiDou for long-distance fleet management services [43, 44].

The basic performance for services is shown in Table 11.5 [43, 44]:

11.2.9 RDSS Navigation Signals

The BNTS satellite broadcasts to the users at 2,492 MHz (S-band). The user equipment transmits a short-burst, spread-spectrum response at 1,616 MHz (L-band). The signals are modulated with 4.08-Mbps spread-spectrum signals (8-MHz bandwidth). At the time of this writing, there was no publicly available ICD or similar document defining the BeiDou signal structure [43, 44].

Table 11.5   BeiDou Service Performance

Function	Advertised Performance
RDSS positioning accuracy	20–100m (two-dimensional) within vicinity of benchmarks
GPS/GLONASS enhancement	2–5m (two-dimensional)
Text messaging	120 Chinese characters; 480 numeric characters
Chinese time dissemination	20 ns (two-way communications mode); 100 ns (one-way communications mode)
Communications for GPS-based tracking and fleet management	5–10m (two-dimensional)

11.2.10   System Coverage and Accuracy

The BNTS RDSS service provides continuous, all-weather, day-night coverage in the Northern Hemisphere, focused on China and the surrounding area for mid-latitudes where the system provides optimal satellite geometry for a position fix. The coverage footprints depend on type of service used. For navigation and positioning, two satellites are required to be in view in order to obtain a position fix, thus limiting coverage to the overlapping footprints of the satellites. The Chinese advertise the coverage as being between 5°N and 55°N latitude and 70°E and 140°E longitude. In this area, the BNTS should provide approximately up to 20m. The accuracy typically degrades as much as several factors of ten for southern latitudes within BNTS coverage area or in rugged terrain. For text messaging and broadcast of GPS and GLONASS corrections, only one of the satellites is required to be in view in order to communicate, thus expanding the coverage to the composite of the satellite footprints [43, 44].

The Chinese advertise the BeiDou RDSS accuracy ranging from 20m to 100m. However, this level of performance can only be obtained in areas where calibration sites called benchmarks are deployed. With other RDSS implementations, altitude is determined at the master control station by using digital maps in the course of calculating the user's location. Any errors in the altitude estimated would result in additional corresponding errors in the user's position [43, 44].

11.2.11   Future Developments

11.2.11.1   BeiDou-1 SBAS Service

In addition to BNTS RDSS service, the Chinese are in the process of establishing an indigenous SBAS using the L-band transponder carried on the third BeiDou-1 satellite (110°E longitude). At the time of writing, little information was available on the service's status or Chinese future plans. What is known is that the Chinese filed radio frequency registrations with the International Telecommunication Union (ITU) for L1 (1,559–1,610 MHz) and L2 (1,215–1,260 MHz) in 1999 for an SBAS service. Subsequent filings indicated that the Chinese planned for the SBAS payload to be nadir pointing and provide coverage in both the Northern and Southern Hemispheres. In addition, from 2000–2002, the Chinese purchased SBAS ground monitoring equipment from Canadian company Novatel, the supplier of ground equipment for the U.S. WAAS, the EGNOS, and Japanese MSAS. The SBAS service will likely share the GPS monitoring structure currently transmitting corrections via the S-band signals. Potentially, the SBAS will augment both GPS and GLONASS. At the time of this writing, the Chinese had not released an ICD [51–59].

11.2.11.2   BeiDou-2

Beyond the current BeiDou-1 system, the Chinese are in the late stages of designing a follow-on system designated BeiDou-2. The Chinese announced 2005 as the target date to complete research and finalize the design. Based on the history of the BeiDou-1 program, the Chinese will likely take about 5 years to begin launching the BeiDou-2 satellites and will take 3 to 6 years to fully populate the full constellation [60].

In an apparent competing initiative to BeiDou-2, the Chinese also joined the GALILEO program in late 2003. However, it is clear from the Chinese perspective that cooperation with the GALILEO program will not replace or hinder plans for the Chinese to deploy their own indigenous system; these efforts are complementary, not competitive, options.

As part of the development of the BeiDou-2 program, the Chinese have filed for radio frequency allocation by the ITU Radio Board under the "Chinasat" and "Compass" designations. At the time of this writing, the Chinese had filed for a total of 61 satellites, apparently in an effort to secure orbital slots and radio frequency allocations for potential design options for BeiDou-2. Based on the information contained in the request to the ITU and the Chinese press, there are apparently four design options under consideration. These are outlined in Table 11.6 [61–64].

In 1997, the Chinese filed for a follow-on to BeiDou-1 under the Chinasat-34 and Chinasat-35 designators. The ITU filing indicated that they planned a constellation of satellites similar to BeiDou-1c (Chinasat-33) supporting both an RDSS and SBAS capabilities. However, in this case, they planned to place two or three satellites in the two orbital slots currently occupied by BeiDou-1a (140°E longitude) and BeiDou-1b (80°E longitude). No satellites were planned to fill the middle orbital slot, currently occupied by BeiDou-1c (110°E longitude). Although the Chinese have

Table 11.6 Chinese Design Options for BeiDou-2

	Design Option 1	Design Option 2	Design Option 3	Design Option 4
ITU designators	Chinasat-34a and b and Chinasat-35a, b, and c	Compass-GEOs and Compass-highly elliptical orbit (HEO)	Compass-GEOs and Compass-medium Earth orbit (MEO)	Compass-MG
ITU filing date	1997 with continued coordination in Dec. 2003	2000 and amended in Nov. 2003	2000 and amended in Nov. 2003	Registered in 2003
Constellation design	2 GEO + 2–3 GEO	4 GEO + 9 inclined geosynchronous	4 GEO + 12 MEO	30 MEO
Orbit	80°E and 140°E longitude	55°E, 80°E, 110°E, 140°E, and 160°E longitude 6 orbital planes at 50° inclination × 36,000-km circular orbits	55°E, 80°E, 110°E, 140°E, and 160°E longitude 6 orbital planes at 55° inclination × 20,200-km circular orbits	3 orbital planes at 56° inclination × 21,363-km circular orbits
Navigation techniques	Two-dimensional RDSS GPS augmentation	Two-dimensional active RDSS GPS augmentation Three-dimensional passive navigation	Two-dimensional active RDSS GPS augmentation Three-dimensional passive navigation	Three-dimensional active RDSS Three-dimensional passive navigation
Planned radio frequencies	S-band and L-band communication links Two L-band navigation links	S-band and L-band communication links Four L-band navigation links	S-band and L-band communication links Four L-band navigation links	S-band and L-band communication links Four L-band navigation links
Service area	Asian-Pacific region	Asian-Pacific region	Asian-Pacific region	Worldwide

continued to file paperwork with the ITU in support of this option, Chinese publications on future plans for BeiDou-2 do not present this as an option [61].

In 2000, the Chinese filed for 25 new navigation satellites under the "Compass" designator. Subsequent articles by Chinese experts indicated that they are considering deploying a hybrid constellation composed of either four geostationary and nine inclined geosynchronous satellites, or four geostationary and 12 MEO satellites. Both options are designed to provide regional navigation similar to GPS and carry forward provisions for the legacy-RDSS service. In late 2003, the Chinese added a fifth geostationary satellite to both constellation options [62].

Also in late 2003, the Chinese filed for an additional 30-satellite constellation under the "Compass-MG" designator. The 30-satellite "Compass-MG" proposal is more ambitious than previous 5-, 14-, or 17-satellite alternatives and is designed to provide world navigation support like GPS, but also carries forward provisions for the legacy-RDSS service. The Compass-MG design is very similar to the plan for the European GALILEO, and it is likely that the Chinese hope to benefit from lessons learned and cooperation with the European GALILEO program [64].

The Chinese were scheduled to likely complete their design decision around 2005 as planned, but it is unclear what impact, if any, GALILEO will have on the fabrication and deployment schedule of BeiDou-2. However, as noted earlier, the cooperation is not expected to replace or hinder plans for the Chinese to deploy their own indigenous system. It is thus reasonable to assume that the cooperation will help China to gain the experience to facilitate its own program.

11.3   The Japanese QZSS Program

11.3.1   Introduction

At the time of this writing, the Japanese were developing an indigenous satellite navigation augmentation to the U.S. GPS under the QZSS program. The concept has been under development in Japan for more than 6 years and is the result of several independent government and industry initiatives. Under current plans, the QZSS constellation will be designed to support both mobile communications and GPS augmentation services, but the size and orbit remain incompletely defined. Specifically, the Japanese intend the navigation services to address shortfalls in GPS satellite visibility in urban canyons and mountainous terrain, which the Japanese assess to be a problem in 80% of the country. In addition, the Japanese have expressed the need for an independent regional navigation capability in times of crisis in order to protect the Japanese economy and its extensive use of GPS [65].

11.3.2   Program Overview

Originally, the QZSS was an initiative of a joint industry effort under the (then) Japanese Communications Research Laboratory. A number of national and consortium projects in Japan have developed concepts for a satellite-based augmentation to GPS with a funding and marketing base broadened by providing both a navigation and a communications capability. The QZSS program appears to be the first such program to be moving forward with both government and industry support.

The intent is to bring the navigation service on line in coordination with GPS upgrades. A U.S.-Japanese working group was established in October 2002 and is working toward this goal. When the GPS-QZSS Technical Working Group met in January 2004, problems related to interoperability were addressed through formal documents on configuration management [66, 67].

11.3.3 Organizational Structure

Support from industry in the earliest stages of planning in the late 1990s was focused on the goal of improving mobile communications in the rural areas as well as the urban canyons of metropolitan areas. Joining this activity, the government developed a plan to provide through the public sector improvements to the satellite navigation service available from GPS. A variety of commercial, economic, and political influences have swayed the program during the course of development. The allocation of resources and responsibilities for spacecraft deployment as well as operation of the constellation on a daily basis remains a topic of discussion. Progress in the QZSS program is nearly assured, owing to the clear benefits it brings in stimulating the national space technology industries. This progress may occur slowly, however, as the various stakeholders sort out the opportunities it presents. A directive coming from the Japanese Council on Science Technology Policy on September 9, 2004, gave further structure. The four basic ministries involved, as well as the major industries comprising the Advanced Space Business Corporation hope to sort out the particulars. The QZSS program has been under development long enough to see both the founding agency the Communications Research Laboratory (CRL) and Japan's National Aeronautics and Space Development Agency renamed and reorganized into the National Institute of Information and Communications Technology and the Japanese Aerospace Exploration Agency, respectively [68, 69].

11.3.4 Constellation and Orbit

To meet the requirements for having a system with satellites operating predominantly over Japan, an inclined geosynchronous or semisynchronous orbit is being planned. The inclination will give, for at least part of the orbit, the desired high viewing altitude over the 2,500-km range stretch of Japanese islands running from 27°N to 45°N. The synchronous orbit will keep the satellites in the appropriate longitude so they are in view from Japan. In the case of GPS, the difficulty has been in accessing four visible satellites in a geometry that is optimal for an accurate navigation fix, as seen from such terrain. Additionally, the QZSS concept will alleviate difficulties in using communications services provided by geostationary satellites, which have low elevation of no higher than 45° when viewed from central Japan [65, 70].[1]

The first concept for an indigenous Japanese constellation of geosynchronous satellites in inclined orbits producing the figure 8 pattern for regional access was promoted by CRL for communications alone. In fact the plan in 1998 was for an "EFSAT" (eight-figure satellite) system. Though there were several advantages, the idea was to provide high-quality communications services to Japan and Australia

---

1.   Okinawa is at 27°; Iwo Jima, off somewhat to the East, is actually further south yet at 25°.

using only three or four satellites. An initial design called for these to be placed in circular orbits at the full 35,800-km geosynchronous altitude with 45° inclination. This design has carried over to the current QZSS concept for navigation services as well, with the exception that the new design now calls for orbits with high eccentricity [71].

A number of possible constellation designs have been considered for placing three satellites in HEO. The original plan for a 45° inclination and symmetrical figure 8 (circular orbit) was dropped due to the hazard of crossing the geostationary belt (evidently not addressed in the original concept). The currently favored HEO design will miss the belt by 400 km and remain near apogee for 12 hours a day, above 70° elevation-from central Japan. This design calls for three satellites, all tracing the same elliptical orbit with timing to make the apparent intersection of the resultant figure eight trace directly over Tokyo for hand-off of services from one satellite to the next [72, 73].

At the time of this writing, the Japanese Aerospace Exploration Agency presented an updated concept for the QZSS constellation at an international conference. In an apparent reversal, the agency proposed a constellation of three distinct and separate inclined HEO orbits, complemented by a return to as many as five spacecraft at geostationary positions instead of the minimal three-satellite design. This new design may conceivably rely on existing or new communications satellites to host the additional navigation payloads [68].

11.3.5   Spacecraft Development

Specifications for the spacecraft and the letting of contracts were on hold at the time of this writing, awaiting allocation of funding. The question of which governmental element or industry consortium will assume the task of operating the QZSS system once it is launched remains at an impasse. Monies expected from the private sector in the amount of approximately $47 million needed in 2005 to start the spacecraft design will likely be available when the question is settled as to who will fund and administer operations. Success in this unstructured negotiation is doubly important because it will establish guidelines for future public-private space projects. The government's share of the overall program cost has been estimated at $814 million for the overall program, anticipating a first launch sometime after 2008, but none of four ministries seen as stakeholders in QZSS has stepped forward to submit the first year's increment in their budget proposal [69].

The spacecraft design itself has not been finalized but a 12-year lifetime is in the current specification. This number and some additional technical requirements for the spacecraft have emerged because they are implicit in the constellation design. As with virtually all other space systems, the 12-year lifetime goal is challenged by the demands of station keeping. Velocity increments required for satellite formation phasing represent part of this challenge, which has already been considered [74, 75].

Not all QZSS concepts rely on having an atomic clock on board, but if one is required, clock reliability and reliability in terms of mean time between failures (MTBF) may be an issue. Parallel development of a hydrogen maser for the program is proceeding under the High Accuracy Positioning Experiment project at the Japanese National Institute of Information and Communications Technology. The ability to meet this lifetime specification will likely determine the choice of clock [76].

Designs for the antenna and power amplifiers for both the communications and navigation services must address the changes in gain and footprint associated with significant eccentricity in the planned elliptical orbits. At the time of this writing, plans for the technical solution to these related problems were not available in the public domain. With plans for mobile communications and audio/video broadcast in S-band, data services and TT&C in the K_u-band, and navigation signals in L-band, each QZSS spacecraft will need to carry an impressive array of antennas [77].

11.3.6 Ground Support

Ideas concerning the satellite signal-monitoring stations essential to GPS augmentation service are three tiered and exceedingly complex. They will, where possible, draw on existing resources and on occasion serve dual or multiple functions. Monitoring of the overall satellite navigation service in Japan will be provided by 1,200 stations with the capability to receive GPS, the augmentation signals from QZSS, and any future independent ranging signal that may be provided by QZSS satellites in the future. These sites already exist in part, in association with a network of locations for tracking GPS carrier phase under Japan's Geographical Survey Institute [72].

11.3.7 User Equipment

Little or nothing has been said about development of user equipment capable of addressing consumer demand for both the mobile (principally automotive) communications market as well as the augmented GPS service. With the whole force of the Japanese consumer electronics industry at hand, however, it is highly unlikely that either quality or manufacturing of user equipment will cause a stumble in the program.

11.3.8 Reference Systems

The QZSS system plans to use the Japanese Geodetic Datum JGD-2000, based on regional measurements taken in support of the ITRF. Much existing documentation in Japan still relies on the Tokyo-1927 datum, requiring a corresponding transformation for these users where needed. Timing corrections and a match-up to WGS-84 datum for complete GPS overlay and compatibility are planned.[2]

11.3.9 Navigation Services and Signals

Services provided by QZSS may actually emphasize communications, with S-band for broadcast of audio and video, K_u-band for data and TT&C, and L-band for the navigation signals. No explicit specification has been given yet for data bandwidth, though filings with the ITU in 2002 set some limitation [72].

News about the status of QZSS in late 2004 suggested some decisions remain unsettled about what services will be offered. An impasse between the Japanese gov-

2.   Japanese Geodetic Datum JGD-2000 is derived from the ITRF.

ernment and industry over who will assume responsibility for operation of the deployed QZSS constellation and ground infrastructure has resulted in an announcement by the government that the planned communications and broadcasting features will be dropped, and only a positioning and navigation service will be provided. With the potential for consumer market, it is doubtful that the government will defend this new go-it-alone position without industry and without a communication service. However, plans for an expanded constellation for communications services as well as navigation under a follow-on project called the Japanese Regional Advanced Navigation Satellite system, which looked well supported in mid-2003, may not be brought forward by the business sector [66, 78]. No signal design information or signal specifications have yet appeared.

11.3.10   System Coverage and Accuracy

Exactly what regions of the Far East beyond Japan will benefit from QZSS depends critically on the choice of orbit inclination, eccentricity, and argument of perigee. Sharing Japan's longitude, it is nearly certain Australia will enjoy some coverage, though the coverage will not be symmetric above and below the equator, and the satellites in view will not linger at the zenith over any particular Australian city. Ultimately, system performance in Australia, as well as Taiwan and the coastal regions of China, will depend on the implementation of supporting ground infrastructure in those areas. One recent compendium on QZSS shows notional sites for tracking facilities as well as satellite signal monitoring in Bangkok, Hawaii, Tsukuba (Tokyo), Okinawa, and Australia. These sites are under consideration in simulations of system performance [72].

11.3.11   Future Development

It is not certain whether the QZSS satellites will provide an independent, GPS-like ranging signal from the outset, but this has been a feature desired as a measure enhancing the number of pseudoranging satellites available, as well as protection against a feared but never occurring GPS outage. In addition to providing corrections to GPS for accuracy, a likely next step that has been mentioned is to follow developments under GPS III and provide similar corrections for the new signals. It is likely that a similar service will be provided for current and future GLONASS signals, as well as GALILEO signals when the program comes into service around the same time as QZSS itself (2008 and beyond).

After resolution of the impasse between government and industry on who will become the operator of the deployed QZSS constellation, it is possible that interest will be renewed in the Japanese Regional Advanced Navigation Satellite concept or some measure like it. Details provided in public forum by the corporate interests involved reflect careful consideration to one possible enhancement to QZSS, but draw from proprietary research and development. These may change with ongoing alterations in the final QZSS configuration and are outside the scope of this brief review of the QZSS program.

Acknowledgments

The information on GLONASS was a revised and updated version of material published originally in the first edition of this book (Chapter 10 of *Understanding GPS—Principles and Applications*, pp. 439–465). The coauthors of Chapter 10 were Scott Feairheller, Richard Clark, and Jay Purvis, all of whom worked for the U.S. Air Force in 1996. The primary source for former Chapter 10 was "Russia's Global Navigation Satellite System," which was produced under U.S. Air Force Contract Number F33657-90-D-0096. The authors would like to thank all the contributors and participants involved in that effort. The contract was performed by ANSER (Washington, D.C.) with some assistance from the Russian Space Agency. ANSER assembled a team of Russian GLONASS experts in Russia to compile and author the report. The Russian authors included: V. F. Cheremisin, V. A. Bartenev, and M. F. Reshetnov of the NPO Prikladnoy Mekhaniki (Applied Mechanics); Y. G. Gouzhva and V. V. Korniyenko of the Russian Institute of Radio Navigation and Time; N. E. Ivanov and V. A. Salishchev of the Scientific Research Institute of Space Device Engineering; Y. V. Medvedkov of the Russian Space Agency; V. N. Pochukaev of the Central Scientific Research Institute of Machine Building; M. N. Krasilshikov and V. V. Malyshev of the Moscow Aviation Institute; V. I. Durnev, V. L. Ivanov, and M. Lebedev of the Russian Space Forces; and V. P. Pavlov of the Flight Control Center. The team from ANSER included E. N. O'Rear and R. Turner from the Arlington office and S. Hopkins, R. Dalby, and D. Van Hulle from the Moscow office. In addition, the authors would like to thank the following navigation experts who reviewed the initial draft of the ANSER report and provided many valuable comments: P. Misra of Lincoln Laboratory; L. Chesto, former Chairman of RTCA Special Committee 159; and J. Danaher and Jacques Beser, formerly of 3S.

References

[1]   ANSER, "Russia's Global Navigation Satellite System," Arlington, VA, U.S. Air Force Contract Number F33657-90-D-0096, May 1994.

[2]   Kazantsev, V. N., et al., "Overview and Design of the GLONASS System," *Proc. of Intl. Conference on Satellite Communications*, Volume II, Moscow, Russia, October 18–21, 1994, pp. 207–216.

[3]   Technical Description and Characteristics of Global Space Navigation System GLONASS-M—Information Document, International Telecommunications Union, Documents 8D/46-E and 8D/ 46(Add.1)-E, November 22, 1994, and December 6, 1994, respectively.

[4]   "On the Activity on Application of the Global Navigation Satellite System GLONASS," Russian Federation Governmental Decree 237, March 7, 1995, http://www.glonass-center. ru/decree.html.

[5]   "Global Navigation Satellite System—GLONASS, Interface Control Document (Version 5.0)," Moscow, 2002, http://www.glonass-center.ru/icd02_e.zip.

[6]   "The Decree of the President of the Russian Federation," Decree 38-RP, February 18, 1999, http://www.glonass-center.ru/38rp_e.html.

[7]   "Declaration of the Government of the Russian Federation," Russian Federation Governmental Decree 346, March 29, 1999, http://www.glonass-center.ru/decl_e.html.

[8] "On the Federal Target Program—Global Navigation System," Russian Federation Governmental Decree 587, August 20, 2001. (Decree is not publicly available—information deduced from briefings and papers presented by Russians on the decree.)

[9] Kulik, S. V., "Status and Development of GLONASS," *First United Nations/United States of America Workshop on the Use of Global Navigation Satellite Systems*, Kuala Lumpur, Malaysia, August 20–24, 2001, http://www.jupem.gov.my/gnss_bm.htm (removed from the Internet in 2004).

[10] Kulik, S. V., "GLONASS: Status and Progress," Second United Nations/United States of America Regional Workshop on the Use of Global Navigation Satellite Systems, Vienna, Austria, November 26–30, 2001, http://www.oosa.unvienna.org/SAP/act2001/gnss2/presentations/index.html.

[11] Revnivych, S., "Status and Development of GLONASS," *Third UN/USA Workshop on the Use and Applications of Global Navigation Satellite Systems, for the Benefit of Latin America and the Caribbean*, Santiago, Chile, April 1–5, 2002, http://www.oosa.unvienna.org/SAP/act2002/gnss1/presentations/index.html.

[12] Revnivych, S., "Status and Development of GLONASS," *Fourth UN/USA Workshop on the Use of Global Satellite Positioning Systems, for the Benefit of Africa, Lusaka, Zambia*, July 15–19, 2002, http://www.oosa.unvienna.org/SAP/act2002/gnss2/presentations/index.html.

[13] Feairheller, S., "The Russian GLONASS System: A U.S. Air Force/Russian Study," *Proc. of 7th Int. Technical Meeting of Satellite Division of U.S. Institute of Navigation*, Salt Lake City, UT, September 20–23, 1994, pp. 293–304.

[14] Lebedev, Colonel M., "Space Navigation System 'GLONASS'—Application Prospective," Scientific Information Coordination Center for Military Space Forces, *Proc. of RTCA 1994 Symposium*, Reston, VA, November 30–December 1, 1994, pp. 199–210.

[15] Gouzhva, Y. G., A. G. Gevorkyan, and V. V. Korniyenko, "Atomic Frequency Standards for Satellite Radionavigation Systems," *Proc. of 45th Annual Symposium on Frequency Control*, Los Angeles, CA, May 29–31, 1991, pp. 591–593.

[16] Polischuk, G., et al., "The Global Navigation Satellite System GLONASS: Development and Usage in the 21st Century," *34th Annual Precise Time and Time Interval (PTTI) Meeting*, http://www.tycho.usno.navy.mil/ptti/ptti2002/paper13.pdf.

[17] Revnivych, S., "Developments and Plans of the GLONASS System," UN/USA International Meeting of Experts the Use and Applications of Global Navigation Satellite Systems, Vienna, Austria, November 11–15, 2002, http://www.oosa.unvienna.org/SAP/gnss/expert_meeting/presentations/index.html.

[18] Revnivych, S., "Developments of the GLONASS System and GLONASS Service Interface," *Joint Meeting of Action Team on Global Navigation Satellite Systems and Global Navigation Satellite Systems Experts of UN/USA Regional Workshops and International Meeting 2001–2002*, Vienna, Austria, December 8–12, 2003.

[19] Koshelyaevsky, N. B., and S. B. Pushkin, "National Time Unit Keeping over a Long Interval Using an Ensemble of H-Maser," *Proc. of 22nd Annual Precise Time and Time Interval Applications and Timing Meeting*, Vienna, VA, December 14–6, 1990, pp. 97–116.

[20] Boykov, V. V., V. F. Galazin, and Y. V. Korablev, "Geodesy: Application of Geodetic Satellites for Solving the Fundamental and Applied Problems," *Geodeziya i Katografiya*, No. 11, November 1993, pp. 8–11.

[21] Boykov, V. V., et al., "Experiment of Compiling the Geocentric System of Coordinates PZ-90," *Geodeziya i Katografiya*, No. 11, November 1993, pp. 18–21.

[22] Beser, J., and J. Danaher, "The 3S Navigation R-100 Family of Integrated GPS/GLONASS Receivers: Description and Performance Results," *Proc. of U.S. Institute of Navigation National Technical Meeting*, San Francisco, CA, January 20–22, 1993, pp. 25–45.

[23] Stein, B., and W. Tsang, "PRN Codes for GPS/GLONASS: A Comparison," *Proc. of U.S. Institute of Navigation National Technical Meeting*, San Diego, CA, January 23–25, 1990, pp. 31–35.

[24] "Technical Description and Characteristics of Global Space Navigation System GLONASS-M—Information Document," International Telecommunications Union, Document 8D/46-E, November 22, 1994.

[25] "Technical Description and Characteristics of Global Space Navigation System GLONASS-M—Information Document," International Telecommunications Union, Document 8D/ 46(Add.1)-E, December 6, 1994.

[26] Misra, P., "Integrated Use of GPS and GLONASS in Civil Aviation," *MIT Lincoln Laboratory Journal*, Vol. 6, No. 2, Summer/Fall 1993.

[27] Misra, P., M. Pratt, and R. Muchnik, "GLONASS Performance in 1994: A Review," *Massachusetts Institute of Technology Lincoln Laboratory Report: ATC Project*, Memorandum No. 42PM-SATNAV- 0100, February 8, 1995.

[28] GLONASS System Information, First Consultation Meeting Forum, Geneva, Switzerland, December 8–9, 2003, International Telecommunication Union Web site, http://www.itu.int/jive/forum.jspa?forumID=300&start=0.

[29] Polishchuk, G. M., et al., "The Creation of Differential Correction Systems and the Systems of Global Navigation Satellite System Monitoring," *34th Annual Precise Time and Time Interval Meeting*, 2002, http://www.tycho.usno.navy.mil/ptti/ptti2002/paper15.pdf.

[30] Kharisova, V. N., A. I., Perov, and V. A. Boldin, (eds.), "Global Satellite Radio-Navigation System," *Journal of Radio Engineering*, 1998, pp. 1–400.

[31] Solov'yev, Yu. A., *Satellite Navigation Systems*, Moscow: Eko-Trendz Press, 2000, pp. 1–267.

[32] http://www.glonass-center.ru/icd02_e.zip.

[33] http://www.glonass-center.ru/frame_e.html.

[34] http://www.mcc.rsa.ru/IACKVO/homepage1.html.

[35] http://rniikp.ru/en/abilities.

[36] http://www.mte.ru/www/navig.nsf.

[37] Ma, J., "Space Eye—Famous Satellite Telemetry Expert Chen Fangyun," in *Collection of Literary Biographies of Chinese National Defense Science and Technology Scientists*, Beijing, China: People's Liberation Army Publishing House, 2000.

[38] Fangyun, C., et al., "Development of Satellite Positioning Determination and Communication Systems," *Chinese Space Science and Technology*, 1987.

[39] Foley, T. M., "Space Operations Begin Using Geostar Payload," *Aviation Week and Space Technology*, July 25, 1988, pp. 55–56.

[40] Zhihao, P., "A New Era in Satellite Navigation and Positioning Systems—The GEOSTAR System," *Aerospace China* (in Chinese), No. 1, January 1992, pp. 20–23.

[41] Kean, H., "Radio Determination and Communication Experimental System (RDCES) Using Two Satellites," *Proc. of GLOBECOM 93*, November 29–December 3, 1993, pp. 579–582.

[42] "BeiDou Navigation Experiment Satellite (BeiDou-1)," Chinese Academy of Space Technology, http://www.cast.ac.cn/cpyyy/htqzt.htm.

[43] "CTC—Civilian Service Provider BeiDou Navigation System" and associated Web sites in English, China Top Communications Web site, http://www.chinatopcom.com/english/gsii.htm, September 8, 2003.

[44] "BDStar Navigation—BeiDou Application the Omni-Directional Service Business" and associated Web sites in Chinese, BDStar Navigation Web site, http://www.navchina.com/pinpai/beidou.asp.

[45] "BeiDou System Synopsis," Web sites in English, Xi'an Astronautics Star Science and Technology Ltd. (SpaceStar), CAST 504th, http://www.spacestar.com.cn/product/show.asp?id=285&kind=4.

[46] "BeiDou Navigation Experiment Satellite (BeiDou-1)," Chinese Academy of Space Technology, http://www.cast.ac.cn/cpyyy/htqzt.htm.

[47] "CHINASAT-31, -32 and -33" International Telecommunication Union Radio AR11/A, IFIC 1211, January 24, 1995.

[48] Zhu, Y., "CAST's Satellite Common Platforms," IAF-98-U.5.07, *49th International Astronautical Congress*, Melbourne, Australia, September 28–October 2, 1998.

[49] "DFH-3 Satellite Platform" Web site in English, Chinese Academy of Space Technology (CAST), July 31, 2004, http://www.cast.ac.cn/en/ShowArticle.asp?ArticleID=47.

[50] "Satellite Subsystems," and associated Web sites in English, China Aerospace Corporation Space Products Web site, July 31, 2004, http://www.spaceproducts.com.cn.

[51] "CHINASAT-33," International Telecommunication Union Radio AR11/C, IFIC 2676, March 18, 1997.

[52] "CHINASAT-33," International Telecommunication Union Radio RES/47 MOD-1, IFIC 2513, November 18, 2003.

[53] "CHINASAT-33," CR/C/885, IFIC 2490, International Telecommunication Union Radio, March 8, 2001.

[54] "NovAtel Supplies GPS Receivers for Chinese WAAS Program," Press Release, July 6, 2000.

[55] "Satellite Navigation Enhancement System—More Than Ten Million Yuan Supply Agreement Evaluates Once More on November 28, 2001," Web site in Chinese, BDStar Navigation, http://www.navchina.com/news/23.asp.

[56] Murfin, T., "NovAtel Delivers GPS Receivers for Phase 2 of Chinese WAAS Program," Press Release, January 17, 2002, NovAtel Web site, http://www.novatel.com/about-us/archive/20020117.html.

[57] "NovAtel Inc. Ships More GPS Receivers for Chinese WAAS Program," Press Release, December 5, 2002.

[58] "The China Satellite Navigation Enhancement System (SNAS) Construction," Web site in Chinese, BDStar Navigation, http://www.navchina.com/apption/1.asp.

[59] Liu, J., and L. Xia, "GNSS Activities in China—Application and Advancement," *2003 International Symposium on GPS/GNSS,* Tokyo, Japan, November 15–18, 2003.

[60] Kai, T., "Chinese Navigation Localization Satellite System Progress," *Aerospace China,* Issue 8, 2002.

[61] "CHINASAT-34A, -34B, -35A, -35B, and –35C," API/A 515-519, published June 8, 1999, International Telecommunication Union (ITU) Radio Frequency Filing submitted by China to the ITU in 1997.

[62] "COMPASS-58.75E, -80E, 110E, -140E, -M and -H," API/A 1300-1305, published May 3, 2000, International Telecommunication Union Radio Frequency Filing submitted by China.

[63] "COMPASS-160E," published November 16, 2003, International Telecommunication Union Radio Frequency Filing submitted by China.

[64] "COMPASS-MG," published November 18, 2003, International Telecommunication Union Radio Frequency Filing submitted by China.

[65] Maeda, H., "Status of the Japanese QZSS Satellite System," *Munich Satellite Navigation Summit,* March 23–25, 2004.

[66] Takahashi, H., "The Future of JRANS Concept (Japanese Regional Advanced Navigation Satellite System)," *SATNAV 2003 Symposium,* Melbourne, Australia, July 23, 2003.

[67] Karner, J., "GPS International Activities—Briefing by U.S. State Dept.," *43rd Meeting of the CGSIC IIS,* March 2004.

[68] Makota, K., "The Quasi-Zenith Satellite System (Japanese Satellite Positioning System)," *International Aerospace Federation Conference (IAC) 2004,* Vancouver, Canada, 2004.

[69] Kallender, P., "Impass over Japan's QZSS System Persists," *SPACE NEWS,* November 1, 2004, p. 9.

[70] Kon, M., "System Overview and Applications of Quasi-Zenith Satellite Systems," *21st ICSSC,* as AIAA 2003-2302, Yokohama, Japan, April 15–19, 2003.

[71] Kimura, K., et al., "Quasi-Zenithal Satellite Communications System Using Inclined Synchronous Orbits," *49th Astronautical Congress*, Melbourne, Australia, September 28–October 2, 1998, IAF-98-M.4.03.

[72] Petrovski, I. G., et al., "QZSS—Japan's New Integrated Communication and Positioning Service for Mobile Users," *GPS World*, June 2003.

[73] Kawano, I., et al., "Japanese Experimental GPS Augmentation Using Quasi-Zenith Satellite System (QZSS)," *ION GNSS 2004*, Long Beach, CA, September 2004.

[74] Kallender-Umezu, P., "Japanese Quasi-Zenith Satellite System May Face Delays," *SPACE NEWS*, August 9, 2004, p. 8.

[75] Kimura, K., and M. Tanaka, "Required Velocity Increment for Formation Keeping of Inclined Geo-Synchronous Constellation," *51st International Astronautical Congress (IAF '00)*, Rio de Janeiro, Brazil, October 2–6, 2000.

[76] Hama, S., et al., "Space Borne Hydrogen Maser and Time Keeping System for the Quasi-Zenith Satellite System (QZSS)," National Institute of Information and Communication Technology, *ION GNSS 2004 Conference*, Long Beach, CA, September 2004.

[77] Petrovski, I. G., et al., "QZSS—Japan's New Integrated Communication and Positioning Service for Mobile Users," *GPS World*, June 2003.

[78] "Government to Focus Quasi-Zenith Satellite Project on GPS-Type Services," Tokyo Nikkei Telecom 21, October 2, 2004, http://telecom21.nikkei.com.jp.

CHAPTER 12

GNSS Markets and Applications

Len Jacobson
Global Systems and Marketing, Inc.

12.1 GNSS: A Complex Market Based on Enabling Technologies

The only thing more difficult than describing the GNSS market is predicting its future growth. Until there is a deployed GALILEO satellite constellation late in this decade, the GNSS market will consist largely of the GPS market and its space-based and ground-based augmentations. Even more tenuous is the market potential for China's BeiDou and Russia's GLONASS, despite a formal agreement between the United States and Russia to foster cooperation in their respective national satellite navigation systems. BeiDou is just getting started as a test program, and GLONASS has largely been ignored by the world's civil user community in favor of GPS. Thus, these systems, along with the Japanese QZSS and the Indian GAGAN, are necessarily excluded from any marketing considerations due to the uncertainty of their schedules and viability. But if they are fielded, perhaps by the 2012–2015 time frame, they could influence the overall market potential of GNSS beyond just GPS and GALILEO.

Market definitions usually start by counting the sales of the goods and services loosely associated with a technology. But how does one aggregate and quantify an ensemble of goods such as GPS receivers that range from the $2 chips that are components of a GPS receiver for use inside cell phones to large $300,000, nuclear-hardened navigation sets inside a submarine? And how do you account for all the value-added applications enabled by GPS? Are they part of the GNSS market? A public presentation by THALES Research put the total world market for GNSS equipment at $68 billion by 2010 [1]. At the time of this writing, the United States enjoyed about a 50% share of the world GPS user equipment market, based on reported sales of U.S. GPS companies, while the remaining 50% is primarily European and Asian, split about 25% each. Canada has a small (less than 5%) market share and is included in the U.S. total [2]. The U.S. share will likely decline as GALILEO comes on line and more European competition enters the market.

GPS market forecasts and growth rates have varied significantly depending on which segments or which geographic areas are included in the total. A 1991 study predicted the total market to be $5.7 billion in 1996 [3]. That value could grow to $68 billion by 2010, with just a 16.5% growth rate. The early forecast was significantly wrong, as the actual total for the 1996 market was only about $2 billion, as shown in a study by ABI Research [4]. This is not surprising, as anytime one tries to forecast 5 years ahead, a small change in assumed growth rate can lead to significant differences five years out. At the time of the 1991 forecast, there was very little experience with GPS applications, the industry was infantile, and the future cost of GPS receivers was almost impossible project. Additionally, SA was expected to remain in place for the foreseeable future. Using a more likely growth rate of 20% as experienced over the past several years, the 1996 figure of $2 billion could grow to $26 billion by 2010. The ABI Research study predicted global GPS equipment revenue of $22 billion by 2008. Extrapolating the fairly constant growth rate in the data leads to a $25 billion prediction for 2010. Beyond 2010, market predictions become even more uncertain and dependent on GALILEO deployment. However, by 2018, ABI Research expects a GNSS market of over $150 billion. Forecasts from European organizations estimate 2018 product sales to be 150 billion Euros ($175 billion) and the total sales of both products and services at 250 billion Euros ($290 billion). That same publication predicts the GNSS market to approach 265 billion Euros ($310 billion) by 2020 with at least 3 billion chipsets in use [5, 6]. Another 2004 presentation at the International Satellite and Communications Conference (ISCe) in Long Beach, California, predicted 2.5 billion GALILEO users by 2020. They also predicted that by 2012 users will opt for a GNSS receiver that will likely be a combined GALILEO/GPS receiver [7]. What all this conflicting data indicates is that it is very difficult to predict the GNSS market 5 years ahead with any confidence of certainty, let alone to do it when GALILEO is included. The dollar/Euro conversion factor (1.2 used herein) itself could vary 20% or more. However, all forecasts agree that the GNSS market will be both large and growing as the myriad of emerging applications, with some still in a conceptual stage, come to fruition.

The likely future of GPS in the United States is fairly clear as the modernization program is underway and the GPS III architecture is being defined. New GPS capabilities such as L5 have been confidently factored into market projections, but how much credence should one put into 2004 projections of a GALILEO market that won't even begin to emerge until at least 4 or 5 years from now? One way to approach this is to understand just why GALILEO is being developed, when GPS devoid of user charges is already so imbued in the world. First, it's a question of European sovereignty—GPS is developed and operated by the U.S. Department of Defense with input from the U.S. Department of Transportation, whereas GALILEO is run by a strictly civil organization. Second, GPS does not guarantee service or take responsibility or liability for any damages, while GALILEO will provide a certified service. Having their own system provides some political influence, especially in areas such as air transportation and potential military exploitation. And probably the most important reason is that GALILEO will improve the level of European space technology and enable European industry to be a more effective competitor in the world GNSS marketplace.

Defining and quantifying a market segment for GNSS services is no less a challenge. Consider services such as developing receivers for the government, designing filtering software in order to integrate GPS with other sensors in a commercial or military aircraft, testing the products, installing and integrating them into vehicles and aircraft, and services that rely on GPS information like surveying. Classic definitions of the GPS market have first split the market into military and commercial (or civil, as these two terms will be used interchangeably) segments. Market studies are usually performed by researchers versed in consumer electronics markets. Organizations performing market studies can count users, rely on sales projections of similar products, draw upon earlier experiences with those products, use existing modeling, and make educated guesses as to the potential for growth. In most cases, these studies are weak in one or more areas (e.g., aviation and marine), but strong in others like consumer products or mobile location services. This is not surprising, as most of these research firms are likely to specialize more in some particular market segments than in others. They do a great job in a micro sense with demographics, historical data, focus groups, surveys, competitive analyses, and such. Their results are used to decide on investments in new products and new ventures, but in a macro sense they just cannot accurately describe, let alone forecast, the totality of something as multifaceted as the GPS market. It is doubtful that anyone could perform a comprehensive forecast with high confidence. The attempt provided herein provides a starting point for delving deeper into particular market segments.

Almost all previous studies have relegated the military market to a small fraction of the civil market. While it is true that the total dollars expended in the military market is small compared to the total for civil markets, it is nonetheless significant (over $25 billion spent to date) [8]. It endures and provides seed money for developments that often lead to new or enhanced civilian applications. Even more importantly, the military value of GPS is the primary reason why it remains funded, supported, and sustained, thus enabling the civil market. Because the civil component has become so important, there is no doubt that civil GPS services will be maintained even if the military eventually migrates to some new technology to satisfy its navigation, positioning, and timing needs. Furthermore, the military is planning on using GPS at least until 2030. While there are significant differences between commercial and military markets, consider that in the commercial marketplace:

- The market size varies smoothly.
- The seller bears the development risk.
- There are many buyers.
- There are many competitors for market share.
- There are many similar products.
- Prices are set by marginal utility.

While in the military market:

- We see erratic buying behavior due to changing requirements and budgets.
- The government usually bears any development risk.
- There are relatively few buyers.
- In most cases, there are few competitors for market share.
- Product requirements vary significantly among customers.
- Performance is more important than price.

The most important difference is probably that in the military market there is a substantial return on investment (ROI) because a company's investment is relatively low. Profitability is certainly also lower in military markets as the amount allowed is usually limited by legislation but still the real ROI is much higher than in civil markets. In addition, the risk associated with the investment is much lower for the military market.

Yet many military products and technologies eventually find their way into the commercial market. These are called dual-use systems. After the Internet, GPS is likely the second greatest modern dual-use DOD system in terms of impact on our civilization.

In the first edition of this book in 1996, GPS was described as an enabling technology. It certainly is that but it is also a ubiquitous technology. With the hindsight of recent history, one can see how GPS has not only enabled new applications heretofore unknown, but it has permeated almost all aspects of commerce, agriculture, leisure, travel, and of course, warfare (e.g., GPS-equipped "smart bombs"). At the 2004 Institute of Navigation, GNSS Conference, Frank Kreuse, head of the Chicago Transit System, said that "GPS is quietly permeating the infrastructure." What he meant is that GPS is becoming a critical piece of the U.S. and other nations' structural underpinning as more and more people and functions depend upon it.

12.1.1 Market Scope, Segmentation, and Value

The definition of the GPS market that is used here is the dollar value of all the goods (such as GPS receivers, antennas, and chipsets) and services (such as software development, testing, integration, and location-based services) provided to users of GPS or to applications that incorporate GPS receivers. We cannot logically include such things as flight management systems or the total value of an integrated GPS/INS, but the GPS receiver and integrating software is included. What is not included in any of the forecasts for GPS or for GALILEO are the costs to develop, deploy, and maintain the satellite constellations or the control segments. For example, GPS has cost about $24 billion for the satellites and control segment through fiscal year 2004, with another $8 billion to get to a modernized GPS and to the first GPSIII in fiscal year 2011 or fiscal year 2012 [8]. GALILEO will probably cost nearly $10 billion for these elements by the time it is fielded [2]. These funds provided by governments are also part of the overall GNSS market, as they will be mostly spent via contracts with private industry. In the case of GALILEO, it is expected that a concessionaire will fund part of the costs of the system in the hope of recouping that investment through user fees for the regulated services. Whether that will come to pass remains to be seen. Estimating this market segment is difficult, as it depends on future governments' plans to maintain, improve, and operate GNSS. At least for GPS, there is a high confidence of continued funding. In the case of GALILEO, we will have to wait until it is deployed and operating. In any case, the companies that benefit from this market segment generally are not the same companies that serve the market segments that deal with equipment or services for users of GNSS.

The GPS component of the GNSS market is obviously global, since users are all over the world, yet much of the potential for global GPS market growth is dependent on U.S. government actions and policy, particularly export policy. While highly unlikely, the return of SA or possible imposition of fees for use of GPS would be a deterrent to all civil market growth. Neither of these contingencies has been factored into any projections given herein, as the probabilities of occurrence are extremely low. Expected deployments of new signals such as L5 for civilian users could be delayed, as many government programs have been, and in turn delay market growth in several civilian sectors. By contrast, policies such as the E-911 mandate from the U.S. FCC that require cell phone operators to pinpoint their users who call 911 has spurred growth of GPS chips for cell phones as one way to satisfy the mandate. There were over 450 million cell phones in use in 2002, with an expectation of almost 700 million by 2007. In the same period, PDA quantities are expected to rise from 48 million to 140 million [9].

The GPS user-oriented market as defined earlier has been growing at 18–20% compound annual growth rate (CAGR) [2]. This is expected to continue for the next several years until GALILEO signals are available. Then the CAGR for the combined GPS and GALILEO GNSS market could increase to about 30%. Some aspects will remain the same, notably that civil users will continue to outnumber military users by more than 1,000 to 1, with that ratio increasing. The current ratio is over 100 to 1. About 80 of the world's militaries use GPS in one way or another, but approximately 50 of those countries must rely on ruggedized civil receivers. The others have executed memoranda of understanding with the U.S. DOD and therefore have access to the GPS military signals.

Because of the vast difference in number of users, the civil market value will always be greater than the military market value. However, as GALILEO deploys, it will have to be left for a future prognosticator to determine the new ratio. This is because the extent that the military will use GALILEO is yet to be determined.

12.1.2 Unique Aspects of GNSS Market

Markets can be thought of in a hierarchical way with the total market subsuming an addressable market subsuming an achievable market. A company interested in entering the market or concerned with forecasting possible sales will start with the total market, which includes all of the goods and services described earlier. It includes both military and civilian and as noted, is global in nature. From that is derived an *addressable* market and within that an *achievable*, or an expected, market. An example might be the market addressed by a civil GPS chip maker. This addressable market would eliminate the military market but consider all civil receiver manufacturers and chipset adapters as potential customers. Another approach is to come at it from the number of possible users of the technology. This is done by just counting the ships, aircraft, hikers, autos, trucks, laptops, cell phones, and so forth. Afterwards, an educated guess is used to try and quantify what portion of these users of these products will need a GPS or GNSS chipset. The GNSS chipset can be thought of now as GPS + WAAS or GPS + EGNOS. In a few years, that definition would be expanded to include GALILEO and any other civil satellite navigation system or augmentation. With flexible software-based digital signal processing, it is well within the state of the art to develop products that can utilize any signals in view.

Once the determination of the addressable market is firm, the sales and marketing people will agree on the achievable market. This is a very important goal because it establishes the sales forecast from which all budgeting in a corporation begins. Much activity, employment, and capital expenditures are driven by this forecast, which in fact is really a guess as to how many sales can be made from a market definition that is fuzzy at best. Yet that is the best data from which to start. Fortunately, there is history and competitive information that lends credence to such a forecast.

Forecasting in the military is much simpler, although not built up with any more confidence. The data provided by government budgets provide a starting point that in general is fairly accurate, at least in the short term. Budgets traditionally cover five or more years so the military GPS equipment forecast is available to a potential supplier. In the United States, Congress and defense priorities often change these forecasts but usually not more often than annually. Projects and procurements span several years, so there is a built-in inertia that keeps the forecast somewhat stable.

12.1.3   Market Limitations, Competitive Systems, and Policy

GNSS market growth is highly dependent on U.S. and EU government actions and policy. Some possible changes are:

- *The return of SA or possible fees for use of GPS*. Both seem highly unlikely to occur.
- *Time to deploy new signals*, including L2C and L5 for GPS and all of the GALILEO signals. The overall schedules for both of these capabilities are likely to slip to the right as most such endeavors usually do.
- *Export rule changes and regulatory demands*. While U.S. export limits on GPS may never be any more stringent; the use of GALILEO receivers or hybrid GPS/GALILEO receivers could be mandated for use in Europe. There could also be charges in the form of tariffs or royalties imposed on these receivers, thus limiting the market for them, although recent U.S./EU agreements would militate against that.
- *E-911 mandate and its equivalent in Europe*, which should actually increase the market worldwide as it has done in the United States.

In late 2004, President Bush of the United States issued a new policy on space-based positioning, navigation, and timing. It created a new National Space-Based Position, Navigation, and Timing Executive Committee and dissolved the existing IGEB created under the Clinton administration.

The policy stressed the military value of GPS to the United States by mentioning the importance of navigation warfare training, testing, and exercises in several places. However, it also maintained the commitment to discontinue the use of SA.

The GNSS market can only expand as nascent satellite navigation systems mature. Besides GALILEO, there could be a GLONASS renaissance as well as the fielding of GAGAN from India, BeiDou from China, and MTSAT from Japan. While some of this added market potential will be related to SBAS applications, there also could be new combined receiver products business for many of the world's chipmakers and receiver suppliers.

Like any venture, there are always risks to success. The GNSS market looks extremely promising, but there are concerns that any prudent entrepreneur should be aware of. As GPS receivers embed themselves in our cars, cell phones, PDAs, laptops, watches, and cameras, and they become wedded to wireless communications links therein, a potential backlash from consumers could limit market growth. More and more we are becoming a society where privacy rights are being eroded by fear of crime and terrorism abetted by technology that fosters the erosion. Telematics, or the provision of services to mobile users, is one area where the line between location awareness by the service provider can easily become location awareness by unwelcome surveillers.

Governments have made use of covert tracking techniques for many years. GPS with communications just makes it easier. As small, inexpensive wearable GPS/communications devices become more prevalent, the opportunity to impinge on privacy grows and, if abused, could lead to a backlash that could prompt legislation limiting the market [10].

12.2 Civil Navigation Applications of GNSS

Commercial use of GPS has its roots in the predecessor program, the Transit Satellite Navigation System. It was fielded by the U.S. Navy in the early 1960s and used by nuclear submarines to fix their positions in the open ocean. A satellite came into view only every 90 minutes (approximately), so the system was not very useful to aircraft. Just as Navy ships were the primary users, large commercial vessels also became users as receiver prices dropped. This drop was spurred by new emerging technology and by the oil crisis of 1973. By then, equipment prices were in the $100,000 range and could actually be justified by large oil tankers as a cost offset to wasted bunker fuel caused by inaccurate navigation. Then prices dropped even further, and large fishing vessels became the growing market. This was accompanied by markets in land and ocean survey.

When GPS concepts were being explored in the 1965–1973 time frame as a solution for aircraft navigation, Congress demanded that in exchange for funding it, there would be two conditions: the GPS had to be a joint service program, and it had to have a civil signal. These roots of commercial GPS are shown in Figure 12.1.

As soon as there were GPS satellites in the sky, there was a commercial market. The first satellites were launched in the late 1970s, and it became possible to find one's time very accurately knowing one's location whenever a satellite was visible. With three satellites in view, periods of two-dimensional positioning and velocity determination were possible. With four satellites, this increased to three dimensions. As more satellites were added, the daily periods of good navigation (i.e., low GDOP) grew longer until full 24-hour coverage was achieved in the early 1990s. As GPS use increased and technology marched forward, the prices of user equipment came down, fueling even greater usage. The primary technological advances that spurred this were large-scale integrated circuits, monolithic microwave integrated circuits, dense memory chips, and microprocessors [2].

The first companies to offer commercial GPS products were the same ones developing military equipment (e.g., Magnavox and Rockwell Collins). Magnavox

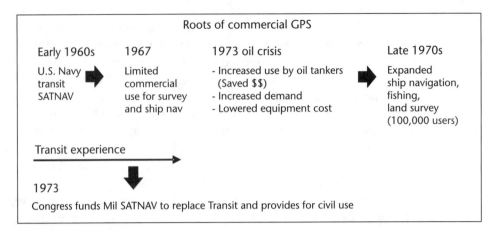

Figure 12.1   Roots of commercial GPS.

developed the first GPS set to use only the L1 C/A signal. It was a sequencing receiver and could handle low flight dynamics. It was tested by NASA and the FAA. Another early civil GPS developer was Trimble Navigation. In Europe, THALES has a substantial GPS business that developed internally and from acquisitions that date back many years.

The established, public, pure GPS commercial companies Trimble, NovAtel, and GARMIN were joined on the stock market in 2004 by SiRF, which has been developing GPS chipsets since 1995. SiRF described its current competition in its Securities and Exchange Commission filing [9]: "For chip sets, the main competitors include SiRF, Analog Devices, Motorola, Philips, QUALCOMM, Sony, STMicroelectronics, Texas Instruments and Trimble, as well as some start-up companies. For modules, the main competitors are Furuno, JRC, Motorola, Sony, GARMIN, THALES and Trimble. For licensed intellectual property (IP) cores, competitors include QUALCOMM and Trimble."

12.2.1 Marine Navigation

While not the largest market segment, marine navigation was the first to embrace satellite navigation. Today the market is maturing. Along with radios and radar, a GPS receiver is a piece of standard equipment on any boat operating far from shore. There are about 20 million boats in North America, and 50 million worldwide. Of these, almost 98% are pleasure craft. Commercial coastal and inland vessels comprise about 1 million potential platforms for GPS, and there are more than 90,000 registered merchant vessels worldwide, most of which are involved in fishing.

The International Loran Association estimates that there are currently well over one million Loran-C receivers installed in North America alone. Most of these are in ships and boats, and all, shipborne or not, are candidates for replacement with GPS.

The U.S. Coast Guard's system of differential correction broadcasts (discussed in Section 12.6) has been widely accepted, and other countries have similar systems, particularly in the North Sea and Scandinavian waters. These systems provide accuracy in the 1-m–3-m range within about 150 miles of a correction beacon, and they yield speed over ground (SOG) accuracy of about one-tenth of a knot. This can be a benefit to commercial fishermen in providing the ability to monitor small changes in speed caused by a dragged net's snagging, allowing rapid response to prevent serious damage. There is also obvious application in sailboat and yacht racing for this kind of speed accuracy. The combination of SOG with wind speed and speed through the water gives information about set and drift and apparent wind speed and direction. Accurate speed of advance is also available, aiding the yachting tactician in finding the fastest route to the mark.

Figure 12.2 shows a marine navigator with database management capability and graphical display of position and speed information. In this market, ease of use and the ability to manage a large database of waypoints and sophisticated cartography are key requirements.

Ferries and cruise lines are also prime candidates for accurate navigation systems. There are almost 1,000 ferries operating in North America and over 100 major cruise ships. On any major cruise ship you can usually visit the bridge and see a plethora of GPS navigators, electronic chart displays, and other equally impressive electronics. Since the grounding of the oil tanker Exxon Valdez in March 1989 and the resulting oil-spill damage, there has been a time-tabled mandate to provide ADS capabilities to all oil carriers using the Port of Valdez in Alaska. Similar requirements are found in other world harbors. These systems derive a ship's position from GPS and transmit it via a radio link to a control station on the shore. The ship's position can then be monitored by the Coast Guard or other agency, and dangerous situations can be alarmed and rectified. Because of the critical nature of this radio link, and the development of new long-range communications technologies, communications carriers such as INMARSAT are heavily involved in ADS systems and are the primary market for this positioning technology. Most of the world's 6,000 oil tankers are now fitted with GPS/ADS equipment.

Figure 12.2   Typical GPS marine navigator. (Courtesy of GARMIN.)

Fisheries management is a worldwide mandate requiring swift action by governments when a sea boundary is intruded upon. Dwindling fish stocks have prompted the establishment of strict guidelines for fishermen and the closure of entire grounds. The situation is also making countries that share sea boundaries more and more sensitive to foreign fishing in their waters. These tensions engender the need for accurate position determination and recording to prove or disprove a boundary violation. Many of the 40,000 North American–registered fishing vessels, and those in most other countries, are subject to mandatory ADS. Even where not mandated, the 45,000 vessels that fish near international boundaries find it prudent to carry such gear for their own protection against false accusations.

GPS can aid in the berthing and docking of large vessels, by means of position, attitude, and heading reference systems. These installations use multiple antennas aboard the vessel to determine an accurate representation of the ship's orientation. Combined with appropriate reference cartography, this can be an immense aid in the handling of large vessels in close quarters. The more than 80,000 seagoing merchant vessels worldwide are candidates for this type of system. There is a market for extremely accurate positioning for seismic survey and oil exploration activities, as well as in dredging, buoy laying, and maintenance. There are about 2,500 dredges and 300 buoy tenders in operation around the world. Dredge operators are paid based on the amount of material they remove from a harbor or shipping channel, so accurate measurement of position can optimize the operation, reducing cost and wasted effort.

The availability of GPS and accurate DGPS has proven a boon to the development of precise seismic maps and location of drill sites with respect to identified geologic structure, especially in the offshore case, where exploration teams have paid significant revenue per day for accurate satellite positioning services. The availability of such accurate systems for navigation has enabled much resurveying of published marine chart information. A good portion of the data currently represented on marine charts are more than 50 years old, and hydrographic services are involved in the production of digital databases to an agreed-upon international format (DX90). This information is being used in a navigational aid known as an Electronic Chart Display and Information System (ECDIS). A typical ECDIS can cost nearly $100,000 per installation and provide almost autonomous operation of the vessel. Simpler ECDIS installations costing from $4,000 to $10,000 are used primarily as aids to situational awareness in conjunction with radar and visual references. A third class of marine charting device is becoming very popular, due to very low unit cost. Navigators with simple built-in or disc-updatable databases allow a vector map of a selected area to be drawn on a screen. These systems are excellent for providing a degree of situational awareness to a recreational boater, but in general are not certifiable for use on commercial vessels.

The rise of worldwide terrorism has spurred the development of means of tracking of large container ships as they ply the seas. GPS plays an important role in these kinds of systems, which also rely on satellite communications and electronic tagging.

Marine use of GPS has been widely accepted, and differential services are well established. Recreational vessels make good use of basic GPS for navigation, and the early acceptance of differential GPS bodes well for the health of that sector. The huge number of vessels and the value of GPS in marine navigation, fishing, and waterway maintenance, coupled with strong economic activity, will allow steady growth to a level of nearly $200 million annually by 2008. This segment, however, has a fairly low growth rate due to the maturity of the market [11].

12.2.2   Air Navigation

There are essentially two kinds of markets and two regimes of operation to consider in the airborne area. There are 224,000 GA aircraft registered in the United States and Canada. The U.S.-based Aircraft Owners and Pilots Association asserts that this represents 77% of the world GA aircraft population, so there would be an additional 67,000 in the rest of the world. These aircraft are privately owned by individuals or companies for personal or corporate transportation, or recreational flying. The second category is the air carrier industry, which employs just over 5,000 aircraft in North America and a similar number worldwide. Both of these markets will have a high demand for GPS as a long-range area navigation system, since phaseout of current VOR and NDB navigation aids is slated to begin in 2010 [12].

Loran-C provides effective coverage over most of North America, and coverage is growing in Northern Europe, the Middle East, and parts of Asia. Of course, none of these land-based systems can provide contiguous coverage over uninhabited or oceanic areas, as does GPS. For this regime of navigation, most transoceanic airliners currently rely on INS and GPS. GPS capability is routinely installed in all new Boeing and Airbus aircraft.

In the GA aircraft market, Loran-C navigators used to dominate, but penetration by GPS into this market is phenomenal, especially as GPS-aided approach capabilities become standard at most airfields. Figure 12.3 is representative of this equipment.

GPS now provides commercial and GA airborne systems with sufficient integrity to perform NPA. NPA is the most common type of instrument approach performed by GA pilots. The FAA has instituted a program to implement NPA. This so-called overlay program allows the use of a specially certified GPS navigator in place of a VOR or NDB receiver to fly the conventional VOR or NDB approach. New NPA overlays that define waypoints independent of ground-based facilities and that simplify the procedures required to be flown are being put into service at the rate of about 500 to 1,000 approaches per year and are almost complete at the

Figure 12.3   Typical general aviation GPS navigator. (Courtesy of GARMIN.)

5,000 public use airports in the United States. Other countries are implementing such procedures, and there is almost universal acceptance of some sort of GPS approach capability at most of the world's major airports.

In the execution of an NPA, the pilot or autopilot is given direction to enable the aircraft to be maneuvered into the appropriate position for a descent toward the runway. The descent is made with reference to an approach *plate*, which dictates minimum safe altitudes for each phase of the approach. Altitude information is provided by a separate instrument—a barometric altimeter. DGPS is required to provide the performance required for vertically guided approaches. Traditional category I, II, and III approaches involve guidance to the runway threshold in all three dimensions. Local area differential corrections, broadcast from an airport-based GBAS reference station (see Section 8.6.1.3), are anticipated to meet all requirements for even the most demanding (category III) approaches.

In 2003, the FAA declared WAAS operational for instrument flight operations. WAAS broadcasts on the GPS L1 frequency, so signals are accessible to GPS receivers without the need for a dedicated DGPS corrections communications link. The performance of this system is sufficient for NPA and new types of vertically guided approaches that are only slightly less stringent than category I.

The GA market is seeing a surge of activity after publication of GPS NPA at the busiest airports and most of the others. As described in Chapter 8, other SBASs are being fielded or considered to provide services equivalent to WAAS in other regions of the world. Also, as GALILEO is deployed, the use of GNSS by aviation for en-route, approach and landing is expected to become even more widespread.

12.2.3   Land Navigation

By far, the most promising navigation market for GNSS in terms of sheer size is for land navigation products. At the 2003 Civil GPS Service Interface Committee meeting, it was reported by the DOT that there are more than 420 million cars and 130 million trucks in the world, with 150 million cars and 40 million trucks in North America. (Americans drive or ride a total of 11 billion miles per day.) Initial use of GPS technology for land navigation was for fleet tracking applications, but its use for individual vehicle navigation is growing rapidly. In 2004, there were approximately 8 million GPS receivers in automobiles in the United States. At that same meeting, it was forecast that safety improvements made via the application of GNSS technologies will reduce the national annual traffic death rate to below 1 per 100 million miles driven, or about a 30% reduction from current levels.

The value of current fleet information provided by GNSS is evident for delivery, emergency vehicle, and scheduled service fleet dispatch and control. AVLS are being developed or installed in many of North America's 10.3 million trucking and emergency fleets, currently involving about a million vehicles in North America. Qualcomm Corp. is a pioneer of fleet tracking, with over 500,000 trucks and other fleet vehicles tracked via its OmniTRACS System. Many of these are GPS equipped, primarily outside of the United States and particularly in South America. Urban transit buses are finding application of GPS for schedule maintenance and safety enhancement. The drive toward increasing the capacity of the existing transportation infrastructure has spawned the emerging concept of intelligent transportation systems (ITS). These systems are meant to modify traffic flow according to demand and other factors. One way to do this involves the monitoring of the progress of vehicles that are transmitting their position to a central location. Traffic signals or rerouting signs can then be used to respond to situations where a particular *probe* vehicle is not progressing as it should under optimum conditions. Another aspect of ITS involves the automatic collection of highway and other tolls and tariffs. This eliminates the need for vehicles to stop at state lines or at toll booths on toll roads and bridges if their position is being reported and appropriate accounting arrangements are made between the tariff-collecting authority and the vehicle's operator. This is most appropriate for commercial operations, but it is not inconceivable that private automobiles could be subject to the same kind of system. It would be possible in early implementation to provide a through lane at toll booths for appropriately equipped vehicles. GPS is not central to this kind of technology. Since the location of the required toll payment is always known, the vehicle's passing of a local code reader would initiate toll billing. Yet there are other potential tariff systems where total road usage could be tracked and taxed rather than just on given roadways, as is done now. While the United States is unlikely to adopt such a revenue collection system, the EU may be more apt to do so in order to raise revenue from the use of GALILEO.

In the United States, the Americans with Disabilities Act requires that municipal transport facilities announce and display location information to passengers with sight and hearing disabilities. This requires that both audible and visual presentations be provided. Many transit systems do not fully comply with this requirement. Systems to provide this information automatically are attractive and low cost. GPS enables them.

Land navigation opportunities for GPS are enormous. The incorporation of moving maps and databases into private passenger vehicles will generate more demand for GPS products than all other vehicle markets combined. Early land-based adapters of the technology, of course, are the fleet operators, who can gain significant benefits from more efficient tracking and dispatch operations with integrated navigation and communications facilities. One concept employed is called *geofencing*, where a vehicle's GPS is programmed with a fixed geographical area and alerts the fleet operator whenever the vehicle violates the prescribed "fence."

The largest operator of a GPS-based land navigation service is OnStar, a General Motors subsidiary. In 2004, over 4 million vehicles were equipped with GPS receivers that communicate with OnStar operators via cell phone to provide either voice commands or map guidance to the driver.

12.3   GNSS in Surveying, Mapping, and Geographical Information Systems

For several reasons, GPS receiver technology owes much to its early application in the business of land surveying. The production of maps and charts and the georeferencing of data using GPS are natural outgrowths of the accurate and reliable techniques developed for the land-survey market.

12.3.1 Surveying

The huge economic advantage of using GPS in surveying applications drove the development of very sophisticated GPS equipment and tools to predict GPS coverage and derive position with centimeter accuracy. Delays in the launch of GPS satellites caused by the Challenger disaster in 1986 further strengthened the head start that surveying applications got over navigational uses of the system, and significant refinements in the use of carrier-phase, dual-frequency, postprocessed, differential positions were made. Extreme accuracy is possible by applying information on satellite positions available after the fact to the data obtained in the field. The value of the technology in the surveying business stems from the availability of absolute positions with respect to a universal coordinate system (WGS-84) and from the fact that they can be determined with a much smaller survey crew. A single surveyor can collect data in the field, where it would take a two- or three-person crew to achieve the same results using some conventional methods. Collected data can be processed to the required accuracy using inexpensive computing facilities, and the GPS equipment in the field can be used by the surveyor for rough surveys or the location of benchmarks or other features. Differential and kinematic techniques can provide accurate real-time information in the field and obviate the need for postprocessing the data, further reducing the cost of surveying operations. A great deal of sophistication has been brought to products in this area, and to a large extent the market is mature, with a handful of suppliers well entrenched. While the market for simple surveying by GPS may well be saturated, the use of GPS as an aid for position-based data collection for geographical information systems (GIS) continues to fuel growth in the market for sophisticated receivers.

12.3.2 Mapping

A major early implementation of GPS was in the provision of ground truthing, or orientation of aerial photogrammetry. Aircraft or spacecraft are used to photograph large areas of the Earth's surface. Index marks are often surveyed on the ground to provide reference locations on these photographs, which can be used in determining their scale and orientation. GPS can be used to survey these references. Further, the use of these references can be eliminated altogether if the position of the camera can be known accurately enough at the precise moment it took the picture. This technology has been developed using GPS augmented by accurate INS. Inertial systems have excellent short-term stability but tend to drift over time and require recalibration. By contrast, GPS has its inherent absolute referencing capabilities and can provide excellent augmentation for an INS. The two can be used together in this kind of application; the INS to help resolve cycle ambiguities inherent in the kinematic method of GPS use and to carry positioning duties over the short periods of GPS outage that may occur. The generation of road maps, or any other kind of feature map, is now extremely easy, achieved simply by recording a series of positions as a receiver is moved over the area to be mapped. Any degree of postprocessing necessary to achieve desired accuracy is available. Specific locations recorded may be annotated with location-specific information, such as street address, elevation, or vegetation type. This type of data collection is particularly useful for the building of data for GIS.

12.3.3   GIS

Anyone charged with the responsibility of managing a distributed inventory, such as might be the case with a utility, municipality, or steelyard, might appreciate the ability to locate and identify this inventory quickly and accurately. This is the role played by GPS in conjunction with GIS. The last decade has seen a proliferation of GIS software packages and programs. Government agencies and utilities have been eager to adopt this technology, but find that the initial input of data and timely updating thereof is a huge task using conventional means of data collection. With GPS, it is possible to capture position-referenced data in the field with a simple handheld computer. The situation is best illustrated by the example of the management of a municipality's streetlights. There may be a mix of fluorescent, sodium, mercury, and incandescent lights, with several varieties of each. The maintenance engineer capable of recognizing the types can be dispatched with a GPS-based data collector to log the location of each type of installation. This information can be loaded into a central database, so that when maintenance is necessary, the appropriate replacements can be ordered, stocked, and dispatched. Steel mills store large quantities of product in huge yards, stacked in such a way as to prevent warping. The stacks must be rotated periodically, on a set schedule. Further, there are different types of products that are indistinguishable from one another, except for the record of where each was put. The layout of these yards does not lend itself to physical marking, so accurate GPS can be used to locate each stack and reference its contents to a central database. The management of other yard inventory items such as shipping containers or lumber is similar, and GPS applications have been investigated here also.

A rapidly growing and highly visible endeavor is the management of natural resources. Environmental impact studies involve the collection of large amounts of position-related data, and GIS is prevalent here, too. GPS is instrumental in collecting data to provide input to animal population studies and the like.

Finally, a whole new discipline, referred to as precision farming, or farming by the foot, has emerged. The application of pesticides, herbicides, and fertilizers is becoming an increasingly exacting science. Many farm implement manufacturers are producing variable-rate application equipment that is controlled by sophisticated electronics coupled to a sort of GIS. It has been shown that material input costs can be reduced by 40%, and yield enhancements of a similar magnitude can be expected. Furthermore, the harmful effects of the runoff of unneeded fertilizers can be mitigated. It is possible that the variable application of fertilizers might be legislated for this reason. GPS of course is central to the soil mapping to determine requirements and to the control of application vehicles.

Several firms offer products to guide airborne applicators of pesticides. These systems involve customized mapping routines to direct the pilot of crop duster swath by swath over a particular field. This allows the replacement of the flagperson, who would direct the pilot from the ground (a job in a very hazardous environment), with more accurate electronic guidance. This reduces the amount of overspray and can significantly decrease the amount of time and material used.

12.4 Recreational Markets for GNSS-Based Products

Some obvious recreational applications of global positioning technology include hiking and orienteering. SAR teams can also make good use of the technology. Some applications are not so obvious, and it is here that the assertion that there are more uses for GPS than we can imagine is put to the test. Several organizations are developing positioning systems for golfing applications. Differential corrections are required, as accuracy of a few feet is needed. Course managers are attracted to the idea as a method to speed up play and improve the utilization of an existing resource. Receivers have been put on golf carts to display from a database the distance to the green, to the pin, and to any hazards that may be of interest from a given location.

At outdoor parks, tourists can use a GPS device that will allow them to conduct a self-guided tour without any external signs or references. At each designated spot, vignettes can be automatically triggered by the GPS unit and direct tourists based on their present position and knowledge of where they have been previously. Recently, recreational and commercial users were able to display digital maps on their GPS-equipped cell phones via a service provided by Cellular Telephone Industry Association members.

GPS receivers are small enough to be worn on the wrist. This has opened up applications for joggers to keep track of their location, speed, and distance, as well as for keeping track of children and for blind people to navigate [13, 14].

12.5 GNSS Time Transfer

The fact that GPS is based on accurate time references implies that the signals can be used for the synchronization of very accurate clocks and timing standards. Each satellite has multiple atomic clocks on board, and each is frequently updated to system time. A prime application of this accurate timing capability is in the control of data communications networks like the Internet, where data packets time-share the same communications bandwidth. Receivers and transmitters can be synchronized, reducing the data overhead required of the system. Other applications include synchronized switching of power grids and timing of racecars. An example of this was reported in August 2004 in *Network World* at the July 2004 NASCAR race at the New Hampshire International Speedway. Over 90,000 fans watched as GPS was used to time the racecars' performances. Data from each car, including its speed, position, time, braking, throttle position, and rpm, were sent five times per second to a BS and thence over the Internet and pay-per-view TV. There are several manufacturers of equipment dedicated solely to the extraction of accurate time from the GPS signal.

12.6 Differential Applications and Services

Perhaps the largest submarket involves the provision and use of differential corrections.

Stationary users can derive their own differential corrections and transmit them to specific locations using almost any means of communications, from the Internet to cellular to VLF-HF-microwave radios to satellite links. It makes better sense, however, to share such a system with other users, and there are market opportunities in providing such signals. In addition to the freely provided satellite transmitted corrections of the FAA's WAAS, the U.S. Coast Guard provides correction signals, broadcast over an existing network of nondirectional beacon transmitters around the coast of the United States and in the Great Lakes. This NDGPS system is being expanded to cover all of the U.S. landmass so it can be used by vessels in all inland waterways and by railroads for positive train control. The latter application alone is expected to accrue $3 billion/year in economic benefits for the railroad industry and its customers. NDGPS has many U.S. government participants; notably, the U.S. Army Corps of Engineers in conjunction with the Coast Guard provides similar coverage for the Mississippi and Ohio River valleys, and other countries' authorities are implementing similar systems. These broadcasts are provided free of charge, but require the purchase of specialized receivers and demodulators to decode the correction signals, sent at 283–325 kHz.

12.6.1   Precision Approach Aircraft Landing Systems

Most instrument approaches carried out by commercial air carriers are precision approaches.

Unlike NPA, these procedures give glideslope guidance to the aircraft on approach. The lack of signal integrity precludes the use of unaided GPS for demanding aviation applications. These applications require the use of either code differential or kinematic carrier-phase tracking techniques. Precision landing systems require not only better integrity (warnings of system failure or inaccuracy within 6 seconds or less) but also better accuracy than is provided by the basic GPS service. The FAA's WAAS provides this warning, and sufficient accuracy to perform close to category I precision landing requirements. This allows about 90% of the airline approaches currently performed to use a GPS approach augmented in this way. Category II and III approaches, involving lower weather minima, also require improved accuracy and integrity warnings, which will be provided by airport-based differential stations broadcasting GPS corrections directly to the aircraft on approach (i.e., LAAS). It is expected that when GPS III and GALILEO are deployed, there will be both an improvement in overall accuracy and additional integrity.

12.6.2   Other Differential Systems

Surveyors, cartographic and hydrographic agencies, as well as a host of other users require accuracy better than that available from GPS's SPS. These users can either set up their own BSs and datalink facilities or purchase correction signals from a supplier or cooperative of similar users. Many services are presently available from which one can purchase or otherwise obtain differential corrections. Some of these services operate in real time, broadcasting their signals to users, and some provide time-tagged data with which one can correct field data after gathering it. This is known as postprocessing and is common in surveying applications. State survey and geodetic organizations are using GPS to form *active control networks* that rely on GPS to tie together positions rather than referencing them back to fixed monuments by conventional surveying means. California has established an earthquake monitoring system along these lines.

12.6.3 Attitude Determination Systems

While a limited market segment, GPS receivers have been proven to be useful in determining the attitude of host vehicles. Examples include pointing a long artillery gun barrel, finding an aircraft's attitude, outputting ship's heading, pitch, and roll, and particularly determining spacecraft attitude. These applications go back to the 1980s with the military funding the research and development. In the mid-1990s, a unit was introduced called the Trimble Advanced Navigation System Vector Attitude Determination System, which many researchers applied to various attitude determination problems, including NASA/Stanford's Gravity Probe-B spacecraft. All of these systems make use of either multiple antennas for three-dimensional solutions or at least a linear array to determine a pointing vector. Honeywell obtained one of the earliest patents (6088653) for a vehicle application, where a three-antenna GPS receiver is integrated with a vehicle inertial sensor. Today, integrations between GPS receivers and inertial sensors are a very high-tech market area requiring software development that uses sophisticated Kalman filtering algorithms. In 2002, a similar integration was used for a typical space application of GPS attitude determination aboard NASA's Thermosphere, Ionosphere, Mesosphere Energetics and Dynamics (TIMED) spacecraft by Johns Hopkins University Applied Physics Laboratory. The TIMED mission studied the influences of the Sun and humans on the least explored and understood portion of Earth's atmosphere—the mesosphere and lower thermosphere/ionosphere.

12.7 GNSS and Telematics and LBS

A truly exciting and major growth area for GNSS equipment and services is in what is euphemistically called *transport telematics*, or vehicle location-awareness services. Driven mainly by service providers looking for steady income streams, these services rely heavily on knowing where a user is located and being able to communicate with that user. Estimates of this market segment range between $1 billion and $11 billion by 2008. The uncertainty is due to the difficulty allocating the revenue to the telecommunications companies and to the actual location awareness service provider. Nonetheless, as the world's cell phone population approaches the half billion mark and GPS chips proliferate, the technology is available to satisfy the basic elements of a telematics service. In its infancy now, there are the standard vehicle tracking services, most notably QUALCOMM's OmniTRACS for commercial vehicles and GM's OnStar for consumers. They make use of OnStar's primary service, which is safety and stolen vehicle recovery. Typical OnStar services include contacting the dispatcher of emergency vehicles in an accident and remotely unlocking the car of a user who has lost his keys. This is besides the normal route guidance functions used regularly by most customers.

A major input to ITS is location awareness, and therefore many automatic toll roads will be relying on GNSS for that basic information. A study by the Telematics Research Group concluded that by 2010 there will be over 40 million Telematics-enabled automobiles in the United States alone. There would be a similar number overseas. However in Europe, it is expected that drivers would be encouraged to use a GALILEO-only or a combined GALILEO/GPS receiver.

Keeping track of vehicles' whereabouts is a lucrative market. This GNSS application area was pioneered by QUALCOMM with OmniTRACS (though at first OmniTRACS did not use GPS—but it is now a standard component), and similar systems are now prevalent throughout the world from many companies. At the time of this writing, C. J. Driscoll and Associates, a noted GNSS market research firm, predicted about 1.3 million automatic vehicle trackers installed in fleet vehicles. Another research firm, ABI Research, examined the U.S.–non-U.S. market split for this area and concluded that between 2003 and 2008, the U.S. share would drop from 89% to 55%, while the European share would rise from 6% to 17%. Japan and the rest of the world would carve the balance off the market [15].

Rental car companies have a strong incentive to offer navigation information to their customers. Hertz relies on the NeverLost System, while AVIS chose to go with a cellular solution whereby the customer can remove the phone from the vehicle and continue to receive downloaded maps and guidance. A similar system has been offered by NEXTEL to any driver with a NEXTEL phone through a company called Telenavigation, Inc. Rental car companies have also been experimenting with surreptitious vehicle tracking to help in recovering stolen vehicles and for enforcing contract provisions against speeding or driving in areas prohibited by the rental agreement. This has caused a backlash from privacy advocates and is expected to be a major issue for LBS in the future until legislation is in place to protect consumers' privacy rights [16]. Responding to these concerns, the state of California passed a law in 2004 prohibiting rental car companies from using GPS to fine renters for speeding or crossing state lines. About 25% of all rental cars have some sort of tracking technology installed in them. Hertz had pioneered in the use of GPS in rental cars with their NeverLost system, a product originally developed by Rockwell-Collins over 20 years ago [17].

These location awareness applications can be generally classified into four groups: convenience, safety and security, productivity, and mobile information access. As quoted in [5]: "Personal safety and security can be enhanced through the ability to locate and track lost persons using a specifically designed device with GPS and wireless connectivity or a mobile telephone with GPS. An example of an enterprise productivity improvement application is the use of location information to more efficiently route work teams or assets between multiple job sites. Mobile devices that can access wireless data can use location awareness capabilities to filter information relevant to the user based on his or her location, such as the closest gas station, or to share that information with a group of users for coordination purposes."

Personal GPS applications have unique design issues due to the limitations and preferences for a human installation. Products in the "child tracking" business include from Wherify Wireless, Inc., a GPS Locator for Kids, Digital Angel Personal Safety and Location System, and the National Scientific Urban Tracker IIK [18].

12.8   Creative Uses for GNSS

Location awareness is the ability to know where one is or where someone else is at a given time. This knowledge can be applied in untold unique ways to provide service, to understand the environment, to keep an eye on someone or something. The only limitation is human ingenuity, which so far has proven to be unlimited when it comes to GPS. Consider the following varied location awareness uses: tracking sheep; guiding blind people; tracking the movement of ice floes; and *geocaching*, which is a sport where people find hidden packages at given GPS coordinates and then add something of their own to the package. Other creative uses include plowing roads hidden by snow; tracking race cars; mapping the location of victims of disasters, such as was the case on September 11, 2001; keeping track of children and teenage drivers and adults with dementia. As receivers shrink to the size of a single chip with concomitant low-power wireless communications, location awareness is provided by wearable devices like watches, pocket PDAs, or cell phones. Many new applications become feasible, like tracking toddlers in an amusement park, Alzheimer's patients, and teenage drivers [19, 20].

Another unique GNSS application involves the use of EGNOS and the Internet [13]. Here, the GPS receiver takes corrections from EGNOS received via a wireless Internet connection and combines them with the pseudorange measurements in order to improve accuracy and availability. This is similar to assisted GPS, except that SBAS data sent over the Internet is used to assist the GNSS receiver. Originally, assisted GPS used the cellular network to provide acquisition and tracking aiding to the GPS receiver. Qualcomm's SnapTrack System is prototypical of this type of operation.

At the time of this writing, achieving GPS usage indoors remained a challenge. Because of its weak signal, most commercial GPS receivers a decade ago did not function well when the antenna did not have a clear view of the sky. This limitation is being addresses in a variety of ways (see Sections 5.13 and 9.3).

12.9   Government and Military Applications

GPS is first and foremost a military system. Since its inception in the late 1960s, GPS was designed to satisfy military requirements for a worldwide positioning, navigation, and timing service. Only a satellite-based system could ensure global coverage. The signals had to enable very accurate fixes yet be resistant to enemy jamming. Thus, the military developed user receivers that relied on what was called the P code. This code was later encrypted to be today's Y code. Modernized GPS will transmit the Y code for existing receivers and transmit the M code for new receivers. M code is an even more robust signal whose dispersed spectrum properties allow for Allied forces to jam in the band center to interfere with adversary receivers that are trying to use C/A code signals, without disturbing their own use of M code.

Today, military use of other GNSS is limited primarily to the Russian GLONASS. However, many of the world's militaries are using the C/A code of GPS. Authorized users such as NATO forces and other countries with agreed-to access are using the GPS P(Y) code for their military activities. It is expected that there will also be military use of GALILEO signals. Though conceived as a civil system, GALILEO contains an encrypted PRS that could be used militarily.

The first military applications were with man-operated receivers on ships and other vehicles. As coverage increased with every new satellite launch, additional applications emerged until GPS became not only a useful tool; it became an essential capability for modern, network-centered warfare.

12.9.1   Military User Equipment—Aviation, Shipboard, and Land

The original development of GPS receivers was accomplished at the Magnavox Research Laboratories (later acquired by Hughes Aircraft and subsequently by Raytheon). Some typical receivers were produced for aircraft first in a standard avionics package known as a 3/4 ATR size (Collins 3A) shrinking its width in half later to a 3/8 ATR (Collins and Raytheon MAGR) and to man-portable units like the Collins PLGR and finally to today's DAGR, which approaches the size and weight of a commercial handheld receiver. Figure 12.4 shows an airborne military receiver. At the time of this writing, prototype M code receivers were under development by these companies.

As many military aircraft already had inertial navigation systems installed, work began to marry the long-term stability of GPS by virtue of its atomic timing to the short-term stability of the inertial system to create integrated navigation systems that could maintain very accurate solutions regardless of short outages to GPS caused by signal interference, vehicle dynamics, or antenna shading. Similar but far simpler integrations were performed for today's car navigation systems using heading sensors, wheel counters, and map matching. The integrations became even more

Figure 12.4   Raytheon MAGR2000 airborne GPS receiver. (Courtesy of Raytheon.)

symbiotic as technology allowed for faster processors, smaller receivers, and lower cost, strapped-down inertial measurement units. The age of GPS guided missiles and other smart weapons had dawned.

12.9.2 Autonomous Receivers—Smart Weapons

Modern warfare attempts to minimize civilian casualties while maximizing the effectiveness of destroying intended targets. This requires pinpoint accuracy, on the order of a few feet in some cases. A December 2004 test of a 155-mm artillery shell guided by GPS landed 3m from its intended target. GPS is once again the enabling technology. By combining GPS measurements with those of an on-board inertial sensor, a weapon can provide the required probability of kill with a smaller warhead than would otherwise be necessary. It is no longer a question of how many sorties will be necessary to kill a target, as was the case in World War II. Today, military planners speak in terms of how many targets can be killed in a single sortie using GPS-equipped weapons. GPS receivers have found their way into ballistic missiles, guided missiles like the Tomahawk, smart bombs like the Joint Attack Direct Munitions (JDAM), artillery shells, and autonomous air, land, and sea vehicles. Recent applications include guiding unmanned combat air vehicles and reconnaissance drones. Use of GPS in combat, however, begs the question about jamming vulnerability. For these applications, antijam techniques are employed, such as nulling antennas and ultratight coupling of the GPS and the inertial sensors. In the future, higher military signal power from the satellites will further mitigate the possibility of disruption due to enemy jamming.

GPS-equipped precision guided munitions quantities will total over 300,000 in the U.S. Air Force alone. JDAM accounts for about 80% of these [21]. The Army and Navy will buy even more units as artillery and naval gun shells become GPS-guided. Figure 12.5 shows a typical munitions GPS receiver with its SAASM.

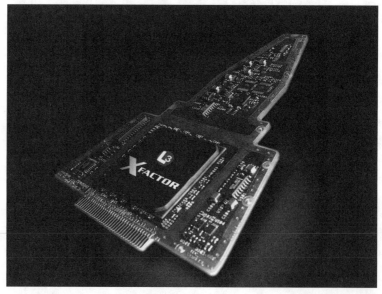

Figure 12.5   L-3 Communications munitions GPS receiver. (Courtesy of L-3 Communications.)

12.9.3   Space Applications

In the early 1980s, GPS receivers were flying on NASA's LANDSAT. This marked the beginning of the use of GPS in a spacecraft. Pictures from LANDSAT of the Yucatan peninsula, coupled with a GPS-equipped airborne survey, enabled a *National Geographic* expedition to find ruins of several heretofore unknown Mayan cities. Space use of GPS expanded on the Shuttle and the Space Station and on many other civilian and military low- to mid-orbital satellites. GPS receivers are quite useful on spacecraft in orbit up to about 10,000 nmi, although some visibility is still present at synchronous altitudes. Typically, GPS receivers are used in LEO and MEO satellites, where attitude determination is required. Further discussion on this topic is contained in [22].

12.9.4   Other Government Applications

Within the United States, many government agencies make use of GPS. The Department of Agriculture funds some research in precision farming, and both the Department of the Interior and the Bureau of Land Management routinely use GPS in our national forests. NASA looks after civilian space applications. The Department of Homeland Security uses GPS in its law enforcement role to covertly track the movements of suspects and through the Coast Guard's efforts to control our shores.

NGS and NOAA are heavy users of GPS reference stations' data and compute high-accuracy, postprocessed orbital data for use by GPS surveyors and others. One major supplier/user of this data is IGS. A major IGS center is located at the JPL in Pasadena, California, but IGS is international in scope with other centers in Europe.

Numerous law enforcement agencies rely on GPS for tracking applications, especially for surveillance on suspected criminals or for recovering GPS-equipped stolen vehicles. More and more accident investigators from the National Transportation Safety Board are incorporating GPS data into their findings. Automobiles and trucks are being equipped with "black box" recorders such as those required on commercial aircraft in order to have information about all vehicle systems as well as the speed and location at the time of an accident.

The Department of Transportation in Minnesota ran an experimental program that showed that a DGPS-equipped snow remover could accurately plow roads completely obscured by several feet of snow.

12.10   User Equipment Needs for Specific Markets

On a system level, civil GNSS users have different priorities than military users. The civil community expects high accuracy, availability, coverage, integrity, and robustness. The latter will be obtained from redundant signals and more power than in the premodernized GPS. These same users have been the drivers to require second and third civil signals in the modernized GPS and in GALILEO. For SOL applications, they clamor for spectrum protection from other systems such as ultrawideband and telecommunications that covet GNSS bandwidths.

The military users desire many of the same system attributes but are more concerned about improving the jamming resistance. While unlikely that they will be a regular user of GALILEO, they understand its potential for military applications, as many countries have done with the GPS C/A code. The military also wants shorter TTFFs and direct signal acquisition without any reliance on civil signals.

With these user desires in mind, user equipment manufacturers have addressed various segments of the market with products that are useful to the customers and profitable to the companies involved. From the low-powered receiver chip or chipset to complete stand-alone receivers, there is a product to fit all end users of the GNSS. Some of the manufacturers offer both chipsets for others to incorporate into products and complete GNSS receivers for sale directly to end users. Some sample products are shown in Figure 12.6.

Note that most of these products have the ability to receive both GPS and WAAS signals so they are truly GNSS receivers. Future models will include GALILEO capability as well. NovAtel has already begun a GALILEO proof-of-concept receiver development program under contract to the Canadian Space Agency (see Figure 12.7).

Each market segment has unique requirements over and above various environmental requirements and emission and safety standards set by regulatory bodies such as the FCC and Underwriters Laboratory. GNSS chipsets for incorporation into cell phones or PDAs must be very low power, low cost, and small. They also must be able to make use of assisted-GPS signals delivered to them over the cellular network itself. Handheld receivers must also have low power and low cost. Receivers that are part of car navigation systems operate off vehicle power, so they can draw more current than the handheld units. However, these receivers are usually

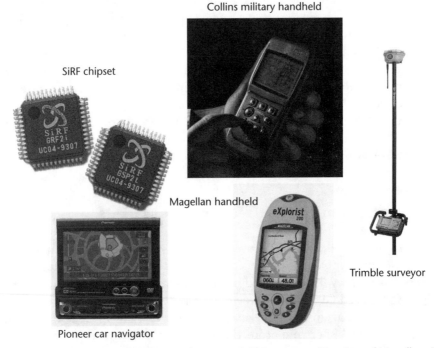

Figure 12.6   Chipset, handheld, car navigator, and GPS surveyor. (Courtesy of Magellan, Pioneer, Rockwell-Collins, SiRF, and Trimble.)

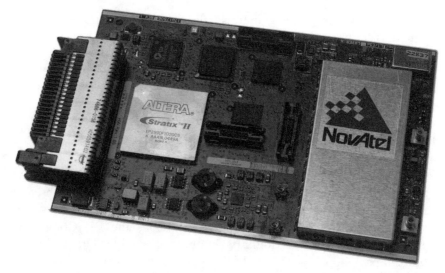

Figure 12.7   NovAtel GPS L5 FPGA card modified for GALILEO L5. (Courtesy of NovAtel.)

part of an integrated navigation system, so they may have very different interfaces than the chipsets.

Receivers for the marine navigator have very different outputs than ones found in aircraft. Typical marine outputs are used to guide ships over great circle, rhumb line routes, and ocean sea lanes. Most marine receivers include the capability to process corrections from the NDGPS system through a serial port connection or via an internal low-frequency radio. Calculations of latitude and longitude, speed, and the like are standard outputs for maritime equipment.

Aircraft outputs are typically those found in any flight management system, such as range and bearing to the next VOR station. In addition, aircraft receivers must meet very stringent hardware and software standards set down by the FAA. They are designed to receive WAAS broadcasts and LAAS data.

Survey receivers are a different breed. They are sometimes known as RTK receivers and rely on carrier-phase measurements, usually in some sort of a differential mode of operation. Here the most important requirements are for accuracy, often subcentimeter and for very rapid reacquisition of signals whenever there is an outage. Chapter 8 provides extensive details on RTK.

Still more rigorous requirements are found in military receivers. Manufacturers in this segment tend to serve only this segment. Some commercial manufacturers, notably Trimble Navigation and GARMIN also sell ruggedized units to the military. However, their military offerings, for the most part, are derived from their SPS equipment, with little special development for the military. Timble's Y code cards are an exception to that generalization.

Like all military equipment, GPS receivers must meet stringent environmental specifications as well as high-accuracy, antijam, fast fix, security, and so on. Military receivers operate on C/A and Y code on both the L1 and L2 frequencies. Future versions will receive M code as well.

An important receiver component is the GPS antenna. Oftentimes it limits performance of the receiver. Some installations, such as cell phones and handhelds, compromise coverage and gain for small size and low cost. Reference stations utilize antennas designed especially to mitigate multipath, while some military systems prescribe an antenna with adaptive, multijammer nulling and beam steering capabilities. There is quite a range of antenna sizes, shapes, and capabilities associated with the myriad of GPS applications.

12.11   Financial Projections for the GNSS Industry

GPS and soon GNSS companies that make up the industry enjoy a growing demand for their products and services. These companies vary from chipset providers like SiRF to receiver suppliers like GARMIN and Trimble, to multidivisional and military suppliers like THALES, Collins, Raytheon, and L-3 Communications. The industry also includes the military suppliers of satellites like Boeing and Lockheed Martin, payload suppliers like ITT, and control segment software and user equipment developers. There are many opportunities for all of them, as every market segment is growing. Financial results for most of these companies are freely available, as they are public companies with openly traded stock. Most are enjoying good profitability from sales of GNSS receivers and other GPS products and services. In January 2004, GPS World's receiver survey listed 77 companies offering GPS receivers [23]. Whether or not all can develop and deliver new products successfully will depend on various factors, including their abilities to:

- Accurately predict market requirements and evolving industry standards for the GNSS-based applications industry they are addressing;
- Anticipate changes in technology standards, such as wireless technologies;
- Develop and introduce new products that meet market needs in a timely manner;
- Attract and retain engineering and marketing personnel and required capital investment.

A major market determinate for all of these companies will be the deployment schedules of modernized GPS and GALILEO. In the first instance, GPS IIR-M satellites will transmit the new M code and L2C signals. Soon, the IIF satellites will add L5. Sometime between 2007 and 2010, GALILEO signals should appear, opening up still more possibilities for new products—but exactly when is still debatable. These schedules are highly dependant on both continued, stable government funding and effective contractor performance to establish not only the spacecraft but also the ground control environment that operates them. These are large, complicated undertakings, so all projected schedules need be watched closely for signs of slippage. Companies jumping in too soon may find that their products cannot be sold, as the signals they were designed to use are not yet available. In short, the next few years are the critical ones that will determine just how accurate all the market projections will turn out to be.

Currently, many companies are offering other GNSS products and services associated with particular niches or application areas. A partial list includes accessories such as car adapters, carrying cases, and earphones; antennas; antijam/interference suppression units; differential services; digital compasses; electronic charts/maps; GLONASS receivers; integrated instrumentation with GPS; ionospheric calibrators; photogrammetry/GPS; precise ephemeris information; receiver components; signal simulators; and training [23]. These niche/application companies are all part of the GNSS market. Taking all of their business into account in addition to the main user receiver manufacturing market makes the GNSS market a fabulous growth area for the foreseeable future.

References

[1] Dutton, L., "GNSS Presentation," *THALES Research, ION GPS 2002*, Portland, OR.

[2] Jacobson, L., "The Business of GNSS," *Navtech Seminars, ION-GNSS 2004*, Long Beach, CA, September 2004.

[3] Simon, S., "The GPS Markets and Applications," Decision Resources, Inc., November 1991.

[4] "GPS Market to Navigate North of $22 Billion by 2008, Says ABI," Press Release, ABI Research, Oyster Bay, New York, October 1, 2003.

[5] Onidi, O., et al., "Directions 2004," *GPS World*, December 2003, p. 16.

[6] "Business in Satellite Navigation," *GALILEO Joint Undertaking*, Brussels, Belgium 2003.

[7] Hein, G. W., "GNSS Market," *Presentation, ISCe Conference*, Long Beach, CA, June 2003.

[8] Ballenger, W., "GPS Presentation," SMC Industry Days, Joint Forces Training Base, Los Alamitos, CA, April 2003.

[9] SEC Filing for SiRF Inc., March 2004.

[10] Warrior, J., et al., "They Know Where You Are," *IEEE Spectrum*, July 2003.

[11] Kaplan, E., et al., *Understanding GPS: Principles and Applications*, Norwood, MA: Artech House, 1996.

[12] "Navigation and Landing Transition Strategy," Office of Architecture and Investment Analysis, ASD-1, Federal Aviation Administration, Washington, D.C., June 30, 2002.

[13] Mossberg, W., "Track Your Morning Jog Via Satellite," *Wall Street Journal*, March 17, 2004.

[14] Prince, M., "GPS Technology Helps Blind Find Way," *Wall Street Journal*, March 17, 2004.

[15] "Two Studies Gauge AVL/LBS," *GPS World*, July 2003, p. 50.

[16] "When You Rent a Car, Does the Company Secretly Track You?" *Los Angeles Times*, April 4, 2004, p. L3.

[17] Elliott, C., "Some Rental Cars Keep Tabs on the Drivers," *New York Times*, January 13, 2004.

[18] Kinnersley, H. K., "Tracking Kids by GPS," *Wall Street Journal*, 2002.

[19] Byler, J., "Location-Based Services Are Positioned for Growth," *Wireless System Design*, September 2003.

[20] Toran, F., et al., "Position Via Internet," *GPS World*, April 2004, p. 28.

[21] Tirpak, J., "Precision: The Next Generation," *Air Force Magazine*, November 2003.

[22] Parkinson, B., et al., *GPS Theory and Applications*, Vol. 2, Washington, D.C.: AIAA, 1996.

[23] "Buyers Guide," *GPS World*, June 2004.

APPENDIX A
Least Squares and Weighted Least Squares Estimates

Christopher J. Hegarty
The MITRE Corporation

Let $\mathbf{x} = [x_1 x_2 \ldots x_M]^T$ be a column vector containing M unknown parameters that are to be estimated and $\mathbf{y} = [y_1 y_2 \ldots y_N]^T$ be a set of noisy measurements that are linearly related to $\mathbf{x}$ as described by the expression:

$$\mathbf{y} = \mathbf{Hx} + \mathbf{n} \tag{A.1}$$

where $\mathbf{n} = [n_1 n_2 \ldots n_N]^T$ is a vector describing the errors corrupting the N measurements, and $\mathbf{H}$ is an $N \times M$ matrix describing the connection between the measurements and $\mathbf{x}$.

The *maximum likelihood* estimate of $\mathbf{x}$, denoted as $\hat{\mathbf{x}}$, is defined as (see, for example, [1]):

$$\hat{\mathbf{x}} = \arg \max_{\mathbf{x}} p(\mathbf{y}/\mathbf{x}) \tag{A.2}$$

where $p(\mathbf{y}/\mathbf{x})$ is the probability density function of the measurement $\mathbf{y}$ for a fixed value of $\mathbf{x}$.

If the measurement errors, $\{n_i\}$, for $i = 1, \ldots, N$, are identically Gaussian distributed with zero-mean and variance σ^2, and furthermore if errors for different measurements are statistically independent, then (A.2) becomes:

$$\hat{\mathbf{x}} = \arg \max_{\mathbf{x}} \frac{1}{(2\pi\sigma)^{N/2}} e^{-\frac{1}{2\sigma^2}\|\mathbf{y}-\mathbf{Hx}\|^2}$$

$$= \arg \min_{\mathbf{x}} \|\mathbf{y} - \mathbf{Hx}\|^2 \tag{A.3}$$

The solution to (A.3) can readily be found by first differentiating $\|\mathbf{y} - \mathbf{H}\hat{\mathbf{x}}\|^2$ with respect to $\hat{\mathbf{x}}$:

$$\frac{d}{d\hat{\mathbf{x}}}\|\mathbf{y} - \mathbf{H}\hat{\mathbf{x}}\|^2 = 2\mathbf{H}^T\mathbf{H}\hat{\mathbf{x}} - 2\mathbf{H}^T\mathbf{y} \tag{A.4}$$

and then setting this quantity equal to zero to obtain:

$$\hat{x} = \left(H^T H\right)^{-1} H^T y \tag{A.5}$$

where it is assumed that the matrix inverse involved exists (i.e., that $H^T H$ is not singular).

The estimate described by (A.5) is referred to as a *least squares estimate*, since, as shown in (A.3), it results in the minimum square error between the measurement vector y and Hx, where the latter is the expected measurement vector based upon the estimate of x.

Next, consider the more general case where the measurement errors are still Gaussian distributed with zero-mean but are not necessarily identically distributed or independent of each other. In this case, the maximum likelihood estimate can be expressed as

$$\hat{x} = \arg\max_x \frac{1}{(2\pi)^{N/2} |R_n|^{1/2}} e^{-\frac{1}{2}(y-Hx)^T R_n^{-1}(y-Hx)}$$
$$= \arg\min_x (y - Hx)^T R_n^{-1}(y - Hx) \tag{A.6}$$

where R_n is the covariance matrix associated with the measurement errors and $|R_n|$ is its determinant.

Proceeding as before, (A.6) can be solved to yield:

$$\hat{x} = \left(H^T R_n^{-1} H\right)^{-1} H^T R_n^{-1} y \tag{A.7}$$

The estimate in (A.7) is referred to as a WLS solution.

Reference

[1]   Stark, H., and J. W. Woods, *Probability, Random Processes, and Estimation Theory for Engineers*, Englewood Cliffs, NJ: Prentice-Hall, 1986.

Stability Measures for Frequency Sources

Lawrence F. Wiederholt
The MITRE Corporation

B.1 Introduction

The principle of employing satellite navigation systems for position and time determination requires the satellite clocks to be in synchronism to a common timebase.

High-accuracy AFS are required to meet the stringent stability and drift rate requirements so that the common time base can be maintained. Stability is also important for the less accurate crystal-based oscillators that are typically employed in user equipment.

Frequency sources are subject to systemic errors, such as frequency offsets, aging, and random frequency errors. Random frequency errors are a primary concern, especially when characterizing the performance of an AFS. There are a number of important random frequency noise processes (i.e., frequency fluctuations): random walk frequency modulation, flicker frequency modulation, white frequency modulation, flicker phase modulation, and white phase modulation, as described in [1].

B.2 Frequency Standard Stability

The stability of a frequency source can be described by starting with an oscillator whose output voltage $V(t)$, is given by:

$$V(t) = \left(V_0 + \varepsilon(t)\right)\left(\sin\left(2\pi\nu_0 t + \phi(t)\right)\right) \tag{B.1}$$

where V_0 and ν_0 are the nominal amplitude and frequency, respectively, with corresponding errors $\varepsilon(t)$ and $\varphi(t)$.

The instantaneous phase is defined by

$$\Phi(t) = 2\pi\nu_0 t + \phi(t) \tag{B.2}$$

and the instantaneous frequency is defined by

$$\nu(t) = \nu_0 + \frac{1}{2\pi}\frac{d\phi(t)}{dt} \tag{B.3}$$

665

A common method used to measure oscillator stability is based on the instantaneous fractional frequency deviation from the nominal frequency v_0 given by

$$y(t) = \frac{\dot{\phi}}{2\pi v_0}$$

The power-law spectral densities of the five random frequency noise processes mentioned in Section B.1 can be represented in the frequency domain by the sum of five independent noise processes as [1]:

$$S_y(f) = \sum_{\alpha=-2}^{+2} b_\alpha f^\alpha \qquad \text{for} \quad 0 < f < f_h$$
$$= 0 \qquad \text{for } f \geq f_h$$

where:

b_α = constant

α = integer

f_h = high-frequency cutoff of an infinitely sharp lowpass filter

This power spectral density is visually represented in Figure B.1 for the five random frequency noise processes: random walk frequency, flicker frequency, white frequency, flicker phase, and white phase.

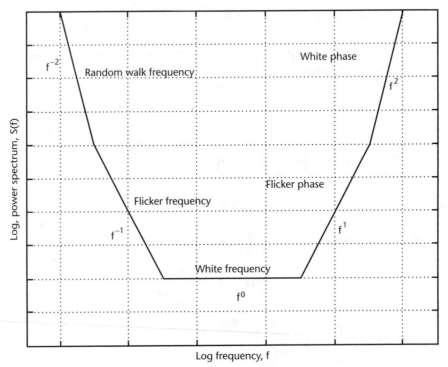

Figure B.1   Power spectral densities for five random frequency noise processes: random walk frequency, flicker frequency, white frequency, flicker phase, and white phase.

B.3   Measures of Stability

Two basic approaches can be taken to analyze the stability of an oscillator: a frequency domain approach and a time domain approach. One can map from one to the other. The time domain approach is more commonly used for stability analysis.

The interest in oscillators and the common measurement of their stability became such an item of interest that the IEEE Standards Committee 14 developed a standard in the 1980s. With this standard in place, oscillator stability evaluations could be performed on a common basis using standard definitions and evaluation techniques. The latest revision of this standard was published in 1999 [1].

B.3.1   Allan Variance

One common measure of oscillator stability based on the instantaneous fractional frequency deviation is the *Allan variance*, $\sigma_y^2(\tau)$, defined by

$$\sigma_y^2(\tau) = \frac{1}{2}E\left[\left(\bar{y}_{k+1} - \bar{y}_k\right)^2\right]$$

where:

$$\bar{y} = \frac{\phi(t_k + \tau) - \phi(t_k)}{2\pi v_0 \tau}$$

τ = sampling interval

E is the expected value operator. In theory, E is an infinite sum of elements, but in practice the sum is limited to a large but finite number.

The square root of the Allan variance is referred to as the *Allan deviation*.

B.3.2   Hadamard Variance

The Allan variance works well for cesium-based AFS with no linear drift effects. It is also often used to characterize the stability of quartz crystal oscillators. Rubidium-based AFS have a significant linear drift above the random noise, which degrades the fidelity of the Allan variance and thus does not provide an accurate measure of stability. The linear drift can be removed by a separate processing step, but an alternate measure of stability has been defined which overcomes this inherent limitation of the Allan variance. This measure is referred to as the Hadamard variance, which removes any linear drift and is thus not effected by linear drift. Thus, the Hadamard variance is a good measure of stability for rubidium AFS.

The Hadamard variance, $_H\sigma_y^2(\tau)$, is defined by

$$_H\sigma_y^2(\tau) = \frac{1}{2}E\left[\left(\bar{y}_{k+2} - 2\bar{y}_{k+1} + \bar{y}_k\right)^2\right]$$

As in the Allan variance, E is the expected value operator. In theory, E is an infinite sum of elements, but in practice the sum is limited to a large but finite number.

Note that the Allan variance is a two-sample variance requiring two time sample values for each point, while the Hadamard variance is a three-sample variance requiring three time samples for each point. Thus, the Hadamard variance requires more computations.

The GPS MCS uses the Hadamard variance and its variations to measure oscillator stability [2–4]. This is appropriate considering that the constellation will have a predominance of rubidium standards in the near future (Blocks IIR, IIR-M, and IIF).

References

[1]   "IEEE Standard Definitions of Physical Quantities for Fundamental Frequency and Time Metrology—Random Instabilities," *IEEE Std. 1139-1999*, IEEE Standards Coordinating Committee 27 on Time and Frequency, approved March 26, 1999.

[2]   Howe, D., et al., "A Total Estimator of the Hadamard Function Used for GPS Operations," *Proc. of 32nd Annual Precise Time and Time Interval (PTTI) Applications and Planning Meeting*, November 2000.

[3]   Hutsell, S., "Relating the Hadamard Variance to MCS Kalman Filter Clock Estimation," *Proc. of 27th Annual Precise Time and Time Interval (PTTI) Applications and Planning Meeting*, November 29–December 1, 1995, pp. 291–302.

[4]   Hutsell, S., et al., "Operational Use of the Hadamard Variance in GPS," *Proc. of 28th Annual Precise Time and Time Interval (PTTI) Applications and Planning Meeting*, December 1996, pp. 201–213.

Free-Space Propagation Loss

John W. Betz
The MITRE Corporation

C.1 Introduction

Calculating propagation loss is a fundamental tool in systems engineering for GNSS, since this loss relates the power at a source (e.g., a satellite transmitter or an interferer) to the power at a destination (e.g., a GNSS receiver). The propagation loss typically depends on the distance between source and destination, as well other factors.

The simplest common expression for propagation loss is called *free-space propagation loss*, since it applies in free space (source and receiver are located in a vacuum or equivalent, with no other objects in the vicinity). Although this expression is often employed, there are widespread misunderstandings of its applicability (under what conditions does it apply?) and its technical characteristics (e.g., in what sense is free-space propagation loss frequency dependent?).

Entire texts (e.g., [1]) are devoted to radio wave propagation—predicting, measuring, and compensating for its effects. This appendix only touches on one simple and common model for radio wave propagation—free-space propagation loss. It also addresses a related topic—how to convert back and forth between power flux densities (PFDs) and power spectral densities (PSDs).

C.2 Free-Space Propagation Loss

Propagation loss is defined as the ratio of the power transmitted in the direction of the receive antenna to the power at the terminals of a receive antenna, for a unity-gain receive antenna. If the receive antenna has gain other than unity, the received power is divided by the receive antenna gain in taking this ratio. The transmit antenna actually radiates P_T watts, and has a gain of G_T (dimensionless), producing an EIRP of $P_T G_T$ watts. The receive antenna has a gain of G_R. The power at the receive antenna terminals is denoted P_R, so that the propagation loss is the dimensionless quantity

$$\Lambda = \frac{P_T G_T}{(P_R / G_R)} = \frac{P_T G_T G_R}{P_R} \tag{C.1}$$

Since (C.1) is merely a definition, it could also be defined as the reciprocal of what is shown. The particular definition was selected so that the numerator is typically greater than the denominator, making the propagation loss usually a quantity greater than unity, or positive when expressed in decibels. This corresponds with common usage (e.g., "a 180-dB propagation loss").

It is often convenient to perform calculations for a receive antenna having unit gain ($G_R = 1$), calculating the received isotropic power (RIP).

The free-space propagation loss model described in this appendix applies when the transmitting antenna and receiving antenna are located in free space (ideally, a vacuum) where there are no other nearby conductive objects and no obstructions. In practice at L-band at least, it is sufficient that the LOS path between transmitter and receiver is not obstructed, that there are no obstructions even near the LOS path, and that the transmitter to receiver LOS path is far from conducting surfaces, even the Earth's surface. If one of these conditions do occur, actual propagation loss may be much greater than predicted using the free-space model.

Furthermore, the transmitting antenna and receiving antennas must be separated by many wavelengths so that they are not within each other's near fields. At L-band, several meters of separation are adequate for antennas having modest gain.

Detailed criteria for quantifying the conditions under which free-space propagation applies and ways to predict propagation losses under conditions other than free space can be found in [1] and are beyond the scope of this appendix. In many cases, free-space propagation is a good first-order model for L-band propagation from space to a terrestrial or airborne receiver, from an airborne transmitter to an airborne receiver, or from an airborne transmitter to the ground (or for these same paths with transmitter and receiver exchanged). These situations are clearly of interest to GNSS.

Consider a transmitter radiating an EIRP of $P_T G_T$. As the electromagnetic wave propagates, its power spreads out in a spherical pattern, so that the same amount of power remains in a given solid angle measured from the transmit antenna. The PFD, however, which is the power per unit area in the surface of the sphere, diminishes as the radius of the sphere increases with increasing distance from the transmitter.

Now assume that the solid angle is small and the radius of the sphere is large enough that the solid angle can be approximated by a flat patch tangent to the sphere and thus normal to the LOS between transmit antenna and receiver.

The effective area of an antenna, A, is given by

$$A = \frac{\lambda^2 G}{4\pi} \tag{C.2}$$

where $\lambda = c/f$ is the wavelength, with c the speed of propagation, f is the frequency, and G is the antenna gain. When the receive antenna gain is G_R, the effective area of the receive antenna is

$$A_R = \frac{G_R \lambda^2}{4\pi} = \frac{G_R c^2}{f^2\, 4\pi} \tag{C.3}$$

Observe that the effective area of an antenna having a given gain is inversely proportional to the square of the frequency. For the same antenna gain with increasing frequency, the antenna's area must become smaller.

Returning to the earlier discussion of an electromagnetic wave emanating outward from a transmitter, the power spatial density (having units of W/m^2) at a point on a sphere with radius d from the transmit antenna is

$$\Phi = \frac{P_T G_T}{4\pi d^2} \tag{C.4}$$

The power spatial density is also known as the *power flux density* (PFD). Observe that the PFD decreases with the square of the distance from the transmitter, so that the PFD (the received power per unit area) is independent of frequency and depends only on the distance from the transmitter.

The power at the receive antenna's terminals is given by the product of the PFD at the receive antenna and the effective area of the receive antenna

$$P_R = \Phi A_R \tag{C.5}$$

Substituting (C.3) and (C.4) into (C.5) yields

$$\begin{aligned} P_R &= \left(\frac{P_T G_T}{4\pi d^2}\right)\left(\frac{G_R \lambda^2}{4\pi}\right) \\ &= P_T G_T G_R \left(\frac{\lambda}{4\pi d}\right)^2 \end{aligned} \tag{C.6}$$

Expression (C.6), often called the Friis equation [2], allows calculation of the received power, given the EIRP ($P_T G_T$) and the receive antenna gain (G_R). When (C.6) is calculated for an isotropic receive antenna, for which $G_R = 1$, the result is the RIP.

Sometimes the free-space propagation model is generalized to account for an excess propagation loss beyond the free-space loss. This excess propagation loss could be caused by attenuation due to the atmosphere, foliage penetration, building penetration, or polarization mismatch. The effect of this excess power loss is modeled by a dimensionless multiplicative factor L that takes on values between unity and infinity, with unity indicating no excess loss and infinity indicating complete blockage. As in the definition of propagation loss, L is defined to match common terminology (e.g., "an excess loss of 2 dB"). The resulting expression for received power is

$$P_R = \frac{P_T G_T G_R}{L}\left(\frac{\lambda}{4\pi d}\right)^2 \tag{C.7}$$

Computation of the received power is commonly performed in decibels. Denoting the quantities of units as subscripts allows (C.7) to be rewritten in decibels as

$$
\begin{aligned}
\left(P_R\right)_{dBW} &= \left(P_T\right)_{dBW} + \left(G_T\right)_{dB} + \left(G_R\right)_{dB} - L_{dB} + 20\log_{10}\left(\frac{\lambda}{4\pi d}\right) \\
&= \left(P_T\right)_{dBW} + \left(G_T\right)_{dB} + \left(G_R\right)_{dB} - L_{dB} - 21.98 - 20\log_{10}\left(\frac{d}{\lambda}\right)
\end{aligned}
\tag{C.8}
$$

The latter expression is particularly simple, using a constant and the separation between transmitter and receiver expressed as the number of wavelengths.

Finally, the generalized free-space propagation loss (which includes excess loss) is found from (C.1) and (C.7) to be

$$
\Lambda = L\left(\frac{4\pi d}{\lambda}\right)^2
\tag{C.9}
$$

with

$$
P_R = \frac{P_T G_T G_R}{\Lambda}
$$

and

$$
\left(P_R\right)_{dBW} = \left(P_T\right)_{dBW} + \left(G_T\right)_{dB} + \left(G_R\right)_{dB} - \Lambda_{dB}
$$

where

$$
\Lambda_{dB} = 10\log_{10}\left(\Lambda\right)
$$

While (C.9) is a very compact expression for free-space propagation loss, simplistic interpretation of this expression leads to the faulty conclusion that, since free-space propagation loss increases with frequency, there is a frequency-dependent attenuation mechanism in free space. The correct interpretation is that the loss in PFD (in W/m^2) with distance from the transmitter does not depend on frequency, as seen in (C.4). However, free-space propagation loss is defined to include the effects of a receive antenna having a gain (often unity) that remains constant over frequency. Since an antenna of given gain has smaller effective area at higher frequencies, the fixed-gain antenna collects a smaller fraction of the PDF at higher frequencies, resulting in lower received power at higher frequencies.

Since the antenna area contributes to the free-space propagation loss as commonly defined, free-space propagation loss increases with frequency. If free-space propagation loss were instead defined for fixed effective area of the receive antenna rather than fixed gain of the receive antenna, (C.5) shows that the free-space propagation loss would then be independent of frequency (but the antenna would become increasingly directive at higher frequencies, since it would remain the same physical size).

C.3   Conversion Between PSDs and PFDs

While PFDs arise often in documents involving spectrum protection and radio frequency interference, most signal theory is written in terms of PSDs. This section describes how to convert between the two quantities.

Recall that a PFD describes the power per unit area (often a square meter) normal to a propagating electromagnetic wave, while a PSD describes the power per bandwidth (often 1 Hz, but sometime 1 kHz, 4 kHz, or 1 MHz) in a signal. These are very different concepts and quantities, and conversion between them requires an intermediate quantity—power—as well as definition of the receive antenna's effective area and of the normalized (unit power) PSD for the unit-power signal, in units of seconds (or reciprocal hertz).

To convert from PFD to PSD, first use (C.5) and the given effective area of the receive antenna. Often, a unity-gain antenna is assumed. Note from (C.3) that at frequencies greater than $\dfrac{c}{\sqrt{4\pi}} \cong 84.3$ MHz, the effective area of a unity-gain antenna is less than unity, so for calculations involving GNSS, the effective area is typically negative when expressed in decibels. The result is power, in units of watts. Multiply the power by the normalized (unit area) PSD to obtain the actual PSD in units of W/Hz. To find the PSD in a given bandwidth centered at a given center frequency, merely integrate the actual PSD over that bandwidth at that frequency. In many cases, the latter step can be approximated by evaluating the PSD at the center frequency and then multiplying it by the bandwidth. As long as the actual PSD is well approximated by a straight (not necessarily horizontal) line over the given bandwidth, the result is valid.

To convert from PSD to PFD, integrate the PSD over all frequencies to determine the total power. Then, using (C.5), divide the total power by the effective area of the receive antenna (for frequencies of typical interest in GNSS, this involves adding a positive quantity in decibels) to obtain the PFD.

References

[1]   Parsons, J. D., *The Mobile Radio Propagation Channel*, 2nd ed., New York: John Wiley and Sons, 2000.

[2]   Friis, H. T., "A Note on a Simple Transmission Formula," *Proc. IRE*, Vol. 34, 1946, pp. 254–256.

About the Authors

John W. Betz is a fellow at The MITRE Corporation. He received his B.S.E.E. from the University of Rochester and his master's and doctorate degrees in electrical and computer engineering from Northeastern University. His work at MITRE, and before that at The Analytical Sciences Corporation and RCA Corporation, has involved the development and analysis of signal processing for sonar, radar, communications, navigation, and other applications. Dr. Betz led the Modulation and Acquisition Design Team for M code signal design, contributing to many aspects of M code signal design and evaluation, including developing the BOC modulation. He has made contributions to many other aspects of modernized GNSS, including participating in technical and expert working groups concerning GPS and GALILEO, as well as GPS and QZSS. Dr. Betz is a member of the U.S. Air Force Scientific Advisory Board and received the Institute of Navigation's Burka Award in 2001.

J. Blake Bullock is the product manager of location solutions at Motorola Mobile Devices. He has been with Motorola for 10 years, where he has worked on GPS receivers and applications, telematics systems, and distributed navigation solutions. Mr. Bullock received his B.Sc. and M.Sc. in geomatics engineering from the University of Calgary, Canada. He has received nine patents and has authored several papers, articles, and a thesis in the areas of GPS, navigation, traffic, and digital mapping. Mr. Bullock is a member of the Institute of Navigation and is currently pursuing an M.B.A. at Arizona State University.

Richard Clark received a B.S. in physics from the University of Illinois and an M.S. in physics from Northern Illinois University. After teaching physics and mathematics at the secondary level in the United States and Europe in 1977, Mr. Clark joined the Air Force, developing technology assessments on electronics and spacecraft.

Rob Conley is the chief engineer at Overlook Systems Technologies, Inc. He has worked in various aspects of the GPS program for 24 years. He began his career in GPS in the GPS JPO, where he served as a user equipment flight test engineer and managed the development of interfaces between the GPS operational control system and the Block II satellites. Mr. Conley spent 4 years at Schriever Air Force Base overseeing the development and integration of GPS command and control software, and directing the test program for the first operational GPS satellites. He has worked at Overlook for more than 15 years, where he has focused much of his efforts on the improvement of GPS services being provided to the military and civil GPS community. Mr. Conley served as the first program director for the GPS Support Center and developed the original GPS SPS signal specification for the Office of the Assistant Secretary of Defense for C3I. He is currently serving as the program manager for the GPS Operations Center. Mr. Conley is a graduate of the U.S. Air Force Academy, with a degree in astronautical engineering.

Ronald J. Cosentino received a B.E.E. from the Polytechnic Institute of Brooklyn and an M.A. in mathematics from Fordham University. He contributed to the development of radar systems at the General Electric Company and at Cornell Aeronautical Labs. His efforts focused on radar and communications systems at the Cincinnati Electronics Corporation. While at The MITRE Corporation, Mr. Cosentino made technical contributions in several areas, including radar and communications systems, signal processing algorithms, architectures for VLSI, air traffic management systems, and precision landing systems. The latter areas included the GPS and the Microwave Landing System for navigation and instrumented landing.

David W. Diggle is the associate director of the Avionics Engineering Center at Ohio University in Athens, Ohio. He joined the center in 1994 as a research scientist shortly after receiving his Ph.D. in electrical and computer engineering from Ohio University. His areas of expertise include real-time precise positioning using GPS with application to land surveying and to aircraft precision approach and landing. Based on the research performed for his doctoral dissertation, the RTCA honored him with its Jackson Award. The award is given annually for the outstanding contribution to the field of avionics. Dr. Diggle is a member of the Institute of Electrical and Electronic Engineers, the Institute of Navigation, the International Loran Association, Sigma Xi, and the Eta Kappa Nu and Tau Beta Pi engineering honoraria. In addition, he holds a private pilot certificate completed through the Ohio University Aviation Department.

Arthur J. Dorsey is a senior engineer with Lockheed Martin Information Systems and Services. He has more than 20 years of professional experience in research, design, and development of GPS and Air Traffic Control automation systems, with expertise in GPS navigational accuracy and air traffic control radar data processing and conflict detection. He was involved in the initial algorithm design of the GPS CS navigation processing, its development and fielding, and the recent L-AII development and fielding. He participated in the development of the rearchitecture, distributed workstation GPS control segment implementation (AEP); performed analysis and characterization of the GPS monitoring station receivers, and participated in the development of a Lockheed Martin wide-area GPS differential system. He designed and developed a Lockheed Martin wide-area GPS differential service volume modeling tool and a DOD GPS service-level planning tool for accessing navigational performance. Recently, Dr. Dorsey performed the fundamental analysis in the new improved clock and ephemeris message definition of the modernized signals. He was involved in the design of air traffic control tracking and maneuver detection algorithms. He holds a B.S., an M.S., and a Ph.D., all in electrical engineering, from the University of Maryland.

Philippe Erhard holds a master of science and engineering in aerospace and radionavigation from the French National School for Civil Aviation (Ingénieur–Ecole Nationale de l'Aviation Civile). After 6 years of industrial experience at Alcatel Space (Toulouse, France) and Astrium Space (Stevenage, England), respectively, in both communication and navigation space systems, he joined the ESA in 2001 as GALILEO Navigation system engineer and signal expert in the GALILEO Project Office at ESA/ESTEC. He coordinated GALILEO signal design, performance, and validation activities, and he was the project manager for the design and procurement of related validation test bed hardware [GALILEO Signal Validation Facility (GSVF)], including the GALILEO constellation simulator, RF signal generator, and breadboard navigation receiver. Among his duties, Mr. Erhard provided support to the European Commission (EC) as the technical coordinator of the GALILEO Signal Task Force, chaired by the EC, in particular in the frame of EU/U.S. negotiation and cooperation on GALILEO and GPS. He has since been appointed to the Director General's Office for Policy at ESA Headquarters in Paris, France.

Marco Falcone is the system engineering manager for the ESA GALILEO Project Office. His main task is to define the GALILEO requirements and interfaces at the system level and to ensure that the GALILEO system fulfills the required navigation and integrity performance. Mr. Falcone has worked for ESA since 1991, serving first on the ESA/CNES Hermes Joint Team as Hermes space vehicle electrical ground support equipment engineer and subsequently at the ESA Research and Technology Centre as the payload data engineer for the ENVISAT Ground Segment Team. Prior to this, Mr. Falcone was employed in the Software Engineering Section/Space Programs Group at Intecs Sistemi, working with the COLUMBUS and Hermes Projects. He holds an M.S. in computer science from the University of Pisa in his native Italy and another M.S. in space systems engineering from the University of Delft in the Netherlands.

Scott Feairheller has more than 22 years of experience in international satellite navigation systems and international space policy. From 1989 through 1997, he served as the Department of Defense technical representative to the GPS-GLONASS portion of the 1988 U.S.-U.S.S.R. Transportation Agreement and the 1994 U.S.-Russia Transportation Agreement. Since 1999, Mr. Feairheller has supported the U.S.-EU GPS-GALILEO negotiations. He currently works for the U.S. Air Force as an aerospace engineer. He received a B.S. from the University of Dayton in 1982 and an M.S. from the Joint Military College in 1997. Mr. Feairheller has been a member of the U.S. Institute of Navigation since 1987.

Michael Foss holds a B.S.E.E. and an M.S.E.E. from Northeastern University. He has been working in the field of real-time systems for the last 20 years and in the field of integrating GPS and inertial sensors for the last decade developing various GPS/inertial navigation systems. His work has included the design, development, and evaluation of aided GPS receivers. This effort extends to problems associated with integrating various receivers with low-cost inertial components. Mr. Foss is currently the president of Vehicle Guidance, Inc., a manufacturer of GPS/inertial systems for use in land applications.

Peter M. Fyfe is a technical fellow with The Boeing Company in Anaheim, California. He received his B.E. in electrical engineering from the Stevens Institute of Technology and his M.S.E.E. from the University of Southern California. He has more than 18 years of GPS systems engineering analysis and test experience in all three GPS segments. Mr. Fyfe worked on GPS IIF from 1995 to 2003 and was a contributor to the development and implementation of the new M code and L5 signals.

G. Jeffrey Geier is a member of the technical staff with the Motorola Personal Communications Sector. He has more than 36 years of experience with integrated navigation systems, GPS navigation and signal processing, and integrity monitoring. His experience base in GPS and INS technology includes both military (C.S. Draper Laboratory, TASC, Intermetrics, and The Aerospace Corporation) and commercial (Trimble Navigation and Motorola) applications. At Motorola, he developed signal processing and navigation algorithms for cell phone–based positioning in support of the FCC E-911 mandate, and he led efforts to integrate its GPS receiver technology with dead-reckoning sensors for automotive applications. In recognition of his technical leadership, he was named to Motorola's Science Advisory Board. Mr. Geier has been an instructor for NavTech Seminars, teaching a two-day course in GPS integration with inertial systems nationwide, and has taught short courses in GPS integration with low-cost sensors at the University of Calgary, Canada, as an invited lecturer. He is a member of the Institute of Navigation and the Institute of Electrical and Electronic Engineers, and holds 28 GPS-related patents. Mr. Geier received a B.S. and an M.S. in aeronautics and astronautics from the Massachusetts Institute of Technology.

Christopher J. Hegarty is a senior principal engineer with The MITRE Corporation's Center for Advanced Aviation System Development. He received his B.S. and M.S. in electrical engineering from Worcester Polytechnic Institute and a D.Sc. in electrical engineering from The George Washington University. From September 1999 until October 2000, he served as the FAA's Civil GPS Modernization Project Leader under an Intergovernmental Personnel Act assignment. Dr. Hegarty is a member of the Program Management Committee of RTCA, Inc., and also serves as cochair of RTCA Special Committee 159. Since 1997, he has been the editor of *NAVIGATION: Journal of The Institute of Navigation*. He has taught graduate-level courses in digital communications at The George Washington University and seminars on GPS for Navtech. He was the program chair of the Institute of Navigation GNSS 2004 and is the general chair of Institute of Navigation GNSS 2005. Dr. Hegarty was a recipient of the Institute of Navigation Early Achievement Award (1998), The MITRE Corporation President's Award (1999), Air Traffic Control Association Chairman's Citation of Merit (2000), FAA Appreciation Award (2000), RTCA Certificate of Appreciation (2001 and 2005), and the Department of State Superior Honor Award (2005).

Guenter Hein is a professor and the director of the Institute of Geodesy and Navigation of the University FAF Munich, Germany. He studied surveying engineering and satellite geodesy at the Universities in Mainz, Stuttgart, and Darmstadt, where he received his Ph.D. and worked as a scientific research associate. After his habilitation (Dr.-Ing. habil.) in gravity gradiometry, he became a Privatdozent. At the age of 33, Dr. Hein was appointed full professor at the University FAF Munich. His work in GPS had already started when he formed a research group that did pioneering research and development in the field of RTK GPS positioning and GPS/INS integration. For this work, he and his team received a Best Paper Award from the Institute of Navigation in 1988. Dr. Hein has contributed to more than 200 scientific publications in Geodesy and Satellite Navigation, has received over 100 research grants, was a visiting senior scientist at the U.S. National Geodetic Survey and a visiting professor at the University of New South Wales in Sydney and at the University of Maine, and is a member of various national and international associations. He is currently the European technical representative on the Institute of Navigation's Satellite Division Executive Committee, an instructor for Navtech

Seminars, Inc., and a guest professor in the Space Science Master Program of Delft University (Toptech Studies). Dr. Hein is a member of the European Commission GALILEO Signal Task Force and joined as a German delegate and technical expert in the negotiations between the EU and the United States on the interoperability of GPS and GALILEO in the last years. In September 2002, he received the prestigious Johannes Kepler Award, the highest worldwide award in satellite navigation, from the U.S. Institute of Navigation.

Len Jacobson is a technical, management, and business development consultant to the GPS industry, the U.S. government, and the legal profession through his own company, Global Systems and Marketing, Inc. He earned his B.S.E.E. from the City College of New York and his M.S.E.E. from the Polytechnic Institute of New York and did postgraduate work at UCLA and at the Stanford Executive Institute. He was a systems engineer in satellite communications and navigation at ITT, Hughes Aircraft, and the Magnavox Research Laboratories before becoming a vice president at Interstate Electronics. He was elected to the NATO Industrial Advisory Group and served on a Defense Science Board Panel considering international defense trade policies. He was elected to the Institute of Navigation Council serving as space representative and twice as western regional vice president as well as holding the chairs for finance and sections. Mr. Jacobson twice chaired the Institute of Navigation National Technical Meeting and served as program chair. He has been an editorial advisor to *GPS World* magazine since its inception and also served as vice president of the Board of Directors of the Los Angeles National Defense Industrial Association Chapter. Among his other affiliations are AFCEA and the Institute of Electrical and Electronic Engineers. He has testified in civil and criminal cases several times as a GPS expert witness. Len has written extensively on GPS and other defense matters and has appeared on CBS television's *60 Minutes*.

Elliott D. Kaplan is a principal engineer at The MITRE Corporation in Bedford, Massachusetts. He earned his B.S.E.E. from the Polytechnic Institute of New York and M.S.E.E. from Northeastern University. Mr. Kaplan has been participating in GPS-related government programs since 1986. He is currently supporting GPS JPO system engineering activities. Prior to that, Mr. Kaplan led the MITRE GPS III team during the System Architecture/Requirements Definition phase. He edited and coauthored the first edition of *Understanding GPS: Principles and Applications*, published by Artech House in 1996. Mr. Kaplan is also an active member of the Institute of Navigation.

Michael King has a B.S. and M.S. in electrical engineering from Arizona State University. Since 1984 and while at Motorola, he worked in the GPS technology development field. His efforts included receiver architecture, signal processing, algorithm design, efficient ASIC design, and software development. Mr. King developed receiver architectures, algorithms, and over-the-air standards for assisted GPS cellular telephone positioning to support the FCC E-911 mandate and to enable a family of handset-hosted position-based services. Prior to that, he led the technology roadmap, architecture, and development of GPS sensor chipsets used in the telematics and timing industries. In recognition of his technical leadership, he was elected to Motorola's Science Advisory Board in 1998 and appointed a Dan Noble Fellow in 2003, Motorola's highest honor for a technologist. After retiring from Motorola in 2004, Mr. King joined the space division of General Dynamics Corporation, where he is leading the development of modernized GPS sensors for future DOD space missions. He is a member of the Institute of Navigation and of the Institute of Electrical and Electronic Engineers and holds 35 GPS-related patents.

Joseph L. Leva holds a B.S. in engineering physics from the University of Michigan and an M.S. in mathematics from Carnegie Mellon University. At The MITRE Corporation, he has worked on a number of defense-related projects. His strengths and interests lie in mathematical analysis, digital signal processing, and algorithm development. He has worked on radar and position location system projects and has over 20 years experience in time of arrival and time difference of arrival processing. Mr. Leva has published a number of papers in the GPS field dealing with the probabilistic treatment of DOP and closed-form solution to the pseudorange equations. He served as editor for navigation systems for the *IEEE Transactions for Aerospace and Electronic Systems* from 1999 to 2005. He is a member of the Institute of Navigation.

Willard A. Marquis is a senior staff engineer with Lockheed Martin's GPS IIR Flight Operations Group in Colorado Springs, Colorado. He received a B.S. and an M.S. in aeronautics and astronautics from the Massachusetts Institute of Technology. He has pursued further graduate work at the University of Colorado at Boulder. At Lockheed Martin since 1982, Mr. Marquis has worked on several rocket, upper stage, and satellite programs. In 1994, he joined the GPS Block IIR Flight Operations Group at Schriever Air Force Base in Colorado in the following capacities: as a navigation subsystem expert, as the modernization and special studies lead, and as a mission planner during launch and early orbit operations. Mr. Marquis is a member of the Institute of Navigation and the American Astronautical Society and is a senior member of the American Institute of Aeronautics and Astronautics. He is a past member of the AIAA Guidance, Navigation, and Control Technical Committee.

Dennis Milbert received a B.S. in physics from the University of Colorado and an M.S. and a Ph.D. in geodetic science from Ohio State University. He worked for more than 29 years at the National Geodetic Survey of the National Oceanic and Atmospheric Administration, where he was promoted to the position of chief geodesist. In his federal career, he developed accuracy standards, adjustment software, gravity and geoid models, GPS kinematic surveys, and vertical datum transformations. He served on numerous federal technical and policy working groups, including a recent Department of Transportation Radionavigation Task Force and the Federal Radionavigation Plan Working Group, and he was an alternate representative to the Senior Steering Group of the Interagency GPS Executive Board. Dr. Milbert served for 8 years on the joint editorial board for *Manuscripta Geodetica/Bulletin Geodesique* and the *Journal of Geodesy*. He is a recipient of the Kaarina and Weikko A. Heiskanen Award, the NOAA Administrator's Award, the Department of Commerce Bronze Medal, and two Department of Commerce Silver Medals. He is a member of the American Geophysical Union, the International Association of Geodesy, and the Institute of Navigation. Dr. Milbert recently retired from government service and is pursuing research in GPS carrier-phase positioning.

Jim Nagle is the chief of the communication, navigation and surveillance section for the ICAO. He has more than 35 years of experience in the design, management, operations, and international coordination of both terrestrial and space-based radio navigation and communication systems. Prior to joining ICAO, his career activities focused on the assessment of satellite-based technologies to support communications, navigation, surveillance/air traffic management systems and infrastructure. Mr. Nagle was the group leader for Inmarsat's navigation program activities. This program developed the Inmarsat-3 navigation payloads. These satellites provide the space segment of the U.S. WAAS, the EGNOS, and the basis for other international space-based augmentation systems.

Mike S. Pavloff received a B.S. in physics at Harvard and an M.S. in aeronautics and astronautics at the Massachusetts Institute of Technology. Mr. Pavloff joined The MITRE Corporation in 1988, where he was a member of the Space Systems Analysis Specialty Group. From 1988 to 1994, he was also on the faculty at Harvard, where he taught calculus and linear algebra, and helped to design and write a new calculus curriculum as well as a textbook under a National Science Foundation grant. Mr. Pavloff joined Hughes Space and Communications (subsequently acquired by Boeing) in 1995 and supported a number of satellite navigation programs, including GPS IIF, GPS III, and a navigation payload for the ICO program. In 2004, he joined Raytheon Santa Barbara Remote Sensing (also formerly Hughes) to manage the Visible Infrared Imager Radiometer Suite program, which will fly on the National Polar-Orbiting Operational Environmental Satellite System program.

Maarten Uijt de Haag is an associate professor of electrical engineering and computer science and a principal investigator with the Avionics Engineering Center at Ohio University. He obtained an M.S.E.E. from Delft University in the Netherlands in 1994 and a Ph.D. in electrical engineering from Ohio University in 1999. His areas of expertise are the development of advanced signal processing techniques for GPS software-defined radios, GPS/INS integrated systems, terrain-referenced navigation systems, and enhanced and synthetic vision systems. The latter includes the development of data integrity monitors as an enabling technology. Since 2002, Dr. Uijt de Haag has been an associate editor with *NAVIGATION: Journal of The Institute of Navigation*. He is a member of the Institute of Navigation, the Institute of Electrical and Electronic Engineers, the International Society for Optical Engineering, and Sigma Xi.

Karen Van Dyke is an electrical engineer with the U.S. Department of Transportation Volpe Center. Ms. Van Dyke has conducted availability and integrity studies for aviation applications of GPS for all phases of flight, including precision approach. She was the project lead of a Volpe Center team that designed, developed, and implemented GPS RAIM outage reporting systems for both the U.S. Air Force and the FAA, which are used to brief GPS availability to pilots during preflight planning. Ms. Van Dyke has worked with Australian, German, Brazilian, and Chilean aviation authorities on the implementation of similar systems for use by pilots and air traffic control in these countries. She also supported the FAA in development of the Notice to Airmen system for WAAS. More recently she has been the project lead for the IGEB GPS Integrity Failure Modes and Effects Analysis. Ms. Van Dyke has served as the president of the Institute of Navigation, and she received a B.S. and an M.S. in electrical engineering from the University of Massachusetts at Lowell.

Phillip W. Ward is the president of NAVWARD GPS Consulting, which he founded in 1991 in Dallas, Texas. From 1960 to 1991, he was a senior member of the technical staff at Texas Instruments, Inc., in the Defense Systems and Electronics Group. During a 1967–1970 educational leave of absence from Texas Instruments, he was a member of the technical staff at the Massachusetts Institute of Technology Instrumentation Lab (now the Draper Lab). Mr. Ward earned a B.S.E.E. from the University of Texas at El Paso in 1958 and an M.S.E.E. from Southern Methodist University in 1965. He has also taken postgraduate courses in computer science at the Massachusetts Institute of Technology. Mr. Ward has been involved in the field of navigation since 1958 and with GPS receiver design since 1976. He served as the lead systems engineer on several of Texas Instruments' advanced GPS receiver development programs. He developed five generations of GPS receivers for Texas Instruments, including the TI 4100 NAVSTAR Navigator Multiplex Receiver, the first commercial GPS receiver. For his pioneering work in the development of TI 4100, Mr. Ward received the Colonel Thomas L. Thurlow Navigation Award in 1989, the highest award given by the Institute of Navigation. At the MIT Instrumentation Lab, he worked with the Apollo Guidance Computer design team. He was the president of the Institute of Navigation (1992–1993) and the chair of the Institute of Navigation Satellite Division (1994–1996). Mr. Ward was the first Congressional Fellow of the Institute of Navigation (2001–2002) and is a Fellow member of the Institute of Navigation. He is also a senior member of the Institute of Electrical and Electronic Engineers.

Lawrence F. Wiederholt has worked on precision approach and landing systems for the military using GPS since his employment at The MITRE Corporation in 2000. During his employment at Intermetrics in Cambridge, Massachusetts, from 1976–2000, he worked on a variety of navigation systems with the principal focus being GPS. Most of that time, he worked with GPS receivers and user navigation solution formation using Kalman filtering and least squares estimation techniques. Integration of GPS with other sensors, such as inertial navigation systems, baro-altimeter, and Doppler radars was a part of this experience. The work entailed analysis, simulation, real-time software development, field test, and evaluation. This work included the Autonomous Navigation function for the GPS Block IIR satellites. Dr. Wiederholt has also performed assignments for the Calspan Corporation in Buffalo, New York, and the Aerospace Corporation in El Segundo, California. Dr. Wiederholt has a Ph.D., an M.S., and a B.S. in electrical engineering from the University of Wisconsin–Madison and a B.A. from Loras College. He is a member of the Institute of Navigation.

Index

Recent Titles in the Artech House
Mobile Communications Series

John Walker, Series Editor

Personal Wireless Communication with DECT and PWT, John Phillips and
Gerard Mac Namee

Practical Wireless Data Modem Design, Jonathon Y. C. Cheah

Prime Codes with Applications to CDMA Optical and Wireless Networks,
Guu-Chang Yang and Wing C. Kwong

QoS in Integrated 3G Networks, Robert Lloyd-Evans

Radio Engineering for Wireless Communication and Sensor Applications,
Antti V. Räisänen and Arto Lehto

Radio Propagation in Cellular Networks, Nathan Blaunstein

Radio Resource Management for Wireless Networks, Jens Zander and
Seong-Lyun Kim

RDS: The Radio Data System, Dietmar Kopitz and Bev Marks

Resource Allocation in Hierarchical Cellular Systems, Lauro Ortigoza-Guerrero and
A. Hamid Aghvami

RF and Baseband Techniques for Software-Defined Radio Peter B. Kenington

RF and Microwave Circuit Design for Wireless Communications,
Lawrence E. Larson, editor

Sample Rate Conversion in Software Configurable Radios, Tim Hentschel

Signal Processing Applications in CDMA Communications, Hui Liu

Smart Antenna Engineering, Ahmed El Zooghby

Software Defined Radio for 3G, Paul Burns

Spread Spectrum CDMA Systems for Wireless Communications, Savo G. Glisic and
Branka Vucetic

Third Generation Wireless Systems, Volume 1: Post-Shannon Signal Architectures,
George M. Calhoun

Traffic Analysis and Design of Wireless IP Networks, Toni Janevski

Transmission Systems Design Handbook for Wireless Networks, Harvey Lehpamer

UMTS and Mobile Computing, Alexander Joseph Huber and Josef Franz Huber

Understanding Cellular Radio, William Webb

Understanding Digital PCS: The TDMA Standard, Cameron Kelly Coursey

Understanding GPS: Principles and Applications, Second Edition, Elliott D. Kaplan
and Christopher J. Hegarty, editors

Understanding WAP: Wireless Applications, Devices, and Services, Marcel van der
Heijden and Marcus Taylor, editors

Universal Wireless Personal Communications, Ramjee Prasad

WCDMA: Towards IP Mobility and Mobile Internet, Tero Ojanperä and Ramjee Prasad, editors

Wireless Communications in Developing Countries: Cellular and Satellite Systems, Rachael E. Schwartz

Wireless Intelligent Networking, Gerry Christensen, Paul G. Florack, and Robert Duncan

Wireless LAN Standards and Applications, Asunción Santamaría and Francisco J. López-Hernández, editors

Wireless Technician's Handbook, Second Edition, Andrew Miceli

For further information on these and other Artech House titles, including previously considered out-of-print books now available through our In-Print-Forever® (IPF®) program, contact:

Artech House
685 Canton Street
Norwood, MA 02062
Phone: 781-769-9750
Fax: 781-769-6334
e-mail: artech@artechhouse.com

Artech House
46 Gillingham Street
London SW1V 1AH UK
Phone: +44 (0)20 7596-8750
Fax: +44 (0)20 7630-0166
e-mail: artech-uk@artechhouse.com

Find us on the World Wide Web at: www.artechhouse.com